Shanghai

"All you've got to do is decide to go and the hardest part is over.

So go!"

TONY WHEELER, COFOUNDER – LONELY PLANET

THIS EDITION WRITTEN AND RESEARCHED BY
Damian Harper, Christopher Pitts

Contents

Plan Your Trip 4

Explore Shànghǎi 46

Understand Shànghǎi 203

Survival Guide 239

Shànghǎi Maps 278

IMAGEMORE CO, LTD / GETTY IMAGES ©

ATLANTIDE PHOTOTRAVEL / CORBIS ©

(left) Oriental Pearl TV Tower (p138)

(above) Jade Buddha Temple (p122)

(right) Food for sale at Yùyuán Bazaar (p76)

LAURIE NOBLE / GETTY IMAGES ©

Welcome to Shànghǎi

The engine of China's future, Shànghǎi dazzles, beckoning millions with promises of reinvention and glamour.

Architecture

Pǔdōng wasn't built in a day, but it sure didn't take much longer than that. And while Shànghǎi may be renowned for its record-setting skyscrapers – there was nothing but farmland on the other side of the river in the early 1990s – it's the sheer diversity of building styles that makes the city unique. By no means should you skip out on a night in one of the world's highest hotels, but don't forget to do some exploration at ground level too: from Jesuit cathedrals, Jewish synagogues and Buddhist temples to streamlined art-deco apartment blocks and the home-grown *lòngtáng* laneway housing, Shànghǎi's architectural heritage is like nowhere else.

Cuisine

Shànghǎi is most alive at the end of the day, when workers pour out of the offices, the neon lights flicker on and the restaurants begin to fill up. As in the rest of China, food is at the centre of social life. It's over a meal that people catch up with friends, celebrate and clinch business deals, and – newsflash – Shànghǎi has the most exciting culinary scene in the Middle Kingdom. So whatever it is you're hungry for, make sure you do as the Shanghainese do and dig in with those chopsticks.

Shopping

As modern China's ground zero, the city exudes a style that's unlike anywhere else in the country. Often portrayed as a blend of East and West, Shànghǎi, with its voracious appetite for new styles and trends, is above all cosmopolitan and cutting edge. Pop-up boutiques, bustling markets and new brands created by the aspiring young designers flocking to the city – these are only some of the pleasures of shopping in China's fashion capital. There's no doubt you could create an entire itinerary devoted solely to the art of retail therapy: the question is, what are you waiting for?

Entertainment & the Arts

Běijīng often takes all the credit as China's cultural nexus, but for what is essentially a town of wheelers and dealers, Shànghǎi is surprisingly creative. Many art galleries are first-rate, offering a window into the contemporary Chinese art scene, while nightlife offerings have expanded exponentially in the past decade. Massage is always a favourite with visitors, as is the inevitable acrobatics show. Even Shànghǎi's music and club scene has made great strides: from unpretentious jazz and indie venues to all-night hip-hop and electro dance parties, the city swings with the best of them.

DANITA DELIMONT / GETTY IMAGES ©

Why I Love Shànghǎi

By Christopher Pitts, Author

My favourite thing to do in Shànghǎi is to roll out of bed, grab my notebook and maps and head straight for the nearest hand-pulled noodle stall. Like all megacities, Shànghǎi can be overwhelming at times, but it's while watching the crowds hurry by as I plan my day that I feel most connected to the place and the people in it. It's that rare moment of early morning tranquillity, when the day feels ripe with promise, and you think: anything could happen today. And then I finish my noodles, scribble a few more notes, take one last look at the map and dive in.

For more about our authors, see p304.

Taichi practitioners on the Bund

Shànghǎi's Top 13

PETER STUCKINGS / GETTY IMAGES ©

The Bund *(p52)*

1 Mainland China's most iconic concession-era backdrop and a source of intense local pride, the Bund is Shànghǎi's standout spectacle. A gorgeous curve of larger-than-life heritage architecture, the buildings here may be dwarfed by the city's modern high-rises, but they carry in their stones an old-fashioned gravity that simply can't be matched. As a monument to the unbridled pursuit of wealth, it's no surprise that the Bund was left to languish during the communist years, but with China's economic renaissance it has once again found its place among the city's most stylish destinations.

The Bund & People's Square

Shànghǎi Museum *(p57)*

2 Shànghǎi has never been a city to bother with the rear-view mirror, and this obvious disregard for tradition is what most distinguishes it from the rest of the country. The one glaring exception, however, is the standout Shànghǎi Museum, a marvellous tribute to the path of beauty throughout the millennia, from ancient bronzes to gorgeous ceramic masterpieces from the Qing dynasty. Come here for Chinese landscape paintings, sea-green celadon jars, Buddhist statuary and a taste of a world that has since disappeared.

The Bund & People's Square

1

KEREN SU / GETTY IMAGES © ARCHITECT XING TONGHE

2

3

5

CHRISTIAN KOBER / GETTY IMAGES ©

French Concession Fashion *(p113)*

3 In the early 20th century, Shànghǎi single-handedly shaped the image of the modern Chinese woman through calendar posters, which were printed in the millions and distributed throughout the rural hinterland and beyond. Ever since, it has worn the crown of China's most fashionable city, and there's no better place to get a feel for the latest trends than the French Concession. Browse boutiques for sequin-covered shoes, Tibetan-inspired jewellery, silky summer dresses and the hip new styles of a growing crop of local and international designers.

French Concession

Hángzhōu's West Lake *(p171)*

4 Whizz down to Hángzhōu on the high-speed train in a shot, but whatever you do, take your time dawdling around willow-fringed West Lake, one of the nation's top sights. The most famous city lake in China, it's vast, placid and beautiful in equal measure and best savoured in a very low gear. With its undulating range of pagoda-capped hills to the north, picturesque causeways and lakeside gardens and parks, West Lake is even more spellbinding come nightfall, when couples come out to walk languorously along its shores. Aim for sundown for spectacular photographs across the water to the setting sun.

Day Trips

Yùyuán Gardens & Bazaar *(p76)*

5 Sūzhōu is forever associated with traditional Chinese gardens, but the Yùyuán Gardens – in Shànghǎi's Old Town – is one of the nation's best examples. With its ponds, trees, flowers, bridges, pavilions and harmonic compositions, the gardens encourage contemplation and reflection, elusive moods in today's frantic Shànghǎi. The gardens are popular though, so get here early in the day while it's still quiet, before joining the hectic throb of shoppers in the attached bazaar, an excellent place to pick up skilfully made handicrafts and keepsakes.

Old Town

Dining in the French Concession *(p96)*

6 An incomparable melange of regional Chinese restaurants, stylish Shanghainese eateries, international restaurateurs and no-frills street food, the French Concession is the epicentre of the city's culinary revolution. On a single strip you might find explosively hot Sichuanese, a Hong Kong–style diner, Shanghainese seafood and MSG-free noodles – venture just a little bit further and you can travel to the end of the Middle Kingdom and back.

French Concession

Markets *(p86)*

7 Shànghǎi's air-conditioned malls can be a haven on a hot day but if you want to see locals in their true shopping element, drop by a market. Get your haggling hat on and your elbows out and join the push and shove – among all the jostling and banter, endless fakes and tricks of the trade, you might just find exactly what you're looking for and don't forget, prices aren't fixed. For starters, roll up your sleeves in the Shíliùpù Fabric Market or cast a shrewd eye over the goods at the Dongtai Road Antique Market in the Old Town. DONGTAI ROAD ANTIQUES MARKET

Old Town

6

Jade Buddha Temple *(p122)*

8 While Shànghǎi and materialism fit together like hand and glove, the city's connection to spiritual matters may seem more tenuous, to say the least. Despite first impressions, however, the city does have a strong current of religious tradition, best observed in the main courtyard of this century-old Buddhist temple, which is witness to a continual stream of worshippers throughout the day. Housed on the top floor of a rear building is the temple's centrepiece, a 1.9m-high statue of Sakyamuni made of pure Burmese jade.

Jìng'ān

M50 *(p123)*

9 Shànghǎi has traditionally eschewed the arts in favour of more commercial pursuits, but the escalating value of Chinese artwork has led to the emergence of a busy gallery scene. Located in a former cotton mill, the industrially chic M50 is the city's main creative hub and Shànghǎi's answer to the 798 Art District in Běijīng. Dozens of edgy galleries, a handful of studios and occasional events make this an absorbing place to wander.

Jìng'ān

Modern Architecture *(p228)*

10 Through its occasionally debauched history, Shànghǎi has become synonymous with both excess and success. Today is no different. It's hard to talk about Shànghǎi without references to skyscrapers, as they have become *the* defining architectural style (even eclipsing art deco). Urban Shànghǎi's high-altitude topography is entirely man-made: walk around Lùjiāzuǐ at night and be blown away by the visuals. There's nowhere else in mainland China quite like it. VIEW FROM SHÀNGHǍI WORLD FINANCIAL CENTER

Architecture in Shànghǎi

Nightlife *(p39)*

11 The one-time city of sin, Shànghǎi's heady mix of lipstick-smudged martini glasses and flashing neon lights doesn't always match expectations, but there's no doubt that the place loves to party. You don't need to knock back shots of green tea and whisky or dance till dawn to have a good time, though. The nightlife scene continues to mature, and whether you prefer theatre, jazz or punk rock, you can be sure that the midnight hour will always have something in store. TMSK BAR

Drinking & Nightlife

9

Lǐlòng & Lòngtáng *(p234)*

12 When Shànghǎi's superscale buildings leave you feeling totally dwarfed, get down to the city's traditional *lǐlòng* and *lòngtáng* lanes. Exploring this charming realm allows you to discover a more personable aspect to the city, so go slow. This is where you can find Shànghǎi's homey and more intimate side: narrow alleys, classic three-storey buildings, a warm community spirit, history, heritage and a lethargic tempo entirely at odds with the roar of the main drag.

Architecture in Shànghǎi

LO MAK / REDLINK / CORBIS ©

Zhūjiājiǎo *(p185)*

13 The nearest decent-sized water town to Shànghǎi, Zhūjiājiǎo is ideal for a day trip. Easily reached by bus, there are quintessential traditional bridges, pinched lanes, ancient streets, hoary Qing-dynasty temples, waterside views and even some pretty fine cafes. It's fun losing your bearings, but Zhūjiājiǎo is small enough to mean you never get entirely lost. If you take to the water-town culture, you can carry on from Zhūjiājiǎo to other canal towns in neighbouring Jiāngsū province.

Day Trips

What's New

Fairmont Peace Hotel

Reopened after years of renovations, the Peace has recaptured the art-deco magic of a bygone era. Pop in to gaze at the gorgeous rotunda or swing with the jazz band. (p53)

The Bund

Several other heritage buildings along the Bund have been given a new lease on life, including the former British Consulate, the Swatch Art Peace Hotel, the Jardine Matheson building and the old Shànghǎi Club, now the plush Waldorf Astoria. (p52)

The North Bund

This area (aka the Rockbund) is finally coming into its own following the restoration of Yuanmingyuan Rd. Luxury shops and restaurants have moved in with the aim of making it the next big lifestyle destination. (p64)

Rockbund Art Museum

One block back from Yuanmingyuan Rd is the former Royal Asiatic Society building, completed in 1933 and now home to this bold contemporary Chinese art museum. (p61)

Shànghǎi Tower

Although not due to be completed until 2014, there's no doubt that this massive skyscraper – set to top out at 632m – will redefine the Pǔdōng skyline.

China Art Palace & Former Expo Area

There's no telling what will become of the former World Expo area, but the star attraction, the China Art Palace (formerly the China Pavilion), is touting itself as the next big museum to hit the city, with an emphasis on modern art. (p141)

Liúli China Museum

Wonderfully quirky, this Taiwanese museum showcases ancient and contemporary glass sculpture from around the world, with an emphasis on the Buddhist-inspired creations of its founder, Loretta Yang. (p94)

Jìng'ān Temple

A skyscraper only needs a few years to go up in Shànghǎi, but rebuilding this temple has been an eternal work in progress. Miraculously enough it's now almost complete, its curved teak eaves set majestically against the modern Jìng'ān skyline. (p124)

The Metro

The Shànghǎi metro is the world's fastest-growing underground rail network, and recent developments continue to be a boon for visitors. New extensions to lines 11 and 13 should be complete by the time this book is in print, with more stations set to open by the end of 2014. (p245)

Hóngqiáo Railway Station

Shànghǎi now has high-speed rail connections with Běijīng, Hángzhōu, Nánjīng and other destinations throughout China, all of which leave from this new station, the largest in Asia.

For more recommendations and reviews, see **lonelyplanet.com/shanghai**

Need to Know

Currency
Renminbi (RMB); basic unit is the yuan (¥).

Languages
Mandarin
Shanghainese

Visas
Needed for all visits to Shànghǎi except 48-hour transits.

Money
ATMs widely available. Credit cards less widely used; always carry cash.

Mobile Phones
Inexpensive pay-as-you-go SIM cards can be bought locally for most mobile phones. Buying a local mobile phone is also cheap.

Time
Běijīng time (GMT/UTC plus eight hours).

Tourist Information
Tourist and Information Service Centre (Map p280; ☎6357 3718; 518 Jiujiang Rd; 九江路518号; ⏰9.30am-8pm; Ⓜ East Nanjing Rd) Free maps and basic info.

Your Daily Budget
The following are average costs per day:

Budget under ¥200
- Dorm bed ¥50-60
- Cheap hole-in-the-wall restaurants, food markets and street food ¥50
- Affordable internet access, bike hire or other transport ¥20-30
- Some free museums
- Sundries ¥40-60

Midrange ¥200–1600
- Double room in a midrange hotel ¥200-1300
- Lunch and dinner in decent local restaurants ¥150-200
- Entertainment ¥80
- Travelling in comfort ¥80

Top end over ¥1600
- Double room in a top-end hotel from ¥1300
- Lunch and dinner in excellent restaurants from ¥300
- Shopping at top-end shops ¥300

Advance Planning
Three months Book a room at a popular hotel.

One month Book a table at a popular restaurant; check listings on entertainment sites such as Time Out Shanghai (www.timeoutshanghai.com) for art exhibitions, live music, festivals, shows and book tickets.

A few days Check the weather online (www.bbc.co.uk/weather/1796236)

Websites & Blogs
- **Lonely Planet** (www.lonelyplanet.com/shanghai) Destination information, hotel bookings, traveller forum and more.
- **Time Out Shanghai** (www.timeoutshanghai.com) Authoritative, in-the-know entertainment listings.
- **City Weekend** (www.cityweekend.com.cn/shanghai) Comprehensive listings website of popular expat magazine. News stories can be weak.
- **Shanghaiist** (www.shanghaiist.com) Excellent source for news and reviews.
- **Smart Shanghai** (www.smartshanghai.com) Quality listings website with forum.
- **Shanghai Scrap** (www.shanghaiscrap.com) Well-researched blog from American writer/journalist Adam Minter.

WHEN TO GO

Summer is peak season but it's hot and sticky with heavy rain; spring and late September to October are optimal (neither too hot nor rainy). Winter is cold and clammy.

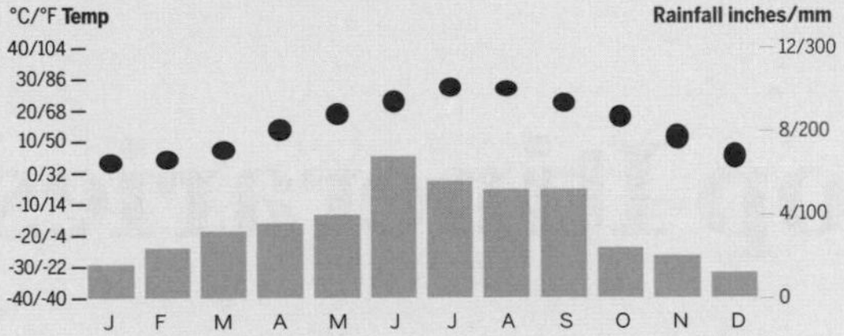

Arriving in Shànghǎi

Pǔdōng International Airport Metro into town 6am to 10pm ¥3-10; Maglev to Longyang Rd metro station between 6.45am and 9.40pm ¥50; airport buses into town from 7am to 11pm ¥16-30; taxi into town ¥160.

Hóngqiáo International Airport Metro into town 6.05am to 10.50pm ¥3-10; airport buses run into town from 6am to 11pm ¥4-30; taxi into town ¥70.

Shànghǎi Railway Station Metro into town 5.30am to 11pm ¥3-10; taxi into town ¥20-30.

Shànghǎi Hóngqiáo Railway Station Metro into town 5.30am to 11pm ¥3-10; taxi into town ¥70.

Shànghǎi South Railway Station Metro into town 5.30am to 11pm ¥3-10; taxi into town ¥50.

For much more on **arrival**, see p240.

Getting Around

The easiest way to get around Shànghǎi is by metro or taxi. A Transport Card or travel pass (see p248) is useful for avoiding ticket queues at metro stations.

Metro The most cost-effective and fastest way to get around town. Runs from around 5.30am to 10.30pm or 11pm.

Taxi Cheap and plentiful, especially if tied in with metro; can be hailed on the street; traffic gridlock can slow progress.

Bus Slow-going but OK views; difficult to use for foreigners and distances can be huge. Sightseeing buses recommended.

Bike OK for shorter distances and cycling around neighbourhoods.

Walking OK for shorter distances within neighbourhoods and for some central sightseeing.

For much more on **getting around**, see p245.

Sleeping

Sleeping in Shànghǎi is rarely a cheap proposition unless you snag a dorm bed or move into the suburbs. You'll need to book your room in advance to secure your top choice and avoid the national holiday periods.

There's a great deal of choice in the main, fashionable and sight-heavy areas but some neighbourhoods, such as Pǔdōng, strictly favour the top end. Finding accommodation within reach of a metro station is rarely hard. Hotels range from budget hostels and express business hotels, through heritage hotels and boutique choices to five-star towers.

Useful Websites

For general traveller information on Shànghǎi and hotel bookings, try:

➡ **Lonely Planet** (www.lonelyplanet.com/shanghai) Hotel bookings and forum.

➡ **CTrip** (☎400 619 9999; http://english.ctrip.com) An excellent online agency, good for hotel bookings.

➡ **eLong** (www.elong.net) Hotel bookings.

For much more on **sleeping**, see p189.

TOURIST INFORMATION

Oddly, Shànghǎi is not well served with tourist information offices so get chummy with your hotel concierge/reception staff for travel pointers. Pop their number into your mobile phone to communicate with taxi drivers or for any situation requiring an interpreter. Youth hostels often offer great advice and are generally well attuned to the needs of travellers. The Shànghǎi Call Centre (☎962 288) is a handy 24-hour English-language hotline.

Top Itineraries

Day One

The Bund (p52)

First stop, follow the sweep of architectural pomp along the **Bund** and savour the art-deco grandness of the **Fairmont Peace Hotel**, before walking along the riverside promenade to pixelate **Pǔdōng** across the Huángpǔ River. Art lovers can swoop upon the **Rockbund Art Museum**, while architecture fans can revel in the highlights of **Yuanmingyuan Road**. Head west along East Nanjing Rd past shoppers to **People's Square**.

Lunch Lost Heaven (p66): all the flavours of far-off Yúnnán province.

People's Square (p65)

Immerse yourself in the outstanding collection of the **Shànghǎi Museum** before weighing up the **Shànghǎi Urban Planning Exhibition Hall** or finding a pocket of greenery in People's Park. The **Shànghǎi Art Museum** blends art and concession-era architecture; for views, shoot up in the lift to the lobby of the JW Marriott on the 38th floor of **Tomorrow Square**.

Dinner Kitchen Salvatore Cuomo (p141): have a table booked.

Lùjiāzuǐ (p138)

Hop on the metro (or a sightseeing bus) from People's Square to Lùjiāzuǐ to wander round the walkway in front of the **Oriental Pearl TV Tower**. Choose between the observation towers of the **Jinmao Tower** and the **Shànghǎi World Financial Center**, or settle for an evening cocktail at **Flair** or **Cloud 9**.

Day Two

French Concession East (p92)

Relish the architecture and boutiques of **Xīntiāndì** and pop into the **Shíkùmén Open House Museum** for a lowdown on *shíkùmén* (stone-gate house) architecture before tracking down **St Nicholas Church**, the fairy-tale **Moller House** or taking a seat to watch locals relaxing in French-designed **Fùxīng Park**.

Lunch Din Tai Fung (p97): classic, moreish Shànghǎi dumplings.

French Concession West (p95)

Admire the dazzling glass creations at the **Liúli China Museum** and the photographs at the **Beaugeste** gallery before totally disappearing among **Tiánzǐfáng's** warren of lanes. Boutique window-shop around Tiánzǐfáng, take your hat off to the collection in the **Propaganda Poster Art Centre** and hunt down contemporary art at **James Cohan**, **Art Labor** and **Space**.

Dinner Spicy Joint (p100): fantastic Sìchuān restaurant (but book ahead).

The Bund (p70)

Zip up the day in style sipping cocktails and dining on the **Bund**, but most of all enjoying the mind-altering neon views. Select from a long list: the **Glamour Bar**, **New Heights**, the **Long Bar**, **Jiao Bar**, **Bar Rouge** or **Captain's Bar** – or don your best togs for views, booze and moves at **M1NT**. Die-hard traditionalists can lend an ear to the jazz band in the **Fairmont Peace Hotel Jazz Bar**.

Day Three

Old Town (p77)

Reach the Old Town's **Yùyuán Gardens** early in the day, before the crowds arrive. Sift through the handicrafts on sale in the **Yùyuán Bazaar** before tracking down bargain collectibles along **Old Street** and **Dongtai Road Antiques Market**. Head east past **Dǒngjiādù Cathedral** to the **Cool Docks** for its appealing blend of *shíkùmén* and riverside warehouse architecture (plus views).

Lunch Nánxiáng Steamed Bun Restaurant (p83): celebrated dumplings.

Jìng'ān (p124)

Weave some Buddhist mystery into your afternoon at the **Jade Buddha Temple** before sprinkling contemporary art into the mix at the fascinating galleries of **M50**. Consider a cruise along **Sūzhōu Creek** or explore the **Jìng'ān Temple** before seeking out the *lǐlòng* lanes of the **Bubbling Well Road Apartments** and shopping along West Nanjing Rd.

Dinner Fu 1088 (p101): fine Shànghǎi cuisine in dapper villa surrounds.

French Concession (p105)

Round off your day ticking off some of Shànghǎi's best bars, all handily located in the French Concession: chill out at **Bell Bar**, seek out specialist beers at **Kaībā** or **Boxing Cat Brewery**, sink a drink in the garden of **Cotton's** or corner your perfect cocktail at **el Cóctel**.

Day Four

Xújiāhuì & South Shànghǎi (p158)

Spend the morning admiring the former Jesuit sights of Xújiāhuì, in particular the **St Ignatius Cathedral** and the **Tousewe Museum**. Pay your respects to the Buddhist **Lónghuá Temple & Pagoda**; the green-fingered can explore the foliage of the **Shànghǎi Botanical Gardens**.

Lunch Xīnjiāng Fēngwèi Restaurant (p160): feast on Uighur lamb.

Hóngkǒu & North Shànghǎi (p150)

Pay a visit to the **Ohel Moishe Synagogue** and the surrounding former Jewish neighbourhood, walk up **Duolun Road Cultural Street**, track down some of the neighbourhood's best architecture and relax in **Lu Xun Park**. In the late afternoon, head back south to the North Bund area of Hóngkǒu, which puts you within easy reach of the Bund.

Dinner Guǒyúan (p152): super-duper spice-infused dishes from Húnán.

Pǔdōng (p138)

Get haggling at the **AP Xīnyáng Fashion & Gifts Market** before getting a handle on local history at the **Shànghǎi History Museum**, followed by an evening walk along the **Riverside Promenade**, gazing over to the Bund. For fine Pǔdōng views, jump on a ferry across the river to toast the skyline from **Char Bar** in the South Bund or **The Waterhouse** by the Cool Docks.

If You Like...

Views

The Bund Walk the promenade for views of Pŭdōng's soaring skyline on one side and concession-era magnificence on the other. (p52)

Shànghăi World Financial Center The city's highest observation deck, until it's surpassed by the Shànghăi Tower. (p140)

Flair An outdoor terrace gives this sky-high Pŭdōng bar the edge. (p144)

New Heights This top-floor cafe-bar at Three on the Bund is a good spot to stop on a stroll. (p70)

Vue An outdoor Jacuzzi and views of both Pŭdōng and the Bund. (p154)

JW Marriott Tomorrow Square Lobby Pop up to the 38th floor for stupendous vistas over People's Square. (p192)

Cloud 9 This cool bar at the top of the Jinmao Tower is another great alternative to the observation decks. (p144)

West Lake Hángzhōu's main attraction is the very definition of classical beauty in China. (p171)

Modern Architecture

Shànghăi Tower With an estimated completion date of 2014, this 632m-high skyscraper will be the undisputed king of the Shànghăi skyline. (p145)

Tomorrow Square The People's Square supertower could easily

LOOK DIE BILDAGENTUR DER FOTOGRAFEN GMBH / ALAMY ©

Reception of the Fairmont Peace Hotel (p53 and p192)

double as the headquarters for a sci-fi corporation. (p66)

Jinmao Tower No longer the tallest, but still one of the city's most graceful buildings. (p139)

China Art Palace The upturned red pyramid was the symbol of the 2010 World Expo. (p141)

Oriental Art Center Way out in Pŭdōng, this classical music venue was designed to resemble the five petals of a butterfly orchid. (p146)

Shànghǎi Grand Theatre The curving eaves of this theatre recall traditional Chinese architectural design. (p72)

Oriental Pearl TV Tower Not so subtle perhaps, but this poured-concrete tripod is nonetheless a Shànghǎi icon. (p138)

Boutique Shopping

Spin Imaginative ceramics from a new generation of designers. (p134)

NuoMi Stylish women's wear that's ecofriendly too. (p116)

Brocade Country Jewellery, clothing and handicrafts from the Miao of Guìzhōu province. (p117)

Annabel Lee An elegant shop that specialises in embroidery and sells accessories in silk, linen and cashmere. (p72)

William the Beekeeper The city's best vintage, with organic honey sticks too. (p116)

PCS (Pop Classic Sneakers) Come here to pick up the latest canvas-shoe styles. (p115)

Heirloom An elegant range of clutches, satchels and shoulder bags. (p115)

Chouchou Chic Kids' clothes from a joint French-Chinese brand. (p115)

Urban Tribe Local fashion label inspired by the ethnic minorities of China's southwest. (p118)

Ba Yan Ka La Natural beauty products with a traditional Chinese medicine slant. (p117)

Street Food

Qībǎo Poke a straw in a coconut, sample barbecued squid or indulge in sweet dumplings – Qībǎo corners the market for Shànghǎi street food. (p164)

Yunnan Road Food Street One of the best strips for unpretentious regional Chinese restaurants. (p69)

Wujiang Road Food Street The most modern snack street in the city, with Japanese and Korean options too. (p131)

Huanghe Road Food Street Near People's Park, this strip has some big traditional restaurants, but it's most famous for its dumplings. (p69)

Yùyuán Bazaar It's crowded and overpriced, but famous spots like the Nánxiáng Steamed Bun Restaurant make this a can't-miss option for many. (p76)

Raffles City A good primer to mall-style food courts, with the popular Food Republic on the top floor and nonstop snacking options in the basement. (p73)

Art-Deco Architecture

Fairmont Peace Hotel Built as the legendary Cathay Hotel, this is the best surviving example of art-deco style in Shànghǎi. (p53)

Park Hotel The tallest building in Shànghǎi until the 1980s and an early inspiration for IM Pei. (p66)

For more top Shànghǎi spots, see

➡ Eating (p29)

➡ Drinking & Nightlife (p39)

➡ Entertainment (p41)

➡ Shopping (p43)

Embankment Building An art-deco landmark now housing private studios that travellers can rent out. (p153)

Shànghǎi Art Museum Former British racecourse club building with period features such as art-deco chandeliers and horse-head balustrades. (p65)

Art Deco Artsy boutique in the M50 complex containing a trove of period furnishings. (p134)

Cathay Theatre Catch a movie in this original 1930s French Concession theatre. (p112)

Broadway Mansions A 1934 apartment block north of Sūzhōu Creek that today is home to a hotel. (p153)

China Baptist Publication Society One of many buildings designed by Ladislaus Hudec, a Czech-Hungarian who became one of Shànghǎi's most prolific architects. (p64)

Paramount Ballroom (p133) This art-deco dance hall was once Shànghǎi's biggest concession-era nightclub.

Art Galleries

M50 Former manufacturing space now housing the largest collection of art galleries in the city. (p123)

Propaganda Poster Art Centre Collection of 3000 original posters from the golden age of Maoist propaganda. (p95)

Beaugeste Superb photography gallery tucked away in Tiánzǐfáng. (p95)

James Cohan Edgy New York gallery set in a French Concession villa. (p96)

Art Labor Independent French Concession gallery representing Chinese and international artists. (p96)

Shànghǎi Gallery of Art Conceptual Chinese art on the Bund. (p56)

Leo Gallery Works by young Chinese artists. (p96)

Space Modern art gallery housed in a former Russian Orthodox church. (p95)

Temples & Churches

Jade Buddha Temple Shànghǎi's most active Buddhist temple. (p122)

Língyǐn Temple Hángzhōu's main Buddhist temple, with a remarkable series of cliff-side carvings. (p173)

Chénxiānggé Nunnery This Old Town temple shelters a gorgeous effigy of the Buddhist goddess of compassion. (p77)

Confucian Temple A tranquil spot with old trees and a Sunday book market, located in an atmospheric part of the Old Town. (p78)

Jìng'ān Temple Downtown Buddhist temple constructed of Burmese teak and holding several enormous statues. (p124)

Ohel Moishe Synagogue One-time heart of Shànghǎi's Jewish ghetto, now home to the Jewish Refugees Museum. (p151)

Lónghuá Temple & Pagoda The oldest and largest monastery in the city, though it's a hike to get here. (p159)

Temple of the Town God Shànghǎi is one of the few cities in China whose Taoist town god weathered the vicissitudes of the 20th century. (p77)

Dǒngjiādù Cathedral Shànghǎi's oldest church, established by Spanish Jesuits in 1853. (p78)

St Ignatius Cathedral This Xújiāhuì landmark and Jesuit cathedral dates back to 1904. (p158)

Shěshān Basilica Magnificently crowning a hilltop southwest of the city (p188).

Museums

Shànghǎi Museum Extraordinary overview of traditional Chinese art through the millennia, from ancient bronzes to Qing-dynasty ink paintings. (p57)

Sūzhōu Museum Local artefacts – jade, ceramics and carvings – housed in a gorgeous new building. (p179)

Shànghǎi History Museum Fun and accessible introduction to old Shànghǎi. (p138)

Shànghǎi Urban Planning Exhibition Hall The highlight here is an incredible scale model of the megalopolis c 2020. (p65)

Rockbund Art Museum Contemporary Chinese art installations in a gorgeous 1930s building, once home to Shànghǎi's first museum. (p61)

Liúli China Museum This unusual edifice is dedicated to the art of glass sculpture, with both ancient and contemporary pieces on display. (p94)

Post Museum Surprisingly good museum covering the history of the Chinese postal service. (p150)

Mínshēng Art Museum Excellent line-up of contemporary Chinese art exhibits. (p165)

China Art Palace (p141) Former World Expo China Pavilion reconfigured as a mammoth five-floor art museum, Pǔdōng-side.

Power Station of Art (p141) Shànghǎi's take on London's Tate Modern, with contemporary art hung within a riverside power station.

Markets

AP Xīnyáng Fashion & Gifts Market The city's largest market sells everything from tailor-made clothes to counterfeit bags. (p147)

Flower, Bird, Fish & Insect Market Pick up your city-sized pets at one of Shànghǎi's only traditional markets. (p78)

Dōngtái Road Antique Market Always a fun browse, Dōngtái has Mao memorabilia, old calendar posters and mass-produced 'antiques'. (p87)

Shíliùpù Fabric Market Have a suit, dress or blouse tailor-made for a song. (p86)

Ghost Market Climb up to the top floors of the Fúyòu Antique Market on weekends when sellers from the countryside hawk their wares. (p87)

Yùyuán Bazaar The ultimate Shànghǎi souvenir market, the Old Town bazaar is slightly tacky and extremely crowded, but always entertaining. (p76)

Qīpǔ Market Push through the crowds at this popular clothing outlet – everything must go now! (p154)

Electronics Market DVD players, speakers and various computer parts for sale. It's cheap, but there's no receipt. (p155)

Month by Month

TOP EVENTS

Chinese New Year, February

Lantern Festival, February

JUE Festival, March

Shanghai International Literary Festival, March

Lónghuá Temple Fair, April

January

The Western New Year is celebrated in bars citywide.

Western New Year

Lónghuá Temple has excellent New Year (元旦; Yuándàn) celebrations, with dragon and lion dances. On 1 January the abbot strikes the bell 108 times while the monks beat on gongs and offer prayers for the forthcoming year.

February

Preparations for the festive Chinese New Year are well under way as hundreds of millions of people get ready to journey home, so if you plan to do any travelling, make sure you reserve your tickets as far in advance as possible.

Chinese New Year

Commonly called the Spring Festival (春节; Chūn Jié), Chinese New Year is the equivalent of Christmas. Families get together to feast on dumplings, vegetate in front of the TV, hand out *hóngbāo* (red envelopes stuffed with money) and take a week-long holiday. New Year's Eve fireworks can be a chaotic but good show.

The festival traditionally commences on the first day of the first moon of the traditional lunar calendar (31 January 2014, 19 February 2015, 8 February 2016), but a high-octane month-long build-up – featuring a crescendo of red and gold decorations festooning shopping malls and the inescapable onset of seasonal Cantopop ditties – gets everyone hyped up much earlier.

Lantern Festival

Lantern Festival (元宵节; Yuánxiāo Jié) falls on the 15th day of the first lunar month (14 February 2014; 5 March 2015; 22 February 2016). Families get together, make *yuán xiāo* (also called *tāng yuán;* delicious dumplings of glutinous rice with a variety of sweet fillings) and sometimes hang paper lanterns. It's a colourful time to visit Yùyuán Gardens.

Valentine's Day

Valentine's Day (情人节; Qíngrén Jié) is taken seriously by Shànghǎi suitors as an occasion for a massive blowout: it's the chance to get their true love that Cartier wristwatch or diamond ring she has been hankering for, although a bunch of 11 roses could do the trick.

March

March in Shànghǎi is usually grey, cold and clammy, though hints of spring usually appear by the end of the month.

JUE Festival

Two-week arts-and-music festival (www.juefestival.com) held in both Shànghǎi and Běijīng. This is one of the best times of the year for music lovers and creative types. There's no single venue in town; anyone can host an event.

Shanghai International Literary Festival

To counter Shànghǎi's drift towards philistinism, this highly popular festival for book lovers is staged in the Glamour Bar in March or April, with a range of famous names in attendance.

Birthday of Guanyin

The Buddhist goddess of mercy celebrates her birthday (观世音生日; Guānshìyīn Shēngrì) on the 19th day of the second lunar month (19 March 2014; 7 April 2015; 27 March 2016), an excellent time to visit Buddhist temples.

April

Countrywide, transport and hotels are booked solid on Tomb Sweeping Day and Labour Day (1 May); both are often extended into a long weekend.

Tomb Sweeping Day

Now a public holiday, Qīngmíng Jié (清明节) is held every 5 April (4 April in leap years), when more than six million Shanghainese visit the graves of their dearly departed relatives. The other 15 million head out of town on vacation.

Lónghuá Temple Fair

The two-week fair (龙华寺庙会; Lónghuá Sìmiào Huì) coincides with the blossoming of the local peach trees and kicks off on the third day of the third lunar month (12 April 2013, 2 April 2014, 21 April 2015).

Formula One (F1)

The slick Shànghǎi International Circuit has hosted F1's Chinese Grand Prix (www.formula1.com) every year since 2004. The race usually comes to town for three days in mid-April.

June

The sweltering summer heat begins to kick in and rainfall in Shànghǎi hits its peak.

Dragon Boat Festival

This public holiday (端午节; Duānwǔ Jié) is celebrated on the fifth day of the fifth lunar month (12 June 2013, 2 June 2014, 20 June 2015) with boat races along the Huángpǔ River, Sūzhōu Creek and Diànshān Lake.

Shanghai International Film Festival

With screenings at various cinemas around Shànghǎi, the moviegoing festival (www.siff.com) brings a range of international and locally produced films to town in June.

September

The tail end of summer, this is one of the best times to visit as temperatures drop from August highs, although rainfall is still abundant.

Mid-Autumn Festival

The Mid-Autumn Festival (中秋节; Zhōngqiū Jié) is the time to give and receive delicious moon cakes stuffed with bean paste, egg yolk, coconut, walnuts and the like. The festival, now a one-day public holiday, takes place on the 15th day of the eighth lunar month (19 September 2013, 8 September 2014, 27 September 2015).

October

The week-long holiday beginning 1 October (National Day) wreaks havoc throughout China. Like Chinese New Year and Labour Day, it's best to avoid travelling at this time. If you're headed to Shànghǎi, book your hotel well in advance.

Hairy Crabs

Now's the time to sample delicious hairy crabs *(dàzháxiè)* in Shànghǎi. They're at their best between October and December.

Halloween

One of a handful of imported Western festivals, spooky Halloween is increasingly popular with young Chinese. Pumpkins, seasonal outfits and masks pile up at large supermarkets and stores, while parties are held at expat-oriented bars and restaurants.

Shanghai Biennale

Held once every two years (October to March 2014–15), this popular international arts festival (www.shanghaibiennale.org) takes place on the former World Expo grounds.

(Top) Choosing decorations for Chinese New Year
(Bottom) Lónghuá Temple Fair

TAO IMAGES LIMITED / GETTY IMAGES ©

GETTY IMAGES ©

November

Autumn's last gasp before winter begins.

China International Arts Festival

A month-long program (www.artsbird.com) of cultural events in October and November, which includes the Shanghai Art Fair, a varied program of international music, dance, opera and acrobatics, and exhibitions of the Shanghai Biennale.

Shanghai International Marathon

Usually held on the last Sunday of November, this annual event (www.shmarathon.com) attracts around 20,000 runners. It starts at the Bund and events include a half-marathon and a 4.5km 'health race'.

December

Shànghǎi winters are generally unpleasant, with temperatures that are cold enough to cut to the bone, but rarely chilly enough for snow.

Christmas

Not an official Chinese festival, Christmas (圣诞节; Shèngdàn Jié) is nevertheless a major milestone on the commercial calendar, and Shànghǎi's big shopping zones sparkle with decorations and glisten with fake snow.

With Kids

Shànghǎi isn't exactly at the top of most kids' holiday wish list, but the new Disney theme park in Pǔdōng (estimated completion date 2015) will no doubt improve its standing. In the meantime, if you're passing through the city with children, the following sights will keep the family entertained.

Need to Know

- In general, 1.4m (4ft 7in) is the cut-off height for children's tickets. Children under 0.8m (2ft 7in) normally get in for free.
- Holidays and weekends see traffic peak, but in China, 'crowded' takes on a new meaning. Try to schedule your visits for weekdays if possible.
- For more information on events and activities, grab a copy of *That's Shanghai* or *City Weekend*.

Observation Decks

Zipping to the top of a Pǔdōng skyscraper for a bird's-eye view of the city is one of Shànghǎi's top draws. The Shànghǎi World Financial Center, Jinmao Tower and Oriental Pearl TV Tower are all good options.

Museums

Shànghǎi History Museum

Waxworks and interactive exhibits make this museum a fun day out for everyone.

Science & Technology Museum

There are loads of things for kids to explore here, from volcano and space exhibits to sports activities and robots that can solve Rubik's cubes before your eyes. It also has IMAX and 4D theatres.

Madame Tussauds

This waxworks museum is aimed at locals (the family admission ticket only includes one child), though it could make do if you get caught in a downpour near People's Square.

Animal Parks

Shànghǎi Zoo

As far as Chinese zoos go, this is just about the best there is. In addition to the animals, there's plenty of green space to run around in.

Shànghǎi Ocean Aquarium

One of the top aquariums in China, this Pǔdōng attraction is surprisingly good, with an impressively long shark tunnel and intelligent exhibits organised by region. Avoid the weekends if possible.

Acrobatics Shows

An evening with the acrobats will certainly keep most kids (and adults) entertained, with plate spinning, contortionism and even daredevil motorcycle feats performed to *Star Wars* theme music.

Amusement & Water Parks

Happy Valley

China's best amusement park by a long shot, Happy Valley has scores of roller coasters, dive machines and other heart-thumping rides, but there are also mellower attractions for younger kids. A new water park is set to open here in 2013.

Dino Beach

This water park boasts Asia's largest wave pool and is a fun-filled way to beat the summer heat.

Like a Local

On the surface Shànghǎi appears more Western than anywhere else in China, bar Hong Kong. But don't be fooled by appearances – even if the Shanghainese are known for their embrace of foreign tastes, engaging in local life will reveal a culture that is captivatingly unique.

Learn Chinese

True, Mandarin isn't something you can simply pick up overnight, but learning the basics – or at least trying to – will take you a long way. It's also good for your ego, because you only need to master a handful of words before you start receiving enthusiastic compliments about your language skills. On that note, it's good form to return the compliment when someone speaks to you in English.

If you've been hankering to learn some Shanghainese, well, we won't discourage you, but make sure you've got Mandarin down first.

Eat Like a Local

This is actually a little trickier than it sounds. If you're wondering how you could not eat like a local, you only need to step into a Western restaurant or bar any night of the week – in Shànghǎi, the temptation to stay in your comfort zone is everywhere. Eating Shanghainese-style may require an initial leap of faith (you want me to eat *what*?), but be brave and travel your taste buds: with specialities like freshly pulled noodles, braised pork belly and quick-fried shrimp, you won't regret it.

Practise Taichi

The elderly in China are admirably active, but you don't have to be a retiree to join them. Head out to the nearest park in the early morning and look for the group that seems to be moving in slow motion. That's the martial art known as taichi (actually pronounced *tàijí quán*), and if you want to try to follow along, you'll usually be welcomed. While you won't really learn anything if you're just in town for a few days, it's a fun experience nonetheless. If you are in Shànghǎi for the long haul, there are plenty of places to study.

Shop till You Drop

Shopping is Shànghǎi's official pastime and it doesn't matter whether you prefer the see-and-be-seen scene of megamalls or true browsing in independent boutiques, creating your own individual style – no matter how crazy the look – is an essential part of Shanghainese identity. Guys, take note: many Shanghainese women expect their boyfriends to accompany them on shopping excursions and, just as importantly, to carry their purse or handbag.

Get on the Bus

The prevalence of cheap taxis makes it all too easy to steer clear of public transport, but hopping on a bus is an easy way to become part of the local fabric and is generally more interesting than the metro. Note that a sense of adventure and specific instructions (the name of your destination written down in Chinese) are required.

For Free

Shànghǎi is a surprisingly pricey destination. And as inflation and the value of the yuan continue to climb, it's only going to become more expensive. If you're on a budget or just want to save your máo, be sure to check out these recommendations.

Museums

Shànghǎi Museum

Shànghǎi's premier museum, this excellent venue walks you through the pages of Chinese history as depicted in various art forms such as porcelain and landscape painting. The number of daily visitors is limited, so don't show up too late.

Bund History Museum

Located beneath the uninspired Monument to the People's Heroes at the north end of the Bund, this museum introduces the history of the area through a selection of old photographs and maps.

M50

The largest complex of modern art galleries in Shànghǎi, housed in an industrial setting.

Shànghǎi Museum of Public Security

Original gangsta paraphernalia from the 1930s as well as assorted police weaponry.

Shànghǎi Arts & Crafts Museum

Almost free (but not quite), this gorgeous building features live displays of traditional arts and crafts.

Post Museum

Head up to the rooftop of the Post Museum for fabulous panoramas of the city.

CY Tung Maritime Museum

Learn more about the great 15th-century explorer Zheng He here.

Communist Heritage

Make sure you have your passport with you to gain access to the Site of the 1st National Congress of the CCP, Zhou Enlai's Former Residence and the Former Residence of Mao Zedong.

Walks

The Bund

The Bund is the first port of call for most visitors to Shànghǎi. Thankfully, strolling the promenade and peeking inside the historic buildings here doesn't cost a cent. Restaurants and bars here are mostly upscale; for the cheapest pit stops with a view, head to either the Captain's Bar or Atanu.

Walking Tours

Follow one of our walking tours as they guide you around the backstreets and historic neighbourhoods of the Bund, Old Town, French Concession and Jìng'ān.

Parks

Shànghǎi parks are great for people watching. There is almost always something going on, whether it's people practising *qìgōng*, playing chess or holding impromptu music concerts.

Food for sale at Yùyuán Bazaar (p76)

Eating

Brash, stylish and always on the move, Shànghǎi's culinary scene is a reflection of the city's craving for foreign trends and tastes. As much an introduction to regional Chinese cuisine as it is a magnet for talented chefs from around the globe, Shànghǎi has staked a formidable claim as the Middle Kingdom's trendiest dining destination.

NEED TO KNOW

Price Ranges

$	up to ¥60 a meal
$$	¥60–160 a meal
$$$	over ¥160 a meal

Opening Hours

In general, the Chinese eat earlier than Westerners. Restaurants serve lunch from 11am to 2pm and then often close until 5pm, when the dinner crowd starts arriving, and then carry on serving until 11pm. Smaller restaurants are more flexible though, and if you're hungry out of hours they're often happy to accommodate you.

Ordering

Almost all of the places listed in this guide have English and/or picture menus unless noted, although they aren't always as comprehensive (or comprehensible) as the Chinese version. In any case, if you see a dish on someone else's table that looks absolutely delicious, just point at it when the waiter comes – no one will think you're being rude. For a Menu Decoder, see p267.

Tipping

Tipping is not done in the majority of restaurants. High-end international restaurants are another matter and while tipping is not obligatory, it is encouraged. Hotel restaurants automatically add a 15% service charge.

Reservations

At high-end restaurants or smaller places, it's sometimes necessary to book a week ahead, particularly if you want a decent table with a view. Otherwise, a couple of days in advance is fine.

Shanghainese Cuisine

Shànghǎi cuisine has been heavily influenced by the culinary styles of the neighbouring provinces, and many of the techniques, ingredients and flavours originated in the much older cities of Yángzhōu, Sūzhōu and Hángzhōu. Broadly speaking, dishes tend to be sweeter and oilier than in other parts of China.

Dim sum

The eastern provinces around the Yangzi River Delta produce China's best soy sauces, vinegars and rice wines, and the method of braising (known as 'red cooking'), using soy sauce and sugar as a base, was perfected here. As a general rule, the regional cuisine emphasises the freshness of ingredients, using sauces and seasonings only to enhance the original flavours.

DUMPLINGS

Dumplings are the easiest way to become acquainted with Shanghainese cuisine. They're simple, delicious, and have no annoying bones or unusual ingredients that might otherwise deter the naturally squeamish. The city's favourite dumpling is the *xiǎolóngbāo* ('little steamer buns'), copied everywhere else in China but only true to form here. There's an art to eating them as they're full of a delicious but scalding gelatinous broth: the trick is to avoid both burning your tongue and staining your shirt. Tradition actually attributes the invention of the dumpling – filled with pork, and in more upmarket establishments with pork and crab – to Nánxiáng, a village north of Shànghǎi city. *Xiǎolóngbāo* are normally bought by the *lóng* (steamer basket) and dipped in vinegar.

Another Shanghainese speciality is *shēngjiān,* scallion-and-sesame-seed-coated dumplings that are fried in an enormous flat-bottomed wok, which is covered with a wooden lid. These are also pork-based; again, watch out for the palate-scorching scalding oil.

On the sweet side are *tāng yuán* (also known as *yuán xiāo*), a small glutinous

Top: Food preparation at street stall

Right: Nánxiáng Steamed Bun Restaurant (p83)

GARDEL BERTRAND / GETTY IMAGES ©

rice ball filled with sweet fillings such as black-sesame paste or red-bean paste and traditionally eaten during the Lantern Festival; they're utterly delectable. You can find them easily in Qībǎo (p164) at any time of year.

APPETISERS

Many visitors unfamiliar with Chinese cuisine tend to skip right through the first part of the menu, which is always dedicated to cold starters. This is a mistake, however, as these tiny servings are not only delicious, they also provide a refreshing counterpoint to the heavier dishes that follow. Some of Shànghǎi's most popular cold starters are marinated in rice wine or liquor – these are referred to as 'drunken' dishes, and can include anything from raw crab or live shrimp to steamed chicken. Obviously you should use your own judgement when eating raw shellfish, but in reputable restaurants this should be fine. Other popular starters include cucumber and garlic salad, as well as smoked fish and different bean-curd and mushroom combinations. If you've never tasted 'black fungus' (wood-ear fungus) before, this is your chance.

FISH & SEAFOOD

The city's position as a major port at the head of the Yangzi River Delta means that you'll find plenty of fish and seafood, especially crab, river eel and shrimp. The word for fish *(yú)* is a homonym for 'plenty' or 'surplus', and fish is a mandatory dish for most banquets and celebrations. Fish commonly appearing on Shànghǎi's menus include *guìyú* (Mandarin fish), *lúyú* (Songjiang perch), *chāngyú* (pomfret) and *huángyú* (yellow croaker). Fish is usually *qīngzhēng* (steamed) but can be stir-fried, pan-fried or grilled. Squirrel-shaped Mandarin fish is one of the more famous dishes from Sūzhōu.

Dàzháxiè (hairy crabs) are a Shànghǎi speciality between October and December. They are eaten with soy, ginger and vinegar and downed with warm Shàoxīng rice wine. The crab is thought to increase the body's *yīn*, or coldness, and so rice wine is taken lukewarm to add *yáng*.

Sichuanese

Perhaps China's most famous regional cuisine, Sìchuān cooking relies on six basic tastes, which can be combined together to form over 20 distinct flavours, including favourites like 'numbing spicy', 'sour spicy', 'fish-flavour spicy' and 'chilli-oil spicy'. One of the key ingredients of Sichuanese cuisine is the Sìchuān peppercorn, which creates a characteristic tingling sensation (known as *má*) when eaten. Although there are obviously a lot of spicy dishes, the key to a good meal, as with all Chinese cuisines, is to balance the different flavours, so even those who don't like it hot will find something to savour.

Sichuanese cuisine uses ingredients that are inexpensive and relatively easy to find, hence a lot of restaurants across China – particularly tiny family-run places – have incorporated the standards in their menus. Look for classics such as kung pao chicken *(gōngbǎo jīdīng)*, mapo tofu *(mápó dòufu)*, fish-flavoured eggplant *(yúxiāng qiézi)*, twice-cooked pork *(huíguōròu)* and dandan noodles *(dàndàn miàn)*. In Shànghǎi, one of the most popular Sichuanese dishes is a giant bowl of tender pieces of catfish or frog suspended in hot chilli oil.

CHEAP EATS

Shànghǎi's restaurants are in a whole other ballpark when compared to the rest of China – meal prices here even exceed Běijīng, and to top it off, the portions are smaller! Thankfully, you can still eat cheaply if you know where to look. Malls are always a good place to begin; they may lack atmosphere, but you will always find food inside – check the basement or top floors. The larger malls are best as they often have decent food courts.

Street food is another sure thing, though in some neighbourhoods tiny restaurants and backstreet stalls can be hard to find. Look for corner noodle shops or dumpling vendors – we've listed the most popular places in this guide, which include stalwarts such as Yang's Fry Dumplings, Jiājiā Soup Dumplings, Wúyuè Rénjiā, Ajisen and Noodle Bull. When in doubt, head to one of the official food streets for a good selection of restaurants that won't empty your wallet.

More and more restaurants catering to office workers offer good-value weekday lunch specials – to take advantage, ask for a *tàocān* (套餐).

Hunanese

Known as Xiāngcài in Chinese, Hunanese is another chilli-driven cooking tradition from China's heartland. It differs from Sichuanese cooking notably for its use of fresh chilli peppers (Sìchuān cuisine often makes use of chilli paste), which are ladled liberally onto many dishes. The heat from the peppers helps to drive moisture out of the body, helping to combat high humidity in summer. Chicken, frog, freshwater fish and pork are key ingredients; some of the all-time classics include cumin spare ribs *(zīrán páigǔ)* and smoked-pork drypot *(gānguō tuìròu)*.

COOKING SCHOOLS

Learn how to make your own *xiǎolóngbāo* at the following Shànghǎi institutions.

The Kitchen at... (www.thekitchenat.com) Great culinary school offering courses in regional Chinese and Western cuisines; good for both long-term residents and short-term visitors.

Chinese Cooking Workshop (www.chinesecookingworkshop.com) Learn different Chinese cooking styles from dim sum to Sichuanese. It also offers market tours and courses for kids.

Cantonese

Cantonese cuisine shares some similarities with Shànghǎi cuisine, notably light seasoning, an emphasis on natural flavours and lots of seafood. Many of the fanciest restaurants in Shànghǎi (generally located in hotels) are Cantonese, though these cater primarily to Hong Kong tourists and businesspeople. The Cantonese restaurants that are most popular among everyday Shanghainese are entirely different; these are based on Hong Kong–style cafeterias known as 'tea restaurants' *(chá cāntīng)*. Tea restaurants have a casual, downmarket atmosphere that's somewhat similar to an American diner, and feature an incredibly eclectic menu that ranges from Cantonese comfort food (beef with oyster sauce) to Italian pasta, Malaysian curries, sandwiches and an endless array of rice and noodle dishes.

Beef and pepper noodle dish

The other famous tradition associated with Cantonese cuisine is, of course, dim sum, which is served in a number of places in Shànghǎi, often incorporating local specialities (eg *xiǎolóngbāo*) in addition to Cantonese standards.

Muslim

Most of Shànghǎi's Muslim restaurants are run by Uighurs – Central Asians from Xīnjiāng, in China's far northwest. A refreshing alternative to the seafood and sweetness of Shanghainese cuisine, Xīnjiāng dishes consist of lots of mutton (though chicken and fish dishes are available), peppers, potatoes, cumin and delicious naan bread. Charcoal-grilled lamb kebabs are the staple here. It's not unusual for Uighur restaurants to offer evening performances of some kind (usually karaoke-style singing).

Shànghǎi's other main Muslim food vendors are tiny noodle stalls that specialise in *lāmiàn* (hand-pulled noodles), which are made fresh to order and can be served either in broth or fried.

Street Food

Shànghǎi's street food is excellent and usually quite safe to eat. It generally consists of tiny dumpling and noodle shops along with vendors selling snacks like green onion pancakes *(cōngyóu bǐng)*, steamed buns *(bāozi)*, stinky tofu *(chòu dòufu)* and baked sweet potatoes *(dìguā)*. The city's food streets are also great places to browse for snacks. Try the following destinations:

- Yunnan Rd (p69)
- Huanghe Rd (p69)
- Wujiang Rd (p131)
- Qībǎo (p164)
- North Jiangxi Rd (p152)

Hotpot

A hugely popular winter meal is *huǒguō* (hotpot), with several chain restaurants cornering the market. There are two varieties of hotpot: Sìchuān and Mongolian. A typical Sìchuān version is the circular *yuānyāng* hotpot, compartmentalised into hot (red) and mild (creamy-coloured) sections, into which you plunge vegetables and meats. Plucking the cooked chunks from the broth,

Vegetables for sale at a street market

diners dip them in different sauces and then tuck in. It's a sweat-inducing experience that is best with a group. Mongolian hotpot differ in both appearance and flavour. These are typically a brass pot with a central stove, focusing on thin slices of lamb and vegetables with a nonspicy broth. Again, they are accompanied by sauces.

Ordering for first-timers can be confusing: first you order the stock, then you order the ingredients by ticking off your choices from a long list of items (each with a different price). If there's no English list, wander to other tables with your server and point to whatever tempts you.

International

Shànghǎi is quite popular with both global superchefs and less-established international talents trying to make a name for themselves, and it's worth taking note of their presence; there are some fantastic meals to be had here. Many gastronomic destinations are not adverse to incorporating local ingredients and flavours; it's not exactly fusion cuisine, but it's not something you're likely to get back home either.

Much lower down on the food chain are Shànghǎi's pubs, which are seriously happening dining destinations, both because of the convivial atmosphere and the huge servings of comfort food. Burgers, plates of pasta and countless sandwich variations are offered by the majority of big-name drinking destinations, and while the food is neither cheap nor particularly memorable, the venues are almost always packed with locals and expats alike.

Vegetarians

Chīzhāi (vegetarianism) became something of a snobbish fad in Shànghǎi in the 1930s, when it was linked to Taoist and Buddhist groups. It's now undergoing a minor revival, although there's nothing like the huge vegetarian and vegan populations in countries such as the UK or the USA. Beyond Buddhist reasons, very few Chinese give up meat as an ethical choice. But there is a growing band of vegetarian restaurants in Shànghǎi, while monasteries all have good nonmeat restaurants.

The Chinese are masters at adding variety to vegetarian cooking and, to the bemusement of Western vegetarians, they like to create so-called 'mock meat' dishes. Chinese vegetarian food is based on *dòufu*

ANDREW ROWAT / GETTY IMAGES ©

EMANUELE CICCOMARTINO / GETTY IMAGES ©

OUROBOROS / GETTY IMAGES ©

Top: Steamed buns at food stall
Middle: Diners with Sichuanese dishes
Bottom: Spicy wok-fried dish

GARDEL BERTRAND / GETTY IMAGES ©

Nánxiáng Steamed Bun Restaurant (p83)

(bean curd or tofu), to which crafty chefs add their magic. Not only is it made to taste like any meaty food you could possibly think of, it's also made to resemble it; dishes can be made to look like everything from fish to spare ribs.

Etiquette

Strict rules of etiquette don't apply to Chinese dining; table manners are relaxed and get more so as the meal unfolds and the drinks flow. Meals commence in Confucian fashion – with good intentions, harmonic arrangement of chopsticks and a clean tablecloth – before spiralling into total Taoist mayhem, fuelled by incessant toasts with *báijiǔ* (hard liquor) or beer and furious smoking all round. Large groups in particular wreak havoc wherever they dine, with vast quantities of food often strewn across and under the table at the end of a meal.

A typical dining scenario sees a group of people seated at a round table, often with one person ordering on everyone's behalf. At Chinese restaurants, group diners never order their own dishes, but instead a selection of dishes embracing both *ròu* (meat) and *cài* (vegetables) are chosen for everyone to share. At large tables, dishes are placed on a lazy Susan, so the food revolves to each diner, occasionally knocking over full glasses of beer and causing consternation. Rice normally comes at the end of the meal. If you want it before, just ask.

The mainland Chinese dig their chopsticks into communal dishes, although some dishes are ladled out with spoons. Don't worry too much about your chopstick technique; many Chinese are equally fazed by knives and forks. Regardless of your skill, remember not to point them at people or stick them upright in bowls of rice; it's a portent of death.

TRY THIS!

Some of the most common Shanghainese dishes include the following:

Smoked fish (*xūn yú*; 熏鱼) This cold appetiser is gingery sweet and absolutely succulent when prepared correctly.

Drunken chicken (*zuìjī*; 醉鸡) Another cold appetiser that consists of steamed chicken marinated overnight in Shàoxīng rice wine.

Braised pork (*hóngshāo ròu*; 红烧肉) The uncontested king of Shanghainese home-cooking, this dish consists of tender, fatty pieces of pork stewed in sweet soy sauce.

Crystal shrimp (*shuǐjīng xiārén*; 水晶虾仁) They may not look like much, but these quick-fried shrimp undergo an elaborate preparation that results in a unique texture that's both crispy and tender.

Lion's head meatball (*shīzi tóu*; 狮子头) A large creamy meatball made of crab and minced pork, often presented as a single serving.

Crab and tofu casserole (*xièfěn dòufu*; 蟹粉豆腐) Another dish that emphasises texture, this is a good way to indulge in crab without having to spend over-the-top prices.

Peking duck

Service

If there's one thing that drives foreigners in Shànghǎi crazy, it's the service. To be fair, some waiters and waitresses really are completely disorganised and indifferent, but the real underlying problem here is twofold: first, Chinese and Westerners have completely different expectations when it comes to what constitutes good service; second, overcoming the language barrier is no trifling matter. Remember that many waitstaff will only have a minimal command of English (if they speak it at all), and unless you are able to hold your own in Mandarin, there will inevitably be a few mix-ups and scowling faces somewhere along the way. Occasionally a waiter or waitress will be so intimidated by a non-Chinese-speaking customer that they will, unfortunately, completely ignore you, especially if it's a busy night. If you're having trouble, shout out *Fúwùyuán!* (Waiter/Waitress!) loudly – don't be shy – and someone will usually appear.

If you're eating at a smaller place without a menu, be sure to clarify the total price *before* you finalise your order.

Eating by Neighbourhood

- ➡ **The Bund & People's Square** (p66) From superchefs to food streets.
- ➡ **Old Town** (p82) Famous dumplings.
- ➡ **French Concession** (p96) The epicentre of Shànghǎi dining.
- ➡ **Jìng'ān** (p125) Popular vegetarian restaurants and sumptuous Chinese.
- ➡ **Pǔdōng** (p140) Dinner with a view.

Lonely Planet's Top Choices

Yang's Fry Dumplings (p68) Simple, greasy and oh-so-good.

Dī Shuǐ Dòng (p97) Country cookin' and Húnán chilli peppers.

Spicy Joint (p100) Blistering hot Sìchuān classics.

Din Tai Fung (p129) Glorified street food from the renegade province.

Lost Heaven (p101) A taste of paradise, from Yúnnán with love.

Fu 1039 (p101) Old-fashioned charm, succulent Shanghainese.

Best by Budget

$

Noodle Bull (p102)

Cha's (p98)

Sìchuān Citizen (p102)

South Memory (p68)

Wagas (p130)

Guǒyuán (p152)

$$

Yīn (p101)

Southern Barbarian (p97)

Gǔyì Húnán Restaurant (p101)

Haiku (p101)

Crystal Jade (p129)

Kebabs on the Grille (p83)

$$$

Ultraviolet (p67)

el Willy (p83)

M on the Bund (p67)

Xīndàlù (p153)

Best Stylish Shanghainese

Jesse (Xīnjíshì) (p101)

Shànghǎi Min (p105)

Diǎn Shí Zhāi Xiǎo Yàn (p98)

1221 (p166)

Lynn (p129)

Lè Shēng (p103)

Best Hole-in-the-Wall Shanghainese

Lánxīn Cāntīng (p97)

Bai's Restaurant (p104)

Bǎoluó Jiǔlóu (p103)

Wǒ Jiā Cāntīng (p104)

Grape Restaurant (p105)

Best Gastronomic

Mr & Mrs Bund (p67)

T8 (p97)

Jean Georges (p67)

Shintori Null II (p102)

Best Dumplings

Nánxiáng Steamed Bun Restaurant (p83)

Jiājiā Soup Dumplings (p69)

Shaanxi Dumplings (p69)

Lóngpáo Xièhuáng Tāngbāo (p167)

Best Noodles

Kungfu Noodles (p102)

Ajisen (p68)

Wúyuè Rénjiā (p69)

Wèixiāng Zhāi (p99)

Best Vegetarian

Vegetarian Lifestyle (p129)

Gōngdélín (p130)

Jade Buddha Temple Vegetarian Restaurant (p131)

Jen Dow Vegetarian Restaurant (p130)

Sōngyuèlóu (p84)

Best Cafes

Ginger (p103)

Ferguson Lane (p103)

Kommune (p99)

Element Fresh (p105)

Baker & Spice (p130)

Best by Cuisine

Sichuanese

Yúxìn Chuāncài (p67)

Pǐnchuān (p102)

South Beauty (p104)

Shǔ Dì Làzi Yú Guǎn (p104)

Nina's Sìchuān House (p69)

Cantonese

Tsui Wah (p102)

Vivi Kitchen (p98)

Charme (p68)

Xian Yue Hien (p103)

Southeast Asian

Pho Real (p102)

Simply Thai (p104)

Coconut Paradise (p105)

Food Fusion (p98)

Bali Laguna (p130)

Japanese

Kagen (p101)

Bankura (p98)

Hotpot

Hǎi Dǐ Lāo (p129)

Qímín Organic Hotpot (p129)

Dolar Shop (p68)

Uighur

Xīnjiāng Fēngwèi Restaurant (p160)

Afanti Restaurant (p154)

Xībó Grill (p102)

Drinking & Nightlife

Shànghǎi loves its lychee martinis and cappuccinos to go, and with such exclusively minded tastes, it's no surprise that even former basketball star Yao Ming has decided to get in on the action with his own cabernet sauvignon brand. But don't be intimidated by the glitzy exterior: underneath is a happening nightlife scene that keeps everyone – VIP or not – plenty entertained.

Bars

While bars today are frequented predominantly by expats and internationally minded locals, the race is on to capture the domestic market. In Běijīng there's a more populist approach, but Shànghǎi has stayed true to its roots: it's all about looking flash, sipping craft cocktails or imported wine, and tapping into the insatiable appetite for new trends. As might be expected, new bars pop up and disappear with impressive rapidity, but the upside to the intense competition is that weekly specials and happy hours (generally from 5pm to 8pm) manage to keep Shànghǎi affordable.

Cafes

Cafe culture is the latest rage to sweep Shànghǎi and though you'd be hard-pressed to find a decent teahouse within a 20km radius, lattes and sandwiches served at hip wireless hangouts - some familiar names, some not - are all over the place. Another common sight are the street stalls selling bubble tea *(zhēnzhū nǎichá),* a fabulously addictive Taiwanese milk tea with tapioca balls, and all sorts of related spin-offs, like hot ginger drinks or freshly puréed papaya smoothies.

Clubbing

Shànghǎi's clubs are mostly big, glossy places devoted to playing mainstream house, techno and hip hop. The offerings are getting better, and each year sees at least one new opening that strives to go beyond mainstream expectations. A number of big-name DJs are flying in these days, which has helped boost interest among the locals, although the crowds are still predominantly made up of Westerners, Hong Kong and Taiwanese expats, and young, rich Shanghainese. Unsurprisingly, there's a lot of turnover here; check the local listings for the latest up-to-date hotspots.

Drinking & Nightlife by Neighbourhood

- **The Bund & People's Square** (p50) The Bund has glamour and gorgeous views in equal measure.
- **French Concession East** (p105) Nice crop of cafes and bohemian hideaways.
- **French Concession West** (p109) The most alcohol-saturated stretch of the city, with plenty of clubs, pubs and microbreweries.
- **Jìng'ān** (p131) Sports bars and a few divey faves.
- **Pǔdōng** (p144) It's all about the views in Pǔdōng.

NEED TO KNOW

Opening Hours

➡ Many bars offer a full dining menu and open for lunch at 11am, and even earlier for weekend brunch. Bars that only serve drinks are more erratic; they might open anywhere between 4.30pm and 8pm.

➡ For the most part, last call at bars is 2am, but there are a handful of places that stay open till 4am or 5am.

➡ Clubs generally don't get going until 10pm at the earliest and stay open until 2am on weekdays and 5am on weekends. Most close on Sunday and Monday.

➡ Sports bars will sometimes open around the clock, depending on what time the big game is on. You can even get a pancake breakfast at some places.

Prices

➡ On average, expect to spend roughly ¥35 for bottled beer, ¥70 for cocktails, ¥25 for coffee and ¥15 for tea and juice.

Event Listings

➡ **Smart Shanghai** (www.smartshanghai.com)

➡ **Time Out** (www.timeoutshanghai.com)

➡ **City Weekend** (www.cityweekend.com.cn/shanghai)

Lonely Planet's Top Choices

Glamour Bar (p70) Iconic views, great drinks and a first-rate events line-up.

Bell Bar (p105) The place to kick back in Tiánzǐfáng.

Apartment (p110) Loft-style bar with drinks, dining and dancing.

Shelter (p110) Cold War relic turned underground dance floor.

Cotton's (p109) The French Concession villa that everyone wants to call home.

Best Views

Flair (p144)

Cloud 9 (p144)

Vue (p154)

M1NT (p71)

New Heights (p70)

Best Brews

Boxing Cat Brewery (p108)

Kāibā (p132)

Shànghǎi Brewery (p111)

Brew (p146)

Abbey Road (p110)

Best Design

Long Bar (p70)

Bar Rouge (p71)

Barbarossa (p71)

TMSK (p109)

People 7 (p111)

Old Shanghai Teahouse (p85)

Best Dives

I Love Shànghǎi (p132)

Time Passage (p111)

Jiao Bar (p70)

B&C (p132)

Captain's Bar (p71)

Best Cocktails

el Cóctel (p109)

Constellation (p110)

Alchemist (p108)

Fennel Lounge (p131)

Glo Lounge (p111)

Best Cafes

Café 85°C (p133)

Citizen Café (p108)

Lòushì (p108)

Vienna Café (p108)

Best Clubs

No 88 (p111)

Dada (p110)

Lola (p111)

Shiva (p111)

Geisha (p108)

Muse (p71)

Best Wine

Dr Wine (p110)

Franck (p103)

Café des Stagiaires (p108)

Enoterra (p109)

Fat Olive (p84)

Best Gay Bars

Eddy's Bar (p110)

Shànghǎi Studio (p111)

390 Bar (p112)

Entertainment

Shànghǎi is no longer the city of sin that went out dancing as the revolution shot its way into town, but the entertainment options have blossomed again over the past decade. Plug into the local cultural scene for a stimulating shot of gallery openings, music concerts and laid-back movie nights at the local bar.

Acrobatics

The Shànghǎi troupes are among the best in the world and spending a night watching them spinning plates on poles and contorting themselves into unfeasible anatomical positions never fails to entertain. See www.shanghaiacrobaticshow.com for an overview of performances around town.

Karaoke

Karaoke is by far China's favourite leisure activity and karaoke places, ranging from the seedy to upmarket, probably outnumber the bars and clubs in town. If you're up for crooning a few Mandopop tunes or you need to close out a business deal, why not start the night at Partyworld (p112)?

Music

Shànghǎi had a brief heyday in the jazz spotlight, back in the 1920s and '30s when big-band swing was the entertainment of choice. It remains a popular genre – there are more jazz clubs than rock venues – and even if you won't catch many household names, there are some surprisingly good musicians here.

Classical music is also big, with both local and foreign orchestras performing regularly. For traditional Chinese music, check out the programs at the Oriental Art Center or Shànghǎi Grand Theatre.

Shànghǎi's rock scene continues to evolve, though it is somewhat hamstrung by a lack of good venues. Nevertheless, a dedicated local following means that shows are often packed.

Chinese Opera

The shrill falsetto, crashing cymbals, expressive masks and painted faces of Běijīng opera are what most people have in mind when they think of Chinese opera, though the art form actually has a number of different styles. A local predecessor to Běijīng opera is the melodic Kūnjù or Kūnqǔ (Kun opera, from nearby Kūnshān), one of the oldest existing forms of Chinese opera, and best known for its 19-hour-long adaptation of the 16th-century, erotic-love ghost story *The Peony Pavilion*. One of the only Kun opera troupes in the country is based in Shànghǎi.

The main problem with going to see a traditional opera in Shànghǎi is that there are no English surtitles and certain performances can be, well, quite lengthy. But the plotlines are relatively simple, which makes following the action not impossible. Nonetheless, before snatching up tickets for *A Dream of Red Mansions* at the Shànghǎi Grand Theatre, try the Běijīng opera highlights show in the Yìfū Theatre first.

NEED TO KNOW

Tickets

➡ Tickets for all of Shànghǎi's performing-arts events can be purchased at the venues where the performances take place.

➡ Tickets are also available from **Smart Ticket** (www.smartshanghai.com/smartticket)

➡ **Shanghai Cultural Information & Booking Centre** (上海文化信息票务中心; Shànghǎi Wénhuà Xìnxī Piàowù Zhōngxīn; Map p294; ☎6217 2426; www.culture.sh.cn; 272 Fengxian Rd; 奉贤路272号; Ⓜ West Nanjing Rd), which is directly behind the Westgate Mall on West Nanjing Rd, also sells tickets. It often has tickets available when other places have sold out.

➡ The Shanghai Cultural Information & Booking Centre office carries a handy monthly bilingual *Calendar of Performances in Shanghai*, although you can find the same information in the local press.

Lonely Planet's Top Choices

Shànghǎi Centre Theatre (p133) Spend an evening with the acrobats.

Fairmont Peace Hotel Jazz Bar (p71) Swing with Shànghǎi's most famous – and oldest – jazz band.

Shànghǎi Grand Theatre (p72) Ballet, opera and classical music on the biggest stage in town.

Yùyīntáng (p167) Shànghǎi's premier indie venue, where the amps get cranked up to 11.

Best Jazz & Rock Venues

Cotton Club (p112)

JZ Club (p113)

Brown Sugar (p112)

House of Blues & Jazz (p71)

MAO Livehouse (p112)

Best Classical Venues

Yìfū Theatre (p71)

Oriental Art Center (p146)

Shànghǎi Concert Hall (p72)

Shànghǎi Conservatory of Music (p113)

Shànghǎi Gǔqín Cultural Foundation (p113)

Best Cinemas

Cathay Theatre (p112)

UME International Cineplex (p112)

Peace Cinema (p72)

Kodak Cinema World (p161)

Studio City (p133)

Shànghǎi Film Art Centre (p167)

Best Movie Screenings

Vienna Café (p90)

Alliance Française (p250)

Apartment (p110)

Dada (p110)

Old Film Café (p154)

Best Chinese Opera & Theatre

Yìfū Theatre (p71)

Kūn Opera House (p161)

Daguan Theater (p146)

Píngtán Museum (p179)

Qībǎo Shadow Puppet Museum (p164)

Xīntiāndì branch of Shanghai Tang (p115)

KARL JOHAENTGES / GETTY IMAGES ©

Shopping

No economic recession here – after the austerity of the communist years, the Shanghainese have returned to consumer culture with a vengeance. 'Shop, shop, shop' has become the unofficial mantra, and everyone, from trendy 20-somethings to store-minding grandmothers, is eager to make up for lost time. All the better for visitors: Shànghǎi shopping has never been so good.

Boutiques

The boutiques in the French Concession are where the most interesting finds are going to be, though given the sheer number of tiny shops, it can be hard to separate the wheat from the chaff. Start with our recommended shopping strips (p117) to get a feel for local fashion before you cross town for a specific store. Keep in mind that unless you are petite, finding the right size can be a potential stumbling block.

Tailor-Made Clothes

If you're worried about finding the right size, the Old Town fabric markets may be the solution. All manner of textiles can be found here, from synthetic to silk and cashmere – compare fabric and prices at different stands to ensure no one is blatantly ripping you off. Suits, trousers, shirts, dresses and scarves can be made at such places in as little as 24 hours (expect to pay extra), though a one-week turnaround is more realistic. For traditional Chinese *qípáo*

NEED TO KNOW

Opening Hours

Most shops are open from 10am to 10pm daily, though government-run stores often close at 6pm while smaller boutiques may not open until noon. Nonstandard opening hours are listed in the reviews. Yùyuán Bazaar and Dongtai Road Antique Market are best visited early in the day.

Haggling

If negotiating in pidgin Chinese, be very careful of similar-sounding numbers, like 14 *(shísì)* and 40 *(sìshí)*, and 108 *(yībǎilíngbā)* and 180 *(yībǎibā)*, as these offer great potential for misunderstanding, deliberate or otherwise.

Customs

Technically, nothing over 200 years old can be taken out of China, but you'll be very lucky if you come across any antiques in Shànghǎi that old. If you are buying a reproduction, make sure the dealer provides paperwork stating that it is not an antique. Dealers should also provide the proper receipts and paperwork for any antiques. Keep the receipts along with the business card of the dealer, just in case.

Phrases to Know

- *Duōshao qián?* – How much?
- *Tài guì le!* – Too expensive!
- *Tài xiǎo.* – Too small.
- *Tài dà.* – Too big.
- *Bù yào.* – I don't want it.

(cheongsam) and jackets, head to South Maoming Rd or Tiánzǐfáng in the French Concession.

Counterfeits

'In Shànghǎi, everything can be faked except for your mother', or so the saying goes. Counterfeit goods are ubiquitous; even if you've set out to buy a genuine item, there's no guarantee that's what you're going to get. Antiques in particular are almost always reproductions: the best word of advice is to buy something because you like it, not because you think it has historic value.

DVD stores and fake markets are popular destinations for visitors and can make for a fun browse, but remember that although your purchases might not cost much (provided you're a decent bargainer), they most likely break international copyright law, and they might not last that long either.

Haggling

In the markets, haggling over prices is all part of the shopping experience. The most common method of haggling is for the vendor to display the price on a calculator and hand the calculator to you. You then laugh and punch in 10% to 25% of their price, the vendor shakes their head and emits a cry that suggests you just insulted their ancestors, comes down a little and gives the calculator back to you. This goes on until the price drops by at least 50%. At some of the more touristy places, like Yùyuán Bazaar, vendors will go as low as 25% of the original price. But at stores where a discount is not normally offered, you may only get 10% or 20% off.

It often pays to smile, shrug and walk away to a nearby stall selling exactly the same thing. Most times the vendor will chase you down and get you to agree to a deal. Do bear in mind, though, that the point is to achieve a mutually acceptable price and not to screw the vendor into the ground. It's always best to smile, which will help keep negotiations light even if you don't ultimately agree on a sale.

Shipping

Most reputable shops will take care of insurance, customs and shipping for larger items, though find out first exactly what the dealer covers. Separate charges may materialise for handling, packaging, customs duty and quarantine, driving the shipping charges above the price of the item! Also consider how much it will cost to get the goods from the shipping port to your home.

Shipping clothing, curios and household items on your own is generally not a problem and China Post has an excellent packing system for airmailing light items.

Lonely Planet's Top Choices

Tiánzǐfáng (p113) Great collection of shops in an artsy enclave.

Old Street (p87) All your souvenir needs, from calendar posters to Mao-era kitsch.

Spin (p134) The coolest china in China.

AP Xīnyáng Fashion & Gifts Market (p147) The mother of all fake markets.

Amy Lin's Pearls (p134) Fresh- and saltwater pearls at unbeatable prices.

Best Boutiques

NuoMi (p116)

William the Beekeeper (p116)

Heirloom (p115)

XinleLu.com (p117)

Ba Yan Ka La (p117)

Chouchou Chic (p115)

Best Souvenirs & Antiques

Dongtai Road Antique Market (p87)

Fúyòu Antique Market (p87)

Art Deco (p134)

Lòushì (p108)

Yùnhóng Chopsticks Shop (p72)

Best Art

Shànghǎi Museum Art Store (p73)

Liúli China Museum Shop (p113)

Propaganda Poster Art Centre (p95)

Duǒyúnxuān Art Shop (p72)

Best Shoes

PCS (Pop Classic Sneakers) (p115)

Sūzhōu Cobblers (p72)

100 Change & Insect (p115)

The Thing (p116)

Best Teaware

Pottery Workshop (p118)

Yú (p117)

Zhēnchálín Tea (p114)

Blue Shànghǎi White (p72)

Tiānshān Tea City (p167)

Jǐngdézhèn Porcelain Artware (p134)

Best Jewellery & Handicrafts

Brocade Country (p117)

Nine (p115)

Paramita (p117)

Best Local Fashion

Annabel Lee (p72)

Xīntiāndì Style (p115)

Madame Mao's Dowry (p117)

la vie (p114)

Urban Tribe (p118)

Best Markets

Shíliùpù Fabric Market (p86)

South Bund Fabric Market (p87)

Qīpǔ Market (p154)

Flower, Bird, Fish & Insect Market (p78)

Han City Fashion & Accessories Plaza (p134)

Best Bookstores

Foreign Languages Bookstore (p167)

Garden Books (p116)

Shànghǎi Book Traders Used Books (p73)

Best Electronics

Cybermart (p116)

Electronics Market (p155)

Apple Store (p116)

Metro City (p161)

Xīngguāng Photography Equipment (p116)

Explore Shànghǎi

SHÀNGHĂI'S TOP SIGHTS

Neighbourhoods at a Glance

❶ The Bund & People's Square (p50)

Shànghǎi's most famous landmark is the Bund, the magnificent stretch of colonial-era buildings that lines the western bank of the Huángpǔ River. It's the first stop for visitors, and the historic architecture here is home to an array of exclusive restaurants, bars, shops and hotels.

Running perpendicular from the waterfront is East Nanjing Rd – a maelstrom of shoppers, department stores and neon lights – which eventually gives way to the city's heart, People's Square. The de facto centre of town, this large open space is studded with museums and ringed by skyscrapers.

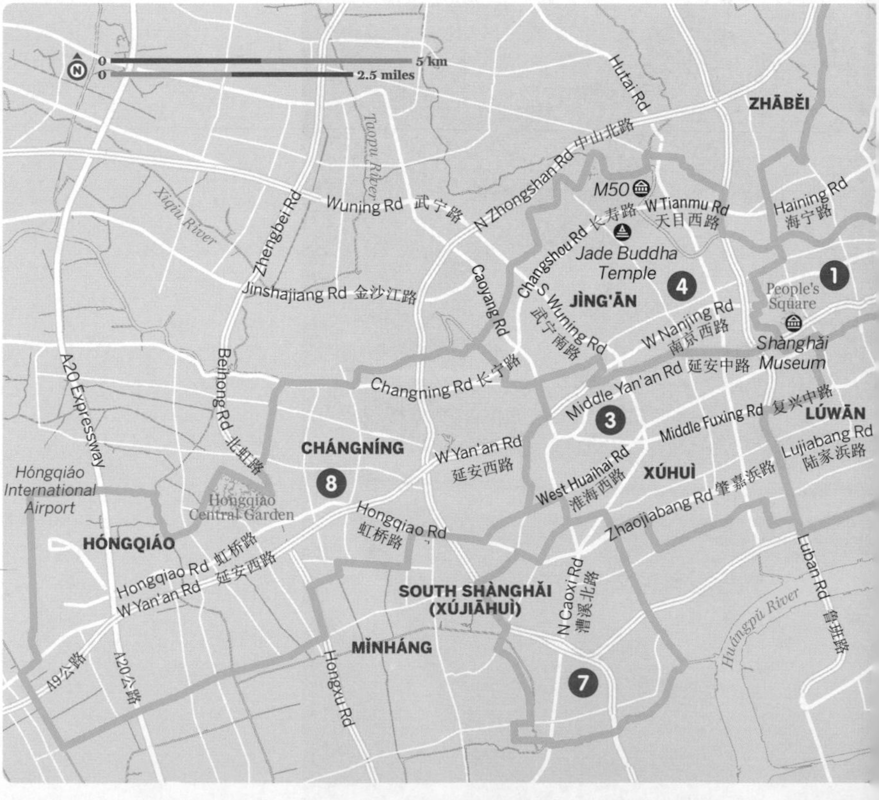

❷ Old Town (p74)

The original city core and the only part of Shànghǎi to predate the 1850s, the Old Town is a favourite with visitors hoping to get a glimpse of 'traditional' China. Many of the older buildings have been replaced with modern apartment blocks, but there are still more temples here than in the rest of the city combined, and pockets of atmosphere remain.

❸ French Concession (p88)

The most stylish part of town, the former French Concession is where the bulk of Shànghǎi's disposable income is spent. The low-rise leafy backstreets are all about shopping, dining and entertainment, but a scattering of museums make the former concession – now an amalgam of several distinct neighbourhoods – a cultural destination as well.

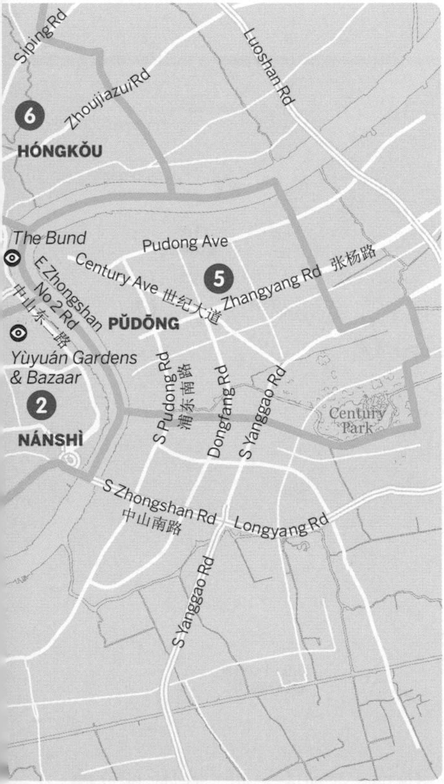

❹ Jìng'ān (p120)

North of the French Concession extends the vibrant commercial district of Jìng'ān, an expat-friendly domain focused on the bustling West Nanjing Rd, with an abundance of period architecture, malls, top-end hotels and appealing *lòngtáng* (laneway) architecture. Further away is the grittier railway station area, where the city's most famous Buddhist temple and art enclave are located.

❺ Pŭdōng (p136)

Needing little introduction, Pŭdōng is new Shànghǎi, sprawling east from the Huángpǔ River's opposite bank. A dazzling panorama of high-altitude five-star hotels, banks, Maglev trains, giant TV screens and, less glamorously, faceless residential towers, it's all set to the constant roar of traffic and construction work.

❻ Hóngkǒu & North Shànghǎi (p148)

Hóngkǒu extends north from Sūzhōu Creek and the Bund, and is a less polished realm of old lanes and working-class textures. The former American- and later Japanese-controlled concession, Hóngkǒu is slowly building up speed as a redevelopment area – the biggest project to open here recently was the International Cruise Terminal.

❼ Xújiāhuì & South Shànghǎi (p156)

An extension of the French Concession, Xújiāhuì's Jesuit history and the prestigious Jiāotōng University contrast spectacularly with the huge shopping centres that now surround its main intersection.

❽ West Shànghǎi (p162)

You don't get a sense for just how vast the city is until you start to head west, where the residential and office towers, conference centres and busy highways of Shànghǎi's suburban districts stretch into the horizon. The focal point here is Hóngqiáo's airport and railway station, though the old canal town of Qībǎo is worth a visit.

The Bund & People's Square

THE BUND | PEOPLE'S SQUARE

Neighbourhood Top Five

❶ Stroll along the **Bund** (p52) promenade, then watch Pŭdōng light up through a martini glass.

❷ Contemplate the masterpieces on display at the **Shànghǎi Museum** (p57).

❸ Propel your consciousness into the year 2020 at the **Shànghǎi Urban Planning Exhibition Hall** (p65).

❹ Catch up on the latest in contemporary Chinese art at the **Rockbund Art Museum** (p61).

❺ Plunge into the neon-lit crowds on **East Nanjing Road** (p61).

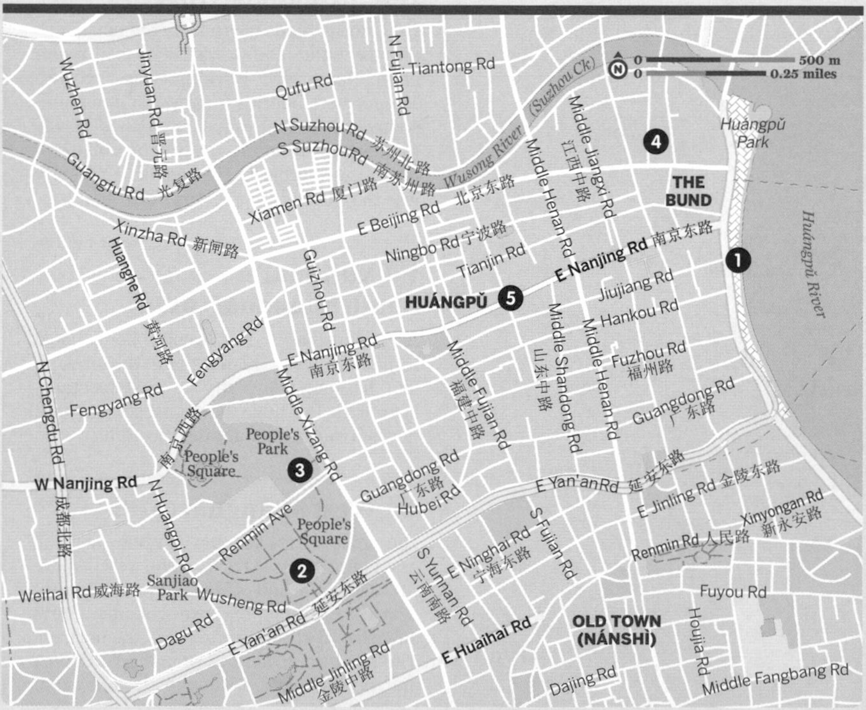

For more detail of this area, see Map p280 ➡

Explore: The Bund & People's Square

Shànghǎi's standout spectacle, the Bund (外滩) has emerged as a designer retail and dining zone, and the city's most exclusive boutiques, restaurants and hotels see the strip as the only place to be. The optimum activity here is to simply stroll, contrasting the bones of the past with the futuristic geometry of Pǔdōng's skyline.

The streets west from the waterfront form a gritty commercial district housed in the shells of concession-era buildings, mixed with newer skyscrapers and office towers. Even the most casual of wanders divulge sudden architectural gems; see our walking tour (p64) for an introduction to the area known as the Rockbund.

Beyond this is People's Square (人民广场), a rare swathe of open space ringed by skyscrapers. The de facto city centre, it's home to a clutch of museums, entertainment venues, malls, a park and the city hall. Much less austere than Běijīng's Tiān'ānmén Square, People's Square is free of the rigid geometry and paranoia of the capital's better-known rectangle, but crowds can be intense.

Linking the Bund with People's Square is East Nanjing Rd, once China's most famous shopping street. Mostly pedestrian, it's now home to a bonanza of department stores, gaudy neon signs and determined English-speaking girls latching onto foreign men, seeking kick-backs from cafes they drag their victims to. If you don't mind the crowds, it's a fun walk.

Local Life

- **Dumplings** Sample *shēngjiān* at Yang's Fry Dumplings (p68) or *xiǎolóngbāo* at Jiājiā Soup Dumplings (p69) or Nánxiáng Steamed Bun Restaurant (p69).
- **Museum Hopping** Spend a rainy day checking out the museums at People's Square (p65).
- **Shopping** Join the throngs strolling East Nanjing Rd (p72), crowding into malls like Raffles City (p73) or browsing for discounts in the subterranean stalls around the People's Sq metro station.

Getting There & Away

- **Metro** The Bund is a 10-minute walk east from the East Nanjing Rd stop (lines 2 and 10). People's Sq, one of the city's busiest stations, is served by lines 1, 2 and 8.
- **Pedicabs** Drivers hang out in side streets along the Bund and charge ¥10 (total) to Yùyuán Gardens.
- **Bund Sightseeing Tunnel** Runs from the Bund to Pǔdōng under the Huángpǔ River; see p61 for details.
- **Tourist Train** Runs the length of East Nanjing Rd's pedestrianised section (tickets ¥2) from Middle Henan Rd to the Shànghǎi No 1 Department Store.

Lonely Planet's Top Tip

Watch out for young people posing as out-of-town students who work the main tourist drags, approaching visitors and engaging them in conversation. At first, they seem friendly enough. You help them take a picture, chat about China and then they invite you to a traditional tea ceremony. It sounds intriguing, but don't do it. You'll get the tea all right, but you'll also get a bill for about US$100 and a private escort to the closest ATM machine.

Best Places to Eat

- Lost Heaven (p66)
- Yang's Fry Dumplings (p68)
- Mr & Mrs Bund (p67)
- Yúxìn Chuāncài (p67)
- M on the Bund (p67)

For reviews, see p66

Best Places to Drink

- Glamour Bar (p70)
- New Heights (p70)
- Long Bar (p70)
- Jiao Bar (p70)
- Barbarossa (p71)

For reviews, see p70

Best Shopping

- Annabel Lee (p72)
- SūzhōuCobblers (p72)
- Shànghǎi Museum Art Store (p73)
- Shànghǎi No 1 Food Store (p73)
- Yùnhóng Chopsticks Shop (p72)

For reviews, see p72

PETER ADAMS / GETTY IMAGES ©

TOP SIGHTS THE BUND

Symbolic of colonial Shànghǎi, the Bund (外滩; Wàitān) was the city's Wall St, a place of feverish trading and fortunes made and lost. Originally a towpath for dragging barges of rice, it's remained the first port of call for visitors since passengers began disembarking here over a century ago, although today it's the trendy restaurants and views of Pǔdōng that beckon the crowds.

DON'T MISS...

- The Promenade
- Fairmont Peace Hotel
- HSBC Building
- Dining or drinks with a view

PRACTICALITIES

- Map p280
- East Zhongshan No 1 Rd; 中山东一路
- MEast Nanjing Rd

Promenade

The Bund offers a horde of things to do, but most visitors head straight for the riverside promenade to pose for photos in front of Pǔdōng's ever-changing skyline. The area is essentially open around the clock, but it's at its best in the early morning, when locals are out practising taichi, or in the early evening, when both sides of the river are lit up and the majesty of the waterfront is at its grandest. The promenade begins at Huángpǔ Park; you can follow it 1km to the Bund's south end at the Meteorological Signal Tower.

Huángpǔ Park

China's first public **park** (黄浦公园; Huángpǔ Gōngyuán; Map p280; MEast Nanjing Rd) was laid out in 1886 by a Scottish gardener shipped out to Shànghǎi especially for that purpose. Located at the northern end of the Bund, the park's anachronistic **Monument to the People's Heroes** hides the entrance to the **Bund History Museum** (外滩历史纪念馆; Wàitān Lìshǐ Jìniànguǎn; admission free; 9am-4pm Mon-Fri), which contains a collection of old maps and photographs.

Jardine Matheson

Standing at No 27 on the Bund is the former headquarters of early opium traders Jardine Matheson, which went on to become one of the most powerful trading houses in Hong Kong and Shànghǎi. Also known as EWO, it was the first foreign company to erect a building on the Bund in 1851, and later invested in China's earliest railways and cotton mills, and even operated a popular brewery. The current building was completed in 1922. In 1941 the British Embassy occupied the top floor, facing the Germany Embassy across the road in the Glen Line Building, at No 28. Jardine Matheson now holds the House of Roosevelt, which is quite possibly China's largest wine cellar and bar.

Bank of China

Originally established in 1897, the Bank of China (Map p280), at No 23, relocated its headquarters from Běijīng to Shànghǎi in the 1920s, undergoing a major transformation from state bureaucracy to a market-driven business. Although the bank has occupied this address since 1923, the present building was only begun in 1935 and was originally designed to be the tallest building in the city at 33 storeys high. The Sino-Japanese War interrupted construction, however, and when it was finally opened in 1942, it was only 17 storeys in height, its blue-tiled roof one metre shorter than its neighbour.

Fairmont Peace Hotel

Lording it over the corner of East Nanjing Rd and East Zhongshan Rd is the most famous building on the Bund, the landmark Fairmont Peace Hotel (Map p280), constructed between 1926 and 1929. It was originally built as Sassoon House, with Victor Sassoon's famous Cathay Hotel on the 4th to 7th floors. It wasn't for the hoi polloi, with a guest list running to Charlie Chaplin, George Bernard Shaw and Noel Coward, who penned *Private Lives* here in four days in 1930 when he had the flu. Sassoon himself spent weekdays in his personal suite on the top floor, just beneath the green pyramid. The building was renamed the Peace Hotel in 1956.

Even if you aren't a guest, pop in to admire the wonderful art-deco lobby and magnificent rotunda or listen to the old jazz band (see p71) in the evening. It's also possible to arrange an hour-long tour (¥100) of the premises through the **Peace Gallery** (☎6321 6888, ext 6751; ⏲10am-7pm), a small, museum-like space that contains hotel memorabilia and is hidden up a flight of stairs near the main entrance. It's recommended you book a half-day in advance.

WHAT'S IN A NAME?

The Bund gets its Anglo-Indian name from the embankments built up to discourage flooding (a *band* is an embankment in Hindi). There's some debate over how to say the word, though given its origins, it's likely the correct pronunciation is 'bunned', not 'booned'.

The Shànghǎi Club, at No 2 on the Bund, originally had 20 rooms for residents, but its most famous accoutrement was its bar – at 34m said to be the longest in Asia. Once one of the most exclusive spots in the city, the building lost considerable face in the 1990s when a KFC set up inside, but has recently found redemption with the opening of the Waldorf Astoria.

RIVER CRUISE

The Bund's monumental facades presented an imposing – if strikingly un-Chinese – view for those arriving in the busy port. For a glimpse of how it might have looked, take a river cruise (p65) departing from the docks in either Pǔxī or Pǔdōng.

The best way to get acquainted with Shànghǎi is to take a stroll along the Bund. The waterfront was the seat of colonial power from the mid-19th century onward, and the city's landmark hotels, banks and trading houses all established themselves here, gradually replacing their original buildings with even grander constructions as the decades passed.

The Bund had its golden age in the 1920s and '30s before the turmoil of war and occupation brought an end to the high life enjoyed by Shànghǎi's foreign residents. Mothballed during the communist era, it's only in the past 15 years that the strip has sought to rekindle its past glory, restoring one heritage building after another. Today, it has become China's showcase lifestyle destination, and many of the landmarks here house designer restaurants, swish cocktail bars and the flagship stores of some of the world's most exclusive brands.

Once you've wandered the promenade and ogled at the Pŭdōng skyline opposite, return to examine the Bund's magnificent facades in

CHRIS MELLOR/GETTY ©

LYNDON GIFFARD IMAGES/ALAMY ©

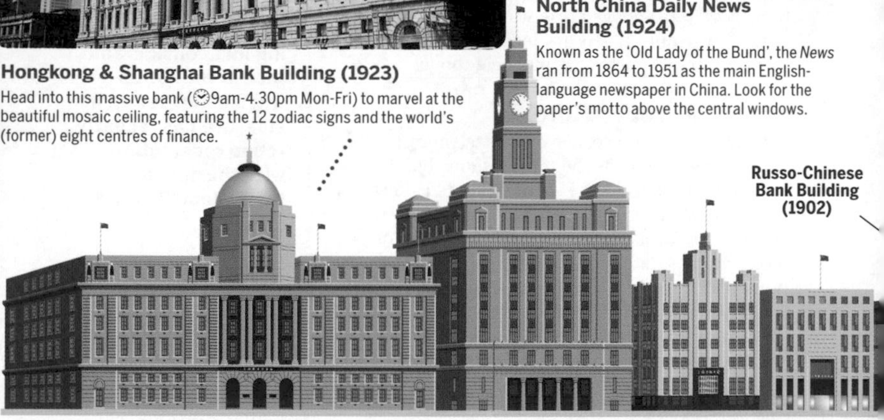

North China Daily News Building (1924)

Known as the 'Old Lady of the Bund', the *News* ran from 1864 to 1951 as the main English-language newspaper in China. Look for the paper's motto above the central windows.

Hongkong & Shanghai Bank Building (1923)

Head into this massive bank (⌚9am-4.30pm Mon-Fri) to marvel at the beautiful mosaic ceiling, featuring the 12 zodiac signs and the world's (former) eight centres of finance.

Russo-Chinese Bank Building (1902)

Custom House (1927)

One of the most important buildings on the Bund, Custom House was capped by the largest clock face in Asia and 'Big Ching', a bell modelled on London's Big Ben.

Former Bank of Communications (1947)

Bund Public Service Centre (2010)

KEITH LEVIT/ALAMY ©

Top Tip

The promenade is open around the clock, but it's at its best in the early morning, when locals are out practising taichi, or in the early evening, when both sides of the river are lit up and the majesty of the waterfront is at its grandest.

more detail and visit the interiors of those buildings open to the public.

This illustration shows the main sights along the Bund's central stretch, beginning near the intersection with East Nanjing Road. The Bund is 1km long and walking it should take around an hour. Head to the area south of the Hongkong & Shanghai Bank Building to find the biggest selection of prominent drinking and dining destinations.

FACT FILE

- **Number** of remaining heritage buildings on the Bund: 22
- **Date** the first foreign building on the Bund was constructed: 1851
- **The year** in which M on the Bund, the first high-profile Bund restaurant, opened: 1999
- **Approximate** number of wooden piles supporting the Fairmont Peace Hotel: 1600

CHRISTOPHER PITTS

Bank of China (1942)

This unusual building was originally commissioned to be the tallest building in Shànghǎi, but, probably because of Victor Sassoon's influence, wound up being one metre shorter than its neighbour.

Former Palace Hotel (1909)

Now known as the Swatch Art Peace Hotel (an artists' residence and gallery, with a top-floor restaurant and bar), this building hosted Sun Yatsen's 1911 victory celebration following his election as the first president of the Republic of China.

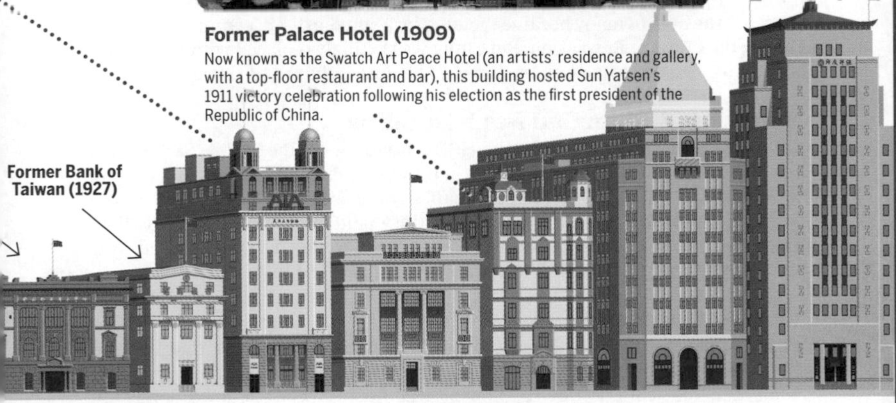

Former Bank of Taiwan (1927)

Former Chartered Bank Building (1923)

Reopened in 2004 as the upscale entertainment complex Bund 18, the building's top-floor Bar Rouge is one of the Bund's premier late-night destinations.

CHRISTOPHER PITTS

Fairmont Peace Hotel (1929)

Originally built as the Cathay Hotel, this art deco masterpiece was *the* place to stay in Shànghǎi and the crown jewel in Sassoon's real estate empire.

ASIATRAVELCOLLECTION/ALAMY ©

WINING & DINING ON THE BUND

There's no shortage of bars and restaurants on the Bund, many of which sport fabulous views. Top choices:

- **Fairmont Peace Hotel** Visit its old-fashioned Jazz Bar (p71) and street-side cafe Victor's (p68).
- **Former Palace Hotel rooftop** Part of Shook! (p68).
- **Bund 18** Features Bar Rouge (p71) and Mr & Mrs Bund (p67).
- **Five on the Bund** Home to M on the Bund (p67) and the Glamour Bar (p70).
- **Three on the Bund** With Jean Georges (p67) and New Heights (p70).
- **Waldorf Astoria** At No 2, with the Long Bar (p70).

For something more low-key, head to the Captain's Bar (p71) or Atanu (p71).

Former Palace Hotel

The Palace Hotel was China's largest hotel when completed (1909), though it was ravaged by fires in the early years and then hit by stray Chinese bombs in 1937 (one of the Bund's most tragic moments, when 720 passers-by were killed). Now owned by Swatch, it's home to an artists' residency program, with a gallery planned.

Custom House

The Custom House (No 13), established at this site in 1857 and rebuilt in 1927, is one of the most important buildings on the Bund. Capping the Custom House is Big Ching, a bell modelled on London's Big Ben. Clocks were by no means new to China, but Shànghǎi was the first city in which they gained widespread acceptance and the lives of many became dictated by a standardised, common schedule. During the Cultural Revolution, Big Ching was fittingly replaced with loudspeakers that blasted out revolutionary songs ('The East is Red') and slogans.

Hongkong & Shanghai Bank Building

Adjacent to the Custom House, the **HSBC building** (12 The Bund; ⌚9am-4.30pm Mon-Fri) was constructed in 1923. The bank was first established in Hong Kong in 1864 and in Shànghǎi in 1865 to finance trade, and soon became one of the richest in Shànghǎi, arranging the indemnity paid after the Boxer Rebellion. Enter and marvel at the beautiful mosaic ceiling, which was plastered over until its restoration in 1997. Photography is not allowed inside.

Three on the Bund

With its opening in 2004, Three on the Bund became the strip's first lifestyle destination and the model that many other Bund edifices followed. Upscale restaurants and bars occupy the upper three floors, while the lower levels are anchored by Armani, the Evian Spa and the conceptually minded **Shànghǎi Gallery of Art** (上海沪申画廊; Shànghǎi Hùshēn Huàláng; Map p280; 3rd fl, Three on the Bund, 3 East Zhongshan No 1 Rd; 中山东一路3号3楼; ⌚11am-9pm; Ⓜ East Nanjing Rd).

Meteorological Signal Tower

This **signal tower** (外滩信号台; Wàitān Xìnhào Tái; Map p280; 1 East Zhongshan No 2 Rd; 中山东二路1号; admission free; ⌚10am-5pm; Ⓜ East Nanjing Rd) was built in 1907 to replace the wooden original as well as to serve as a meteorological relay station for the tireless Shànghǎi Jesuits. The ground floor contains a small scattering of historical photographs, while the upper floors house the cafe Atanu.

PETER STUCKINGS / GETTY IMAGES © ARCHITECT XING TONGHE

TOP SIGHTS
SHÀNGHǍI MUSEUM

One of the world's premier repositories of Chinese art, the Shànghǎi Museum (上海博物馆; Shànghǎi Bówùguǎn) introduces one masterpiece after another while guiding visitors through the pages of Chinese history. Whether you prefer the meditative beauty of a landscape painting or the exquisite perfection of a Song-dynasty bowl, the luxurious curves of a Ming chair or the expressive face of a Nuo mask, this is the one museum in Shànghǎi you just can't miss.

Although you could easily spend an entire day here, many people only come with a half-day to spare. Thus, in order to get the most out of your visit, make sure to identify your interests ahead of time. It's best to arrive in the morning, as only 8000 people are allowed in daily and the lines can get long once the tour groups arrive.

Ancient Chinese Bronzes Gallery

On the ground floor is the museum's star attraction, a collection of ancient bronzes, some dating back to the 21st century BC. Many visitors are unfamiliar with this early aspect of Chinese art and for this reason the exhibit may seem less appealing than others, but Asian art enthusiasts should make a point of stopping by this unrivalled collection.

These bronzes were created during a long shamanistic period that saw the development of ancestor worship and ritual – two facets of life that would go on to dominate Confucianism.

Their diversity of shapes and versatility are striking, revealing the significance of bronze in important rituals and, later, everyday life. Objects range in shape from wine bottles and jars to goblets, weapons and even two-toned bells, once China's chief musical

DON'T MISS...

- Ancient Chinese Bronzes Gallery
- Ancient Chinese Ceramics Gallery
- Chinese Painting Gallery
- Minority Nationalities Art Gallery

PRACTICALITIES

- Map p280
- www.shanghaimuseum.net
- 201 Renmin Ave (entrance on East Yan'an Rd); 人民大道201号
- admission free
- 9am-5pm Mon-Fri (last entry 4pm)
- M People's Sq

ARCHITECTURAL INSPIRATION

Before you enter the museum, admire the exterior of the building. Designed to recall an ancient bronze *dǐng* (a three-legged cooking vessel), the building also echoes the shape of a famous bronze mirror from the Han dynasty, exhibited within the museum.

The audio guide is well worth the ¥40 (¥400 deposit, or your passport). It highlights particularly interesting items within an exhibit and offers good gallery overviews and general background information.

SEAL GALLERY

Although obscure, this gallery on the 3rd floor provides a fascinating glimpse into the niche art form of miniature carving. Seals (chops) are notable both for the intricacy of their design and the special script used on the underside, which is known to only a handful of artisans and calligraphers. Look for the two orange soapstone seals that feature incredibly detailed landscapes in miniature.

instrument. The most important ritual bronzes were *dǐng* (three- or four-legged food vessels used for cooking and serving) – one highlight in the collection is an enormous 10th-century *dǐng* weighing 200kg. Look for inscriptions on the vessels and you'll be able to witness the early evolution of Chinese writing.

Decoration is an intrinsic element of the beauty of ancient bronzes. The most common design is the stylised animal motif, depicting dragons, lions and the phoenix. This was replaced in the 10th century BC by zigzags (representing thunder) and cloud designs, and later by geometric shapes. As bronzes lost their ritual significance, decorative scenes from daily life made an appearance. Later still, stamped moulds, lost wax techniques and piece moulds enabled designs to become ever more complex.

When appreciating the bronzes, remember that they would have originally been a dazzling golden colour. Oxidisation has given them their characteristic dull green patina.

Ancient Chinese Sculpture Gallery

Also on the ground floor is the Ancient Chinese Sculpture Gallery, whose exhibits range from the funeral sculptures of the Qin and Han dynasties to the predominantly Buddhist sculptures of the following centuries, which were heavily influenced by the Indian and Central Asian styles that came to China via the Silk Road. If you're interested in Buddhism and the various representations of bodhisattvas, disciples and fierce-looking *lokapalas* (Buddhist protectors), it's certainly worth a visit. Note that the sculptures displayed were almost all painted, but only scraps of pigment survive.

Ancient Chinese Ceramics Gallery

On the 2nd floor, this is one of the largest and most fascinating galleries in the museum. The exhibits include so much more than the stereotypical blue-and-white porcelain that many think of when they hear the word 'China', and even if you don't consider yourself a fan, this is one gallery that everyone should at least take a look at.

It begins with 6000-year-old pottery excavated from just outside Shànghǎi before leapfrogging ahead to the figurines of Han times, the *sāncǎi* (polychrome) pottery of the Tang, the marvellously diverse and elegant tableware of the Song, and the sea-green celadon jars, Yíxīng teapots and vast collection of porcelain produced under the Ming and Qing.

Don't worry if you don't know your 'ewer with overhead handles in *dòucǎi*' from your 'brush-holder with *fěncǎi* design', it's all part of a luxurious learning curve. Look out for the 'celadon vase with ancient

SHÀNGHĂI MUSEUM

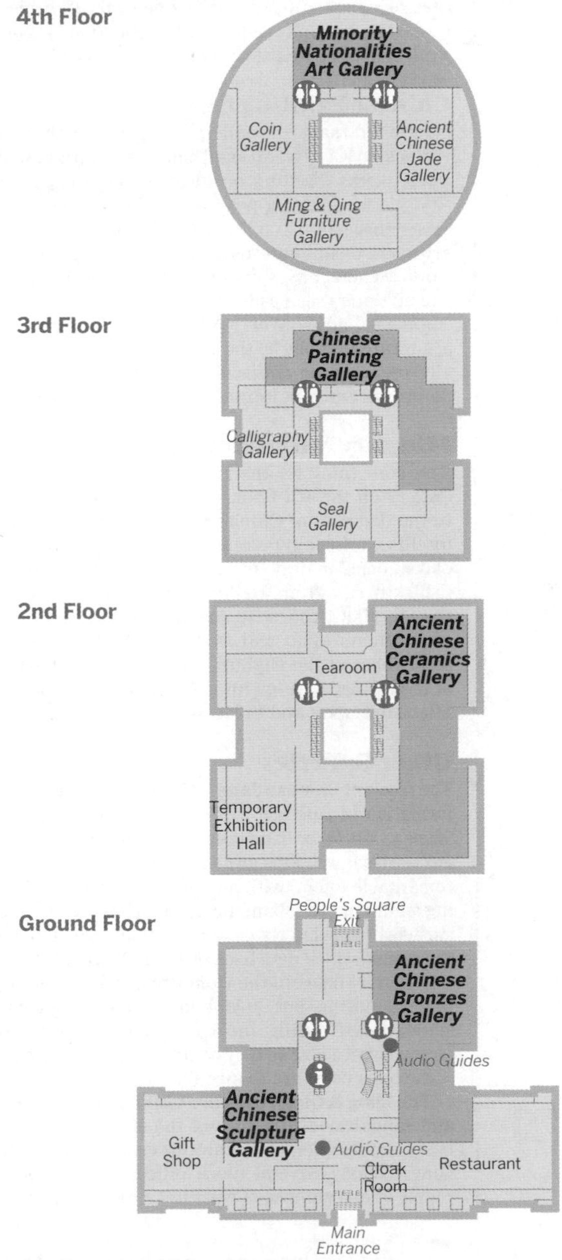

CALLIGRAPHY GALLERY

Chinese characters, which express both meaning as a word and visual beauty as an image, are one of the most fascinating aspects of the Chinese language. While the full scope of this 3rd-floor gallery may be unfathomable for those who don't read Chinese, anyone can enjoy the purely aesthetic balance of Chinese brush artistry.

There's a simple restaurant on the ground floor and a tearoom and cafe on the 2nd floor if you need a break, but the best place for a real meal is outside the museum at the nearby Yunnan Road Food Street.

THE FOUR TREASURES OF THE SCHOLAR'S STUDY

The basic tools of Chinese painting are the brush, ink, ink-stone (on which the ink is mixed) and paper. The brush, which is not only used for visual arts but also for writing, was instrumental in influencing the closely intertwined development of painting, poetry and calligraphy.

bronze design' and the delightful Ming-dynasty white-glazed porcelain statues of Guanyin, the goddess of mercy. Angled mirrors beneath each piece reveal the mark on the foot. A reproduction kiln and workshop is located at the end of the gallery.

Chinese Painting Gallery

On the 3rd floor, this gallery leads visitors through various styles of traditional Chinese painting, with many works dwelling on idealised landscapes. At first glance many appear to be similar, but upon closer inspection you'll realise that there is a vast array of techniques used to depict the natural world. There are some true masterpieces here, from painters such as Ni Zan (1301–74), Wang Meng (1308–85) and Wu Wei (1459–1508). Although works are rotated regularly, the Ming collection is generally regarded as containing the best selection of paintings. Scroll paintings are 'read' right to left.

Minority Nationalities Art Gallery

Save something for the Minority Nationalities Art Gallery on the 4th floor, which introduces visitors to the diversity of China's non-Han ethnic groups, totalling (officially) some 40 million people. Displays focus mainly on dress: from the salmon fish-skin suit from Hēilóngjiāng and the furs of the Siberian Oroqen, to the embroidery and batik of Guìzhōu's Miao and Dong, the Middle-Eastern satin robes of the Uighurs and the wild hairstyles of the former slave-owning Yi. Handicrafts include Miao silverware and Yi lacquer work.

Other Galleries

The **Ancient Chinese Jade Gallery** reveals the transformation of jade use from early mystical symbols (such as the *bì*, or 'jade discs', used to worship heaven) to ritual weapons and jewellery. Exhibit 414 is a remarkable totem, with an engraved phoenix carrying a human head. Bamboo drills, abrasive sand and garnets crushed in water were used to shape some of the pieces, which date back over 5000 years.

When it comes to the **Coin Gallery**, it's tempting to keep moving. But do look for the *bànliáng* coins, standardised during the Qin dynasty, which are pierced with a hole so they could be carried by string. Some older coins are shaped like keys or knives.

The **Ming & Qing Furniture Gallery** features rose- and sandalwood furniture of the elegant Ming dynasty, and heavier, more baroque examples from the Qing dynasty. Several mock offices and reception rooms offer a glimpse of wealthy Chinese home life.

SIGHTS

The Bund

THE BUND ARCHITECTURE

See p48.

HUÁNGPŬ PARK PARK

See p48.

EAST NANJING ROAD ARCHITECTURE

Map p280 (南京东路; Nánjīng Dōnglù; MEast Nanjing Rd) Linking the Bund with People's Square is East Nanjing Rd, formerly known as Nanking Rd. This was where the first department stores in China were opened in the 1920s, and where the modern era – with its new products and the promise of a radically different lifestyle – was ushered in.

A glowing forest of neon at night, it's no longer the cream of Shànghǎi shopping, but its pedestrian strip is still one of the most famous and crowded streets in China. Shànghǎi's reputation as the country's most fashionable city was forged in part here, through the new styles and trends introduced in department stores such as the Sun Sun (1926), today the Shànghǎi No 1 Food Store (p66), and the Sun Company (1936), now the Shànghǎi No 1 Department Store (p66).

ROCKBUND ART MUSEUM MUSEUM

Map p280 (上海外滩美术馆; Shànghǎi Wàitān Měishùguǎn; www.rockbundartmuseum.org; 20 Huqiu Rd; 虎丘路20号; adult ¥15; ⌚10am-6pm Tue-Sun; MEast Nanjing Rd) Housed in the former Royal Asiatic Society building (1933), this private museum behind the Bund focuses on contemporary Chinese art, with rotating exhibits year-round. Opened in 2010 to mark the opening of the Rockbund (North Bund) renovation project – funded by the Rockefeller Group – the museum has since become one of the city's top modern-art venues.

In addition to the art museum, there are a number of other architectural gems in this area that are part of the project, including the former British Consulate; see the walking tour (p57) for details. The most extensively renovated section is along Yuanmingyuan Rd, a magnet for the latest crop of high-profile restaurants and luxury brands to come to Shànghǎi. Additional landmark buildings in the area are slated for redevelopment, including the wonderful curved facade of the art-deco Capitol Theatre (1928), at the north end of Huqiu Rd.

BUND SIGHTSEEING TUNNEL TUNNEL

Map p280 (外滩观光隧道; Wàitān Guānguāng Suìdào; 300 East Zhongshan No 1 Rd; 中山东一路300号; one way/return ¥50/60; ⌚8am-10pm; MEast Nanjing Rd) A 647m voyage with entertainment from budget effects, garish lighting and dreadful props, the Bund Sightseeing Tunnel is a transport mode that guarantees to get you to Pǔdōng in an altered state. Stepping from the trains at the terminus, visitors are visibly nonplussed, their disbelief surpassed only by those with return tickets. Connoisseurs of unabashed cheesiness will love it.

SHÀNGHǍI GALLERY OF ART GALLERY

See p50.

NO DOGS OR CHINESE

A notorious sign at Huángpŭ Park, then called the Public Gardens, apocryphally declared 'No dogs or Chinese allowed'. Although this widely promoted notice never actually existed, the general gist of the wording hits the mark. A series of regulations was indeed posted outside the gardens listing 10 rules governing use of the park. The first regulation noted that 'The gardens are for the use of the foreign community.' while the fourth ruled that 'Dogs and bicycles are not admitted.' Chinese were barred from the park (as expressed in the first regulation), an injustice that gave rise to the canard. The bluntly worded sign has, however, become firmly embedded in the Chinese consciousness. Bruce Lee destroys a Shànghǎi park sign declaring 'No dogs and Chinese allowed' with a flying kick in *Fist of Fury* and Chinese history books cite the insult as further evidence of Chinese humiliation at the hands of foreigners. For a thorough academic examination of the subject, hunt down *Shanghai's 'Dogs and Chinese not Admitted' Sign: Legend, History and Contemporary Symbol* by Robert A Bickers and Jeffrey N Wasserstrom, published in the *China Quarterly,* No 142 (June 1995).

LONELY PLANET / GETTY IMAGES ©

LONELY PLANET / GETTY IMAGES ©

1. Glamour Bar (p70)
Iconic views, great drinks and a first-rate events line-up draw crowds to Glamour Bar.

2. Huángpǔ River Cruise (p65)
An evening boat cruise offers outstanding illuminated views of the Bund and Pǔdōng.

3. Custom House (p56)
Capping the 1927 Custom House is Big Ching, a bell modelled on London's Big Ben.

4. Shànghǎi Museum (p57)
This standout museum offers an extraordinary overview of traditional Chinese art through the millennia.

DENNIS WU / GETTY IMAGES ©

START **BROADWAY MANSIONS**
END **ROCKBUND ART MUSEUM**
DISTANCE **800M**
DURATION **45 MINUTES**

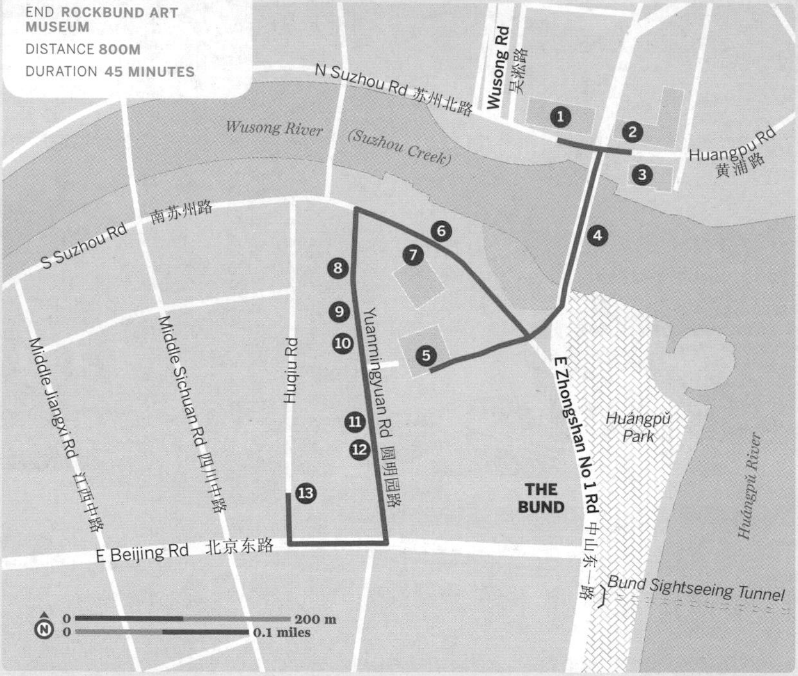

Neighbourhood Walk

The North Bund

Begin in Hóngkǒu, where the American Settlement was established in 1848. First stop is the Orwellian brick pile ❶ **Broadway Mansions** (1934), originally an apartment block that later became a favourite with military officers and journalists because of its commanding views over the harbour. The Japanese occupied the building from 1937 until the end of WWII. Not far from here is the ❷ **Astor House Hotel**, established in 1846 as the Richards Hotel. It was Shànghǎi's most prestigious hotel until the completion of the Cathay Hotel in 1929, and from 1990 to 1998 its ballroom served as the location of the Shànghǎi Stock Exchange. Across the street is the original ❸ **Russian Consulate**, still in use today. Head south over ❹ **Wàibáidù Bridge** (Garden Bridge; 1906), the first steel bridge in China, over which trams used to glide.

From here, cross the street to the grounds of the ❺ **former British Consulate** (1873), whose gardens are also home to the former consul's residence (1884). The consulate was one of the first foreign buildings to go up in Shànghǎi in 1852, although the original was destroyed in a fire in 1870. Continue west past the ❻ **former Shànghǎi Rowing Club** (1905) and ❼ **former Union Church** (1886) to arrive at the restored Yuanmingyuan Rd. This street was once home to several godowns – buildings that served as both warehouses and office space. Such buildings were shared by traders and missionaries, such as the ❽ **China Baptist Publication Society**, whose Gothamesque offices at No 187 (1932) were designed by the prolific Ladislaus Hudec.

Further along is the Italian Renaissance ❾ **Lyceum Building** (1927), the multi-denominational ❿ **Missions Building** (1924; No 169), the lovely ⓫ **YWCA Building** (1932; No 133) and the red-brick ⓬ **Yuanmingyuan Apartments** (No 115).

Turn onto Huqiu Rd to end the tour at the ⓭ **Royal Asiatic Society Building** (1933). Once Shànghǎi's first museum, it now houses the Rockbund Art Museum.

For another walk along the Bund, see p54.

METEOROLOGICAL SIGNAL TOWER MUSEUM

See p50.

HUÁNGPǓ RIVER CRUISE CRUISE

Map p280 (黄浦江游览; Huángpǔ Jiāng Yóulǎn; 219-239 East Zhongshan No 2 Rd; 中山东二路219-239号; tickets ¥128; Ⓜ East Nanjing Rd) The Huángpǔ River offers intriguing views of the Bund, Pǔdōng and riverfront activity. The night cruises are arguably more scenic, though boat traffic during the day is more interesting – depending on when you go, you'll pass an enormous variety of craft, from freighters, bulk carriers and roll-on roll-off ships to sculling sampans and massive floating TV advertisements.

Most cruises last 90 minutes and include not one, but two trips up to the International Cruise Terminal and back. The whole experience is a bit long, and if you can find one of the rarer 40- or 60-minute cruises (¥100), book that instead.

Departures are from the docks on the south end of the Bund (near East Jinling Rd), or, less conveniently, from the **Shíliùpù Docks** (十六铺; Shíliùpù), a 20-minute walk south of the Bund. Buy tickets at the departure points or from the Bund tourist information centre, next to the Bund Sightseeing Tunnel entrance. Departure times vary, but cruises usually run from 11am to 8.30pm.

Six 40-minute cruises also depart from the **Pearl Dock** (明珠码头; Míngzhū Mǎtou; 1 Century Ave; tickets ¥100) in Lùjiāzuǐ between 10am and 1.30pm.

SHÀNGHǍI MUSEUM OF NATURAL HISTORY MUSEUM

Map p280 (上海自然博物馆; Shànghǎi Zìrán Bówùguǎn; 260 East Yan'an Rd; 延安东路260号; admission ¥5; ⏲9am-4.30pm Tue-Sun, last tickets 3.30pm; Ⓜ East Nanjing Rd) Located in the former Cotton Exchange Building (built in 1923), the exhibits at this dusty and gloomy museum haven't been touched since the 1950s. It is easily the city's most forlorn attraction and horribly out of date, but, like the Bund Sightseeing Tunnel, it's a bizarre experience and it has its fans.

It's all expected to go at some point, though, as the new natural history museum is planned to open in Jìng'ān in 2014.

⊙ People's Square

SHÀNGHǍI MUSEUM MUSEUM

See p51.

SHÀNGHǍI URBAN PLANNING EXHIBITION HALL MUSEUM

Map p280 (上海城市规划展示馆; Shànghǎi Chéngshì Guīhuà Zhǎnshìguǎn; 100 Renmin Ave, entrance on Middle Xizang Rd; 人民大道100号; adult ¥30; ⏲9am-5pm Tue-Sun, last entry 4pm; Ⓜ People's Sq) Some cities romanticise their past, others promise good times in the present, but only in China are you expected to visit places that haven't even been built yet. The highlight is the 3rd floor, where you'll find Shànghǎi's idealised future (c 2020), with an incredible model layout of the megalopolis-to-come, plus a dizzying Virtual World 3D wraparound tour.

Balancing out the forward-looking exhibits are photos and maps of historic Shànghǎi.

SHÀNGHǍI MUSEUM OF CONTEMPORARY ART (MOCA SHÀNGHǍI) MUSEUM

Map p280 (上海当代艺术馆; Shànghǎi Dāngdài Yìshùguǎn; www.mocashanghai.org; People's Park; 人民公园; admission ¥30; ⏲10am-9.30pm; Ⓜ People's Sq) This nonprofit museum collection has an all-glass home to maximise natural sunlight when it cuts through the clouds, a tip-top location in People's Park and a fresh, invigorating approach to exhibiting contemporary artwork. Exhibits are temporary only; check the website to see what's on. On the top floor is the funky Art Lab Café with terrace.

FREE **SHÀNGHǍI ART MUSEUM** MUSEUM

Map p280 (上海美术馆; Shànghǎi Měishùguǎn; www.sh-artmuseum.org.cn; 325 West Nanjing Rd; 南京西路325号; ⏲9am-5pm, last entry 4pm; Ⓜ People's Sq) This museum is located within the former British racecourse club building next to People's Park. Refreshingly cool in summer, the interior galleries are suited to appreciating art, displayed in well-illuminated alcoves and with a voluminous sense of space. It's also worth noting the ceiling details and other period features original to the 1933 building. Unfortunately, the quality of the exhibitions is inconsistent. English captions are sporadic at best.

PEOPLE'S PARK PARK

Map p280 (人民公园; Rénmín Gōngyuán; admission free; ⏲6am-6pm; Ⓜ People's Sq) Occupying the site of the colonial racetrack (which became a holding camp during WWII), People's Park is a green refuge from Shànghǎi's fume-ridden roads, with its Shànghǎi Museum of Contemporary Art and pond-side bar, Barbarossa, all overlooked by Tomorrow Square, the Shànghǎi Art Museum and the Park Hotel.

If you're in Shànghǎi in June, join the photographers ringing the gorgeous pink lotuses that flower in the pond.

TOMORROW SQUARE SKYSCRAPER

Map p280 (明天广场; Míngtiān Guǎngchǎng; 399 West Nanjing Rd; 南京西路399号; Ⓜ People's Sq) This stupendous tower seizes the Shànghǎi zeitgeist with dramatic aplomb. Resembling a sci-fi corporation headquarters, the stratospheric building is given further lift by the stylistic awkwardness of nearby rivals. Tomorrow Sq houses Shànghǎi's highest serviced apartments while the foyer of the JW Marriott Tomorrow Square hotel debuts on the 38th floor. Pop up to put People's Square in the proper perspective.

PARK HOTEL HISTORIC BUILDING

Map p280 (国际饭店; Guójì Fàndiàn; 170 West Nanjing Rd; 南京西路170号; Ⓜ People's Sq) Designed by Hungarian architect Ladislaus Hudec and erected as a bank in 1934, the Park Hotel was Shànghǎi's tallest building until the 1980s, when shoulder-padded architects first started squinting hopefully in the direction of Pǔdōng. Back in the days when building height had a different meaning, it was said your hat would fall off if you looked at the roof.

Peruse the foyer for its art-deco overture and wander further east along Nanjing Rd to the Pacific Hotel, formerly the China United Apartment Building, also equipped with some lovely lobby details.

MADAME TUSSAUDS MUSEUM

Map p280 (上海杜莎夫人蜡像馆; Shànghǎi Dùshā Fūrén Làxiàngguǎn; West Nanjing Rd; 南京西路; adult ¥150, 1 adult plus 1 child ¥190; ⌚10am-9pm; Ⓜ People's Sq) The waxworks at Madame Tussauds are largely aimed at locals and cost a lot, but could make do when one of Shànghǎi's notorious summer downpours inundates town.

EATING

The Bund is Shànghǎi's epicentre of global chic, where international superchefs and hotel restaurants vying for China's first Michelin star have established themselves. While the settings are often spectacular, there's less diversity here than in the French Concession. Many local eateries are in malls or designated food streets; try Huanghe Rd or Yunnan Rd for an old-school Shànghǎi atmosphere.

The Bund

TOP CHOICE **LOST HEAVEN** YUNNANESE $$$

Map p280 (花马天堂; Huāmǎ Tiāntáng; ☎6330 0967; www.lostheaven.com.cn; 17 East Yan'an Rd; 延安东路17号; dishes ¥38-180; ⊗; Ⓜ East Nanjing Rd) Lost Heaven might not have the views that keep its rivals in business, but why go to the same old Western restaurants when you can get sophisticated Bai, Dai and Miao folk cuisine from China's mighty

LOCAL KNOWLEDGE

SHANG ART

Leo Li, curator of the stylish Leo Gallery (p96), introduced us to his favourite modern art museums and galleries in Shànghǎi.

➡ **Rockbund Art Museum** (p61) A trip to this museum is recommended not only for the monumental art installations, but also for the well-restored heritage building in which it is located.

➡ **ShanghART** I love visiting this contemporary art institution (p123). It always has avant-garde shows and exhibitions of great contemporary Chinese artists.

➡ **James Cohan** This was the first gallery (p96) from New York to establish itself in mainland China in 2008. Its gorgeous garden villa in the heart of the French Concession is always a pleasure to visit.

➡ **Hong Merchant Gallery** This beautiful gallery (p96) is another gallery housed in a historical villa, and displays Chinese furniture and sculpture alongside China-inspired contemporary art. Each time I come here, it feels like my ideal home.

southwest? Specialities are flowers (banana and pomegranate), wild mushrooms, chillies, Burmese curries, Bai chicken and superb pu-erh teas, all served up in gorgeous Yúnnán-meets-Shànghǎi surrounds.

MR & MRS BUND FRENCH $$$

Map p280 (☎6323 9898; www.mmbund.com; 6th fl, Bund 18, 18 East Zhongshan No 1 Rd; 中山东一路18号6楼; mains ¥150-600, 2-/3-course set lunch ¥200/250; ⏲lunch & dinner, to 4am Tue-Sat; ⊜; Ⓜ East Nanjing Rd) French chef Paul Pairet opened this casual eatery in 2008, aiming for a space that's considerably more playful than your average fine-dining restaurant. The mix-and-match menu has a heavy French bistro slant, but reimagined and served up with Pairet's ingenious presentation.

But it's not just the food you're here for: it's the post-midnight meals (discounted), the Bingo nights and the wonderfully wonky atmosphere. Reserve.

ULTRAVIOLET GASTRONOMIC $$$

(www.uvbypp.cc; dinner from ¥2000; ⏲dinner Tue-Sat) You've probably paired food and wine before, but what about pairing an illuminated apple-wasabi communion wafer with purple candles, *Hell's Bells* on the stereo and a specially designed cathedral scent? No? Sounds like it might be time to visit Ultraviolet, China's most conceptual dining experience.

A meal consisting of 22 courses – each accompanied by a different sensory mood (sounds, scents and images) – this is Paul Pairet's masterpiece, years in the making. Revolving around his signature mischievous creations, a dinner here is bound to be unlike anything you've ever experienced before.

Reservations must be made online; there's only one table with 10 available seats, so book well in advance. The evening's diners gather first at Mr & Mrs Bund for an apéritif before they're whisked away to a secret location.

M ON THE BUND EUROPEAN $$$

Map p280 (米氏西餐厅; Mǐshì Xīcāntīng; ☎6350 9988; www.m-onthebund.com; 7th fl, 20 Guangdong Rd; 广东路20号7楼; mains ¥188-288, 2-/3-course set lunch ¥186/254; ⊜; Ⓜ East Nanjing Rd) M exudes a timelessness and level of sophistication that surpasses the flash and fireworks of many other upscale Shànghǎi restaurants. The menu isn't radical, but that's the question that it seems to ask you – do you really need to break new culinary ground just to enjoy dinner? Crispy suckling pig and a chicken tajine with saffron are, after all, simply delicious just the way they are.

The art-deco dining room and 7th-floor terrace are equally gorgeous. Finish off with drinks in the Glamour Bar downstairs and reserve well in advance.

JEAN GEORGES FUSION $$$

Map p280 (法国餐厅; Fǎguó Cāntīng; ☎6321 7733; 4th fl, Three on the Bund, 3 East Zhongshan No 1 Rd; 中山东一路3号4楼; mains ¥248-318, 3-course lunch/dinner ¥238/638; ⊜; Ⓜ East Nanjing Rd) Somewhere between Gotham City and new Shànghǎi is Jean Georges Vongerichten's dimly lit, copper-appliquéd temple to gastronomy. Head chef Lam Ming Kin has some divine palate-pleasers on the menu, such as foie gras brûlée with sour cherries and candied pistachios, black cod with sesame and citrus confit, and seared lamb with cardamom crumbs.

It's divided into the **Nougatine bar** (3-course dinner ¥218), with an early-bird special from 6pm to 7pm, and the formal dining room (set menu only) at night, but not for lunch, when you can get a window table with relatively little hassle. Reserve.

SHÀNGHǍI UNCLE SHANGHAINESE $$$

Map p280 (海上阿叔; Hǎishàng Āshū; ☎6339 1977; Basement, 222 East Yan'an Rd; 延安东路222号; dishes ¥48-168; Ⓜ East Nanjing Rd) This restaurant is what Shànghǎi is all about: brash, bustling and just a little tacky. The owner is the son of a *New York Times* food critic and the dishes mix Western and Asian influences with Shanghainese cooking to surprising and succulent effect. The seafood dishes are particularly good – a steamed Yangzi sole, gingery-sweet smoked fish – but the pine-seed pork ribs in a soy, Worcester and red wine sauce is excellent too.

YÚXÌN CHUĀNCÀI SICHUANESE $$

Map p280 (渝信川菜; ☎6361 1777; 5th fl, Huasheng Tower, 399 Jiujiang Rd; 九江路399号华盛大厦5楼; dishes ¥18-98; 📶; Ⓜ East Nanjing Rd) A regular contender for Shànghǎi's best Sichuanese, Yúxìn pulls no punches when it comes to the blistering chillies and numbing peppercorns. Menu all-stars include the 'mouthwatering chicken' starter (口水鸡; *kǒushuǐ jī*), spicy frog legs, tea-smoked duck, hot-stone beef and catfish in chilli oil.

CHARME HONG KONG $

Map p280 (港丽餐厅; Gǎnglì Cāntīng; ☎6360 7577; 4th fl, Hóngyī Plaza, 299 East Nanjing Rd; 南京东路299号宏伊国际广场4楼; dishes ¥20-68; MEast Nanjing Rd) Charme is a rip-roarin' Canto-style cafe that's all over the map, with dishes that range from spicy Sichuanese and Hong Kong curries to Cantonese seafood, Italian pasta and, of course, milk tea. Reserve or come prepared to wait; service can be spotty. It's one of several choices located in the Hóngyī Plaza mall, above the East Nanjing Rd metro station.

SOUTH MEMORY HUNANESE $

Map p280 (望湘园; Wàng Xiāng Yuán; ☎6360 2797; 6th fl, Hóngyī Plaza, 299 East Nanjing Rd; 南京东路299号宏伊国际广场6楼; dishes ¥26-88; MEast Nanjing Rd) This popular Húnán place is a stone's throw from the waterfront and has a range of spicy drypots (served in a personal mini wok), including favourites like bamboo shoots and smoked pork, and chicken and chestnuts. Also on the menu are other Húnán classics (steamed pork served in a bamboo tube); it's absolutely jammed at lunchtime, so arrive early to get a window seat.

DOLAR SHOP HOTPOT $$

Map p280 (豆捞坊; Dòulāo Fáng; ☎6351 7077; 5th fl, Hóngyī Plaza, 299 East Nanjing Rd; 南京东路299号宏伊国际广场5楼; hotpot from ¥70; MEast Nanjing Rd) Hotpot is a favourite across China, especially in the winter months, but this top-notch chain is popular no matter what the season because of the quality ingredients and the big range of sauces, essential to hotpot dining, which you can mix yourself at the sauce bar. Unusual soup bases include the fire-purging pot and the pickled-fish pot.

The procedure is simple: you select a variety of ingredients from the menu (thinly sliced lamb, mushrooms, fish balls, noodles), cook them in the hotpot at your table and then dip in the sauce(s) of your choice.

SHOOK! SOUTHEAST ASIAN $$$

Map p280 (☎2329 8522; www.shookshanghairestaurant.com; 5th fl, Bund 18, 23 East Zhongshan No 1 Rd; 中山东一路23号5楼; 2-course set lunch ¥123, set dinner for 2 people ¥988; ⊜; MEast Nanjing Rd) Like most of its Bund-side brethren, Malaysian Shook! sports trendy design and fabulous views, particularly from its rooftop terrace. There are some good ideas on the menu, which stretches from Southeast Asian classics to Japanese and Western, but the lack of a culinary focal point is telling – the kitchen's execution can be inconsistent.

WAGAS CAFE $

Map p280 (沃歌斯; Wògēsī; 1st fl, Hóngyī Plaza, 288 Jiujiang Rd; 九江路288号宏伊国际广场1楼; mains ¥48-58; ⊙6.30am-10pm; ⊜; MEast Nanjing Rd) Convenient branch of the city's favourite cafe (p130).

AJISEN NOODLES $

Map p280 (味千拉面; Wèiqiān Lāmiàn; Basement, Hóngyī Plaza, 299 East Nanjing Rd; 南京东路299号宏伊国际广场地下一层; noodles ¥23-35; ⊙11am-10pm; ⊜; MEast Nanjing Rd) Simply hopping come meal time, this Japanese ramen chain escorts diners to the noodle dish of their choice via easy-to-use photo menus and diligent squads of staff in regulation black T-shirt and jeans. This is possibly the most popular chain in Shànghǎi, with over 100 locations around town.

SHÀNGHǍI GRANDMOTHER CHINESE $

Map p280 (上海姥姥; Shànghǎi Lǎolao; ☎6321 6613; 70 Fuzhou Rd; 福州路70号; dishes ¥20-52; MEast Nanjing Rd) This packed home-style eatery is within easy striking distance of the Bund and perfect for a casual lunch or dinner. You can't go wrong with the classics here: fried tomato and egg, Grandmother's braised pork and three-cup chicken rarely disappoint. It may look touristy from the outside, but even the local foodies on dianping.com give it the thumbs up.

VICTOR'S CAFE $$

Map p280 (西饼屋; Xībǐng Wū; Peace Hotel Lobby, 20 East Nanjing Rd; 南京东路20号; mains from ¥68, plus 15% service charge; ⊙7am-10pm; ⊜; MEast Nanjing Rd) When you need a break from the push and pull of the Bund, refuel at this exceedingly *réposant* French cafe, whose large windows overlook East Nanjing Rd. It's pricey, but there's no faulting the location at the entrance to the Peace Hotel, or the menu of quiches, salads, freshly baked pastries and coffee.

People's Square

TOP CHOICE **YANG'S FRY DUMPLINGS** DUMPLINGS $

Map p280 (小杨生煎馆; Xiǎoyáng Shēngjiān Guǎn; 101 Huanghe Rd; 黄河路101号; per liǎng ¥6 (两; 4 dumplings); MPeople's Sq) The city's

LOCAL KNOWLEDGE

PEOPLE'S SQUARE FOOD STREETS

The following two streets are lined with an amazing variety of Chinese restaurants, each with its own speciality.

Huanghe Road Food Street (黄河路美食街; Huánghé Lù Měishí Jiē; MPeople's Sq) With a prime central location near People's Park, Huanghe Rd covers all the bases from cheap lunches to late-night post-theatre snacks. You'll find large restaurants like the always popular **Táishèngyuán Restaurant** (苔圣园中华料理; 50 Huanghe Rd), but Huanghe Rd is best for dumplings – get 'em fried at Yang's (No 97) or served up in bamboo steamers across the road at **Jiājiā Soup Dumplings** (佳家汤包; 90 Huanghe Rd).

Yunnan Road Food Street (云南路美食街; Yúnnán Lù Měishí Jiē; MDashijie) Yunnan Rd has some great speciality restaurants and is just the spot for an authentic meal after museum hopping at People's Square. Look out for Shaanxi dumplings and noodles at No 15 and five-fragrance dim sum at **Wǔ Fāng Zhāi** (五芳斋; 28 Yunnan Rd). You can also get salted duck (盐水鸭; *yán shuǐ yā*) and steamed dumplings at **Xiǎo Jīn Líng** (小金陵; 55 Yunnan Rd), Mongolian hotpot and Yunnanese here.

most famous sesame-seed-and-scallion-coated fried dumplings (生煎; *shēngjiān*) unquestionably belong to Yang's. Lines here can stretch to the horizon as eager diners wait for their scalding *shēngjiān* to be dished out onto vintage communist-era enamel dishes – this isn't some sort of retro fashion statement, they just never bothered to upgrade the tableware.

Order at the left counter – eight dumplings and a soup (汤; *tāng*) should be enough – then join the queue on the right to pick up your order.

NÁNXIÁNG STEAMED BUN RESTAURANT — DUMPLINGS $

Map p280 (南翔馒头店; Nánxiáng Mántou Diàn; 2nd fl, 666 Fuzhou Rd; 福州路666号2楼; steamer 8 dumplings ¥25-50; MPeople's Sq) Pleasant branch of Shànghǎi's most famous dumpling restaurant (p83) overlooking Fuzhou Rd.

SPICY JOINT — SICHUANESE $

Map p280 (辛香汇; Xīnxiānghuì; ☎400 100 1717; 4th fl, Yalong International Plaza, 500 East Jinling Rd; 金陵东路500号亚龙国际广场4楼; dishes ¥12-58; ⊙11am-10pm; wi-fi; MDashijie) Branch of one of Shànghǎi's best Sichuanese joints (p100). Be warned that waits can be excruciatingly long at peak times; you'll need a mobile number to secure a place in the queue.

KEBABS ON THE GRILLE — INDIAN $$

Map p280 (☎3315 0132; 227 North Huangpi Rd, inside Central Plaza; 黄陂北路227号; dishes ¥40-90, lunch sets from ¥55; 🖉; MPeople's Sq) Handy branch of the excellent north Indian restaurant (p83).

FOOD REPUBLIC — FOOD COURT $

Map p280 (大食代; Dàshídài; meals ¥40; ⊙10am-10pm) The most successful food court in Shànghǎi, Food Republic has several locations around town – this one, on the 6th floor of the Raffles City mall, is kind of cool. Choices range from teppanyaki and curry to hotpot and noodles. Pay up-front at the entrance (¥50 or ¥100; ¥10 deposit; refunds granted) and hand over your card to the vendor of your choice.

For quick snacks, desserts and juices, head to the equally bustling food court in the mall basement.

WÚYUÈ RÉNJIĀ — NOODLES $

Map p280 (吴越人家; 479 East Nanjing Rd; 南京东路479号; noodles ¥12-38; MEast Nanjing Rd) Hidden in a side street basement off East Nanjing Rd, this unassuming little place serves great bowls of Sūzhōu noodles in an old-style teahouse. Choose between *tāng* (soupy) or *gān* (dry) noodles; in either case, the flavouring comes on a side plate. The excellent *xiābào shànbēi miàn* comes with shrimp and fried eels.

NINA'S SÌCHUĀN HOUSE — SICHUANESE $$

Map p280 (蜀菜行家; Shǔcài Hángjiā; 227 North Huangpi Rd, inside Central Plaza; 黄陂北路227号; dishes ¥19-88; MPeople's Sq) Nina's is as authentic as they come, with lines out the door and few foreigners in on the secret. For those who can take the heat, the good news is that chilli peppers and Sichuanese peppercorns are ladled liberally on everything, from the mapo tofu to the giant bowl of spicy catfish.

WÁNG BǍOHÉ JIǓJIĀ SHANGHAINESE $$$
Map p280 (王宝和酒家; ☎6322 3673; 603 Fuzhou Rd; 福州路603号; dishes ¥18-148, set menu from ¥450; Ⓜ People's Sq) Over 250 years old, this restaurant's fame rests on its extravagant selection of crab dishes; its popularity reaches an apex during hairy-crab season (October to December). Most diners opt for one of the all-crabs-must-die banquets, but if you're new to hairy crab, you might want to give it a try elsewhere before shelling out for an eight-course meal. Reserve.

DRINKING & NIGHTLIFE

The Bund is home to some of Shànghǎi's premier drinking spots that jump at the weekends. These are places to get dressed up for and the drinks don't come cheap. But a trip to at least one of these bars is obligatory, if only for the stunning night-time view of the Huángpǔ River and the glittering lights of Pǔdōng.

The Bund

TOP CHOICE **GLAMOUR BAR** BAR
Map p280 (魅力酒吧; Mèilì Jiǔbā; www.m-onthebund.com; 6th fl, 20 Guangdong Rd; 广东路20号6楼; ⏲5pm-2am; Ⓜ East Nanjing Rd) The Glamour Bar is more than just one of Shànghǎi's most popular watering holes, it's a cultural institution. It hosts the annual literary festival, chamber music performances and China-related book launches and talks. Of course, none of that would hold up if the martinis weren't so good. Get here before midnight on weekends or be prepared to queue to get in.

NEW HEIGHTS BAR
Map p280 (新视角; Xīn Shìjiǎo; ☎6321 0909; 7th fl, Three on the Bund, 3 East Zhongshan No 1 Rd; 中山东一路3号7楼; ⏲11.30am-1.30am; Ⓜ East Nanjing Rd) The most amenable of the big Bund bars, this splendid roof terrace has the choicest angle on Pǔdōng's hypnotising neon performance. There's always a crowd, whether for coffee, cocktails or meals (¥158 to ¥298).

LONG BAR BAR
Map p280 (廊吧; Láng Bā; ☎6322 9988; 2 East Zhongshan No 1 Rd; 中山东一路2号; ⏲4pm-1am; 📶; Ⓜ East Nanjing Rd) For a taste of colonial-era Shànghǎi's elitist trappings, you'll do no better than the Long Bar. This was once the members-only Shànghǎi Club, whose most spectacular accoutrement was a 34m-long wooden bar. Foreign businessmen would sit here according to rank, with the taipans (foreign heads of business) closest to the view of the Bund.

Now part of the Waldorf Astoria, the bar's original wood-panelled decor has been painstakingly recreated from old photographs. There's a good selection of old-fashioned cocktails as well as an oyster bar.

JIAO BAR BAR
Map p280 (1st fl, 68 East Jinlong Rd; 金陵东路68号1楼; ⏲7pm-2am Tue-Sun; Ⓜ Yuyuan Garden) There are few bars in Shànghǎi as endearingly quirky as this one: the Japanese owners rock to a reggae soundtrack while serving a head-spinning variety of *shōchū*, liquor distilled from rice, sweet potato or barley. Order it straight or mixed with fresh fruit, and appreciate the price tag: you won't find many other ¥35 drinks by the Bund.

IDENTITY & THE SHÀNGHǍI DIALECT

Older Shanghainese are very conscious of the disappearance of their cherished Shànghǎi dialect (Shànghǎihuà), under assault from the increased promotion of the Mandarin (Pǔtōnghuà) dialect and the flood of immigrant tongues. As a deeply tribal element of Shànghǎi culture and heritage, the disappearance of the slightly Japanese-sounding dialect equals a loss of identity. Fewer and fewer young Shanghainese are now able to speak the pure form of the dialect. Youngsters might not care, but older Shanghainese agonise over the dialect's slow extinction. The most perfectly preserved forms of Shànghǎihuà survive in rural areas around Shànghǎi, where Mandarin has less of a toehold. The Shanghainese may remind themselves of the Chinese idiom – *jiùde bù qù, xīnde bù lái* (旧的不去新的不来; 'If the old doesn't go, the new doesn't arrive') – but it may offer scant consolation.

BAR ROUGE BAR

Map p280 (7th fl, Bund 18, 18 East Zhongshan No 1 Rd; 中山东一路18号7楼; ⏲6pm-2am Sun-Thu, to 4.30am Fri & Sat; Ⓜ East Nanjing Rd) Bar Rouge attracts a cashed-up party crowd who come for the fantastic views from the terrace and the all-night DJ parties. The lipstick-red decor is slick and the crowd is slicker, so ordinary mortals can sometimes struggle to get served on busy nights. Cover is charged on Fridays and Saturdays after 10pm.

CAPTAIN'S BAR BAR

Map p280 (船长青年酒吧; Chuánzhǎng Qīngnián Jiǔbā; 6th fl, 37 Fuzhou Rd; 福州路37号6楼; ⏲8am-2am; 📶; Ⓜ East Nanjing Rd) Don't let the crummy lift up to the top floor of the Captain Hostel put you off. This is the only bar in the area that offers both a decent, if slightly restricted, view of Pǔdōng's lights from the outside terrace and drinks that don't cost a bomb. It serves pizza too.

M1NT CLUB

Map p280 (☎6391 2811; 24th fl, 318 Fuzhou Rd; 福州路318号24楼; ⏲lounge 6pm-late daily, club 9pm-late Wed-Sat; Ⓜ East Nanjing Rd) Exclusive penthouse-style club with knockout views, snazzy fusion food and not a lot of dance space. Dress to impress or you'll get thrown into the shark tank.

ATANU BAR

Map p280 (阿塔努咖啡酒吧; Ātǎnǔ Kāfēi Jiǔbā; 1 Zhongshan East No 2 Rd; 中山东二路1号; ⏲10am-2am; Ⓜ East Nanjing Rd) Located on the top two floors of the former signal tower, this cafe-bar is an ideal pit stop for those strolling the Bund.

MUSE CLUB

(5th fl, Yi Feng Galleria, 99 East Beijing Rd; 北京东路99号5楼; Ⓜ East Nanjing Rd) One of the hottest clubs in the city for over six years now – and that's no small feat – Muse has moved downtown to this swanky Bund-side location. Don't go looking for a lot of dance space; just squeeze into the crowd or jump up on a private table (minimum ¥4000 per night).

🍷 People's Square

BARBAROSSA BAR

Map p280 (芭芭露莎会所; Bābālùshā Huìsuǒ; People's Park, 231 West Nanjing Rd; 南京西路231号人民公园内; ⏲5pm-2am; 📶; Ⓜ People's Sq) Set back in People's Park alongside a pond, Barbarossa is all about escapism. Forget Shànghǎi, this is Morocco reimagined by Hollywood set designers. The action gets steadily more intense as you ascend to the roof terrace, via the cushion-strewn 2nd floor, where the hordes puff on fruit-flavoured hookahs. At night, use the park entrance just east of the Shànghǎi Art Museum.

☆ ENTERTAINMENT

☆ The Bund

TOP CHOICE FAIRMONT PEACE HOTEL JAZZ BAR LIVE MUSIC

Map p280 (费尔蒙和平饭店爵士吧; Fèi'ěrmēng Hépíng Fàndiàn Juéshì Bā; ☎6138 6883; 20 East Nanjing Rd; 南京东路20号; ⏲5.30pm-1am; Ⓜ East Nanjing Rd) Shànghǎi's most famous hotel features Shànghǎi's most famous jazz band, a septuagenarian sextet that's been churning out nostalgic covers like 'Moon River' and 'Summertime' since time immemorial. The original band takes the stage from 7pm to 9.45pm; afterwards it's Theo Croker's smokin' **contemporary group** (⏲10pm-1am Tue-Sat). Entrance is ¥100; reserve on weekends.

HOUSE OF BLUES & JAZZ LIVE MUSIC

Map p280 (布鲁斯乐爵士之屋; Bùlǔsī Yuè Juéshì Zhīwū; ☎6323 2779; 60 Fuzhou Rd; 福州路60号; ⏲5pm-1am; Ⓜ East Nanjing Rd) This is a classy restaurant and bar for music lovers. The owner, a Chinese TV celebrity, has plastered the walls with old photos of jazz legends, and the in-house band (which changes regularly) delivers live music from 9.30pm to 1am. Sunday night is a free-for-all jam.

☆ People's Square

YÌFŪ THEATRE CHINESE OPERA

Map p280 (逸夫舞台; Yìfū Wǔtái; ☎6322 5294; www.tianchan.com; 701 Fuzhou Rd; 人民广场福州路701号; Ⓜ People's Sq) One block east of People's Square, this is the main opera theatre in town and recognisable by the huge opera mask above the entrance. The theatre presents a popular program of Běijīng, Kun and Yue (Shaoxing) opera. A Běijīng opera highlights show is performed several times a week at 1.30pm and 7.15pm; pick up a brochure at the ticket office.

TOP CHOICE **SHÀNGHĂI GRAND THEATRE** CLASSICAL MUSIC

Map p280 (上海大剧院; Shànghǎi Dàjùyuàn; ☎6386 8686; www.shgtheatre.com; 300 Renmin Ave; 人民广场人民大道300号; Ⓜ People's Sq) Shànghǎi's state-of-the-art concert venue hosts everything from Broadway musicals to symphonies, ballets, operas and performances by internationally acclaimed classical soloists. There are also traditional Chinese music performances here. Pick up a schedule at the ticket office.

PEACE CINEMA CINEMA

Map p280 (和平影都; Hépíng Yǐngdū; 290 Middle Xizang Rd; 西藏中路290号; Ⓜ People's Sq) People's Square cinema with an attached IMAX theatre (巨幕影院; Jùmùyǐngyuàn).

SHÀNGHĂI CONCERT HALL CLASSICAL MUSIC

Map p280 (上海音乐厅; Shànghǎi Yīnyuè Tīng; ☎6386 2836; 523 East Yan'an Rd; 人民广场延安东路523号; Ⓜ People's Sq, Dashijie) In 2003 the government moved this classic 1930s building (all 5650 tonnes of it) 66m away from busy East Yan'an Rd to a quieter park-side setting, a relocation that actually cost more than building a brand-new concert hall. It features smaller-scale concerts and local and international soloists.

SHOPPING

The Bund is all about luxury shopping, while underneath People's Square is a maze of former bomb shelters that have been transformed into a downmarket shopping centre known as D-Mall. Linking the two is East Nanjing Rd, which reached its peak as the most famous shopping strip in East Asia in the 1920s.

ANNABEL LEE ACCESSORIES

Map p280 (安梨家居; Ānlí Jiājū; No 1, Lane 8, East Zhongshan No 1 Rd; 中山东一路8弄1号; Ⓜ East Nanjing Rd) This elegant shop sells a range of soft-coloured accessories in silk, linen and cashmere, many of which feature delicate and stylish embroidery. Peruse the collection of shawls, scarves, table runners and evening bags.

SŪZHŌU COBBLERS ACCESSORIES

Map p280 (上海起想艺术品; Shànghǎi Qǐxiǎng Yìshùpǐn; unit 101, 17 Fuzhou Rd; 福州路17号101室; ⏲10am-6.30pm; Ⓜ East Nanjing Rd) Right off the Bund, this cute boutique sells exquisite, hand-embroidered silk slippers, bags and hats. Patterns and colours are based on the fashions of the 1930s, and as far as the owner, Huang Mengqi, is concerned, the products are one of a kind.

YÙNHÓNG CHOPSTICKS SHOP SOUVENIRS

Map p280 (韵泓筷子店; Yùnhóng Kuàizi Diàn; 387 East Nanjing Rd; 南京东路387号; Ⓜ East Nanjing Rd) The Běijīng arts-and-crafts people have opened up this smart little shop selling designer chopsticks for everyone from your four-year-old to the sophisticated aunt who loves to throw extravagant dinner parties. You might even find a set for yourself.

BLUE SHÀNGHĂI WHITE CERAMICS

Map p280 (海晨; Hǎi Chén; unit 103, 17 Fuzhou Rd; 福州路17号103室; ⏲10.30am-6.30pm; Ⓜ East Nanjing Rd) Just off the Bund, this little boutique is a great place to browse for a contemporary take on a traditional art form. It sells a tasteful selection of hand-painted porcelain teacups, teapots and vases, displayed together with the store's ingeniously designed wooden furniture.

SHIATZY CHEN CLOTHING

Map p280 (夏姿; Xià Zī; 9 East Zhongshan No 1 Rd; 中山东一路9号; Ⓜ East Nanjing Rd) One of the top names in Asian haute couture, Taiwanese designer Shiatzy Chen finds her inspiration in traditional Chinese aesthetics. The exclusive collections (women's and men's apparel) at her Bund 9 flagship store display a painstaking attention to detail and cross cultural boundaries with grace.

SILK KING FABRIC

Map p280 (真丝大王; Zhēnsī Dàwáng; 136 East Nanjing Rd; 南京东路136号; Ⓜ East Nanjing Rd) The city's largest fabric chain is good for a quick browse to see a typical selection of Chinese prints and fabric designs. In-store tailors can make you a custom-fit *qípáo* (cheongsam), shirt or jacket in three to 10 days for around ¥1800. Twenty-four-hour rush jobs are also possible.

DUǑYÚNXUĀN ART SHOP ART

Map p280 (朵云轩; Duǒyún Xuān; 422 East Nanjing Rd; 南京东路422号; ⏲9.30am-9.30pm; Ⓜ East Nanjing Rd) A multistorey, traditional-

GREAT WORLD

If you were passing through Shànghǎi in the 1920s or '30s, chances were you'd wind up at **Great World** (大世界; Dà Shìjiè; cnr East Yan'an & Middle Xizang Rds; Ⓜ People's Sq) sooner rather than later – no place better epitomised the city's reputation as a den of escapism and vice, and at its peak it allegedly saw some 20,000 visitors per day. The six-storey building initially opened in 1917 as a place for acrobats and nightclub stars, rivalling the existing New World on Nanjing Rd. For the first decade or so it was relatively tame, gradually incorporating a movie theatre, fortune tellers and Chinese opera shows. By the time Pockmarked Huang got ahold of it in 1931, however, it had become a centre for the bizarre and burlesque, its floors a mixture of singsong girls, gambling, opium and prostitution.

It's been in a state of perpetual renovation since 2002, and while it is rumoured that it will one day reopen as an entertainment centre, nothing so far has materialised.

looking building (look for the two enormous calligraphy brushes outside) with an excellent selection of art and calligraphy supplies. The 2nd floor is one of the best places for heavy art books, both international and Chinese, and the 3rd floor houses antiques and some excellent calligraphy and brush-painting galleries. You can get your own chop (seal) made here.

FOREIGN LANGUAGES BOOKSTORE BOOKS

Map p280 (外文书店; Wàiwén Shūdiàn; 390 Fuzhou Rd; 福州路390号; ⌚9.30am-6pm; Ⓜ East Nanjing Rd) The days when the selection of titles at these government-sponsored bookstores ran from Dickens to Sherlock Holmes are long gone. There's now an ever-expanding range of fiction and nonfiction upstairs, as well as an impressive selection of Lonely Planet guides on the ground floor. It's a good place to come for titles and maps on Shànghǎi.

SHÀNGHǍI BOOK TRADERS USED BOOKS BOOKS

Map p280 (上海外文图书公司; Shànghǎi Wàiwén Túshū Gōngsì; 36 Shaanxi Rd; 山西路36号; ⌚9am-5.30pm; Ⓜ East Nanjing Rd) This used bookstore has back issues of *Time, Elle* and *Vogue*, along with three walls of used English-language books, from Balzac to Dan Brown. Prices start at a mere ¥8.

SHÀNGHǍI MUSEUM ART STORE ART

Map p280 (上海博物馆艺术品商店; Shànghǎi Bówùguǎn Yìshùpǐn Shāngdiàn; 201 Renmin Ave; 人民大道201号; ⌚9.30am-5pm; Ⓜ People's Sq) Attached to the Shànghǎi Museum and entered from East Yan'an Rd, this high-quality store offers refreshing variety from the usual tourist souvenirs. Apart from the excellent range of books on Chinese art and architecture, there is a good selection of quality cards, prints and slides. The annexe shop sells fine imitations of some of the museum's ceramic pieces, as well as scarves and bags.

SHÀNGHǍI NO 1 FOOD STORE FOOD

Map p280 (上海市第一食品商店; Shànghǎi Shì Dìyī Shípǐn Shāngdiàn; 720 East Nanjing Rd; 南京东路720号; Ⓜ People's Sq) Brave the crowds here to check out the amazing variety of dried mushrooms, ginseng and sea cucumber, as well as more tempting snacks like sunflower seeds, nuts, dried fruit, moon cakes and tea. Built in 1926 and redone in 2012, this used to be Sun Sun, one of Shànghǎi's big department stores.

SHÀNGHǍI NO 1 DEPARTMENT STORE CLOTHING

Map p280 (上海市第一百货商店; Shànghǎi Shì Dìyī Bǎihuò Shāngdiàn; 800 East Nanjing Rd; 南京东路800号; ⌚9.30am-10pm; Ⓜ People's Sq) Opened in 1936, the Shànghǎi No 1 Department Store was formerly known as the Sun Company and was one of East Nanjing Rd's big department stores (with Wing On, Sun Sun and Sincere) and the first equipped with an escalator. Today it averages 150,000 shoppers a day over 11 levels of merchandise.

RAFFLES CITY MALL

Map p280 (来福士广场; Láifúshì Guǎngchǎng; 268 Middle Xizang Rd; 西藏中路268号; ⌚10am-10pm; Ⓜ People's Sq) This seven-floor, non-smoking, Singapore-owned mall is the most popular shopping destination by People's Square, with everything from clothes to electronics and toys. Like most Shànghǎi malls, it's also a big-time dining destination: food courts, restaurants and juice bars occupy the basement and upper levels.

Old Town

Neighbourhood Top Five

❶ Lose your bearings in the labyrinthine **Yùyuán Gardens & Bazaar** (p76), but avoid the weekend surge.

❷ Browse for handicrafts, faux antiques, tailor-made clothes and souvenirs in the Old Town's **shops, markets and bazaars** (p86).

❸ Explore the traditional **backstreets** of the Old Town on our walking tour (p79).

❹ Quaff a cup of Iron Guanyin tea in one of the Old Town's **teahouses** (p84).

❺ Get **temple hopping** (p77) among the Old Town's quaint and historic brood of Buddhist, Taoist, Confucian, Christian and Muslim shrines.

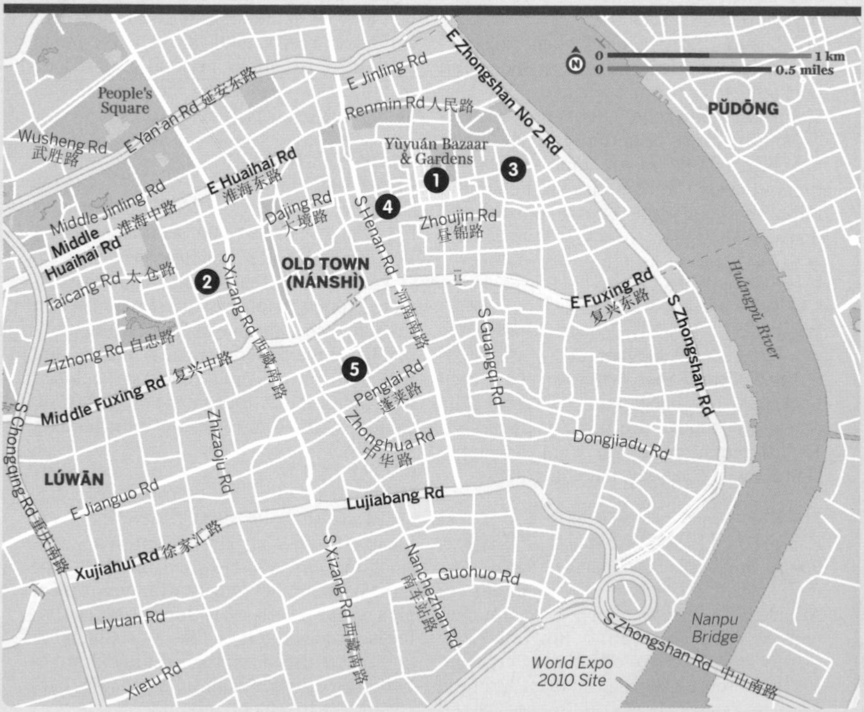

For more detail of this area, see Map p284 ➡

Explore: Old Town

Known to locals as Nánshì (Southern City), the Old Town (南市) is the most traditionally Chinese area of Shànghǎi, along with Qībǎo. For long a concoction of old-fashioned textures, tatty charm and musty temples, developers long ago started mining the area's lucrative real estate potential, so today expect a mishmash of old and new. For glimpses of old Shànghǎi (that of the Chinese, not the foreigners), however, the surviving Old Town backstreets with their narrow, pinched and crowded lanes, dark alleyways and overhanging laundry are great to explore.

The oval layout of the Old Town follows the footprint of its old 5km-long city walls, flung up to defend against marauding Japanese pirates. The 16th-century city wall was eventually torn down in 1912, but its outline remains along Renmin and Zhonghua Rds.

Temple buffs will love the area's modest Confucian, Taoist, Buddhist, Christian and Muslim shrines but most visitors are here for the traditional Chinese charms of the Yùyuán Gardens. You can also down pots of Chinese tea, haggle at the attached bazaar and sift through knick-knacks on Old Street and Dongtai Road Antique Market.

East of the Old Town, the riverside Cool Docks and South Bund 22 have added pizzazz to formerly run-down areas, bringing in a steady stream of diners and drinkers to their Westerner-oriented bars and restaurants.

Local Life

➡ **Local Lanes** Jostle with Shànghǎi locals wandering along the pinched Old Town back lanes.

➡ **Chinese Medicine** Forage for the best panaceas at the Tóng Hán Chūn Traditional Medicine Store (p86).

➡ **Religious Devotion** Fathom the profound Buddhist mysteries of the Chénxiānggé Nunnery (p77).

➡ **Local Markets** Join the critter-loving Shanghainese browsing the Flower, Bird, Fish & Insect Market (p78).

Getting There & Away

➡ **Metro** Line 10 runs from East Nanjing Rd to the French Concession, passing under the Old Town. The Yuyuan Garden station is close to most sights. Line 8, which runs south from People's Sq to the World Expo grounds, intersects with line 10 at Laoximen (near the Confucian Temple), line 9 at Lujiabang Rd, and line 4 at South Xizang Rd. Line 9 runs along the Old Town's southern edge and into Pǔdōng with a station at Xiaonanmen.

➡ **Bus** Route 11 circles the Old Town, following Renmin Rd and Zhonghua Rd; bus 66 travels along Henan Rd, connecting the Old Town with East Nanjing Rd.

Lonely Planet's Top Tip

Development has largely prevailed over preservation in Shànghǎi's Old Town. The most intriguing areas to wander are well off the main drag: the alleys north of the Confucian Temple (old roads like Zhuangjia St) retain their old flavour, as do some of the alleys off Dajing Rd (such as Changsheng St) and the western stretch of Dongjiadu Rd.

Best Places to Eat

➡ Kebabs on the Grille (p83)

➡ Nánxiáng Steamed Bun Restaurant (p83)

➡ Char (p83)

➡ el Willy (p83)

➡ Stiller's Restaurant & Cooking School (p83)

➡ Table No 1 by Jason Atherton (p83)

For reviews, see p82 ➡

Best Places to Drink

➡ Char Bar (p84)

➡ Zeal (p84)

➡ Old Shanghai Teahouse (p85)

➡ Moonlight Teahouse (p85)

For reviews, see p84 ➡

TOP SIGHTS
YÙYUÁN GARDENS & BAZAAR

With its shaded corridors, glittering pools churning with carp, pavilions, pines sprouting wistfully from rockeries, whispering bamboo, jasmine clumps, potted flowering plants and stony recesses, the labyrinthine Yùyuán Gardens (豫园; Yùyuán) are a delightful escape from Shànghǎi's hard-edged concrete modernity. The attached bazaar (豫园商城; Yùyuán Shāngchéng) is a treasure trove of handicrafts, souvenirs and snacking opportunities, but brace for a powerful onslaught of visitors and the hard sell.

DON'T MISS...

- Hall of Heralding Spring
- Exquisite Jade Rock
- Shopping and snacking in the bazaar area

PRACTICALITIES

- Map p284
- Anren Jie; 安仁街
- admission ¥40
- 8.30am-5.30pm (last tickets sold at 5pm)
- Ⓜ Yuyuan Garden

The Yùyuán Gardens

The Yùyuán Gardens were founded by the Pan family, who were rich Ming-dynasty officials. The gardens took 18 years (from 1559 to 1577) to be nurtured into existence, only to be ransacked during the Opium War in 1842, when British officers were barracked here, and again during the Taiping Rebellion, this time by the French in reprisal for attacks on their nearby concession.

Today the restored gardens are a fine example of Ming garden design. The gardens are small, but seem much bigger thanks to an ingenious use of rocks and alcoves. A handy map depicting the layout of the gardens can be found just inside the entrance. Keep an eye out for the **Exquisite Jade Rock** (玉玲珑; Yù Línglóng), which was destined for the imperial court in Běijīng until the boat carrying it sank outside Shànghǎi, and the **Hall of Heralding Spring** (点春堂; Diǎnchūn Táng), which in 1853 was the headquarters of the Small Swords Society. Note also the beautiful stage, dating from 1888.

Spring and summer blossoms bring a fragrant and floral aspect to the gardens, especially in the heavy petals of its *Magnolia grandiflora,* Shànghǎi's flower. Other trees include the luohan pine, bristling with thick needles, along with willows, towering ginkgos, cherry trees and fine-needled dawn redwoods.

Over a thousand visitors stream into the gardens daily, so early birds get the worm; turn up at midday and you'll be sidestepping camera-toting tour groups (weekends are also overpowering).

The Bazaar

Next to the Yùyuán Gardens entrance rises the **Mid-Lake Pavilion Teahouse** (湖心亭; Húxīntíng; tea downstairs/upstairs ¥25/50; 8.30am-9.30pm), once part of the gardens and now one of the most famous teahouses in China. The zigzag causeway is designed to thwart spirits, who can only travel in straight lines.

Surrounding all this is the restored bazaar area, where scores of speciality shops and restaurants – including the Nánxiáng Steamed Bun Restaurant (p83) – jostle over narrow laneways and small squares in a mock 'ye olde Cathay' setting. There are some choice gift-giving ideas in the souvenir shops, from painted snuff bottles to paper and leather silhouette cuttings, delightful Chinese kites, embroidered paintings and clever palm-and-finger paintings. Despite the skill on display, the hard sell is off-putting.

SIGHTS

At the time of writing, the former Pavilion of the Future (the disused Nánshì Power Plant) in the World Expo site on this side of the river was being unveiled as the Power Station of Art, a huge gallery space showcasing post-1980s contemporary Chinese art and venue of the Shanghai Biennale. For further details on the World Expo sites, see p141.

CHÉNXIĀNGGÉ NUNNERY BUDDHIST TEMPLE

Map p284 (沉香阁; Chénxiāng Gé; 29 Chenxiangge Rd; 沉香阁路29号; admission ¥10; ⌚7am-5pm; Ⓜ Yuyuan Garden) Sheltering a community of dark brown-clothed nuns from the *chénhǎi* (Sea of Dust) – what Buddhists call the mortal world, but which could equally refer to Shànghǎi's murky atmosphere – this lovely yellow-walled temple is a tranquil respite from the mania of Shànghǎi. The **Hall of Heavenly Kings** (天王殿; Tiānwáng Diàn) envelops four gilded Heavenly Kings and a slightly androgynous form of Maitreya. Muttered prayers and chanted hymns fill the **Great Treasure Hall** (大雄宝殿; Dàxióng Bǎodiàn), where a statue of Sakyamuni (Buddha) is flanked by two rows of nine *luóhàn* (arhat). At the rear, the **Guanyin Tower** (观音楼; Guānyīn Lóu; admission ¥2; ⌚7am-3pm) guides you to a glittering effigy of the male-looking goddess upstairs within a resplendent gilded cabinet. Carved from *chénxiāng* wood (Chinese eaglewood) and seated in *lalitasana* posture, head tilted and with one arm resting on her leg, this version is a modern copy (the original disappeared during the Cultural Revolution).

TEMPLE OF THE TOWN GOD TAOIST TEMPLE

Map p284 (城隍庙; Chénghuáng Miào; Yùyuán Bazaar (off Middle Fangbang Rd); admission ¥10; ⌚8.30am-4.30pm; Ⓜ Yuyuan Garden) Chinese towns traditionally came with a Taoist Temple of the Town God, but many fell victim to periodic upheaval. Originally dating to the early 15th century, this particular temple was badly damaged during the Cultural Revolution and later restored. Note the fine carvings on the roof as you enter the main hall, dedicated to Huo Guang, a Han-dynasty general, flanked by rows of

MOUNTAIN-WATER GARDENS

Classical Chinese gardens can be hard to come to grips with: there are no lawns, few flowering plants, and misshapen, huge rocks are everywhere. Yet a stroll in the Yùyuán Gardens is a walk through many different facets of Chinese civilisation, and this is what makes them so unique. Architecture, philosophy, art and literature all converge, and a background in some basics of Chinese culture helps to fully appreciate the garden design.

The Chinese for 'landscape' is *shānshǔi* (山水), literally 'mountain-water'. Mountains and rivers constitute a large part of China's geography, and are fundamental to Chinese life, philosophy, religion and art. So the central part of any garden landscape is a pond surrounded by rock formations.

This also reflects the influence of Taoist thought. Contrary to geometrically designed formal European gardens, where humans saw themselves as masters, Chinese gardens seek to create a microcosm of the natural world through an asymmetrical layout of streams, hills, plants and pavilions (they symbolise humanity's place in the universe – never in the centre, just a part of the whole).

Symbolism works on every level. Plants are chosen as much for their symbolic meaning as their beauty (the pine for longevity, the peony for nobility), the billowy rocks call to mind not only mountains but also the changing, indefinable nature of the Tao (the underlying principle of the universe in Taoist thought), and the names of gardens and halls are often literary allusions to ideals expressed in classical poetry. Painting, too, goes hand in hand with gardening, its aesthetics reproduced in gardens through the use of carefully placed windows and doors that frame a particular view.

Finally, it's worth remembering that gardens in China have always been lived in. Generally part of a residence, they weren't so much contemplative (as in Japan) as they were a backdrop for everyday life: family gatherings, late-night drinking parties, discussions of philosophy, art and politics – it's the people who spent their leisure hours there that ultimately gave the gardens their unique spirit.

effigies representing both martial and civil virtues. Exit the hall north and peek into the multifaith hall on your right dedicated to three female deities: Guanyin (Buddhist), Tianhou and Yanmu Niangniang (Taoist). Gazing fiercely over offerings of fruit from the rear hall is the red-faced and bearded Town God himself.

CONFUCIAN TEMPLE — CONFUCIAN TEMPLE

Map p284 (文庙; Wén Miào; 215 Wenmiao Rd; 文庙路215号; adult/student ¥10/5; ⏲9am-5pm, last entry 4.30pm; Ⓜ Laoximen) A modest and charming retreat, this well-tended temple to Confucius is cultivated with maples, pines, magnolias and birdsong. Originally dating to 1294, when the Mongols held sway through China, the temple moved to its current site in 1855, at a time when Christian Taiping rebels were sending much of China skywards in sheets of flame. The layout is typically Confucian, its few worshippers complemented by ancient and venerable trees, including a 300-year-old elm. The towering **Kuíxīng Pavilion** (Kuíxīng Gé) in the west is named after the god of the literati. The main hall for worshipping Confucius is **Dàchéng Hall** (Dàchéng Diàn), complete with twin eaves and a statue of the sage outside. In line with Confucian championing of learning, a busy secondhand market of (largely Chinese language) books is held in the temple every Sunday morning (admission ¥1; 7.30am to 4pm).

FLOWER, BIRD, FISH & INSECT MARKET — MARKET

Map p284 (万商花鸟鱼虫市场; Wànshāng Huā Niǎo Yú Chóng Shìchǎng; South Xizang Rd; 西藏南路; Ⓜ Laoximen) One of few remaining traditional markets in town, this spot is a fascinating experience. Wander among the roar of crickets, interlaced with snatches of birdsong, to a backdrop of multicoloured fish flitting about. Crickets come in a variety of sizes and are sold in woven bamboo cages; nab one for under ¥30.

FREE DǑNGJIĀDÙ CATHEDRAL — CHURCH

Map p284 (董家渡教堂; Dǒngjiādù Jiàotáng; 185 Dongjiadu Rd; 董家渡路185号; Ⓜ Nanpu Bridge) Just outside the Old Town and once known as St Francis Xavier Church, this magnificent whitewashed cathedral is Shànghǎi's oldest church, built by Spanish Jesuits in 1853. A splendid sight, the church was located within a famously Catholic area of Shànghǎi and is generally open if you want to view the well-kept interior (ring the bell at the side door). Look out for the oil painting of a Chinese-looking infant Jesus and the Virgin Mary. Follow Dongjiadu Rd west for an absorbing stroll through the bustling garment district.

COOL DOCKS — ARCHITECTURE

Map p284 (时尚老码头; Shíshàng Lǎomǎtou; www.thecooldocks.com; 479 South Zhongshan Rd; 中山南路479号; Ⓜ Xiaonanmen) Billed as Xīntiāndì 2, the riverside Cool Docks consist of several *shíkùmén* (stone-gate houses) surrounded by red-brick warehouses, near (but not quite on) the waterfront. Now full of restaurants and bars and all lit up at night, the Cool Docks for long looked like a damp squib without the vibe, buzz or visitor numbers of Xīntiāndì, largely because of little artfulness or style in its conception. After a rash of high-profile and trendy restaurant, bar and hotel openings, business has picked up.

SUNNY BEACH — BEACH

Map p284 (老码头阳光沙滩; Lǎomǎtou Yángguāng Shātān; ☎133 1167 3735; South Zhongshan Rd; incl 1 soft drink ¥50; ⏲10am-10pm; Ⓜ Xiaonanmen) Life's a beach, even in the middle of Shànghǎi. If the sun comes out, pop down to this amusing artificial strip of sand right by the river and north of the Cool Docks with a backdrop of Lùjiāzuǐ, a bar, deckchairs, beach volleyball, Frisbee, tents and other fun beach activities (and no jellyfish).

DÀJÌNG PAVILION — HISTORIC SITE

Map p284 (大境阁; Dàjìng Gé; 259 Dajing Rd; 大境路; admission ¥5; ⏲9am-4pm; Ⓜ Dashijie) Dating from 1815, this pavilion contains the only preserved section of the 5km-long city walls. They were originally erected in 1553, to protect the city against pirates, but were toppled in 1912. A Chinese-language-only exhibition on the history of the Old Town is on the ground floor, along with an interesting scale model depicting the walled district during the reign of Qing emperor Tongzhi. You can climb up to the restored battlements and wander through a collection of halls, but otherwise there's not much to see.

BÁIYÚN TEMPLE — TAOIST TEMPLE

Map p284 (白云观; Báiyún Guàn; 239 Dajing Rd; 大境路239号; admission ¥5; ⏲8am-4.30pm; Ⓜ Dashijie) Immediately west of a hulking

START **CHÉNXIĀNGGÉ NUNNERY**
END **SHÍLIÙPÙ FABRIC MARKET**
DISTANCE **1KM**
DURATION **TWO HOURS**

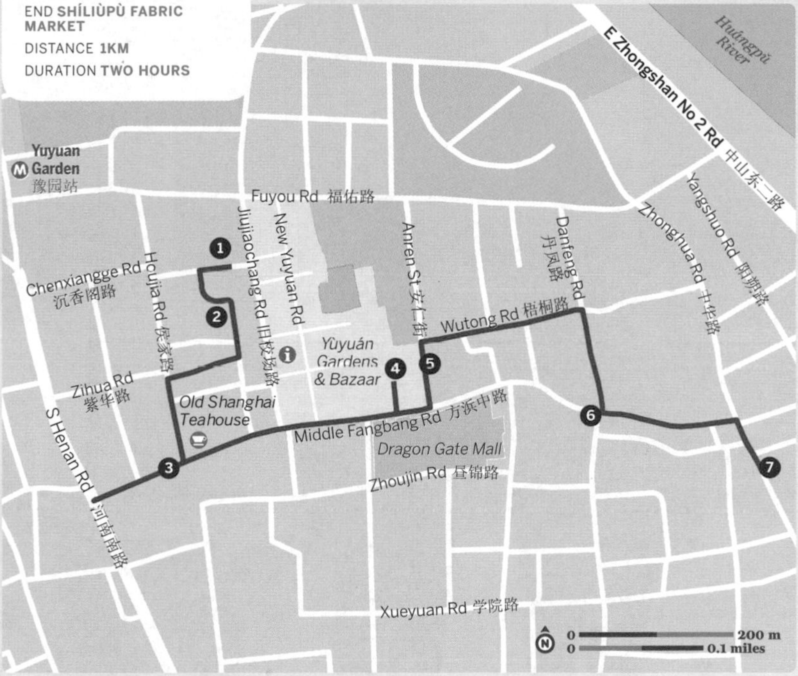

Neighbourhood Walk

Old Town

Begin by visiting the charming **1 Chénxiānggé Nunnery** on Chenxiangge Rd (沉香阁路), a Buddhist retreat from the surrounding clamour.

Clarity attained, exit the temple and weave south down **2 Wangyima Alley** (王医马弄), a small and typical Old Town alley immediately facing you. Follow the alley, then turn west along Zhongwangyima Alley (中王医马弄) to follow Zihua Rd (紫华路) before turning south onto Houjia Rd (侯家路).

Wander along Middle Fangbang Rd (方浜中路) – once a canal and also known as **3 Old Street** – and browse for Tibetan jewellery, teapots and prints of 1930s poster advertisements. Alternatively, break for a pot of refreshing oolong tea at the Old Shanghai Teahouse.

Head east down Old Street, passing the Yùyuán Bazaar, to pay your respects to the red-faced town protector at the **4 Temple of the Town God**.

Upon exiting, continue east down Middle Fangbang Rd and then turn north at the KFC onto **5 Anren Street** (安仁街). Wend your way past the outdoor mah jong and Chinese chess matches, then turn east onto Wutong Rd (梧桐路) and then south on Danfeng Rd (丹凤路), a pinched lane frequently dressed with hanging washing. Note the lovely old doorways on Danfeng Rd, such as the carved red-brick gateway at No 193.

Exit Danfeng Rd, turning east onto Middle Fangbang Rd at the old **6 stone archway** (四牌楼; *sì páilou*). Stroll down the boisterous shopping street, filled with snack stands, clothing shops and booming stereo systems. As long as the eastern part of town remains standing over the next few years, there are plenty of little alleyways to explore here, particularly off to the south. When you reach the end of Middle Fangbang Rd, cross Zhonghua Rd (which marks the eastern boundary of the old city wall) to the **7 Shíliùpù Fabric Market** for a tailor-made shirt, dress or jacket.

1

4

GREG ELMS / GETTY IMAGES ©

3

MICHELE FALZONE / GETTY IMAGES ©

1. Old Town streetlife (p79)
Old Town backstreets, with their crowded lanes and overhanging laundry, are great to explore.

2. Confucian Temple (p78)
This modest and tranquil temple was lovingly restored in the 1990s after taking a hammering during the Cultural Revolution.

3. Shíliùpù Fabric Market (p86)
If you're in search of inexpensive fabric or tailor-made clothes, make a beeline for this market.

4. Flower, Bird, Fish & Insect Market (p78)
Crickets come in a variety of sizes and are sold in woven bamboo cages at this fascinating traditional market.

2

LONELY PLANET / GETTY IMAGES ©

new shopping centre, the port-red and recently built Taoist Báiyún (White Cloud) Temple is fronted by an entrance with twin eaves and separated from Dàjìng Pavilion by Dajing Lane.

FĂZÀNGJIĂNG TEMPLE BUDDHIST TEMPLE

Map p284 (法藏讲寺; Făzàngjiăng Sì; 271 Ji'an Rd; 吉安路271号; admission ¥5; ⏲7.30am-4pm; Ⓜ Laoximen) This simple but very active temple is curiously accessed from the west rather than the south, where the entrance to Buddhist temples usually lies. The main hall, restored with new doors, encloses a large modern statue of Sakyamuni, seated lily-top between two walls glinting with gilded *luóhàn*. Other lesser halls include a trinity of golden Buddhist effigies and a small shrine to the Buddhist god of the underworld, Dizang Wang.

PEACH GARDEN MOSQUE MOSQUE

Map p284 (小桃园清真寺; Xiăotáoyuán Qīngzhēnsì; 52 Xiaotaoyuan Rd; 小桃园路52号; ⏲8am-7pm; Ⓜ Laoximen, Yuyuan Garden) Originally dating to 1917, this famous mosque is the main place of worship for Shànghăi's Muslims. Fridays are the best time to visit, when the faithful stream in to pray at lunch and a large market is held outside the entrance.

LÚPŬ BRIDGE BRIDGE

(卢浦大桥; Lúpŭ Dàqiáo; 909 Luban Rd; 鲁班路909号; adult/student ¥80/40; ⏲8.30am-5pm; Ⓜ Luban Rd, then bus 17, 1 stop) For aerial views of the World Expo grounds or for those seeking to measure the extent of Shànghăi's urban sprawl, climb up to a viewing platform at the apex of the city's longest suspension bridge. The entrance is located at the end of Luban Rd (under the bridge). It's one elevator ride and an additional 367 wind-blown steps to the top. If you take a taxi, insist on the address; the bridge is 4km long and the driver will probably have no idea what you are looking for.

EATING

The Yùyuán Gardens area is hardly a dining destination in itself, but if you're visiting the Old Town you needn't go hungry as there's snack food a plenty and several famous old restaurants, while a collection of zestful and stylish new openings in South Bund 22 and the Cool Docks makes it easy to tie in the area's sights with dinner and drinks by the river.

NAVIGATING SHÀNGHĂI ON FOOT

Unlike in other Chinese cities where street signs are in Chinese (sometimes accompanied by Pinyin), all street signs in Shànghăi display the name of the road in Chinese script and its English translation. Throughout this book we have used road names as they appear on street signs, to aid navigation on foot. But we have also added road names in Chinese in the text to assist you in your journey around town.

By far the majority of roads in Shànghăi are affixed with the word *lù* (路), which means 'road', as in Huashan Lu (Huashan Rd). Occasionally the word *jiē* (街) is used, which means 'street', as in Menghua Jie (Menghua St). The other convention you may see is *dàdào* (大道), which means 'avenue' or 'boulevard', as in Shiji Dadao (Century Ave). Alleys are called *lòng* (弄).

Many road names are also compound words that place the road in context with others in the city, by using the points of the compass. These are:

běi	north	北
nán	south	南
dōng	east	东
xī	west	西
zhōng	middle	中

So, Nanjing Donglu (南京东路) literally means East Nanjing Rd, while Huaihai Zhonglu (淮海中路) means Middle Huaihai Rd. Other words you may see are *huán* (环; ring, as in ring road) and numbers, such as Ruijin Erlu (瑞金二路), or Ruijin No 2 Rd.

NÁNXIÁNG STEAMED BUN RESTAURANT DUMPLINGS $$

Map p284 (南翔馒头店; Nánxiáng Mántou Diàn; 378 Fuyou Rd, Yùyuán Bazaar; 豫园商城福佑路378号; 16 dumplings takeaway ¥12-20, 6 dumplings upstairs from ¥25, set menu ¥60; ⏲10am-9pm; Ⓜ Yuyuan Garden) Shànghǎi's most famous dumpling restaurant divides the purists, who love the place, from the younger crowd, who reckon it's an overrated tourist trap. Decide for yourself how the *xiǎolóngbāo* rate, but be forewarned that hordes of visitors descend on the place and you won't even get near it on weekends. There are three dining halls upstairs, with the prices escalating (and crowds diminishing) in each room. The takeaway deal (including crab meat) is comparable to what you pay elsewhere for *xiǎolóngbāo,* but the queue snakes halfway around the Yùyuán Bazaar.

CHAR STEAKHOUSE $$$

Map p284 (恰餐厅; Qià Cāntīng; ☎3302 9995; www.char-thebund.com; 29-31 fl, Hotel Indigo, 585 East Zhongshan No 2 Rd; 中山东二路585号29-31楼; steaks from ¥390, burgers ¥290, other mains from ¥140; ⏲6-10pm; 🚭 📶; Ⓜ Xiaonanmen) Atop the Hotel Indigo, Char has become a Shànghǎi steakhouse sensation. Park yourself on a sofa against the window or a comfy chair facing Lùjiāzuǐ for optimum views or keep one eye on the open kitchen to see how your Tajima Wagyu rib-eye steak, grilled black cod or seafood tower is coming along. There's a choice of six different steak knives, bookings are recommended and the views continue in spectacular fashion from the terrace of the supremely chilled-out upstairs bar (p84).

EL WILLY SPANISH $$

Map p284 (www.el-willy.com; 5th fl, South Bund 22, 22 East Zhongshan No 2 Rd; 中山东二路22号5楼; tapas/paella from ¥45/195; ⏲lunch & dinner Mon-Sat; 🚭; Ⓜ Yuyuan Garden) Ensconced in the stunningly converted South Bund 22, bright, vivacious, bubbly and relocated from the French Concession, Willy Trullas Moreno's fetching and fun restaurant is a more relaxed counterpoint to many other overdressed Bund operations. Seasonally adjusted scrumptious tapas and paellas are Willy's forte, paired with some serene Bund views beyond the windows. Chopsticks encourage the communal Chinese dining approach.

KEBABS ON THE GRILLE INDIAN $$

Map p284 (☎6152 6567; No 8, Cool Docks, 505 South Zhongshan Rd; 中山南路505号老码头8号; mains from ¥45, set lunch Mon-Fri ¥58; ⏲11am-10.30pm; Ⓜ Xiaonanmen) This immensely popular and busy Cool Docks restaurant is a genuine crowd-pleaser, with al fresco seating by the pond outside. The Boti mutton (barbecued lamb pieces) is adorable, there's a delicious range of tandoori dishes, live table-top grills, an excellent range of vegetarian and smooth and spicy daal options plus an all-you-can-eat Sunday brunch (¥150). Another central branch can be found west of People's Square (p69).

STILLER'S RESTAURANT & COOKING SCHOOL EUROPEAN $$$

Map p284 (☎6152 6501; 6th fl, Bldg 13, Cool Docks, 505 South Zhongshan Rd; 中山南路505弄老码头13号楼6楼; mains from ¥215; ⏲6-10.30pm daily, lunch noon-2.30pm Sun; 🚭 📶; Ⓜ Xiaonanmen) Prices are certainly decadent at Stiller's (restaurant, bar, deli and cooking school), but dishes are sublime, the evening Bund views are delicious and the ambience is classy, but relaxing. Tuck into a turbot fillet with parsley crust or a Mongolian lamb rack, make a start on the ample wine list and round things off with a glass or two on the rooftop bar. Vegetarian menu available. Book ahead.

TABLE NO 1 BY JASON ATHERTON EUROPEAN $$

Map p284 (☎6080 2918; www.tableno-1.com; The Waterhouse at South Bund, 1-3 Maojiayuan Rd; 毛家园路1-3号; mains from ¥148, 3-course lunch & dinner ¥158; ⏲lunch & dinner; 🚭 📶; Ⓜ Xiaonanmen) On the ground floor of the Waterhouse by the Cool Docks, English chef Jason Atherton's Table No 1 commences with a distressed industrial-chic lobby perked up with eclectic furniture before giving way to a casual and smooth interior of candlelit wooden tables arranged in communal dining fashion with a courtyard beyond. The excellent menu (seared sea bass, broccolini and Spanish rice or roasted lamb, smoked eggplant and tomato) is backed up by an impressive wine list.

DRAGON GATE MALL CHINESE $

Map p284 (豫龙坊; Yùlóngfáng; Middle Fangbang Rd; 方浜中路; dishes from ¥10; ⏲9am-11pm; Ⓜ Yuyuan Garden) True, eating in a mall isn't *quite* the same as wandering amid the chaos of the Yùyuán Bazaar, but if you've had enough of the push and pull of the crowds, this spot is a lifesaver. Noodle restaurants, a food court and juice bar are on the basement level while a branch of **Din Tai Fung** is on the 2nd floor, thumbing its nose at Nánxiáng's *xiǎolóngbāo* across the way. The enormous dragon-arch fountain marks the entrance.

FAT OLIVE MEDITERRANEAN **$$**

Map p284 (6334 3288; 6th fl, 228 South Xizang Rd, enter through the Fraser Residence on Shouning Rd; 西藏南路228号6楼; wine per glass from ¥35, meze from ¥28, pita burgers ¥68; 11am-1pm; Dashijie) Nestled among office towers and residential suites, the Fat Olive has a cosy outdoor deck overlooking the Old Town to the south. The brainchild of chef David Laris, it serves Greek-style meze (olives, feta, tzatziki and pita burgers) accompanied by a decent selection of New World wines that go for as low as ¥100 a bottle. This is a prime summer-lounging locale.

SŌNGYUÈLÓU CHINESE **$**

Map p284 (松月楼; 6355 3630; 23 Bailing Rd; 百灵路23号 ; dishes from ¥10; 7am-7.30pm; Yuyuan Garden) Dating to 1910, this place has decent-value vegie cheap eats like wonton (*tānghúndùn;* ¥10) and tofu masquerading as meat such as black pepper beef noodle soup (¥35). Upstairs has an English menu, spotless tablecloths and a price hike. Downstairs is Mandarin-only busy canteen style where you order first, get a receipt and share tables.

ELEMENT FRESH SANDWICHES **$**

Map p284 (新元素; Xīnyuánsù; www.elementfresh.com; 6th fl, Fraser Residence, 228 South Xizang Rd; 西藏南路228号6楼; breakfast from ¥38, meals ¥60-100; Dashijie) Handy Old Town outpost of the health-conscious chain (see p144) dedicated to pick-me-up breakfasts, crisp salads, sandwiches and feel-good juices and smoothies.

DRINKING & NIGHTLIFE

CHAR BAR BAR

Map p284 (恰酒吧; Qià Jiǔbā; www.char-thebund.com; 30th fl, Hotel Indigo, 585 East Zhongshan No 2 Rd; 5pm-1.30am Mon-Thu, 5pm-2.30am Fri & Sat, 2pm-1am Sun; Xiaonanmen) One of Shànghǎi's supreme al fresco bar experiences, Char Bar – above its namesake restaurant on the top floors of the Hotel Indigo – is a top spot for a cocktail and neon gazing. The terrace packs some of the finest views over the Bund, the Huángpǔ River and Pǔdōng, while inside it's chilled out and hip. Drinks are ¥50 between 6pm and 9pm from Monday to Thursday.

ZEAL CLUB

Map p284 (6328 8668; www.zeal-shanghai.com; 6th fl, South Bund 22, 22 East Zhongshan No 2 Rd; 中山东二路22号6楼; beer/cocktail ¥50/70; 5pm-late; Yuyuan Garden) At the top of the stylishly converted South Bund 22 complex, crowd-pulling club/bar Zeal lures clubbers and drinkers alike to its

SEDUCTION AND THE CITY

Shànghǎi owes its reputation as the most fashionable city in China to calendar posters, whose print runs once numbered in the tens of millions and whose distribution (they were given out as bonus gifts, a practice that began at the Shànghǎi racecourse in the late 1890s) reached from China's interior to Southeast Asia. The basic idea behind the posters – associating a product with an attractive woman to encourage subconscious desire and consumption – today sounds like Marketing 101, but in the early 20th century it was revolutionary. Calendar posters not only introduced new products to Chinese everywhere, their portrayal of Shànghǎi women – wearing makeup and stylish clothing, smoking cigarettes and surrounded by foreign goods – set the standard for modern fashion that many Chinese women (trapped in rural lives with little freedom and certainly no nearby department stores) would dream of for decades. Today, reproduction posters are sold throughout the Old Town for as little as ¥10, though finding a bona fide original is quite a challenge. For an in-depth look at calendar posters and Shànghǎi's role in modern China, see Wen-Hsin Yeh's *Shanghai Splendor*.

OLD SHÀNGHǍI STREET NAMES

The naming of streets in Shànghǎi once depended on which concession they belonged to, French or English, except for the central area of the city where the streets were given the names of Chinese cities and provinces. While the foreign names have disappeared, streets named after Chinese places have been retained: those named after other Chinese cities are oriented east–west and those named after provinces north–south. Below are some of Shànghǎi's former street names:

Now	Then
East Yan'an Rd	Edward VII Ave
Fanyu Rd	Columbia Rd
Fenyang Rd	Rue Pichon
Gaolan Rd	Rue Corneille
Guangdong Rd	Canton Rd
Huaihai Rd	Ave Joffre
Jiangsu Rd	Edinburgh Rd
Jinling Rd	Ave Foch
Jinshan Rd	Astor Rd
Tongren Rd	Hardoon Rd
West Nanjing Rd	Bubbling Well Rd
Xiangshan Rd	Rue Molière
Xinhua Rd	Amherst Rd

fabulous outside terrace (exceptional views) and neat interior dance space with video mapping projected onto the wall, live bands and DJ (house, hip hop, electro).

YAWARAGI BAR

Map p284 (3rd fl, South Bund 22, 22 East Zhongshan No 2 Rd; 中山东二路22号3楼; cocktail ¥70; ⏲11am-2am; Ⓜ Yuyuan Garden) Luring patrons with exquisite Japanese chocolate cakes and a delectable Japanese menu, stylish Yawaragi sees the sophisticated cocktail crowd arriving come evening to cherry-pick from its generous list of Bund-priced alcoholic infusions and fruity cocktails.

BRIX BAR

Map p284 (www.brix-shanghai.com; 5th fl, South Bund 22, 22 East Zhongshan No 2 Rd; 中山东二路22号5楼; ⏲5.30pm-late; Ⓜ Yuyuan Garden) A further addition to the burgeoning South Bund 22 development, Brix zeroes in on a casual/urban feel with steel girders, ducts, pipework, grey leather seats and novel table-top Carlsberg and San Miguel beer taps, plus live music. There's a big menu of meat-laden food with a pronounced Austro-Hungarian lean (such as Wiener schnitzel, Hungarian goulash soup).

OLD SHANGHAI TEAHOUSE TEAHOUSE

Map p284 (老上海茶馆; Lǎo Shànghǎi Cháguǎn; ☎5382 1202; 385 Middle Fangbang Rd; 方浜中路385号; tea from ¥45; ⏲9am-9pm; Ⓜ Yuyuan Garden) This wonderfully decrepit 2nd-floor teahouse, overlooking Old St, is a shrine to the 1930s, with music on scratched records, period typewriters, aged photos, an old fireplace, sewing machines, electric fans, an ancient fridge and oodles of charm. It's a bit like barging into the attic of an eccentric aunt.

MOONLIGHT TEAHOUSE TEAHOUSE

Map p284 (耕月人茶馆; Gēngyuèrén Cháguǎn; 4th fl, 235 Middle Fangbang Rd; 方浜中路235号4楼; ⏲10am-11pm; Ⓜ Yuyuan Garden) Squirrelled away on the 4th floor and accessed by lift, the Qing-dynasty setting of stone carvings, Chinese lions and antiques is unrepentantly faux, but this is a relaxing place caressed by traditional Chinese music and infused with the aroma of tea. It's next to the Temple of the Town God, on the corner of Anren St (安仁街).

SHOPPING

Although not originally set up as a shopping district, Yùyuán Bazaar has become exactly that. All souvenirs can be found here or on the bordering Old Street (Middle Fangbang Rd), along with 'antiques' and shops specialising in things such as fans, scissors and walking sticks. The Shíliùpù Fabric Market and the South Bund Fabric Market are both fine places to go in search of inexpensive fabric or to have a dress or shirt tailor-made.

TÓNG HÁN CHŪN TRADITIONAL MEDICINE STORE CHINESE MEDICINE

Map p284 (童涵春堂; Tóng Hán Chūn Táng; ☎6355 0308; 20 New Yuyuan Rd; 上海豫园新路20号; ⏰8am-9pm; Ⓜ Yuyuan Garden) A fantastic old emporium of elixirs, infusions and remedies, this place has been selling Chinese medicinal cures since 1783. There's a vast range here, including modern medications, but it's all labelled in Chinese and little English is spoken so take along a translator. On the 3rd floor, traditional Chinese medicine (TCM) doctors offer consultations (you'll need an appointment).

SHÍLIÙPÙ FABRIC MARKET FABRIC

Map p284 (十六铺面料城; Shíliùpù Miànliào Chéng; ☎6330 1043; 2 Zhonghua Rd; 中华路2号; ⏰8.30am-6.30pm; Ⓜ Xiaonanmen) Having silk shirts, dresses and cashmere coats

LOCAL KNOWLEDGE

SHÀNGHǍI STRUCTURES: THE A LIST

Canadian-born architects Sacha Silva and Raefer Wallis established the innovative and successful Shànghǎi-based firm A00 Architecture in 2004. Here are some of their top architectural picks in Shànghǎi:

Jinmao Tower

Although rather crowded in by two new towers, the Jinmao (p139) is a beautiful, iconic tower – enjoyable from a distance or up close. Remember: bigger is not always better and the Jinmao is sure to go down as a classic with its subdued pagoda-influenced silhouette.

Waterhouse Hotel

To see cutting-edge work by Shànghǎi's leading firm NHDRO, the Waterhouse hotel (p195) is well worth a visit with its perfect combination of industrial and modern aesthetics.

Embankment Building

On North Suzhou Rd, Shànghǎi's contribution to the art-deco style is detailed in the beautiful terrazzo entries and stairways of the Embankment Building (Map p298) that seem frozen in time. Steeped in history, there are many stories tied in with this building; walk up into the endless corridors and imagine yourself back in Shànghǎi's heyday.

Lane 1025

Today West Nanjing Rd is a bustling commercial road, but slip into Lane 1025 (Bubbling Well Rd Apartments) – there are many entry points – and you can see one of the best examples of how British and Asian housing vernacular combined to create the *lǐlòng* housing style unique to Shànghǎi. Well preserved and picturesque, these lane communities are the essence of life in Shànghǎi (see our walking tour on p128).

URBN

The award-winning URBN (p198) hotel on Jiaozhou Rd has been making waves in China and internationally for its ground-breaking push into sustainability, along with its unique take on Shànghǎi's local aesthetic. Always a crowd favourite, take a break from the hectic street bustle and refresh in its garden or lobby restaurant.

tailor-made for a song is one of Shànghǎi's great indulgences. This three-storey building, one of several fabric markets in the city, is conveniently located near the Yùyuán Bazaar. It's a far cheaper source of silk than many shops, with prices no higher than ¥200 per metre. There are many other types of fabric here, from wool and velvet to synthetic, but the quality of the material varies, so shop around. Most places can fill an order in 24 hours if needed, but it's best to count on at least three days.

SOUTH BUND FABRIC MARKET FABRIC

Map p284 (南外滩轻纺面料市场; Nán Wàitān Qīngfǎng Miànliào Shìchǎng; 399 Lujiabang Rd; 陆家浜路399号; ⌚8.30am-6pm; Ⓜ Nanpu Bridge) This old building with over 100 stalls has an atmospheric location not far from the markets and tailoring shops along Dongjiadu Rd. It's further out of the way, but more popular with expats.

DONGTAI ROAD ANTIQUE MARKET SOUVENIRS

Map p284 (东台路古玩市场; Dōngtái Lù Gǔwán Shìchǎng; ☎5582 5254; Dongtai Rd; 东台路; ⌚9am-6pm; Ⓜ Laoximen) A block west of South Xizang Rd, this market street has over 100 stalls strewn along both Dongtai Rd and Liuhekou Rd. It's a long sprawl of miniature terracotta warriors, Guanyin figures, imperial robes, walnut-faced *luóhàn* statues, twee lotus shoes, fake old tin cars, helicopter pilot helmets and Mao-era knick-knacks; generally only recent stuff such as art-deco ornaments (and later) are genuine. Get haggling (a good rule of thumb: if you like the look of something and can get a fair price for it, buy it for what it is and not as an antique).

FÚYÒU ANTIQUE MARKET ANTIQUES, SOUVENIRS

Map p284 (福佑工艺品市场; Fúyòu Gōngyìpǐn Shìchǎng; 459 Middle Fangbang Rd; 方浜中路459号; Ⓜ Yuyuan Garden) There's a permanent antique market here on the 1st and 2nd floors, but the place really gets humming for the 'ghost market' on Sunday at dawn, when sellers from the countryside fill up all four floors and then some. The range is good, but there's a lot of junk, so you need a shrewd eye if you don't want to pay too much over the odds.

TOP CHOICE OLD STREET SOUVENIRS

Map p284 (老街; Lǎo Jiē; Middle Fangbang Rd; 方浜中路; Ⓜ Yuyuan Garden) A renovated Qing-dynasty stretch of Fangbang Rd lined with specialist tourist shops, this is an excellent place for souvenirs and vendors are less pushy than at Yùyuán Bazaar. Shops spill forth with shadow puppets, jade jewellery, embroidered fabrics, old illustrated books and calligraphy manuals, kites, horn combs, chopsticks, *zǐshā* teapots, old poster advertisements, bank notes, Tibetan jewellery, the usual knock-off Mao trash, repro 1930s posters and surreal three-dimensional dazzle photos of kittens.

French Concession

FRENCH CONCESSION EAST | FRENCH CONCESSION WEST

Neighbourhood Top Five

❶ Delve into the lived-in charm and trendy shops of **Tiánzǐfáng** (p90).

❷ Go on a shopping spree in the city's best shopping strips along **Nanchang** or **Xinle Roads** (p117).

❸ Savour home-style Shanghainese cuisine at **Jesse** (p101) or **Diǎn Shí Zhāi Xiǎo Yàn** (p98).

❹ Explore the interior of a stone-gate house at **Xīntiāndì** (p91).

❺ Shake off the stress with massages at **Dragonfly** (p119), clubbing at **Shelter** (p110) or cocktails at **el Cóctel** (p109).

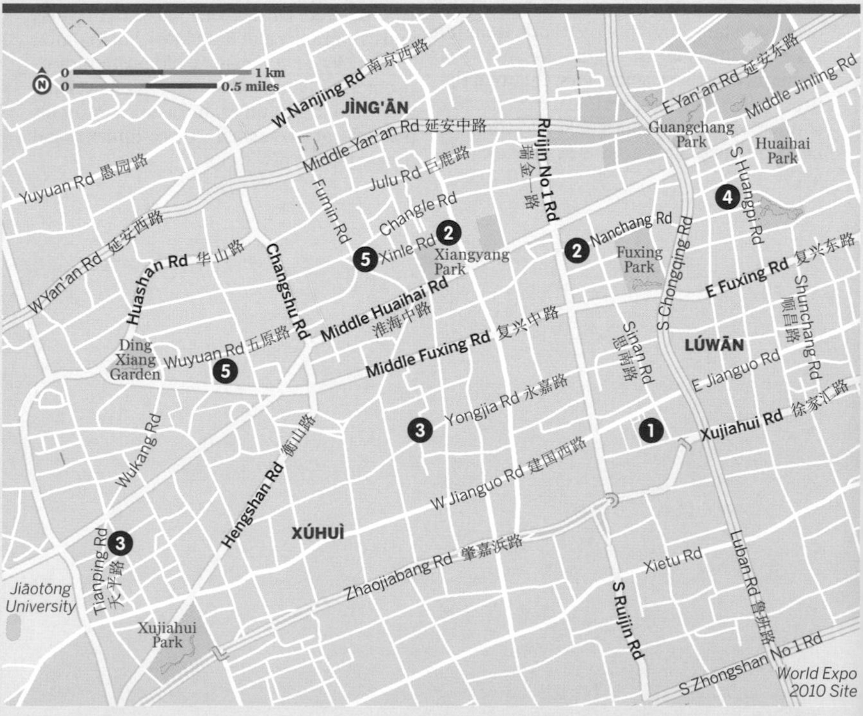

For more detail of this area, see Maps p290 & p286 ➡

Explore: French Concession

If you want to see the city's best profile, the French Concession (法租界) is Shànghǎi sunny side up, at its coolest, hippest and most elegant. Once home to the bulk of Shànghǎi's adventurers, revolutionaries, gangsters, prostitutes and writers – though ironically many of them weren't French – the former concession (also called Frenchtown) is the most graceful part of Pǔxī. Shànghǎi's erstwhile reputation as the 'Paris of the East' largely stems from this area's tree-lined avenues, 1920s mansions and French-influenced architecture.

While sights are few in number, the concession's leafy backstreets and distinct personality make exploration a delight. Most first-time visitors start off in Xīntiāndì, which offers a quick introduction to the local *shíkùmén* (stone-gate house) architecture alongside delicious dining and shopping options. South from here is the former concession's other big draw: Tiánzǐfáng, a less-polished warren of lanes and artsy boutiques that can keep you wandering indefinitely.

The French Concession's real attraction, however, is not sightseeing. Like Shànghǎi itself, the area thrives on its endless quest for sophistication, and its tirelessly inventive restaurant and bar scene, coupled with pop-up boutiques and diverse entertainment options, means that you should come prepared to expand your tastes – just make sure you have cash to spend.

Local Life

- **Shopping** Follow the crowds to the nearest sale or boutique hop from one local designer to another.
- **Foot massages** Sink into an armchair (and maybe catch some Hong Kong action on the tube) while a masseuse kneads your tension away.
- **Snacks** Dumplings, noodles, haute cuisine, Sichuanese, Hunanese, stinky tofu and lychee ice cream – no matter the time of day or the location, you'll always find something to eat.

Getting There & Away

- **Metro** Two main lines serve the French Concession area, both running east–west past Xīntiāndì: line 1 and line 10. Line 1 continues on to People's Square, while line 10 serves the Old Town and East Nanjing Rd (the Bund). The two lines meet at the South Shaanxi Rd metro stop. At the southern edge of the concession is line 9, which serves Tiánzǐfáng. The north–south line 7 provides a handy link between the French Concession and the Jìng'ān neighbourhood; it connects with line 1 at Changshu Rd and line 9 at Zhaojiabang Rd.

Lonely Planet's Top Tip

Although this guide uses the colonial-era term French Concession as a matter of convenience, the name will bring blank looks from many Shanghainese. Locals refer to most of the eastern area as either Lúwān (卢湾) or Huángpǔ (黄浦), while the area west of South Shaanxi Rd is known as Xúhuì (徐汇), a district that extends southwest into Xújiāhuì. If you're in Shànghǎi for more than a short visit, it's worth familiarising yourself with these official district names.

Best Places to Eat

- Spicy Joint (p100)
- Yīn (p101)
- Jesse (p101)
- Dī Shuǐ Dòng (p97)
- 18 (p97)

For reviews, see p96

Best Places to Drink

- el Cóctel (p109)
- Cotton's (p109)
- Abbey Road (p110)
- Boxing Cat Brewery (p110)
- Dr Wine (p110)

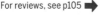

For reviews, see p105

Best Shopping

- Tiánzǐfáng (p113)
- NuoMi (p116)
- Brocade Country (p117)
- Xīntiāndì Style (p114)
- PCS (Pop Classic Sneakers) (p115)

For reviews, see p113

LO MAK / REDLINK / CORBIS ©

TOP SIGHTS
TIÁNZǏFÁNG

Tiánzǐfáng (田子坊) and Xīntiāndì are based on a similar idea – an entertainment complex housed within a layout of traditional *lòngtáng* alleyways – but when it comes to genuine charm and vibrancy, Tiánzǐfáng is the one that delivers. A community of design studios, local families, wi-fi cafes and start-up boutiques, this is the perfect antidote to Shànghǎi's oversized malls and intimidating skyscrapers.

Galleries
There are three main north–south lanes (Nos 210, 248 and 274) crisscrossed by irregular east–west alleyways, which makes exploration slightly disorienting and fun. On the main lane is the **Deke Erh Art Centre** (Map p286; No 2, Lane 210; ⌚9am-10pm), owned by local photographer Deke Erh, who also runs the Old China Hand Reading Room (p108). A good range of books on Shànghǎi are on display. Another gallery to seek out is Beaugeste (p95), which has excellent contemporary photography exhibits that are in a league of their own when compared with the digitally enhanced photos for sale everywhere else.

Just outside the complex on Taikang Rd, an enormous peony bloom covers the exterior of the Liúli China Museum (p94), dedicated to the art of glass sculpture.

Shopping & Drinking
Of course the real activity here is shopping, and the recent explosion of creative start-ups makes for some interesting finds (see p113), from local fashion brands to Běijīng-style messenger bags. An increasing number of stalls selling mass-produced souvenir dross have moved in, so you'll need to hunt for the genuine boutiques, but rest assured, they're still here.

Elsewhere, a growing band of cool cafes – such as Kommune (p99), the Bell Bar (p105), Kāibā (p108) and Origin (p99) – can sort out lunch or drinks, provide a wi-fi connection and take the weight off your feet.

DON'T MISS
- Boutique hunting
- Liúli China Museum
- Drinks or a meal at an alleyway cafe

PRACTICALITIES
- Map p286
- Lane 210, Taikang Rd; 泰康路210弄
- Ⓜ Dapuqiao

LONELY PLANET / GETTY IMAGES ©

TOP SIGHTS
XĪNTIĀNDÌ

Xīntiāndì (新天地) has only been around for a decade and already it's a Shànghǎi icon. An upscale entertainment complex modelled on traditional alleyway *(lòngtáng)* homes, this was the first development in the city to prove that historic architecture does, in fact, have economic value. Elsewhere that might sound like a no-brainer, but in 21st-century China, which is head-over-heels for the bulldozer, it came as quite a revelation.

Well-heeled shoppers and al fresco diners keep the place busy until late, and if you're looking for a memorable meal (p97) or a browse through some of Shànghǎi's more fashionable boutiques (p114), you're in the right place.

DON'T MISS

- Shíkùmén Open House Museum
- Al fresco dining
- Window shopping

PRACTICALITIES

- Map p286
- www.xintiandi.com
- 2 blocks enclosed within Taicang, Zizhong, Madang & South Huangpi Rds
- M South Huangpi Rd, Xintiandi

Museums, Restaurants & Shops

The heart of the complex, divided into a pedestrianised north and south block, consists of largely rebuilt traditional *shíkùmén* houses, brought bang up-to-date with a stylish modern spin. (For more on *shíkùmén* see p234.) But while the layout suggests a flavour of yesteryear, you should not expect much in the cultural realm. Xīntiāndì doesn't deliver any of the lived-in charm of the Tiánzǐfáng or the creaking, rickety simplicity of the Old Town. Beyond the two sights located in the North Block – the Shíkùmén Open House Museum (p92) and the Site of the 1st National Congress of the CCP (p92) – it's best for strolling the prettified alleyways and enjoying a summer evening over drinks or a meal.

Serious shoppers – and diners – will eventually find their way to the malls at the southern tip of the South Block. Beyond the first, which holds three top-notch restaurants on the 2nd floor (Din Tai Fung, p97; Crystal Jade, p98; and Shànghǎi Min, p98), is the newly constructed mall Xīntiāndì Style, showcasing local brands at the vanguard of Shanghainese fashion.

SIGHTS

French Concession East

XĪNTIĀNDÌ LANDMARK

See p91.

SHÍKÙMÉN OPEN HOUSE MUSEUM MUSEUM

Map p286 (石库门屋里厢; Shíkùmén Wūlǐxiāng; Xīntiāndì North Block, Bldg 25; 太仓路181弄新天地北里25号楼; admission ¥20; ⏰10.30am-10.30pm; Ⓜ South Huangpi Rd, Xintiandi) Arranged over two floors and entered via Xingye Rd in Xīntiāndì, this fascinating exhibition invites you into a typical *shíkùmén* household, decked out with period furniture. The ground-floor arrangement contains a courtyard, entrance hall, bedroom, study and lounge, small kitchen to the rear and natural illumination spilling down from light wells *(tiānjǐng)* above.

The small and frequently north-facing wedge-shaped *tíngzijiān* room on the landing almost at the top of the stairs between the 1st and 2nd floors was a common feature of *shíkùmén*, and was often rented out. The main bedrooms are all on the 2nd floor, linked together by doors.

FREE **SITE OF THE 1ST NATIONAL CONGRESS OF THE CCP** HISTORIC BUILDING

Map p286 (中共一大会址纪念馆; Zhōnggòng Yīdàhuìzhǐ Jìniànguǎn; Xīntiāndì North Block, 76 Xingye Rd; 兴业路76号; ⏰9am-5pm; Ⓜ South Huangpi Rd, Xintiandi) On 23 July 1921 the Chinese Communist Party (CCP) was founded in this French Concession building (then 106 rue Wantz), and in one fell swoop converted this unassuming *shíkùmén* block into one of Chinese communism's holiest shrines.

The dizzying Marxist spin of the museum commentary is a salutary reminder that Shànghǎi remains part of the world's largest communist nation. The certainties of that era – whether you sympathise with *Mǎlièzhǔyì* (Marxist-Leninism) or not – exude a nostalgic appeal in today's Shànghǎi, where ideology of any shade is fervently shunned. Beyond the communist narcissism, there's little to see, although historians will enjoy ruminating on the site's historic momentousness.

On the ground floor you can be present in the room where the whole party began, actually the house of the delegate Li Hanjun. Up the marble stairs in the 'Exhibition of Historical Relics Showing the Founding of the Communist Party of China' is a highly patriotic hymn to early Chinese communist history with exhibits such as the Chinese translation of Mary E Marcy's *The ABC of Das Kapital by Marx*.

A passport is required for entry; last admission is at 4pm.

SUN YATSEN'S FORMER RESIDENCE HISTORIC BUILDING

Map p286 (孙中山故居; Sūn Zhōngshān Gùjū; 7 Xiangshan Rd; 香山路7号; admission ¥20; ⏰9am-4pm; Ⓜ South Shaanxi Rd, Xintiandi) China is awash with Sun Yatsen (Sun Zhongshan) memorabilia and this is one of several former dwellings nationwide. Countless Chinese cities evoke the celebrated Father of Modern China with a Zhongshan Park, Zhongshan Rd, or both. Sun lived here on rue Molière for six years from 1918 to 1924, supported by overseas Chinese funds.

After Sun's death, his wife, Song Qingling (1893–1981; see p94), continued to live here until 1937, constantly watched by Kuomintang plain-clothes officers and the French police. The two-storey house is set back from the street and is furnished as it was back in Sun's day, though it was looted by the Japanese during WWII. The entry price gets you a brief tour of the house in English.

FREE **FÙXĪNG PARK** PARK

Map p286 (复兴公园; Fùxīng Gōngyuán; ⏰5am-6pm; Ⓜ South Shaanxi Rd, Xintiandi) This leafy park, laid out by the French in 1909 and later used by the Japanese as a parade ground in the late 1930s, remains one of the city's more pleasant. There is always plenty to see here: the park is a refuge for the elderly and a practising field for itinerant musicians, chess players, people walking backwards and slow-moving taichi types.

Heavily shaded by big-leafed wutong trees, it's an excellent place to take a seat and escape the summer sun and there's even a popular kiddies' playground. Wreathed in the laughter of children, the huge stony-faced busts of Karl Marx and Friedrich Engels gaze out from a seemingly redundant epoch, and nobody seems to notice.

ST NICHOLAS CHURCH CHURCH

Map p286 (圣尼古拉斯教堂; Shèngnígǔlāsī Jiàotáng; 16 Gaolan Rd; 皋兰路16号; Ⓜ South Shaanxi Rd) A short walk west along

START **XINTIANDI METRO STATION**
END **CATHAY THEATRE**
DISTANCE **2.5KM**
DURATION **75 MINUTES**

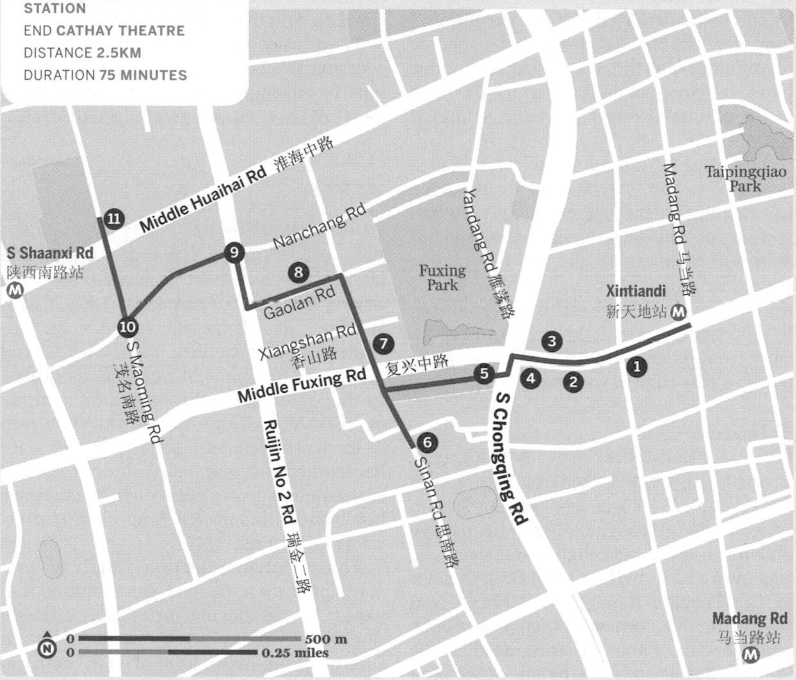

Neighbourhood Walk
French Concession Stroll

Begin walking west on Middle Fuxing Rd (formerly rue Lafayette), first passing the red-brick Italianate ❶ **All Saint's Church** (1925) and then the ❷ **Park Apartments** (1926) and smaller private villas fronted by palm trees, which date to the same era. On the northern side of Middle Fuxing Rd at No 512 is the ❸ **Former Residence of Liu Haisu** (1896–1994), a 20th-century artist who revolutionised traditional Chinese art by introducing Western painting styles. Opposite, at the corner with South Chongqing Rd, is the ❹ **Dubail Apartment Building** (1931), the one-time home of US journalist and communist sympathiser Agnes Smedley (1892–1950). Smedley reported extensively on the Chinese civil war in the '30s; her return to the US the following decade was marred by accusations of her being a Soviet spy.

Turn into ❺ **Sinan Mansions**, a complex of luxurious 1920s private villas that were built south of French Park (now Fùxīng Park) and recently renovated as an upscale lifestyle destination; today it houses numerous cafes and restaurants, as well as ultra-exclusive short-term residences to the south. Exit on Sinan Rd (route Massenet) and turn south to see ❻ **Zhou Enlai's Former Residence**, which served primarily as the Communist Party's Shànghǎi office. Retrace your footsteps and return north up leafy Sinan Rd and its lovely stretch of old villas to reach ❼ **Sun Yatsen's Former Residence**, where the father of modern China lived from 1918 to 1924. On Gaolan Rd (route Cohen) is the Russian Orthodox ❽ **St Nicholas Church**, built in 1934 in dedication to the murdered tsar of Russia.

Continue on to ❾ **Nanchang Road** (rue Vallon), a shopping strip where you'll find boutiques selling jewellery, shoes, antiques and clothing. Turn onto ❿ **Maoming Road** (route Cardinal Mercier), another shopping hotspot that specialises in *qípáo* (figure-hugging dresses) and other Chinese-style clothes. Across busy Huaihai Rd is the landmark art-deco ⓫ **Cathay Theatre** (1932).

Gaolan Rd from Fùxīng Park is rewarded by the distinctive shape of the vacant, and now derelict, St Nicholas Church, one of Shànghǎi's small band of Russian Orthodox houses of worship, built to service the huge influx of Russians who arrived in Shànghǎi in the 1930s.

The church, dating from 1934, has a typically varied CV, ranging from shrine to washing-machine factory and French restaurant (the latter recalled by the inscription 'Ashanti Dome' on the plaque embedded above the door). It was spared destruction during the Cultural Revolution by a portrait of Mao Zedong, hung strategically from its dome. It was not open to the public at the time of writing.

FREE ZHOU ENLAI'S FORMER RESIDENCE — HISTORIC BUILDING

Map p286 (周恩来故居; Zhōu Ēnlái Gùjū; 73 Sinan Rd; 思南路73号; ⏲9am-4pm; ⓂSouth Shaanxi Rd, Xintiandi) In 1946 Zhou Enlai, the urbane and much-loved (although some swear he was even more sly than Mao) first premier of the People's Republic of China, lived briefly in this former French Concession Spanish villa. Zhou was then head of the Communist Party's Shànghǎi office and spent much of his time giving press conferences and dodging Kuomintang agents who spied on him from across the road.

There's not much to see these days except spartan beds and stern-looking desks, but the charming neighbourhood, with its lovely old houses, is a great place to stroll.

TIÁNZǏFÁNG — LANDMARK

See p90.

LIÚLI CHINA MUSEUM — MUSEUM

Map p286 (琉璃艺术博物馆; Liúli Yìshù Bówùguǎn; www.liulichinamuseum.com; 25 Taikang Rd; 泰康25号; admission ¥20; ⏲10am-5pm Tue-Sun; ⓂDapuqiao) Founded by Taiwanese artists Loretta Yang and Chang Yi, the Liúli China Museum is dedicated to the art of glass sculpture (*pâte de verre* or lost-wax casting). Peruse the collection of ancient artefacts – some of which date back over 2000 years – to admire the early craftsmanship of pieces such as earrings, belt buckles and even a Tang-dynasty crystal *wéiqí* (go) set.

The collection transitions fluidly to more contemporary creations from around the world, before moving on to Yang's serene Buddhist-inspired creations, including a sublime 1.6m-high, 1000-armed Guanyin, which was modelled on a Yuan-dynasty mural in the Mògāo Caves near Dūnhuáng.

THE SOONG FAMILY

The Soongs probably wielded more influence and power over modern China than any other family. The father of the family, Charlie Soong, grew up in Hǎinán and after an American evangelical education, finally settled in Shànghǎi. He began to print bibles and money, becoming a wealthy businessman and developing ties with secret societies, during which time he became good friends with Sun Yatsen (Sun Zhongshan). Charlie had three daughters and a son.

Soong Ailing – said to be the first Chinese girl in Shànghǎi to own a bicycle – married HH Kung, the wealthy descendent of Confucius, Bank of China head and later finance minister of the Republic of China. Soong Meiling (May-ling) became the third wife of Chiang Kaishek (Kuomintang leader and future president of the Republic of China) in 1928. She went to the USA during the Japanese occupation of China and fled to Taiwan with Chiang after the communist victory. Much to the disapproval of her father, Soong Qingling (more commonly known as Song Qingling) married Sun Yatsen, 30 years her elder, studied in Moscow and was the only member of the family to live in China after 1949, until her death in 1981. TV Soong, Charlie's only son, served as the Republic of China's finance minister and premier, becoming the richest man of his generation.

Mainland Chinese say that of the three daughters, one loved money (Ailing), one loved power (Meiling) but only Qingling loved China. Among them, the siblings stewed up a heady brew of fascism and communism.

Song Qingling died in Běijīng and is buried at the Song Qingling Mausoleum (p165) in Shànghǎi. Her sister Meiling declined the invitation to return to China to attend the funeral; she died in the USA in October 2003, aged 105.

The museum is free for children under 18 and seniors over 65. On the 1st floor is a vegan-friendly **cafe** (⏲10am-11pm; 📶) and a shop (p113) selling *liúli* crystal.

FREE **BEAUGESTE** GALLERY

(比极影像; Bǐjí Yǐngxiàng; www.beaugeste-gallery.com; 5th fl, No 5, Lane 210, Taikang Rd; 泰康路210弄5号520室田子坊; ⏲10am-6pm; ⓂDapuqiao) One of the best galleries in Shànghǎi, this small space is concealed high above the street-level crowds. Curator Jean Loh focuses on humanistic themes in contemporary Chinese photography, and his wide range of contacts and excellent eye ensure exhibits that are always both moving and thought provoking. You can also pick up previous exhibition catalogues here.

FREE **SHÀNGHǍI MUSEUM OF PUBLIC SECURITY** MUSEUM

off Map p286 (上海公安博物馆; Shànghǎi Gōng'ān Bówùguǎn; 518 South Ruijin Rd; 瑞金南路518号; ⏲9am-4pm Mon-Sat; ⓂDapuqiao) It may sound turgid and dull, but this museum has some gems among the inevitable displays on traffic control and post-Liberation security milestones. The gold pistols of Sun Yatsen and 1930s gangster Huang Jinrong (p213) are worth hunting down amid the fine collection of Al Capone–style machine- and pen-guns, and look out for the collection of hand-painted business cards once dispensed by the city's top *jìnǚ* (prostitutes).

MOLLER HOUSE HISTORIC BUILDING

Map p286 (马勒别墅; Mǎlè Biéshù; 30 South Shaanxi Rd; 陕西南路30号; ⓂSouth Shaanxi Rd) One of Shànghǎi's most whimsical buildings, the Scandinavian-influenced gothic peaks of the Moller House could double as the Munsters' holiday home. The Swedish owner and horse-racing fan, Eric Moller, owned the Moller Line. Previously home to the Communist Youth League, the building now houses a hotel, the Héngshān Moller Villa (p196).

Fancifully perhaps, legend attests that a fortune teller warned Moller that tragedy would befall him on the house's completion, so the tycoon dragged out its construction (until 1949). Moller clung on for a few more years before dying in a plane crash in 1954.

French Concession West

PROPAGANDA POSTER ART CENTRE GALLERY

Map p290 (宣传画年画艺术中心; Shànghǎi Xuānchuánhuà Yìshù Zhōngxīn; ☎6211 1845; Room B-OC, President Mansion, 868 Huashan Rd; 华山路868号B-OC室; admission ¥20; ⏲10am-5pm; ⓂShanghai Library) If phalanxes of red tractors, bumper harvests, muscled peasants and lantern-jawed proletariats fire you up, this small gallery in the bowels of a residential block should intoxicate. The collection of 3000 original posters from the 1950s, '60s and '70s – the golden age of Maoist poster production – will have you weak-kneed at the cartoon world of anti-US defiance.

The centre divides into a showroom and a shop featuring posters and postcards for sale. Once you find the main entrance, a guard will pop a small business card with a map on it into your hands and point you the way. Head around the back of the apartment blocks to Building B and take the lift to the basement. It's a good idea to phone ahead (they speak some English) before heading out here to make sure it's open.

SHÀNGHǍI ARTS & CRAFTS MUSEUM MUSEUM

Map p290 (上海工艺美术博物馆; Shànghǎi Gōngyì Měishù Bówùguǎn; 79 Fenyang Rd; 汾阳路79路; admission ¥8; ⏲9am-4pm; ⓂChangshu Rd) Repositioned as a museum, this arts and crafts institute displays traditional crafts such as embroidery, paper cutting, lacquer work, jade cutting and lantern making. Watch traditional crafts being performed live by craftspeople and admire the wonderfully wrought exhibits, from jade, to ivory to ink stones and beyond.

It's hard not to suspect that the collections were arranged to herd visitors through the overpriced ground-floor shops (foreign exchange assisted). The highlight is quite possibly the building itself, built in 1905, which once served as the residence for Chen Yi, Shànghǎi's first mayor after the founding of the CCP.

FREE **RUSSIAN ORTHODOX MISSION CHURCH** CHURCH

Map p290 (东正教圣母大堂; Dōngzhèngjiào Shèngmǔ Dàtáng; 55 Xinle Rd; 新乐路55号; ⏲10.30am-6pm Tue-Sun; ⓂSouth Shaanxi Rd) Built in 1934, the lovely blue-domed church was designed for the huge influx of Russian worshippers to Shànghǎi in the 1930s. Faded murals grace the cupola, but the real reason to visit today is for a meander through the contemporary art gallery **Space** (www.espace-sh.com), which shows four to five exhibits in the interior each year.

SONG QINGLING'S FORMER RESIDENCE
HISTORIC BUILDING

Map p290 (宋庆龄故居; Sōng Qìnglíng Gùjū; 1843 Middle Huaihai Rd; 淮海中路1843号; admission ¥20; ⌚9am-4.30pm; Ⓜ Jiaotong University) Built in the 1920s by a Greek shipping magnate, this building became home to the wife of Dr Sun Yatsen from 1948 to 1963 (see boxed text, p94). Size up two of her black limousines (one a gift from Stalin) in the garage and pad about the house, eyeing its period furnishings.

A few personal belongings are also on display, including autographed books from American journalists Edgar Snow and Agnes Smedley, and a collection of old photographs depicting the Soong sisters and various heads of state. The highlight is the gorgeous garden out back, with tall magnolias and camphor trees towering over a delightful lawn, where Song entertained her guests with conversation and tea.

FREE WUKANG ROAD TOURIST INFORMATION CENTER
ARCHITECTURE

Map p290 (武康路旅游咨询中心; Wǔkāng Lù Lǚyóu Zīxún Zhōngxīn; 393 Wukang Rd; 武康路393号; ⌚9am-5pm; Ⓜ Shanghai Library) On one of the area's best-preserved streets, this centre displays scale-model concession buildings, photos of historic Shànghǎi architecture and maps for self-guided walking tours of Wukang Rd. It's in the former residence of Huang Xing (1874–1916), a revolutionary who co-founded the Republic of China together with Sun Yatsen.

FREE LEO GALLERY
GALLERY

Map p290 (狮语画廊; Shīyǔ Huàláng; 376 Wukang Rd; 武康路376号; ⌚11am-7pm; Ⓜ Shanghai Library, Jiaotong University) Spread across two buildings in the charming Ferguson Lane complex, the Leo Gallery focuses on works by young Chinese artists. See also p66.

FREE HONG MERCHANT GALLERY
GALLERY

Map p290 (☎6283 2696; www.hongmerchant.com; No 3, Lane 372, Xingguo Rd; 兴国路372弄3号; ⌚11am-6pm; Ⓜ Jiaotong University) An elegant showroom combining antique furniture and contemporary art. Open by appointment only.

FREE ART LABOR
GALLERY

Map p290 (www.artlaborgallery.com; Bldg 4, Surpass Court, No 570 Yongjia Rd; 永嘉路570号4号楼; ⌚11am-7pm Tue-Sat, noon-6pm Sun; Ⓜ Hengshan Rd) An independent gallery representing a balance of Chinese and international artists. Exhibits often focus on the question of identity in contemporary Shànghǎi.

FREE JAMES COHAN
GALLERY

Map p290 (www.jamescohan.com; Bldg 1, Lane 170, Yueyang Rd; 岳阳路170弄1号楼; ⌚10am-6pm Tue-Sat, noon-6pm Sun; Ⓜ Hengshan Rd) Excellent New York gallery representing international artists; their provocative Shànghǎi branch is set in a lovely art-deco villa.

FREE BA JIN'S FORMER RESIDENCE
HISTORIC BUILDING

Map p290 (巴金故居; Bājīn Gùjū; 113 Wukang Rd; 武康路113号; ⌚10am-3pm Tue-Sat; Ⓜ Shanghai Library) Probably for literary buffs only, this French Concession house is where the acclaimed author Ba Jin (1904–2005) lived from 1955 to the mid-90s. Ba was the author of dozens of novels and short stories (the most famous of which is *Family*), many of which were published during the peak of his career in the 1930s. His house today contains a collection of old photos, books and manuscripts. Like many intellectuals, he was persecuted mercilessly during the Cultural Revolution, during which time his wife died after being denied medical treatment. Passport may be needed for entry.

EATING

The French Concession is where it's at when it comes to eating, and whatever it is that you're craving, you'll probably be able to find it here. Fancy fusion food? Check. Wild Yunnanese mushrooms? Check. Wacky *maki* rolls? Check. Tongue-tingling Sichuanese? Double check. Taojiang Rd, Dongping Rd, Fumin Rd and Xīntiāndì are the main culinary hotspots in town, and with dozens of choices between them, you'd have to eat out every night for a year to try them all. Well, what are you waiting for?

French Concession East

TOP CHOICE **DĪ SHUǏ DÒNG** HUNANESE $$

Map p286 (滴水洞; ☎6253 2689; 2nd fl, 56 South Maoming Rd; 茂名南路56号2层; dishes ¥25-88; ⏰11am-12.30am; ⓂSouth Shaanxi Rd) It's hard to imagine Mao as a restaurateur, but he may have liked this place (named after a cave in his home village) with its unpretentious, down-home atmosphere and killer chilli pepper-infused cuisine. Join the waitresses decked out in blue calico and red-faced diners talking it up over an increasingly raucous meal for a taste of Hunanese done right.

The claim to fame is the Húnán-style cumin-crusted ribs, but there's no excuse not to sample the *làzi jīdīng* (fried chicken with chillies), one of the excellent claypot dishes or even the classic boiled frog. Cool down with plenty of beers and the crowd-pleasing caramelised bananas for dessert.

LÁNXĪN CĀNTĪNG SHANGHAINESE $

Map p286 (兰心餐厅; 130 Jinxian Rd; 进贤路130号; dishes ¥12-65; ⏰11am-2pm & 5-9pm; ⓂSouth Shaanxi Rd) The best Shanghainese kitchens are the hole-in-the-walls along Jinxian Rd. These aren't design-heavy spots started by savvy investors or international superchefs; they're unpretentious and family-run – the last of a dying breed. Dishes to savour include the classic *hóngshāo ròu* (红烧肉; braised pork), the delectable *gānshāo chāngyú* (干烧鲳鱼; quick-fried pomfret fish) and even the *xiǎopái luóbo tāng* (小排萝卜汤; spare-rib-and-radish soup).

For total immersion, order a bottle of warm *huáng jiǔ* (黄酒; traditional Chinese wine). If the wait is too long, **Hǎijīnzī** (海金滋; 240 Jinxian Rd) at the western end of the street is a comparable experience. No reservations, no English and cash only.

DIN TAI FUNG DUMPLINGS $$

Map p286 (鼎泰丰; Dǐng Tài Fēng; ☎6385 8378; Xīntiāndì South Block, 2nd fl, Bldg 6; 兴业路123弄新天地南里6号楼2楼; 10 dumplings ¥58-88; ⏰10am-midnight; ⊖; ⓂSouth Huangpi Rd, Xintiandi) To-die-for dumplings and classy service from Taiwan's most famous chain (p160). It's on the 2nd floor, in the mall. Reserve.

TOP CHOICE **T8** FUSION $$$

Map p286 (☎6355 8999; Xīntiāndì North Block, Bldg 8; 太仓路181弄新天地北里8号楼; mains ¥248-598, 2-/3-course set lunch ¥168/238; ⏰closed lunch Mon; ⊖; ⓂSouth Huangpi Rd, Xintiandi) T8 is designed for seduction, which it does exceptionally well. The renovated grey-brick *shíkùmén* is the perfect setting for the dark, warm interior, decorated with antique Chinese cabinets, carved wooden screens and the striking feng shui–driven entrance. Catalan chef Jordi Servalls Bonilla is now at the helm, bringing along a preference for molecular cuisine: sample dishes like watermelon salad 2.0, *tataki* of sesame-crusted tuna and Sìchuān high pie. Reserve.

ECSTASY IN XTD

The best dining options in Xīntiāndì.

Crystal Jade (p98) Join the queue for dim-sum delicacies.

Din Tai Fung (p97) Glorified street food from the renegade province.

Kabb (p100) Sandwiches, wraps and salads for a taste of home.

Shànghǎi Min (p98) Chic, affordable chain specialising in Shanghainese cuisine.

T8 (p97) A feng shui fusion masterpiece.

Xīnjíshì (p99) Home-style Shanghainese in all its sweet and oily glory.

Yè Shànghǎi (p99) 1930s class and delectable Shànghǎi cooking.

SOUTHERN BARBARIAN YUNNANESE $$

Map p286 (南蛮子; Nánmánzi; ☎5157 5510; 2nd fl, Gourmet Zone, 56 South Maoming Rd; 茂名南路56号生活艺术空间2楼; dishes ¥25-68; ⓂSouth Shaanxi Rd) Despite the alarming name, there's nothing remotely barbaric about the food here. Instead, you get fine, MSG-free Yúnnán cuisine served by friendly staff in a laid-back (though somewhat noisy) atmosphere. It's hard to fault any of the dishes, but the barbecued freshwater snapper with a cumin-and-peppercorn glaze is a sublime explosion of flavours. The stewed beef and mint casserole is almost as good, as is the incomparable 'grandmother's mashed potatoes'. It's essential to make room for the chicken wings too, which come covered in a seriously addictive secret sauce. To top it off, they have an impressively long imported beer list. You can also enter at 169 Jinxian Rd.

CRYSTAL JADE DIM SUM $$

Map p286 (翡翠酒家; Fěicuì Jiǔjiā; ☎6385 8752; Xīntiāndì South Block, 2nd fl, Bldg 6; 兴业路123弄新天地南里6号2楼; dim-sum dishes ¥16-24, noodles from ¥32; ⏲10.30am-11pm; Ⓜ South Huangpi Rd, Xintiandi) Long one of Xīntiāndì's most popular Chinese restaurants, Crystal Jade still draws lines out the door. What distinguishes it from other dim-sum restaurants is the dough: dumpling skins are perfectly tender, steamed buns come out light and airy, and the freshly pulled noodles are just plain delicious. Go for lunch, when both Cantonese and Shanghainese dim sum are served. It's in the mall; reserve ahead.

CHA'S CANTONESE $

Map p286 (查餐厅; Chá Cāntīng; 30 Sinan Rd; 思南路30号; dishes ¥20-50; ⏲11am-2am; Ⓜ South Shaanxi Rd) This absolutely packed Cantonese diner does its best to teleport you to 1950s Hong Kong, with old-style tiled floors, whirring ceiling fans and even an antique Coca-Cola ice box to set the scene. You'll need to wait to get a table, so use the time wisely and peruse the menu of classic comfort food (curries, sweet-and-sour pork) in advance.

BANKURA JAPANESE $$

Map p286 (万藏; Wànzàng; ☎6215 0373; 344 Changle Rd; 长乐路344号; noodles ¥30-45, lunch sets ¥39; Ⓜ South Shaanxi Rd) Pull up a seat at this underground Japanese noodle bar, where you'll find an array of soba (thin buckwheat noodles, often served cold) and udon (thick wheat noodles, often served in broth) choices, as well as delectable extras such as grilled shiitake mushrooms, curried shrimp and fried-eel rice bowls. In the evening, the drinks menu – *shōchū* cocktails and plum wine – provides further incentive for a visit.

VIVI KITCHEN CANTONESE $

Map p286 (维园悦谱; Wéiyuán Yuèpǔ; 396 South Shaanxi Rd; 陕西南路396号; dishes ¥26-48; Ⓜ South Shaanxi Rd) This soothing Cantonese restaurant is low on attitude and high on quality cuisine. Sitting in the shadow of the Geisha (p108), Vivi provides a calming antidote to its high-profile neighbour with relaxing background music and simple, understated decor. Shrimp in XO sauce, beef with vegies and fungus, dim-sum standards and fresh juices are all first-rate.

SHÀNGHǍI MIN SHANGHAINESE $$

Map p286 (小南国; Xiǎo Nán Guó; ☎400 820 9777; Xīntiāndì South Block, 2nd fl, Bldg 6; 兴业路123弄新天地南里6号楼2楼; dishes ¥38-158; Ⓜ South Huangpi Rd, Xintiandi) Even with the smart banquet halls and classy presentation, this is still one of Shànghǎi's more affordable (and delicious) chains. First-rate dishes include tofu and crab casserole, lion's head meatballs, pork trotters braised for six hours and the usual run of Shanghainese dumplings and noodles. Finish off with sweet rice dumplings in osmanthus juice. It's in the mall.

BELLAGIO CAFÉ CHINESE $$

Map p286 (鹿港小镇; Lùgǎng Xiǎozhèn; ☎6386 5701; 68 Taicang Rd; 太仓路68号; dishes ¥29-69; ⏲11.30am-4am; Ⓜ South Huangpi Rd) Nope, not another pizza place – this Bellagio has nothing to do with Lake Como (or Las Vegas). It's actually a trendy Taiwanese restaurant popular with the 20-something crowd, where waitresses are dressed to match the black-and-white decor. Taiwanese specialities on offer include three-cup chicken and pineapple fried rice, but when the mercury rises it's the shaved-ice desserts and smoothies that bring in the crowds.

DIǍN SHÍ ZHĀI XIǍO YÀN SHANGHAINESE $$

Map p286 (点石斋小宴; ☎5465 0270; 320 Yongjia Rd; 永嘉路320号; dishes ¥48-168; Ⓜ South Shaanxi Rd, Jiashan Rd) Shànghǎi cuisine can be cloyingly sweet when improperly prepared, but this elegant restaurant hits the mark with its delicate flavours and a wonderful range of cold appetisers and seafood dishes. Be sure to look out for the excellent Zhèjiāng dishes on the menu, including Shàoxīng drunken chicken and individual portions of tender *dōngpō ròu* (stewed pork fat).

FOOD FUSION MALAYSIAN $$

Map p286 (融合; Rónghé; 8th fl, Parkson Plaza, 918 Middle Huaihai Rd; 淮海中路918号百盛8楼; dishes ¥30-98, lunch sets from ¥30; Ⓜ South Shaanxi Rd) Secreted away on the 8th floor of one of Huaihai Rd's numerous shopping malls is this authentic Malaysian option. Join the throng of office workers crowding into the lift and ascend to some stellar Southeast Asian flavours: sample classics such as *rendang* beef (slow cooked with coconut milk), chilli-flecked laksa (coconut curry noodle soup), chicken satay and fish curry.

MELANGE OASIS CAFE $$

Map p286 (www.melange-oasis.com; Bldg D, No 37, Lane 550, South Shaanxi Rd; 陕西南路550弄37号D栋; mains ¥45-65; 9am-10pm; South Shaanxi Rd) Anchoring the Jiāshān Market development is this community cafe, which relies on organic, seasonal produce to fill out the standard cafe menu of salads and sandwiches. With an outdoor terrace that opens onto a flower-filled courtyard, it's no surprise that Mo Cafe also serves as Shànghǎi's centre of ecofriendly living: come here to pick up biodegradable baby wipes, flyers on raw food seminars or to arrange a date with the preschool playgroup.

ART SALON RESTAURANT SHANGHAINESE $$

Map p286 (屋里香食府; Wūlǐxiāng Shífǔ; 5306 5462; 164 Nanchang Rd; 南昌路164号; dishes ¥58-98; South Shaanxi Rd) Run by two brothers, this eccentric, artsy space is a rarity in Shànghǎi, distinguishing itself with a funky, colourful interior full of kitschy antique furnishings, old-school porcelain tableware and contemporary paintings. And hey, if you like that green Ming-dynasty chair – it's all for sale. The food is predominantly Shanghainese, with a few Sìchuān favourites thrown in to spice things up.

YÈ SHÀNGHǍI SHANGHAINESE $$

Map p286 (夜上海; 6311 2323; Xīntiāndì North Block, 338 South Huangpi Rd; 黄陂南路338号新天地北里; dishes ¥38-88, set lunch menu ¥58; 11.30am-2.30pm & 6-10.30pm; South Huangpi Rd, Xintiandi) Yè offers sophisticated, unchallenging Shanghainese cuisine in classy surroundings, which makes it a favourite with visitors. The drunken chicken and smoked fish starters are an excellent overture to local flavours, the crispy duck comes with thick pancakes and the sautéed string beans and bamboo shoots doesn't disappoint either. It also features an affordable wine list.

ORIGIN CAFE $$

Map p286 (源于自然; Yuányú Zìrán; 159 2183 2324; Tiánzǐfáng, No 39, Lane 155, Middle Jianguo Rd; 建国中路155弄39号田子坊; mains ¥48-72; 10.30am-11pm; Dapuqiao Rd) Serving Shànghǎi's locavores, Origin is an upbeat Italian-run cafe that uses seasonal ingredients to create a clever menu of salads (tuna tartar), sandwiches (sweet potato and chèvre) and, of course, pasta and homemade gelato. Not everything on the menu appears to come from within a 160km radius, but hey, they're trying. Arrive early for seats on the upstairs terrace.

INFINITI PLAZA MALL $

Map p286 (无限度广场; Wúxiàndù Guǎngchǎng; 138 Middle Huaihai Rd; 淮海中路138号; meals from ¥30; 10am-10pm; Dashijie) Closer to People's Square than the actual French Concession, Infiniti is an impressively popular lunch destination. Topping the list of choices are 4th-floor South Memory, Teppanyaki Xiang – a Húnán-meets-teppanyaki dining concept – and the Soup Expert, where you can give your yin or yang a boost with five-element medicinal soups (watch out for the ox penis variety though). Also here are Korean barbecue (Han Shan Gong; 5th floor) and a branch of the omnipresent Wagas (p130) on the 1st floor.

XĪNJÍSHÌ SHANGHAINESE $$

Map p286 (新吉士; 6336 4746; Xīntiāndì North Block, Bldg 9; 新天地北里9号楼; dishes ¥38-88; 11am-2.30pm & 5-10pm; South Huangpi Rd, Xintiandi) A branch of classic Shanghainese restaurant Jesse (p101).

VEGETARIAN LIFESTYLE CHINESE, VEGETARIAN $$

Map p286 (枣子树; Zǎozishù; 6384 8000; 77 Songshan Rd; 嵩山路77号; dishes ¥22-68; South Huangpi Rd) Head into a courtyard off Songshan Rd to find a branch of this popular vegetarian restaurant (p129).

WÈIXIĀNG ZHĀI NOODLES $

Map p286 (味香斋; 14 Yandang Rd; 雁荡路14号; noodles ¥8; South Huangpi Rd, Xintiandi) There aren't that many places left in Shànghǎi where you can get a bowl of savoury sesame noodles (麻酱面; *májiàng miàn*) for a mere ¥8, and for this reason Wèixiāng Zhāi is consistently packed, even at four in the afternoon.

KOMMUNE CAFE $$

Map p286 (公社; Gōngshè; Tiánzǐfáng, the Yard, No 7, Lane 210, Taikang Rd; 泰康路210弄7号田子坊; meals from ¥58; 7am-1am; Dapuqiao Rd) The original Tiánzǐfáng cafe, Kommune is a consistently bustling hangout with outdoor seating, big breakfasts, sandwiches and barbecue on the menu.

LOCAL KNOWLEDGE

A SHÀNGHǍI CHEF'S FAVOURITE EATS

Shànghǎi chef Wang Xinhai, who teaches Chinese cuisine at The Kitchen at... (p33), filled us in on his favourite restaurants in the city.

Xīnjiāng Fēngwèi Restaurant (p160) I really like Xīnjiāng food and the staff at our cooking school often comes here for dinner. The lamb in particular is excellent; what I like the most is the whole roast sheep (烤全羊; *kǎo quányáng*).

Diǎn Shí Zhāi Xiǎo Yàn (p98) This is a cosy restaurant that offers quality Shanghainese cuisine. My favourite dish is the slow-roasted river carp with deep-fried spring onions (葱烤河鲫鱼; *cōng kǎo héjìyú;* a cold dish served as an appetiser).

Tsui Wah (p102) I also like to cook Cantonese cuisine and I think the kitchen at Tsui Wah produces authentic flavours. I love their pineapple bun (菠萝包; *bōluó bāo*) – a sweet pastry that's served warm with a slab of cold butter inside.

Hǎi Dǐ Lāo (p129) From a Chinese point of view, this hotpot restaurant has the best service in Shànghǎi. You can get snacks, drinks and even a manicure while you wait for a table, and the staff's attention to detail and their upbeat attitude is remarkable. It's an excellent place to come in a group simply because it's so entertaining. Make sure to order the noodles, which are pulled into shape with a special performance.

NEW YORK STYLE PIZZA PIZZA $

Map p286 (比萨; Bǐsà; Tiánzǐfáng, No 23, Lane 248, Taikang Rd; 泰康路248弄23号田子坊; slices ¥16, whole pizza ¥112/122; ⏲11.30am-9pm; Ⓜ Dapuqiao) Shànghǎi's pizza-by-the-slice Tiánzǐfáng outlet (p131).

KABB AMERICAN $$

Map p286 (凯博西餐厅; Kǎibó Xīcāntīng; ☎3307 0798; Xīntiāndì North Block, Bldg 5; 太仓路181弄新天地北里5号楼; mains ¥65-95; ⏲7am-midnight; 📶; Ⓜ South Huangpi Rd, Xintiandi) For those times when the desire to chew becomes overpowering, this smart grill hits the spot, delivering authentic American-portioned comfort food at midrange prices. There's a good selection of main-course salads, burgers and wraps. The outdoor cafe-style seating is particularly popular for a slower-paced weekend brunch, when the menu stretches to French toast with bananas and eggs Benedict.

SIMPLY THAI THAI $$

Map p286 (天泰餐厅; Tiāntài Cāntīng; www.simplythai-sh.com; ☎6326 2088; Xīntiāndì North Block, cnr Madang Rd & Xingye Rd; 马当路与兴业路路口; dishes ¥48-68; ⏲11am-10.30pm; 🚭; Ⓜ South Huangpi Rd, Xintiandi) A branch of Shànghǎi's favourite Thai (p104).

BÌ FĒNG TÁNG DIM SUM $

Map p286 (避风塘; ☎6467 0628; 175 Changle Rd; 长乐路175号; dim sum ¥17-22; ⏲24hr; Ⓜ South Shaanxi Rd) At busy times, this popular wicker-and-bamboo-clad dim-sum joint resonates to the constant clatter of porcelain dishes and waitstaff shouting back and forth to each other. This 24-hour branch is still bustling in the early hours as the late-night crowd staggers in to fill up on steamed shrimp-and-chive dumplings, duck noodle soup and barbecued pork buns.

CITY SHOP SUPERMARKET

Map p286 (城市超市; Chéngshì Chāoshì; ☎400 811 1797; www.cityshop.com.cn; B1, New World Printemps Department Store, 939 Middle Huaihai Rd; 淮海中路939号巴黎春天百货; ⏲10am-10pm; Ⓜ South Shaanxi Rd) For all those imported goodies you just can't get anywhere else – at a price. They deliver too.

French Concession West

TOP CHOICE **SPICY JOINT** SICHUANESE $

Map p290 (辛香汇; Xīnxiānghuì; ☎400 100 1717; 3rd fl, K Wah Center, 1028 Middle Huaihai Rd; 淮海中路1028号嘉华中心3楼; dishes ¥12-58; 📶; Ⓜ South Shaanxi Rd) If you only go to one Sìchuān joint in Shànghǎi, you might as well make it this one, where the blistering heat is matched only by its scorching popularity. Dishes are inexpensive by the city's standards; favourites include massive bowls of spicy catfish in hot chilli oil, an addictive garlic-cucumber salad, smoked-tea duck and chilli-coated lamb chops. Be forewarned that the wait can be excruciatingly long at peak times; you'll need a mobile number to secure a place in the queue.

TOP CHOICE YĪN CHINESE $$

Map p290 (音; ☎5466 5070; 2nd fl, 4 Hengshan Rd; 衡山路4号2楼; dishes ¥38-108; ⊜; ⓂHengshan Rd) A throwback to the 1930s, Yīn emanates soft, jazzy decadence with its antique furnishings, Song-dynasty-style tableware and Ella Fitzgerald on the stereo. But they're as much visionaries as they are traditionalists. The kitchen has adopted older cooking techniques – back from the days before MSG – and prepares standout regional dishes from across China, including the superbly named 'squid lost in a sandstorm'.

TOP CHOICE JESSE SHANGHAINESE $$

Map p290 (吉士酒楼; Jíshì Jiǔlóu; ☎6282 9260; 41 Tianping Rd; 天平路41号; dishes ¥28-98; ⓂJiaotong University) Jesse specialises in packing lots of people into tight spaces, so if you tend to gesture wildly when you talk, watch out with those chopsticks. This is Shanghainese home-cooking at its best: crab dumplings, Grandma's braised pork and plenty of fish, drunken shrimp and eel. There are several branches around town – such as the one at **28 Taojiang Road** (新吉士; Xīnjíshì; ☎6445 0068; ⓂChangshu Rd) – though serious foodies should make the effort to trek out to the original.

TOP CHOICE FU 1039 SHANGHAINESE $$$

Map p290 (福一零三九; Fú Yào Líng Sān Jiǔ; ☎5237 1878; 1039 Yuyuan Rd; 愚园路1039号; dishes ¥48-108; ⓂJiangsu Rd) Set in a three-storey 1913 villa, Fu attains an old-fashioned charm uncommon in design-driven Shànghǎi. Foodies who appreciate sophisticated surroundings and Shanghainese food on par with the decor, take note – Fu is a must. The succulent standards here won't let you down: the smoked fish starter and stewed pork in soy sauce are recommended, with the sautéed chicken and mango and sweet-and-sour Mandarin fish coming in close behind.

Take note that the entrance, down an alley and on the left, is unmarked and the staff speak little English. There's a minimum charge of ¥200 per head here.

HAIKU JAPANESE $$

Map p290 (隐泉之语; Yǐnquán Zhī Yǔ; ☎6445 0021; 28B Taojiang Rd; 桃江路28号乙; maki rolls ¥68-98; ⊜; ⓂChangshu Rd) Though the name may suggest the minimalist beauty of a butterfly perched upon a temple bell, Haiku is anything but. Rather, it's all about 'let's see how many different things we can fit into a maki roll'. On this count they have definitely succeeded: the Ninja wraps up shrimp and crab with a killer spicy sauce, while the Moto-roll-ah is a deep-fried spicy tuna, crab and avocado combo. Can't make up your mind? Pimp My Roll may be the one for you – it's loaded with everything. Reserve.

KAGEN TEPPANYAKI $$$

Map p290 (隐泉源铁板烧; Yǐnquán Yuán Tiěbǎnshāo; ☎6433 3232; 28D Taojiang Rd; 桃江路28号丁; all you can eat teppanyaki ¥258; ⏲lunch Fri-Sun, dinner daily; ⊜; ⓂChangshu Rd) Opened by the folks at Haiku next door, super-sleek Kagen takes Shànghǎi's all-you-can-eat-and-drink teppanyaki craze into the upper echelon. Wagyu beef, tiger prawns and foie gras are some of the finer ingredients on the menu, and quality sushi, sashimi, sake and wine are all part of the buffet deal. Reserve.

LOST HEAVEN YUNNANESE $$

Map p290 (花马天堂; Huāmǎ Tiāntáng; ☎6433 5126; 38 Gaoyou Rd; 高邮路38号; dishes from ¥48-88; ⊜; ⓂShanghai Library) In a town of notoriously fickle diners, Lost Heaven has maintained its fashionable status longer than many restaurants have managed to stay open. Located on a quiet street in Shànghǎi's most desirable neighbourhood, it's stylish and atmospheric with subdued red lighting and a giant Buddha dominating the main dining area.

The Yunnanese food is delicately flavoured and nicely presented, although purists will bemoan the way some dishes, such as the Dali chicken, aren't as spicy as they should be. The Yunnan vegetable cakes come with a salsa-like garnish and make a fantastic starter. There's another branch on the Bund, p66. Reserve.

GǓYÌ HÚNÁN RESTAURANT HUNANESE $$

Map p290 (古意湘味浓; Gǔyì Xiāngwèinóng; ☎6247 0758; 87 Fumin Rd; 富民路87号; dishes ¥28-98; ⊜; ⓂJing'an Temple, Changshu Rd) Shànghǎi's foodies divide into those who back this place to the hilt and others who prefer the more laid-back charms of Dī Shuǐ Dòng (p97). Gǔyì is certainly better for a romantic dinner and the classy atmosphere is equalled by the comprehensive menu, which includes great *huǒguō* (hotpot) featuring beef, chicken, crab or frog and, once again, those delectable cumin ribs. Reserve.

TSUI WAH CANTONESE $

Map p290 (翠华餐厅; Cuìhuá Cāntīng; ☎6170 1282; 291 Fumin Rd; 富民路291号; dishes ¥32-68, set lunch ¥42; ⏰11am-1am; 🚭; Ⓜ Changshu Rd, South Shaanxi Rd) The famous Hong Kong tea restaurant has finally set up shop in Shànghǎi, garnering instant acclaim not only among homesick Hong Kongers but pretty much everyone else in the 'hood. Notable dishes include Hǎinán chicken and the Malaysian curries, but the menu skips from Cantonese to club sandwiches to Italian pasta without missing a beat. And what would a tea restaurant be without milk tea?

NOODLE BULL NOODLES $

Map p290 (狠牛面; Hěnniú Miàn; ☎6170 1299; unit 3b, 291 Fumin Rd; 富民路291号3b室; noodles ¥28-35; 🖉; Ⓜ Changshu Rd, South Shaanxi Rd) Noodle Bull has all the makings of a cult favourite: it's far cooler than your average street-corner noodle stand (minimalist concrete chic and funky bowls), it's inexpensive, and boy is that broth slurpable. It doesn't matter whether you go vegetarian or for the roasted beef noodles, it's hard not to find satisfaction. The cherry on the cake? No MSG. Enter on Changle Rd.

SHINTORI NULL II FUSION $$$

Map p290 (新都里无二店; Xīndūlǐ Wú'èr Diàn; ☎5404 5252; 803 Julu Rd; 巨鹿路803号; dishes ¥80-160, tasting menu ¥380; ⏰6-10.30pm; 🚭; Ⓜ Jing'an Temple) The industrial-chic interior here resembles a set from a Peter Greenaway film, from the eye-catching open kitchen, which looks like it should house Hannibal Lector, to the sleek staff running around like an army of ninjas. The dishes (Běijīng duck rolls, cold noodles served in an ice bowl, beef steak on *pu-erh* leaves) are excellent, but they maintain the minimalist theme, so make sure to order enough. Finish with black-sesame-seed ice cream. Reserve.

PHO REAL VIETNAMESE $$

Map p290 (166 Fumin Rd; 富民路166号; noodles ¥48-60, set lunch ¥55-68; Ⓜ Changshu Rd, Jing'an Temple) This ultra-hip pint-sized eatery, decked out with woven fishing traps suspended from the ceiling and a bright blue-and-white colour scheme, serves what many believe to be the best *pho* (beef noodle soup flavoured with mint, star anise and cilantro) and spring rolls in town. It only seats about 20 and there are no reservations, so show up early and come prepared to wait. There's another branch at **1465 Fuxing Road** (☎6437 2222; 复兴中路1465号; Ⓜ Changshu Rd), which does take reservations.

PǏNCHUĀN SICHUANESE $$

Map p290 (品川; ☎400 820 7706; 47 Taojiang Rd; 桃江路47号; dishes ¥39-90; 🚭; Ⓜ Changshu Rd) Fire fiends love Sìchuān cooking, where the sophistication goes far beyond merely smothering everything with hot peppers. The telltale blend of chillies and peppercorns is best summed up in two words: *là* (spicy) and *má* (numbing). Even though Pǐnchuān has hit the upscale button repeatedly in the past few years, this is still a fine place to experience the tongue tingling. Try the sliced beef in spicy sauce, baked spare ribs with peanuts or *làzi jī* (spicy chicken). The duck with sticky rice will help mitigate the damage to your tastebuds. Reserve.

KUNGFU NOODLES NOODLES $

Map p286 (武当功夫牛肉面; Wǔdāng Gōngfu Niǔròumiàn; 100 North Xiangyang Rd; 襄阳北路100号; noodles ¥26-36; Ⓜ South Shaanxi Rd) No need to drop into a praying mantis stance to get into this funky little noodle shop, just make sure you get here before the lunch-hour rush. The rich MSG-free broth in the beef noodle soup takes the top prize, though other noodle dishes, including the Sichuanese classic *dàndàn miàn*, also get high marks. The drink list is equally good, with Belgian and German beer, barley tea and a Taiwanese sour plum drink.

XĪBÓ GRILL CENTRAL ASIAN $$

Map p290 (锡伯餐厅; Xībó Cāntīng; ☎5403 8330; www.xiboxinjiang.com; 3rd fl, 83 Changshu Rd; 常熟路83号3楼; dishes ¥52-98, lunch sets ¥38-50; Ⓜ Changshu Rd) You'll have to come to Shànghǎi to find a stylish Xīnjiāng joint, because this is not the type of place you're likely to find in Kashgar (or, for that matter, the Xībó Autonomous County on the border with Kazakhstan). But who's complaining? When you need a mutton fix or some spicy 'big plate chicken', Xībó will do you right.

SÌCHUĀN CITIZEN SICHUANESE $

Map p290 (龙门阵茶屋; Lóngménzhèn Cháwū; ☎5404 1235; 30 Donghu Rd; 东湖路30号; dishes ¥28-98, set lunch ¥38-58; 📶; Ⓜ South Shaanxi Rd) Citizen has opted for the 'rustic chic' look, the wood panelling and whirring ceiling fans conjuring up visions of an old-style Chéngdū teahouse that's been made over for an *Elle* photo shoot. But the food is the real stuff, prepared by a busy Sìchuān kitchen crew to ensure no Shanghainese sweetness creeps into the peppercorn onslaught. If you're new to Sichuanese, this is a great place to try the classics, including twice-cooked pork, mapo tofu and kung pao shrimp.

FERGUSON LANE ITALIAN, FRENCH **$$**

Map p290 (武康庭; Wǔkāng Tíng; www.fergusonlane.com.cn; 376 Wukang Rd; 武康路376号; mains ¥48-130; Ⓜ Shanghai Library, Jiaotong University) On those rare days when Shànghǎi's skies are cloud free, the secluded Ferguson Lane courtyard fills up in the blink of an eye with sun-starved diners. There are several tempting options here, including the **Coffee Tree** (9am-10pm; wi-fi), which features panini, pasta, salads and organic coffee, and **Franck** (☎6437 6465; lunch & dinner Sat & Sun, dinner Tue-Fri), which serves delicate French bistro fare and also doubles as a wine bar from Wednesday to Sunday.

AZUL TAPAS **$$$**

Map p290 (☎6433 1172; 8th fl, 378 Wukang Rd; 武康路378号8楼; tapas ¥40-80, weekend brunch ¥138-148; noon-midnight; Ⓜ Shanghai Library, Jiaotong University) Peruvian restaurateur Eduardo Vargas specialises in hip fusion food with the flavours of South America prominent. Relaunched in 2012 with a new location on the top floor of Ferguson Lane's extension – terrace included – Azul keeps the tapas tradition going strong with temptations that run from prawn ceviche (marinated raw prawns) to reinvented standards such as *patatas bravas*. The weekend brunch, pisco sours and margaritas remain as popular as ever.

GINGER CAFE **$$**

Map p290 (www.gingercorp.asia; 91 Xingguo Rd; 兴国路91号; dishes ¥48-88; 11am-9.30pm; wi-fi, English menu; Ⓜ Shanghai Library) Shades of yellow cloak this secluded chill-out space, which does Asian standards, salads, French cafe fare and gingery desserts with equal panache. Try the quiches or tandoori chicken wrap, or skip straight to the sweet stuff (cranberry cheesecake), to go with afternoon coffee.

BǍOLUÓ JIǓLÓU SHANGHAINESE **$$**

Map p290 (保罗酒楼; ☎6279 2827; 271 Fumin Rd; 富民路271号; dishes ¥20-68; 11am-3am; Ⓜ Changshu Rd, Jing'an Temple) Gather up a boisterous bunch of friends and join the Shanghainese night owls who queue down the street well into the early hours to get into this amazingly busy venue. Bǎoluó is typically chaotic, cavernous and packed – a great place to get a feel for Shànghǎi's famous buzz. The English menu is only of minor help here so follow your nose and see what other tables are ordering. Try the excellent baked eel (保罗烤鳗; *bǎoluó kǎomán*) or pot-stewed crab and pork.

LÈ SHĒNG SHANGHAINESE **$$$**

Map p290 (乐生; ☎5406 6011; leshengsh.com; 308 Anfu Rd; 安福路308号; dishes ¥38-138; no smoking; Ⓜ Changshu Rd) For those looking for a high-end introduction to Shanghainese cuisine, Lè Shēng will certainly fit the bill. Intimate enough to be romantic and with haute cuisine presentation, it caters well to couples and provides a refreshing change from Shànghǎi's larger banquet halls. No surprise, perhaps, that it was opened by an Australian (David Laris), but don't translate this to mean inauthentic – the food is on par with expectations.

NEPALI KITCHEN NEPALESE **$$**

Map p290 (尼泊尔餐厅; Níbó'ěr Cāntīng; ☎5404 6281; No 4, Lane 819, Julu Rd; 巨鹿路819弄4号; set lunch ¥45, set dinner ¥110-170; 11am-2pm & 6-11pm; English menu; Ⓜ Jing'an Temple, Changshu Rd) Reminisce about that Himalayan trek over a plate of Tibetan *momos* (dumplings) or a *choila* (spicy chicken) amid prayer flags in this homey, lodge-like place. For a more laid-back meal, take your shoes off and recline on traditional cushions, surrounded by colourful *thangkas* and paper lamps. Prices are higher than the Annapurna Circuit, but then again, you're not just eating *dhal bhat* (lentils and rice). Both the set lunch and dinner are a good bet, with traditional Nepali dishes such as *sekuwa* (grilled beef) and *sikarni* (yoghurt).

XIAN YUE HIEN DIM SUM **$$**

Map p290 (申粤轩酒楼; Shēnyuèxuān Jiǔlóu; ☎6251 1166; 849 Huashan Rd; 华山路849号; dim sum ¥17-24; 11am-2.30pm & 5.30-11pm Mon-Fri, from 9am Sat & Sun) The Ding Xiang Garden, originally built for the concubine of a Qing-dynasty mandarin, is now reserved for retired Communist Party cadres, so the only way you'll get to peek behind the undulating dragon wall is to eat at this serene restaurant. Stroll past the octogenarian officials in wheelchairs reminiscing about the good old days to sample classic Shanghainese and Cantonese dishes. The seafood dishes can get very expensive, but the real draw is the dim sum, served overlooking the lawn on mornings and afternoons. Take a taxi here and reserve ahead.

SHǓ DÌ LÀZI YÚ GUǍN — SICHUANESE $

Map p290 (蜀地辣子鱼馆; ☎5403 7684; 187 Anfu Rd; 安福路187号; dishes from ¥16-58; MChangshu Rd) Most celebrity-owned restaurants in China are temples of style over substance. Not this place, which is the brainchild of a famous Sìchuān actor. Both the prices and decor are decidedly downmarket, but there's nothing cut-rate about the food. An intriguing mix of Sìchuān and northeastern classics with a dash of Shanghainese flavour, they're consistently tasty. Try the fried shredded beef with preserved chillies or the spicy fish if you can handle the heat.

BAI'S RESTAURANT — SHANGHAINESE $$

Map p290 (白家餐厅; Báijiā Cāntīng; ☎6437 6915; No 12, Lane 189, Wanping Rd; 宛平路189弄12号; dishes ¥24-78; MHengshan Rd, Zhaojiabang Rd) Hidden down an alley off Wanping Rd is this family-style restaurant (based out of what appears to be the living room) with tasty, authentic Shanghainese food. The *hǔpí jiānjiāo* (虎皮煎椒; tiger-skin chillies) are mild and sweet and there are plenty of affordable delicacies like the steamed yellow croaker in soy sauce. The *suànxiāng bàngbànggú* (蒜香棒棒骨; fried pork ribs in garlic) are a house speciality, but a little pricey. There are only five tables, so book ahead.

EATING ORGANIC

The organic movement in China has only just sprouted, but it has quickly spread its leaves in Shànghǎi. With the quality of produce and manufactured products becoming increasingly dubious, there's been enough negative publicity (including the discovery of bean sprouts being soaked in a banned chemical solution at local markets, glass noodle samples that contained aluminium, and mutated eggs that bounced 'like ping-pong balls') that Shanghainese are starting to get interested. Organic farms in the area have gone from five to 30 in just three years. Upscale restaurants (el Willy, Jean Georges) usually use at least some organic produce, while the following restaurants specialise in local organic ingredients:

- Melange Oasis (p99)
- Organic Kitchen (p105)
- Qímín Organic Hotpot (p129)
- Origin (p99)
- Vegetarian Lifestyle (p99, p129)

GLO LONDON — BRITISH $$

Map p290 (☎6466 6565; www.glolondon.com; 1 South Wulumuqi Rd; 乌鲁木齐南路1号; mains ¥98-168, 2-/3-course set lunch ¥83/110; ⊙7am-midnight; ⊖; MChangshu Rd, Hengshan Rd) This four-storey behemoth wants to be everything to everyone, and, amazingly enough, it seems to be working. The 1st floor is a casual bakery and cafe (sandwiches, pastries, smoothies), while the slick 2nd floor (the Gastro Grill) dishes out the greatest hits of British cuisine: chicken tikka pizza, tandoori lamb chops, beer-battered cod (and chips) and the like. The 3rd floor is the swish Glo Lounge (p111), while the top-floor terrace is set to become the hickory-smoked BBQ ribs hangout in warmer weather.

SIMPLY THAI — THAI $$

Map p290 (天泰餐厅; Tiāntài Cāntīng; ☎6445 9551; 5c Dongping Rd; 东平路5号C座; dishes ¥48-68; ⊙11am-10.30pm; MChangshu Rd) This popular branch of Shànghǎi's favourite Thai has a tree-shaded patio, perfect for al fresco dining. Expect reasonably priced classics such as green and red curries, tom yum soup and fiery green papaya salad.

WǑ JIĀ CĀNTĪNG — SHANGHAINESE $

Map p290 (我家餐厅; ☎6279 3985; No 7, Lane 229, Huashan Rd; 华山路229弄7号; dishes ¥18-40; MJing'an Temple) Tucked down an old alley lined with yellow stucco homes is this hidden home-style Shanghainese eatery, one of the few still remaining in the neighbourhood. Expect lots of seafood and a simple, unpretentious atmosphere.

SOUTH BEAUTY — SICHUANESE, CANTONESE $$

Map p290 (俏江南; Qiào Jiāngnán; ☎6445 2581; 28 Taojiang Rd; 桃江路28号; dishes from ¥18; MChangshu Rd) Popular branch of the stylish, upmarket Sichuanese chain (p141).

DĪ SHUǏ DÒNG — HUNANESE $$

Map p290 (滴水洞; ☎6415 9448; 5 Dongping Rd; 东平路5号; dishes ¥25-88; ⊙10am-12.30am; MChangshu Rd) Branch of the spicy Húnán favourite (p97).

CANTINA AGAVE MEXICAN $$

Map p290 (☎6170 1310; unit A2, 291 Fumin Rd; 富民路291号A2室; burritos from ¥60; ; ⓂChangshu Rd, South Shaanxi Rd) It used to be that if you went out for a burrito in Shànghǎi, it would taste like cardboard and you'd pay up the wazoo, but no longer. Kelley Lee's Cantina Agave has come to the rescue, and oh, what a rescue – flavour-filled chicken and salsa verde burritos, vegie or beef *machaca* soft tacos, an extensive list of margaritas and a fresh salsa bar.

ORGANIC KITCHEN CAFE $$

Map p290 (www.organickitchenshanghai.com; 57 West Fuxing Rd; 复兴西路57号; mains from ¥50, breakfast sets ¥58-65; ⏲8am-10pm; ; ⓂShanghai Library, Changshu Rd) A cosy brick-walled cafe, the Organic Kitchen is a welcome change from the usual coffee chains that dominate the Shànghǎi landscape. The focus is on health-conscious comfort food, and the menu stretches from all-day breakfast sets and salads to falafel wraps, Indian curries and banana muffins.

DA MARCO ITALIAN $$

Map p290 (大马可餐厅; Dàmǎkě Cāntīng; ☎6210 4495; 103 Dong Zhu'anbang Rd, inside Metro Park Apartments; 东诸安浜路103号; pasta & pizza ¥64-78, mains ¥108-158; ⏲noon-11pm; ⓂJiangsu Rd) This homey spot is one of the most popular Italian restaurants in town and remains a steal after over a decade in business (which, it should be noted, is an eternity in Shànghǎi). Daily specials such as pear-and-gorgonzola pizza and fettuccine porcini are chalked up on the blackboard. Reserve.

COCONUT PARADISE THAI $$

Map p290 (椰香天堂; Yēxiāng Tiāntáng; ☎6248 1998; 38 Fumin Rd; 富民路38号; dishes ¥50-98; ⓂJing'an Temple) Coconut Paradise is a tropical delight, its lush garden seating and dimly lit interior making for a decidedly romantic venue. Curries, fish salads and Chiang Mai soup will bring back memories of days spent lazing around in northern Thailand, and by the end of the meal on a good night, you might even forget you're in Shànghǎi. No MSG. Reserve.

GRAPE RESTAURANT SHANGHAINESE $

Map p290 (葡萄园酒家; Pútáoyuán Jiǔjiā; ☎5404 0486; 55 Xinle Rd; 新乐路55号; dishes ¥18-58; ⓂSouth Shaanxi Rd) This long-standing fave from the 1980s still serves up reliable and inexpensive Shanghainese in its bright premises beside the old Russian Orthodox church. Try the delicious *yóutiáo chǎoniúròu* (油条炒牛肉; dough sticks with beef) or any of the crab dishes – you won't find them any cheaper than here.

WAGAS CAFE $

Map p290 (沃歌斯; Wògēsī; 7 Donghu Rd; 东湖路7号; mains ¥48-58; ⏲7am-10pm; ; ⓂSouth Shaanxi Rd) Convenient branch of the city's favourite cafe (p130).

ELEMENT FRESH CAFE $$

Map p290 (新元素; Xīnyuánsù; ☎6279 8682; 4th fl, K Wah Centre, 1028 Middle Huaihai Rd; 淮海中路1028号嘉华中心4楼; sandwiches & salads ¥45-98, dinner from ¥128; ⏲7am-11pm; ; ⓂSouth Shaanxi Rd) French Concession branch of the hip, health-conscious eatery (p144).

SHÀNGHǍI MIN SHANGHAINESE $$

Map p290 (小南国; Xiǎo Nán Guó; ☎400 820 9777; 4th fl, Dichan Bldg, 9 Donghu Rd; 东湖路9号地产大厦4楼; dishes ¥38-158; ⏲11am-2pm & 5-10pm; ⓂSouth Shaanxi Rd) Branch of the popular Shanghainese restaurant (p98).

DRINKING & NIGHTLIFE

Home to the largest concentration of bars and cafes in the whole of Shànghǎi, the French Concession offers drinkers a choice between elegant bars housed in colonial-era villas, foreign pubs around the north end of Hengshan Rd, as well as a brand-new crop of places springing up along the alcohol-sodden Yongfu Rd.

French Concession East

TOP CHOICE **BELL BAR** BAR, CAFE

Map p286 (bellbar.cn; Tiánzǐfáng, back door No 11, Lane 248, Taikang Rd; 泰康路248弄11号后门田子坊; ⏲11am-2am; ; ⓂDapuqiao) Perhaps the most discreet of Tiánzǐfáng's drinking options, this dimly lit den is the perfect spot to chill for an hour or three. Sink into a couch on the upper levels and order a hookah, or peruse the selection of books (inquire about exchanges) lining the brick walls. It's in the second alley (Lane 248) on the right.

1

LONELY PLANET / GETTY IMAGES ©

2

4

MAISANT LUDOVIC / HEMIS / CORBIS ©

1. Shíkùmén Open House Museum (p92)
Take a look inside a typical *shíkùmén* household, decked out with period furniture.

2. Mao memorabilia
Shopping in the French Concession will answer all your retail needs, from high-end fashion to revolution-era kitsch.

3. Tiánzǐfáng shopping (p113)
Burrow into the alleyways for a rewarding haul of creative boutiques, selling everything from hip jewellery and yak-wool scarves to funky footware.

4. Shanghai Sideways (p248)
Take a tour with Shanghai Sideways to see the sights from a motorcycle sidecar.

LONELY PLANET / GETTY IMAGES ©

CAFÉ 85°C CAFE

Map p286 (85度C咖啡店; Bāwǔ Dù C Kāfēidiàn; 117 South Shaanxi Rd; 陕西南路117号; ⏲24hr; Ⓜ South Shaanxi Rd) This Taiwanese chain offers the cheapest caffeine fix in town, with quality coffee (try the trademark 'sea salt') and nearly a dozen milk tea drinks. If you want to experience a modern-day Chinese breakfast on the go, sampling some of the bizarre pastries in the bakery section is a must. Alas, seating is extremely limited.

CITIZEN CAFÉ CAFE

Map p286 (天台餐厅; Tiāntái Cāntīng; 222 Jinxian Rd; 进贤路222号; ⏲11am-12.30am; 📶; Ⓜ South Shaanxi Rd) The perfect place to hide out with a cappuccino and netbook on a rainy day, Citizen's burgundy-and-cream colours, antique ceiling fans and well-worn parquet offer calming respite from the Shànghǎi crush. Recharge with a club sandwich or sit back with one of the much-loved ginger cocktails while watching street scenes unfold from the 2nd-floor terrace.

VIENNA CAFÉ CAFE

Map p286 (维也纳咖啡馆; Wéiyěnà Kāfēiguǎn; ☎6445 2131; 25 Shaoxing Rd; 绍兴路25号; ⏲8am-8pm, to 10pm Thu-Sat; 📶; Ⓜ Jiashan Rd) Highly at ease with itself, this old-world spot is ideal for unwinding with Kafka and a coffee and tuning out from Shànghǎi's frantic tempo. Movie nights are held every Thursday at 7.30pm; call to reserve a spot. No wi-fi connection on weekends.

KĀIBĀ BAR

Map p286 (开巴; www.kaiba-beerbar.com; Tiánzǐfáng, 2nd fl, 169 Middle Jianguo Rd; 建国中路169号2楼田子坊; ⏲11am-2am; 📶; Ⓜ Dapuqiao) This branch of the Kāibā beer specialists (p132) is one of Tiánzǐfáng's most popular bars. You'll need to explore to find it.

BOXING CAT BREWERY MICROBREWERY

Map p286 (拳击猫啤酒屋; Quánjīmāo Píjiǔwū; unit 26a, Sinan Mansions, 519 Middle Fuxing Rd; 复兴中路519号思南公馆26a; ⏲11am-2am; Ⓜ Xintiandi) A branch of the popular three-floor microbrewery (p110) in the Sinan Mansions complex.

GEISHA BAR, CLUB

Map p286 (www.thegeisha-shanghai.com; 390 South Shaanxi Rd; 陕西南路390号; ⏲5pm-2am; Ⓜ South Shaanxi Rd) Although the Geisha unfortunately falls well short of its claim to provide a 'surreal high-class brothel atmosphere' (sorry guys), it's definitely on the radar for a fun evening out, with a dance club on the 2nd floor, sake lounge on the 3rd floor and an equally popular California-style Japanese restaurant on the 1st.

LÒUSHÌ CAFE

Map p286 (陋室; www.loushispace.com; 145 Nanchang Rd; 南昌路145号; ⏲10am-11pm; 📶; Ⓜ South Shaanxi Rd) An antique store-cum-cafe, this homey space is cluttered with Shànghǎi antiques of every conceivable nature, from the chairs you sit in to stone bodhisattvas, art-deco light fixtures and even waffle irons. Regardless of whether or not you're in the market for home furnishings, it's a great place to get off your feet for a spell.

CAFÉ DES STAGIAIRES BAR, CAFE

Map p286 (54-56 Yongkang Rd; 永康路54-56号; dishes ¥48-168; ⏲8am-11pm Tue-Sun; 📶; Ⓜ South Shaanxi Rd) A hip oasis of Francophilia, the Café des Stagiaires offers a time-honoured tour of French geography via the wine list: Languedoc, Provence, Côte du Rhône, Loire, Alsace, Bourgogne, Bordeaux and, *bien sûr*, Rest of the World. If you're feeling hungry, sample the quality charcuterie (deli meats), cheese and pizzas.

CONSTELLATION 2 BAR

Map p286 (酒池星座; Jiǔchí Xīngzuò; 33 Yongjia Rd; 永嘉路33号; ⏲7pm-2am; Ⓜ South Shaanxi Rd) Larger branch of the classy Japanese whisky bar (p110), with old leather armchairs and herringbone parquet floors.

ALCHEMIST BAR

Map p286 (www.alchemistbar.cn; Bldg 32, Sinan Mansions, 45 Sinan Rd; 思南路45号思南公馆32号楼; ⏲5pm-2am; Ⓜ Xintiandi) Molecular is the name of the game here, from the truffled oxtail sliders and curry frites to the magically imbued drinks that look like they were concocted in the Hogwarts School of Cuisine. The Alchemist Kir (sprinkled with Amaretto dust) is unlike anything you'll ever find in Paris, while the Dark Mystic contains a dash of lapsang souchong tea smoke. Seeing is believing.

OLD CHINA HAND READING ROOM CAFE

Map p286 (汉源书店; Hànyuán Shūdiàn; 27 Shaoxing Rd; 绍兴路27号; ⏲10am-midnight; Ⓜ Jiashan Rd; 📶) Opened by Shànghǎi photographer and publisher Deke Erh, the

Old China Hand Reading Room is a bright cafe stuffed with antique furnishings and bookshelves.

TMSK BAR

Map p286 (透明思考; Tòumíng Sīkǎo; Xīntiāndì North Block, Bldg 11; 太仓路181弄新天地北里11号楼; 11.30am-1am; South Huangpi Rd, Xintiandi) A place to visit as much for the decor as for the drinks, TMSK is designed within an inch of its life. The whole place is full of swirled pastel-coloured glass (*liúli*; p94), but the interior design pales into insignificance once the house band gets going with its unholy fusion of techno and traditional Chinese music (Friday and Saturday at 8.30pm).

ENOTERRA WINE BAR

Map p286 (58 Taicang Rd; 太仓路58号; 10am-2am; ; South Huangpi Rd) Branch of the casual wine bar (p111) near Xīntiāndì.

YY'S BAR

Map p286 (轮回酒吧; Lúnhuí Jiǔbā; Basement, 125 Nanchang Rd; 南昌路125号; 6pm-4am; South Shaanxi Rd;) Once home to the Shànghǎi underground scene (way back in the 1990s), YY's has successfully remained on the fringes of the city's consciousness without ever becoming too hip. Now relegated to the basement, it continues to attract an alternative crowd and has its own rough-edged appeal, which increases as night blurs into dawn.

French Concession West

TOP CHOICE **COTTON'S** BAR

Map p290 (棉花酒吧; Miánhuā Jiǔbā; 6433 7995; www.cottons-shanghai.com; 132 Anting Rd; 安亭路132号; 11am-2am; ; Hengshan Rd, Zhaojiabang Rd) This excellent bar is perhaps the most pleasant spot in the Concession for a libation or two. Situated in a converted 1930s villa, the interior has cosy sofas and fireplaces to snuggle around in the winter and a tiny outdoor terrace on the 2nd floor. The real draw, though, is the garden, which is intimate yet still big enough not to feel cramped. The drinks and bar snacks, pizzas, burgers, salads and sandwiches are reasonably priced and the crowd is a good mix of locals and expats. You'll have to get here early on weekends to grab a table outside, or book ahead.

TOP CHOICE **EL CÓCTEL** BAR

Map p290 (6433 6511; el-coctel.com; 2nd fl, 47 Yongfu Rd; 永福路47号; 5pm-3am; Shanghai Library) What do you get when you cross the ever-creative el Willy (p83) with a perfectionist bartender from Japan? el Cóctel, of course – an artsy, retro cocktail lounge that mixes up some damn fine drinks. The mixology list goes beyond the usual suspects: sample old-school temptations like the Black Manhattan or the Bermuda Mule, but come with cash to spare. If you don't reserve you might find it hard to

TEA TASTING

It may be a rather clichéd choice, but there's no doubt that a Yíxīng teapot and a package of oolong tea makes for a convenient gift. But how do you go about a purchase? Two things to remember: first, taste (品尝; *pǐncháng*) and compare several different teas – flavours vary widely, and there's no point in buying a premium grade if you don't like it. Tasting is free (免费; *miǎnfèi*) and fun, but it's good form to make some sort of purchase afterwards. Second, tea is generally priced by the *jīn* (500g; 斤), which may be more tea than you can finish in a year. Purchase several *liǎng* (50g; 两) instead – divide the list price by 10 for an idea of the final cost. Some of the different types of tea for sale include oolong *(wūlóng)*, green *(lǜ)*, flower *(huā)* and *pu-erh (pǔ'ěr)* – true connoisseurs have a different teapot for each type of tea.

Try the following stores.

Huìfēng Tea Shop (汇丰茶庄; Huìfēng Cházhuāng; Map p286; 124 South Maoming Rd; 茂名南路124号; 9am-9.30pm; South Shaanxi Rd)

Yányè Míngchá (严叶茗茶; Map p290; 170 Fumin Rd; 富民路170号; 8am-10pm; Jing'an Temple)

Tiānshān Tea City (p167)

Zhēnchálín Tea (p114)

get in, but don't worry, as there's a line of bars downstairs, including a surprisingly popular French pirate rum bar (Bounty Rhumerie).

TOP CHOICE SHELTER CLUB

Map p290 (5 Yongfu Rd; 永福路5号; ⏲9pm-4am Wed-Sat; Ⓜ Shanghai Library) The darling of the underground crowd, Shelter is a reconverted bomb shelter where you can count on great music, cheap drinks and a nonexistent dress code. They bring in a fantastic line-up of international DJs and hip-hop artists; the large barely lit dance area is the place to be. Cover for big shows is usually around ¥30.

TOP CHOICE APARTMENT BAR

Map p290 (☎6437 9478; 3rd fl, 47 Yongfu Rd; 永福路47号; ⏲11am-2am; 📶; Ⓜ Shanghai Library) This trendy loft-style bar is designed to appeal to the full spectrum of 30-something professionals, and proof of the point is that the standard food and drinks menu is complemented by a surprisingly artsy events program, with everything from Chinese cinema nights to locally directed English-language plays. They even host erotic-lit readings. A dance space is located across from the bar, while the top-level terrace is the centre of the summer BBQ action.

TOP CHOICE BOXING CAT BREWERY MICROBREWERY

Map p290 (拳击猫啤酒屋; Quánjīmāo Píjiǔwū; www.boxingcatbrewery.com; 82 West Fuxing Rd; 复兴西路82号; ⏲5pm-2am Mon-Fri, 11am-2am Sat & Sun; 📶; Ⓜ Shanghai Library, Changshu Rd) A deservedly popular three-floor microbrewery, with a rotating line-up of fresh beers that range from the Standing 8 Pilsner to the Right Hook Helles. But that's not all – the omnipresent restaurateur Kelley Lee has paired southern classics (gumbo) and sandwiches (Cali-Cajun chicken club) to go with the drinks. Come for a pint, stay for dinner.

TOP CHOICE ABBEY ROAD BAR

Map p290 (艾比之路; Àibǐ Zhī Lù; 45 Yueyang Rd; 岳阳路45号; ⏲4pm-2am Mon-Fri, 10am-2am Sat & Sun; 📶; Ⓜ Changshu Rd) The cheap beer–classic rock combination works its stuff again, attracting plenty of regulars to this neighbourhood pub. Once the weather gets nice, the tree-shaded outdoor patio adds the final ingredient to make Abbey Road an irresistible favourite. There are gigantic portions of Swiss pub food too.

DADA CLUB

off Map p290 (115 Xingfu Rd; 幸福路115号; ⏲8pm-late; Ⓜ Jiaotong University) This friendly no-frills place out by Jiāotōng University is one of Shànghǎi's most popular dives, specialising in cheap drinks, Tuesday night slasher flicks (free popcorn) and popular weekend dance parties.

CONSTELLATION BAR

Map p290 (酒池星座; Jiǔchí Xīngzuò; 86 Xinle Rd; 新乐路86号; ⏲7pm-2am; Ⓜ South Shaanxi Rd) The bow-tied staff at the Japanese-run Constellation (or, as the original name translates, 'Constellations in a pool of liquor') take their drinks seriously – you're not going to get any watered-down cocktails here. A choice selection of whiskies (including a samurai-helmeted Nikka), Van Gogh prints on the walls and overhead black lights make this a classy yet appealingly eccentric place.

TOP CHOICE DR WINE WINE BAR

Map p290 (177 Fumin Rd; 富民路177号; ⏲11am-2am; 📶; Ⓜ Jing'an Temple) Black-leather armchairs, salvaged *shíkùmén* brick walls and worn-in tables set the mood at this casual, two-storey wine bar on Fumin Rd. Wines are sold by both the glass and bottle, and the prices are reasonably affordable. The usual French accompaniments – cheese and charcuterie (saucisson, pâté etc) – are on the menu, as well as set lunch deals during the week.

CAMEL SPORTS BAR

Map p290 (www.camelsportsbar.com; 1 Yueyang Rd; 岳阳路1号; ⏲9am-3am Tue-Sat; Ⓜ Changshu Rd) The French Concession's go-to sports bar, Camel has pool tables, foosball and big screens everywhere. Pints are sensibly priced and they often stay open at odd hours so that fans can catch that crucial 4am game.

EDDY'S BAR BAR

Map p290 (嘉浓休闲; Jiānóng Xiūxián; 1877 Middle Huaihai Rd; 淮海中路1877号, 近天平路; ⏲8pm-2am; Ⓜ Jiaotong University) Shànghǎi's longest-running gay bar is a friendly place with a flash, square bar to sit around, as well as a few corners to hide away in. It attracts both locals and expats, but it's mostly for the boys rather than the girls. The entrance is on Tianping Rd.

NO 88 CLUB

Map p290 (搜浩88酒吧; Sōuhào Bābā Jiǔbā; www.no88bar.com; 2nd fl, 291 Fumin Rd; 富民路291号; ⌚9pm-6am; Ⓜ South Shaanxi Rd, Changshu Rd) This nationwide chain is the place to go when you're ready to get down Chinese-style, with over-the-top baroque decor, West Coast beats, nonstop drinking games and lots of whisky and green tea. One of the city's most popular party spots.

LOLA CLUB

Map p290 (www.lolaclubshanghai.com; Bldg 4, Surpass Court, 570 Yongjia Rd; 永嘉路570号4号楼; ⌚10pm-3am Tue-Sat; Ⓜ Hengshan Rd) A superior sound system and wall-to-ceiling video projections that sync with the beat pull in the crowds at this first-rate club, opened by a trio of Catalan DJs. Plus, they serve tapas.

SHÀNGHǍI BREWERY MICROBREWERY

Map p290 (www.shanghaibrewery.com; 15 Dongping Rd; 东平路15号; ⌚10am-2am; 📶; Ⓜ Changshu Rd, Hengshan Rd) Hand-crafted microbrews, a huge range of comfort food, pool tables and sports on TV...this massive two-storey hangout might have it all. Well, not quite, but it certainly has enough to make an impression on a strip already bursting with established names. Try the Czech-style People's Pilsner or the Hong Mei Amber Hefeweizen, which start at a mere ¥20 during happy hour (2pm to 8pm).

GLO LOUNGE BAR

Map p290 (www.glolondon.com; 1 South Wulumuqi Rd; 乌鲁木齐南路1号; ⌚5pm-2am; Ⓜ Changshu Rd, Hengshan Rd) Glo London's lounge bar is angling to become the neighbourhood's sophisticated option – no rowdy guys cheering on their favourite teams here. Instead you get an extensive mojito list, proper dry martinis, candlelit tables and all the requisite PYTs.

PEOPLE 7 BAR

Map p290 (人间荧七; Rénjiān Yíngqī; 803 Julu Rd; 巨鹿路803号; ⌚11.30am-2pm & 6pm-midnight; Ⓜ Jing'an Temple, Changshu Rd) Getting into this super-stylish bar is an achievement in itself. That's not because there's a door policy, rather it's because the shiny steel doors will only open if you insert your hand into one of the nine holes set into the wall. Once inside, there's a long steel bar on which to rest the oddly shaped glass your cocktail will arrive in. With white armchairs scattered throughout the darkly lit interior and bathrooms that are even harder to work out than the front door, this place could be oppressively trendy. But it isn't. They do affordable Chinese food too.

ENOTERRA WINE BAR

Map p290 (53-57 Anfu Rd; 安福路53-57号; ⌚10am-2am; 📶; Ⓜ Changshu Rd) Wine bars are the latest fad to hit Shànghǎi, and Enoterra was the first to provide a winning formula, with its convivial atmosphere and affordable wines by the glass and bottle. There's a definite focus on French wines – from sunny Corbières to powerful Vacqueyras – but there's a good selection of New World wines as well. Meals are also served.

SHÀNGHǍI STUDIO BAR

Map p290 (嘉浓休闲; Jiānóng Xiūxián; www.shanghai-studio.com; No 4, Lane 1950, Middle Huaihai Rd; 淮海中路1950弄4号; ⌚9pm-2am; Ⓜ Jiaotong University) This hip addition to the Shànghǎi gay scene has transformed the cool depths of a former bomb shelter into a laid-back bar, art gallery and men's underwear shop (MANifesto; open 2pm to 2am). There's a ¥100 open bar on Thursday.

SHIVA CLUB

Map p290 (47 Yongfu Rd; 永福路47号; ⌚8pm-6am Tue-Sat; Ⓜ Shanghai Library) Three in the morning, nowhere to go? The Indian-themed Shiva is one of the city's better after-hours clubs, where like-minded night owls stay up partying till dawn. Fresh-fruit cocktails and quality DJs.

TIME PASSAGE BAR

Map p290 (昨天今天明天; Zuótiān Jīntiān Míngtiān; No 183, Lane 1038, Caojiayan Rd; 曹家堰路1038弄183号; ⌚4.30pm-2am; 📶; Ⓜ Jiangsu Rd) Tucked down a small street, Time Passage is that rare thing in Shànghǎi, a pub that could be your local back home. With friendly staff, cheap drinks and a faithful clientele of local musos, students and expat teachers, it's a businessman-free zone. There's live music on Friday and Saturday nights, and a daily happy hour from 5.30pm to 7.30pm.

BLARNEY STONE BAR

Map p290 (上海岩烧; Shànghǎi Yánshāo; 5a Dongping Rd; 东平路5号a座; ⌚4pm-2am Mon-Fri,

11am-2am Sat & Sun; 📶; Ⓜ Changshu Rd) This authentically Irish spot has low ceilings, a stone floor and wood panelling to give it a genuine pub feel. It's a friendly place that attracts a slightly older expat crowd, who enjoy the fish and chips and pints of Guinness and Kilkenny.

SASHA'S BAR

Map p290 (萨沙; Sàshā; ☎6474 6628; 11 Dongping Rd, cnr Hengshan Rd; 东平路11号, 近衡山路; ⏲11am-2am; 📶; Ⓜ Changshu Rd, Hengshan Rd) Housed in a fine old mansion that once belonged to the Soong family, Sasha's large garden is one of Shànghǎi's most splendid summer spots. There's a pricey expat restaurant on the premises, but this place is renowned not so much for blowout dinners as it is for the weekend brunches and outdoor lounging in warmer weather.

390 BAR CLUB

Map p290 (www.390shanghai.com; 390 Panyu Rd; 番禺路390号; ⏲6pm-late; 📶; Ⓜ Jiaotong University) One of the only LGBT clubs in Shànghǎi, the 390 Bar was opened up by the owner of Shànghǎi Studio (p111) and his partner, who runs local vinyl store Uptown Records. The club is divided into several sections, with live music, a dance floor and two bars.

O'MALLEY'S BAR

Map p290 (欧玛莉爱尔兰酒吧; Ōumǎlì Ài'ěrlán Jiǔbā; 42 Taojiang Rd; 桃江路42号; ⏲24hr; 📶; Ⓜ Changshu Rd) With ¥25 pints of Carlsberg on Monday and Tuesday, an all-day breakfast menu, live music three days a week and nonstop sport on the many TVs, O'Malley's spares no effort to pack in the punters. Families like the lawn area and kids' playground. It's a bit pricey, so don't miss happy hour from 4pm to 8pm.

MURAL BAR

Map p290 (摩砚酒吧; Móyàn Jiǔbā; basement, 697 Yongjia Rd; 永嘉路697号底层; ⏲6pm-2am; Ⓜ Hengshan Rd) If those crazy Buddhist monks ever had a raging 8th-century party out in Dūnhuáng's Thousand Buddha Caves, this is probably what it would have looked like, minus the salsa and reggae of course. Mural's big claim is not really the Silk Road decor, but the all-you-can-drink ¥100 bar every Friday night (10pm to 2am).

☆ ENTERTAINMENT

☆ French Concession East

MAO LIVEHOUSE LIVE MUSIC

Map p286 (www.mao-music.com; 3rd fl, 308 South Chongqing Rd; 重庆南路308号3楼; Ⓜ Madang Rd) One of the city's best and largest music venues, MAO is a stalwart of the Shànghǎi music scene, with acts ranging from rock to pop to electronica. Check the website for schedules and ticket prices.

PARTYWORLD KARAOKE

Map p286 (钱柜; Qián Guì; ☎5306 3888; 109 Yandang Rd; 雁荡路109号, 复兴公园内; ⏲2pm-dawn; Ⓜ South Huangpi Rd) Partyworld is the nation's leading karaoke chain and this monster branch gets going early in the afternoon for those who just can't wait to belt out a tune or two. There are plenty of English-language songs to choose from. Prices run according to the number of people, size of the room you want and the time of day.

CATHAY THEATRE CINEMA

Map p286 (国泰电影院; Guótài Diànyǐngyuàn; 870 Middle Huaihai Rd; 淮海中路870号; Ⓜ South Shaanxi Rd) This 1932 art-deco theatre is one of the cheaper and more centrally located French Concession cinemas.

UME INTERNATIONAL CINEPLEX CINEMA

Map p286 (国际影城; Guójì Yǐngchéng; Xīntiāndì South Block, 5th fl, Bldg 6; 新天地南里6号楼5楼; Ⓜ South Huangpi Rd) Modern cinema complex at Xīntiāndì.

BROWN SUGAR LIVE MUSIC

Map p286 (红糖爵士餐厅; Hóngtáng Juéshì Cāntīng; ☎5382 8998; Xīntiāndì North Block, Bldg 15; 太仓路181弄新天地北里15号楼; ⏲6pm-3am; Ⓜ South Huangpi Rd) Brown Sugar is an upscale jazz-and-blues establishment set in the heart of Xīntiāndì. The focus here is on female vocalists (eg Aretha Franklin and Ella Fitzgerald covers), but there's also a salsa band on Sundays.

☆ French Concession West

COTTON CLUB LIVE MUSIC

Map p290 (棉花俱乐部; Miánhuā Jùlèbù; www.thecottonclub.cn; 8 West Fuxing Rd; 复兴西路8号; ⏲7.30pm-2am Tue-Sun; Ⓜ Changshu Rd)

Harlem it ain't, but this is still the best and longest-running bar for live jazz in Shànghǎi and features blues and jazz groups throughout the week. Wynton Marsalis once stepped in to jam, forever sealing the Cotton Club's reputation as the best live-music haunt in town. The music gets going around 9pm.

JZ CLUB LIVE MUSIC

Map p290 (www.jzclub.cn; 46 West Fuxing Rd; 复兴西路46号; ⏲9pm-2am; Ⓜ Changshu Rd) Together with the Cotton Club, JZ is one of the best places in town for serious music lovers. The schedule rotates local and international groups, with sounds ranging from fusion, Latin and R&B to Chinese folk-jazz; music generally gets going around 9pm. There's a ¥50 cover on Monday, Friday and Saturday nights. They also organise the annual **JZ Shànghǎi Jazz Festival**.

SHÀNGHǍI GǓQÍN CULTURAL FOUNDATION CULTURE CENTRE

Map p290 (上海古琴文化会; Shànghǎi Gǔqín Wénhuà Huì; ☎6437 4111; www.yhgy-guqin.com; 1801 Middle Huaihai Rd; 淮海中路1801号; ⏲9am-5pm; Ⓜ Shanghai Library) This cultural centre offers classes in a handful of traditional arts: Chinese ink painting, *wéiqí* (go) and the *gǔqín* (seven-string zither). It's possible to drop by just to visit the old 1930s villa, and on Friday nights there are sometimes free music performances at 7pm (call first).

SHÀNGHǍI CONSERVATORY OF MUSIC CLASSICAL MUSIC

Map p290 (上海音乐学院; Shànghǎi Yīnyuè Xuéyuàn; ☎6431 1792; 20 Fenyang Rd; 汾阳路20号; Ⓜ South Shaanxi Rd) The auditorium here holds classical music performances (Chinese and Western) daily at 7.15pm and the musicians are often the stars of the future. The ticket office (售票处; *shòupiàochù*; open 9am to 5pm) is in the southern part of the campus. Ask for directions once you're at the school.

SHOPPING

Huaihai Rd in the French Concession area is definitely *the* modern shopping street in Shànghǎi. It's unlikely, however, that the avenue's towering department stores and global chains will appeal to most travellers. Instead, seek out local boutiques along leafy backstreets such as Nanchang or Xinle Rds. Xīntiāndì has plenty of high-end brands, but for sheer diversity, nothing beats Tiánzǐfáng, one of the best shopping destinations in the city.

French Concession East

TOP CHOICE **TIÁNZǏFÁNG** CLOTHING, SOUVENIRS

Map p286 (田子坊; Taikang Rd; 泰康路; ⏲10am-8pm; Ⓜ Dapuqiao) Burrow into the *lǐlòng* (alleys) here for a rewarding haul of creative boutiques, selling everything from hip jewellery and yak-wool scarves to retro communist dinnerware. **Shànghǎi 1936** (unit 110, No 3, Lane 210; ⏲10am-8pm) is the place to pick up a tailored *wàitào* (Chinese jacket) or *qípáo* (figure-hugging Chinese dress); they also have a nearby **men's store** (unit 910, No 9, Lane 210).

Further along is **Harvest** (International Artists Factory, unit 118, No 3, Lane 210), which sells Miao embroidery from southwest China and the courtyard at No 7, Lane 210 (aka the Yard): look for Himalayan jewellery and tapestries at **Joma** (unit 6) and local fashion designers at la vic (p114) and **Woo** (unit 7). **Jip** (No 51, Lane 210) comes in with eye-catching, modern jewellery for men, while **Not Just Silver** (No 10, Lane 210) sells its jewellery from a lovely old residence with a magnificent tiled floor. Just next door you can find 1960s propaganda prints and old calendar posters at the **Unique Hill Gallery** (No 10, Lane 210). The vibrant and colourful selection of crafts at **Esydragon** (No 20, Lane 210) makes for excellent gifts; Zhēnchálín Tea (p114) has Chinese herbal teas in nifty packaging. Other standout stores are Shokay (p114), **Chouchou Chic** (No 47, Lane 248), see p115, and **Urban Tribe** (No 14, Lane 248), see p118.

LIÚLI CHINA MUSEUM SHOP ART

Map p286 (琉璃艺术博物馆商店; Liúli Yìshù Bówùguǎn Shāngdiàn; 25 Taikang Rd; 泰康25号; ⏲10am-10pm Tue-Sun; Ⓜ Dapuqiao) If you like the decor at TMSK (p109) or the collection of artefacts at the Liúli China Museum (p94), you'll definitely want to check out this crystal art shop. Marvel at iridescent cast-glass creations such as contemplative monks, majestic dragons or exquisite earrings and pendants, or browse through the quality collection of English-language books and other knick-knacks.

ZHĒNCHÁLÍN TEA TEA

Map p286 (臻茶林; Zhēnchálín; Tiánzǐfáng, No 13, Lane 210, Taikang Rd; 泰康路210弄13号田子坊; ⌚10am-8.30pm; Ⓜ Dapuqiao) From the entrance this looks like just another tea shop, but poke around inside and you'll find specially blended herbal teas from Ayako, a traditional Chinese medicine–certified nutritionist. Peruse the hand-wrapped *pu-erh* teas, ceramic and crystal teaware, and watercolour postcards of Shànghǎi while staff ply you with tiny cups of ginseng oolong to keep you lingering.

SHOKAY CLOTHING

Map p286 (Tiánzǐfáng, No 9, Lane 274, Taikang Rd; 泰康路274弄9号田子坊; ⌚10am-8.30pm; Ⓜ Dapuqiao) If the sign outside ('100% yak!') doesn't catch your attention, we don't know what will. Shokay is one of the few places in the world where you can pick up hand-knit clothing made entirely out of, yup, yak wool – which is a surprisingly soft, supple material.

A nonprofit organisation, they support Tibetan herders (who gather the wool) and Chóngmíng Island farmers (who do the knitting) and use revenue to help Chinese minority groups start their own businesses.

LA VIE CLOTHING

Map p286 (生; Shēng; Tiánzǐfáng, the Yard, No 7, Lane 210, Taikang Rd; 泰康路210弄7号13室; ⌚10.30am-8.30pm; Ⓜ Dapuqiao) Local designer Jenny Ji has made a name for herself with her stylish take on street fashion, including patterned jeans and nicely cut shirts. None of it comes cheap, though: even the T-shirts go for a couple thousand *kuài*. Another shop is at **306 Changle Road** (长乐路306号; ⌚1-10pm; Ⓜ South Shaanxi Rd).

POTTERY WORKSHOP CERAMICS

Map p286 (乐天陶社; Lètiān Táoshè; www.potteryworkshop.com.cn; Tiánzǐfáng, 220 Taikang Rd; 泰康路220号田子坊; ⌚10am-8pm; Ⓜ Dapuqiao) Originally founded in Hong Kong, the Pottery Workshop is a community arts centre offering classes in ceramic design. The diverse creations of the workshop's resident artists – including those in China's ceramics capital Jǐngdézhèn – are on display in this shop at the entrance to Tiánzǐfáng.

TOP CHOICE XĪNTIĀNDÌ ACCESSORIES, CLOTHING, SOUVENIRS

Map p286 (新天地; cnr Taicang & Madang Rds; 太仓路与马当路路口; ⌚11am-11pm; Ⓜ South Huangpi Rd, Xintiandi) There are few bargains to be had at Xīntiāndì, but even window shoppers can make a fun afternoon of it here. The North Block features embroidered accessories at Annabel Lee (p115),

LOCAL KNOWLEDGE

SHÀNGHǍI'S BEST BOUTIQUES

Sandy Chu, who writes the blog **Shanghai Style** (www.shanghaistyle.onsugar.com), gave us the lowdown on Shànghǎi's best designer boutiques.

NuoMi (p116) This is my favourite Shànghǎi-based boutique chain for womenswear. Led by a team of Filipino designers, NuoMi's silhouettes are figure conscious, feminine, well designed and stylish without being trendy. Ecofriendly fabrics are incorporated and many pieces are quite luxurious – think silk and super-soft jerseys. With several boutiques across town it's easy to reach a shop, and prices are on par with Zara.

William the Beekeeper (p116) While the city's not known for its vintage, there are still a few gems out there. William the Beekeeper is my go-to place. They offer vintage collected from places like California, Hong Kong, Korea and Japan in an affordable price range. Indie designers are also stocked alongside their own vintage-inspired label, Kaileeni.

Heirloom (p115) This is probably my favourite place to window shop. With classy, stylish handbags for the city miss, Heirloom's designs are colourful and fun.

Mayumi Sato (p118) This Japanese-run boutique offers colourful, cute clothing in Western sizes, which are still a bit difficult to find in Shànghǎi. Pieces are more relaxed and girly, so don't expect to see anything too revealing in the shop.

high-end fashion from Shanghai Tang and mod jewellery from **NoD** (Bldg 25), in addition to home furnishings at Simply Life and a few scattered souvenir shops. In contrast, the South Block has not one, but two malls.

Serious shopaholics should make for the one known as **Xīntiāndì Style** (新天地时尚; Xīntiāndì Shíshàng; 245 Madang Rd; 马当路245号), which features a handful of local designers including la vie (p114), Heirloom, The Thing (p116), Shànghǎi Trio, Woo and Even Penniless.

ANNABEL LEE ACCESSORIES

Map p286 (安梨家居; Ānlí Jiājū; Xīntiāndì North Block, Bldg 3; 太仓路181弄新天地北里3号楼; ⏲10.30am-10.30pm; Ⓜ South Huangpi Rd, Xintiandi) The local designer's (p72) Xīntiāndì branch, with an emphasis on cashmere and silk.

SHANGHAI TANG CLOTHING

Map p286 (上海滩; Shànghǎi Tān; Xīntiāndì North Block, Bldg 15; 太仓路181弄新天地北里15号楼; Ⓜ South Huangpi Rd) Hong Kong–based Shanghai Tang flies the flag for the Middle Kingdom in the world of high-end fashion. The designs are classic Chinese with a twist, incorporating fluorescent colours, traditional motifs and luxury fabrics like silk and cashmere into the clothes and accessories. More affordable items include the slinky tops and the scarves, but if you have to ask the price of an item here, you can't afford it.

SHÀNGHǍI TRIO ACCESSORIES, CLOTHING

Map p286 (上海组合; Shànghǎi Zǔhé; Store 129, Xīntiāndì Style, 245 Madang Rd; 马当路245号新天地时尚129屋; ⏲10am-10pm; Ⓜ Xintiandi) *Ravissant! C'est tout moi!* French women go crazy for the chic ecofriendly fabrics here, which incorporate traditional Chinese motifs into much of the collection. Among the finds: cute children's clothes, purses, scarves and quilt (duvet) covers. It's located in the mall by the Xintiandi metro stop.

SIMPLY LIFE HOMEWARES

Map p286 (逸居生活; Yìjū Shēnghuó; ☎6387 5100; Xīntiāndì North Block, unit 101, 159 Madang Rd; 马当路159号新天地北里101单元; ⏲10.30am-10pm; Ⓜ South Huangpi Rd, Xintiandi) Come here for upmarket household knick-knacks, including hand-painted tea sets, crockery and pottery, all of which is locally made.

HEIRLOOM ACCESSORIES

Map p286 (78 Xinle Rd; 新乐路78号; ⏲10.30am-10.30pm; Ⓜ South Shaanxi Rd) Founded in 2008 by two Asian American designers, Heirloom specialises in a range of bold, stylish clutches, satchels and shoulder bags, as well as smaller accessories such as leather wallets and bracelets. Prices range from ¥190 to around ¥4000.

CHOUCHOU CHIC CLOTHING

Map p286 (喆缤豆小童生活馆; Zhébīndòu Xiǎotóng Shēnghuó Guǎn; 162-8 South Shaanxi Rd; 陕西南路162-8号; Ⓜ South Shaanxi Rd) French-Chinese hybrid Chouchou Chic sells kids' clothes (up to age eight) that are infinitely cuter than what you find at the souvenir stalls. Most of the clothing is Western-style, but you can find some attractive floral-patterned fabrics and Chinese-style cotton dresses as well. Prices start at ¥148; the entrance is on Changle Rd.

100 CHANGE & INSECT SHOES

Map p286 (百变虫; Bǎibiànchóng; 318 Nanchang Rd; 南昌路318号; ⏲10.30am-10.30pm; Ⓜ South Shaanxi Rd) Strange name, funky footwear – this is the place for those who want their heels to be seen in the dark. Browse Hong Kong designs covered in rhinestones, sequins, pink glitter, and silver and gold accents. Another branch is at **76 Xinle Road** (新乐路76号; Ⓜ South Shaanxi Rd).

NINE JEWELLERY

Map p286 (142 Nanchang Rd; 南昌路142号; Ⓜ South Shaanxi Rd) Drop by this incense-filled boutique to peruse the collection of handmade Tibetan-themed jewellery, fashioned from mother-of-pearl, red coral and turquoise.

PCS (POP CLASSIC SNEAKERS) SHOES

Map p286 (130 Nanchang Rd; 南昌路130号; ⏲1-10pm; Ⓜ South Shaanxi Rd) This tiny shoebox of a store has a fantastic collection of men's canvas sneakers, all sold at unbeatable prices. Try on a pair of original Feiyue, Warrior or spruced-up Ospop worker boots; owner Jacob Wang will doubtless find the style that suits you best.

HÉPÍNG FINERY CLOTHING

Map p286 (和平旗袍专卖店; Hépíng Qípáo Zhuānmài Diàn; 161 South Maoming Rd; 茂名南路161号; ⏲9.30am-9.30pm; Ⓜ South Shaanxi Rd) This tiny store offers cheaper tailor-made *qípáo* than most of its nearby competitors.

It does silk shirts, dresses and jackets as well, with most of the patterns incorporating large embroidered flowers in their design. Custom-fit clothing can be made in as little as three days, though the average wait is closer to 10 days.

HUĀYÀNG NIÁNHUÁ CLOTHING

Map p286 (花样年华; 145 South Maoming Rd; 茂名南路145号; ⌚11am-9pm; Ⓜ South Shaanxi Rd) Huāyàng Niánhuá takes its name from the Chinese title of the Wong Kar Wai movie *In the Mood for Love*, which featured Hong Kong actress Maggie Cheung in an array of stunning *qípáo*. Fittingly, they make fine tailor-made *qípáo* here from ¥1200, but there's no guarantee you'll look like Ms Cheung once you slip one on.

GARDEN BOOKS BOOKS

Map p286 (韬奋西文书局; Tāofèn Xīwén Shūjú; 325 Changle Rd; 长乐路325号; 📶; Ⓜ South Shaanxi Rd) This is the French Concession's sole English-language bookshop, which makes up for the fact that the ice-cream parlour inside occupies about as much space as the bookshelves. Stock up on Shànghǎi-related books, travel guides, foreign magazines and as much Harry Potter and John Grisham as you can read.

THE THING CLOTHING

Map p286 (276 Changle Rd; 长乐路276号; Ⓜ South Shaanxi Rd) The Thing specialises in Shànghǎi urbanwear, selling hoodies, messenger bags, shoes and Chinglish T-shirts.

APPLE STORE ELECTRONICS

Map p286 (Hong Kong Plaza North Block, 282 Middle Huaihai Rd; 淮海中路282号香港广场北座; ⌚10am-10pm; 📶; Ⓜ South Huangpi Rd) Stop by the Genius Bar for advice or troubleshooting, get online or browse the latest wonders of the tech world in this two-floor Apple outlet.

CYBERMART ELECTRONICS

Map p286 (赛博数码广场; Sàibó Shùmǎ Guǎngchǎng; 1 Middle Huaihai Rd; 淮海中路1号; ⌚10am-8.30pm; Ⓜ Dashijie) Cybermart is the most central and reliable location for all sorts of gadgetry, including DVD players, iPods, laptops, digital cameras and camcorders, as well as blank CDs, memory sticks and software. It's essentially two floors of independent stalls so you won't get a store guarantee, but you may find some deals. You can definitely bargain, but don't expect enormous discounts.

XĪNGGUĀNG PHOTOGRAPHY EQUIPMENT ELECTRONICS, PHOTOGRAPHY

off Map p286 (星光摄影器材城; Xīngguāng Shèyǐng Qìcái Chéng; 288 Luban Rd; 淮海中路288号; ⌚7am-7pm; Ⓜ Dapuqiao, Luban Rd) There are three main floors of photography equipment here, and while prices vary (you need to bargain; no guarantees) you can still expect to find some good buys. Digital cameras are everywhere, but photography buffs will be most interested in sorting through the various lenses, tripods and bags. A real find is the **Shen-Hao** (申豪; 4th fl), which sells its hard-to-find field cameras. A repair shop is on the 3rd floor.

YĚ HUǑ HÙWÀI YÒNGPǏN DIÀN OUTDOOR EQUIPMENT

Map p286 (野火户外用品店; 296 Changle Rd; 长乐路296号; ⌚10.30am-10pm; Ⓜ South Shaanxi Rd) A great store for outdoor gear. Osprey packs and Vasque boots are available, in addition to quality Gore-Tex clothing, tents and sleeping bags.

French Concession West

TOP CHOICE NUOMI CLOTHING

Map p290 (糯米; Nùomǐ; www.nuomishanghai.com; 196 Xinle Rd; 新乐路196号; Ⓜ Changshu Rd) This Shànghǎi-based label seems to do everything right: gorgeous dresses made from organic cotton, silk and bamboo, eye-catching jewellery fashioned from recycled materials, a sustainable business plan that gives back to the community and even an irresistible line of kids' clothes.

WILLIAM THE BEEKEEPER CLOTHING

Map p290 (www.williamthebeekeeper.com; 84 Fenyang Rd; 汾阳路84号; ⌚11.30am-7.30pm Tue-Sun; Ⓜ Changshu Rd) Size isn't everything, a point emphatically made by this clever boutique, which American Cairn Wu Reppun opened in 2010. Satisfy your sweet tooth with an organic honey stick (fresh from the family farm in Honolulu) before browsing through the vintage duds, indie designer labels (including Reppun's own Kaileeni) and a tasteful collection of secondhand furniture and books. There's another branch sharing space with XinleLu.com.

BEST SHOPPING STRIPS

Looking for the best spots to wander and window shop? Around the South Shaanxi Rd metro station are a few blocks that are a must for serious clothes shoppers. Afternoon and evening are the best hours for browsing: some smaller shops don't open their doors until noon, but most stay open until 10pm.

Nanchang Road (Map p286) A good street for general browsing, with shoes, antiques, and men's and women's clothing.

Changle Road (Map p286) Young designers and emerging local brands have taken over a one-block stretch of Changle Rd east of Ruijin No 1 Rd. Check out la vie (p114), The Thing (p116), **Elbis Hungi** (No 139-18) and **Even Penniless** (No 139) to see where local fashion is headed.

Xinle Road (Map p290 and Map p286) This two-block stretch has less high-end fashion than Changle Rd but ultimately greater variety. Pop into Heirloom (p115), 100 Change & Insect (p115), **Source** (No 158) and NuoMi (p116) for a taste of the 'Hai's urban style.

South Maoming Road (Map p286) South of Huaihai Rd is custom-tailored traditional women's clothing (like *qípáo*); north of Huaihai Rd is tailored men's suits and dress shoes.

XINLELU.COM — CLOTHING

Map p290 (www.xinlelu.com; 87 Wuyuan Rd; 五原路87号; ⌚noon-10pm Tue-Sun; Ⓜ Changshu Rd) Local style mavens XinleLu.com have finally ventured out into the offline world with this original showroom, displaying the best of their handpicked bags, shoes and dresses from local designers.

TOP CHOICE BROCADE COUNTRY — HANDICRAFTS

Map p290 (锦绣纺; Jǐnxiù Fǎng; 616 Julu Rd; 巨鹿路616号; ⌚10am-7.30pm; Ⓜ South Shaanxi Rd) Peruse an exquisite collection of minority handicrafts from China's southwest, most of which are secondhand (ie not made for the tourist trade) and personally selected by the owner Liu Xiaolan, a Guìzhōu native. Items for sale include embroidered wall hangings (some of which were originally baby carriers), sashes, shoes and hats, as well as silver jewellery.

The butterfly, a homonym for 'mother' in the Miao language, is a popular motif.

BA YAN KA LA — BEAUTY

Map p290 (巴颜喀拉; Bā Yán Kā Lā; 1221 Changle Rd; 长乐路1221号; ⌚10am-9pm; Ⓜ Changshu Rd) Taking its name from the Tibetan mountain range that separates the Yellow and Yangzi watersheds, Ba Yan Ka La offers a line of natural beauty products derived from Chinese herbs. Goji berry (skin revitalisation), lotus seed (skin nourishment) and mulberry (detoxification) are all familiar ingredients in traditional Chinese medicine, and match well with Ba Yan Ka La's natural elegance. The scented candles, shampoos, Tibetan (crystal of wisdom) bath salts and facial scrubs can also be found in several hotels around town.

PARAMITA — HANDICRAFTS

Map p290 (波罗蜜多西藏工艺品; Bōluómìduō Xīzàng Gōngyìpǐn; 850-1 Julu Rd; 巨鹿路850-1号; Ⓜ Changshu Rd, Jing'an Temple) If you can't make it to Tibet, at least swing by Paramita for its inspiring collection of souvenirs, including yak-bone amulets, masks, jewellery, framed mandalas and other Buddhist treasures from the Himalayas. It's a nonprofit organisation, founded to help Tibetans with minimal education find employment.

MADAME MAO'S DOWRY — CLOTHING, SOUVENIRS

Map p290 (毛太设计; Máotài Shèjì; madame maosdowry.com; 207 Fumin Rd; 富民路207号; ⌚10am-7pm; Ⓜ Jing'an Temple) Everyone needs some revolution-era collector's items somewhere in the house. What better way to brighten up the foyer than with a bust of the chairman? Or why not make a statement in the kitchen with a poster of happy socialist workers? If reminiscing about the Mao days leaves you cold, peruse the store's collection of locally designed clothing and jewellery.

YÚ — CERAMICS

Map p290 (萸; 164 Fumin Rd; 富民路164号; ⌚11am-9pm; Ⓜ Changshu Rd) Man Zhang and her husband create the personable porcelain at this tiny shop, the latest link in the Shànghǎi-Jǐngdézhèn connection, which is an excellent place to browse for handmade and hand-painted teaware, bowls and vases.

POTTERY WORKSHOP CERAMICS

Map p290 (乐天陶社; Lètiān Táoshè; www.potteryworkshop.com.cn; 176 Fumin Rd; 富民路176号; 10am-8pm; M Jing'an Temple) A second retail shop from Shànghǎi's community ceramics centre (p114).

URBAN TRIBE CLOTHING

Map p290 (城市山民; Chéngshì Shānmín; 133 West Fuxing Rd; 复兴西路133号; M Shanghai Library) Urban Tribe is the only contemporary Shànghǎi label to draw inspiration from the ethnic groups of China and Southeast Asia. The collection of loose-fitting blouses, pants and jackets are made of natural fabrics and are a refreshing departure from the city's on-the-go attitude and usual taste for flamboyance. Don't miss their collection of silver jewellery and the lovely tea garden behind the store.

CHINESE PRINTED BLUE NANKEEN EXHIBITION HALL FABRIC

Map p290 (中国蓝印花布馆; Zhōngguó Lán Yìnhuābù Guǎn; No 24, Lane 637, Changle Rd; 长乐路637弄24号; 9am-5pm; M Changshu Rd) Follow the blue signs through a maze of courtyards until you see bolts of blue cloth drying in the yard. Originally produced in Jiāngsū, Zhèjiāng and Guìzhōu provinces, this blue-and-white cotton fabric (sometimes called blue calico) is similar to batik, and is coloured using a starch-resist method and indigo dye bath. This museum and shop, started by Japanese artist Kubo Mase, displays and sells items made by hand, from the cloth right down to the buttons. It has been in business for over 20 years, takes pride in quality and does not give discounts.

MAYUMI SATO CLOTHING

Map p290 (www.mayumisato.com; 169 Anfu Rd; 安福路169号; noon-8pm; M Changshu Rd) Japanese designer Mayumi Sato uses organic cotton, silk and wool to create a playful collection of limited-edition skirts, dresses and tops. Nothing is mass produced and off-cuts are recycled into her line of signature accessories.

SIMPLY LIFE HOMEWARES

Map p290 (逸居生活; Yìjū Shēnghuó; 9 Dongping Rd; 东平路9号; M Changshu Rd) A branch of the local home furnishings store (p115).

PROPAGANDA POSTER ART CENTRE ART, SOUVENIRS

Map p290 (上海宣传画艺术中心; Shànghǎi Xuānchuánhuà Yìshù Zhōngxīn; 6211 1845, 1390 184 1246; Room B-OC, 868 Huashan Rd; 华山路868号B-OC房间; admission ¥20; 10am-5pm; M Shanghai Library) If socialist art is your thing, check out this gallery, which houses a huge collection of propaganda posters. Increasingly prized by collectors, some of them are very rare and prices are correspondingly high. See p95 for more details.

TRADITIONAL CHINESE MASSAGE

In the 17th and 18th centuries, Qing-dynasty barbers developed the current form of Chinese massage, known as *tuīná* (推拿; literally push-grab). In addition to cutting hair, skilled barbers learned to use acupressure points to treat different ailments and the practice, which was cheaper, less painful and safer than acupuncture, soon became quite popular – even late Qing emperors employed *tuīná* masseurs. In 1822, the Daoguang emperor decried acupuncture as unsafe and banned the practice, helping *tuīná* to secure its position as an integral part of Chinese medical treatment.

The general idea behind Chinese massage is that it stimulates your *qì* (vital energy that flows along different pathways or meridians, each of which is connected to a major organ) and removes energy blockages, through which you can treat specific ailments, from muscular and joint pain to the common cold.

Interestingly, the hairdresser-massage association is still quite common in China, though the roles have again changed: many businesses that advertise themselves as hairdressers are now nothing more than brothels, with rows of young girls seated beneath lurid pink lighting waiting to provide 'massage services' to their clients. This doesn't mean that *tuīná* has disappeared – getting a real massage has never been easier, and in Shànghǎi, they come at a fraction of the price that you'd pay at home.

SPORTS & ACTIVITIES

French Concession East

TOP CHOICE DOUBLE RAINBOW MASSAGE HOUSE — MASSAGE

Map p286 (双彩虹保健按摩厅; Shuāng Cǎihóng Bǎojiàn Ànmó Tīng; 45 Yongjia Rd; 永嘉路45号; ⏲noon-midnight; Ⓜ South Shaanxi Rd) Perhaps Shànghǎi's best neighbourhood massage parlour. The visually impaired masseuses here will have you groaning in agony in no time as they seek out those oft neglected pressure points. The rates are a steal: only ¥45 for a 45-minute foot or back massage (throw in an extra ¥10 for the herbal foot soak).

GREEN MASSAGE — MASSAGE

Map p286 (青专业按摩; Qīng Zhuānyè Ànmó; ☎5386 0222; www.greenmassage.com.cn; 58 Taicang Rd; 太仓路58号; massages & spa treatments ¥118-528; ⏲10.30am-2am; Ⓜ South Huangpi Rd) Calming fragrances envelop guests at this plush midrange spa, which offers foot, *tuīná* (see p118) and shiatsu massages. In addition to traditional practices such as cupping and moxibustion, they also provide waxing and other beauty treatments. Reserve.

LÓNGWǓ KUNG FU CENTER — MARTIAL ARTS

Map p286 (龙武功夫馆; Lóngwǔ Gōngfu Guǎn; ☎6287 1528; www.longwukungfu.com; 1 South Maoming Rd; 茂名南路1号; Ⓜ South Shaanxi Rd) Coaches from Shànghǎi's martial-arts teams give classes in Chinese, Japanese and Korean martial arts. The largest centre in the city, it also offers children's classes on weekend mornings and lessons in English.

WǓYÌ CHINESE KUNGFU CENTRE — MARTIAL ARTS

Map p286 (武懿国术馆; Wǔyì Guóshù Guǎn; ☎137 0168 5893; room 311, 3rd fl, International Artists' Factory, No 3, Lane 210, Taikang Rd; 法租界泰康路210弄3号3楼311; Ⓜ Dapuqiao) English-language taichi classes on Thursday and Sunday and *wǔshù* classes on Wednesday and Sunday for adults and kids. Call for the latest schedules and prices.

HATHA YOGA CENTER — YOGA

Map p286 (哈达瑜伽会所; Hādá Yújiā Huìsuǒ; ☎6218 0955; www.cnyoga.com; 1 South Maoming Rd; 茂名南路1号; Ⓜ South Shaanxi Rd) Attached to the Lóngwǔ Kung Fu Center, this is one of Shànghǎi's premier yoga spaces. Sign up for intro classes or a range of more advanced styles, from Hatha and Bikram to Ashtanga and Pilates.

French Concession West

SUBCONSCIOUS DAY SPA — MASSAGE

Map p290 (桑格水疗会所; Sāngkē Shuǐliáo Huìsuǒ; ☎6415 0636; www.subconsciousdayspa.com; 183 Fumin Rd; 富民路183号; ⏲10am-midnight; Ⓜ Changshu Rd, Jing'an Temple) The scent of lemongrass fills the air as you enter this serene ecofriendly spa. A veritable centre for mind-body rejuvenation, Subconscious offers an array of traditional massages (¥150/225 per 60/90 minutes), from *tuīná* and hot stone to Thai, as well as six-person yoga classes, nutrition counselling and beauty treatments such as manicures and waxing.

DRAGONFLY — MASSAGE

Map p290 (悠庭保健会所; Yōutíng Bǎojiàn Huìsuǒ; ☎5405 0008; www.dragonfly.net.cn; 20 Donghu Rd; 东湖路20号; ⏲10am-2am; Ⓜ South Shaanxi Rd) One of the longest-running massages services in Shànghǎi, the soothing Dragonfly offers Chinese body massages, foot massages and Japanese-style shiatsu (¥168/252 per 60/90 minutes) in addition to more specialised services such as aroma oil massages (¥420) and beauty treatments. Prices include a private room and a change of clothes. Reserve. There's another French Concession branch at **206 Xinle Road** (☎5403 9982; 新乐路206号; Ⓜ South Shaanxi Rd).

Jìng'ān

WEST NANJING ROAD | SHÀNGHĂI RAILWAY STATION

Neighbourhood Top Five

❶ Delve into the divine at Shànghǎi's busiest place of worship, the **Jade Buddha Temple** (p122).

❷ Discover the latest trends in the art world at the post-industrial **M50** (p123).

❸ Explore the *lǐlòng* lanes of the **Bubbling Well Road Apartments** on our walking tour (p128).

❹ Snap some shots of the **Jìng'ān Temple** (p124) juxtaposed against a skyscraper background.

❺ Catch the acrobats at the **Shànghǎi Centre Theatre** (p133).

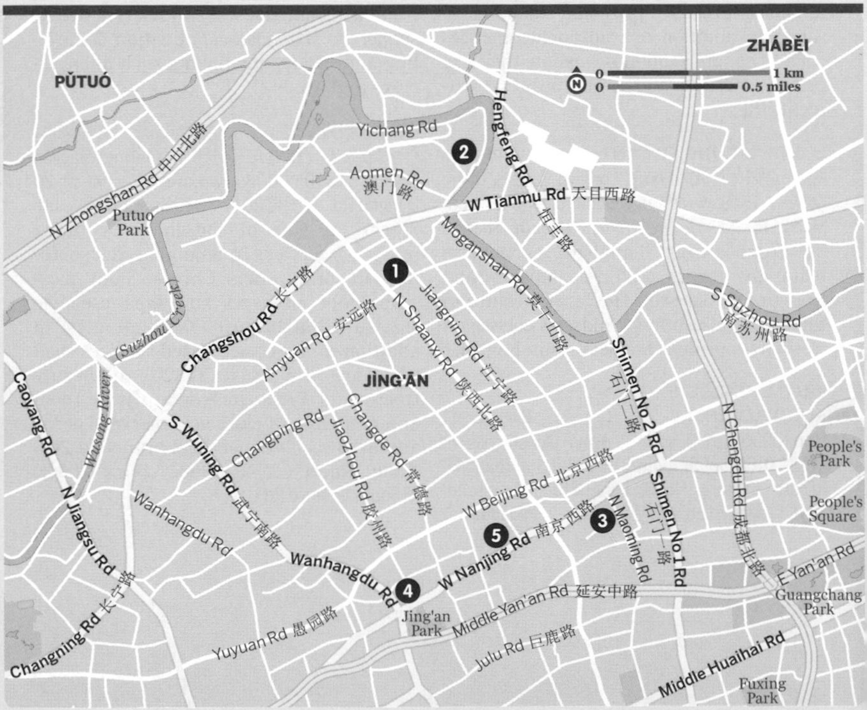

For more detail of this area, see Map p294 and p293 ➡

Explore: Jìng'ān

In the early days of the International Settlement, West Nanjing Rd was known as Bubbling Well Rd and its far western end marked where the city stopped and the countryside began. By the 1920s, the fields were being swallowed up by the rapidly expanding city and Bubbling Well Rd was one of Shànghǎi's busiest and most exclusive streets. Apart from its name, not much has changed since then. The main thoroughfare of today's Jìng'ān district (静安), West Nanjing Rd is now home to some of the city's priciest malls, high-end shops and five-star hotels.

Pudong may have taller towers and the French Concession more charisma, but this part of Jìng'ān is still the city's most exclusive neighbourhood. Even the skyscrapers here exhibit harmony – a change from the disjointed skyline in other districts – while the traditional *lǐlòng* (alleyways) are unexpectedly well preserved. The heart of all the consumer action is the Shànghǎi Centre, a focal point both for tourists and the many expats who work in the district.

But head north of West Nanjing Rd and you're plunged into a grittier and more absorbing area. The first stop on many tours of Jìng'ān is the Jade Buddha Temple; a short hike to the north from here are the M50 art galleries along Sūzhōu Creek. Good streets to explore for a taste of an authentic working-class Shànghǎi neighbourhood include the bustling Jiangning and North Shaanxi Rds.

Local Life

- **Temple Life** Join the worshippers at the Jade Buddha (p122) and Jìng'ān (p124) Temples, followed by an authentic vegetarian meal.
- **Art** Explore the labyrinth of galleries at M50 (p123).
- **Snack Attack** When the munchies strike, follow the crowds to Wujiang Road Food Street (p131).

Getting There & Away

- **Metro** Line 2 runs parallel to West Nanjing Rd, stopping at People's Sq, West Nanjing Rd, Jing'an Temple and Jiangsu Rd. Line 7 runs north–south and intersects with line 2 at Jing'an Temple and line 1 at Changshu Rd in the French Concession. The new line 13 links Changshou Rd in north Jìng'ān with West Nanjing Rd.
- **Bus** Bus 19 links the North Bund area to the Jade Buddha Temple area; catch it at the intersection of Tiantong and North Sichuan Rds. Bus 112 zigzags north from the southern end of People's Sq to West Nanjing Rd, and up Jiangning Rd to the Jade Buddha Temple.

Lonely Planet's Top Tip

Jìng'ān has some remarkably well-preserved *lǐlòng* (alleyways). The gentrified Bubbling Well Rd Apartments, covered in our walking tour, are a great place to start exploration, but architecture buffs should also seek out the handful of lanes off Yuyuan Rd in the west of the district, particularly those at Nos 395 and 361, near the intersection with West Beijing Rd.

Best Places to Eat

- Wujiang Road Food Street (p131)
- Hǎi Dǐ Lāo (p129)
- Vegetarian Lifestyle (p129)
- Lynn (p129)
- Fu 1088 (p129)

For reviews, see p125

Best Places to Drink

- Fennel Lounge (p131)
- Kāibā (p132)
- Roof Club (p133)
- Big Bamboo (p132)
- B&C (p132)

For reviews, see p131

Best Sports & Activities

- Apsara Spa (p135)
- Green Massage (p135)
- Aromassage (p135)
- Oz Body Fit (p135)

For reviews, see p135

ATLANTIDE PHOTOTRAVEL / CORBIS ©

TOP SIGHTS
JADE BUDDHA TEMPLE

One of Shànghǎi's few active Buddhist monasteries, this temple was built between 1918 and 1928. The highlight is a transcendent Buddha made of pure jade, one of five shipped back to China by the monk Hui Gen at the turn of the 20th century. In February, during the Lunar New Year, the temple is very busy, as some 20,000 Chinese Buddhists throng to pray for prosperity.

Entrance Courtyard

Festooned with red lanterns, the first courtyard is located between the **Hall of Heavenly Kings** (the main entrance hall) and the twin-eaved **Great Treasure Hall**, where worshippers pray to the past, present and future Buddhas. Also lodged within the main hall are the temple's drum and bell, which would normally be hung within separate towers, and a copper-coloured statue of Guanyin dispensing holy water at the rear entrance.

Jade Buddha Hall

Follow the right-hand corridor past the Hall of Heavenly Kings and the Guanyin Hall to arrive at the **Jade Buddha Hall** (admission ¥10). The absolute centrepiece of the temple is the 1.9m-high pale green jade Buddha, which is seated upstairs. Visitors are not able to approach the statue, but can admire it from a distance. Photographs are not permitted.

Ancestral Hall

On your right as you exit the Jade Buddha Hall is the Ancestral Hall, where Buddhist services are held. Heading back towards the entrance will then take you past a similarly elegant jade **reclining Buddha**, opposite a larger copy made from marble.

DON'T MISS...

- Hall of Heavenly Kings
- Great Treasure Hall
- Jade Buddha Hall

PRACTICALITIES

- Map p293
- cnr Anyuan & Jiangning Rds; 安远路和江宁路拐角
- admission ¥20
- ⌚8am-4.30pm
- 🚌19 from Broadway Mansions along Tiantong Rd
- Ⓜ Changshou Rd

TOP SIGHTS
M50

Chinese contemporary art has been the hottest thing in the art world for over a decade, and there's no sign of the boom ending, with collectors around the globe paying record prices for the work of top artists. Běijīng may dominate the art scene, but Shànghǎi has its own gallery subculture, centred on this complex of industrial buildings down dusty Moganshan Rd in the north of town.

Although the artists who originally established the M50 enclave (M50创意产业集聚区; M Wǔshí Chuàngyì Chǎnyè Jíjùqū) are long gone, it's worth putting aside a half-day to poke around the galleries here. There's a lot of mass-produced commercial prints (especially in buildings three and four), but there are also some challenging, innovative galleries if you're willing to look for them. Most galleries are open from 10am to 6pm; some close on Monday.

DON'T MISS...

- ShanghART
- island6
- m97

PRACTICALITIES

- Map p293
- 50 Moganshan Rd; 莫干山路50号
- Ⓜ Shanghai Railway Station or taxi

Galleries

The most established gallery here, the 10-year-old **ShanghART** (Xiānggénà Huàláng; www.shanghartgallery.com; Bldg 16 & 18) has a big, dramatic space to show the work of some of the 40 artists it represents. The top-notch and provocative **island6** (www.island6.org; 2nd fl, Bldg 6) focuses on collaborative works created in a studio behind the gallery. **OFoto** (2nd fl, Bldg 13) features China-related photography exhibitions. Other notable galleries include **Other Gallery** (Bldg 9) and **twocities** (www.twocitiesgallery.com; 2nd fl, Bldg 0). Across the street is **m97** (www.m97gallery.com; 2nd fl, 97 Moganshan Rd), an innovative photography gallery.

Cafes

When your legs finally give way, order a drink or simple snack at the Roof Club (p133) or Bandu Cabin (p133), which also hosts Chinese music concerts.

Entertainment includes Image Tunnel (p133), which screens independent Chinese films, and twocities, which occasionally holds improv jazz concerts.

SIGHTS

West Nanjing Road

JÌNG'ĀN TEMPLE BUDDHIST TEMPLE

Map p294 (静安寺; Jìng'ān Sì; 1686-1688 West Nanjing Rd; 南京西路1686-1688号; admission ¥30; ⏲7.30am-5pm; Ⓜ Jing'an Temple) After over a decade of restoration, Jìng'ān Temple is finally coming together as one of the city's most eye-catching temples. Although it lacks an air of venerability and there are fewer devotees than at the Jade Buddha Temple, there can be no denying its spectacular location among the district's soaring skyscrapers.

Constructed largely of Burmese teak, the temple has recently installed some gorgeous statues, including a massive 8.8m-high, 15-tonne silver Buddha in the main Mahavira Hall, and a 6.2m-high camphor Guanyin and 3.86m-high white jade Sakyamuni in the side halls. At the time of writing, the rear hall and other parts of the temple were still undergoing renovation.

Khi Vehdu, who ran Jìng'ān Temple in the 1930s, was one of the most remarkable figures of the time. The nearly 2m-tall abbot had a large following as well as seven concubines, each of whom had a house and a car. During the Cultural Revolution the temple was shorn of its Buddhist statues and turned into a plastics factory before burning to the ground in 1972.

Good times to visit include the Festival of Bathing Buddha on the eighth day of the fourth lunar month and at the full moon.

FREE FORMER RESIDENCE OF MAO ZEDONG HISTORIC BUILDING

Map p294 (毛泽东旧居; Máo Zédōng Jiùjū; Nos 5-9, 120 North Maoming Rd; 茂名北路120弄5-9号; ⏲9-11am & 1-4pm; Ⓜ Jing'an Temple) Mao lived here in the latter half of 1924 with his second wife (Yang Kaihui) and their two children at the time, Anying and Anqing. The residence has old photos and newspaper clippings on display, but for many foreigners the real highlight is the building itself, a beautiful example of *shíkùmén* (stone-gate house) architecture. A passport or mobile telephone number is required to enter.

SHÀNGHĂI CHILDREN'S PALACE ARCHITECTURE

Map p294 (少年宫; Shàonián Gōng; West Nanjing Rd; 南京西路; admission weekday/weekend ¥20/50; ⏲9-11.30am & 1.30-5pm Wed-Sun; Ⓜ Jing'an Temple) A striking, white, two-storey 1920s building, this was formerly Kadoorie House, named after its wealthy Jewish owner. Architecture detectives can still peek in the rooms of Elly Kadoorie's 1920s mansion, once the site of Shànghǎi's most extravagant balls. It now hosts activities for children.

SHÀNGHĂI EXHIBITION CENTRE ARCHITECTURE

Map p294 (上海展览中心; Shànghǎi Zhǎnlǎn Zhōngxīn; 1000 Middle Yan'an Rd; 延安中路1000号; Ⓜ Jing'an Temple) The hulking great monolith of the Shànghǎi Exhibition Centre can be seen from West Nanjing Rd. It was built as the Palace of Sino-Soviet Friendship, a friendship that soon turned to ideological rivalry and even the brink of war in the 1960s. Architectural buffs will appreciate its monumentality and unsubtle, bold Bolshevik strokes – there was a time when Pǔdōng was set to look like this.

The site of the Exhibition Centre was originally the gardens of the Jewish millionaire Silas Hardoon.

Shànghǎi Railway Station

JADE BUDDHA TEMPLE BUDDHIST TEMPLE

See p122.

M50 GALLERIES

See p123.

SŪZHŌU CREEK BOAT TOURS BOAT CRUISES

(苏州河游览船; Sūzhōu Hé Yóulǎn Chuán; www.sz-river.com; Changhua Rd Dock; 昌化路码头; day/evening ¥130/150) The Sūzhōu Creek boat tours have been promoted for several years now, with little to show, but as this book went to press they appeared to be finally getting under way. The cruise is fairly low-key; however, there are development plans for several sites along the route, including a former matchbox factory and – no kidding – a Jackie Chan Museum.

The original tour runs from the Danba Rd Dock out in Pǔtuó (West Shànghǎi) to either the Xikang Rd Dock or Changhua Rd Dock (both off Yichang Rd), near M50, and

THE GREAT JEWISH FAMILIES

The Sassoon family consisted of generations of shrewd businesspeople from Baghdad to Bombay, whose achievements brought them wealth, knighthoods and far-reaching influence. Though it was David Sassoon who initiated cotton trading out of Bombay (now Mumbai) to China, and son Elias Sassoon who had the ingenuity to buy and build his own warehouses in Shànghǎi, it was Sir Victor Sassoon (1881–1961) who finally amassed the family fortune and enjoyed his wealth during Shànghǎi's heyday. Victor concentrated his energies on buying up Shànghǎi's land and building offices, apartments and warehouses, at one time owning an estimated 1900 buildings in Shànghǎi. Victor left the city in 1941, returning only briefly after the war to tidy up the business, and then he and his assets relocated to the Bahamas. He had plenty of affairs but remained a bachelor until he finally married his American nurse when he was 70.

Today the Sassoon legacy lives on in the historic Fairmont Peace Hotel (p53) and Sassoon Mansion (known to Sassoon as 'Eve') – now the Cypress Hotel in Hóngqiáo – each the site of some infamously raucous Sassoon soirées. For one of his celebrated fancy dress parties, he requested guests to come dressed as if shipwrecked.

The company of David Sassoon & Sons gave rise to several other notables in Shànghǎi, among them Silas Hardoon and Elly Kadoorie. Hardoon began his illustrious career as a night guard and later, in 1880, as manager of David Sassoon & Sons. Two years later he set out to do business on his own and promptly went bust. His second independent business venture in 1920 proved successful and Silas Hardoon made a name for himself in real estate. In his father's memory he built the Beth Aharon Synagogue near Sūzhōu Creek, which later served as a shelter for Polish Jews who had fled Europe. It has since been demolished. Once a well-respected member of both the French and International Councils, Hardoon's reputation turned scandalous when he took a Eurasian wife, Luo Jialing, and adopted a crowd of multicultural children. He then began to study Buddhism. His estate, including the school he had erected (now the grounds of the Shànghǎi Exhibition Centre), went up in smoke during the Sino-Japanese War. At the time of his death in 1931, he was the richest man in Shànghǎi.

Like Silas Hardoon, Elly Kadoorie began a career with David Sassoon & Sons in 1880 and he too broke away and amassed a fortune – in real estate, banking and rubber production. His famous mansion is the result of too much money left in the hands of an unreliable architect; after returning from three years in England, Kadoorie found a 19.5m-high ballroom aglow with 5.4m chandeliers and enough imported marble to warrant the name Marble Hall. Architecture detectives can still visit the staircases and peek at the ballroom of the former mansion, once the site of Shànghǎi's most extravagant balls and now home to the Children's Palace. Kadoorie died the year the communists took power; you can visit his mausoleum in the International Cemetery (p165).

With their immense wealth, many Jewish families were pivotal in aiding the thousands of refugees who fled to Shànghǎi. The Kadoorie family now resides in Hong Kong and is still involved in charity work.

lasts roughly 1½ hours round trip. Both are currently closed, though you should be able to buy tickets for cruises at the Changhua Rd Dock in the near future. Additionally, by the time this book is in print, the route may extend all the way to Wàibǎidù Bridge on the Bund, which could make for an interesting way to travel to and from the art galleries at M50.

Cruises currently run at 1.30pm, 3pm and 7pm.

EATING

Although business lunches and after-dinner drinks are the rule in Jìng'ān, most of the dining options here have long been first-rate, and those on a culinary tour of Shànghǎi should definitely squeeze the area into their itinerary.

1

KYLIE MCLAUGHLIN / GETTY IMAGES ©

2

1. I Love Shànghǎi (p132)
A cool dive bar that expresses its love for the city via strong drinks and theme nights.

2. Temple worshipping
The layout of temples allows the *qì* (energy) to circulate, aided by the liberal burning of incense.

3. Jìng'ān Temple (p124)
Find peace among the district's skyscrapers at this restored Buddhist temple.

4. M50 (p123)
Full of contemporary art galleries, industrially chic M50 is the city's main creative hub.

4

JUSTIN GUARIGLIA / NATIONAL GEOGRAPHIC SOCIETY / CORBIS©

START **WEST NANJING RD METRO STATION**

END **OHEL RACHEL SYNAGOGUE**

DISTANCE **1.7KM**

DURATION **1½ HOURS**

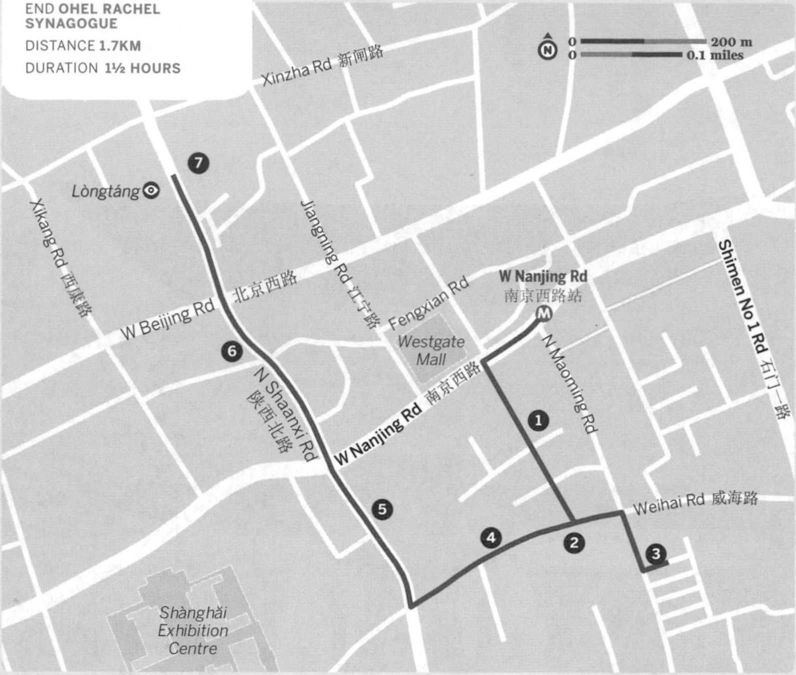

Neighbourhood Walk

Jìng'ān Walking Tour

Begin by walking through the ❶ **Bubbling Well Road Apartments** (静安别墅; Jìng'ān Biéshù), which you can enter off West Nanjing Rd. One of the most delightful surviving new-style *lǐlòng* housing complexes in Shànghǎi, with three-storey red-brick houses built between 1928 and 1932, it's a great spot to observe daily residential life – people walking their dogs, playing cards or hanging out laundry to dry. This is all mixed in with a new crop of tiny ground-floor cafes, boutiques and old-fashioned barber shops – look for places such as Fàn Jiā (梵家) at No 61 (open from noon to 8pm), which sells Tibetan Buddhist–themed jewellery.

Exit at the south end of the complex, which faces ❷ **Sun Court**, a 1928 apartment block, and turn left onto Weihai Rd. Continue right onto North Maoming Rd and explore the lovingly preserved *shíkùmén* (stone-gate) architecture of the ❸ **Former Residence of Mao Zedong**, where a 30-year old Mao once lived for several months in 1924.

Retrace your steps and return to Sun Court, continuing west down Weihai Rd and passing a ❹ **tea shop** (小叶名茶; Xiǎoyè Míngchá) at No 686, with a fabulous collection of aged *pǔ'ěr* cakes lining the walls. Turn right onto North Shaanxi Rd, where you'll eventually get a glimpse of an enormous ❺ **garden residence** (1918) at No 186, which once belonged to Wúxī native Rong Zongjing, one of Shànghǎi's most powerful industrialists at the time. Rong Zongjing's nephew, Rong Yiren, was one of the rare individuals with a capitalist background to succeed in communist China, becoming vice mayor of Shànghǎi in 1957 and later vice president of the PRC from 1993 to 1998.

Follow Shaanxi Rd north, past ❻ **Grace Baptist Church** at No 375 (moved here in 1942), until you reach the Sassoon-built ❼ **Ohel Rachel Synagogue** (1920) at No 500, the first of seven synagogues built in Shànghǎi (only two remain). It is closed to the public.

West Nanjing Road

TOP CHOICE FU 1088 SHANGHAINESE $$$

Map p294 (5239 7878; 375 Zhenning Rd; 镇宁路375号) Sister restaurant to Fu 1039 (p129), the more exclusive Fu 1088 consists of 17 rooms filled with Chinese antiques. Rooms are rented out privately, with white-gloved service and an emphasis on elegant Shanghainese fare such as shredded crab and drunken chicken. There's a minimum charge of ¥300 per person. Reserve.

VEGETARIAN LIFESTYLE CHINESE, VEGETARIAN $$

Map p294 (枣子树; Zǎozishù; 6215 7566; 258 Fengxian Rd; 奉贤路258号; dishes ¥22-68; ; West Nanjing Rd) These folks are surely improving their karma by making organic, vegetarian fare fashionable for the masses. There's a wide range of clever dishes, including soup served in a pumpkin, but best are the sweet Wúxī spare ribs, stuffed with lotus root of course, and the diverse claypots. No MSG is used and cooks go light on the oil.

HǍI DǏ LĀO HOTPOT $$

Map p294 (海底捞; 6258 9758; 3rd fl, 1068 West Beijing Rd; 北京西路1068号3楼; hotpot per person from ¥60; ; West Nanjing Rd) This Sichuanese hotpot restaurant is all about service, and the assault begins the minute you walk in the door. Predining options include complimentary shoe shines, manicures and trays of fresh fruit; once you've actually sat down, the buzz of activity continues with the donning of matching red aprons and a YouTube-worthy noodle-stretching dance performance (order *lāo miàn*; 捞面).

Hǎi Dǐ Lāo sets the standard for sauce bars across the country – make sure your table has enough bowls to fully appreciate the range of flavours available. While it's great for group meals, this is definitely not a place to dine alone or to go on a date.

LYNN SHANGHAINESE $$

Map p294 (琳怡; Lín Yí; 6247 0101; 99-1 Xikang Rd; 西康路99-1号; dishes ¥48-125; 11.30am-10.30pm; West Nanjing Rd) Another one of the growing number of restaurants pushing the boundaries between Shanghainese and Cantonese cuisine, Lynn offers consistently good, cleverly presented dishes at reasonable prices in plush but unfussy surroundings. The lunch dim-sum menu offers a range of delicate dumplings, while for dinner there are more traditional Shanghainese dishes, like eggplant with minced pork in a garlic and chilli sauce.

More adventurous standouts include the sautéed chicken with sesame pockets and deep-fried spare ribs with honey and garlic. Weekends feature all-you-can-eat dim sum for brunch. Reserve.

QÍMÍN ORGANIC HOTPOT HOTPOT $$$

Map p294 (齐民有机中国火锅; Qímín Yǒujī Zhōngguó Huǒguō; 6258 8777; 407 North Shaanxi Rd; 陕西北路407号; set menu lunch Mon-Fri ¥78/98, dinner ¥178/238; ; West Nanjing Rd) Hotpot aficionados may scoff at the idea of healthy *huǒguō* (hotpot) and iced organic vinegar drinks, but if Alice Waters ever comes to Shànghǎi, we recommend she make this one of her first stops. True, the renovated art-deco villa, low-fat lamb and local vegies are a long way from what generally passes for hotpot in the rest of the country, but Qímín does make use of a 6th-century treatise on agriculture and food preparation (the *Qímín Yàoshù*), effectively taking an old tradition in a new direction.

GǓYÌ HÚNÁN RESTAURANT HUNANESE $$

Map p294 (古意湘味浓; Gǔyì Xiāngwèinóng; 6232 8377; 8th fl, City Plaza, 1618 West Nanjing Rd; 南京西路1618号8楼久百城市广场; dishes ¥28-98; ; Jing'an Temple) Classy Hunanese dining and mouth-watering cumin ribs next to Jìng'ān Temple.

TOP CHOICE DIN TAI FUNG DUMPLINGS $$

Map p294 (鼎泰丰; Dǐng Tài Fēng; 6289 9182; Shànghǎi Centre, 1376 West Nanjing Rd; 南京西路1376号; 10 dumplings ¥58-88; ; Jing'an Temple, West Nanjing Rd) To-die-for dumplings and flawless service from Taiwan's most famous chain. Reserve.

PǏNCHUĀN SICHUANESE $$

Map p294 (品川; 6288 8389; 5th fl, Plaza 66, 1266 West Nanjing Rd; 南京西路1266号恒隆广场5楼; dishes ¥39-90; ; West Nanjing Rd) Located on the top floor of the swish Plaza 66 shopping mall is this excellent, fine-dining Sichuanese restaurant.

CRYSTAL JADE DIM SUM $$

Map p294 (翡翠酒家; Fěicuì Jiǔjiā; 5228 1133; 7th fl, Westgate Mall, 1038 West Nanjing Rd; 静安南京西路1038号7楼; dim-sum dishes ¥16-24, noodles from ¥32; 10.30am-11pm; West Nanjing Rd) Branch of the stellar Singapore dimsum restaurant.

LEGEND TASTE
YUNNANESE $$

Map p294 (滇道; Diān Dào; 5228 9961; 1025 Kangding Rd; 康定路1025号; dishes ¥28-68; Changping Rd) Although not quite at the same level as Shànghǎi's more established Yúnnán restaurants, this is perhaps the only one that's as popular with the locals as it is with foreigners. Specialities are wild mushrooms and medicinal plants such as ferns; standouts include Dai hot-and-sour chicken and the chilli-infused mashed potatoes.

GŌNGDÉLÍN
CHINESE, VEGETARIAN $

Map p294 (功德林; 6327 0218; 445 West Nanjing Rd; 南京西路445号; dishes ¥18-48; ; People's Sq) Shànghǎi's second-oldest vegetarian restaurant (opened in 1922), Gōngdélín never fails to perplex Western vegetarians – close to everything on the menu is prepared to resemble meat! Don't worry though, the beef with *shacha* sauce and the sesame chicken rolls are actually made of tofu, no matter how convincing they look.

The interior is a mix of stone and wood with Venetian blinds, honeycombed lamps and a couple of Buddhist statues thrown in for good fortune.

JEN DOW VEGETARIAN RESTAURANT
CHINESE, VEGETARIAN $

Map p294 (人道素菜小吃; Réndào Sùcài Xiǎochī; Yuyuan Rd; 愚园路; 9am-midnight; ; Jing'an Temple) This well-known Taiwanese vegetarian restaurant was preparing to open a branch behind Jìng'ān Temple as this book went to press. Renowned for its excellent buffets, it has another Shànghǎi location near Lónghuá Temple (p159).

ELEMENT FRESH
CAFE $$

Map p294 (新元素; Xīnyuánsù; 6279 8682; www.elementfresh.com; Shànghǎi Centre, 1376 West Nanjing Rd; 南京西路1376号; sandwiches & salads ¥45-98, dinner from ¥128; 7am-11pm; ; Jing'an Temple, West Nanjing Rd) Perennially popular, Element Fresh hits the spot with its tempting selection of healthy salads, pasta dishes (Western and Asian) and hefty sandwiches. Vegetarians may well faint with excitement at the roasted eggplant on ciabatta bread or the Italian tofu sandwich smothered in pesto. Then there are the imaginative smoothies, big breakfasts, coffee and after-work cocktails.

BAKER & SPICE
CAFE $

Map p294 (Shànghǎi Centre, 1376 West Nanjing Rd; 南京西路1376号; dishes from ¥40; 7am-10pm; ; Jing'an Temple, West Nanjing Rd) This jam-packed cafe at the Shànghǎi Centre has long wooden tables and a tempting array of fresh pastries, bread, salads and sandwiches – don't miss the nutty carrot cake.

GOLDEN POT
HOTPOT $

Map p294 (金涮盘; Jīn Shuànpán; 142 Yuyuan Rd; 愚园路142号; lunch sets/meals from ¥29/40; Jing'an Temple) You'll be sure to receive an enthusiastic welcome at this personal hotpot place, which is full to bursting during the lunch rush. Pull up a stool at the central counter and select your broth, dipping sauce and whatever ingredients you're in the mood for: thinly sliced Mongolian lamb, squid, crunchy lotus roots, mushrooms, potato slices…the list goes on.

Feeling thirsty? Wash it all down with a carafe of kumquat-lemon juice.

WAGAS
CAFE $

Map p294 (沃歌斯; Wògēsī; B11A, Citic Sq, 1168 West Nanjing Rd; 南京西路1168号中信泰富地下一层11A室; mains ¥48-58; 7am-10pm; ; West Nanjing Rd) Breakfasts are 50% off before 10am, the pasta is ¥38 after 6pm, and you can hang out here for hours with your laptop and no one will shoo you away – need we say more? Wagas is the best and most dependable of the local cafes, with tantalising wraps, salads and sandwiches, perfect for a quick bite at any time.

Locations abound (this one is hidden behind a McDonald's).

PIZZA MARZANO
ITALIAN $$

Map p294 (比萨马上诺; Bǐsà Mǎshàngnuò; 6289 8733; Shànghǎi Centre, 1376 West Nanjing Rd; 南京西路1376号; pizza ¥79-120; ; Jing'an Temple, West Nanjing Rd) Pizza Marzano serves a tempting selection of delicious thin-crust Neapolitan pizzas and even thinner-crust Roman-style pizzas that are definite contenders for the city's best. From the Quattro Formaggi and the Sicilia to the Peking Duck, toppings are excellent quality and sprinkled on liberally. It also has pasta and bruschetta.

BALI LAGUNA
INDONESIAN $$

Map p294 (巴厘岛; Bālí Dǎo; 6248 6970; 1649 West Nanjing Rd; 南京西路1649号; mains ¥78-105; ; Jing'an Temple) This restaurant has a tranquil lakeside setting in Jìng'ān Park, and the open long-house interior decked out in dark wood and rattan has a genuine tropical feel. Waiters in sarongs serve up excellent dishes, such as seafood curry in a fresh pineapple, gado gado (vegetable salad with peanut sauce) and *kalio dagging* (beef in coconut milk, lemongrass and curry sauce).

MÉILÓNGZHÈN JIǓJIĀ CHINESE **$$**

Map p294 (梅陇镇酒家; ☎6253 5353; No 22, Lane 1081, West Nanjing Rd; 南京西路1081弄22号; dishes ¥30-120; ⓂWest Nanjing Rd) Shànghǎi has a host of famous local restaurants, none more so than this fantastic old building, which has been churning out food since the 1930s. The rooms once housed the Shanghai Communist Party headquarters, but are now bedecked in woodcarvings, huge palace lamps and photos of foreign dignitaries.

The menu mixes Sìchuān and Shanghainese tastes and ranges from the pricey (crab with tofu) to the more reasonable, such as the fish slices with tangerine peel.

NEW YORK STYLE PIZZA PIZZA **$**

Map p294 (比萨; Bǐsà; ☎6247 2265; J16 Jìng'ān Temple Plaza, 1699 West Nanjing Rd; 南京西路1699号静安寺广场J16; slice ¥16, whole pizza from ¥112; ⓂJing'an Temple) This isn't some fancy pseudo-Italian wood-burning-oven pizza, this is the real deal: gooey, greasy, calorie laden and utterly delicious. Perfect for a lunch on the run. It's located outside exit No 5 of the Jing'an Temple metro station.

CITY SHOP SUPERMARKET **$**

Map p294 (城市超市; Chéngshì Chāoshì; ☎400 811 1797; www.cityshop.com.cn; B1, Shànghǎi Centre, 1376 West Nanjing Rd; 南京西路1376号; ⏲8am-10.30pm; ⓂJing'an Temple) For all those imported goodies you just can't get anywhere else – at a price. The Shànghǎi Centre branch offers 50% off bakery items after 7pm.

Shànghǎi Railway Station

JADE BUDDHA TEMPLE VEGETARIAN RESTAURANT CHINESE, VEGETARIAN **$**

Map p293 (玉佛寺素斋; Yùfó Sì Sùzhāi; 999 Jiangning Rd; 江宁路999号; dishes ¥18-36; 🚭📝; ⓂChangshou Rd) Pull up a seat alongside the monks, nuns and lay worshippers at this two-storey Buddhist banquet hall for a vegetarian feast.

DRINKING & NIGHTLIFE

Jìng'ān drinking options don't match the diversity of the area's restaurants, catering almost exclusively to the expat and business crowd.

West Nanjing Road

FENNEL LOUNGE BAR

off Map p294 (回香; Huí Xiāng; ☎3353 1773; 217 Zhenning Rd, entrance on Dongzhu'anbang Rd; 镇宁路217号; ⓂJiangsu Rd) Fennel is a classy cocktail lounge divided into three areas: a dining room, a cosy living-type room with a tiny stage, and the lounge area, which features a sunken bar and casual seating.

LOCAL KNOWLEDGE

WUJIANG ROAD FOOD STREET

The original food street (吴江路休闲街; Wújiāng Lù Xiūxián Jiē) may have been replaced by a more sanitised pedestrian area in the run up to the World Expo, but when it comes to snack food, Wujiang Rd has still got the goods. If you can beat the mealtime rush, the first spot to go scavenging is the multistorey building at No 269 (above one of the West Nanjing Rd metro exits). The 2nd floor here has two of the city's most famous chains: the **Nánxiáng Steamed Bun Restaurant** and a much-too-small outlet of **Yang's Fry Dumplings**.

Down at street level, you'll find plenty of cafes, ramen chains, ice-cream vendors and stalls selling more-traditional snacks like roasted chestnuts. Also look out for the famous Japanese treat *takoyaki* (ball-shaped octopus waffles) at No 122, and Korean noodles and *bibimbap* (a rice bowl topped with seasoned vegetables and an egg) at No 200.

Decent drinks and an eclectic line-up of live acoustic performances (everything from jazz to traditional Chinese music) have made this a favourite with hip 30-somethings with cash to spare.

KĀIBĀ BAR

Map p294 (开巴; www.kaiba-beerbar.com; 479 Wuding Rd; 武定路479号; ⏲4pm-2am; Ⓜ Changping Rd) Beer-o-philes who have suffered through too many bottles of Shànghǎi's watery Reeb will be thrilled at the impressive selection of Trappist brews and other imported micro beers served in a chill setting.

BIG BAMBOO BAR

Map p294 (132 Nanyang Rd; 南阳路132号; 📶; ⏲9.30am-2am; Ⓜ Jing'an Temple) Big Bamboo is a popular sports bar on two floors that serves up decent Western food, while offering pool, darts and all the big games on TV.

SPOT BAR

Map p294 (331 Tongren Rd; 铜仁路331号; ⏲11am-late; 📶; Ⓜ Jing'an Temple) The Spot is the district's upscale watering hole, with two sections: dining (nonsmoking) and the bar (smoking). It's much slicker than the competition, with fluorescent-coloured chairs and fancier dining options (with a distinctly German slant), but when push comes to shove, it's still a sports bar, best for catching football and rugby matches in the middle of the night.

MALONE'S BAR

Map p294 (www.malones.com.cn; 255 Tongren Rd; 新闸路255号; ⏲11am-3am; Ⓜ Jing'an Temple) This American-style grill is the founding member of Jìng'ān's sports bar triumvirate and still going strong after more than a decade in business. There's nothing mysterious about the formula here: it's the burgers, beer and 13 TV screens that keep the customers coming through the door.

B&C BAR

Map p294 (940 Changde Rd; 常德路940号; ⏲6pm-2am; Ⓜ Changping Rd) While you definitely wouldn't wander into this back-alley place by accident (even on purpose you might hesitate), for cash-strapped Shànghǎi veterans the B&C is an ideal spot to head to for an evening of cheap drinks and a few rounds of Jenga or darts with friends.

A dated disco ball hangs from the ceiling, while Bon Jovi and Duran Duran take everyone back to the good old days of bad hairstyles. The two barkeeps are quite welcoming – expect hugs on arrival.

I LOVE SHÀNGHĂI BAR

Map p294 (我爱上海; Wǒ Ài Shànghǎi; 3rd fl, 1788 Xinzha Rd; 新闸路1788号3楼; ⏲5pm-2am; Ⓜ Jing'an Temple) Despite the name, this bar

SHÀNGHĂI'S COMMUNIST VESTIGES

In its bid to totally refashion itself as a Brave New World futuropolis, Shànghǎi is deeply at odds with its more mundane communist heritage. The colourless residue of the communist period – still nominally the presiding epoch lest we forget – still lurks among the swell and neon of the town like a record at the bottom of the pile that no one plays any more. Nonetheless, nostalgic middle-aged Chinese on the 'Red Tour' (红色旅游; Hóngsè Lǚyóu) of town get dewy eyed at several places of note.

China's communist bandwagon first rolled out from the Site of the 1st National Congress of the CCP (p92), one of communist China's holiest places of pilgrimage, possibly on par with Mao Zedong's birthplace at Sháoshān in Húnán province.

A palpable reverence hangs over the Former Residence of Mao Zedong (p124), a pretty *shíkùmén* (stone-gate house) that includes his bedroom, study and photos of the ex-Chairman doing his thing. Others on the Chairman Mao trail can check out the building at 168 Anyi Rd (安义路168号) where the Great Helmsman once stayed in 1920.

Visits to Fùxīng Park (p92) turn up anachronistic statues of Karl Marx and Friedrich Engels, godfathers to China's communist dry run. Astonishingly, the effigies were only carved in 1985, when Marxist dogma in Shànghǎi was already irreversibly pear-shaped.

The Shànghǎi Exhibition Centre (p124) is a classic example of socialist bravado, and for a lavish blast of hardcore communist spin, pop into the Propaganda Poster Art Centre (p95). Then visit another notable stop on the heritage trail (though the architecture may be concession era), Zhou Enlai's Former Residence (p94).

has little to do with Shànghǎi and everything to do with getting hammered and having fun along the way. Pitchers of beer, Strong Island Tea and absinthe shots are all the ammo you'll need. Each night is a theme night of some sort, the climax coming with Saturday's open bar (¥100). It's above the Orchard Restaurant.

CAFÉ 85°C CAFE

Map p294 (85度C咖啡店; Bāwǔ Dù C Kāfēidiàn; 408 North Shaanxi Rd; 陕西北路408号; 24hr; West Nanjing Rd) This Taiwanese chain offers the cheapest caffeine fix in town.

Shànghǎi Railway Station

BANDU CABIN CAFE

Map p293 (半度音乐; Bàndù Yīnyuè; 6276 8267; www.bandumusic.com; Bldg 11, 50 Moganshan Rd; 莫干山路50号11号楼; 10am-6.30pm Sun-Fri, to 10pm Sat; Shanghai Railway Station) Tucked away in M50, this laid-back cafe-cum-record label serves up noodles, drinks and snacks, along with traditional Chinese music concerts on Saturday at 7.30pm (¥50). Phone ahead on Friday to reserve seats. It also sells a quality selection of Chinese folk music CDs.

ROOF CLUB CAFE

Map p293 (3rd fl, Bldg 17, 50 Moganshan Rd; 莫干山路50号17号楼3楼; 11am-7pm; Shanghai Railway Station) In nice weather, the best place to pull up a chair in M50 is the roof of Building 17, which features appropriately industrial views over muddy Sūzhōu Creek and the surrounding high-rises. Coffee, tea and barbecued snacks are on offer.

JUICE ME UP, SCOTTY

Fresh juice (果汁; *guǒzhī*) made on the spot sells for as little as ¥10 a cup and is vital for staying hydrated in the sweltering summer heat. Of course, you could be predictable with an orange juice or a mango smoothie, but why not try something a little more adventurous? Here are some of Shànghǎi's more adventurous creations:

- Dragon fruit and pear
- Aloe and cucumber
- Bittermelon
- Durian and yoghurt
- Pineapple and cabbage

ENTERTAINMENT

West Nanjing Road

TOP CHOICE SHÀNGHǍI CENTRE THEATRE ACROBATICS

Map p294 (上海商城剧院; Shànghǎi Shāngchéng Jùyuàn; 6279 8948; www.pujiangqing.com; Shànghǎi Centre, 1376 West Nanjing Rd; 南京西路1376号; tickets ¥100-280; Jing'an Temple) The Shànghǎi Acrobatics Troupe has popular performances here most nights at 7.30pm. It's a short but fun show and is high on the to-do list of most first-time visitors. Buy tickets a couple of days in advance from the ticket office on the right-hand side at the entrance to the Shànghǎi Centre.

PARAMOUNT BALLROOM BALLROOM DANCING

Map p294 (百乐门; Bǎilèmén; 6249 8866; 218 Yuyuan Rd; 豫园路218号; tea dances ¥80, ballroom dancing ¥100; tea dances 1-4.30pm, ballroom dancing 4.30-8pm; Jing'an Temple) This old art-deco theatre was the biggest nightclub in the 1930s, and today has sedate tea dances in the afternoon to the sounds of old-school jazz and tango, followed by ballroom dancing. It makes for a nice nostalgia trip for those with a sense of humour. Dance partners are ¥35 to ¥45 for 10 minutes.

STUDIO CITY CINEMA

Map p294 (环艺电影城; Huányì Diànyǐngchéng; 10th fl, Westgate Mall, 1038 West Nanjing Rd; 静安南京西路1038号10楼; West Nanjing Rd) Modern cinema complex in the Westgate Mall.

Shànghǎi Railway Station

IMAGE TUNNEL CINEMA

Map p293 (影像隧道; Yǐngxiàng Suìdào; 159 2101 9461; www.imagetunnel.com; 2nd fl, Bldg 19, 50 Moganshan Rd; 莫干山路50号19号楼2楼; 2pm Sat; Shanghai Railway Station) This small art salon, run by the indefatigable Han Yuqi, screens hard-to-find independent Chinese films on Saturday afternoons (among other projects), though English subtitles are not guaranteed.

SHOPPING

West Nanjing Rd is more upmarket and elitist than the eastern end. It's home to the high-end Western fashion brands and luxury items, as well as Shànghǎi's most exclusive malls, like Plaza 66. Behind People's Square is Dagu Rd, which has a number of large DVD stores.

TOP CHOICE SPIN — CERAMICS

Map p294 (旋; Xuán; 360 Kangding Rd; 康定路360号; ⊙11am-9.30pm; Ⓜ Changping Rd) Chinese porcelain hasn't developed artistically since at least the Qing dynasty, and much of the mass-produced stuff you see for sale these days is clunky and devoid of originality. Fortunately, a new generation of designers has started picking up the slack, trying to restore artistic integrity to Jǐngdézhèn ceramics.

Spin, which provides the chinaware for Shintori Null II (see p102), does an excellent job of bringing China up to speed with its oblong teacups, twisted sake sets and all manner of cool plates, chopstick holders and 'kung fu' and 'exploded pillar' vases.

TOP CHOICE AMY LIN'S PEARLS — PEARLS

Map p294 (艾敏林氏珍珠; Àimǐn Línshì Zhēnzhū; Room 30, 3rd fl, 580 West Nanjing Rd; 南京西路580号3楼30号; ⊙10am-8pm; Ⓜ West Nanjing Rd) The most reliable retailer of pearls of all colours and sizes. Both freshwater pearls (from ¥80), including prized black Zhèjiāng pearls (from ¥3000), and saltwater pearls (from ¥200) are available here. The staff speak English and will string your selection for you. It sells jade and jewellery too.

Another outlet is in the AP Xīnyáng Fashion & Gifts Market (p147) in Pǔdōng.

HAN CITY FASHION & ACCESSORIES PLAZA — CLOTHING

Map p294 (韩城服饰礼品广场; Hánchéng Fúshì Lǐpǐn Guǎngchǎng; 580 West Nanjing Rd; 南京西路580号; ⊙9am-9pm; Ⓜ West Nanjing Rd) This unassuming-looking building is a popular location to pick up knock-offs, with hundreds of stalls spread across two floors. Scavenge for bags, belts, jackets, shoes, suitcases, sunglasses, ties, T-shirts and electronics. Amy Lin's Pearls is located here. Prices are more inflated than at the AP Xīnyáng Fashion & Gifts Market in Pǔdōng, so bargain hard.

MASSAGE & SPAS

In Shànghǎi, a body or foot massage will come at a fraction of the price that you'd pay at home. Options range from neighbourhood foot massage parlours – where everyone kicks back on an armchair and watches TV – to midrange and luxury hotel spas, which offer private rooms, a change of clothes and a wonderfully soothing atmosphere. The latter two usually offer beauty treatments (waxing, manicures etc) as well. Just remember, traditional massage (*tuīná*) is not particularly gentle. As your masseuse might very well tell you: no pain, no gain. Here are our favourites:

- Double Rainbow Massage House (p119)
- Green Massage (p135)
- Dragonfly (p119)
- Subconscious Day Spa (p119)
- Apsara Spa (p135)
- Aromassage (p135)

ART DECO — ANTIQUES

Map p293 (凹凸家具库; Āotū Jiājù Kù; Bldg 7, 50 Moganshan Rd; 莫干山路50号7号楼; ⊙10am-6pm Tue-Sun; Ⓜ Shanghai Railway Station) For stylish period furnishings that match the Peace Hotel's streamlined aplomb, stop by artist Ding Yi's gallery in the M50 complex. His standout antique collection includes folding screens, armoires, tables and chairs, with a few vintage poster girls on the walls to help recapture the 1930s magic.

JǏNGDÉZHÈN PORCELAIN ARTWARE — PORCELAIN

Map p294 (景德镇艺术瓷器; Jǐngdézhèn Yìshù Cíqì; 212 North Shaanxi Rd; 陕西北路212号; Ⓜ West Nanjing Rd) This is one of the best places for high-quality traditional Chinese porcelain. Blue-and-white vases, plates, teapots and cups are some of the many choices available. Credit cards are accepted, and shipping overseas can be arranged.

ZHANG'S TEXTILES — ANTIQUES

Map p294 (花张; Huā Zhāng; 2nd fl, Shànghǎi Centre, 1376 West Nanjing Rd; 南京西路1376号; Ⓜ Jing'an Temple) Some of the brightly coloured antique embroideries on display at Zhang's date to the early Qing dynasty, including divine floral embroidery from the reign of Jia Qing and dragon pattern embroidery from the reign of Dao Guang. Heads of state have dropped by here for souvenirs in the past, so expect accordingly high price tags.

PLAZA 66 MALL

Map p294 (恒隆广场; Hénglóng Guǎngchǎng; 1266 West Nanjing Rd; 南京西路1266号; M West Nanjing Rd) Staff outnumber shoppers at this upmarket mall, featuring fake palms, a live pianist and an entire line-up of haute couture fashion brands straight from Paris' Triangle d'or. Even if you're not in the market for a little pick-me-up from Chanel or Hermès, there are some decent dining options here on the top floor.

SPORTS & ACTIVITIES

APSARA SPA MASSAGE

Map p294 (馨园水疗; Xīnyuán Shuǐliáo; ☎6258 5580; www.apsara.com.cn; 457 North Shaanxi Rd; 陕西北路457号; massages & spa treatments ¥190-980; ⏲10am-10pm; M West Nanjing Rd) Angkor-style massage therapy with treatments such as a 60-minute *qì* re-energising massage, facials (Tibetan black mud purification), body wraps, manicures and waxing.

GREEN MASSAGE MASSAGE

Map p294 (青专业按摩; Qīng Zhuānyè Ànmó; ☎6289 7776; www.greenmassage.com.cn; 2nd fl, Shànghǎi Centre, 1376 West Nanjing Rd; 南京西路1376号2楼; massages & spa treatments ¥118-528; ⏲10.30am-2am; M Jing'an Temple, West Nanjing Rd) Soothing midrange spa, with foot, *tuīná* and shiatsu massages. Reserve.

AROMASSAGE MASSAGE

Map p294 (茗之荟; Míng Zhī Huì; ☎6267 0783; 38 Changhua Rd; 昌化路38号; massages from ¥88; ⏲11am-1am; M West Nanjing Rd) Inexpensive but excellent foot and body massages from an all-male staff.

ONE WELLNESS GYM

Map p294 (咪猫健身; Mīmāo Jiànshēn; ☎6267 1550; www.onewellness.com.cn; 2nd fl, 98 Yanping Rd; 静安区延平路98号2楼; ⏲6am-11pm; M Jing'an Temple) A boutique fitness club located in a renovated factory, One Wellness has a gourmet cafe on the premises and in-house massage therapy. Classes range from yoga and taichi to bodypump and aerobics, and the equipment is all state-of-the-art. It also boasts the claim of being China's first carbon-neutral gym. The day rate is ¥300; a month-long membership starts at ¥1588.

OZ BODY FIT MARTIAL ARTS

Map p293 (www.ozbodyfit.com; 717 Huai'an Rd; 淮安路717号; M Hanzhong Rd) Popular Thai kickboxing workouts, for those who want to keep fit using martial-arts training.

Pǔdōng

PǓDŌNG | CENTURY AVENUE AREA

Neighbourhood Top Five

❶ View Shànghǎi from low-orbit altitude on the observation decks of the **Shànghǎi World Financial Center** (p140).

❷ Sink an evening al fresco cocktail and bathe yourself in Pǔdōng's neon glow at **Flair** (p144).

❸ Point your telephoto lens westwards from the **Riverside Promenade** (p138) as the sun sets over Pǔxī.

❹ Wrap yourself in the sensations of old Shànghǎi in the **Shànghǎi History Museum** (p138).

❺ Take a crash course in haggling at the Science & Technology Museum metro station's **AP Xīnyáng Fashion & Gifts Market** (p147).

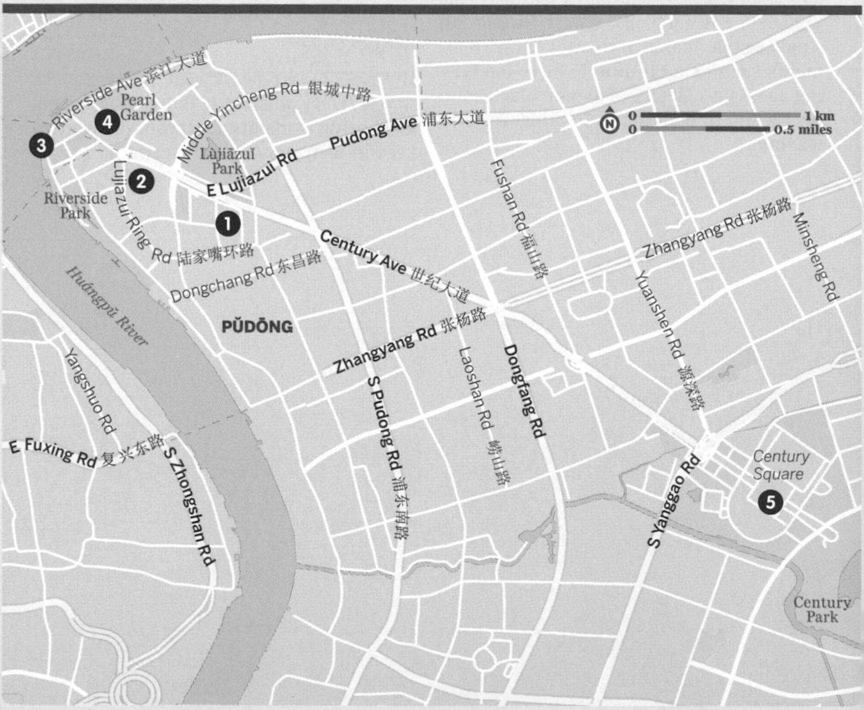

For more detail of this area, see Map p296 and p297

Explore: Pǔdōng

With its neck-craning tourists, scurrying suits and dazzling evening neonscapes, Pǔdōng is a place name many Westerners know before setting foot in China. Over 1.5 times bigger than urban Shànghǎi, the economic powerhouse of the Pǔdōng New Area (浦东新区; Pǔdōng Xīnqū) swallows up the eastern bank of the Huángpǔ River.

The high-rise area directly across from the Bund is the Lùjiāzuǐ Finance and Trade Zone, where China's largest stock market (the Shànghǎi Stock Exchange) makes or breaks China's nouveau riche. There's no obvious focal point where people congregate, although a swirlpool of sightseers rotates around the elevated walkway by the Oriental Pearl TV Tower.

For visitors, the main attractions are the high-altitude observation decks, hotels, restaurants and bars in the rocketing towers, offering ringside seats onto some of China's most mind-altering urban panoramas.

And what of the next top sight? Aiming for a 2014 completion date, the Shànghǎi Tower will one day dwarf the rest of Lùjiāzuǐ at a towering height of 632m.

Local Life

➡ **Shop** Flee the slick malls and make a beeline to the AP XīnyángFashion & Gifts Market (p147) to haggle your socks off.

➡ **Take a Ferry** Hop aboard the ferry (p144) across the Huángpǔ River with local Shanghainese (and take your bike with you).

Getting There & Away

➡ **Metro** Line 2 can whisk you through several stations in Pǔdōng, including Lujiazui, Century Ave and the Science & Technology Museum. Line 9 runs through the southern part of the French Concession and on to Century Ave. Lines 4 and 6 also cut through Pǔdōng, but are less useful for travellers. All four lines meet at Century Ave.

➡ **Ferry** Ferries run regularly between Pǔxī and Pǔdōng for the six-minute trip across the river (¥2). It's a 10-minute walk to the Jinmao Tower from the dock.

➡ **Bus** Both City Sightseeing Buses and Big Bus Tours (p247) have lines to Lùjiāzuǐ from Pǔxī.

➡ **Taxi** A taxi ride will cost you around ¥25, as you'll have to pay the ¥15 tunnel toll heading eastwards. There is a useful taxi queue in front of the Science & Technology Museum.

➡ **Bund Sightseeing Tunnel** Travel underneath the Huángpǔ River in a tunnel (p61) dedicated to kitsch.

Lonely Planet's Top Tip

The best time to see Lùjiāzuǐ's modern architecture is during late afternoon or at twilight/early evening, especially during summer (the wide Pǔdōng roads make the sun merciless), when sky-high views from the observation decks, bars or restaurants allow you to contrast day, dusk and evening views. Walk around the elevated walkway by the Oriental Pearl TV Tower for knockout evening visuals.

Best Places to Eat

➡ Hǎi Dǐ Lāo (p144)

➡ On 56 (p140)

➡ Yi Cafe (p141)

➡ Kitchen Salvatore Cuomo (p141)

➡ South Beauty (p141)

For reviews, see p140 ➡

Best Places to Drink

➡ Cloud 9 (p144)

➡ Flair (p144)

➡ 100 Century Avenue (p144)

➡ Brew (p146)

For reviews, see p144 ➡

SIGHTS

Pǔdōng

ORIENTAL PEARL TV TOWER BUILDING

Map p296 (东方明珠广播电视塔; Dōngfāng Míngzhū Guǎngbō Diànshì Tǎ; ☎5879 1888; ⏲8am-10pm; Ⓜ Lujiazui) Love it or hate it, it's hard to be indifferent to this 468m-tall poured-concrete tripod tower. Sucking in a vortex of visitors, the Deng Xiaoping–era design is inadvertently retro (1950s atom age or thereabouts), but socialism with Chinese characteristics was always cheesy in those days. The tower is dazzling when illuminated at night: toast the big bauble with a cocktail on the terrace at Flair (p144) for the best visuals. You can join the long queues for high-rise views of Shànghǎi, but there are better views elsewhere. For sightseeing, the tower stands out most for its excellent Shànghǎi History Museum, in the basement. The tower's long lines are matched by a tortuous ticketing system.

Boat tours on the Huángpǔ River operate from the **Pearl Dock** (明珠码头; Míngzhū Mǎtou; 1 Century Ave), next to the tower.

SHÀNGHǍI HISTORY MUSEUM MUSEUM

Map p296 (上海城市历史发展陈列馆; Shànghǎi Chéngshì Lìshǐ Fāzhǎn Chénlièguǎn; ☎5879 8888; Oriental Pearl TV Tower basement; admission ¥35, English audio tour ¥30; ⏲8am-9.30pm; Ⓜ Lujiazui) The entire family will enjoy this sophisticated and informative museum with a fun presentation on old Shànghǎi. The city's transport history gets a look-in, where you can size up an antique bus, an old wheelbarrow taxi and an ornate sedan chair. Learn how the city prospered on the back of the cotton trade and junk transportation, when it was known as 'Little Sūzhōu'. Life-size models of traditional shops are staffed by realistic waxworks, and a wealth of historical detail abounds, including a boundary stone from the International Settlement and one of the bronze lions that originally guarded the entrance to the HSBC bank on the Bund. Some exhibits are hands-on or accompanied by creative video presentations.

RIVERSIDE PROMENADE RIVER

Map p296 (滨江大道; Bīnjiāng Dàdào; ⏲6.30am-11pm; Ⓜ Lujiazui) Hands down the best stroll in Pǔdōng, the sections of promenade alongside Riverside Ave on the eastern bank of the river offer splendid views to the Bund across the way and choicely positioned cafes looking out over the water.

SHÀNGHǍI OCEAN AQUARIUM AQUARIUM

Map p296 (上海海洋水族馆; Shànghǎi Hǎiyáng Shuǐzúguǎn; ☎5877 9988; www.sh-aquarium.com; 1388 Lujiazui Ring Rd; 陆家嘴环路1388号; adult/child ¥160/110; ⏲9am-6pm, last tickets 5.30pm; Ⓜ Lujiazui) Education meets entertainment in this slick and intelligently

ORIENTAL PEARL TV TOWER TICKETS

Ticket	Price*	Includes
A	¥180	bottom, middle & top bauble plus Shànghǎi History Museum
B	¥150	bottom & middle bauble plus Shànghǎi History Museum
C	¥120	middle bauble plus Shànghǎi History Museum
Revolving Restaurant	lunch ¥268, dinner ¥298	ticket A plus lunch or dinner (lunch 11am-2pm, dinner 5-9pm)
Boat Tours	¥100-120	boat tours from the dock (10am-8pm)
Package	¥180	top sphere, museum & cruise
Museum	¥35	Shànghǎi History Museum

*Children from 1m to 1.4m are half-price.

designed aquarium that children will love. Join them on a tour through the aquatic environments from the Yangzi River to Australia, South America, the frigid ecosystems of the Antarctic and the flourishing marine life of coral reefs. The 155m-long underwater clear viewing tunnel has gob-smacking views.

NATURAL WILD INSECT KINGDOM MUSEUM

Map p296 (大自然野生昆虫馆; Dà Zìrán Yěshēng Kūnchóng Guǎn; ☎5840 6950; 1 Fenghe Rd; 丰和路1号; adult/child ¥40/25; ⏰9am-5pm; Ⓜ Lujiazui) Aimed at kids, this collection of creepy-crawlies includes a chance to handle the hairy beasts. It's one that could be missed unless your kids have an interest.

WÚ CHĀNGSHUÒ MEMORIAL HALL HISTORIC BUILDING

Map p296 (吴昌硕纪念馆; Wú Chāngshuò Jìniànguǎn; 15 East Lujiazui Rd; 陆家嘴东路15号; admission ¥10; ⏰9.30am-4pm Tue-Sun; Ⓜ Lujiazui) The lack of English captions badly hobbles the displays of this small museum detailing the life and work of artist, poet, calligrapher and seal carver Wu Changshuo (1844–1927), but this place is well worth exploring for the architecture of the historic building itself, once the residence of Chen Guichun, a rich merchant. Built between 1914 and 1917, there's some superb tiling on its floors, an old fireplace, lovely woodwork and carved doorframes plus a gorgeous courtyard.

JINMAO TOWER BUILDING

Map p296 (金茂大厦; Jīnmào Dàshà; ☎5047 5101; 88 Century Ave; 世纪大道88号; adult/student/child ¥120/90/60; ⏰8.30am-9.30pm; Ⓜ Lujiazui) Resembling an art-deco take on a pagoda or the joints of a length of bamboo, the crystalline Jinmao Tower is a beauty. It's essentially an office block (owned by the Ministry of Foreign Trade and Economic Cooperation) with the high-altitude Grand Hyatt renting space from the 53rd to 87th floors. If you want to see what Shànghǎi looks like from a mountain-top perspective, travel in the elevators to the 88th-floor **observation deck**, accessed from the separate podium building to the side of the main tower. Time your visit at dusk for both day and night views. Alternatively, sample the same view through the carbonated fizz of a gin and tonic at Cloud 9 (p144) on the 87th floor of the Grand Hyatt (accessed on the south side of the building), and photograph the hotel's astonishing barrel-vaulted atrium.

LOCAL KNOWLEDGE

A STEP TOO FAR?

Need to burn off some *xiǎolóngbāo* calories? The **Sky Marathon** (☎6064 3584; www.swfc-observatory.com) was held twice in 2012, with a race up 2754 stairs and 100 floors to the top of the Shànghǎi World Financial Center; it's not for the faint-hearted, but it's the ultimate step-master workout. You must be over 16, the event is limited to 300 people and registration is ¥100. You can descend by lift (if you want). Check online for future dates.

Century Avenue Area

SHÀNGHǍI SCIENCE & TECHNOLOGY MUSEUM MUSEUM

Map p297 (上海科技馆; Shànghǎi Kējìguǎn; www.sstm.org.cn; 2000 Century Ave; 世纪大道2000号; adult/student/child under 1.3m ¥60/45/free; ⏰9am-5.15pm Tue-Sun, last tickets 4.30pm; Ⓜ Science & Technology Museum) You need to do a huge amount of walking to get about this seriously spaced-out museum but there are some fascinating exhibits, from relentless Rubik's-cube-solving robots to automated archers and the chance to take penalty kicks against a computerised goalkeeper.

There are four theatres (two IMAX, one 4D and one outer space), which show themed films throughout the day (tickets ¥20 to ¥40; 15 to 40 minutes). When you need a break, there's a good food court for lunch; get your hand stamped with a pass if you want to return to the exhibits.

HIMALAYAS ART MUSEUM MUSEUM

off Map p297 (喜玛拉雅美术馆; Xǐmǎlāyǎ Měishùguǎn; www.himalayasart.cn; Himalayas Center, 1188 Fangdian Rd; 喜玛拉雅中心芳甸路1188弄1号; ⏰10am-6pm Tue-Sun; Ⓜ Huamu Rd) Just moved to the eye-catching Himalayas Center (attached to the Jumeirah Himalayas Hotel) and formerly the Zendai Museum of Art, this art gallery was due to become a major landmark on the Pǔdōng art scene, with an emphasis on contemporary exhibitions in a modern art space.

TOP SIGHTS
SHÀNGHĂI WORLD FINANCIAL CENTER

Soon to be trumped by the nearby Shànghǎi Tower (completion date 2014) as the city's tallest building, the neck-craning 492m-high Shànghǎi World Financial Center (上海环球金融中心; Shànghǎi Huánqiú Jīnróng Zhōngxīn) is an astonishing sight, even more so come nightfall when its 'bottle opener' top dances with lights. There are three **observation decks** here, with head-spinningly altitude-adjusted ticket prices and wow-factor elevators thrown in. The top two (located at the bottom and top of the trapezoid) are known as Sky Walks. It's debatable whether the top Sky Walk (474m) is the best spot for Shang-high views, though. The hexagonal space is bright and futuristic, and some of the floor is transparent glass, but the lack of a 360-degree sweep – windows only face west or east – detracts somewhat in comparison with the facing Jinmao Tower. But you get to look down on the top of the Jinmao, which might be worth the ticket price alone. A clear, smog-free day is imperative. If you want to make a meal (or a cocktail) of it, or if lines are long, you can sashay into restaurant/bar 100 Century Avenue on the 91st floor instead. Access to the observation deck is on the west side of the building off Haixin Rd; access to the Park Hyatt is on the south side of the building.

DON'T MISS...

- Observation Decks
- 100 Century Avenue

PRACTICALITIES

- Map p296
- ☎5878 0101
- http://swfc-shanghai.com
- 100 Century Ave; 世纪大道100号
- observation deck adult 94th/94th, 97th & 100th fl/exclusive tour ¥120/150/300, child under 140cm ¥60/75/300
- ⏲8am-11pm (last entry 10pm)
- Ⓜ Lujiazui

CENTURY PARK PARK

Map p297 (世纪公园; Shìjì Gōngyuán; 1001 Jinxiu Rd; 锦绣路1001号; admission ¥10; ⏲7am-6pm; Ⓜ Century Park) Shànghǎi's largest park at the eastern end of Century Ave is strong on hard edges and synthetic lines, but there's a great central lake with boat hire (¥50 per hour), and a variety of bike and tandem hire (¥50 per hour, ¥100 deposit) for getting around the paths. Children will enjoy themselves, and the spacious paved area between the Science & Technology Museum and the park is great for flying kites (for sale from hawkers) and rollerblading.

QĪNCÌYĂNG TEMPLE TAOIST TEMPLE

Map p297 (钦赐仰殿; Qīncìyǎng Diàn; 476 Yuanshen Rd; 源深路476号; admission ¥5; ⏲6.30am-4pm; Ⓜ Yuanshen Stadium) Shànghǎi's largest Taoist temple is, perhaps surprisingly, in Pǔdōng. It's worth a look for its massive trinity of Taoist gods in the **Hall of the Three Clear Ones** (三清殿; Sānqīng Diàn), although the temple architecture is all recent. At the rear of the temple is the huge **Hall for the Storing of Scriptures** (藏经殿; Cángjīng Diàn) and up the stairs above the side halls is a glittering gathering of 61 Taoist generals.

EATING

Most dining in Pǔdōng is about feasting on priceless views through floor-to-ceiling windows in five-star hotel restaurants. The gargantuan Superbrand Mall in Lùjiāzuǐ has restaurants spread out across 10 floors. For hole-in-the-wall dining, try roads like the eastern end of Dongchang Rd (off South Pudong Rd), where budget *dōngběi* (northeastern) and Xīnjiāng eateries are concentrated. The spectacular new Himalayas Center complex (attached to the Jumeirah Himalayas Hotel) boasts an impressive selection of restaurants.

Pǔdōng

ON 56 INTERNATIONAL **$$$**

Map p296 (意庐; Yìlú; ☎5047 1234; 54th-56th fl, Grand Hyatt, Jinmao Tower, 88 Century Ave; 世纪大道88号君悦大酒店; meals from ¥120; ⏲11.30am-2.30pm & 5.30-10.30pm; 🚭📶; Ⓜ Lujiazui) The Grand Hyatt in the Jinmao Tower offers a swish selection of Western and Asian restaurants, all of which come with breathtaking vistas into the Shànghǎi void. **Cucina** cooks up delectable Italian dishes from Campania and breads and pizzas fresh from the oven. The **Grill** offers fine imported meats and seafood. The Japanese **Kobachi** features excellent sushi, sashimi and yakitori. The flagship **Canton** showcases Cantonese food and afternoon dim sum. You can sit in any restaurant of your choosing and order food from another. After dinner, retire to the **Patio Lounge** (11.30am-11pm Sun-Thu, to midnight Fri & Sat) on the same floor for a drink with the spectacular 33-floor atrium towering above you.

On the 54th floor (the hotel lobby) is the **Grand Café** (24hr) offering stunning panoramas through its glass walls and a good-value lunchtime buffet during the week (¥208), which allows you to choose a main course and have it prepared fresh in the show kitchen. On weekends and in the evening the buffet is ¥278. To reserve a table by the window, book well in advance.

YI CAFE — CAFE/BUFFET $$$

Map p296 (怡咖啡; Yí Kāfēi; 5877 5372; 2nd fl, Pǔdōng Shangri-La, 33 Fucheng Rd; 富城路33号2楼; meals ¥300; breakfast, lunch & dinner; ; M Lujiazui) If you're squabbling over what to eat for lunch, brunch or dinner, settle your differences at smart/casual Yi Cafe. With 10 open kitchens and a walk-through layout, it's a veritable Asian/Southeast Asian/international food fest with endless menus (but cultivate a real hunger before you stop by). The buffet breakfasts easily match Pǔdōng's sightseeing calorific demands.

KITCHEN SALVATORE CUOMO — ITALIAN $$$

Map p296 (5054 1265; Riverside Ave, 2967 West Lujiazui Rd, near Fenghe Lu; 陆家嘴西路2967号滨江大道近丰和路; meals ¥250-300; lunch & dinner; ; M Lujiazui) The hefty wood-fired pizza prices will have your eyes as big as the margaritas at this swish riverside restaurant, while the views of fairy-light-festooned boats gliding up and down the night-time Huángpǔ River could keep them that way. The pizzas are sublime, however, and views go straight through the ample plate glass, and al fresco tables out front beckon for long summer evenings, with the Oriental Pearl TV Tower rocketing overhead.

SOUTH BEAUTY — SICHUANESE, CANTONESE $$

Map p296 (俏江南; Qiào Jiāngnán; 5047 1817; 10th fl, Superbrand Mall, 168 West Lujiazui Rd; 陆家嘴西路168号10楼; dishes from ¥18; 11am-10pm; M Lujiazui) Views, views and more views – while everyone else is gazing at Pǔdōng's lights, you can stare back at them with loaded chopsticks from this elegant Sìchuān-Cantonese combo. The stuffed

WORTH A DETOUR

WORLD EXPO SITE

Most of the pavilions at the **2010 World Expo site** (世博会区; Shìbó Huì Qū; M Yaohua Rd, lines 7 & 8) were dismantled. However, at least five structures on the Pǔdōng side of the river remain standing and continue to host exhibits and events, including the iconic **China Pavilion** (中国国家馆; Zhōngguó Guójiā Guǎn), **Expo Center** (世博中心; Shìbó Zhōngxīn) and the galactically styled UFO **Mercedes-Benz Arena** (梅赛德斯奔驰文化中心; Méisàidésī Bènchí Wénhuà Zhōngxīn; www.mercedes-benzarena.com).

At the time of writing, a handful of structures were open on the Pǔdōng side: the underwhelming **Moon Boat** (月亮船; Yuèliàng Chuán; Mon-Fri ¥60, Sat & Sun ¥80, holiday ¥100; 9am-6pm Tue-Sun) – the former Saudi Pavilion – and the **Shànghǎi Italian Centre** (admission ¥60; 9am-5pm Tue-Sun) in the former Italian World Expo Pavilion.

With 64,000 sq metres of exhibition space, the China Pavilion was relaunched in 2012 as the **China Art Palace** (9am-5pm Tue-Sun; M China Art Museum) and was set to become a landmark art museum. Hosting the Shanghai Biennale, the **Power Station of Art** (上海当代艺术博物馆; Shànghǎi Dāngdài Yìshù Bówùguǎn; Lane 20 Huayuangang Rd; 9am-5pm Tue-Sun; M South Xizang Rd) also opened in late 2012 on the far side of the Huángpǔ River in the disused Nánshì Power Plant (the former Pavilion of the Future).

Engaging highlights of the Expo are displayed in the **Expo 2010 Commemoration Exhibition** (上海世博会纪念展; Shànghǎi Shìbòhuì Jìniànzhǎn; cnr Mengzi & East Longhua Rds; admission ¥30; 9am-5pm Tue-Sun; M Luban Rd) on the Pǔxī side, including exhibits and parts of the original pavilions. Sadly, there are no English captions.

1

DENNIS DEGNAN / CORBIS ©

TAO IMAGES LIMITED / ALAMY ©

1. Oriental Pearl TV Tower (p138)
Love it or hate it, this 468m-tall tripod tower is a Shànghǎi icon.

2. Shànghǎi Ocean Aquarium (p138)
The underwater viewing tunnel at this family-friendly attraction has fabulous fishy panoramas.

3. Shànghǎi History Museum (p138)
Visitors can get a handle on local history at this fun and accessible museum.

4. Riverside Promenade (p138)
Stroll and take in splendid views of the Bund along this waterside path.

PETER STUCKINGS / GETTY IMAGES ©

chillies at the entrance hint at what's to come (spicy beef; ¥58), but for milder flavours, southern dishes such as the crispy chicken (¥58) are more soothing. You'll need to reserve for window seats, but an equally attractive locale is in front of the glass-paned kitchen, where you can watch the 30-plus chefs work the woks. There are several other branches, including in the **French Concession** (Map p290; ☎6445 2581; 28 Taojiang Rd; 桃江路28号).

ELEMENT FRESH SANDWICHES **$**

Map p296 (新元素; Xīnyuánsù; www.elementfresh.com; 1st fl, Superbrand Mall, 168 West Lujiazui Rd; 陆家嘴西路168号正大广场1楼; breakfast ¥38-88, sandwiches & salads ¥45-98; ; Ⓜ Lujiazui) Thanks to the Element Fresh chain for this funky outpost providing healthy eats in Pǔdōng through the day. For early starters there are endless coffee refills on breakfasts like the 'Big American' (¥88) or just go for a simple but healthy yoghurt and fruit (¥38). The rest of the day can be taken up with terrific salads, hefty sandwiches, pastas, smoothies and a kids' menu for the young ones.

Century Avenue Area

HǍI DǏ LĀO HOTPOT **$$**

Map p297 (海底捞; ☎3871 3936; 6th fl, 588 Zhangyang Rd; 张杨路588号6楼; hotpot per person from ¥60; ; Ⓜ Shangcheng Rd) Faultless and resourceful service is the name of the game at this Pǔdōng outpost of the West Nanjing Rd restaurant chain, which concocts an effortlessly enjoyable Sìchuān hotpot experience. Not for solo diners or romantic soirées.

PǓDŌNG TO PǓXĪ FERRY

To get to the Cool Docks in the South Bund area from Pǔdōng, consider taking the Dōngfù Xiàn ferry (东复线; ¥2, every 10 to 20 minutes from 5am to 11pm) from the Dongchang Rd dock to the Fuxing Rd dock. For the Old Town and the Bund, hop on the Dōngjīn Xiàn ferry (东金线; ¥2, every 15 minutes from 7am to 10pm) to the Jinling Rd dock.

DRINKING & NIGHTLIFE

Most Pǔdōng bars are in hotels (where you occasionally have to deal with condescending staff).

CLOUD 9 BAR

Map p296 (九重天酒廊; Jiǔchóngtiān Jiǔláng; ☎5049 1234; 87th fl, Jinmao Tower, 88 Century Ave; 世纪大道88号金茂大厦87楼; wine from ¥65, cocktails ¥90; ⏲5pm-1am Mon-Fri, 11am-2am Sat & Sun; Ⓜ Lujiazui) Cloud 9 is a fantastic place to watch day fade into night as the neon slowly flickers on. Addictive beats provide the soundtrack for the illuminated skyline and, after an espresso martini or two, you'll probably find out what it means to be *shanghaied* in the best sense of the word. The occasional appearance of fortune tellers and magicians adds to the entertainment. Access is through the lobby of the Grand Hyatt.

FLAIR BAR

Map p296 (58th fl, Ritz-Carlton Shànghǎi Pǔdōng, 8 Century Ave; 世纪大道8号58楼; cocktails ¥90; ⏲5am-2am; ; Ⓜ Lujiazui) Wow your date (and your bank manager) at Flair, where Shànghǎi's most intoxicating neon-scape nocturnal views are on show, especially on clear evenings. Slung out on the 58th floor of the Ritz-Carlton, Flair has the highest al fresco terrace in town (at the time of writing), nudging you that bit closer to the shimmering baubles of the nearby Oriental Pearl TV Tower. If it's raining, you'll end up inside, but that's OK as the chilled-out interior is super-cool. Cocktail prices, however, are as sky-scraping as the panoramas and there's a minimum price if you sit outside.

100 CENTURY AVENUE BAR

Map p296 (世纪大道100号; Shìjì Dàdào Yībǎi Hào; ☎3855 1428; 91st & 92nd fl, Park Hyatt, Shànghǎi World Financial Center, 100 Century Ave; 世纪大道100号柏悦酒店91-92楼; coffee/cocktails ¥65/85; ⏲bar & restaurant 4.30pm-1am Mon-Sat, restaurant 4.30-10.30pm Sun; ; Ⓜ Lujiazui) Pǔdōng continues to keep its edge with one of the highest bars in the world at 100 Century Avenue, but this place lacks the ambience of its cross-street competitor, Cloud 9. Still, it's pretty impressive inside (there are six open kitchens in the restaurant area) and may be cheaper than going up to the viewing platforms (unless they hit you with the ¥120 minimum outlay). The restaurant (on the 91st floor) has better

START **LUJIAZUI METRO STATION**
END **SHÀNGHĂI WORLD FINANCIAL CENTER**
DISTANCE **3.5KM**
DURATION **TWO HOURS**

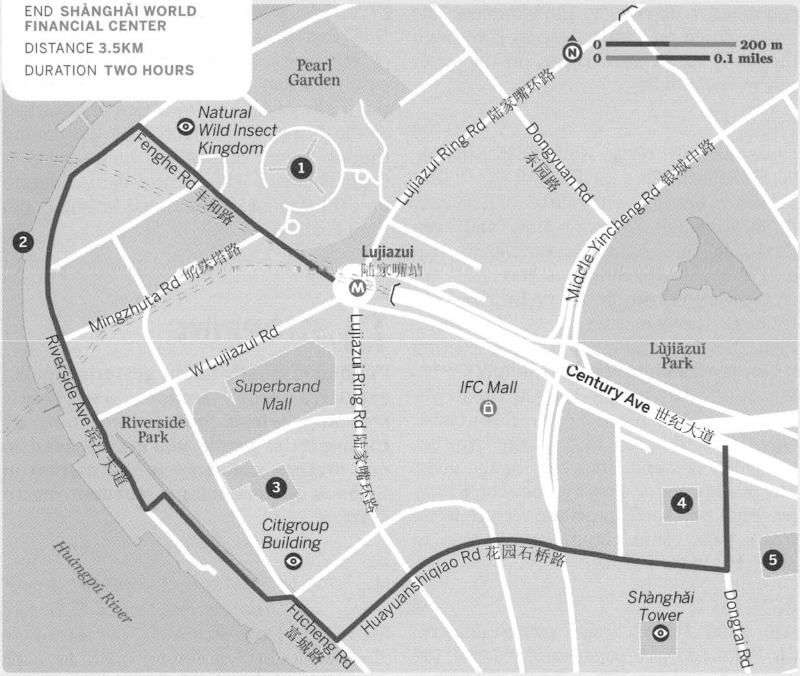

Neighbourhood Walk
Pŭdōng

Looming above you like a sci-fi control tower a short walk from the Lujiazui metro station is the **1 Oriental Pearl TV Tower**, one of Lùjiāzuǐ's most opinion-dividing edifices. Make sure you take a walk around the circular overhead walkway above the main intersection south of the tower, especially at night. Inside the tower, the absorbing Shànghǎi History Museum on the basement level is worth exploration.

Walk up Fenghe Rd (丰和路) past the Natural Wild Insect Kingdom on your right and turn left onto Riverside Park to reach a section of the **2 Riverside Promenade** for glorious images of the Bund across the water.

Follow a further stretch of the Riverside Promenade before cutting through Riverside Park and exiting onto Fucheng Rd (富城路) by the Citigroup Building. Note the dramatic V-form of Tower Two of the **3 Pŭdōng Shangri-La hotel**.

Immediately after the Citigroup Building, turn onto Huayuanshiqiao Rd (花园石桥路) to walk past the twin towers of the IFC (International Financial Centre) on your left; you will see the vast new Shànghǎi Tower on your right (under construction at the time of writing) before reaching the magnificent **4 Jinmao Tower**. You're spoiled for high-altitude views – you can either rocket to the 88th-floor observation deck here or cross the street to the world's second-highest observation deck (100th floor) in the **5 Shànghǎi World Financial Center** (p140), which virtually blots out the sun. Head up to the observation deck or the bar 100 Century Avenue in the Park Hyatt. To return to metro line 2, the Lujiazui metro stop is a short walk west along Century Ave.

views than the bar (on the 92nd floor) as you can get up close to the windows. The bar is closed on Sunday. Access is through the lobby of the Park Hyatt, on the south side of the building.

BREW BAR

off Map p297 (酿; Niàng; ☎6169 8886; Kerry Hotel, 1388 Huamu Rd; 上海浦东嘉里大酒店花木路1388号; beer half/pint ¥48/68; ⏰11am-2am; 📶; Ⓜ Huamu Rd) Pǔdōng-bound (and even Pǔxī-side) ale connoisseurs should trip over themselves heading to this nifty microbrewery bar in the Kerry Hotel, where resident brew-master Leon Mickelson turns his formidable skills to concocting six on-tap handmade beers (Skinny Green, Pils, White Ant, Indian Pale Ale, Dugite Vanilla Stout, Mash) and a cider (Razorback). Otherwise there's a huge range of other bottled beers, and Heineken for the duds. The bar is sleek and cool without being impersonal and you can hit the terrace for al fresco park views. Happy hour is 4pm to 8pm (Monday to Friday).

BLUE FROG BAR

Map p296 (蓝蛙; lánwā; www.bluefrog.com.cn; 2nd fl, Shànghǎi World Financial Center, 100 Century Ave; 世纪大道88号上海环球金融中心2楼; ⏰10am-late) After some stratospheric sightseeing, come down closer to earth at this Pǔdōng Blue Frog chain bolthole near the base of the Shànghǎi World Financial Center for a reassuringly dependable menu of the crucial things in life: good burgers, chilled beer and a relaxing, casual vibe.

☆ ENTERTAINMENT

ORIENTAL ART CENTER CLASSICAL MUSIC

Map p297 (上海东方艺术中心; Shànghǎi Dōngfāng Yìshù Zhōngxīn; ☎6854 1234; www.shoac.com.cn; 425 Dingxiang Rd; 浦东丁香路425号; tickets ¥30-680; Ⓜ Science & Technology Museum) Home of the Shànghǎi Symphony Orchestra, the Oriental Art Center was designed to resemble five petals of a butterfly orchid. There are three main halls that host classical, jazz, dance and Chinese and Western opera performances. Saturday brunch concerts (10am, held on the first and third Saturday of the month) are ¥30 to ¥80. Free tours of the centre are conducted on the first Saturday of the month (1.30pm to 4.30pm).

DÀGUĀN THEATER THEATRE

(大观舞台; Dàguān Wǔtái; Himalayas Center, 1188 Fangdian Rd; 喜玛拉雅中心芳甸路1188弄1号; Ⓜ Huamu Rd) At the time of writing, this new 1100-seat theatre was due to open in the impressive Himalayas Center, attached to the Jumeirah Himalayas Hotel, staging Chinese opera and other traditional performance arts. The theatre is also due to host films from the Shanghai International Film Festival.

SHOPPING

Pǔdōng is mostly about glittering malls, exclusive hotel arcades and heart-stopping prices, but further out, all the material goods you'll ever need in one lifetime converge in the market in Science & Technology Museum metro station.

IFC MALL MALL

Map p296 (上海IFC商场; Shànghǎi IFC Shāngchǎng; www.shanghaiifcmall.com.cn; 8 Century Ave; ⏰10am-10pm; Ⓜ Lujiazui) This incredibly glam and glitzy six-storey mall beneath the Cesar Pelli–designed twin towers of the Shànghǎi International Finance Center hosts a swish coterie of top-name brands, from Armani via Prada to Vivienne Westwood, and a host of dining options. It's rather like an extended version of a customer-free five-star hotel arcade, but it's certainly awesome (and an air-conditioned oasis on a sweltering day).

SHANGHAI TANG CLOTHING

Map p296 (上海滩; Shànghǎi Tān; www.shanghaitang.com; Lobby Level, Pǔdōng Shangri-La, 33 Fucheng Rd; ⏰10am-10pm) Sumptuous Shanghai Tang's shops add splashes of vibrant colour to the greyest of Shànghǎi days: elegant blouses, vivacious silk dresses, gorgeous tops, eye-catching glassware, Chinese-style shirts, scarves, cardigans, handbags, clutches, neat chopsticks, napkin holders, picture frames and more. The main branch is in the French Concession (p115).

CITY SHOP SUPERMARKET

Map p296 (城市超市; Chéngshì Chāoshì; ☎6215 0418; www.cityshop.com.cn; 1st fl, Citigroup Tower, 33 Huayuanshiqiao Rd; ⏰8am-10pm; Ⓜ Lujiazui) Imported goodies from shampoo to champagne, Scrumpy Jack cider, spam, Stolichnaya, Trappist Chimay beer, cheeses, wines and other treats for homesick foreign foodies, at a price. There are seven branches in town, including the main branch in Jìng'ān (p131). Free delivery service.

SUPERBRAND MALL MALL

Map p296 (正大广场; Zhèngdà Guǎngchǎng; 168 West Lujiazui Rd; 陆家嘴西路168号; ⏲10am-10pm; Ⓜ Lujiazui) Always busy, this gargantuan mall is ultra-handy for its dining options, a supermarket in the basement, a kids' arcade on the 6th floor and cinema on the 8th floor.

TOP CHOICE AP XĪNYÁNG FASHION & GIFTS MARKET SOUVENIRS

Map p297 (亚太新阳服饰礼品市场; Yàtài Xīnyáng Fúshì Lǐpǐn Shìchǎng; ⏲10am-8pm; Ⓜ Science & Technology Museum) Well worth a trip, this mammoth underground market by the Science & Technology Museum metro station is Shànghǎi's largest collection of shopping stalls, taking over from where the Xiangyang Rd market of old left off. It includes a branch of the Shíliùpù Fabric Market (p86) and a separate market devoted to pearls, the Yada Pearl Market (Yàdà Zhēnzhū Shìchǎng). **Amy Lin's Pearls** (A3-66) has a shop in the main area. Shop vendors are highly persistent and almost clawing, sending out scouts to wait at the metro exit turnstiles to ensnare shoppers. Haggling is the lingua franca – mixed with much huffing and puffing – so start with a very low offer and take it from there. There's tonnes of merchandise, from suits to moccasins, copy watches glinting from every direction, Darth Vader toys, jackets, English Premier League football strips, T-shirts, Indian saris, Angry Birds bags and so much more.

Hóngkǒu & North Shànghǎi

Neighbourhood Top Five

❶ Explore a prime piece of Jewish heritage at the **Ohel Moishe Synagogue** (p151) and hunt down local heritage along surrounding streets.

❷ Trace Hóngkǒu's historical narrative in its concession-period and art-deco **architecture** (p153).

❸ Poke among the bric-a-brac of **Dàshànghǎi** (p155) and other shops along Duolun Rd.

❹ Escape urban Shànghǎi to the verdant expanses of **Lu Xun Park** (p151).

❺ Raise a glass to the Bund and the Pǔdōng skyline from **Vue** (p154), a bar with a view.

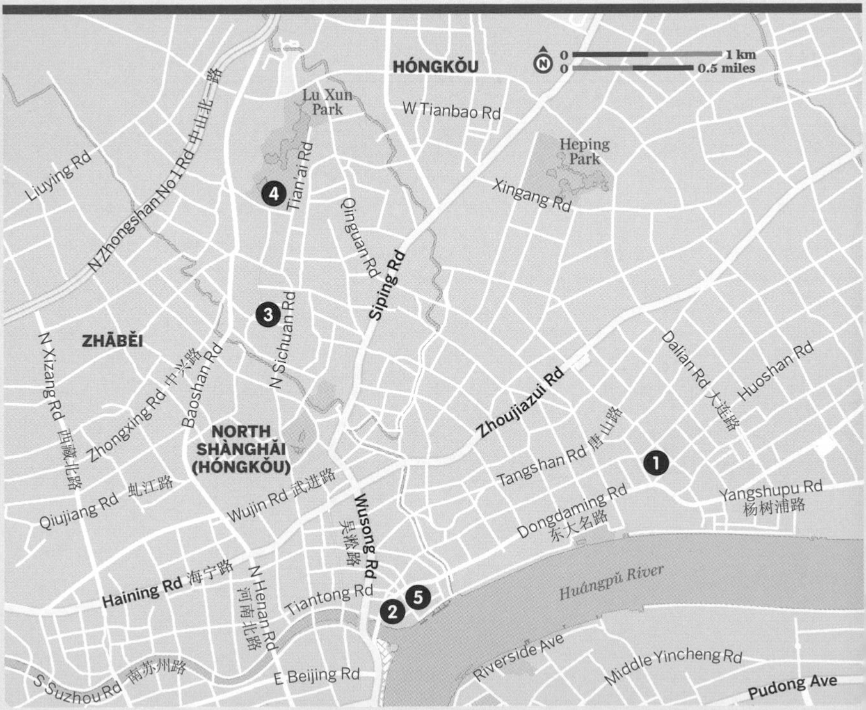

For more detail of this area, see Map p298 ➡

Explore: Hóngkǒu & North Shànghǎi

Hóngkǒu and North Shànghǎi (虹口区、北上海) may not have the lion's share of sights in town, but prize chunks of heritage architecture rise up from the swirl of street life and an authentic grittiness survives.

The up-and-coming North Bund area beyond Sūzhōu Creek is worth exploring for its impressive buildings, including the granddaddy of heritage hotels (the Astor House Hotel), looming art-deco blocks and noteworthy concession-era classics (the Main Post Office). The American Settlement was originally here, merging with the British Settlement in 1863 to form the prosperous International Settlement. To the west, Zháběi became infamous for its sweatshops and factories and was later flattened by the Japanese in 1932.

A rich vein of Jewish heritage survives towards Yángpǔ in the east, dating from the days when Hóngkǒu was home to thousands of Jewish refugees, mostly from Germany, who transformed 'Little Tokyo' (where 30,000 Japanese lived) into 'Little Vienna'. The Ohel Moishe Synagogue stands as a testament to this era. Wander round this neighbourhood and you'll also find examples of Shànghǎi's trademark terrace-style *shíkùmén* (stone-gate house) architecture, *lòngtáng* (alleyway) houses and narrow alleyways filling in the gaps.

Hóngkǒu has some excellently positioned accommodation options and while notable restaurants may seem thin on the ground, work your shoe leather and you can track down excellent options from across China.

Local Life

➡ **Snacking** Join locals along North Jiangxi Rd (p152) for a profusion of local titbits and hunger-busting bites.

➡ **Hóngkǒu Backstreets** Wander the lanes around the Ohel Moishe Synagogue (p151) to soak up local flavour.

➡ **Park Life** Catch the locals performing taichi or honing ballroom dancing spins in Lu Xun Park (p151).

➡ **Shopping** Roll up your sleeves to sift for bargain threads with throngs of shoppers at Qīpǔ Market (p154).

Getting There & Away

➡ **Metro** Line 10 runs north from East Nanjing Rd up to Fùdàn University, passing the Tiantong Rd, North Sichuan Rd and Hailun Rd stations. Line 3 also runs north, offering access to Duolun Rd and Lu Xun Park. Lines 4 and 8 loop east-west. Main interchange stations are Baoshan Rd (lines 3 and 4), Hailun Rd (lines 4 and 10) and Hongkou Football Stadium (lines 3 and 8).

➡ **Bus** Buses 22, 37 and 135 run up Dongdaming Rd and back down Changyang and Dongchangzhi Rds.

Lonely Planet's Top Tip

Basing yourself in south Hóngkǒu – at the Astor House Hotel or Chai Living Residences – allows you to hang your Shànghǎi hat within easy reach of the Bund across Wàibáidù Bridge and the nearby concession architecture of the North Bund district. Join the walking tour (p64) in the Bund & People's Square chapter to walk between these districts.

Best Places to Eat

➡ Guǒyúan (p152)

➡ Xīndàlù (p153)

➡ San Gines (p153)

➡ Yang's Fry Dumplings (p154)

For reviews, see p152 ➡

Best Shopping

➡ Qīpǔ Market (p154)

➡ Dàshànghǎi (p155)

➡ Details Gallery (p155)

➡ Duolun Rd (p150)

For reviews, see p154 ➡

SIGHTS

FREE **POST MUSEUM** MUSEUM

Map p298 (邮政博物馆; Yóuzhèng Bówùguǎn; 2nd fl, 250 North Suzhou Rd; 北苏州路250号2楼; ⌚9am-5pm Wed-Thu, Sat & Sun, last entry 4pm; Ⓜ Tiantong Rd) This interesting museum in the Main Post Office building explores postal history in imperial China, which dates back to the 1st millennium BC and used an extensive pony express to relay messages; Marco Polo estimated there were 10,000 postal stations in 13th-century China. Check out the collection of pre- and post-Liberation stamps (1888–1978) in a special climate-controlled room. On the 5th floor (after you exit) is a rooftop garden (being restored at the time of writing) with panoramic views of the Shànghǎi skyline.

DUOLUN ROAD CULTURAL STREET STREET

Map p298 (多伦文化名人街; Duōlún Wénhuà Míngrén Jiē; Ⓜ Dongbaoxing Rd) Rather like a Xīntiāndì that came too early, this pleasantly restored but rather sleepy street of fine old houses, just off North Sichuan Rd, was once home to several of China's most famous writers (as well as several Kuomintang generals), when the road was known as Doulean Rd. Today it is lined with art-supply stores, curio and Burmese jade shops, galleries, teahouses and cafes. The main appeal of the street is its galleries and antique shops, including Dàshànghǎi (see p155).

The **Shànghǎi Duōlún Museum of Modern Art** (上海多伦现代美术馆; Shànghǎi Duōlún Xiàndài Měishùguǎn; ☎6587 6902; 27 Duolun Rd; 多伦路27号; adult/student ¥10/5; ⌚10am-5pm Tue-Sun) has a focus on experimental contemporary art. Further along the street, you may find the 1928 **Hóngdé Temple** (鸿德堂; Hóngdé Táng; ☎5696 1196; 59 Duolun Rd; 多伦路59号) open, its grey brick interior adorned with pictures of the Stations of the Cross and simple wooden pews; upstairs is a lovely hall with a wooden ceiling. The church was built in a Chinese style as the Great Virtue Church.

The League of Left-Wing Writers was established down a side alley on 2 March 1930. Today the building serves as a **political museum** (No 2, Lane 201, Duolun Rd; 多伦路201弄2号; adult/student ¥5/3; ⌚9am-4pm Tue-Sun), perhaps worth a look for the architecture alone.

Duolun Rd ends in another Kuomintang residence, the Moorish-looking, private **Kong Residence** (孔公馆; Kǒng Gōngguǎn; 250 Duolun Rd; 多伦路250号), built in 1924.

If you need a break, try the Old Film Café (p154), next to the 18.2m-high **Xīshí Bell Tower** (Xīshí Zhōnglóu) at the bend in the road. There's a statue of Charlie Chaplin outside.

LOCAL KNOWLEDGE

HISTORIC HÓNGKǑU

For a mini walking tour of the streets surrounding the Ohel Moishe Synagogue, turn right outside the synagogue, then right again past the former Jewish tenements of Zhoushan Rd, once the commercial heart of the district. At Huoshan Rd (formerly Wayside Rd), head southwest past the art-deco facade of the former **Broadway Theatre** (Map p298) at No 57, to the Ocean Hotel. Turn right up Haimen Rd (Muirhead Rd), past Changyang Rd, to what was once a row of Jewish shops and a kosher delicatessen.

At the top of the road (the crossing with Kunming Rd) you'll see the largely rebuilt **Xiàhǎi Buddhist Monastery** (Xiàhǎi Miào; Map p298; Kunming Rd; 昆明路; admission ¥5; ⌚7am-4pm). Take a right turn, then another right, down Zhoushan Rd (formerly Ward Rd) once again to complete the circle back to the synagogue.

Zhoushan Rd is also home to the British-built **Ward Road Jail** (Map p298), once Shànghǎi's biggest. Used by the Japanese during WWII, it's still functioning as a prison and is probably as close as you'll get, or would want to get, to a Chinese detention facility. You can catch bus 33 here from the Bund.

If you're interested in learning more about Hóngkǒu's Jewish heritage, contact Dvir Bar-Gal, an Israeli Shànghǎi resident who offers informative English and Hebrew **tours** (☎130 021 467 02; www.shanghai-jews.com; half-day tour ¥400) of the area.

TOP SIGHTS
OHEL MOISHE SYNAGOGUE

This synagogue (摩西会堂; Móxī Huìtáng) was built by the Russian Ashkenazi Jewish community in 1927 and lies in the heart of the 1940s Jewish ghetto. Today it houses the **Shànghǎi Jewish Refugees Museum**, a moving introduction to the lives of the approximately 20,000 Central European refugees who fled to Shànghǎi to escape the Nazis. Slip a pair of shower caps over your shoes to look at the synagogue itself (in the main building) and the exhibitions upstairs. The photographs and exhibits on the Holocaust are graphic, but highly educational. Considerable emphasis falls on the Soviet Red Army's liberation of death camps, but seems to skip mention of US and allied efforts. Two other halls in the courtyard below detail the individual stories of notable Jewish refugees in Shànghǎi through their photographs and possessions. The exhibition is rounded off with a moving quote from the writer, Nobel Laureate and Holocaust survivor Elie Wiesel: 'The past is in the present, but the future is still in our hands.' English-language **tours** (⏲9.30am-4.15pm, every 45min) are included in the admission price.

DON'T MISS...

- Synagogue
- Upstairs exhibition
- Courtyard exhibition halls

PRACTICALITIES

- Map p298
- ☎6512 6669
- 62 Changyang Rd; 长阳路62号
- admission ¥50
- ⏲9am-5pm, last entry 4.30pm
- Ⓜ Dalian Rd

FREE LU XUN MEMORIAL HALL MUSEUM
Map p298 (鲁迅纪念馆; Lǔ Xùn Jìniànguǎn; ☎6540 2288; Lu Xun Park, 2288 North Sichuan Rd; 鲁迅公园内, 四川北路2288号; ⏲9am-4pm; Ⓜ Hongkou Football Stadium) An excellent museum, this modern hall charts the life and creative output of Lu Xun with photographs, first editions, videos and waxworks. Detailed English captions throughout.

LU XUN FORMER RESIDENCE HISTORIC BUILDING
Map p298 (鲁迅故居; Lǔxùn Gùjū; ☎5666 2608; No 9, Lane 132, Shanyin Rd; 山阴路132弄9号; adult/child ¥8/4; ⏲9am-4pm; Ⓜ Dongbaoxing Rd) Lu Xun buffs will adore ferreting around this three-floor domicile on lovely Shanyin Rd, where an English-speaking guide can fill you in on all the bits and bobs. Don't overlook wandering along Shanyin Rd and peeking into its lovely alleyways and traditional *lòngtáng* houses (for example at Nos 41 to 50, Lane 180, Shanyin Rd).

LU XUN PARK PARK
Map p298 (鲁迅公园; Lǔ Xùn Gōngyuán; 146 East Jiangwan Rd; 江湾东路146号; admission free; ⏲6am-6pm; Ⓜ Hongkou Football Stadium) Particularly photogenic in spring and summer when the trees are in blossom, Lu Xun Park is one of the city's most pleasant parks, with elderly Chinese practising taichi or ballroom dancing, and even the occasional retired opera singer giving a free performance. The English corner on Sunday mornings is one of the largest in all of Shànghǎi and a good place to chat to locals in English. You can take boats out onto the small lake. It's a big shame about the fenced-in lawn, but the **Plum Garden** (admission ¥15; ⏲7.30am-6pm) is an attractive diversion.

The park used to be called Hóngkǒu Park but was renamed because it holds **Lu Xun's Tomb**, moved here from the International Cemetery in 1956, on the 20th anniversary of his death.

FREE GALLERY MAGDA DANYSZ GALLERY
(www.magda-gallery.com; 188 Linqing Rd; 临青路188号; ⏲11am-6pm Tue-Sun; Ⓜ Huangxin Rd) Twinned with its Paris gallery and bringing further artistic frisson to Yángpǔ district in north Shànghǎi, the Gallery Magda Danysz is a bold and vibrant art space for both emerging and established Chinese and international names. Exhibitions range through an inspiring and thoughtful spectrum of visual media – check the website for details.

EATING

For local Shànghǎi snacks and eats from across China, North Jiangxi Rd (江西北路) is stuffed with chefs wilting over steamers, noisy kebab sellers and red-cheeked *málàtàng* (麻辣烫; spicy soup with meat and vegetables) vendors. Also on sale here are Shāndōng *dàbǐng* (山东大饼; Shāndōng flatbread; ¥2) and the ever-scrummy *ròujiāmó* (肉夹馍; ¥6; bun stuffed with pork and peppers). Several Buddhist vegetarian restaurants selling meat-free pot-stickers and other vegie dishes are flung out down Haimen Rd from the Xiàhǎi Buddhist Monastery.

GUǑYÚAN HUNANESE $

(果园; 520 Dongjiangwan Rd; 东江湾路520号; meals from ¥30; Ⓜ Hongkou Football Stadium) The cool lime-green tablecloths do little to calm the red-hot flavours of this fantastic Húnán restaurant located not too far north of Hongkou Football Stadium metro station. Hunanese is another chilli-driven cooking tradition from China's heartland. The *tiěbǎn niúròu* (铁板牛肉; sizzling beef platter; ¥30) here is a magnificent dish, but its fiery flavours are almost eclipsed by the enticing *xiāngwèi qiézibāo* (湘味茄子煲; Húnán aubergine hotpot). No English menu.

SHÀNGHǍI'S JEWS

Shànghǎi has two centuries of strong Jewish connections. Established Middle Eastern Sephardic Jewish families such as the Hardoons, Ezras, Kadoories and Sassoons built their fortunes in Shànghǎi, establishing at least seven synagogues and many Jewish hospitals and schools. It was Victor Sassoon who famously remarked: 'There is only one race greater than the Jews and that's the Derby.'

A second group of Jews, this time Ashkenazi, arrived via Siberia, Hā'ěrbīn and Tiānjīn from Russia after anti-Jewish pogroms in 1906. The biggest influx, however, came between 1933 and 1941, when 30,000 mostly Ashkenazi Jews arrived from Europe by boat from Italy or by train via Siberia. Many had been issued with visas to cross China by Ho Fengshan, Chinese consul-general in Vienna, who was recently honoured as the 'Chinese Schindler'.

Shànghǎi was one of the few safe havens for Jews fleeing the Holocaust in Europe as it required neither a passport nor visa to stay. Gestapo agents followed the refugees and, in 1942, tried to persuade the Japanese to build death camps on Chongming Island. Instead, in 1943, the Japanese forced Jews to move into a 'Designated Area for Stateless Refugees' in Hóngkǒu.

The Jewish ghetto (stateless Russians didn't have to live here) became home to Jews from all walks of life. It grew to shelter a synagogue, schools, a local paper, hospitals and enough cafes, rooftop gardens and restaurants to gain the epithet 'Little Vienna'. Those Jews who held jobs in the French Concession had to secure passes from the Japanese, specifically the notoriously unpredictable and violent Mr Goya. Poorer refugees were forced to bunk down in cramped hostels known as *Heime*, and had to rely on the generosity of others. As the wealthy Anglophile Jewish trading families left in 1941, the situation grew even tighter. Still, the refugees heard of events in distant Europe and realised that they were the lucky ones.

Today there are a few remainders of Jewish life in Shànghǎi, such as the Ohel Moishe Synagogue and the former Jewish Club (1932) in the grounds of the Conservatory of Music, where concerts are still performed. The **Ohel Rachel Synagogue** (Yóutài Jiàotáng; Map p294; 500 North Shaanxi Rd) was built by Jacob Elias Sassoon in the early 20th century. Unfortunately, it remains closed to the public. Nearby are the remains of the school founded on the grounds by Horace Kadoorie.

For information and pricey tours of Jewish Shànghǎi, contact the **Centre of Jewish Studies Shànghǎi** (上海犹太研究中心; Shànghǎi Yóutài Yánjiū Zhōngxīn; Map p286; ☎5306 0606, ext 2476; www.cjss.org.cn; room 476, No 7, Lane 622, Middle Huaihai Rd; 淮海中路622弄7号476屋; tour US$80; ⏰9am-4pm). The centre offers one-day tours (for groups only) of Jewish Shànghǎi with English- and Hebrew-speaking guides and also has a fine library of books and periodicals.

LOCAL KNOWLEDGE

HÓNGKǑU ARCHITECTURE

Hóngkǒu has a rich crop of architectural gems, from run-down terraced houses and dilapidated *shíkùmén* (stone-gate houses) to riverside art-deco structures, noble concession-period classics, heritage hotels and converted abattoirs.

1933 (上海1933老场坊; Shànghǎi 1933 Lǎochǎngfáng; Map p298; 10 Shajing Rd; 沙泾路10号) A magnificent concrete slaughterhouse transformed into a shopping complex (the shops themselves are of less interest), with very photogenic 'air bridges' intact.

Hongkew Methodist Church (景灵堂; Jǐnglíng Táng; Map p298; 135 Kunshan Rd; 昆山路135号) Dating from 1923, this is the church where Chiang Kaishek married Soong Meiling. It's generally closed to the public, but the caretaker may let you in.

New Asia Hotel (新亚大酒店; Xīnyà Dàjiǔdiàn; 422 Tiantong Rd; 天潼路422号) One of Shànghǎi's rich brood of art-deco wonders.

Main Post Office (国际邮局; Guójì Yóujú; Map p298) Overlooking Sūzhōu Creek, this supremely grand building dates from 1924, is topped with a cupola and clock tower, and ornamented with bronze statues coated in a green patina.

Broadway Mansions (上海大厦; Shànghǎi Dàshà; 20 North Suzhou Rd; 苏州北路20号) Looming over Sūzhōu Creek, this classic brick pile (resembling a Ministry of Truth) was built to great fanfare in 1934 as an apartment block and later used to house American officers after WWII. Today it's a hotel.

Astor House Hotel (浦江饭店; Pǔjiāng Fàndiàn; Map p298) Bursting with history, this classic old-timer has a yarn or two to tell and a lot of fans: it's an excellent place to base oneself for swift access to the Bund (see p201).

Embankment Building (河滨大厦; Hébīn Dàshà; Map p298; 400 North Suzhou Rd; 苏州北路400号) Designed by architects Palmer & Turner, dating from 1935 and home to Chai Living Residences.

Russian Consulate (俄罗斯领事馆; Éluósī Lǐngshìguǎn; Map p298) This grand red-roofed concession building rises up just north of Wàibáidù Bridge.

Shíkùmén Architecture Examples can be found if you stroll north along Zhapu Rd from Kunshan Rd and pop into the first pinched alley at No 313 (乍浦路313弄) on your left, where a line of typical *shíkùmén* awaits, decorated with distinctively carved lintels. Emerging from the alley, turn right along Baiguan Jie (百官街) for a short walk north to admire a further cluster of *shíkùmén* through the archway on your right. Other areas that are good for *shíkùmén* buildings are Zhoushan Rd, especially at its southern end. The market street of Dongyuhang Rd (东余杭路), which it crosses, also has some interesting *shíkùmén* entrances. Shanyin Rd is a pleasant tree-lined street with a number of *shíkùmén*-filled alleyways branching off it.

XĪNDÀLÙ — PEKING DUCK, ZHÈJIĀNG $$$

Map p298 (新大陆; ☎6393-1234, ext 6318; 1st fl, Hyatt on the Bund, 199 Huangpu Rd; 黄浦路199号外滩茂悦大酒店1楼; roast duck half/whole ¥138/198, dishes from ¥48; ⏲11.30am-2.30pm & 6-11pm; Ⓜ Tiantong Rd) Shànghǎi's premier *kǎoyā* (roast duck) experience, this upscale hotel restaurant pulls out all the stops, importing all the necessary ingredients (including the chefs and a special brick oven) direct from the capital. In addition to the sleek open kitchen, it's unusually intimate inside. Other first-rate dishes on offer include beggar's chicken (a Hángzhōu speciality), which needs to be ordered at least four hours in advance. Reserve.

SAN GINES — SPANISH $

Map p298 (圣吉诺; Shèng Jínuò; Basement 2, Hóngkǒu Plaza, 388 West Jiangwan Rd; 西江湾路388号B2楼; churros ¥10 for 6; ⏲10am-10pm; Ⓜ Hongkou Football Stadium) Snacking can be sorted in a flash at San Gines (China's first branch of the Madrid cafe dating to 1894), where glistening, deep-fried *churros* await. They may not catch on with older *yóutiáo*-chewing Shanghainese, who will stick to their fried dough sticks (which some say inspired *churros* in the first place). But more inquisitive younger Chinese are beating a path here to dunk their *churros* in the savoury or warm chocolate sauces or ice creams provided (or chomp them plain).

AFANTI RESTAURANT UIGHUR $$

(阿凡提美食城; Āfántí Měishíchéng; ☎6555 9604; 775 Quyang Rd; 曲阳路775号; dishes from ¥30; ⊙11.30am-11.30pm; Ⓜ Chifeng Rd) Discerning fans of hearty Uighur cuisine will love the delicious *dàpánjī* (fried chicken, peppers and potatoes), *gosh gorma* (fried mutton; *chǎo kǎoròu* in Chinese) and the cumin-rubbed lamb, and don't forget to try the homemade *suān nǎi* (yoghurt). The restaurant is in the basement of the Tiānshān Hotel, next to the Silk Road Hotel. Look for the building with the golden domes.

YANG'S FRY DUMPLINGS DUMPLINGS $

(小杨生煎馆; Xiǎoyáng Shēngjiān Guǎn; 810 Quyang Lu; 曲阳路810号; ¥6 per liǎng (两; 4 dumplings); ⊙6.30am-7.30pm; Ⓜ Quyang Rd) If you need another opportunity to hoover up Yang's signature, time-honoured and much-applauded fried *shēngjiān* dumplings, you're set for brekkie, lunch or (early) dinner.

DRINKING & NIGHTLIFE

VUE BAR

Map p298 (非常时髦; Fēicháng Shímáo; 32nd & 33rd fl, Hyatt on the Bund, 199 Huangpu Rd; 外滩茂悦大酒店黄浦路199号32-33楼; ⊙6pm-1am; Ⓜ Tiantong Rd) Extrasensory nocturnal views of the Bund and Pǔdōng from the Hyatt on the Bund with an outdoor Jacuzzi to go with your raised glasses of bubbly or Vue martinis (vodka and mango purée).

BITES LOUNGE LOUNGE

Map p298 (410 North Suzhou Rd; 苏州北路410号; ⊙5-10pm Tue-Fri, 11.30am-10pm Sat & Sun; 📶) Part of Chai Living, the small and elegant Bites Lounge bar is a short walk along the Embankment Building to the west from Details Gallery.

OLD FILM CAFÉ CAFE

Map p298 (老电影咖啡馆; Lǎodiànyǐng Kāfēiguǎn; ☎5696 4763; 123 Duolun Rd; 多伦路123号; coffee/tea from ¥25/35; ⊙10am-1am; Ⓜ Dongbaoxing Rd) Celebrating the golden age of Shànghǎi cinema, this place is good for a coffee if you're in the Duolun Rd area. There's some fantastic woodwork, comfy armchairs plus an atmospheric loft and photos of Marilyn Monroe and Leonardo DiCaprio plus Chinese legends of the silver screen. There's also screenings of classic films from the '30s, a wide range of teas and alcohol, too.

SHOPPING

Head for the area north of Sūzhōu Creek to see where the masses shop.

QĪPǓ MARKET CLOTHING

Map p298 (七浦服装市场; Qīpǔ Fúzhuāng Shìchǎng; 168 & 183 Qipu Rd; 七浦路168 & 183号; ⊙5am-5pm west side, 7am-7pm east side; Ⓜ Tiantong Rd) Qīpǔ Market is where ordinary Shànghǎi goes shopping for clothes. Consisting of two run-down, rabbit-warren-like department stores surrounding the North Henan Rd intersection, it's one big 'everything must go now' sale here. Do as locals do and push through the hordes of people

WORTH A DETOUR

GÒNGQĪNG FOREST PARK

This vast expanse of forested **parkland** (共青森林公园; Gòngqīng Sēnlín Gōngyuán; www.shgqsl.com; 2000 Jungong Rd; 军工路2000号; adult/child ¥15/7.5; ⊙6am-5pm, last entry 4pm; 👪; Ⓜ Nengjiang Rd) on the western shore of the Huángpǔ River is a leafy, wooded and tranquil slice of countryside in Shànghǎi. This is about as wild as you get in Pǔxī, with acres of willows, luohan pines, magnolias, hibiscus and nary a skyscraper in sight. Aim to spend half if not a whole day picnicking and wandering around this huge area, or hop into one of the buggies (¥10) for express tours around the grounds. For kids there's a roller coaster, rock climbing, horse riding, a zip-liner and other activities. The Nengjiang Rd station near the northern terminus of metro line 8 will get you close to the western edge of the park. If you want to spend the night in the park, check into the **Hongsen Forest Park Hotel** (☎6532 1296; 2300 Jungong Rd; 军工路2300号; r/cabin ¥280/580).

searching for T-shirts, shoes, tank tops, dresses, shorts, pretty much any item of clothing you can find for around ¥50. Haggle here; you should be paying at least 50% below the asking price.

DETAILS GALLERY GALLERY

Map p298 (www.chailiving.com; Embankment Bldg, 370-380 North Suzhou Rd; 苏州北路370-380号; ⊙noon-8pm Tue-Fri, 11am-7pm Sat & Sun; Ⓜ Tiantong Rd) Located on the corner of the Embankment Building, this smart and sedate gallery from Chai Living showcases good-looking antique Chinese chests, wardrobes, silks, art and antiques.

DÀSHÀNGHǍI ANTIQUES

Map p298 (大上海; 181 Duolun Rd; 多伦路181号; Ⓜ Dongbaoxing Rd) Explore keenly at this Duolun Rd shop, where all sorts of historic collectibles from the pre-Liberation era amass: books and catalogues, 1950s maps of Běijīng (¥1500 to ¥8000) and Shànghǎi, genuine posters and authentic memorabilia from the Cultural Revolution, unopened matchboxes and cigarette packs from the 1960s, Republican-era lipsticks, toothbrushes and more. The owner is haggling-resistant (but by all means try).

ELECTRONICS MARKET ELECTRONICS

Map p298 (电子市场; Diànzǐ Shìchǎng; Qiujiang Rd; 虬江路; ⊙9.30am-5.30pm; Ⓜ Baoshan Rd) If you want to put together your own computer, replace a processor, soup up an MP3 player or score a pair of speakers, try this market located right under the elevated train tracks that lead into Baoshan Rd metro. It's a Cybermart for people who don't mind the lack of a guarantee or receipt. Prices are low and negotiable, but how long everything will last is another matter.

LOCAL KNOWLEDGE

SHÀNGHǍI SLOGANS

Unlike Běijīng and other towns and villages across China, Shànghǎi has largely scrubbed away its slogans (政治口号; *zhèngzhì kǒuhào*) from the Cultural Revolution, despite the city's once heady revolutionary zeal. One slogan by Wàibáidù Bridge vanished in recent years during the area's redesign and spruce-up, but an imposing and well-preserved scarlet slogan survives high up on the north wall of the Huángpǔ Hotel (黄浦饭店; Huángpǔ Fàndiàn) at 106 Huangpu Rd (黄浦路), not far from the Hyatt on the Bund. The Maoist slogan is visible through the gate but note that the hotel is for Chinese military and naval guests (foreigners not accepted), so be discreet when looking for it.

Xújiāhuì & South Shànghǎi

XÚJIĀHUÌ | SOUTH SHÀNGHǍI

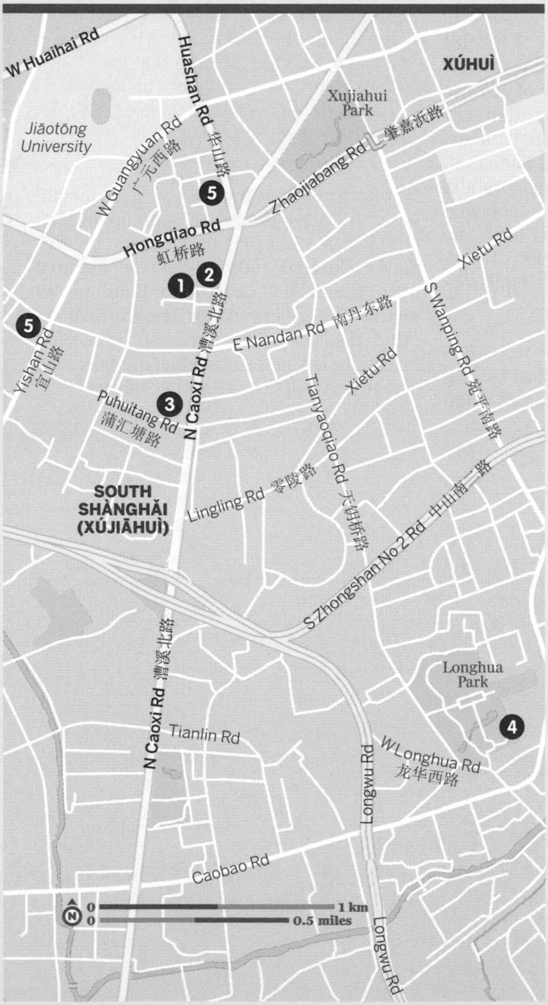

For more detail of this area, see Map p300

Neighbourhood Top Five

❶ Swoon over the brilliant blues and crimsons of the stained glass illuminating **St Ignatius Cathedral** (p158).

❷ Marvel at the astounding Jesuit library in the **Bibliotheca Zi-Ka-Wei** (p158).

❸ Explore the eye-catching fusion of Chinese and Western art within the fascinating **Tousewe Museum** (p158).

❹ Divine the Buddhist heritage of south Shànghǎi in the **Lónghuá Temple & Pagoda** (p159).

❺ Chomp your way through steamers of dumplings at **Din Tai Fung** (p160) or go all out for a Uighur lamb feast at **Xīnjiāng Fēngwèi Restaurant** (p160).

Explore: Xújiāhuì & South Shànghǎi

Bordering the southwestern end of the stylish French Concession and reachable in a zip on the metro from People's Square, Xújiāhuì (徐家汇) was known to 1930s expats as Zicawei or Sicawei. Most locals come here today to shop at the outsize Grand Gateway 66 mall, but Xújiāhuì was originally a low-lying Jesuit settlement dating back to the 17th century. A Catholic flavour still clings to Xújiāhuì, holding firm against the ever-encroaching office blocks and shopping malls. As with elsewhere in Shànghǎi, you have to explore a bit to clutch all the historical threads into once bunch, but if you've an eye for architectural heritage, a trip here makes for rewarding exploration.

Accessed directly on the metro at its namesake station, a day's exploration of Xújiāhuì should suffice. The area is dominated by giant shopping malls and department stores that circle a five-way intersection that's insanely busy even by Shànghǎi standards. It's one of the most popular shopping areas in the city and packed at weekends.

History, heritage architecture, green lawns and academia converge on the tranquil campus of Jiāotōng University along Huashan Rd, north of the main Jesuit sights, while a host of local dining options means you won't be caught hungry at lunch or dinner time. Of course, shopping needs are all met in Xújiāhuì's high-profile malls.

Further out from Xújiāhuì, South Shànghǎi is marked by one of the city's most famous temples, the ancient Lónghuá Temple and its pagoda, as well as an amusement park that can help occupy children rebelling against sightseeing.

Local Life

➡ **Greenery** Join the students relaxing on the lawn of Jiāotōng University (p157).

➡ **Dumplings** Find out what all the fuss is about – follow Shànghǎi's pernickety local diners to Din Tai Fung (p160).

➡ **Shopping** See how the Shanghainese spend, spend, spend at Grand Gateway 66 (p161).

Getting There & Away

➡ **Metro** Lines 1, 3, 4 and 9 run through the district. Xujiahui (lines 1 and 9) and Shanghai Indoor Stadium (lines 1, 3 and 4) are the main interchange stations. Line 1 runs through the French Concession and down to the South Shanghai Railway Station; line 9 can whisk you to Pǔdōng.

Lonely Planet's Top Tip

With its harried shopping hordes and hectic roads, Xújiāhuì can be breathlessly busy. Escape to some of Shànghǎi's best-tended areas of greenery: the gorgeous and inviting lawn a short walk from the main entrance of Jiāotōng University on Huashan Rd, where students lie down on the grass reading and chatting in warm weather.

Best Sights

➡ Bibliotheca Zi-Ka-Wei (p158)

➡ St Ignatius Cathedral (p158)

➡ Tousewe Museum (p158)

➡ Lónghuá Temple & Pagoda (p159)

For reviews, see p158 ➡

Best Places to Eat

➡ Din Tai Fung (p160)

➡ Xīnjiāng Fēngwèi Restaurant (p160)

➡ Kota's Kitchen (p160)

➡ 1001 Noodles House (p161)

For reviews, see p160 ➡

SIGHTS

Xújiāhuì

ST IGNATIUS CATHEDRAL CHURCH

Map p300 (徐家汇天主教堂; Xújiāhuì Tiānzhǔjiàotáng; ☎6438 4632; 158 Puxi Rd; 蒲西路158号; ⏰1-4.30pm Sat & Sun; ⓂXujiahui) The dignified twin-spired St Ignatius Cathedral (1904) is a major Xújiāhuì landmark. A long span of Gothic arches, its nave is ornamented on the outside with rows of menacing gargoyles; note how the church spires find reflection in much of the more recently built local architecture. The original stained glass was destroyed in the Cultural Revolution, but the vivid colours of the recent red, azure and purple replacements (with archaic Chinese inscriptions from the Bible) are outstanding.

Mass is held on Sunday at 6am, 7.30am, 10am and 6pm; on weekdays at 7am and on Saturday at 6pm (and the first Friday of the month at 6pm).

TOUSEWE MUSEUM MUSEUM

Map p300 (土山湾博物馆; Tǔshānwān Bówùguǎn; Tǔshānwān Museum; 55-1 Puhuitang Lu; 蒲汇塘路55-1号; admission ¥10; ⏰9am-4.30pm Tue-Sun; ⓂShanghai Indoor Stadium/Xujiahui) Next to a middle school along Puhuitang Rd, this fascinating museum is dedicated to the arts and crafts of the former red-brick Tousewe Orphanage, established here by the indefatigable Jesuits in 1864. The Catholics taught orphans the techniques of Western art: one of the first things you see as you walk into the museum is a small, exquisite and exact copy of the former Tiānníng Pagoda in Běijīng and a magnificent wooden *páilou* (decorative arch), the Tǔshānwān Archway, carved in 1913. Further along there's a wealth of objects either produced or relating to the orphanage, from religious ornaments to Jesuit literature, including a copy of *Recherches sur les superstitions en Chine*. Woodcraft was particularly productive at the orphanage so some splendid items can be admired; look out for the expertly carved 'Li Kui and his double', fashioned from boxwood, and the Madonna from the 1920s. Filling out the rest of the fascinating collection are paintings and stained glass. Audio tours are available.

FREE **CY TUNG MARITIME MUSEUM** MUSEUM

Map p300 (董浩云航运博物馆; Dǒng Hàoyún Hángyùn Bówùguǎn; ☎6293 3035; Jiāotōng University campus, 1954 Huashan Rd; 华山路1954号交通大学内; ⏰1.30-5pm Tue-Sun; ⓂJiaotong University) Named after the Shànghǎi-born shipping magnate, this small but fascinating museum in Jiāotōng University explores the little-known world of Chinese maritime history, with model ships, maps of early trade routes, and a video. A large portion of the 1st floor is devoted to Zheng He, the 15th-century admiral and explorer who was born a Hui Muslim in Yúnnán, was later captured and made a eunuch at the Ming court, and eventually went on to command vast Chinese fleets on journeys to east Africa, India and the Persian Gulf.

BIBLIOTHECA ZI-KA-WEI

The magnificent St Ignatius Catholic Library, the **Bibliotheca Zi-Ka-Wei** (徐家汇藏书楼; Xújiāhuì Cángshūlóu; Map p300; ☎6487 4095, ext 208; 80 North Caoxi Rd; 漕溪北路80号; ⏰library tour 2-4pm Sat; ⓂXujiahui) is one of several Jesuit monuments defining historic Xújiāhuì. Established in 1847 by the local Jesuit mission and home to 560,000 volumes in Greek, Latin and other languages, the edifice consists of two buildings, with the library itself housed in the lower, two-storey, east-facing building that partially arches over the pavement.

The only way to see its priceless book collection is on a free **guided tour** of the highlight main library (Dà Shūfáng) on Saturday afternoons. English-speaking guides take you through an astonishing collection of antiquarian tomes, arranged in a beautiful historic library laid out on one floor with a gallery above. Wander past rare books on ecclesiastical history, *Philosphica*, *Res Sinenses* (Things Chinese) and other erudite branches of Jesuit learning. The 15-minute tours are limited to 10 people per group, so it's best to phone ahead to book. Photography is not allowed. Adjacent to the magnificent library to the south is the Priest's Residence.

LOCAL KNOWLEDGE

JESUIT XÚJIĀHUÌ

Beyond St Ignatius Cathedral and the Bibliotheca Zi-Ka-Wei, keep your eyes peeled and unearth a small treasure trove of historic architecture around Xújiāhuì. The red-and-grey-brick building on the south side of Hongqiao Rd across from Grand Gateway 66 is the **Xúhuì Public School** (徐汇中学; Xúhuì Zhōngxué), established in 1850 by the Jesuit priest Claude Gotteland. Standing across North Caoxi Rd from St Ignatius Cathedral is the former **St Ignatius Convent**, now a restaurant, once belonging to the Helpers of the Holy Souls. Just south of St Ignatius Cathedral at 166 Puxi Rd is the Jesuit-built **Xújiāhuì Observatory**, currently part of the Shànghǎi Meteorological Bureau. A little further on along East Nandan Rd (南丹东路), you'll see another Jesuit-constructed building on the far side of the road, the former **Major Seminary**.

FREE **QIAN XUESEN LIBRARY & MUSEUM** MUSEUM

Map p300 (钱学森图书馆; Qián Xuésēn Túshūguǎn; Jiāotōng University, 1800 Huashan Rd; 交通大学华山路1800号; ⏰9am-4pm; Ⓜ Jiaotong University) A former graduate of Jiāotōng University, Qian Xuesen (Hsue-shen Tsien) was a pioneering aviation and rocket scientist, trumpeted as the father of China's aeronautical industry and space program. In typical fashion, Qian (who died in 2009) is given a spotlessly patriotic appraisal by this elaborate and overproduced three-floor museum in Jiāotōng University. The displays revel in the milestones of the scientist's life, including his triumphant return to China from the US, where he began his career and had endured house arrest after being labelled a communist during the McCarthy era.

South Shànghǎi

LÓNGHUÁ TEMPLE & PAGODA BUDDHIST TEMPLE

Map p300 (龙华寺、龙华塔; Lónghuá Sì & Lónghuá Tǎ; ☎6457 6327; 2853 Longhua Rd; 龙华路2853号; admission ¥10; ⏰7am-4.30pm; Ⓜ Longcao Rd, 🚌44 from Xujiahui) Southeast, away from Xújiāhuì, is the oldest and largest monastery in Shànghǎi, taking its name (Lónghuá) from the pipal tree under which Buddha achieved enlightenment. The much-renovated temple is said to date from the 10th century, its five main halls commencing with the Laughing Buddha Hall and bell and drum towers rising on either side of the entrance. The temple is particularly famed for its 6500kg bell, cast in 1894.

Several other side buildings can be explored, including the Thousand Luóhàn Hall, sheltering a huge legion of glittering arhat. A large effigy of Sakyamuni seated on a lotus flower resides within the main hall – the Great Treasure Hall. Beyond the main hall is a vegetarian restaurant and a further imposing hall – the Sanshengbao Hall – with a golden trinity of Buddhist statues.

Opposite the temple entrance rises the much-restored seven-storey, 44m-high Lónghuá Pagoda, originally built in AD 977. Visitors are not allowed to climb the pagoda, but a sprawl of stalls selling snacks and souvenirs fans out in the vicinity.

The best time to visit is during the Lónghuá Temple Fair, in the third month of the lunar calendar (usually during April or May).

SHÀNGHǍI BOTANICAL GARDENS GARDENS

(上海植物园; Shànghǎi Zhíwùyuán; ☎5436 3369; 997 Longwu Rd; 龙吴路997号; admission ¥15; ⏰7am-5pm; Ⓜ Shilong Rd) The location just off the busy and polluted Longwu Rd is hardly idyllic, but the Botanical Gardens offer an escape from Shànghǎi's synthetic cityscape. The Tropicarium gives you the chance to get close to tropical flora, and once inside, you can take the lift to the 6th floor for an impressive view of the gardens. Some of the flower arrangements are a little twee, but the place is well maintained and bustling with visitors.

The northern side of the gardens has a dusty memorial temple, originally built in 1728. It's dedicated to Huang Daopo, who supposedly kick-started Shànghǎi's cotton industry by bringing the knowledge of spinning and weaving to the region from Hǎinán.

JǏNJIĀNG AMUSEMENT PARK AMUSEMENT PARK

(锦江乐园; Jǐnjiāng Lèyuán; ☎5421 6858; 201 Hongmei Rd; 虹梅路201号; 2/6 rides ¥50/80;

⏲9am-10pm summer, to 5pm winter; Ⓜ Jinjiang Park) If the kids are in mutiny against sightseeing, the roller coasters, rides and huge Ferris wheel at this amusement park may mollify them. It's a bit out of town, but easy to get to, as it has its own metro station.

MARTYRS MEMORIAL PARK

Map p300 (龙华烈士陵园; Lónghuá Lièshì Língyuán; Longhua Rd; 龙华路; admission ¥1, memorial hall ¥5; ⏲6am-5pm, museum 9am-4pm; Ⓜ Longcao Rd, 🚌44 from Xújiāhuì) Next to Lónghuá Temple, this park marks the site of an old Kuomintang prison, where 800 communists, intellectuals and political agitators were executed between 1928 and 1937. You can take a modern underground tunnel to the original jailhouses and the small execution ground. Scattered throughout the manicured lawns are epic sculptures of workers and soldiers, depicted in true socialist realism style. During WWII this area was a Japanese internment camp and airfield, as depicted in the JG Ballard novel and Spielberg film *Empire of the Sun*.

EATING

The 5th and 6th floors of the Grand Gateway 66 mall and food courts galore cater to the hardened shoppers of Xújiāhuì, but there are also some good restaurants nearby.

DIN TAI FUNG SHANGHAINESE $

Map p300 (鼎泰丰; Dǐng Tài Fēng; 5th fl, Grand Gateway 66; 港汇广场5楼; 🚭; Ⓜ Xujiahui) This capacious, brightly lit and busy Taiwan-owned restaurant chain may still be peddling its 'Top 10 restaurants of the world' mantra after a two-decades-old review in the *New York Times*, but it still delivers some absolutely scrummy Shànghǎi *xiǎolóngbāo* dumplings. Not cheap perhaps (five for ¥29, or 10 for ¥58), but they're worth every jiao. The mildly tangy hot and sour soup with pork and bean curd (¥35) is a great companion dish, or go for the lovely braised ox brisket soup with vegetables (¥50). Service is top-notch and you can watch the chefs prepare your dumplings through sheet glass on arrival. Further branches include the Old Town, Xīntiāndì and the SWFC and Superbrand Mall (both in Pǔdōng).

XĪNJIĀNG FĒNGWÈI RESTAURANT UIGHUR $

Map p300 (维吾尔餐厅; Wéiwú'ěr Cāntīng; ☎6468 9198; 280 Yishan Rd; 宜山路280号; dishes from ¥15; ⏲10am-2am; Ⓜ Yishan Rd/Xujiahui) Kashgar kitsch is the name of the game at this raucous upstairs Uighur restaurant with the bright brass grill out front. Feed an army on the whole roast lamb (¥1388), or just settle down to some *dàpánjī* (small/large ¥45/65) – a spicy stew of chicken, peppers and potatoes – as well as fresh yoghurt, *plov* (mutton pilaf; ¥15), lamb kebabs (four for ¥12), onion-laced tiger salad (¥15) and *naan* (flat bread), and wash it all down with some Xīnjiāng black beer. Things start hopping come evening when the music and dancing kick in.

KOTA'S KITCHEN JAPANESE $$

Map p300 (披头士烤串烧酒吧; Pītóushì Kǎochuànshāo Jiǔbā; ☎6481 2005; 2905 Xietu Rd; 斜土路2905号; ⏲6pm-1am; Ⓜ Shanghai Stadium or

SHÀNGHǍI'S CHRISTIANS

Christianity is the fastest-growing faith in China, and Shànghǎi alone has at least 140,000 Catholics, largely due to its history of Jesuit communities. St Ignatius Cathedral is the largest church in the city proper but Shěshān Basilica, in the suburbs, is even larger. Relations between the government and the Chinese Catholic Church are uneasy, as the Church refuses to disown the Pope as its leader. Nor does China's one-child policy sit well with the Catholic stand on abortion. For this reason, the Vatican maintains diplomatic relations with Taiwan, much to China's consternation.

To see or take part in prayer, Catholics can visit the **Christ the King Church** (君王天主堂; Jūnwáng Tiānzhǔtáng; Map p286; cnr Julu & Maoming Rds), St Ignatius Cathedral or the splendid Catholic Church in Qībǎo. Protestants can visit the lively **Community Church** (Map p290; 53 Hengshan Rd), near South Wulumuqi Rd, with Sunday school for children and a small nursery for toddlers. There is also a growing flock of modern, newly built churches throughout Shànghǎi, including in Pǔdōng. Other marvellous Catholic churches can be found in Zhūjiājiǎo (p185) and Hángzhōu (p170).

Shanghai Indoor Stadium) This entertaining, funky, very welcoming and bijou Beatles-themed Japanese yakitori restaurant/bar cooks up some enticing grilled meat skewers, perfectly accompanied by a heady range of homemade *shochu* spirits. The effect is an enticing blend of '60s musical nostalgia and Japanese culinary skill: book ahead.

ELEMENT FRESH SANDWICHES $

Map p300 (新元素; Xīnyuánsù; www.elementfresh.com; shop 163, 1st fl, Grand Gateway 66; 港汇广场1楼163室; sandwiches & salads ¥45-98, dinner from ¥128; ⏰7am-11pm Mon-Thu, to midnight Fri-Sun; ; Ⓜ Xujiahui) The Grand Gateway branch of the family-friendly health-conscious salads, sandwiches and smoothies restaurant (see also p144) can pep you up with a chilled gazpacho or get you firing on big breakfasts.

1001 NOODLES HOUSE NOODLES $

Map p300 (unit 502, 5th fl, Grand Gateway 66; 港汇广场5楼502室; noodles from ¥22; ⏰10am-10pm; Ⓜ Xujiahui) The *yúxiāng* shredded pork noodles (¥22) or pork chop noodles (¥26) arrive in an ample bowl at this spotless and sophisticated noodle house in Grand Gateway 66. With soft jazzy music, snappy black-and-white decor, thick blue-glass drinking glasses and a long table for solo diners, it's aimed at the dapper window-hopping set and the office crowd but prices are low. Entertainment comes from the occasionally misfiring English menu.

ENTERTAINMENT

KŪN OPERA HOUSE CHINESE OPERA

(上海昆剧团; Shànghǎi Kūnjù Tuán; ☎6437 7756; 295 South Zhongshan No 2 Rd, South Shànghǎi; 中山南二路295号; Ⓜ Damuqiao Rd) Shànghǎi's Kun opera troupe has moved to a new home south of the city. There are usually monthly performances, but you'll have to call ahead for the schedule. No English.

SHOPPING

Xújiāhuì is best known for its collection of department stores and malls that ring an insanely busy intersection. Don't try crossing the roads; use the underground metro tunnels to get to the stores.

XU GUANGQI

Xújiāhuì ('the Xu family gathering') is named after Xu Guangqi (1562–1633), a Chinese renaissance man. Xu was an early student of astronomy, agronomy and the calendar, and he established a meteorological observatory that relayed its information to the tower on the Bund. He was then converted to Catholicism by Matteo Ricci and baptised with the name Paul. Xu became a high official in the Ming court and bequeathed land to found a Jesuit community, which eventually led to the construction of St Ignatius Cathedral. Xu's tomb can still be visited in nearby Guangqi Park (Map p300), next to the modern-day Shànghǎi Meteorological Bureau, and stands as an inspirational symbol of Shànghǎi's openness to foreign ideas.

GRAND GATEWAY 66 MALL

Map p300 (港汇恒隆广场; Gǎnghuì Hénglóng Guǎngchǎng; ☎6407 0111; 1 Hongqiao Rd; 虹桥路1号; ⏰10am-10pm; Ⓜ Xujiahui) Fed by the metro station right below ground and possibly Shànghǎi's most popular mall, Grand Gateway 66 is a vast airy space with a decent range of Western brands like agnès b, Benetton, Diesel, DKNY, Jack Jones and Levi's, as well as a constellation of cosmetics and sports gear outlets. The complex also has an excellent range of restaurants on the 5th and 6th floors, an outside food strip, a cinema and seating for weary shopping legs.

METRO CITY ELECTRONICS

Map p300 (美罗城; Měiluó Chéng; ☎6426 8380; 1111 Zhaojiabang Rd; 肇嘉浜路1111号; ⏰10am-10pm; Ⓜ Xujiahui) Half of this mall is about technology, selling electronics, computers and software; the other half is all about fun, with a Sega arcade, a handy branch of Food Republic on the 6th floor and, on the 5th floor, **Kodak Cinema World** (柯达电影世界; kēdá diànyǐng shìjiè; ☎6426 8181; tickets ¥80-110) with four screens and some English language films. Next door is **Pacific Digital Plaza** (1117 Zhaojiabang Rd; ⏰10am-8pm), another electronics emporium which spreads across two buildings.

West Shànghǎi

CHÁNGNÍNG & GŬBĚI | HÓNGQIÁO AIRPORT AREA

Neighbourhood Top Five

1. Visit the narrow alleyways of old **Qībǎo** (p164) for a glimpse of traditional China.
2. Take in a modern-art exhibit at the often overlooked **Mínshēng Art Museum** (p165).
3. Rock out at **Yùyīntáng** (p167), one of Shànghǎi's premier music venues.
4. Spend a day at the park-like expanse of the **Shànghǎi Zoo** (p165).
5. Sample countless varieties of tea at **Tiānshān Tea City** (p167).

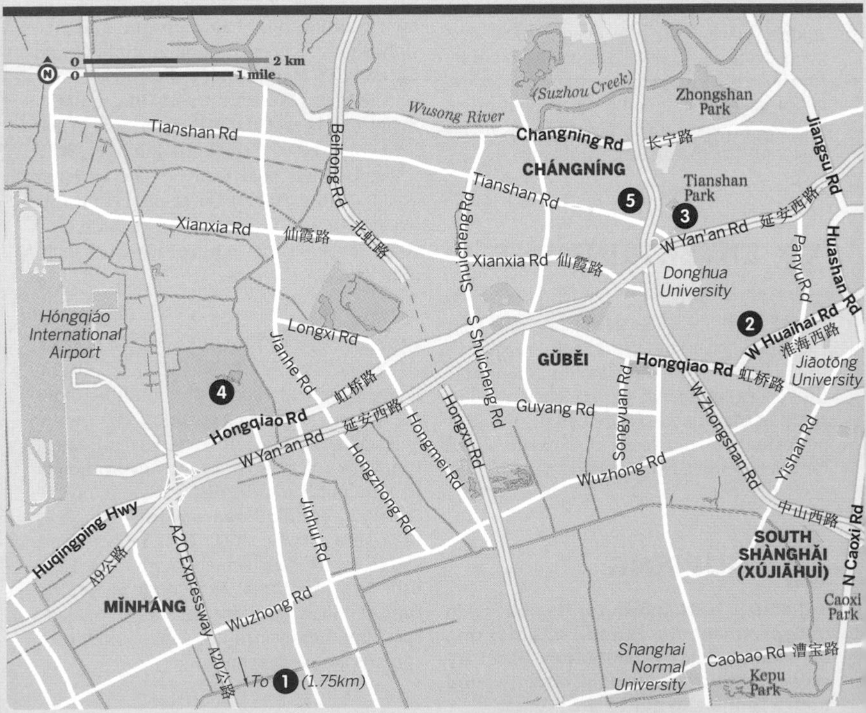

For more detail of this area, see Map p302

Explore: West Shànghǎi

West Shànghǎi (长宁、古北、虹桥) is much more of a residential and business area than a tourist destination, though that's not to say you should immediately scratch the region from your itinerary. Covering a huge swathe of land, it's divided into two main districts (Chángníng and Mǐnháng) and is the site of the Hóngqiáo airport and Hóngqiáo Railway Station (Shànghǎi's high-speed rail link), as well as the ancient town of Qībǎo.

Although Mǐnháng, which runs along the southern and western borders of the Chángníng district, is by far the larger of the two areas, this guidebook focuses primarily on Chángníng, which incorporates important neighbourhoods such as the middle-class and expat enclave of Gǔběi and the Hóngqiáo airport. West Shànghǎi was once countryside and a playground for the rich to retreat to at weekends, and some of the city's largest parks are found here. The old Sassoon country estate is now the Cypress Hotel, while the Shànghǎi Zoo (p165) sits on what was once the British Golf Club.

Parents with kids should investigate the entertainment options here: in addition to the zoo and other pockets of green space, you'll also find an aquarium and fun-filled water park.

Local Life

➡ **Snacks** From stinky tofu and squid on a stick to sweet black-sesame-paste dumplings, Qībǎo has you – and the rest of Shànghǎi – covered.

➡ **Green Space** Escape the relentless concrete sprawl in Zhōngshān Park (p165), the Song Qingling Mausoleum (p165) or the Shànghǎi Zoo (p165).

➡ **Modern Art** Stop by Red Town (p165) for private art galleries and one of the city's top art museums.

Getting There & Away

➡ **Metro** Lines 2 and 10 run east–west through the area (line 10 is more central), converging at Hóngqiáo airport (Terminal 2) and Hóngqiáo Railway Station. Lines 3 and 4 mirror each other, running north–south. Line 9 is to the south, passing through Qībǎo and terminating at Sōngjiāng.

Lonely Planet's Top Tip

Come weekends, the main sights here – Qībǎo and the Shànghǎi Zoo – are absolutely teeming with people, so unless you enjoy crowds, try to plan your visit for a weekday.

Best Places to Eat

➡ 1221 (p166)

➡ Lóngpáo Xièhuáng Tāngbāo (p167)

➡ Hongmei Road Entertainment Street (p167)

➡ Bellagio Café (p166)

➡ Carrefour (p166)

For reviews, see p166 ➡

Best Shopping

➡ Tiānshān Tea City (p167)

➡ Henry Antique Warehouse (p167)

➡ Hóngqiáo International Pearl City (p167)

For reviews, see p167 ➡

Best Sports & Activities

➡ Míngwǔ International Kungfu Club (p168)

➡ Dino Beach (p168)

➡ Mandarine City (p167)

For reviews, see p167 ➡

FENG WEI PHOTOGRAPHY / GETTY IMAGES ©

TOP SIGHTS QĪBǍO

When you tire of Shànghǎi's incessant quest for modernity, tiny Qībǎo (七宝) is only a hop, skip and metro ride away. An ancient settlement that prospered during the Ming and Qing dynasties, it's littered with traditional historic architecture, threaded by small, busy alleyways and cut by a picturesque canal. If you can somehow blot out the crowds, Qībǎo brings you the flavours of old China along with huge doses of entertainment.

DON'T MISS

- Cotton Textile Mill
- Bei Dajie souvenirs
- Nan Dajie snacks

PRACTICALITIES

- off Map p302
- 2 Minzhu Rd, Mǐnháng district; 闵行区民主路2号
- admission ¥45
- ⌚sights 8.30am-4.30pm
- Ⓜ Qibao (line 9)

Sights

There are nine official sights included in the through ticket, though you can also skip the ticket and just pay ¥5 to ¥10 per sight as you go. The best sights here include the **Cotton Textile Mill**, **Old Trades House** (a waxworks museum), **Shadow Puppet Museum** (performances 1pm to 3pm Wednesday and Sunday) and **Zhou's Miniature Carving Gallery**. Half-hour **boat rides** (per person ¥10; ⌚8.30am-5pm) slowly ferry passengers from Number One Bridge to Dōngtángtān (东塘滩) and back. Also worth ferreting out is the **Catholic Church** (天主教堂; 1866), adjacent to a convent off Qibao Nanjie, south of the canal.

Shopping & Snacking

Souvenir hunters and diners will be agog at the choice of shops and eateries stuffed along the narrow streets. Wander along Bei Dajie north of the canal for small shops selling fans, jewellery and wooden handicrafts from traditional two-storey dwellings. You'll eventually arrive at the main bridge, where you'll find excellent crab dumplings at Lóngpáo Xièhuáng Tāngbāo (p167). South of the canal, Nan Dajie is full of snacks and small eateries like No 26, which sells sweet *tāng yuán* (汤圆) dumplings, and No 9, which is a traditional teahouse with **storytelling performances** (admission plus pot of tea ¥2; ⌚12.30-2.30pm).

SIGHTS

Chángníng & Gŭbĕi

MÍNSHĒNG ART MUSEUM — MUSEUM

Map p302 (民生现代美术馆; Mínshēng Xiàndài Měishùguǎn; www.minshengart.org; 570 West Huaihai Rd; 淮海西路570号; admission ¥20, free after 6pm; ⏲10am-9pm Tue-Sun; Ⓜ Hongqiao Rd) Although sponsored mainly by the Mínshēng Bank, this edgy art space also counts the Tate, Centre Pompidou, MoMA and Guggenheim among its partners, so it should come as no surprise that the exhibits (about three per year) are generally excellent. Adding to its street cred is artistic director Zhou Tiehai, one of Shànghǎi's most well-known artists.

RED TOWN — GALLERY

Map p302 (红坊; Hóng Fāng; 570 West Huaihai Rd; 淮海西路570号; ⏲10am-5pm Tue-Sun; Ⓜ Hongqiao Rd) The No 10 Steel Factory has come to life again with an enormous display of large-scale sculpture pieces dotting the lawn, offices and studios of this creative cluster. While the majority of the premises is taken over by the so-so Shànghǎi Sculpture Space, there are a couple of other private galleries here, as well as Red Town's main highlight, the Mínshēng Art Museum.

SONG QINGLING MAUSOLEUM — MAUSOLEUM

Map p302 (宋庆龄陵园; Sōng Qìnglíng Língyuán; 21 Songyuan Rd; 宋园路21号; adult/student ¥20/10; ⏲9am-5pm, last entry 4.30pm; Ⓜ Songyuan Rd) Despite its hard-edged communist layout, this green park is excellent for a stroll and for escaping the relentless Gŭbĕi skyline. Song Qingling (see p94) herself is interred in a low-key tomb here, but she is memorialised in the **Song Qingling Exhibition Hall** (宋庆龄陈列馆; Sòng Qìnglíng Chénlièguǎn) straight ahead from the main entrance, which itself looks like a Chinese imperial tomb.

Among the displays of Song memorabilia (including her black *qípáo* or Chinese-style dress) is a telling photograph of Marxist Westerners reading from Mao's *Little Red Book* back in the days when it was politically fashionable. The **international cemetery** here also contains a host of foreign gravestones, including those of Jewish, Vietnamese and Western settlers of Shànghǎi.

ZHŌNGSHĀN PARK — PARK

Map p302 (中山公园; Zhōngshān Gōngyuán; 780 Changning Rd; 长宁路780号; ⏲6am-6pm; 👪; Ⓜ Zhongshan Park) Known as Jessfield Park to the British, this is a moderately interesting park located in the northeast, in the former 'Badlands' area of 1930s Shànghǎi. Kids will like **Fundazzle** (翻斗乐; Fāndǒulè; admission ¥50; ⏲9am-5pm; 👪), an adventure playground with slides, climbing nets and tunnels.

FREE LIU HAISU ART GALLERY — MUSEUM

Map p302 (刘海粟美术馆; Liú Hǎisù Měishùguǎn; 1660 Hongqiao Rd; 虹桥路1660号; ⏲9am-4pm Tue-Sun; Ⓜ Shuicheng Rd) This hulking gallery exhibits works of the eponymous painter, as well as visiting exhibitions.

CHÁNGFĒNG OCEAN WORLD — AQUARIUM

off Map p302 (长风海底世界; Chángfēng Hǎidǐ Shìjiè; www.oceanworld.com.cn; Gate No 4, Chángfēng Park, 451 Daduhe Rd; 大渡河路451号长风公园4号门; adult/child ¥160/110; ⏲9am-5pm; 👪; Ⓜ Loushanguan Rd, then taxi) Adults may find this subterranean aquarium dank, dingy and dear, but the little people will adore the clownfish and shark tunnel. There are performances every half-hour. Children under 1m get in for free.

Hóngqiáo Airport Area

QĪBĂO — VILLAGE

See p164.

SHÀNGHĂI ZOO — ZOO

Map p302 (上海动物园; Shànghǎi Dòngwùyuán; www.shanghaizoo.cn; 2381 Hongqiao Rd; 虹桥路2381号; adult/child ¥40/20; ⏲6.30am-6pm Apr-Sep, 6.30am-5pm Oct-Mar; 👪; Ⓜ Shanghai Zoo) As Chinese zoos go, this is just about the best there is, and it makes for a good day out for those who have kids in tow. There's a decent selection of beasts – from woolly twin-humped Bactrian camels to spindly legged giraffes, lots of different monkeys and giant pandas – but some of the enclosures they're housed in are less than ideal.

The Shànghǎi folk flock here to enjoy one of the city's most picturesque and well-tended acreages of green grass. Picnicgoers dive onto the lawns for a spot of sun, while electric **tour buggies** (trips ¥15) whirr along shaded paths every 10 to 15 minutes.

The whole menagerie is navigable on foot with a map from the information kiosk at the entrance or by following the signs.

Not far from the zoo, in the grounds of the Cypress Hotel, is the former Sassoon Mansion (see boxed text, p125), now building 1. You can take a peek at the exterior, but there's not much left to see.

EATING

Chángníng & Gǔběi

1221 SHANGHAINESE $$

Map p302 (Yī Èr Èr Yī; ☎6213 6585; 1221 West Yan'an Rd; 延安西路1221号; dishes ¥26-108; taxi) No one has a bad thing to say about this smart expat favourite and rightly so, as it has never let its standards dip over the years. Meat dishes start at ¥50 for the beef and dough strips *(yóutiáo)*, and the plentiful eel, shrimp and squid dishes are around twice that. Other tempting fare includes the roast duck and braised pork. The pan-fried sticky rice and sweet bean paste (from the dim-sum menu) makes a good dessert. It's also worth ordering the eight-fragrance tea just to watch it served spectacularly out of 60cm-long spouts. Reserve.

BELLAGIO CAFÉ CHINESE $$

Map p302 (鹿港小镇; Lùgǎng Xiǎozhèn; 101 South Shuicheng Rd; 水城南路101号; dishes ¥29-69; ⏲11.30am-2am; Ⓜ Shuicheng Rd) Branch of the popular Taiwanese restaurant (p98).

BÌ FĒNG TÁNG DIM SUM $

Map p302 (避风塘; ☎6208 6388; 37 South Shuicheng Rd; 水城南路37号; dim sum ¥17-22; Ⓜ Shuicheng Rd) Branch of the bustling dim-sum chain (p100).

CARREFOUR SUPERMARKET $

Map p302 (家乐福; Jiālèfú; www.carrefour.com.cn; 268 South Shuicheng Rd; 水城路268号; ⏲7.30am-10pm; Ⓜ Shuicheng Rd) This French supermarket chain is the epicentre of Gǔběi, and you can find everything from wine and cheese to cheap bikes and crockery. Also here is a popular food court, with a bakery and branches of Wagas (p130) and Food Republic (p69).

LOCAL KNOWLEDGE

A SHÀNGHǍI PHOTOGRAPHER'S FAVOURITE SPOTS

Based in Shànghǎi since 2005 and a regular press-contributor, internationally published French-Polish photographer Tim Franco (www.timfranco.com) captures the huge changes afoot in China through a mix of urban landscape and documentary portraits. He gives us the lowdown on where to go for Shànghǎi's best photographs.

Sūzhōu River (Sūzhōu Creek; p124) The entire waterway from Wàibáidù Bridge to M50 is fascinating, with a rich assortment of landscapes from old warehouses, to factories, art districts, art-deco buildings and modern high-rises towering over the river.

1933 and Hóngkǒu (p153) The 1933 area is intriguing: the old slaughterhouse with its amazing spaces and rooftops, but Hóngkǒu in general is dressed up with some handsome concession architecture.

Cool Docks and the Old Town (p78) The Cool Docks is a fab spot with a gaggle of restaurants, bars and views of south Pǔdōng; it's fascinating to see how this old area of warehouses and *shíkùmén* buildings has been reclaimed and repackaged. Across the way, access the Old Town through Dongjiadu Rd (gradually being demolished) for traditional Shànghǎi images.

Lùjiāzuǐ Walkway (p145) Quite simply the best way to see modern Shànghǎi, as you wander through a forest of skyscrapers. This is *the* place to come for high-rise Shànghǎi shots.

Tiánzǐfáng (p90) An excellent pocket of old red-brick *shíkùmén* houses, transformed into trendy restaurants and shops: a great place to hang out and take atmospheric photos.

Hóngqiáo Airport Area

LÓNGPÁO XIÈHUÁNG TĀNGBĀO DUMPLINGS $

(龙袍蟹黄汤包; 15 Bei Daijie, Qībǎo; 七宝古镇北大街15号; 8 dumplings ¥12-28; Ⓜ Qibao) This tiny spot at the foot of Qībǎo's main bridge has as many dumpling makers in the kitchen as it does seats. But pay no mind to the cramped premises, as these are by far and away the best *xiǎolóngbāo* on the block. Dumpling fillings include crab, shrimp and pork.

HONGMEI ROAD ENTERTAINMENT STREET FOOD STREET $$

Map p302 (老外街; Lǎowài Jiē; Hongmei Rd Entertainment Street, Lane 3338, Hongmei Rd; 虹梅路3338弄虹梅休闲步行街; Ⓜ Longxi Rd) This popular strip has a selection of Asian and Western restaurants and bars for those who don't want to head into town. In addition to tapas, Indian and Iranian options, there are also branches of Shànghǎi Brewery (p111), Big Bamboo (p132) and Simply Thai (p104) here.

CITY SHOP SUPERMARKET $

Map p302 (城市超市; Chéngshì Chāoshì; ☎400 811 1797; www.cityshop.com.cn; 3211 Hongmei Rd; 虹梅路3211号; ⏰8am-10pm; Ⓜ Longxi Rd) For all those imported goodies you just can't get anywhere else – at a price. They deliver too.

ENTERTAINMENT

TOP CHOICE YÙYĪNTÁNG LIVE MUSIC

Map p302 (育音堂; yytlive.com; 851 Kaixuan Rd; 凯旋路851号; ⏰9pm-midnight Tue-Sun; Ⓜ West Yan'an Rd) Small enough to feel intimate, but big enough for a sometimes pulsating atmosphere, Yùyīntáng has long been one of the top places in the city to see live music. Any Shànghǎi rock band worth its amps plays here, but you can also catch groups on tour from other cities in China and beyond. Rock is the staple diet, but anything goes, from hard punk to gypsy jazz.

SHÀNGHǍI FILM ART CENTRE CINEMA

Map p302 (上海影城; Shànghǎi Yǐngchéng; 160 Xinhua Rd; 新华路160号; taxi) This cinema is the main venue for the Shanghai International Film Festival.

SHOPPING

TIĀNSHĀN TEA CITY TEA

Map p302 (天山茶城; Tiānshān Cháchéng; 520 West Zhongshan Rd; 中山西路520号; ⏰9am-6pm; Ⓜ Zhongshan Park, West Yan'an Rd) Running low on loose-leaf oolong and aged *pu-erh* cakes? This three-storey sprawl is hands down the largest collection of tea shops in the city. You probably won't need to leave the ground level, although you can find a decent selection of teaware and porcelain on the 2nd floor, and teapots and jewellery on the 3rd. See p109 for tea-purchasing tips.

HENRY ANTIQUE WAREHOUSE ANTIQUES

Map p302 (亨利古典家具; Hēnglì Gǔdiǎn Jiājù; ☎6401 0831; www.h-antique.com; 3rd fl, Bldg 2, 359 Hongzhong Rd; 虹中路359号2号楼3层; ⏰9am-6pm) This enormous showroom, with more than 2000 high-quality antique pieces, both large and small, is a good first stop for antique hunters. It's down a lane off Hongzhong Rd in a not-so-obvious location; take a taxi and look for the signs. The Traditional Furniture Research Department of Tongji University is based here.

HÓNGQIÁO INTERNATIONAL PEARL CITY PEARLS

Map p302 (虹桥国际珍珠城; Hóngqiáo Guójì Zhēnzhū Chéng; 2nd fl, Hóngqiáo Craft Market, 3721 Hongmei Rd; 虹梅路3721号虹桥市场2楼; ⏰10am-9pm; Ⓜ Longxi Rd) Popular with local expats, the 2nd floor of this market has a smaller selection of freshwater and saltwater pearls than Amy Lin's Pearls (p134), but is worth a browse. There's a relaxed atmosphere and you can bargain here. On the 1st floor there are clothes and golf gear, on the 3rd floor carpets and luggage.

FOREIGN LANGUAGES BOOKSTORE BOOKS

Map p302 (外文书店; Wàiwén Shūdiàn; 71 South Shuicheng Rd; 水城南路71号; ⏰9.30am-9.30pm; Ⓜ Shuicheng Rd) Small branch of the FLB (p73) stocking foreign-language books and magazines.

SPORTS & ACTIVITIES

MANDARINE CITY SWIMMING

Map p302 (明都城游泳池; Míngdūchéng Yóuyǒng Chí; ☎6405 0404; 788 Hongxu Rd, entrance at cnr

MARTIAL ARTS

Early morning taichi (太极拳; *tàijí quán*) on the Bund is one of the classic images of Shànghǎi. If you're interested in learning either taichi or one of the harder martial-arts (武术; *wǔshù*) styles, there are a number of schools around town offering a range of classes for everyone from kids to adults. There are also aikido, karate and tae kwon do groups. Try these locations:

- Lóngwǔ Kung Fu Center (p119)
- Míngwǔ International Kungfu Club (p168)
- Oz Body Fit (p135)
- Wǔyì Chinese Kungfu Centre (p119)

Guyang & Shuicheng Rds, Hóngqiáo; 虹桥虹许路788号; 7.30am-9pm Jun-Oct; MShuicheng Rd) Popular outdoor pool.

MÍNGWǓ INTERNATIONAL KUNGFU CLUB MARTIAL ARTS

Map p302 (明武国际功夫馆; Míngwǔ Guójì Gōngfu Guǎn; 6465 9806; www.mingwukungfu.com; 3rd fl, Hongchun Bldg, 3213 Hongmei Rd; 虹梅路3213号红春大厦3楼;) This versatile gym offers bilingual classes in a wide range of martial arts, from taichi and *qìgōng* to *wǔshù* and karate, for both children and adults. There's also a shop onsite, selling clothing and weapons.

DINO BEACH SWIMMING

(热带风暴; Rèdài Fēngbào; 6478 3333; www.64783333.com; 78 Xinzhen Rd; 新镇路78号; admission Mon, Tue & Thu ¥120, Wed & Fri ¥120-150, Sat & Sun ¥120-200, child under 0.8m free; 1-11pm Mon, 10am-11pm Wed & Sun, 10am-midnight Tue, Thu, Fri & Sat Jun-Sep; ; MXinzhuang then bus 763 or 173) Way down south in Mǐnháng district, this popular summer place has a beach, a wave pool, water slides and tube hire to beat the Shànghǎi summer heat and keeps going late. But it's absolutely heaving at weekends. To get here, take metro line 1 to Xinzhuang, or catch a cab from Qībǎo.

SHÀNGHǍI YÍNQĪXĪNG INDOOR SKIING SKIING

(银七星市内滑雪场; Yínqīxīng Shìnèi Huáxuěchǎng; www.yinqixing.com; 1835 Qixing Rd, Xīnzhuāng; 莘庄七星路1835号; adults per hr Mon-Thu ¥98, Fri & Sat ¥118, child Mon-Thu ¥80, Fri & Sat ¥100; 9.30am-10.30pm Mon-Thu, to 1am Fri & Sat; ; MXinzhuang) The slope is aimed at first-timers so don't expect anything overly long or steep, but children will love it. The snowboard park is more challenging. To get here take the metro to Xinzhuang (line 1) and then hop in a taxi.

Day Trips from Shànghǎi

Hángzhōu (p170)

Dominated by its huge West Lake, former Southern Song–dynasty capital Hángzhōu is one of China's most picturesque towns.

Sūzhōu (p178)

China's best known water town, Sūzhōu is famed for its classical gardens, canals, bridges, silk and temples.

Tónglǐ (p184)

One of Jiāngsū's best-looking water towns, with a spicy museum dedicated to China's erotic culture.

Zhūjiājiǎo (p185)

Quaint canal-side town, dotted with temples and decorated with ancient bridges and pinched lanes.

Zhōuzhuāng (p186)

Impressive traditional architecture, charming back alleys and bridges make this small Jiāngsū town an eye-catching diversion.

Shěshān (p187)

Incredible views and an imposing hilltop Catholic church, accessible on the metro from Shànghǎi city centre.

Hángzhōu

Explore

One of China's most highly prized tourist drawcards, Hángzhōu's (杭州) dreamy West Lake panoramas and fabulously green and hilly environs have been eulogised by poets and applauded by emperors. Religiously cleaned by armies of street sweepers and litter collectors, its scenic vistas draw you into a classical Chinese watercolour of willow-lined banks, ancient pagodas, mist-covered hills and the occasional *shíkùmén* (stone-gate) building and old *lǐlòng* alleyway. Despite vast tourist numbers, West Lake is a delight to explore, either on foot or by bike.

The Best...

- **Sight** West Lake (p171)
- **Place to Eat** Green Tea Restaurant (p176)
- **Place to Drink** Maya Bar (p177)

Top Tip

Avail yourself of Hángzhōu's excellent public bicycle hire network (see p176) for getting around West Lake. For more info on the town, click on www.morehangzhou.com and www.gotohz.com.

CRUISING WEST LAKE

Cruise boats (游船; yóuchuán; incl entry to Three Pools adult/child ¥45/22.50; ⏲7am-4.45pm) shuttle frequently from four points (Hubin Park, Red Carp Pond, Zhōngshān Park and the Mausoleum of General Yue Fei) to the Mid-Lake Pavilion (Húxīn Tíng) and Xiǎoyíng Island (Xiǎoyíng Zhōu). Trips take 1½ hours and depart every 20 minutes. Alternatively, hire one of the six-person **boats** (小船; xiǎo chuán; per person/boat ¥80/160) rowed by boatmen. Look for them across from the Overseas Chinese Hotel or along the causeways. Paddle boats (¥15 per 30 minutes, ¥200 deposit) on the Bái Causeway are also available for hire.

Getting There & Away

Air Hángzhōu's airport is 30km from the city centre; a taxi will cost ¥100 to ¥130. Shuttle buses (¥20, one hour) run every 15 minutes between 5.30am and 9pm from the Civil Aviation Administration of China office (中国民航; Zhōngguó Mínháng; ☎8666 8666; 390 Tiyuchang Lu; ⏲7.30am-8pm), also stopping at the train station.

Bus Frequent buses (¥68, two hours, regularly from 7.10am to 7.20pm) run from Shànghǎi South long-distance bus station to Hángzhōu's Jiǔbǎo bus station, north bus station and south bus station. In 2012, Hángzhōu's Jiǔbǎo bus station was due to be linked to the centre of town by metro.

Buses (¥68) also run to Hángzhōu from the Shànghǎi long-distance bus station, north of Shànghǎi Railway Station. Hourly buses (¥85, two hours) also run to Hángzhōu from Hóngqiáo International Airport long-distance bus station and six buses daily (¥100) go from Pǔdōng International Airport.

Metro Hángzhōu's new metro line 1 was due to begin operating in 2012, running from the southeast of town, through the main train station, the east side of West Lake and on to the east train station, Jiǔbǎo bus station and the northeast of town.

Train The best way to go. Very regular G-class trains (2nd-/1st-class seat ¥78/124, one hour, 6.38am to 9.32pm) to Hángzhōu depart from Shànghǎi Hóngqiáo Railway Station in Shànghǎi's west. The last G-class train back to Shànghǎi Hóngqiáo Railway Station is at 8.48pm. There are also four G-class trains (2nd-/1st-class seat ¥93/148, 1½ hours) daily to Hángzhōu from Shànghǎi Railway Station.

Need to Know

- **Area Code** ☎0571
- **Location** 170km from Shànghǎi
- **Tourist Office** Hángzhōu Tourist Information Centre (杭州旅游咨询服务中心; Hángzhōu Lǚyóu Zīxún Fúwù Zhōngxīn) At the train station, near Léifēng Pagoda and other locations.

TOP SIGHTS WEST LAKE

West Lake (西湖) didn't appear until the 8th century, when the governor of Hángzhōu had the marshy expanse dredged. As time passed, the lake's splendour was slowly cultivated.

The poet Su Dongpo had a hand in the lake's development, constructing the **Sū Causeway** (苏堤; Sūdī) during his tenure as local governor in the 11th century, to accompany the **Bái Causeway** (白堤; Báidī). Lined by willow, plum and peach trees, today the traffic-free causeways with their half-moon bridges make for excellent outings, particularly by bike.

Connected to West Lake's northern shores by the Bái Causeway is **Gūshān Island** (孤山; Gū Shān), the lake's largest island. It's the site of the modest Zhèjiāng Provincial Museum, Zhōngshān Park (Zhōngshān Gōngyuán) and the intriguing Seal Engravers' Society.

Across from the entrance to the 3km-long Sū Causeway stands Yuè Fēi Temple. At the other end of the Sū Causeway is **Red Carp Pond** (Huāgǎng Guānyú), another collection of gardens on the southern shore, home to a few thousand red carp. East along the shore rises the splendidly eye-catching **Léifēng Pagoda**, across the road from the tranquil Jìngcí Zen Monastery.

DON'T MISS...

- Sū and Bái Causeways
- Léifēng Pagoda
- Gūshān Island

PRACTICALITIES

- Map p172
- tourist buses Y1, Y2 & Y3, K7

SIGHTS

XIǍOYÍNG ISLAND ISLAND

(小瀛洲; Xiǎoyíng Zhōu) Wooden cruise boats shuttle visitors from a number of points to the **Mid-Lake Pavilion** (湖心亭; Húxīn Tíng) and Xiǎoyíng Island, which has a fine central pavilion and 'nine-turn' causeway. From the island you can look over at the **Three Pools Mirroring the Moon** (Sāntán Yìnyuè), a string of three small towers in the water, each of which has five holes that release shafts of candlelight on the night of the Mooncake Festival in midautumn.

YUÈ FĒI TEMPLE TEMPLE

(岳庙; Yuè Miào; Beishan Lu; admission ¥25; 7am-6pm) This temple is bounded by a red-brick wall and dedicated to General Yue Fei (1103–41), whose tomb is here. Commander of the Song armies, Yue was executed after being deceived by Qin Hui, a treacherous court official. More than 20 years later, Song emperor Gao Zong exonerated Yue and had his corpse reburied at the present site.

XĪXIÁLÍNG HILL

The West Lake area is littered with fine walks – just follow the views. For a splendid trek into the forested hills above the lake, however, walk up a lane called Xīxiálíng, immediately west of the Yuè Fēi Temple. The road initially runs past the temple's west wall and enters the shade of towering trees, with stone steps leading you up. At **Zǐyún Cave** (紫云洞; Zǐyún Dòng) the road forks; take the right-hand fork in the direction of the Bàopǔ Taoist Temple, 1km further, and the Bǎochù Pagoda.

At the top of the steps, turn left and, passing the **Sunrise Terrace** (初阳台; Chūyáng Tái), again bear left. Down the steps, look out for the tiled roofs and yellow walls of the striking **Bàopǔ Taoist Temple** (抱朴道院; Bàopǔ Dàoyuàn; admission ¥5; 6am-5pm) below you to your right; head right along a path to reach it.

Come out of the temple's back entrance and turn left towards the **Bǎochù Pagoda** (保俶塔; Bǎochù Tǎ) and, after hitting a confluence of three paths, take the middle track. Squeeze through a gap between some huge boulders (some of which can be climbed for lake views) and the Bǎochù

Hángzhōu

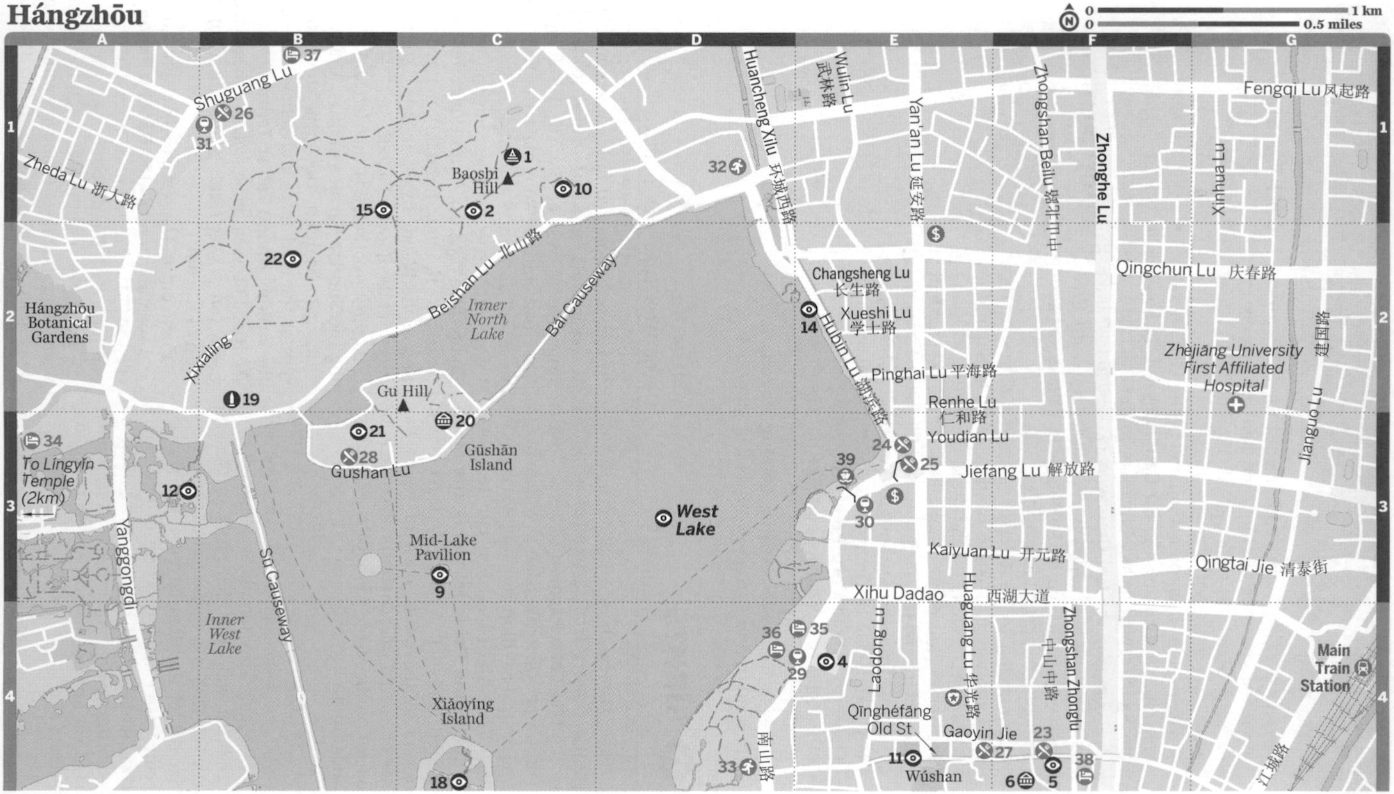
0 1 km
0 0.5 miles
A
B
C
D
E
F
G
1
2
3
4
37
Shuguang Lu
26
31
Zheda Lu 浙大路
Hángzhōu Botanical Gardens
34
To Língyǐn Temple (2km)
12
Yanggongdi
Inner West Lake
Sū Causeway
22
15
Xixialing
19
1
Baoshi Hill
2
10
Beishan Lu 北山路
Inner North Lake
Bái Causeway
Gu Hill
20
21
28
Gushan Lu
Gūshān Island
Mid-Lake Pavilion
9
Xiǎoyíng Island
18
32
Huancheng Xilu 环城西路
West Lake
14
Hubin Lu 湖滨路
39
30
24
25
36
35
29
4
33
南山路
Wulin Lu 武林路
Yan'an Lu 延安路
Changsheng Lu 长生路
Xueshi Lu 学士路
Pinghai Lu 平海路
Renhe Lu 仁和路
Youdian Lu
Jiefang Lu 解放路
Kaiyuan Lu 开元路
Xihu Dadao 西湖大道
Laodong Lu
Huaguang Lu 华光路
Qīnghéfāng Old St
Gaoyin Jie
11
Wúshan
27
23
6
5
38
Zhongshan Beilu 中山北路
Zhongshan Zhonglu 中山中路
Zhonghe Lu
Fengqi Lu 风起路
Xinhua Lu
Qingchun Lu 庆春路
Zhèjiāng University First Affiliated Hospital
建国路
Jianguo Lu
Qingtai Jie 清泰街
Main Train Station
江城路

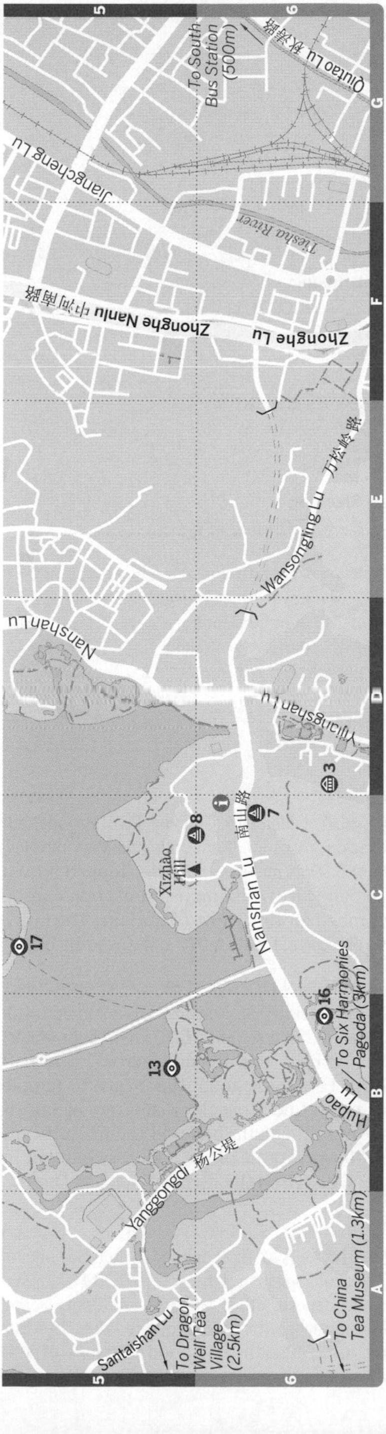

Pagoda rises ahead. Restored many times, the seven-storey brick pagoda was last rebuilt in 1933, although its spire tumbled off in the 1990s.

Continue on down and pass through a **páilou** (牌楼) – or decorative arch – erected during the Republic (with some of its characters scratched off) to a series of stone-carved **Ming-dynasty effigies**, all of which were vandalised in the tumultuous 1960s, save two effigies on the right. Residents in a couple of the old courtyard homes here sell cheap food to weary walkers. Bear right and head down to Beishan Lu, emerging from Baochutaqianshan Lu.

LÍNGYǏN TEMPLE BUDDHIST TEMPLE

(灵隐寺; Língyǐn Sì; Lingyin Lu; 灵隐路; grounds ¥35, grounds & temple ¥65; ⏲7am-5pm) This wonderful collection of buildings is Hángzhōu's principal Buddhist temple. Built in 328, due to war and other calamities it has been destroyed and restored no fewer than 16 times.

The main temple buildings are restorations of Qing-dynasty structures. The **Great Hall** envelops a magnificent 20m-high statue of Siddhartha Gautama (the historical Buddha), sculpted from 24 blocks of camphor wood in 1956. Behind the giant statue is a startling montage of 150 small figures, which charts the journey of 53 children on the road to buddhahood.

The large grounds house other temples too and are also home to **Fēilái Peak** (飞来峰; Fēilái Fēng; Peak Flying from Afar) – magically transported here from India, according to myth – and a stunning series of 470 **Buddhist carvings**, dating from the 10th to 14th centuries. To get a close-up view of the best carvings, including the famous 'laughing' Maitreya Buddha, follow the paths along the far (east) side of the stream.

There are several other temples near Língyǐn Temple that can be explored, including Yǒngfú Temple and Tāoguāng Temple.

Behind the Língyǐn Temple is **North Peak** (北高峰; Běi Gāofēng), which can be scaled via a cable car (*suǒdào;* up/down/return ¥30/20/40) or on foot. From the summit are sweeping views across the lake and city.

To get to Língyǐn Temple, take bus K7 from Beishan Lu, or bus Y1 or Y2 from Nanshan Lu.

Hángzhōu

Top Sights

West Lake ... D3

Sights

Art Gallery ... (see 4)
1 Bǎochù Pagoda ... C1
2 Bàopǔ Taoist Temple ... C1
3 China Silk Museum ... D6
4 Chinese Academy of Art ... E4
5 Huíchūn Táng ... F4
6 Húqìngyú Táng Chinese Medicine Museum ... F4
7 Jìngcí Zen Monastery ... C6
8 Léifēng Pagoda ... C6
9 Mid-Lake Pavilion ... C3
10 Ming-Dynasty Effigies ... C1
11 Qīnghéfáng Old Street ... E4
12 Qūyuàn Garden ... A3
13 Red Carp Pond ... B5
Seal Engravers' Society ... (see 28)
14 Small Boat Hire ... E2
15 Sunrise Terrace ... B1
16 Taiziwan Park ... B6
17 Three Pools Mirroring the Moon ... C5
18 Xiǎoyíng Island ... C4
19 Yuè Fēi Temple ... B2
20 Zhèjiāng Provincial Museum ... C3
21 Zhōngshān Park ... B3
22 Zǐyún Cave ... B2

Eating

23 Dōngyīshùn ... F4
24 Grandma's Kitchen ... E3
25 Green Tea Restaurant ... E3
Jīn Shā ... (see 34)
26 La Pedrera ... B1
27 Lǎo Hángzhōu Fēngwèi ... E4
28 Lóuwàilóu ... B3

Drinking

29 Eudora Station ... E4
30 JZ Club ... E3
31 Maya Bar ... B1

Sports & Activities

32 Bicycle Rental ... D1
33 Bicycle Rental ... D4

Sleeping

34 Four Seasons Hotel Hangzhou ... A3
35 In Lake Youth Hostel ... E4
36 Mingtown Youth Hostel ... D4
37 Tea Boutique Hotel ... B1
38 Wúshānyì International Youth Hostel ... F4

Transport

39 Boats to Xiǎoyíng Island ... E3

FREE **ZHÈJIĀNG PROVINCIAL MUSEUM** MUSEUM
(浙江省博物馆; Zhèjiāng Shěng Bówùguǎn; 25 Gushan Lu; 孤山路25号; audio guide ¥20; ⏲9am-5pm Tue-Sun, noon-5pm Mon) On Gūshān Island, the museum introduces visitors to the region's prehistory and history.

FREE **SEAL ENGRAVERS SOCIETY** CULTURAL BUILDING
(西泠印社; Xīlíng Yìnshè; ⏲9am-5.30pm) Dedicated to the ancient art of carving the name seals (or chops) that serve as personal signatures, this spot on Gūshān Island is housed in beautiful, shaded gardens on the slope of a hill.

QŪYUÀN GARDEN GARDEN
(曲院风荷; Qūyuàn Fēnghé) On the northwest shore of West Lake, this lovely collection of gardens spreads out over numerous islets and is renowned for its fragrant spring lotus blossoms.

LÉIFĒNG PAGODA PAGODA
(雷峰塔; Léifēng Tǎ, Thunder Peak Pagoda; admission ¥40; ⏲7.30am-9pm mid-Mar–mid-Nov, 8am-5.30pm mid-Nov–mid-Mar) Topped with a golden spire, this imposing pagoda can be climbed for fine views of the lake. The original pagoda, built in 977, collapsed in 1924.

JÌNGCÍ ZEN MONASTERY BUDDHIST TEMPLE
(净慈寺; Jìngcí Sì; Nanshan Lu; admission ¥10; ⏲6am-5.15pm summer, 6.30am-4.45pm winter) Set against the hillside across the road from Léifēng Pagoda, this peaceful temple is lovely. Check out the vast effigy of Sakyamuni in the main hall and the magnificent 1000-arm statue of the goddess Guanyin in the **Guanyin Hall** (观音殿; Guānyīn Diàn).

FREE **CHINA SILK MUSEUM** MUSEUM
(中国丝绸博物馆; Zhōngguó Sīchóu Bówùguǎn; 73-1 Yuhuangshan Lu; 玉皇山路73-1号; audio guide deposit ¥100; ⏲8.30am-4.30pm, closed Mon morning) Just south of the lake, the China Silk Museum has good displays of silk

samples, and explains the history and processes of silk production.

TÀIZIWĀN PARK — PARK

(太子湾公园; Tàiziwān Gōngyuán; Nanshan Lu) This exquisite and serene park just south of the Sū Causeway off West Lake offers quiet walks among lush woodland, ponds, lakes, rose gardens and lawns along a wooden walkway. Just take off and explore.

FREE CHINA TEA MUSEUM — MUSEUM

(中国茶叶博物馆; Zhōngguó Cháyè Bówùguǎn; Longjing Lu; ⌚9am-4.30pm Tue-Sun) Not far into the hills southwest of West Lake, you'll begin to see fields of tea bushes planted in undulating rows, the setting for the China Tea Museum – 3.7 hectares of land dedicated to the art, cultivation and tasting of tea. Further up are several tea-producing villages, all of which harvest China's most famous variety of green tea, *lóngjǐng chá* (龙井茶; dragon well tea). Tourist bus Y3 and K27 can get you to the museum.

CHINESE ACADEMY OF ART — GALLERY

(中国美术学院; Zhōngguó Měishùxuéyuàn) This academy on the eastern shore of West Lake houses an excellent **art gallery** (美术馆; měishùguǎn; ⌚9.30am-4.20pm Tue-Thu).

QĪNGHÉFÁNG OLD STREET — STREET

(清河坊历史文化街; Qīnghéfáng Lìshǐ Wénhuà Jiē) At the south end of Zhongshan Zhonglu is this fun, crowded and bustling pedestrian street, stuffed with all manner of shops, stalls and gift shops while snacking alleys branching off from it swarm with diners. It's an entertaining place to browse and there are several traditional medicine shops, including the atmospheric **Húqìngyú Táng Chinese Medicine Museum** (中药博物馆; Zhōngyào Bówùguǎn; 95 Dajing Xiang; admission ¥10; ⌚8.30am-5pm), which is an actual dispensary and clinic. **Huíchūn Táng** (回春堂; 117 Hefang Jie) is another delightful old medicine shop with a swallow's nest inside, high above the entrance.

LÓNGJǏNG VILLAGE — VILLAGE

(龙井村; Lóngjǐng Cūn) Lóngjǐng Village is nestled away in hills southwest of West Lake. Everyone will want to sell you tea, but if you do buy some, do it for the novelty, because prices aren't cheap. Buses 27 and Y3 run to the village from Beishan Lu and Nanshan Lu respectively.

SIX HARMONIES PAGODA — PAGODA

(六和塔; Liùhé Tǎ; 16 Zhijiang Lu; 之江路16号; grounds ¥20, grounds & pagoda ¥30; ⌚6am-6.30pm) Three kilometres southwest of the lake stands an enormous rail-and-road bridge, which spans Qiántáng River. Close by is the 60m-high octagonal Six Harmonies Pagoda, first built in 960 and named after the six codes of Buddhism. The pagoda also served as a lighthouse, and was supposed to have magical powers to halt the tidal bore which thunders up Qiántáng River twice a month (see the boxed text). You can climb the pagoda, while behind it stretches a charming walk, through terraces dotted with sculptures, bells,

HÁNGZHŌU'S INCREDIBLE GIANT WAVE

An often spectacular natural phenomenon occurs every month on Hángzhōu's Qiántáng River, when the highest tides of the lunar cycle send a wall of water – sometimes almost 9m high – thundering up the narrow mouth of the river from Hángzhōu Bay at up to 40km per hour.

Sometimes sweeping astonished sightseers away, this awesome tidal bore (钱塘江潮; *qiántáng jiāngcháo*) is the world's largest and can be viewed from the riverbank in Hángzhōu, but one of the best places to witness it is on the north side of the river at **Yánguān** (盐官), a delightful ancient town about 38km northeast of Hángzhōu. The most popular viewing time is during Mid-Autumn Festival, which falls in September or October, on the 18th day of the eighth month of the lunar calendar, when the International Qiántáng River Tide Observing Festival takes place. However, you can see it throughout the year when the highest tide occurs at the beginning and middle of each lunar month. The Hángzhōu Tourist Information Centre can give you upcoming tide times.

To reach Yánguān, take a bus (¥25, one hour) from Hángzhōu's Jiǔbǎo bus station to Hǎiníng and change to bus 106 (¥8) to Yánguān; alternatively, take a bus from Hángzhōu train station (45 minutes) and change to bus 109 to Yánguān.

HÁNGZHŌU BY BIKE

The best way to hire a bike is to use the public **bike hire scheme** (☎8533 1122; www.hzzxc.com.cn, in Chinese). Stations are dotted in large numbers around the city. You can apply at one of the **booths** (⏲6.30am-9pm Apr-Oct, 6am-9pm Nov-Mar) at certain bike stations (marked on the map) where you will need ¥300 (¥200 for the deposit and ¥100 as credit) and your passport as ID. You will then get a swipecard to hop aboard one of the bright red bikes which you can return to any other station. The first hour on each bike is free, so if you switch bikes within the hour, the rides are free. The second hour on the same bike is ¥1, the third is ¥2 and after that it's ¥3 per hour. Your deposit and unused credit are refunded to you when you return your swipecard. Note you cannot return bikes outside booth operating hours as the swipe units deactivate (you will be charged a whole night's rental). Youth hostels also rent out bikes, but these are more expensive.

shrines and inscriptions. To get to the pagoda, take bus 504 or K4 from Nanshan Lu.

EATING & DRINKING

The top restaurant strip in town is Gaoyin Jie (高银美食街), parallel to and immediately north of Qīnghéfáng Old St. Shuguang Lu (曙光路), northwest of West Lake, is the main place for beers. There are also some bars near the Mingtown Youth Hostel. For a good introduction to what's on and where, grab a copy of *More – Hangzhou Entertainment Guide* (www.morehangzhou.com), available at some bars and hotels.

TOP CHOICE **GREEN TEA RESTAURANT** HÁNGZHŌU $
(绿茶; Lǜchá; 250 Jiefang Lu; 解放路250号; meals ¥70) Doing a brisk trade, this excellent Hángzhōu restaurant has superb food and should be one of your first stops. With a bare brick finish and decorated with rattan utensils and colourful flower-patterned cushions, the dining style is casual. The long paper menu (tick what you want) includes clam soup (¥19) – a plate of mussels that is a salty and moreish dish, spiced up with chilli. The eggplant claypot (¥20) is simply gorgeous while the Green Tea roast chicken (half/whole ¥25/48) is tasty. Avoid the coffee unless you like super-sweet creamer added automatically. Further four branches in town.

GRANDMA'S KITCHEN HÁNGZHŌU $
(外婆家; Wàipójiā; 3 Hubin Lu; 湖滨路3号; mains ¥6-55; ⏲10.30am-2pm & 4-9pm) With all the Hángzhōu classics and more at unbeatable prices, this superb restaurant chain is a huge favourite with the locals. The braised pork (红烧东坡肉; *hóngshāo dōngpō ròu*) is divine.

LA PEDRERA SPANISH $$
(巴特洛西班牙餐厅; Bātèluò Xībānyá Cāntīng; ☎8886 6089; 4 Baishaquan, Shuguang Lu; 曙光路白沙泉4号; tapas from ¥30, meals ¥200; ⏲11am-11pm) This fine two-floor Spanish restaurant just off Shuguang Lu bar street has tapas diners in a whirl, seafood paella aficionados applauding and Spanish wine fans gratified. Prices may take a sizeable bite from your wallet, but the convivial atmosphere and assured menu prove popular and enjoyable.

JĪN SHĀ CHINESE $$$
(金沙厅; Jīn Shā Tīng; ☎8829 8888; www.fourseasons.com/hangzhou; Four Seasons Hotel Hángzhōu, 5 Lingyin Lu; 灵隐路5号; meals ¥300; ⏲lunch & dinner) For fine waterside Hángzhōu, Shànghǎi and Cantonese cuisine in a particularly elegant and well-presented ambience, you can't go far wrong with this signature restaurant at the Four Seasons Hángzhōu Hotel; there's al fresco seating on the terrace outside and a fine selection of teas and wines.

DŌNGYĪSHÙN MUSLIM $
(Dōngyīshùn; 101 Gaoyin Jie; 高银街101号; mains ¥12-50; ⏲11am-9pm) Specialising in food from China's Muslim Hui minority, this is much more than the average Xīnjiāng restaurant you find all over China. It has lamb kebabs (羊肉串; *yáng ròu chuàn;* ¥2), lamb on naan bread (囊包肉; *nángbāo ròu;* ¥50) and fried noodle pieces (炒片; *chǎo piàn;* ¥12) like all the others, but you'll also find hummus dishes, doner kebabs and even felafel (¥20).

LǍO HÁNGZHŌU FĒNGWÈI HÁNGZHŌU $

(老杭州风味; 141 Gaoyin Jie; 高银街141号; mains from ¥20; ⏲11.30am-9pm) This overlit restaurant is one of several along Gaoyin Jie selling traditional Hángzhōu cuisine. Try the flavoursome diced chicken and eggplant pot (*lǎo hángzhōu jīli qiézi bāo;* ¥28), the salty and fatty Hángzhōu style lamb chops (*lǎo hángzhōu kǎoyángpái;* ¥68) or the *dōngpō* pork (*dōngpō ròu;* ¥15 per chunk).

LÓUWÀILÓU HÁNGZHŌU $$

(30 Gushan Lu; 孤山路30号; mains ¥20-200; ⏲10.30am-3.30pm & 4.30-8.45pm) With a choice location on Bai Causeway, and fine lakeside views, the city's most famous restaurant has been going since 1848. It serves up expensive but delicious Hángzhōu favourites such as Lóngjǐng shrimp (龙井虾仁; *Lóngjǐng xiārén;* ¥198) and braised pork (东坡肉; *dōngpō ròu;* ¥14 per chunk), as well as reasonably priced standard Chinese dishes (¥20 to ¥50).

MAYA BAR BAR

(玛雅酒吧; Mǎyǎ Jiǔbā; 94 Baishaquan, Shuguang Lu; 曙光路白沙泉94号; ⏲noon-2am) Jim Morrison, Kurt Cobain, Mick Jagger, Bob Dylan and the Beatles watch on approvingly from the walls of this darkly lit, solid and rock-steady bar. Just as importantly, the drinks are seriously cheap; happy hour sees draught beer costing a risible ¥10 (¥20 at other times). The staff may be morose, but so what?

SLEEPING IN HÁNGZHŌU

If you don't stay in a hotel at least within easy reach of the lake, you'll be kicking yourself afterwards. If calling ahead to book, note that the area code for Hángzhōu is ☎0571.

➡ **Four Seasons Hotel Hángzhōu** (杭州西子湖四季酒店; Hángzhōu Xīzǐ Hú Sìjì Jiǔdiàn; ☎8829 8888; www.fourseasons.com/hangzhou; 5 Lingyin Lu; 灵隐路5号; d ¥3048-3738, ste from ¥6693;) This fabulous 78-room, two-swimming-pool hotel enjoys a seductive position in lush grounds next to West Lake, its low-storey buildings and villas echoing traditional China. The spacious ground-floor deluxe premier rooms come with garden; rooms have lovely bathrooms, walk-in wardrobe and hugely inviting beds.

➡ **Tea Boutique Hotel** (杭州天伦精品酒店; Hángzhōu Tiānlún Jīngpǐn Jiǔdiàn; www.teaboutiquehotel.com; ☎8799 9888; 124 Shuguang Lu; 曙光路124号; d ¥988-1280, ste ¥2688;) Beyond the sinuously shaped reception area, a Japanese minimalist mood holds sway among celadon teacups, muted colours and – interestingly for China – a Bible in each room. Double-glazed windows roadside keep the traffic noise low. Service is excellent and healthy discounts run between 20% and 40%.

➡ **Mingtown Youth Hostel** (明堂杭州国际青年旅社; Míngtáng Hángzhōu Guójì Qīngnián Lǚshè; ☎8791 8948; 101-11 Nanshan Lu; 南山路101-11号; dm/s/d ¥60/185/265;) With its pleasant lakeside location, this friendly hostel is often booked out, so reserve well ahead. It has a relaxing cafe/bar, offers ticket booking, internet access, and rents bikes and camping gear.

➡ **In Lake Youth Hostel** (柳湖小筑青年旅社; Liǔhú Xiǎozhú Qīngnián Lǚshè; ☎8682 6700; 5 Luyang Lu; 绿杨路5号; 6-bed dm with shower ¥70, tw & d ¥368-448;) A few steps from picturesque West Lake off Nanshan Lu, this friendly and amenable hostel radiates a peaceful ambience, with a flower-bedecked courtyard, clean dorms (all with shower), smart doubles and twins, a roof terrace for barbecues, downstairs cafe/bar and welcoming staff.

➡ **Wúshānyì International Youth Hostel** (吴山驿国际青年旅社; Wúshānyì Guójì Qīngnián Lǚshè; 22 Zhongshan Zhonglu; 中山中路22号; d/tr ¥248/320;) With a healthy mix of Chinese and Western travellers, this quiet, unhurried and comfy hostel has clean and well-looked-after rooms and excellent, helpful staff plus a charmingly tucked-away location off Qīnghéfáng Old Street. If it's full, try the **Hofang International Youth Hostel** (荷方国际青年旅社; Héfāng Guójì Qīngnián Lǚshè; ☎8706 3299; 67 Dajing Xiang) round the corner.

EUDORA STATION BAR

(亿多瑞站; Yìduōruìzhàn; 101-107 Nanshan Lu; 南山路101-107号; ⏲9am-2am) A fab location by West Lake, roof terrace aloft, strong menu and a sure-fire atmosphere conspire to make this welcoming watering hole a great choice. There's sports TV, live music, a ground-floor terrace, a good range of beers, and barbecues fire up on the roof terrace in the warmer months. It's right by the Mingtown Youth Hostel.

JZ CLUB CLUB

(黄楼; Huáng Lóu; ☎8702 8298; 6 Liuying Lu, by 266 Nanshan Lu; ⏲6.30pm-2.30am) The folk that brought you JZ Club in Shànghǎi have the live jazz scene sewn up in Hángzhōu with this neat and cultured three-floor venue near West Lake. There's live jazz nightly with international names on the billing.

Sūzhōu

Explore

Famed for its gardens, canals and silk production, Sūzhōu (苏州) is a pleasant, if way overhyped, Jiāngsū canal town. If you don't go expecting an impeccable portrait of traditional China but a melange of modern town planning embedded with picturesque chunks of history, Sūzhōu is a rewarding diversion from Shànghǎi, especially for its traditional walled gardens, excellent museums, riveting temples and charming canal-side streets.

The Best...

- **Sight** Sūzhōu Museum (p179)
- **Place to Eat** Zhūhóngxìng (p183)
- **Place to Drink** Bookworm (p183)

Top Tip

For tips on visiting Sūzhōu, visit www.livingsu.com, www.moresuzhou.com, www.classicsuzhou.com or www.visitsz.com.

Getting There & Away

Bicycle You can rent bikes at hostels or down the alley beside 2061 Renmin Lu (per day ¥20, deposit ¥200; ⏲6.30am-7pm).

Bus Regular buses (¥38, 90 minutes, 6.27am to 7.30pm) to Sūzhōu's south and north long-distance bus stations run from the Shànghǎi south bus station. Regular services (¥38, 7am to 7.40pm) also run to Sūzhōu from the Shànghǎi long-distance bus station north of Shànghǎi Railway Station, Shànghǎi Hóngqiáo Airport long-distance bus station (¥53, 10am to 9pm) and Pǔdōng International Airport (¥84, three hours). Most buses arrive and depart from Sūzhōu's hectic north long-distance bus station, east of the train station, although the south bus station is far better organised and easier to use.

Buses (¥75) also travel from Hángzhōu's north bus station to Sūzhōu's north long-distance bus station, and regular bus services run from Sūzhōu to Tónglǐ (¥9, 50 minutes, every 30 minutes) from both the south and north long-distance bus stations. Take a bus (¥31) from Sūzhōu's north long-distance bus station to Qīngpǔ and change for a bus to Zhūjiājiǎo.

Metro Sūzhōu's spiffing new metro line 1 (tickets ¥2 to ¥4, first/last train 6.45am/10.30pm) runs east–west along Ganjiang Lu. Three more lines are under construction.

Train The best way to reach town, high-speed G-class trains (2nd/1st class ¥40/60, 30 minutes, frequent services) run to Sūzhōu from Shànghǎi Railway Station. G-class trains (2nd/1st class ¥40/60, 30 minutes, frequent) also run to Sūzhōu from Shànghǎi Hóngqiáo Railway Station. The last G-class train back to Shànghǎi is at 10.21pm.

Regular high-speed D-class trains (2nd/1st class ¥26/31, 34 minutes, 6.33am to 8.09pm) run to Sūzhōu from Shànghǎi Hóngqiáo Railway Station; the last D-class train back to Shànghǎi leaves at 10.31pm.

Need to Know

- **Area Code** ☎0512
- **Location** 85km from Shànghǎi
- **Tourist Office** Sūzhōu Tourism Information Centre (苏州旅游咨询中心; Sūzhōu Lǚyóu Zīxún Zhōngxīn; ☎6530 5887; 345 Shiquan Jie) Several branches in town including the bus stations.

SIGHTS

The delightful gardens *(yuánlín)* of Sūzhōu were generally small, private compounds attached to family residences and, in principle at least, they were designed to help achieve the intellectual ideal of balancing Confucian social duties (in the city) with Taoism's worldly retreat (in nature).

Unless stated otherwise, the gardens listed here are open from 7.30am to 5.30pm during high season (March to mid-November) but close at 5pm in winter. Peak prices are from mid-April to October.

FREE SŪZHŌU MUSEUM MUSEUM

(苏州博物馆; Sūzhōu Bówùguǎn; 204 Dongbei Jie; 东北街204号; audio guide ¥30; ⏲9am-5pm, last entry 4pm) The IM Pei–designed Sūzhōu Museum – which stands beside its former building, once the residence of Taiping leader Li Xiucheng – houses jade, ceramics, textiles and other displays in an eye-catching, modern interpretation of a Sūzhōu garden; there's a no thongs (flip-flops) policy.

HUMBLE ADMINISTRATOR'S GARDEN GARDEN

(拙政园; Zhuōzhèng Yuán; 178 Dongbei Jie; 东北街178号; low/high season ¥50/70, audio guide free) The luxuriant 5-hectare Humble Administrator's Garden, dating to 1509, is large enough to be a park. There's also a bonsai *(pénjǐng)* garden, a teahouse and a small museum that explains Chinese gardening concepts.

SŪZHŌU SILK MUSEUM MUSEUM

(苏州丝绸博物馆; Sūzhōu Sīchóu Bówùguǎn; 2001 Renmin Lu; 人民路2001号; admission ¥15; ⏲9am-5pm) The highly recommended Sūzhōu Silk Museum houses live silk worms as well as fascinating exhibitions providing a thorough history of Sūzhōu's silk industry over the past 4000 years. Watch silk workers slaving over looms, walk through an exhibition of silk fashion over the dynasties and amble among mulberry shrubs (the silkworms' favourite meal) sprouting in the garden. There are some outstanding pieces of silk for sale in the shop at the exit.

NORTH TEMPLE PAGODA PAGODA

(北寺塔; Běisì Tǎ; 1918 Renmin Lu; 人民路1918号; admission ¥25; ⏲summer 7.45am-6pm, winter to 5.30pm) The North Temple Pagoda is the tallest pagoda south of the Yangzi River. At nine storeys high, it dominates the northern end of Renmin Lu and can be climbed for city views.

LIONS' GROVE GARDEN

(狮子林; Shīzi Lín; 23 Yuanlin Lu; 园林路23号; low/high season ¥20/30) Around the corner from the Humble Administrator's Garden is the 1-hectare Lions' Grove, constructed in 1350 by the monk Tian Ru and famed for its strangely shaped rocks, meant to resemble lions, protectors of the Buddhist faith.

COUPLE'S GARDEN GARDEN

(耦园; Ǒu Yuán; Cang Jie; 仓街; low/high season ¥15/20; ⏲8am-4.30pm) The less-visited Couple's Garden is in a delightful part of town and has a lovely pond and courtyards, with some good-looking traditional architecture, canals and bridges on nearby Pingjiang Lu.

FREE KŪNQǓ OPERA MUSEUM MUSEUM

(戏曲博物馆; Xìqǔ Bówùguǎn; 14 Zhongzhangjia Xiang; 中张家巷14号; ⏲8.30am-4.30pm) In among the delightful cobblestone, canal-side alleyways in the east of town is the pretty Kūnqǔ Opera Museum, housing a beautiful old stage, musical instruments, costumes and photos. It also stages performances of *kūnqǔ* at 2pm on Sundays.

PÍNGTÁN MUSEUM MUSEUM

(评弹博物馆; Píngtán Bówùguǎn; 3 Zhongzhangjia Xiang; 中张家巷3号; admission ¥4) Right before the Kūnqǔ Opera Museum is the Píngtán Museum where performances of *píngtan* (a Sūzhōu-dialect singing and story-telling art form) are held daily from 1.30pm to 3.30pm.

PÍNGJIĀNG LÙ STREET

(平江路) This lovely stretch of canal-side road (Píngjiāng was the old name for Sūzhōu) on the eastern side of town is brimful of historic charm, with attractive whitewashed architecture, bridges, cafes, teahouses and hostels. The surrounding streets are excellent for slow exploration.

TEMPLE OF MYSTERY TAOIST TEMPLE

(玄妙观; Xuánmiào Guān; Guanqian Jie; 观前街; admission ¥10; ⏲7.30am-5.15pm) At the heart of what was once Sūzhōu Bazaar, the Taoist Temple of Mystery was originally laid out between AD 275 and 279, with many later additions. Its enormous **Three Purities Hall** (三清殿; Sānqīng Diàn), supported by 60 pillars and capped by a double roof with upturned eaves, dates from 1181, and is the

Sūzhōu

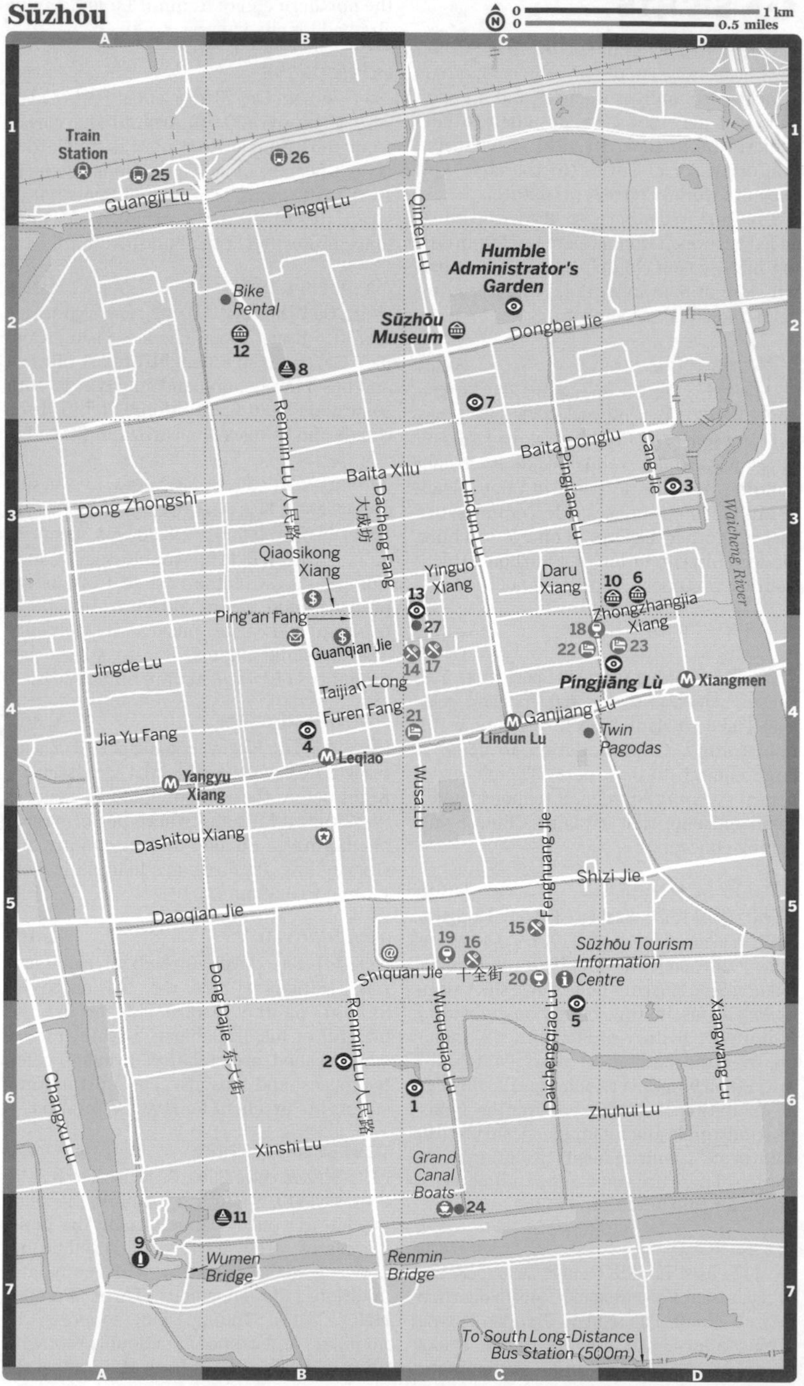
0 1 km
0 0.5 miles
Train Station
25
26
Guangji Lu
Pingqi Lu
Qimen Lu
Humble Administrator's Garden
Bike Rental
12
Sūzhōu Museum
Dongbei Jie
8
Renmin Lu 人民路
7
Baita Donglu
Baita Xilu
Dacheng Fang 大成坊
Lindun Lu
Pingjiang Lu
Cang Jie
3
Dong Zhongshi
Waicheng River
Qiaosikong Xiang
Yinguo Xiang
Daru Xiang
10
6
13
Zhongzhangjia Xiang
Ping'an Fang
27
18
Guanqian Jie
22
23
14
17
Jingde Lu
Taijian Long
Pingjiāng Lù
Xiangmen
Furen Fang
21
Ganjiang Lu
Jia Yu Fang
4
Lindun Lu
Twin Pagodas
Leqiao
Yangyu Xiang
Wusa Lu
Dashitou Xiang
Fenghuang Jie
Shizi Jie
Daoqian Jie
15
19
16
Sūzhōu Tourism Information Centre
Shiquan Jie 十全街
20
Dong Dajie 东大街
Renmin Lu 人民路
Wuqueqiao Lu
Daichengqiao Lu
5
Xiangwang Lu
2
1
Changxu Lu
Zhuhui Lu
Xinshi Lu
Grand Canal Boats
24
11
9
Wumen Bridge
Renmin Bridge
To South Long-Distance Bus Station (500m)
A
B
C
D
1
2
3
4
5
6
7

Sūzhōu

Top Sights

	Humble Administrator's Garden	C2
	Píngjiāng Lù	D4
	Sūzhōu Museum	C2

Sights

1	Blue Wave Pavilion	C6
2	Confucius Temple	B6
3	Couple's Garden	D3
4	Garden of Harmony	B4
5	Garden of the Master of the Nets	C6
6	Kūnqǔ Opera Museum	D3
7	Lion's Grove	C2
8	North Temple Pagoda	B2
9	Pán Gate	A7
10	Píngtán Museum	D3
11	Ruìguāng Pagoda	B7
12	Sūzhōu Silk Museum	B2
13	Temple of Mystery	C3

Eating

14	Déyuèlóu	C4
15	Xīshèngyuán	C5
16	Yàkèxī	C5
17	Zhūhóngxìng	C4

Drinking

18	Bī'àn	C4
19	Bookworm	C5
20	Jane's Pub Bar	C5

Entertainment

	Garden of the Master of the Nets	(see 5)
	Kūnqǔ Opera Museum	(see 6)
	Pīingtán Museum	(see 10)

Sleeping

21	Marco Polo Sūzhōu	C4
22	Píngjiāng Lodge	C4
23	Sūzhōu Mingtown Youth Hostel	D4

Transport

24	Grand Canal Boat Ticket Office	C7
25	Local Buses	A1
26	North Long-Distance Bus Station	B1
27	Train Ticket Office (Guanqian Jie)	C4

only surviving example of Song-era architecture in Sūzhōu.

GARDEN OF THE MASTER OF THE NETS GARDEN
(网师园; Wǎngshī Yuán; low/high season ¥20/30) Accessed via a cute cobbled lane that links Shiquan Jie (十全街) and Daichengqiao Lu (带城桥路), the smallest garden of all, the Garden of the Master of the Nets is also widely considered the best, with a striking use of space. Originally laid out in the 12th century, it was later restored in the 18th century as part of the home of a retired official turned fisherman (hence the name). Architecturally heavy – with residence halls, viewing pavilions and walkways – the garden relies on select landscape arrangements set against whitewashed walls, which are like the blank space of a Chinese ink painting. From March to November, music performances (tickets ¥100) are held here nightly from 7.30pm to 9.30pm for tourist groups.

BLUE WAVE PAVILION GARDEN
(沧浪亭; Cānglàng Tíng; Renmin Lu; 人民路; low/high season ¥15/20) A bit on the wild side, with winding creeks and corridors of bamboo, Blue Wave Pavilion is one of the oldest gardens in Sūzhōu, originally dating from the 11th century. Lacking a northern wall, the 1-hectare garden creates an illusion of space by borrowing scenes from the outside, incorporating the adjacent canal and distant hills.

FREE **CONFUCIUS TEMPLE** CONFUCIAN TEMPLE
(文庙; Wén Miào; Renmin Lu; 人民路; 8.30am-4.30pm) At the southern end of Renmin Lu is the old Confucius Temple; the main hall is being restored but there are some intriguing historical stelae on view.

PÁN GATE GATE
(盘门; Pán Mén; 1 Dong Dajie; 东大街1号; admission ¥25, incl Ruìguāng Pagoda & boat trip ¥40; 7.30am-6pm) By the southwest corner of the outer moat (but entered from Dong Dajie), and part of one of Sūzhōu's few remaining stretches of city wall (which you can walk along), Pán Gate is thought to be China's last remaining land-and-water-gate, dating from 1355.

Inside the same grounds, **Ruìguāng Pagoda** (Ruìguāng Tǎ; admission ¥6) dates from the 3rd century and can be climbed. Further north, **Gold Gate** (Jīn Mén), just inside

SLEEPING IN SŪZHŌU

➡ **Marco Polo Sūzhōu** (苏州玄妙马可波罗大酒店;Sūzhōu Xuánmiào Mǎkěbōluó Dàjiǔdiàn; ☎6801 9888; www.marcopolohotels.com; 818 Ganjiang Donglu; 干将东路818号; d from ¥1688; ❄@📶) For a central location, you can't go wrong with this well-equipped and efficient business hotel right at the heart of town. Hefty discounts of over 50% are frequently in force.

➡ **Píngjiāng Lodge** (平江客栈; Píngjiāng Kèzhàn; ☎6523 3888; www.pingjianglodge.com; 33 Niujia Xiang; 钮家巷33号; r from ¥1988; ❄@) A 400-year-old former residence with quiet courtyards, well-kept gardens and 51 delightful rooms, all with traditional Chinese furniture. Service can be reluctant, though. Discounts of 50% are common.

➡ **Sūzhōu Mingtown Youth Hostel** (苏州明堂青年旅舍; Sūzhōu Míngtáng Qīngnián Lǚshè; ☎6581 6869; mingtown@foxmail.com; 28 Pingjiang Lu; 平江路28号; dm ¥50, tw ¥160-180; ❄@) On the charming canal-side lane of Pingjiang Lu, this decent but busy hostel has good rooms (although some are slightly musty), housed in two equally attractive buildings with a smart cafe next door. There's wi-fi and bike rental.

the western stretch of the city moat, is a plain but charming, unrestored city gate. Take tourist bus Y5 from the train station or Changxu Lu.

GARDEN OF HARMONY — GARDEN

(怡园; Yí Yuán; Renmin Lu; 人民路; admission ¥15) Less busy than other gardens is the small Qing-dynasty Garden of Harmony, which has assimilated many of the features of older gardens and delicately blended them into a style of its own.

TIGER HILL — HILL

(虎丘山; Hǔqiū Shān; ☎6723 2305; Huqiu Lu; 虎丘路; low/high season ¥40/60; ⏲summer 7.30am-6pm, winter to 5pm) In the far northwest of town, Tiger Hill is topped by the leaning **Yúnyán Pagoda** (云岩塔; Yúnyán Tǎ), built in the 10th century. Take tourist bus 1 (游1) from the Renmin Lu end of Jingde Lu. It passes close to the Garden to Linger In and West Garden Temple. Alternatively, it's an interesting cycle along Dongzhong Shi and Fengqiao Lu, passing attractive canal bridges.

GARDEN TO LINGER IN — GARDEN

(留园; Liú Yuán; Liuyuan Lu; 留园路; low/high season ¥30/40) The 3-hectare Garden to Linger In dates from the Ming dynasty and was built by a doctor as a place of relaxation for his recovering patients. Ornamental doorways and windows open onto wisteria-draped rockeries, ivy-covered tiled roofs and overgrown fairyland landscapes. Recuperate from sightseeing in the teahouse. Take tourist bus Y1 from the train station or Renmin Lu.

WEST GARDEN TEMPLE — BUDDHIST TEMPLE

(西园寺; Xīyuán Sì; Xiyuan Lu; 西园路; admission ¥25; ⏲8am-5pm) About 500m west of the Garden to Linger In, to which it once belonged, West Garden Temple was built on a garden donated to the Buddhist community in the 17th century.

Greeting you upon entering the magnificent **Arhat Hall** (罗汉堂; Luóhàn Táng) is a stunning four-faced and thousand-armed statue of Guanyin, leading to mesmerising and slightly unnerving rows of glittering statues of *luóhàn* (Buddhist monks who have achieved enlightenment), each one unique. The Ming-dynasty hall was torched by Taiping rebels in 1860, and rebuilt.

GRAND CANAL — CANAL

(大运河; Dà Yùnhé) The Grand Canal passes to the west and south of Sūzhōu, within a 10km range of the town. Suburban buses 13, 14, 15 and 16 will get you there. In the northwest, bus 11 follows the canal for a fair distance, taking you on a tour of the surrounding countryside.

PRECIOUS BELT BRIDGE — BRIDGE

(宝带桥; Bǎodài Qiáo) Straddling the Grand Canal southeast of Sūzhōu, and boasting 53 arches, the highly impressive Precious Belt Bridge is thought to be a Tang-dynasty construction. It's a 40-minute bike ride. Head south on Renmin Lu, past the south moat, then left at the TV towers, and the bridge will be on your right. If you're heading to Tónglǐ, you'll see the bridge on your right.

TOURS

Hour-long evening boat tours (¥120 per person) do half-circuit return trips along the outer moat. Boats leave every half-hour between 6.30pm and 8.30pm. Buy tickets from the **Suzhou Wharf** (苏州码; Suzhou Mǎtóu; near Renmin Bridge; 人民桥附近).

Eight-person **row boats** (per boat ¥150) ply the canals by Pingjiang Lu where, towards the northern end of the lane, you'll find a ticket office.

EATING

Sūzhōu's most celebrated restaurants are in and around the pedestrianised shopping street of Guanqian Jie (观前街), while loads of cheap restaurants cluster at the eastern end of Shizi Jie (十梓街), immediately south of the university.

For cute canal-side cafes and traditional(ish) teahouses, wander to the charming cobblestone street of Pingjiang Lu. For brash, late-night bars and more wi-fi cafes, head to Shiquan Jie (十全街). A vegetarian restaurant can be found at the West Garden Temple.

ZHŪHÓNGXÌNG NOODLES $

(朱鸿兴; Gong Xiang; 宫巷; dishes from ¥20; 7am-9pm) One of Sūzhōu's most popular noodle joints, this long-standing canteen-style place serves some scrummy and filling noodles. Try the lovely crispy duck noodles (脆皮烧鸭面; *cuìpí shāoyā miàn;* ¥23).

YÀKÈXĪ UIGHUR $$

(亚克西酒楼; Yàkèxī Jiǔlóu; 768 Shiquan Jie; 十全街768号; mains ¥40; 9am-midnight) The Uighur kitsch atmosphere may be a bit cheesy but the Xīnjiāng staples – lamb kebabs (¥3.50), hot and spicy lamb soup (¥16) and *nang* bread (¥3) – are all tasty. Round it off with a bottle of SinKiang beer (¥10) and dream of Kashgar. Lamb kebabs also grilled for takeaway outside.

XĪSHÈNGYUÁN DUMPLINGS $

(熙盛源; 43 Fenghuang Jie; dumplings from ¥8) You can join the crowd outside waiting for *xiǎolóngbāo,* take a seat and order inside, or settle for some tasty wonton dumplings (馄饨; *húntūn;* from ¥6).

DÉYUÈLÓU JIĀNGSŪ $$

(得月楼; 43 Taijian Long; 太监弄43号; dishes ¥30-120; 24hr) For local specialities such as squirrel-shaped mandarin fish (¥140) and Sūzhōu-style fried fish (¥25), try this long-standing restaurant near the Temple of Mystery.

DRINKING

Dicey bars with names like the Drunken Clam, Box Bar, Nowhere Bar or simply the Pub Bar are slung out along Shiquan Jie. Pingjiang Lu is the place for serene cafe culture.

BOOKWORM CAFE

(老书虫; Lǎoshūchóng; www.suzhoubookworm.com; 77 Gunxiu Fang; 滚绣坊77号; beer from ¥20; 9am-1am;) Set back from Shiquan Jie, over the other side of the canal, and housed in an attractive whitewashed, two-storey building with a terrace out back, Bookworm makes a smart choice for a coffee or beer. Like its popular Běijīng branch, this one also has a fantastic range of English-language books, some of which are for sale, and hosts occasional cultural events (check the website for details). The Western-friendly food is pricy; open mic every Wednesday.

BǏ'ÀN CAFE

(彼岸; 36 Pingjiang Lu; 平江路36号; coffee from ¥20; 10am-11pm;) Housed in a gorgeous wooden building that juts out slightly over the water, Bǐ'àn is the cutest of a bunch of canal-side cafes along Pingjiang Lu. There's beer (from ¥18) and a huge selection of tea.

JANE'S PUB BAR BAR

(621 Shiquan Jie; 十全街621号; draught beer from ¥30; 7pm-3am) One of the bars on Shiquan Jie that doesn't have scantily dressed girls beckoning you inside as you walk past, friendly and buzzing Jane's has Guinness on tap (¥55), pie and chips (¥50), a pool table and sports TVs.

Tónglǐ

Explore

With its sights neatly parcelled together in a more picturesque and easily navigable setting than Sūzhōu, the charming canal town of Tónglǐ (同里) is a great day out.

The Best...

- **Sight** Gēnglè Táng (p185)
- **Place to Sleep** Zhèngfú Cǎotáng (p184)

Top Tip

Tónglǐ is best reached by bus from Sūzhōu. Admission to the town covers the sights listed below (apart from the Chinese Sex Culture Museum); however, there is no charge if you just want to wander the old town's streets.

Getting There & Away

Bus Day-trip buses (¥130 return, includes admission to town, 1¾ hours) depart daily from the Shànghǎi Sightseeing Bus Centre (Map p300) at 8.30am, returning from Tónglǐ at 4.30pm. You will be dropped off 2km from town at Tónglǐ Lake, from where there's a shuttle (¥4) to the gate. The boat trip on Tónglǐ Lake is free, though of no particular interest.

Half-hourly public buses (¥36, 6.25am to 3.10pm) leave Tónglǐ bus station for Shànghǎi, dropping you near the main train station. Regular buses (¥9, 50 minutes, every 30 minutes) also run to Tónglǐ bus station from Sūzhōu's north and south long-distance bus stations, from where it's a 15-minute walk to the old town. Frequent buses (¥6, 30 minutes) run between Zhōuzhuāng and Tónglǐ.

Need to Know

- **Area Code** ☎0512
- **Location** 80km from Shànghǎi

SLEEPING IN TÓNGLǏ

Guesthouses (客栈; *kèzhàn*) are in abundance.

- **Zhèngfú Cǎotáng** (正福草堂; ☎6332 0576; www.zfct.net; 138-58 Mingqing Jie; 明清街138-58号; d from ¥480-1180, ste ¥1380; ❄@) Try Zhèngfú Cǎotáng, a beautifully restored courtyard hotel. All 14 rooms are splendidly arrayed with traditional antique-style furniture and underfloor heating.
- **Tónglǐ International Youth Hostel** (同里国际青年旅舍; ☎6333 9311; 210 Zhuhang Jie; 竹行街210号; dm ¥45, r ¥120-150; ❄@📶) In two locations. The main one is off Zhongchuan Beilu (中川北路), with rooms decorated with traditional furniture, and the wooden pillars and stone courtyard ooze atmosphere. The other location beside Taiping Bridge has compact dorms, and shared-bathroom doubles.

SIGHTS

Slow-moving six-person boats (¥90 per person, 25 minutes) ply the waters of Tónglǐ's canal system.

OLD TOWN NEIGHBOURHOOD

(古镇; Gǔzhèn; admission ¥100; ⌚ticket office 7.30am-5.30pm) With its whitewashed houses, laundry hanging out to dry and unhurried canal scenes, the old town is best explored in a lazy meandering loop; bilingual signs guide the way, and maps (地图; *dìtú*) are available at the ticket office, but getting lost is half the fun.

TUÌSĪ GARDEN GARDEN

(退思园; Tuìsī Yuán; ⌚9am-5.30pm) In the east of the old town is this gorgeous 19th-century garden. The Tower of Fanning Delight served as the living quarters while the garden itself is a lovely portrait of pond water churning with outsized goldfish, rockeries and pavilions, caressed by traditional Chinese music. It's a lovely place to find a perch and drift into a reverie, unless you are suddenly outflanked by a marauding tour group.

CHINESE SEX CULTURE MUSEUM MUSEUM

(中华性文化博物馆; Zhōnghuá Xìngwénhuà Bówùguǎn; admission ¥20; ⌚9am-5.30pm) It's definitely not for infant Tónglǐ visitors, but the highly recommended Sex Culture Museum is Tónglǐ's most famous sight and displays ritual sex objects, ancient sex toys and erotic carvings from as far back as 3000 BC.

PEARL PAGODA PAGODA

(珍珠塔; Zhēnzhū Tǎ; ⊙9am-5.30pm) In the north of Tónglǐ is the Pearl Pagoda, originally the home of a Ming-dynasty official, containing a large residential compound, an ancestral hall, a garden and even an opera stage.

GĒNGLÈ TÁNG HISTORIC BUILDING

(耕乐堂; ⊙9am-5.30pm) There are three old residences that you'll pass at some point during your wander, the best of which is this vast Ming-dynasty country estate with 41 rooms and courtyards in the west of town.

Zhūjiājiǎo

Explore

Thirty kilometres west of Shànghǎi, the pleasant canal town of Zhūjiājiǎo (朱家角) is easy as a day trip from Shànghǎi. Even though the settlement is far older, the town prospered during the Ming dynasty, when a commercial centre developed on its network of waterways. What survives today is a charming tableau of Ming- and Qing-dynasty alleys, bridges and old town (古镇; *gǔzhèn*) architecture.

The riverside settlement is small enough to wander completely in three hours. You'll be tripping over souvenir shops and their vocal vendors, and you can buy anything from a pair of children's tiger shoes to 'antique' Chinese eyeglasses. Admission to town, including entry to four/nine of the main sights, is ¥30/90.

The Best...

- **Sight** Fángshēng Bridge (p185)
- **Place to Sleep** Uma Hostel (p186)
- **Tourist Office** Xinfeng Lu, Zhūjiājiǎo (http://en.zhujiajiao.com; English guide half-/whole day ¥120/200; ⊙8am-4.30pm)

Top Tip

Visit Zhūjiājiǎo during the week, as weekends and holidays see the canal town's narrow streets packed with sightseers.

Getting There & Away

Bus The best way to reach Zhūjiājiǎo from Shànghǎi is from Pu'an Rd Bus Station (普安路汽车站; Pǔ'ān Lù Qìchē Zhàn; Ⓜ Dashijie), just south of People's Square, where Hùzhū Gāosù Kuàixiàn buses (沪朱高速快线; ¥12, one hour, every 20 minutes from 6am to 10pm, less frequently in low season) run direct to the town. Nine daily buses (¥15.50, one hour, 8.25am to 4.15pm) run between Tónglǐ bus station and Zhūjiājiǎo; they drop you on the main road, a 10-minute walk from the old town (古镇; *gǔzhèn*).

Need to Know

- **Area Code** ☎021
- **Location** 30km west of Shànghǎi

SIGHTS

FÁNGSHĒNG BRIDGE BRIDGE

(放生桥; Fángshēng Qiáo) Of Zhūjiājiǎo's quaint band of ancient bridges, the standout must be the graceful, 72m long, five-arched Fángshēng Bridge, first built in 1571 with proceeds from a monk's 15 years of alms-gathering.

CITY GOD TEMPLE TAOIST TEMPLE

(城隍庙; Chénghuáng Miào; Caohe Jie; 漕河街; admission ¥10; ⊙7.30am-4pm) Moved here in 1769 from its original location in Xuějiābāng, this temple stands on the west side of the recently built City God Temple bridge.

YUÁNJĪN BUDDHIST TEMPLE BUDDHIST TEMPLE

(圆津禅寺; Yuánjīn Chánsì; Caohe Jie; 漕河街; admission ¥5; ⊙8am-4pm) This Buddhist temple not far from the distinctive **Tài'ān Bridge** (泰安桥; Tài'ān Qiáo) is most notable for its Qīnghuá Pavilion (清华阁; Qīnghuá Gé), a towering hall visible from many parts of town.

ZHŪJIĀJIǍO CATHOLIC CHURCH OF ASCENSION CHURCH

(朱家角耶稣升天堂; Zhūjiājiǎo Yēsū Shēngtiāntáng; 27 Caohe Jie, No 317 Alley; 漕河街27号317弄) Built in 1863, this brick church stands alongside a lovingly cultivated courtyard decorated with a statue of Joseph holding a baby Jesus.

SLEEPING IN ZHŪJIĀJIĀO

➡ **Uma Hostel** (☎189 1808 2961; umahostel@gmail.com; 103 Xijing Jie; 西井街103号; dm/d ¥80/240; 📶) Try the delightful Uma Hostel, by Kèzhí Garden (课植园; Kèzhí Yuán), with its high ceilings, wooden furniture and bohemian feel. There's wi-fi and breakfast, but not many rooms, so book. Otherwise, look out for signs reading '客房' (*kèfáng;* guestrooms).

TOURS

At various points, including Fángshēng Bridge, you can hop aboard six-person **row boats** (per boat 15/30min ¥60/120) for waterborne tours of the town.

EATING & DRINKING

Food sellers line Bei Dajie, flogging everything from pigs' trotters to plump coconuts, above which flail plastic bags of fans to fend off flies. Plentiful cafes have squeezed in along Caohe Jie, Xihu Jie and Donghu Jie, and even a creperie has set up shop near Yongquan Bridge.

Zhōuzhuāng

Explore

Propelled to national fame by Chen Yifei's idyllic old paintings, Zhōuzhuāng (周庄) is Jiāngsū's best-known water town. Sixty kilometres from Shànghǎi, the picturesque canal town is regularly inundated with visitors, but there's no denying the appeal of its waterside views, quaint bridges and ancient households.

If you can steal a lead on the crowds, it's possible to eke out classical red-lantern vignettes of water-town China and some enthralling courtyard architecture. Admission to Zhōuzhuāng is ¥100 (including 16 sights), but there is free access after 8pm.

The Best...

➡ **Sight** Shen's House (p187)

➡ **Place to Drink** Zhōuzhuāng International Youth Hostel bar (p187)

Top Tip

It's straightforward to tie Zhūjiājiǎo, Zhōuzhuāng, Tónglǐ and Sūzhōu together by bus, without having to return to Shànghǎi.

Getting There & Away

Bus Buses (¥140 return, including admission, 90 minutes, from 7am) depart for Zhōuzhuāng regularly from the Shànghǎi Sightseeing Bus Centre (Map p300). From the drop-off at the bus station, turn left and walk for 15 minutes over Zhōuzhuāng Bridge (周庄大桥; Zhōuzhuāng Dàqiáo) to the old town and the ticket office by the gate. A taxi will cost around ¥10; pedicabs charge roughly the same. The last bus back to Shànghǎi is at 5pm. Buses also run from Shànghǎi long-distance bus station (¥25, six per day) and Shànghǎi south long-distance bus station (¥25, two per day). Buses (¥20, 90 minutes, 6.55am to 5.20pm) leave for Zhōuzhuāng every half-hour from the north long-distance bus station in Sūzhōu. Hourly buses (¥10, 50 minutes, 6.30am to 4.30pm) run to Zhōuzhuāng from Zhūjiājiǎo's small bus stand opposite the bus station on Xiangningbang Lu. Frequent buses (¥6, 30 minutes) shuttle between Zhōuzhuāng and Tónglǐ. Boats (single/return ¥180/250, 20 minutes) also run along the waterways to Tónglǐ from Zhōuzhuāng.

Need to Know

➡ **Area Code** ☎0512

➡ **Location** 60km west of Shànghǎi

➡ **Tourist Office** Zhōuzhuāng Visitor Centre (周庄游客中心; Zhōuzhuāng Yóukè Zhōngxīn; ☎5721 1655; Quanfu Lu, near memorial archway)

SIGHTS

TWIN BRIDGES BRIDGE

(双桥; Shuāngqiáo) Of Zhōzhuāng's 14 bridges, this lovely Ming-dynasty double attracts the lion's share of water-colourists and photographers. Prolific artist Chen Yifei consigned them to canvas in the 1980s, forever sealing their – and Zhōuzhuāng's – fame.

ZHANG'S HOUSE HISTORIC BUILDING
(张厅; Zhāngtīng; ⌚8.30am-5.30pm) Of Zhōuzhuāng's impressive households, this 70-room Ming residence south of the Twin Bridges was acquired by the Zhang family in the Qing dynasty and is one of the most beautiful. Hung with *mǎdēng* (old lanterns), the astonishing old building continues to a lovely waterside rockery at the rear.

SHEN'S HOUSE HISTORIC BUILDING
This astonishing old residence seems to go on for ever; in the back hall, dishes are laid out on the tables. At the rear you need a separate ticket to access the **Zǒumǎ Lóu** (走马楼; ⌚8am-4.30pm), where a further six courtyards and 45 rooms await (totally a third of the entire building)!

BOAT RIDES BOATS
(游船; yóuchuán; per boat ¥100) One-hour boat trips float along Zhōuzhuāng's waterways. Speedboats (¥80) tour South Lake from Bàoēn Bridge (报恩桥; Bàoēn Qiáo).

EATING

Impregnated with the clinging smell of stinky *dòufu*, Zhōuzhuāng has no shortage of dining options. Breakfast can be difficult to source, unless you want a glistening hunk of pork; you can get a good cappuccino at the youth hostel, which also cooks up pizza, bacon sandwiches, seafood spaghetti, tuna salad and so forth.

Shěshān

Explore

Easily accessed from the centre of town on the metro, Shěshān is worth a half-day or day trip to its fantastic cathedral, the surrounding views from the hills and Happy Valley amusement park.

Top Tip

At the foot of West Hill is one of several bike stations where you can hire green-coloured bikes (8am to 4.30pm) to explore the Shěshān area. You will need your passport and a deposit of ¥200; the first hour is free, then bike charges are ¥1 per hour.

Getting There & Away

Metro Take metro line 9 to Shěshān station and then hop on free bus 9 (九号线; *jiǔhào xiàn*; every 20 minutes from 9am) to Happy Valley amusement park, which drops off at West Hill; alternatively, jump on bus 92. Both depart from the bus stop outside the metro station.

Need to Know

➡ **Area Code** ☎021

➡ **Location** 35km southwest of Shànghǎi city centre

SLEEPING IN ZHŌUZHUĀNG

Prices peak on Fridays and Saturdays, when the water town is at bursting point, so try to visit on a weekday. There are endless *kèzhàn* (客栈; guesthouses) dotted around the old town, with rooms in the ¥80 to ¥100 mark.

➡ **Zhōuzhuāng International Youth Hostel** (周庄国际青年旅舍; ☎5720 4566; 86 Beishi Jie; 北市街86号; weekday/weekend dm ¥45/45, s ¥100/120, d ¥120/140, tw ¥120/140; ❄@📶) Just along from the old opera stage, this is a lovely place with neat rooms, an OK dorm, a tranquil courtyard setting and a fab bar area.

➡ **Zhèngfú Cǎotáng** (正福草堂; ☎5721 9333; www.zfct.net; 90 Zhongshi Jie; 中市街90号; d ¥480-1080; ❄@) For fine traditional elegance, this charmingly presented hotel has only a handful of rooms decorated with antique-style furniture.

➡ **Gǔzhèn Hotel** (古镇客房; Gǔzhèn Kèfáng; ☎135 1162 7032; 83 Beishi Jie; 北市街83号; d from ¥150) If the youth hostel is booked out, try this handy family-run place next door with clean, tile-floor rooms.

SIGHTS

Sights are contained within the Shěshān National Forest Park, divided into two areas: the West Hill area (西景区; Xījǐngqū) and the East Hill area (东景区; Dōngjǐngqū). The most famous historic attractions can be found in the West Hill area. At the time of writing, access to the West Hill was free, while admission to the East Hill (with a forest park, aviary and butterfly garden) was ¥45.

FREE SHĚSHĀN BASILICA CHURCH

(Shěshān Shèngmǔ Dàdiàn; ⌚8am-4pm) A very pleasant walk up through the trees from the road and the bus drop-off to the top of the hill, this cruciform red-brick and granite church is the highlight of the West Hill area. Glorious views range out from the hill over the suburbs of Shànghǎi. The original Holy Mother Cathedral was built here between 1863 and 1866, and the current Basilica of Notre Dame was finished in 1935. All the stained glass was destroyed during the Cultural Revolution and is being restored; the glass in the church at present is film-coated. Nonetheless, the interior is splendidly illuminated when the sun shines in. Every May sees hordes of local Catholics making a pilgrimage to the church, climbing up the hill along the Via Dolorosa from the south gate.

SHÀNGHǍI ASTRONOMICAL MUSEUM MUSEUM

(上海天文博物馆; Shànghǎi Tiānwén Bówùguǎn; admission ¥12; ⌚8.15am-5pm, last tickets 4.30pm) The Former Shěshān Observatory is right alongside the Shěshān Basilica on West Hill, founded by the Jesuits in 1900. The museum contains exhibitions on the history of observatories and astronomical research in China, as well as a collection of ancient telescopes.

XIÙDÀOZHĚ PAGODA PAGODA

(秀道者塔; Xiùdàozhě Tǎ) Rising from the east flank of West Hill, this graceful 20m-high pagoda dates to the 10th century.

HAPPY VALLEY AMUSEMENT PARK

(欢乐谷; Huānlè Gǔ; adult/child/child under 1.2m ¥200/100/free; ⌚9am-6pm) Happy Valley has the best rides in town, including the epic wooden roller coaster which runs for over 1km, a 90-degree Diving Coaster and a stomach-churning Turbo Drop, but queues can get seriously long, especially during weekends and school holidays. It's huge, so prepare to do some legwork, and it's not much fun in the heat. To reach Happy Valley, take metro line 9 to Sheshan metro station and hop on the free shuttle bus.

Sleeping

There has never been a better time to find a bed in Shànghǎi. From ultrachic, carbon-neutral boutique rooms to slick five-star hotels housed in glimmering skyscrapers, grand heritage names and well-run, down-to-earth backpacker haunts, the range of accommodation in town is just what you would expect from a city of this stature.

Hotels

Top-end stays tend to fall into three categories: trendy boutique hotels, historic heritage hotels where guests can wrap themselves in nostalgia and top-of-the-range modern tower hotels, bursting with the latest amenities and sparkling with highly polished service (and often glorious views).

The less well-developed midrange hotel market, which includes some handy chain hotels, also has some boutique and heritage offerings. Neat, comfortable, but largely soulless express hotels are a budget option, sometimes offering bigger rooms than hostels, but without the Western-friendly facilities or language skills.

Be prepared for reasonably rudimentary English-language skills, except at the very best hotels (and youth hostels). Almost all the hotels we've listed have air-conditioning, and usually have wi-fi (sometimes at pricey daily rates) or broadband.

Learn to treat star rankings in Shànghǎi with a raised eyebrow. Some Shànghǎi hotels have acquired five-star rankings (despite not having a swimming pool).

Hostels

At the budget end, Shànghǎi has a decent choice of youth hostels. Usually staffed by competent English speakers, they offer well-priced dorm beds and private rooms as well as wi-fi, communal internet terminals, bike rental, kitchen and laundry rooms and even the odd table tennis or pool table. Most have small and cheap bar-cafe-restaurant areas. Hostels also provide handy travel advice to guests.

Rates

Rack rates are listed here, but expect discounts of up to 50%. Discounts are offered at most hotels, except during national holiday periods or the Formula One grand prix weekend. Rates can be bargained down at many budget and midrange hotels, but not at express hotels or hostels.

Dorm beds go for around ¥50 or ¥55, but double rooms under ¥200 can be hard to find. Expect to pay at least ¥500 for a midrange room. The fancier boutique hotels will charge more. A standard room in a top-end place will almost certainly top ¥1000, even after discount. Many of the better hotels, especially those aimed at business travellers, have cheaper weekend rates.

For an explanation of the symbols used in this chapter, see How to Use this Book on the inside front cover.

Longer-Term Rentals

The cheapest way to stay in Shànghǎi is to share a flat or rent local accommodation from a Chinese landlord. Classified ads in listings magazines such as *City Weekend* (www.cityweekend.com.cn/shanghai) are a good place to start. You will need to register with the local PSB within 24 hours of moving in.

Some hostels and hotels also rent out long-let rooms. **Chai Living Residences** (Map p298; ☎3366 3209; www.chailiving.com; North Suzhou Rd) is a stylish and recommended option.

NEED TO KNOW

Price Ranges
In our listings, we've used the following codes to represent the price per night of an en suite double room in high season:

$	less than ¥500
$$	¥500–1300
$$$	more than ¥1300

Reservations

➡ Reserve ahead, especially during high season.

➡ Online agencies **CTrip** (☎3406 4880, 800-820 6666; http://english.ctrip.com) and **eLong** (www.elong.com) are handy choices for reservations.

➡ **Lonely Planet** (hotels.lonelyplanet.com) Offers bookings.

Checking In & Out

➡ To check into a hotel, you need your passport and to fill in a registration form (hotels may simply scan your passport instead), a copy of which will be sent to the local Public Security Bureau (PSB; 公安局; Gōng'ānjú) office.

➡ A deposit is required at most hotels; this will be paid either with cash or by providing your credit-card details.

➡ Check-out is usually midday.

Tax
All hotel rooms are subject to a 10% or 15% service charge, but many cheaper hotels don't bother to charge this.

Restrictions
Frustratingly, some very cheap Chinese hotels still refuse to take foreigners, citing the hassles involved with registration as the reason.

Lonely Planet's Top Choices

Fairmont Peace Hotel (p192) The grand dame of the Bund: restored, revitalised and renewed.

Astor House Hotel (p201) Classic old-Shànghǎi heritage and a mere foxtrot from the Bund.

Magnolia Bed & Breakfast (p195) An exquisite French Concession bijou, with only five rooms.

Le Tour Traveler's Rest (p199) Fabulous youth hostel facilities combined with old Shànghǎi textures in a former towel factory.

Waterhouse at South Bund (p195) Swish and chic Cool Docks–boutique style with views to match.

Best by Budget

$

Mingtown E-Tour Youth Hostel (p193)

Mingtown Nanjing Road Youth Hostel (p193)

Blue Mountain Youth Hostel (p197)

Soho People's Square Youth Hostel (p199)

$$

Marvel Hotel (p193)

Kevin's Old House (p196)

$$$

Peninsula Hotel (p192)

Waldorf Astoria (p192)

Ritz-Carlton Shànghǎi Pǔdōng (p200)

Andaz (p195)

Púlì (p198)

Best Boutique Hotels

Langham Yangtze Boutique (p193)

Le Sun Chine (p196)

Urbn (p198)

Jia Shànghǎi (p199)

88 Xīntiāndì (p196)

Best B&Bs

Quintet (p195)

Kevin's Old House (p196)

Best Historic Hotels

Waldorf Astoria (p192)

Mansion Hotel (p196)

Chai Living Residences (p201)

Ruìjīn Hotel (p197)

Best Luxury

Ritz-Carlton Shànghǎi Pǔdōng (p200)

Park Hyatt (p200)

Peninsula Hotel (p192)

Langham Xīntiāndì (p195)

Grand Hyatt (p200)

Best for Views

Park Hyatt (p200)

Grand Hyatt (p200)

Peninsula Hotel (p192)

Les Suites Orient (p192)

JW Marriott Tomorrow Square (p192)

Best for Hotel Restaurants & Bars

Hotel Indigo (p195)

Grand Hyatt (p200)

Waldorf Astoria (p192)

Neighbourhood	For	Against
The Bund & People's Square	Luxury hotels on the Bund; close to the main sights; über-central with good transport links; iconic views and fantastic restaurants	Busy and expensive
Old Town	Traditional part of town; river views from stylish and happening South Bund area	Little choice; transport options limited; busy areas; ramshackle parts
French Concession	Dapper neighbourhood; vibrant, leafy and central; tip-top range of hotels; heritage architecture; standout restaurant choice; fab transport links	Few iconic views; expensive
Jìng'ān	Good transport links; fine range of accommodation choices; shopping zone; central and stylish	Sights light and spread out
Pǔdōng	Luxury, stylish and high-altitude hotels; killer views; fantastic restaurants; good transport links	Few sights, spread out, big distances, little character
Hóngkǒu & North Shànghǎi	Heritage and stylish long-stay options; transport links good; parts close to centre; off beaten trail	Grittier and less fashionable; sprawling area with spread-out sights
West Shànghǎi	Close to Hóngqiáo International Airport; trade zone	Not much character, far from main sights, huge sprawl, non-central

The Bund & People's Square 外滩、人民广场

TOP CHOICE **FAIRMONT PEACE HOTEL** HISTORIC HOTEL **$$$**

Map p280 (费尔蒙和平饭店; Fèi'ěrméng Hépíng Fàndiàn; ☎6321 6888; www.fairmont.com; 20 East Nanjing Rd; 南京东路20号; d ¥2200-3400; ; **M**East Nanjing Rd) If anywhere in town fully conveys the swish sensations of 1930s Shànghǎi, it's the old Cathay, which rises majestically from the Bund. Renamed the Peace Hotel in the 1950s and reopened in 2010 after many years of renovations, it's since reasserted its claim as one of the city's most iconic hotels. Rooms are decked out in art-deco style, from the light fixtures on down to the coffee tables, and the entire hotel is cast in the warm, subdued tints of a bygone era.

Expect all the luxuries of a top-class establishment, though note that wi-fi and broadband access are an extra ¥99 per day. Standard rooms come without a view, deluxe rooms with a street view and suites with the coveted river view. The hotel is also home to a luxury spa, two upscale restaurants and several bars and cafes. Even if you're not staying here, it's worth popping in to admire the magnificent lobby (1929) or take in an evening show at the jazz bar (p71). For more on the history of the hotel, and visiting it, see p53.

PENINSULA HOTEL LUXURY HOTEL **$$$**

Map p280 (半岛酒店; Bàndǎo Jiǔdiàn; ☎2327 2888; www.peninsula.com; 32 East Zhongshan No 1 Rd; 中山东一路32号; d ¥2300-4600; @; **M**East Nanjing Rd) This luxury hotel at the Bund's northern end combines art-deco motifs with Shànghǎi modernity, but it's the little touches that distinguish it from the numerous other five-star places in the neighbourhood: a TV in the tub, valet box, Nespresso machine and fabulous views across the river or out onto the gardens of the former British consulate. Part of the Rockbund development project (p61), it contains an enormous luxury shopping arcade on the ground floor, with a back entrance that leads to the beautifully renovated Yuanmingyuan Rd.

JW MARRIOTT TOMORROW SQUARE LUXURY HOTEL **$$$**

Map p280 (明天广场JW万怡酒店; Míngtiān Guǎngchǎng JW Wànyí Jiǔdiàn; ☎5359 4969; www.jwmarriottshanghai.com; 399 West Nanjing Rd; d ¥2180-3330; 南京西路399号; ; **M**People's Sq) Victor Sassoon probably would have traded in his old digs in a heartbeat if he could have stayed in the chairman's suite here. Housed across the upper 24 floors of one of Shànghǎi's most dramatic towers, the JW Marriott boasts marvellously appointed rooms with spectacular vistas (the view over People's Square from the 38th-floor lobby cafe is something in itself) and showers with hydraulic massage functions to soak away the stress.

Service and facilities are top-class, with two pools (indoor and outdoor) and an excellent spa. Internet costs ¥120 a day for nonmembers.

WALDORF ASTORIA LUXURY HOTEL **$$$**

Map p280 (华尔道夫酒店; Huáěr Dàofū Jiǔdiàn; ☎6322 9988; www.waldorfastoriashanghai.com; 2 East Zhongshan No 1 Rd; 中山东一路2号; d ¥2500-3500; @; **M**East Nanjing Rd) Marking the southern end of the Bund is the stately Shànghǎi Club (1910), once the Bund's most exclusive gentlemen's club. The 20 original rooms here were reconverted in 2010 to house the Waldorf Astoria's premium suites, six of which look out onto the Huángpǔ River. Behind this heritage building is a new hotel tower, which holds 252 state-of-the-art rooms, each featuring luxuries such as touch digital controls, espresso machine, walk-in closet and even a TV in the mirror.

There's a definite New York-meets-Shànghǎi theme here, from the Peacock Lounge to the cocktail list at the Long Bar (p70).

LES SUITES ORIENT LUXURY HOTEL **$$$**

Map p280 (东方商旅酒店; Dōngfāng Shānglǚ Jiǔdiàn; ☎6320 0088; www.hotelsuitesorient.com; 1 East Jinling Rd; 金陵东路1号; d ¥1580-2280; @; **M**Yuyuan Garden) Located at the southern edge of the Bund, Les Suites Orient is notable as the only hotel on the strip with standard rooms (Bund Studio) that have fantastic river and Bund views – in some rooms even the bathtub has a view. It's housed in a modern 23-storey tower, with hardwood floors and minimalist design adding to the appealingly chic interior. Excellent service.

LANGHAM YANGTZE BOUTIQUE
BOUTIQUE HOTEL $$$

Map p280 (朗廷扬子精品宾馆; Lǎngtíng Yángzǐ Jīngpǐn Bīnguǎn; ☎6080 0800; www.langhamhotels.com; 740 Hankou Rd; 汉口路740号; d ¥1300-1800; Ⓜ People's Sq) Originally built in the 1930s, this art-deco beauty was refurbished and reopened in 2010. In addition to period decor, rooms feature deep baths, glass-walled bathrooms (with Venetian blinds) and even tiny balconies – a rarity in Shànghǎi. The hammam and sauna in the fabulous Chuan spa are complimentary for guests; breakfast is served in the Italian restaurant Ciao. Wi-fi costs extra.

TOP CHOICE MARVEL HOTEL
HOTEL $$

Map p280 (商悦青年会大酒店; Shāngyuè Qīngniánhuì Dàjiǔdiàn; ☎3305 9999; www.marvelhotels.com.cn; 123 South Xizang Rd; 西藏南路123号; d ¥1080-1580; Ⓜ Dashijie) Occupying the former YMCA building (1931) just south of People's Square, the Marvel is one of the city's standout midrange hotels. The successful mix of history, a central location and modern comfort (internet access via the TV, soundproofed windows, comfy down pillows) makes it one of Shànghǎi's best-value hotels. Online discounts can slash room rates in half. Wi-fi in the lobby only.

WESTIN SHÀNGHǍI
HOTEL $$$

Map p280 (威斯汀大饭店; Wēisītīng Dàfàndiàn; ☎6335 1888; www.westin.com/shanghai; 88 Middle Henan Rd; 河南中路88号; d from ¥3750; Ⓜ East Nanjing Rd) Partly housed inside one of the most instantly recognisable buildings in Pǔxī – the crown-topped Bund Centre – the Westin boasts more than 500 top-notch rooms. The deluxe doubles are a bit smaller than you'd expect for the price, but are as beautifully decorated as the rest. Beds are heavenly and the bathtubs – some with city views – are nice and deep. There's a gym, a pool and a Thai-style spa. Broadband access is ¥100. Expect at least 50% discounts.

MINGTOWN E-TOUR YOUTH HOSTEL
HOSTEL $

Map p280 (明堂上海青年旅舍; Míngtáng Shànghǎi Qīngnián Lǚshè; ☎6327 7766; 57 Jiangyin Rd; 江阴路57号; dm ¥55, d without/with bathroom ¥160/260; Ⓜ People's Sq) One of Shànghǎi's best youth hostels, E-tour has a historic alleyway setting and pleasant rooms, some with reproduction antique furniture. But it's the tranquil courtyard with fish pond and the split-level bar-restaurant that really sell this one. A superb communal area, it comes with computers, a projector-screen DVD player, free pool table and plenty of outdoor seating on wooden decking. There are both women-only and mixed dorms.

MINGTOWN NANJING ROAD YOUTH HOSTEL
HOSTEL $

Map p280 (明堂上海南京路青年旅舍; Míngtáng Shànghǎi Nánjīng Lù Qīngnián Lǚshè; ☎6322 0939; 258 Tianjin Rd; 天津路258号; dm ¥55, s/d ¥150/220; Ⓜ East Nanjing Rd) This new Mingtown hostel is located halfway between the Bund and People's Square and is just a short hop away from the nearest metro station. The six-bed dorms each have a private bathroom, laminated wood flooring and simple particle-board decor; perks include laundry, a real kitchen, bar-restaurant, DVD room and pool table.

MINGTOWN HIKER YOUTH HOSTEL
HOSTEL $

Map p280 (明堂上海旅行者青年旅馆; Míngtáng Shànghǎi Lǚxíngzhě Qīngnián Lǚguǎn; ☎6329 7889; 450 Middle Jiangxi Rd; 江西中路450号; dm without/with window ¥50/55, s/d ¥160/220; Ⓜ East Nanjing Rd) Far friendlier than its main Bund rival – the Captain Hostel – this justifiably popular hostel is also just a short stroll from the famous esplanade, on the southern corner of the grand old Hengfeng Building. It offers tidy four- and six-bed dorms with pine bunk beds and clean communal shower facilities, as well as a range of decent private rooms, including some cheaper ones with shared bathrooms. There's a pool table, internet and movies as well as a bar-restaurant and useful notice-board in the lobby. Wi-fi in the lobby only.

BLUE MOUNTAIN BUND
HOSTEL $

Map p280 (蓝山国际青年旅舍; Lánshān Guójì Qīngnián Lǚshè; ☎3366 1561; www.bmhostel.com; 6th fl, 350 South Shaanxi Rd; 山西路350号6楼; dm ¥55-65, s ¥150, d ¥200-240; Ⓜ East Nanjing Rd) This Blue Mountain hostel gets kudos for its central location – it's a short hop to the East Nanjing Rd metro station and not much further to the Bund or People's Square. The six-bed dorms are a bit on the small side, but overall the staff are friendly and there's a decent common area/bar with pool table, board games and movies. There are also laundry facilities and an outdoor terrace.

PHOENIX HOSTEL $

Map p280 (老陕客栈; Lǎoshǎn Kèzhàn; ☎6328 8680; www.thephoenixshanghai.com; 17 South Yunnan Rd; 云南南路17号; dm ¥55, d ¥230; ❄@📶; MDashijie) Although the corridors are a bit grotty, the rooms at this friendly place are actually in pretty good shape. Dorms sleep eight people, and the doubles are more appealing than similar choices in many more expensive midrange hotels. The rooftop bar and ground-floor Shaanxi dumpling restaurant add to the appeal. Good location close to People's Square.

MOTEL 168 HOTEL $

Map p280 (莫泰连锁旅馆; Mòtài Liánsuǒ Lǚguǎn; ☎5153 3333; www.motel168.com; 531 East Jinling Rd; 金陵东路531号; d ¥311-338; ❄@; MDashijie) An inviting red-and-orange colour scheme sets the mood at this bright and cheery Motel 168, located just down the road from People's Square. It's in better condition than the Motel 268, though it has fewer amenities. For discounts at any of this chain's branches, buy a ¥50 lifetime member's card (会员卡; *huìyuán kǎ*).

MOTEL 268 HOTEL $

Map p280 (莫泰连锁旅馆; Mòtài Liánsuǒ Lǚguǎn; ☎5179 3333; www.motel168.com; 50 Ningbo Rd; 宁波路50号; d ¥268-308, tr ¥368; ❄@📶; MEast Nanjing Rd) This place has been refurbished and rebranded so that its name matches the price of its new, improved standard doubles. It's still good value for this location with modern doubles coming with huge beds, wood-trimmed furnishings and smartly tiled chrome and glass bathrooms. And for an extra ¥50 you get a room with its own PC. The only quibble: wafer-thin walls mean you need to be lucky with the neighbours you get.

HOME INN HOTEL $

Map p280 (如家酒店; Rújiā Jiǔdiàn; ☎6323 9966; www.homeinns.com; Lane 26, Sijing Rd; 泗泾路26弄; d ¥299-379; ❄@📶; MEast Nanjing Rd) Housed in a delightful *lòngtáng* (lane) which is accessed from Sijing Rd, this is one of the better branches of the dependable Home Inn chain. The pastel interior may not appeal to everyone, but it means clean, functional rooms are nice and bright. The more expensive rooms include a computer.

JǏNJIĀNG INN HOTEL $

Map p280 (锦江之星旅馆; Jǐnjiāng Zhīxīng Lǚguǎn; ☎6326 0505; www.jinjianginns.com; 33 South Fujian Rd; 福建南路33号; s ¥249, d & tw ¥289-309; ❄; MDashijie) This central hotel, which looks like it may have struck a deal with Ikea (think cream bedding, pine-coloured furniture and laminated wood flooring), has bright, spacious, functional rooms with TV, kettle, broadband and clean shower rooms. There are a few doubles and a handful of singles, but most rooms are twins.

CAPTAIN HOSTEL HOSTEL $

Map p280 (船长青年酒店; Chuánzhǎng Qīngnián Jiǔdiàn; ☎6323 5053; www.captainhostel.com.cn; 37 Fuzhou Rd; 福州路37号; dm ¥65, r ¥358-458; ❄@📶; MEast Nanjing Rd) Despite being hands down the least friendly youth hostel in Shànghǎi, this naval-themed backpackers favourite still reels in punters by the boatload with its fantastic location and fine rooftop bar. There's a microwave and washing machine, but all bathrooms are communal. Wi-fi is in the communal area only.

SOFITEL HYLAND HOTEL HOTEL $$$

Map p280 (海仑宾馆; Hǎilún Bīnguǎn; ☎6351 5888; www.sofitel.com; 505 East Nanjing Rd; 南京东路505号; d ¥1150-2110; ❄📶; MEast Nanjing Rd) Standard doubles in this central hotel are a bit dated, but the executive rooms are more modern with chunky wood furnishings and more perks (including wi-fi). Like the standard rooms, they come with mouse-size bathtubs, but also have separate shower cubicles. Facilities include a spa, two restaurants, a bar and a French bakery.

PACIFIC HOTEL HISTORIC HOTEL $$

Map p280 (金门大酒店; Jīnmén Dàjiǔdiàn; ☎6327 6226; pacific.jinjianghotels.com; 108 West Nanjing Rd; 南京西路108号; d ¥988-1988; ❄; MPeople's Sq) Capped by a distinctive clock tower, this historic hotel built in 1926 is strong on both character and style. The neoclassical entrance leads to a marble lobby with attractive ceiling artwork and wood-trimmed corridors with deep-red carpets. The cheaper rooms at the back of the hotel are distinctly ordinary, but the ones overlooking People's Park have nicer furniture and more space.

PARK HOTEL HISTORIC HOTEL $$$

Map p280 (国际饭店; Guójì Fàndiàn; ☎6327 5225; park.jinjianghotels.com; 170 West Nanjing Rd; 南京西路170号; s ¥850 d ¥1350-1950; ❄; MPeople's Sq) Despite the wonderful art-deco building, constructed in 1934 and until the 1980s the tallest building in

Shànghǎi, the rooms here have less character than the nearby Pacific Hotel. Staff members are friendly, though, and 10% discounts are common. For more information on this historic hotel, see p66.

Old Town 南市

TOP CHOICE **WATERHOUSE AT SOUTH BUND** BOUTIQUE HOTEL $$
Map p284 (水舍时尚设计酒店; Shuǐshè Shíshàng Shèjì Jiǔdiàn; ☎6080 2988; www.waterhouseshanghai.com; 1-3 Maojiayuan Rd, Lane 479, South Zhongshan Rd; 中山南路479弄毛家园路1-3号; d ¥1100-2800; ; MXiaonanmen) There are few cooler places to base yourself in Shànghǎi than this 19-room, four-storey South Bund converted 1930s warehouse right by the Cool Docks. Gazing out onto excellent views of Pǔdōng (or into the crisp courtyard), The Waterhouse's natty rooms (some with terrace) are dressed with particularly swish designer furniture. Fittingly for this part of town, the ethos is industrial chic, a lovely rooftop bar caps it all and the trim ground-floor restaurant (p83) throws in a shot or two of culinary excellence for good measure.

HOTEL INDIGO HOTEL $$$
Map p284 (英迪格酒店; Yīngdígé Jiǔdiàn; www.hotelindigo.com; 585 East Zhongshan No 2 Rd; 中山东二路585号; d ¥4546-5006; ; MXiaonanmen) With its bubbly and creatively designed lobby – chairs like birdcages, tree branches trapped in cascades of glass jars, sheets of metal riveted to the wall, modish, sinuously shaped furniture, funky ceiling lights and Apple computers at reception (where Chinese tea awaits guests) – towering Hotel Indigo is a stylish South Bund arrival. The chic and playful rooms are all colourful cushions, whimsical designs, lovely rugs and spotless shower rooms while the infinity pool is a dream. Rooms either look out onto the Old Town (so-so) or the river (stellar). Regular discounts tame prices by up to 60%.

French Concession 法租界

TOP CHOICE **LANGHAM XĪNTIĀNDÌ** LUXURY HOTEL $$$
Map p286 (新天地朗廷酒店; Xīntiāndì Lǎngtíng Jiǔdiàn; ☎2330 2288; xintiandi.langhamhotels.com; 99 Madang Rd, French Concession East; 马当路99号; r ¥1550-2900; ; MSouth Huangpi Rd) Xīntiāndì has become a magnet for luxury hotels and they don't come much nicer than this one. Its 357 rooms all feature huge floor-to-ceiling windows, plenty of space to spread out in, and an attention to the minute details that make all the difference: Japanese-style wooden tubs in suites, heated bathroom floors, internet radio and white orchids in bloom no matter the season.

Amenities include the lauded Cantonese restaurant Ming Court (with a surprisingly affordable business lunch and all-you-can-eat dim sum on the weekends), an indoor pool and the award-winning spa, Chuan.

ANDAZ LUXURY HOTEL $$$
Map p286 (安达仕酒店; Āndáshì Jiǔdiàn; ☎2310 1234; shanghai.andaz.hyatt.com; 88 Songshan Rd, French Concession East; 嵩山路88号; r ¥1820-2820; ; MSouth Huangpi Rd) Housed in one of the twin skyscrapers just north of Xīntiāndì, Andaz (meaning 'personal style' in Hindi) is among the latest luxury hotels to open in the French Concession. Japanese interior designer Super Potato was brought in to lay out the rooms, and the result is a hip, modern space, with clean lines, natural materials (hardwood floors, granite bathrooms) and the signature LED lighting, which can be customised to suit your mood. The building's enormous curving windows are a feature throughout the hotel; you won't be disappointed by the views. Discounts of up to 35% online.

TOP CHOICE **MAGNOLIA BED & BREAKFAST** B&B $$
Map p290 (www.magnoliabnbshanghai.com; 36 Yanqing Rd, French Concession West; 延庆路36号; r ¥650-1200; ; MChangshu Rd) Opened by Miranda Yao of the cooking school The Kitchen at... (p33), this cosy little B&B is located in a 1927 French Concession home. It's Shànghǎi all the way, with an art-deco starting point followed by a stylish quest for modernity in both comfort and design. While the five rooms are on the small side, the place is a true labour of love and you couldn't ask for a better neighbourhood to base yourself in.

QUINTET B&B $$
Map p290 (☎6249 9088; www.quintet-shanghai.com; 808 Changle Rd, French Concession West; 长乐路808号; d ¥850-1200; ; MChangshu Rd) This chic B&B has six beautiful double rooms in a 1930s townhouse not short

on character. Some of the rooms are on the small side, but each is decorated with style, incorporating modern luxuries such as large-screen satellite TVs and laptop-sized safes, with more classic touches such as wood-stripped floorboards and deep porcelain bathtubs. Staff members sometimes get a BBQ going on the roof terrace and there's an excellent restaurant on the ground floor. No sign – just buzz on the gate marked 808 and wait to be let in. Be aware there is no elevator.

KEVIN'S OLD HOUSE B&B $$

Map p290 (老时光酒店; Lǎoshíguāng Jiǔdiàn; ☎6248 6800; www.kevinsoldhouse.com; No 4, Lane 946, Changle Rd, French Concession West; 长乐路946弄4号; ste ¥1180-1280; ❄📶; Ⓜ Changshu Rd) Housed in a secluded 1927 French Concession villa, this lovely boutique hotel has been lovingly restored to create an elegant yet affordable place to stay. Six suites are spread throughout the house; each is decorated with care and comes with wooden floorboards, traditional Chinese furniture, stylish artwork and a few antiques.

LE SUN CHINE BOUTIQUE HOTEL $$$

Map p290 (绅公馆; Shēn Gōng Guǎn; ☎5256 9977; www.lesunchine.com; No 6, Lane 1220 Huashan Rd, French Concession West; 华山路1220弄6号; r ¥1980-4380; ❄📶🏊) Originally the home of the Sun family, this 1932 mansion was completely renovated in 2009 to become one of Shànghǎi's most exclusive boutique properties. Seventeen personalised suites combine an antique-strewn style with all the modern comforts of home. Relax in the Roman-style pool or steam bath before enjoying a Shanghainese banquet in the highly lauded restaurant. The best way to get here is by taxi.

88 XĪNTIĀNDÌ BOUTIQUE HOTEL $$$

Map p286 (88新天地; ☎5383 8833; www.88xintiandi.com; 380 South Huangpi Rd, French Concession East; 黄陂南路380号; r from ¥1700; 🚭❄📶; Ⓜ Xintiandi, South Huangpi Rd) This stylish boutique residence is located in the upscale Xīntiāndì development and has 53 spacious studios, each decorated with red lamps and antique Chinese cabinets. The central feature of each room is the raised sleeping area, enclosed with curtains, but also of note are the kitchenettes (including microwave) and the top-notch home entertainment system that boasts surround-sound speakers, DVD player and satellite TV. There's a small health club overlooking the park; guests also enjoy complimentary access to the indoor pool at the nearby Langham Xīntiāndì.

PÚDǏ BOUTIQUE HOTEL BOUTIQUE HOTEL $$$

Map p286 (璞邸精品酒店; Púdǐ Jīngpǐn Jiǔdiàn; ☎5158 5888; www.boutiquehotel.cc; 99 Yandang Rd, French Concession East; 雁荡路99号; r from ¥1654; ❄@📶; Ⓜ Xintiandi) This trendy, ultra-modern hotel tries so hard to be cool that it sometimes borders on tacky. Unusual flat fish tanks in the dark corridors are neon-lit. Freestanding wooden cabinets with large-screen TV, DVD player and music system revolve to reveal a gaudy minibar, and the digital clocks by the bed use a laser to throw a time display on the ceiling. There is some genuine class, though. The modern artwork above each bed is edgy but dead cool and comes on huge canvasses, guests are given a pillow menu when they arrive so they can choose from a list of scented pillow fillings, and bathrooms, which, like the rooms themselves, are enormous, are beautifully designed and come with a rainforest showerhead as well as a deep bathtub with Jacuzzi jets. Plus, all rooms come with a 24-hour personal butler service.

MANSION HOTEL HISTORIC HOTEL $$$

Map p290 (首席公馆酒店; Shǒuxí Gōngguǎn Jiǔdiàn; ☎5403 9888; www.mansionhotelchina.com; 82 Xinle Rd, French Concession West; 新乐路82号; d from ¥3800; ❄📶; Ⓜ South Shaanxi Rd) This historic landmark is worth a peek even if you're not staying here. Housed in a 1930s building that was originally the residence of Sun Tingsun – a business partner of Huang Jinrong and Du Yuesheng, (two of Shànghǎi's most powerful gangsters; see p213) – stepping inside is like stepping back in time to the city's glorious, notorious past. The Mansion Hotel's concept of combining antique furnishings and modern luxury is a good one, though the place is starting to show some wear and the service is not at the level of Shànghǎi's high-end international hotels. That said, all rooms are huge and come with beautifully upholstered wood furniture, big-screen satellite TVs and, in all but the twins, Jacuzzis big enough for two. Expect discounts of around 50%.

HÉNGSHĀN MOLLER VILLA HISTORIC HOTEL $$$

Map p286 (衡山马勒别墅饭店; Héngshān Mǎlè Biéshù Fàndiàn; ☎6247 8881; www.mollervilla

.com; 30 South Shaanxi Rd, French Concession East; 陕西南路30号; r ¥1500-2800; ❄@📶; Ⓜ South Shaanxi Rd) This fairy-tale castle lookalike, built by Swedish businessman and horse-racing fanatic Eric Moller, was a family home until 1949 when the Communist Youth League took it over. One of Shànghǎi's strangest buildings, it's nonetheless a gorgeous place, with parquet floors in the lobby and a lush garden in the back. A bronze horse stands over the spot where Moller is said to have buried his favourite nag. Rooms feature old Shànghǎi artwork and are well turned out with sumptuous bedding and large-screen TVs that double as computers. Wi-fi access is in the lobby only.

CASA SERENA — BOUTIQUE HOTEL $$$

Map p286 (☎5382 1600; www.lapiscasahotelshanghai.com; 68 Taicang Rd, French Concession East; 太仓路68号; d ¥1500-2500; ❄📶; Ⓜ South Huangpi Rd) Natural textures are a feature of this charming boutique hotel beside Huaihai Park. The paving-stone corridor on the ground floor leads to 18 rooms with antique furniture and granite-tiled bathrooms, while a 2012 renovation has added five new spa rooms (services from the Green Massage spa next door). Expect discounts of 20%.

BLUE MOUNTAIN YOUTH HOSTEL — HOSTEL $

(蓝山国际青年旅舍; Lánshān Guójì Qīngnián Lǚshě; ☎6304 3938; www.bmhostel.com; 2nd fl, Bldg 1, 1072 Quxi Rd, French Concession East; 瞿溪路1072号1号甲2楼; dm ¥55-65, d ¥190, tr ¥240; ❄@📶; Ⓜ Luban Rd) A fabulous hostel, which, although slightly out of the way, is practically next door to Luban Rd metro station so it shouldn't leave you feeling too isolated. Rooms are simple but clean with pine furniture and flooring, TV and kettle. There are women-only, men-only and mixed dorms, and the communal facilities are excellent – a wi-fi–enabled bar-restaurant area with free pool table, free internet and free movie screenings, a kitchen with microwave, washing machines and even hairdryers and irons that you can borrow. Staff members speak English and are very friendly.

RUÌJĪN HOTEL — HISTORIC HOTEL $$$

Map p286 (瑞金宾馆; Ruìjīn Bīnguǎn; ☎6472 5222; www.ruijinhotelsh.com; 118 Ruijin No 2 Rd, French Concession East; 瑞金二路118号; standard/executive d ¥1320/2310; ❄@📶; Ⓜ South Shaanxi Rd) There are four buildings in this lovely garden estate, but the one you want is Building No 1, a 1919 red-brick mansion and the former residence of Benjamin Morris, one-time owner of *North China Daily News*. Dark-wood panelled corridors lead to a series of enormous, executive-class rooms that have attracted guests such as Mao Zedong and President Nixon. The furniture is exquisite – redwood double bed, antique desk and chair – and rooms come with TV, computer, DVD player and bathrooms with deep tubs. Buildings 2, 3 and 4 are more modern and house a mixture of nothing-special standard and executive rooms. Wi-fi in the lobby only; expect discounts of 20%.

OKURA GARDEN HOTEL SHÀNGHǍI — HOTEL $$$

Map p286 (花园饭店上海; Huāyuán Fàndiàn; ☎6415 1111; www.gardenhotelshanghai.com; 58 South Maoming Rd, French Concession East; 茂名南路58号; d from ¥2600; ❄🏊; Ⓜ South Shaanxi Rd) The elegant Japanese-run five-star Okura Garden boasts beautiful grounds, on the site of the old French Club, and an excellent location, close to many of the boutiques in the former concession. Rooms are decorated tastefully in natural colours and the modern bathrooms have Japanese-style seat-warming toilets. Service is top-notch; discounts reach up to 50%.

HILTON HOTEL — HOTEL $$$

Map p290 (静安希尔顿饭店; Jìng'ān Xī'ěrdùn Fàndiàn; ☎6248 0000; www.hilton.com; 250 Huashan Rd, French Concession West; 华山路250号; r from ¥1390; ⊖❄@📶🏊; Ⓜ Jing'an Temple) A favourite with airline crews and tour groups, the Hilton's standard rooms are a bit old-fashioned, but the deluxe versions – only ¥100 to ¥200 more – have had a modern refit, meaning more style (slick furniture, rainforest showers), more comfort (thick carpets, big beds) and better views. Broadband/wi-fi access costs ¥120/160 per day.

HÀNTÍNG HOTEL — HOTEL $

Map p286 (汉庭酒店; Hàntíng Jiǔdiàn; ☎5465 6633; www.htinns.com; 233 South Shaanxi Rd, French Concession East; 陕西南路233号; s ¥299, d from ¥339; ❄@📶; Ⓜ South Shaanxi Rd, Jiashan Rd) Although rooms are a bit on the small side at this midrange chain, they're nonetheless spotless and in good condition, with a sprig of plastic ivy on the air-conditioner to add that special touch. English is limited.

YUÈYÁNG HOTEL HOTEL $

Map p290 (悦阳商务酒店; Yuèyáng Shāngwù Jiǔdiàn; ☎6466 6767; 58 Yueyang Rd; 岳阳路58号; s ¥188, d ¥268-368; ❄; Ⓜ Hengshan Rd) One of the best budget options in the French Concession that's within easy walking distance of a metro station, Yuèyáng has well-kept spacious rooms with big double beds, laminated flooring and free broadband. Shower rooms are clean and modern, although, annoyingly, the hot water isn't always piping hot. Expect only small discounts, if any.

MOTEL 268 HOTEL $

Map p286 (莫泰连锁旅店; Mòtài Liánsuǒ Lǚdiàn; ☎5170 3333; www.motel168.com; 113 Sinan Rd, French Concession East; 思南路113号; d ¥248-298; ❄@; Ⓜ Dapuqiao) This dependable chain on leafy Sinan Rd is ideally located for those wanting to explore the maze of charming alleyways known as Tiánzǐfáng. It's not the best of Shànghǎi's crop of Motel 168s, but rooms are nonetheless in reasonable shape with large desks, comfy chairs and invigorating showers. Note some rooms are windowless. English is limited.

Another **branch** (Map p290; ☎5403 7658; www.motel168.com; 1-3 North Xiangyang Rd, French Concession West; 襄阳北路1-3号; tw from ¥328; ❄@; Ⓜ South Shaanxi Rd) has a central location in French Concession West, although it is more expensive and, at last check, more run-down.

ĀNTÍNG VILLA HOTEL HISTORIC HOTEL $$$

Map p290 (安亭别墅花园酒店; Āntíng Biéshù Huāyuán Jiǔdiàn; ☎6433 1188; 46 Anting Rd; 安亭路46号; r ¥1180-1380; ❄; Ⓜ Hengshan Rd) On a quiet tree-lined street, this pleasant hotel shares its grounds with a 1936 colonial Spanish-style villa. It offers bright, comfortable rooms, with broadband and quality furniture including a chaise longue by the window. Some rooms have fine views over the garden, which is a popular spot for weddings at weekends. Discounts of up to 40% are available.

DŌNGHÚ HOTEL HISTORIC HOTEL $$

Map p290 (东湖宾馆; Dōnghú Bīnguǎn; ☎6415 8158; www.donghuhotel.com; 70 Donghu Rd, French Concession West; 东湖路70号; d US$150-330; ❄📶; Ⓜ South Shaanxi Rd) Once the home of feared Shànghǎi gangster Du Yuesheng (see p213), the historic Dōnghú is divided into several areas and buildings, although only two of them house ordinary guestrooms. The first, an austere 1934 white, concrete building, houses the better rooms, although their colour schemes leave little to be desired. The second, newer building is an ugly, white-tiled affair across the road and has over-priced rooms with cheap carpets and tatty furnishings. Wi-fi in the lobby only. Discounts of up to 50% make this a reliable midrange option.

JǏNJIĀNG HOTEL HISTORIC HOTEL $$$

Map p286 (锦江饭店; Jǐnjiāng Fàndiàn; ☎3218 9888; 59 South Maoming Rd, French Concession East; 茂名南路59号; r from ¥3300, ste from ¥8000; ❄; Ⓜ South Shaanxi Rd) This historic 1931 complex consists of two main buildings – the red-brick Georgian-style Cathay Building which houses the doubles, and the art-deco-style Grosvenor Villa (Guìbīn Lóu) which has the suites. Cathay has huge rooms with large beds, but a dated cream-and-brown colour scheme. The bathrooms are more modern with sparkling showers and deep tubs. All rooms have a TV, a safe and ironing board. Internet access, though, is an extra ¥90 per day. Expect 40% discounts.

Jìng'ān 静安

TOP CHOICE **URBN** BOUTIQUE HOTEL $$$

Map p294 (☎5153 4600; www.urbnhotels.com; 183 Jiaozhou Rd; 胶州路183号; r from ¥1500; 🚭❄📶; Ⓜ Changping Rd) China's first carbon-neutral hotel not only incorporates recyclable materials and low-energy products where possible, it also calculates its complete carbon footprint – including staff commutes and delivery journeys – and offsets it by donating money to environmentally friendly projects. Open-plan rooms are beautifully designed with low furniture and sunken living areas exuding space. Bathtubs are in the bedroom rather than in the bathroom (and sometimes right next to the bed!), while grey slate tiling gives this luxury boutique hotel a distinctly urban vibe.

PÚLÌ LUXURY HOTEL $$$

Map p294 (璞丽酒店; Púlì Jiǔdiàn; ☎3203 9999; www.thepuli.com; 1 Changde Rd; 常德路1号; d from ¥3880; 🚭❄📶🏊; Ⓜ Jing'an Temple) The Púlì is another future-forward Shànghǎi edifice, with open-space rooms divided by hanging silk screens and an understated beige-and-mahogany colour scheme accentuated by the beauty of a few well-placed orchids. The Zen calm and gorgeous design of this 26-storey hotel make another strong case for stylish skyscrapers. Book ahead for discounts of up to 60%.

JIA SHÀNGHǍI BOUTIQUE HOTEL **$$$**

Map p294 (☎6217 9000; www.jiashanghai.com; 931 West Nanjing Rd; 南京西路931号; r from ¥2500; 🚭❄📶; Ⓜ West Nanjing Rd) This stylish boutique hotel is housed in a charming 1920s building that has been re-imagined as a hip short-term residence. Rooms – studios, suites and penthouses – have a slick, sassy, open-plan design with funky furniture and extras such as DVD player and heated towel racks. While all rooms come with a kitchenette, not all have access to the original balconies. Prices – often discounted by nearly 50% – include breakfast as well as afternoon cakes and wine. Note that the hotel entrance is on Taixing Rd.

TOP CHOICE **LE TOUR TRAVELER'S REST** HOSTEL **$**

Map p294 (乐途静安国际青年旅舍; Lètú Jìng'ān Guójì Qīngnián Lǚshè; ☎6267 1912; www.letourshanghai.com; 319 Jiaozhou Rd; 胶州路319号; dm ¥70, d/tr/q ¥260/360/360; ❄@📶; Ⓜ Changping Rd) Housed in a former towel factory, this fabulous youth hostel leaves most others out to dry. You'll pass a row of splendid *shíkùmén* (stone-gate houses) on your way down the alley to get here, and the old-Shànghǎi textures continue once inside, with red-brick walls and reproduced stone gateways above doorways leading to simple but smart rooms and six-person dorms (shared bathrooms). The ground floor has a ping pong table, a pool table and wi-fi, all of which are free to use, while there's a fine rooftop bar-restaurant with outdoor seating. Bicycles can also be rented here.

SOHO PEOPLE'S SQUARE YOUTH HOSTEL HOSTEL **$**

off Map p293 (苏州河畔国际青年旅社; Sūzhōu Hépàn Guójì Qīngnián Lǚshè; ☎5888 8817; 1307 South Suzhou Rd; 南苏州路1307号; dm without/with bathroom ¥55/65, d ¥200-300, tr ¥400; ❄@📶; Ⓜ Xinzha Rd) Set in a former warehouse along Sūzhōu Creek, this spacious hostel features high ceilings, painted murals on the walls and oodles of laid-back common space. It's a bit out of the way, but only a five-minute walk from the Xinzha Rd metro station on line 1, which runs direct through People's Square and the French Concession. Laundry and some kitchen facilities (microwave, fridge) available.

PORTMAN RITZ-CARLTON HOTEL **$$$**

Map p294 (波特曼丽嘉酒店; Bōtèmàn Lìjiā Jiǔdiàn; ☎6279 8888; www.ritzcarlton.com; 1376 West Nanjing Rd; 南京西路1376号; r from ¥4000; 🚭❄@📶🏊; Ⓜ Jing'an Temple) Impeccable service, excellent facilities and a central location make this one of the best business hotels this side of the Huángpǔ River. While it lacks the gorgeous interior design and architectural pizzazz of Shànghǎi's newest crop of five-star hotels, it's nonetheless a first-rate luxury choice. Selling points include two 7th-floor pools, squash and tennis courts, and a gym. The real reason for staying here, of course, is the business amenities and the surrounding Shànghǎi Centre, which has a medical clinic, excellent restaurants and consulates, and, in short, is Shànghǎi's biggest expat hangout since the Peace Hotel c 1931. Discounts can drop rates by as much as 60%.

JǏNJIĀNG INN HOTEL **$**

Map p294 (锦江之星旅馆; Jǐnjiāng Zhīxīng Lǚguǎn; ☎5213 8811; www.jinjianginns.com; 400 Xikang Rd; 西康路400号; s/d from ¥239/299; ❄📶; Ⓜ Changping Rd) Rooms are in excellent shape at this bright and simple chain (there's another branch in the Bund; p194). Wi-fi in the lobby only.

HOLIDAY INN DOWNTOWN HOTEL **$$**

Map p293 (上海广场长城假日酒店; Shànghǎi Guǎngchǎng Chángchéng Jiàrì Jiǔdiàn; ☎6353 8008; www.holidayinn.com.cn; 285 West Tianmu Rd & 585 Hengfeng Rd; 天目西路285号, 恒丰路585号; d from ¥988; ❄@📶; Ⓜ Shanghai Railway Station) Easy to spot as you come out of the train station, the four-star Holiday Inn is made up of two buildings separated by a small pedestrianised street. The Great Wall Wing (长城假日酒店) is accessed from Hengfeng Rd, while the Plaza Wing (广场假日酒店) is accessed from West Tianmu Rd. Prices are the same in both, as are the modern, tastefully decorated rooms which come with TV, broadband (per day ¥60), a safe, fridge and ironing board. Bathrooms are smart but small. Expect 25% discounts; wi-fi in the lobby only.

Pŭdōng 浦东

RITZ-CARLTON SHÀNGHĂI PŬDŌNG LUXURY HOTEL $$$

Map p296 (上海浦东丽思卡尔顿酒店; Shànghăi Pŭdōng Lìsī Kăěrdùn Jiŭdiàn; ☎2020 1888; www.ritzcarlton.com; Shànghăi IFC, 8 Century Ave; 世纪大道8号; d from ¥2800; ; MLujiazui) From the stingray-skin effect wallpaper in the lift to its exquisite accommodation and stunning al fresco bar, the deliciously styled, 285-room Ritz-Carlton in the Shànghăi IFC seizes the much-contested Pŭdōng hotel crown with aplomb. The beautifully designed rooms – a blend of feminine colours, eye-catching art-deco motifs, chic elegance and dramatic Bund-side views – are a stylistic triumph. Divided from the room by a screen, delightful open-plan bathrooms feature deep and inviting freestanding bathtubs. Service is, unsurprisingly, top-notch.

GRAND HYATT LUXURY HOTEL $$$

Map p296 (金茂君悦大酒店; Jīnmào Jūnyuè Dàjiŭdiàn; ☎5049 1234; www.shanghai.grand.hyatt.com; Jinmao Tower, 88 Century Ave; 世纪大道88号金茂大厦; d from ¥3000; ; MLujiazu) This classy 555-room hotel, spanning the top 34 floors of the majestic Jinmao Tower (p139), remains one of Shànghăi's finest. Its once unimpeachable standard for quality high-rise hotel living in Shànghăi attracted inevitable competition, but an ongoing floor-by-floor refurbishment has pepped up rooms. Dramatic-looking Tang-dynasty poems are inscribed in gold above lovely beds, while espresso-making machines, smart tan-leather work desks and inviting bathrooms round out a luxurious picture. Corner rooms are coveted, the neck-craning 33-storey atrium is always astonishing, while service remains highly attentive, restaurants (such as On 56, p140) are outstanding and the views stratospheric.

PARK HYATT LUXURY HOTEL $$$

Map p296 (柏悦酒店; Bóyuè Jiŭdiàn; ☎6888 1234; www.parkhyattshanghai.com; Shànghăi World Financial Center, 100 Century Ave; 世纪大道100号世界金融中心; d from ¥2700; ; MLujiazui) Spanning the 79th to 93rd floors of the towering Shànghăi World Financial Center (p140), this soaring hotel is the world's second highest hotel above ground level (at the time of writing): Pŭdōng's huge towers dwarf into Lego blocks as lobby views graze the tip of the Jinmao Tower. Far smaller than the Grand Hyatt, the 174-room hotel is subdued, with deco touches: high-walled corridors of brown-fabric and grey-stone textures lead to luxurious rooms where quirky features (mist-free bathroom mirror containing a small TV screen, toilet seats that open automatically as you near them) assemble. All rooms come with huge TV, free wi-fi, free fresh coffee, deep bathtubs, leather chaise lounges, sumptuous beds and outrageously good views. Accessed from the south side of the tower.

PŬDŌNG SHANGRI-LA LUXURY HOTEL $$$

Map p296 (浦东香格里拉大酒店; Pŭdōng Xiānggélǐlā Dàjiŭdiàn; ☎6882 8888; www.shangri-la.com; 33 Fucheng Rd; 富城路33号; r from ¥2650; ; MLujiazui) They don't look much from the outside, but the Shangri-La's two towers – one neoclassical, the other much more modern – house an elegance found at few other five-star hotels in Shànghăi. The lobby, corridors, restaurants and rooms are tastefully decorated in natural colours, the beds are sumptuous with pillows galore and the marble bathrooms are exquisite. All rooms have wi-fi and those in the new tower have ceiling-to-floor windows. Discounts bring the standard rooms down to around ¥1800 in the old tower and ¥2000 in the new tower.

JUMEIRAH HIMALAYAS HOTEL LUXURY HOTEL $$$

Map p297 (卓美亚喜玛拉雅酒店; Zhuóměiyà Xǐmălāyă Jiŭdiàn; ☎3858 0888; www.jumeirah.com; 1108 Meihua Rd; 梅花路1108号; d ¥4149, ste ¥5989-6564; ; MHuamu Rd) With its huge lobby hung with traditional Chinese paintings as a vast overhead screen swarms with hypnotic, colourful images and patterns above a Chinese pavilion, this unique hotel is simply jaw-dropping. In fact, it's an event in itself: just perusing the lobby landscape art alone is a diversion in culture-lite Pŭdōng. Feng shui–arranged rooms are gorgeous and spacious, designed with a strong accent on traditional Chinese aesthetics, given a highly contemporary twist. Rooms are stunning with lovely bathrooms, hardwood floors, beds arranged with traditional Chinese pillows, and coffee machines to hand. Service is prompt and assuring, the swimming pool has underwater music and an array of fine restaurants rounds out an already superlative picture. Discounts are good, but book ahead.

BEEHOME HOSTEL HOSTEL $

Map p296 (宾家国际青年旅舍; Bīnjiā Guójì Qīngnián Lǚshè; ☎5887 9801; www.beehome-hostel.com; Lane 490, No 210 Dongchang Rd; 东昌路490弄210号; dm ¥65, tw/tr ¥258/298, d ¥278-360; ❄@📶; ⓂDongchang Rd) This well-tended hostel hidden away behind greenery is a leafy oasis in an otherwise innocuous Pǔdōng housing estate. It offers basic but clean rooms, all with private bathrooms (even the dorms), and excellent communal areas – a bar-restaurant, a balcony seating area and a cute, tree-shaded courtyard garden. There's wi-fi throughout. The hostel is tricky to find as there's no English sign on the road – it's through the first gate past the China Post office by the magazine seller on Dongchang Rd through a wooden gateway marked 东园新村 (Dōngyuán Xīncūn).

Hóngkǒu & North Shànghǎi 虹口区、北上海

TOP CHOICE ASTOR HOUSE HOTEL HISTORIC HOTEL $$$

Map p298 (浦江饭店; Pǔjiāng Fàndiàn; ☎6324 6388; www.astorhousehotel.com; 15 Huangpu Rd; 黄浦路15号; d/ste ¥1280/2800; ❄@📶; ⓂTiantong Rd) Stuffed with history (and perhaps a ghost or two), this august old-timer shakes up an impressive cocktail from select ingredients: a location just off the Bund, old-world, Shànghǎi-era charm, great discounts and colossal rooms. There's enough wood panelling to build an ark, you could shunt a bed into the capacious bathrooms, while the original polished wooden floorboards, corridors and galleries (the forlorn-looking Richard's Bar and massage parlours aside) pitch the mood somewhere between British public school and Victorian asylum. Some of the rooms on the higher floors have river views. Only partial wi-fi cover; broadband is ¥60 per day. Discounts of 40%.

CHAI LIVING RESIDENCES APARTMENT $$$

Map p298 (☎3366 3209; www.chailiving.com; Embankment Bldg, 400 North Suzhou Rd; 苏州北路400号; 3 days/1 week/1 month apt from ¥3300/6000/13,500; 📶; ⓂTiantong Rd) If you need a stylish Shànghǎi address, you can't get much better than these luxurious, beautifully appointed and individually styled apartments in the Embankment Building. The block is a living, breathing residential block and bumping into tenants merely adds authentic charm. There's a minimum three-day stay – just enough time to fully savour the outstanding views and decor. Apartments range from 40 to 200 sq metres, with daily maid service, underfloor heating, kitchens with Nespresso coffee machines and tantalising river views.

NAZA INTERNATIONAL YOUTH HOSTEL HOSTEL $

Map p298 (那宅青年旅舍; Nàzhái Qīngnián Lǚshè; ☎6541 7062; 318 Baoding Rd; 保定路318号; dm ¥75, s/d/tw/f ¥189/229/249/329; ❄@📶; ⓂDalian Rd) Another decent Hóngkǒu youth hostel, quiet Naza comes with a pleasant light-filled courtyard, fine communal spaces including a restful bar area with free pool table and a cute cafe. Rooms are a bit scuffed with basic furniture, but all (apart from some dorms) have TV and en suite bathroom. More expensive rooms come with reproduction antique furniture, including one with a four-poster bed. Internet is free and the ground floor has wi-fi. Long-let rooms are available (per month dorm/single ¥1600/2100).

KOALA GARDEN HOUSE HOSTEL $

Map p298 (考拉花园旅舍; Kǎolā Huāyuán Lǚshè; ☎5671 1038; 240 Duolun Rd; 多伦路240号; dm ¥100, d ¥420-880; ❄@📶; ⓂDongbaoxing Rd) With its high ceilings, brightly painted walls, spacious bar and location on Duolun Rd, this is an OK choice. Rooms, all slightly different, are decorated in a feminine way with flower-patterned wallpaper and gathered-up curtains, and all come with wall-mounted flat-screen TV and small bathroom, but compare rooms as things are getting shabby. The two most expensive – Tulip and Rose – have private balconies. Dorms are small, but quite neat. Internet is free; good discounts.

Xújiāhuì & South Shànghǎi 徐家汇、南上海

ASSET HOTEL HOTEL $

Map p300 (雅舍宾馆; Yǎshè Bīnguǎn; ☎6438 9900; www.asset-hotel.com; 590 South Wanping Rd; 宛平南路590号; r from ¥420; ❄@; ⓂShanghai Stadium) Housed in a charming yellow-and-white building hidden from the main road by apartments, this higher-end budget option offers smart, clean rooms with free broadband, complimentary mineral water, a fridge, TV and kettle. Rates include breakfast, and discounts reach 45%.

West Shànghǎi
长宁、古北、虹桥

HÓNGQIÁO STATE GUEST HOUSE HOTEL $$$
Map p302 (虹桥迎宾馆; Hóngqiáo Yíngbīnguǎn; 6219 8855; www.hqstateguesthotel.com; 1591 Hongqiao Rd; 虹桥路1591号; d from ¥1660; ; Yili Rd) Housed in very pleasant garden grounds, rooms here have a homey feel, decorated in warm colours and benefiting from floor-to-ceiling windows. Although not close to central Shànghǎi and less modern than the downtown choices, it's definitely a possibility for those attending trade fairs in the nearby exhibition centre. The executive rooms, which are far classier than the standard rooms, are located in a more impressive building nearby with a beautiful marble lobby and antiques in the corridors. Facilities include the excellent Clark Hatch Fitness Centre. Discounts of 40% are common.

MARRIOTT HOTEL HÓNGQIÁO HOTEL $$
Map p302 (万豪虹桥大酒店; Wànháo Hóngqiáo Dàjiǔdiàn; 6237 6000; www.marriott.com; 2270 Hongqiao Rd; 虹桥路2270号; r from ¥1024; @; Longxi Rd) This Marriott is a reasonable choice if you're doing business in the Hóngqiáo area. A grand lobby introduces guests to good all-around facilities that include a bright, semicircular swimming pool, tennis court, bar and a number of decent restaurants. While rooms themselves are basic and a bit dated, the rates are reasonable. Broadband in the standard rooms costs extra (¥120 per day).

XĪJIĀO STATE GUEST HOUSE HOTEL $$
Map p302 (西郊宾馆; Xījiāo Bīnguǎn; 6219 8800; www.hotelxijiao.com; 1921 Hongqiao Rd; 虹桥路1921号; r from ¥1168; ; Longxi Rd) This quiet spot, which has hosted guests as esteemed as Queen Elizabeth II and Mao Zedong, claims to be the largest garden hotel in Shànghǎi. Its 80 hectares include huge lawns, streams, mature trees and a large lake. Standard rooms are nothing special, but facilities include indoor and outdoor tennis courts, a delightful indoor pool and a gym.

HOTEL CAROLINA HOTEL $$
Map p302 (美卡商务酒店; Měikǎ Shāngwù Jiǔdiàn; 5258 2000; 643 Xinhua Rd; 新华路643号; d from ¥728; ; West Yan'an Rd) Set back slightly from leafy, historic Xinhua Rd, this midrange business hotel has neat, well-equipped rooms with TV, broadband, safe, fridge and rainforest showers as well as elegant touches such as silk bed-runners. Discounts bring standard doubles down to below ¥400, making it a good-value option. Wi-fi in the lobby.

Understand Shànghǎi

Shànghǎi Today

Rapidly becoming a world metropolis, Shànghǎi somehow typifies modern China while being unlike anywhere else in the land. Awash with cash, ambition and economic energy, Shànghǎi is, for movers and shakers of business (and indeed any job-seeking Chinese migrant), *the* place to be. For all its modernity and cosmopolitanism, however, Shànghǎi is part and parcel of the People's Republic of China, and its challenges are multiplying as fast as cocktails are mixed and served on the Bund.

Best on Film

Shanghai Triad (Zhang Yimou; 1995) Stylish take on Shànghǎi's 1930s gangster scene, starring Gong Li.

Empire of the Sun (Steven Spielberg; 1987) Dramatisation of JG Ballard's account of his internment in WWI Shànghǎi as a child.

Suzhou River (Ye Lou; 2000) A disturbing and obsessive narrative of love in modern Shànghǎi.

Best in Print

Life and Death in Shanghai (Nien Cheng) Classic account of the Cultural Revolution, with a Shànghǎi angle.

Shanghai: The Rise and Fall of a Decadent City 1842–1949 (Stella Dong) Rip-roaring profile of the city's good-old, bad-old days.

Money

The Shanghainese may natter about traffic gridlock and chat about the latest celebrity faux pas or political scandal, but what they really talk about is money. Labelled *xiǎozī* – 'little capitalists' – by the rest of the land, the Shànghǎi Chinese know how to make money *(qián)* and, equally importantly, how to flaunt it. Ever since Shànghǎi first prospered under foreign control, wealth creation has been indivisible from the Shànghǎi psyche. Whether it's the stock market, apartment price tags or the cost of buying a car – money's the talk of the town.

Property

Shànghǎi property prices are talked about in the same way British people chat about the weather. The high prices have ramifications for everyone renting (or owning) floor space, from the lowliest McJobber to the wealthiest property tycoon. Amid dark mutterings of a property bubble, the government has repeatedly tried to tame the runaway market with a raft of tax and ownership measures to stifle speculation, but they have had limited success in Shànghǎi, where property prices in relation to income are higher than London, New York or Tokyo. The average marrying age for Shànghǎi couples has risen with house prices: on average, young Shànghǎi ladies now wait till around 30 before tying the knot (compared to around 26 in 2007).

Economic & Political Uncertainty

The city has been a success story of almost legendary proportions, but the transition of power to the new Chinese leadership in 2012 came at a time of mounting insecurity. Clouds were gathering fast: the speed of economic growth was slowing, political scandals (the fall of disgraced former politician Bo Xilai and the intensifying attention paid to the lavish wardrobes of medium-income officials, for example) were mushrooming and friction with Japan over the Diaoyu (Senkaku) Islands increasing. In September 2012, vociferous anti-Japanese demonstrations across China meant the outlook for the East Asian region looked choppy. In Shànghǎi, as anywhere else in China, the glowing coals of Chinese nationalism are easily stoked. How the new leadership handles this fervour in a time of economic uncertainty will test its mettle.

Greying Shànghǎi

For such a seemingly sprightly city, Shànghǎi is ageing fast. In 2011, 23.4% of the city's population was over 60, but by 2030 this will have leaped to over 30%, with an additional 200,000 people reaching the age of 60 every year. Implemented in 1979, the one-child policy has created a huge bulge of pensioners, around 80% of whom will be looked after by single children.

Growth & Urban Density

Over the past two decades, Shànghǎi has grown faster than any other world city and now houses around 23 million people (a third of the population of the UK). To accommodate the vast influx of economic migrants, the city's size has expanded sixfold since the early 1990s. With four times the number of people per square kilometre living here than in New York, there's not a lot of elbow room. Cars generate 70% to 80% of air pollution, and vehicle numbers continue to multiply, despite the prohibitive costs of buying a registration plate (c ¥40,000).

Us & Them

Shànghǎi has a fraught relationship with the rest of China. The city has lured a vast army of labourers who work on the lowest-paid rung of the employment ladder. Although their city has always been a haven for outsiders, the Shànghǎi Chinese tend to look down on nonlocal Chinese. A non-Shànghǎi accent automatically identifies *wàidìrén* (外地人), who are considered *tǔ* (literally 'earth', meaning rural). Shànghǎi people conversely see themselves as *yáng* (literally 'sea', but meaning 'Western'). This chauvinism is almost an ideology in itself and, despite the glut of immigrant workers, *wàidì* Chinese have to jump through hoops to become a full 'local' (one route is to marry a Shànghǎi person, but you have to stay married for at least 10 years). Even then, if you carry an accent, you remain a misfit.

if Shanghai were 100 people

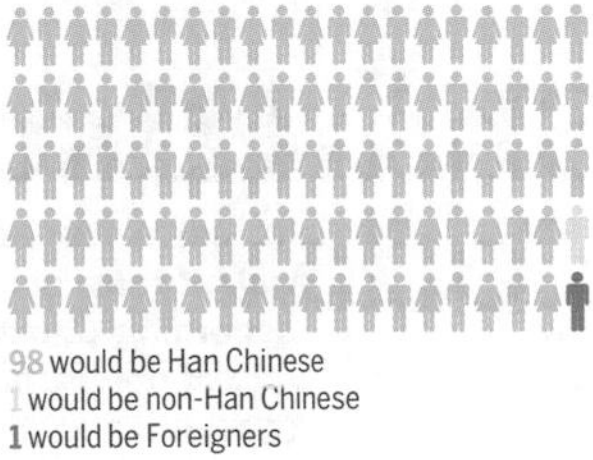

Age of Residents

(% of population by age)

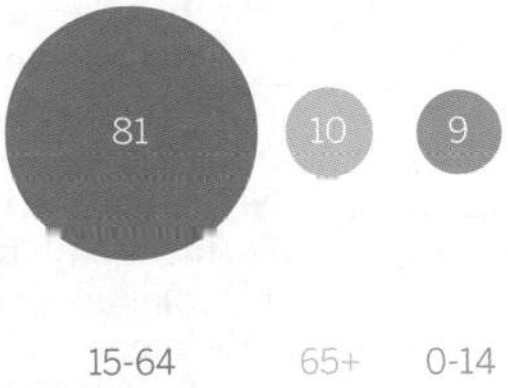

population per sq km

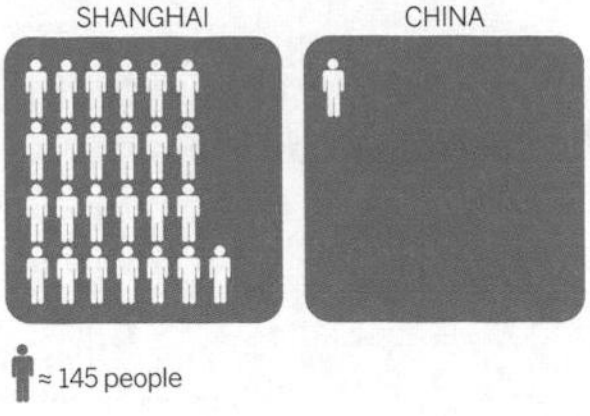

History

In just a few centuries, Shànghǎi went from being an insignificant walled town south of the mouth of the Yangzi River (Cháng Jiāng) to becoming China's leading and wealthiest metropolis. A mesmerising tale of opium, business and trade, foreign control, vice, glamour, glitz, rebellion and restoration, Shànghǎi's story is a rags-to-riches saga of decadence, exploitation and, ultimately, achievement.

SHÀNGHǍI'S MARSHY ROOTS

Up until around the 7th century AD, Shànghǎi was little more than marshland. At that time, the area was known as Shēn, 申, (after Chunshen Jun, 春申君, a local nobleman from the 3rd century BC) or Hù, 沪, (after a type of bamboo fishing trap used by fisherman). The character hù (沪) still identifies the city today – on car number plates, for example – while the city's main football team is known as Shanghai Shenhua (上海申花).

The earliest mention of the name Shànghǎi occurs in the 11th century AD and refers to the small settlement that sprang up at the confluence of the Shanghai River (long since vanished) and the Huángpǔ River (黄浦江; Huángpǔ Jiāng). Upgraded from village status to market town in 1074, Shànghǎi became a city in 1297 after establishing itself as the major port in the area.

By the late 17th century Shànghǎi supported a population of 50,000, sustained on cotton production, fishing and, thanks to its excellent location at the head of the Yangzi River (长江; Cháng Jiāng), trade in silk and tea.

OPIUM

By the 1880s, around 10% of the Chinese population smoked opium. No other commodity became so uniquely associated with all of Shànghǎi's spectacular peaks and troughs.

IT ALL STARTED WITH A LITTLE BIT OF OPIUM

During the early years of the Qing dynasty (1644–1911), the British East India Company and its later incarnations were trading in the only port open to the West: Canton (now Guǎngzhōu; 广州), south of Shànghǎi. British purchases of tea, silk and porcelain outweighed Chinese purchases

TIMELINE

453–221 BC

Warring States period: the earliest imperial records date from this time, although Neolithic discoveries in Qīngpǔ County suggest human settlement of the region 5900 years ago.

AD 242

The original Lónghuá Temple is built during the Three Kingdoms Period.

960–1126

Chinese fleeing the Mongols during the Song dynasty boost the region's population, spurring Shànghǎi on to become the county seat of Jiāngsū in 1291.

of wool and spices, so by the late 18th century the British had decided to balance the books by slipping into India to swap (at a profit) silver for opium with which to purchase Chinese goods. The British passion for tea was increasingly matched by China's craving for opium (鸦片; *yāpiàn*), the drug that would virtually single-handedly create latter-day Shànghǎi and earn the city its bipolar reputation as the splendid 'Paris of the East' and the infamous 'Whore of the Orient'.

From a mercantile point of view, the trade in opium – known as 'foreign mud' in China – was an astonishing success, rapidly worming its way into every nook and cranny of Chinese society. Highly addictive and widely available thanks to the prolific efforts of British traders, the drug – smoked via a pipe – quickly became the drug of choice for all sections of the Chinese public, from the lowliest and most menial upwards. Jardine & Matheson's highly lucrative trade empire was founded on the opium business.

Opium became the driving force behind Shànghǎi's unstoppable rise and its descent into debauchery – from Shànghǎi's affluent taipans (powerful foreign businessmen) and lucrative *hongs* (business houses) to its piercing inequalities: its wanton netherworld of prostitution and vice, violent criminal gangs, corrupt police forces and the city's cartographic constitution of concessions, settlements and Chinese districts.

The Opium War between Great Britain and China was similarly fought in the drug's name and as a pretext to extract the concessions that British opium traders sought from China. The Treaty of Nanking that concluded the First Opium War in 1842 was Shànghǎi's moment of reckoning, for its signing spelled the death of old Shànghǎi and the birth of the wild, lawless and spectacularly prosperous endeavour that would rise up over the Huángpǔ River.

The crossing over Sūzhōu Creek was once undertaken by ferry from three crossing points, until the first proper bridge (Wills' Bridge) was built from wood in 1856, lashing the prosperous British and American settlements together.

THE ILLEGITIMATE BIRTH OF SHÀNGHǍI

The Treaty of Nanking stipulated, among other things: peace between China and Britain; security and protection of British persons and property; the opening of Canton, Fúzhōu, Xiàmén, Níngbō and Shànghǎi, as well as residence for foreigners and consulates in those cities (for the purpose of trade); fair import and export tariffs; the possession of Hong Kong; and an indemnity of US$18 million. Ironically enough, the trade of opium, legal or otherwise, never entered into the treaty.

Following Great Britain's lead, other countries were inspired to join in, including the US and France. In 1843 the first British consul moved into a local house in the Old Town, signalling a foreign presence in the city that would last for the next 100 years.

1553

The city wall around Shànghǎi's Old Town is constructed to fend off Japanese pirates; 9m high and 5km around, the wall stands until the fall of the Qing dynasty, and is demolished in 1912.

1685

A customs house is opened in Shànghǎi for the first time.

1793

Lord Macartney, George III's envoy to China, is rebuffed by the Qianlong emperor in Chéngdé, sinking British hopes of expanding legitimate trade relations with the 'Middle Kingdom'.

1823

The British are now importing roughly 7000 chests of opium annually – with about 140lb of opium per chest, enough to keep one million addicts happy – compared with 1000 chests in 1773.

Of the five port cities in China, Shànghǎi was the most prosperous due to its superb geographical location, capital edge and marginal interference from the Chinese government. Trade and businesses boomed, and by 1850 the foreign settlements housed more than 100 merchants, missionaries and physicians, three-quarters of them British. In 1844, 44 foreign ships made regular trade with China. By 1849, 133 ships lined the shores and by 1855, 437 foreign ships clogged the ports.

Foreigners were divided into three concessions. The original British Concession was north of Bubbling Well Rd (now West Nanjing Rd). The American Concession began life in Hóngkǒu District after Bishop William Boone had set up a mission there. These two concessions later joined to form one large area known as the International Settlement. The French, meanwhile, set up their own settlement south of the British one and to the west of the Old Town, in an area which is still referred to by English speakers as the French Concession.

From regulation to sanitation, everything in Shànghǎi was vested in the foreign oligarchies of the Municipal Council and the Conseil d'Administration Municipale, a pattern that was to last as long as the settlements. It was not until the early 1920s that Chinese and Japanese residents (eventually the two largest groups in the settlements) were allowed even limited representation on the council.

From the start, Shànghǎi's *raison d'être* was trade. Still sailing to the West were silks, tea and porcelain, and 30,000 chests of opium were being delivered into China annually. Soon great Hong Kong trading houses like Butterfield & Swire and Jardine & Matheson set up shop, and trade in opium, silk and tea gradually shifted to textiles, real estate, banking, insurance and shipping. Banks in particular boomed; soon all of China's loans, debts and indemnity payments were funnelled through Shànghǎi. Buying and selling was handled by Chinese middlemen, known as *compradors* (from the Portuguese), from Canton and Níngbō, who formed a rare link between the Chinese and foreign worlds. The city attracted immigrants and entrepreneurs from across

VIRTUAL SHANGHAI

The online resource Virtual Shanghai (www.virtualshanghai.net) is an intriguing treasure trove of old photos, maps, documents, films and specialist information relating to historic Shànghǎi, and includes a blog.

SHANGHAIED

If New York was so good they named it twice, then Shànghǎi was so bad they made it an undesirable verb. To shanghai, or 'render insensible by drugs or opium, and ship on a vessel wanting hands', dates from the habit of press-ganging sailors. Men, many of whom were found drunk in 'Blood Alley' (off modern-day Jinling Rd), were forced onto ships, which then set sail, leaving the comatose sailors no choice but to make up the deficient crew numbers when they sobered up.

1839

Tensions between England and China come to a head when British merchants are arrested and forced to watch three million pounds of raw opium being flushed out to sea.

1842

On 29 August Sir Henry Pottinger signs the Treaty of Nanking aboard the *Cornwallis* on the Yangzi River, prising open China's doors and securing Hong Kong.

1843

A supplement to the Treaty of Nanking, the Treaty of the Bogue regulated trade between Britain and China and the terms under which British people could reside in Shànghǎi.

1847

Shànghǎi's first library, the Bibliotheca Zi-Ka-Wei in Xújiāhuì, opens.

China, and overseas capital and expertise pooled in the burgeoning metropolis.

Foreign ideas were similarly imported. By the 1880s, huge numbers of proselytising American Protestants were saving souls in Shànghǎi, while the erudite Jesuits oversaw a flourishing settlement in Xújiāhuì (徐家汇), called Siccawei (or Zikawei).

Gradually sedan chairs and single-wheeled carts gave way to rickshaws and carriages, the former imported from Japan in 1874. Shànghǎi lurched into the modern age with gaslights (1865), electricity (1882), motorcars (1895), a cinema and an electric tram (1908), and its first bus (1922).

The Manchu in Běijīng gave only cursory glances to the growth of Shànghǎi as all eyes focused on the continued survival of the Qing dynasty, under threat from a barrage of insurgencies that arose from within the rapidly radicalising confines of the Middle Kingdom.

Historical Reads

In Search of Old Shanghai (Pan Ling, 1986)

Secret War in Shanghai (Bernard Wasserstein, 2000)

Shanghai (Harriet Sergeant, 2002)

Shanghai: The Rise and Fall of a Decadent City 1842–1949 (Stella Dong, 2001)

Through the Looking Glass: China's Foreign Journalists from Opium Wars to Mao (Paul French, 2009)

REBELLIOUS YOUTH

Wreathed in opium, sucked dry by local militia, crippled by taxes, bullied by foreign interests and increasingly exposed to Western ideas, Shànghǎi's population was stirring, and anti-Manchu rebellions began to erupt. The first major rebellion to impact on Shànghǎi was the Taiping (太平 – literally, 'Supreme Peace'), led by the Hakka visionary Hong Xiuquan. The uprising, which led to 20 million deaths, went down as the bloodiest in human history.

Hong claimed to have ascended to heaven and received a new set of internal organs by a golden-bearded Jehovah, which he used to battle the evil spirits of the world with his elder brother Jesus Christ. Hong's distorted Christian ideology dates from his contact with Christian missionaries in Canton and an identification of his surname (洪; Hóng, meaning 'flood') with the Old Testament deluge. Believing himself chosen, Hong saw the Manchu as devils to be exterminated and set about recruiting converts to establish a Heavenly Kingdom in China. The rebels burst out of Jīntián village in Guǎngxī (广西) in 1851, swept through Guìzhōu (贵州) and succeeded in taking Nánjīng (南京) three years later, where they established their Heavenly Capital (天京; Tiānjīng).

With the Taiping-inspired Small Swords Society entrenched in the Old Town and fearing the seizure of Shànghǎi, the foreign residents organised the Shanghai Volunteer Corps, a force that would repeatedly protect the interests of foreigners in Shànghǎi.

1849

The French establish their own settlement, known as the French Concession, to the south of the British Concession and beyond the walls of the Chinese Old Town.

HEIDI PRICE / ALAMY ©

Tree-lined streets of the French Concession (p88)

1850

The influential English-language weekly newspaper the *North China Herald* is published for the first time (later published in a daily edition as the *North China Daily News*).

The Taiping threatened again in 1860 but were beaten back by the mercenary armies of Frederick Townsend Ward, an American adventurer hired by the Qing government who was eventually killed in Sōngjiāng in 1862. British and Qing forces joined to defeat the rebels, the Europeans preferring to deal with a corrupt and weak Qing government than with a powerful, united China governed by the Taiping. The Taiping originally banked on the support of the Western powers, but Westerners were ultimately repelled by Hong's heretical concoction.

In the 1920s and '30s, 25,000 White Russians fled their home country for Shànghǎi. By 1935 they formed the city's second-largest foreign community after the Japanese. Ave Joffre (Huaihai Rd) became the heart of the White Russian community, and was lined with Cyrillic signs and cafes serving Shànghǎi borscht, blini and black bread. There were Russian cinemas, printing presses and even rival revolutionary and tsarist newspapers.

As rebellions ravaged the countryside, hundreds of thousands of refugees poured into the safety of Shànghǎi's concessions, setting up home alongside the foreigners and sparking a real-estate boom that spurred on Shànghǎi's rapid urbanisation and made the fortunes of many of Shànghǎi's entrepreneurs.

As imperial control loosened, the encroaching Western powers moved in to pick off China's colonial 'possessions' in Indochina and Korea. National humiliation and a growing xenophobia – partly generated by a distrust of Christian missionaries and their activities – spawned the anti-Western Boxer Rebellion, championed in its later stages by the empress dowager, Cixi.

The Boxers were quelled by Western and Japanese troops – who went on to sack Běijīng's Summer Palace – in 1900, but not before the legation quarter in the capital had been devastated. Empress Cixi and her entourage fled to Xī'ān (西安), but returned to Běijīng to face massive indemnities strapped onto the Qing government by the foreign powers.

The weakened state of the country, the death of the empress dowager and the legion of conspiring secret societies marked the end of the tottering Qing dynasty. Shànghǎi renounced the Qing by declaring independence on the wave of public revolt that swept China in 1911, and all men were instructed to shear off their *queues* (long pigtails that symbolised subjection to Manchu authority). But despite the momentous end to China's final dynasty – one that had ruled China for almost 250 years – insular Shànghǎi carried out business as usual, relatively unaffected by the fall of the Qing or the upheavals of WWI. As the rest of China descended into a bedlam of fighting warlords and plunged into darkness, Shànghǎi emerged as a modern industrial city.

'PARIS OF THE EAST' REACHES ITS PEAK

By the first decade of the 20th century, Shànghǎi's population had swelled to one million. As the most elite and cosmopolitan of China's cities, Shànghǎi ensnared capitalists and intellectuals alike, with

1859

By now half of all British troops stationed in Shànghǎi suffer from venereal disease. The diseases are introduced to Shànghǎi by Westerners and spread by the city's prostitution industry.

1860s

Cotton emerges as Shànghǎi's chief export.

1863

Shànghǎi's first fire engine arrives and enters service, followed by the launch of the Shanghai Volunteer Fire Service three years later.

1882

Shànghǎi's first large beauty pageant for prostitutes is held. The pageant is held every year until 1930.

literature and cinema thriving in the ferment as Chinese intellectuals began to ponder the fate of a modern China.

The foreigners had effectively plucked out prime locations and, using their ever-increasing wealth – the result of cheap labour – they established exclusive communities designed after their own countries and dovetailing with their needs. Vice and crime continued to flourish, assisted by the absence of a paramount police force. The multiple jurisdictions, each representing the laws of the various settlements and the Chinese city, meant that criminals could simply move from one area to another to elude arrest.

Exploited in workhouse conditions, crippled by hunger and poverty, sold into slavery and excluded from the city's high life created by the foreigners, the poor of Shànghǎi developed an appetite for resistance. Intellectuals and students, provoked by the startling inequalities between rich and poor, were perfect receptacles for the many outside influences circulating in the concessions. The *Communist Manifesto* was translated into Chinese and swiftly caught on among secret societies.

In light of the intense dislike that many Chinese felt for foreigners, it seems ironic that fundamental ideals stemmed from overseas inspirations. Shànghǎi, with its vast proletariat (30,000 textile workers alone) and student population, had become the communists' hope for revolution, and the first meeting of the Chinese Communist Party, when Mao Zedong was present, was held in July 1921 in a French Concession house. Elsewhere political violence was growing.

In May 1925 resentment spilled over when a Chinese worker was killed in a clash with a Japanese mill manager. In the ensuing demonstrations the British opened fire and 12 Chinese were killed. In protest, 150,000 workers went on strike, which was later seen as a defining moment marking the decline of Western prestige and power.

Strikes and a curfew paralysed the city as the Kuomintang under Chiang Kaishek (with the help of communist supporters under Zhou Enlai) wrested Shànghǎi from the Chinese warlord Sun Chaofang.

Kaishek's aim was not focused on the settlements or even the warlords, but rather his erstwhile allies the communists, whom he then betrayed in an act of breathtaking perfidy. Backed by Shànghǎi bankers and armed by Shànghǎi's top gangster Du Yuesheng (see boxed text, p213), Chiang Kaishek armed gangsters, suited them up in Kuomintang uniforms and launched a surprise attack on the striking workers' militia. Du's machine guns were turned on 100,000 workers taking to the streets, killing as many as 5000. In the ensuing period, known as the White Terror, 12,000 communists were executed in three weeks. Zhou

FIRST RAILROAD

The first railroad in China was the Woosung Railway which opened in 1876, running between Shànghǎi and Wúsōng (吴淞); it operated for less than a year before being dismantled and shipped to Taiwan.

1882

Shànghǎi – and China – is electrified for the very first time by the British-founded Shanghai Electric Company. The Bund is illuminated by electric lights the following year.

1891

The Shanghai Sharebrokers Association is established, functioning as Shànghǎi's (and China's) first stock exchange.

1895

The Treaty of Shimonoseki (also called the Treaty of Maguan) concludes the First Sino-Japanese War, forcing China to cede territories (including Taiwan) to Japan.

1908

The Shànghǎi–Nánjīng railway is completed. Covering 193 miles of track, the journey takes around 5½ hours.

Enlai and other communists fled to Wŭhàn (武汉), leaving Shànghăi in the hands of the warlords, the wealthy and the Kuomintang.

Nestled away safely in a world of selectively structured law and cruel capitalism, by the 1930s Shànghăi had reached its economic zenith and was soon to begin its fatal downwards slide. Shànghăi had become a modern city replete with art-deco cinemas and apartment blocks, the hottest bands and the latest fashions – a place of great energy where 'two cultures met and neither prevailed'. Chinese magazines carried ads for Quaker Oats, Colgate and Kodak, while Chinese girls, dressed in traditional *qípáo* (Chinese-style dresses), advertised American cigarettes. Shànghăi's modernity was symbolised by the Bund, Shànghăi's Wall Street, a place of feverish trading and an unabashed playground for Western business sophisticates. To this day the strip alongside the Huángpŭ River remains the city's most eloquent reminder that modern Shànghăi is a very foreign invention.

The 'Paris of the East' and 'Whore of the Orient' became an increasingly exotic port of call. Flush with foreign cash and requiring neither visa nor passport for entrance, Shànghăi became home to the movers and the shakers, the down-and-out and on-the-run. It offered a place of refuge and a fresh start, and rejected no one. Everyone who came to Shànghăi, it was said, had something to hide. The city had become three times as crowded as London, and the cosmopolitan mix of people was unequalled anywhere in the world.

THE DEATH OF OLD SHÀNGHĂI

Following Japan's invasion of Manchuria in 1931, with anti-Japanese sentiment inflamed and Chinese nationalistic fervour on the rise, the Japanese seized the opportunity to protect their interests. Warships brought in tens of thousands of Japanese troops, who proceeded to take on and defeat the Chinese 19th Route army in Zhábĕi (闸北). The Japanese conducted an aerial bombing campaign against the district, levelling most of its buildings.

After Japan's full-scale invasion of China in 1937, Chiang Kaishek took a rare stand in Shànghăi – and the city bled for it. The Japanese lost 40,000 men, the Chinese anywhere from 100,000 to 250,000.

The International Settlements were not immune to the fighting, and after Chinese aircraft accidentally bombed the Bund and Nanjing Rd, most foreign residents reacted not by fighting, as perhaps they would have done for a colony, but by evacuation. Four million Chinese refugees were not so lucky.

1910

Shànghăi is hit by mob disturbances (called the Plague Riots) in response to anti-plague measures.

1912

Republicans pull down Shànghăi's ancient city walls to break links with the ousted Qing dynasty. The Provisional Republican Government of China is established in Nánjīng.

1920

Built to serve the city's first influx of Jewish immigrants, Shànghăi's first synagogue, the Ohel Rachel Synagogue, opens.

1921

The first meeting of the Chinese Communist Party, formed by Marxist groups advised by the Soviet Comintern, takes place in Shànghăi.

GREEN GANG GANGSTERS

In Shànghǎi's climate of hedonist freedoms, political ambiguities and capitalist free-for-all, it was perhaps inevitable that the city should spawn China's most powerful mobsters. Ironically, in 1930s Shànghǎi the most binding laws were those of the underworld, with their blood oaths, secret signals and strict code of honour. China's modern-day triads and snakeheads owe much of their form to their Shanghainese predecessors.

One of Shànghǎi's early gangsters was Huang Jinrong, or 'Pockmarked' Huang, who had the enviable position of being the most powerful gangster in Shànghǎi while at the same time holding the highest rank in the French Concession police force. Now sadly closed, Great World (大世界; Dà Shìjiè) opened in 1917 as a place for acrobats and nightclub stars to rival the existing New World building on Nanjing Rd. It soon became a centre for the bizarre and the burlesque under the seedy control of Huang Jinrong in the 1930s before being commandeered as a refugee centre during WWII.

Another famous underworld figure was Cassia Ma, the Night-Soil Queen, who founded a huge empire on the collection of human waste, which was ferried upriver to be sold as fertiliser at a large profit.

The real godfather of the Shànghǎi underworld, however, was Du Yuesheng, or 'Big-Eared' Du as he was known to anyone brave enough to say it to his face. Born in Pǔdōng, Du soon moved across the river and was recruited into the Green Gang (青帮; Qīngbāng), where he worked for Huang. He gained fame by setting up an early opium cartel with the rival Red Gang, and rose through the ranks. By 1927 Du was the head of the Green Gang and in control of the city's prostitution, drug running, protection and labour rackets. Du's special genius was to kidnap the rich and then to negotiate their release, taking half of the ransom money as commission. With an estimated 20,000 men at his beck and call, Du travelled everywhere in a bullet-proof sedan, like a Chinese Al Capone, protected by armed bodyguards crouched on the running boards.

His control of the labour rackets led to contacts with warlords and politicians. In 1927 Du played a major part in Chiang Kaishek's anticommunist massacre and later became adviser to the Kuomintang. A fervent nationalist, his money supplied the anti-Japanese resistance movement.

Yet Du always seemed to crave respectability. In 1931 he was elected to the Municipal Council and was known for years as the unofficial mayor of Shànghǎi. He became a Christian halfway through his life and somehow ended up best known as a philanthropist. When the British poet WH Auden visited Shànghǎi in 1937, Du was head of the Chinese Red Cross!

During the Japanese occupation of Shànghǎi, Du fled to Chóngqìng (Chungking). After the war he settled in Hong Kong, where he died a multimillionaire in 1951. These days you can stay in Du's former Shànghǎi pad, now the Donghu Hotel, or in the building once used as offices by him and Huang, now the exquisite Mansion Hotel. Alternatively, seek out Du's one-time summer retreat in Mògānshān, now a Radisson hotel.

1927

Chiang Kaishek takes control of Shànghǎi, followed by his 'White Terror', a slaughter of communists, left-wing sympathisers and labour leaders, also known as the 'Shànghǎi Massacre'.

1928

Chinese people are finally allowed to visit parks administered by the Shanghai Municipal Council.

1929

A masterpiece of art-deco design, the iconic Peace Hotel – called Sassoon House when built – is completed on the Bund.

Fairmont Peace Hotel (p52)

By 1934 Shànghǎi was the world's fifth-largest city, home to the tallest buildings in Asia, boasting more cars in one city than the rest of China combined, and providing a haven for more than 70,000 foreigners among a population of three million. Its cosmopolitanism and modernity were encapsulated in the architectural style of art deco.

After intense house-to-house fighting, the Japanese invaders finally subdued Shànghǎi in November, allowing their soldiers to proceed to Sūzhōu before advancing on Nánjīng for their infamous occupation of the city. Under Japanese rule the easy glamour of Shànghǎi's heyday was replaced by a dark cloud of political assassinations, abductions, gunrunning and fear. Espionage by the Japanese, the nationalists, the British and the Americans for wartime information was rife. The rich were abducted and fleeced. Japanese racketeers set up opium halls in the so-called Badlands in the western outskirts of the city, and violent gangs ran rabid.

By December 1941 the hostilities between Japan and the allied powers had intensified abroad, giving the Japanese incentive to take over the foreign settlements in Shànghǎi. Suspect foreigners were taken off for interrogation and torture in notorious prisons such as the Bridgehouse, where JB Powell, editor of the *China Weekly Review*, lost all his toes to gangrene. Prisoners were forced to sit for hours in the cold, with heads lowered, facing Tokyo.

The British and American troops had abandoned Shànghǎi in 1942 to concentrate their energies elsewhere, and the British and American governments, unable to overtake the Japanese, signed over their rights of the foreign settlements to Chiang Kaishek in Chóngqìng in 1943, bringing to a close a century of foreign influence.

After the Japanese surrender in 1945, a few foreigners, released from their internment, tried to sweep out their Tudor-style homes and carry on as before, but priorities and politics had shifted. The gangs, conmen, dignitaries, merchants and anyone else who could had already made their escape to Hong Kong. Those who remained had to cope with biting inflation of 1100%.

By 1948 the Kuomintang was on the edge of defeat in their civil war with the communists, and hundreds of thousands of Kuomintang troops changed sides to join Mao Zedong's forces. In May, Chen Yi led the Red Army troops into Shànghǎi, and by October all the major cities in southern China had fallen to the communists.

In Běijīng on 1 October 1949, Mao Zedong stood atop the Gate of Heavenly Peace, announced that the Chinese people had stood up, and proclaimed the foundation of the People's Republic of China (PRC). Chiang Kaishek then fled to the island of Formosa (Taiwan), taking with him China's gold reserves and the remains of his air force and navy, to set up the Republic of China (ROC), naming his new capital Taipei (台北, Táiběi).

1930s

Blood Alley – a sordid domain of whorehouses, seedy bars and all-night vice in the Bund area – is the destination of choice for drunken sailors on shore leave.

1930s

Cosmopolitan Shànghǎi is the world's fifth-largest city (the largest in Asia), supporting a population of four million. Opium use declines as it goes out of fashion.

1931

In September the Japanese invade Manchuria and by December extend control over the entire area. Shànghǎi's Chinese react with a boycott of Japanese goods.

1935

By now 25,000 White Russians have flocked to Shànghǎi, turning the French Concession into Little Moscow.

THE PEOPLE'S REPUBLIC

The birth of the PRC marked the end of 105 years of 'the paradise for adventurers'. The PRC dried up 200,000 opium addicts, shut down Shànghǎi's infamous brothels and 're-educated' 30,000 prostitutes, eradicated the slums, slowed inflation and eliminated child labour – no easy task. The state took over Shànghǎi's faltering businesses, the racecourse became the obligatory People's Park, and Shànghǎi fell uniformly into step with the rest of China. Under Běijīng's stern hand, the decadence disappeared and the splendour similarly faded.

Yet the communists, essentially a peasant regime, remained suspicious of Shànghǎi. The group lacked the experience necessary to run a big city and they resented Shànghǎi's former leadership, which they always regarded as a den of foreign imperialist-inspired iniquity, a constant reminder of national humiliation, and the former headquarters of the Kuomintang.

Perhaps because of this, Shànghǎi, in its determination to prove communist loyalty, became a hotbed of political extremism and played a major role in the Cultural Revolution, the decade of political turmoil that lasted from 1966 to 1976 (although its most ferocious period ended in 1969). Sidelined in Běijīng, it was to Shànghǎi that Mao turned in an attempt to reinvigorate the revolution and claw his way back into power. For most of a decade the city was the power base of the prime movers of the Cultural Revolution, the Gang of Four: Wang Hongwen; Yao Wenyuan (editor of *Shanghai Liberation Army Daily*); Zhang Chunqiao (Shànghǎi's director of propaganda); and Jiang Qing, wife of Mao (and failed Shànghǎi movie actress, formerly known as Lan Ping, who used her position to exact revenge on former colleagues at Shànghǎi Film Studios).

Encouraged by Mao, a rally of one million Red Guards marched through People's Square, a force of anarchy that resulted in the ousting of the mayor. Competing Red Guards tried to outdo each other in revolutionary fervour – Shanghainese who had any contacts with foreigners (and who didn't?) were criticised, forced to wear dunce caps, denounced and sometimes killed.

As the Cultural Revolution unfolded, between 1966 and 1970 one million of Shànghǎi's youth were sent to the countryside. Shànghǎi's industries closed, the Bund was renamed Revolution Blvd and the road opposite the closed Soviet consulate became Anti-Revisionist St. At one point there was even a plan to change the (revolutionary) red of the city's traffic lights to mean 'go'.

In the revolutionary chaos and a bid to destroy the 'four olds' (old customs, old habits, old culture and old thinking), Chinese religion was devastated. Temples were destroyed or converted to factories; priests

Between 1931 and 1941, 20,000 Jews took refuge in Shànghǎi, only to be forced into Japanese war ghettos, and to flee again in 1949. Adding to the mix was a huge influx of Russians seeking sanctuary from the Bolshevik Revolution of 1917. In 1895 the Japanese had gained treaty rights and by 1915 had become Shànghǎi's largest non-Chinese group, turning Hóngkǒu into a de facto Japanese Concession.

1936

Lu Xun, one of China's finest modern novelists and writers, dies of tuberculosis in Shànghǎi.

1937

In an event known as Bloody Saturday, bombs fall onto the foreign concessions for the first time on 14 August, killing more than 2000.

1938

Twenty thousand Jews arrive in Shànghǎi, fleeing persecution in Europe.

1943

The Japanese round up 7600 allied nationals into eight internment camps as the formal foreign presence in Shànghǎi ends.

SHÀNGHĂI VICE

Underneath the glitz and glamour of 1930s Shànghăi lay a pool of sweat, blood and crushing poverty. In the words of a British resident, Shànghăi was violent, disreputable, snobbish, mercenary and corrupt – 'a discredit to all concerned'. 'If God allows Shànghăi to endure,' said the missionaries, 'He will owe Sodom and Gomorrah an apology.' Others agreed: 'Shànghăi is a city of 48-storey skyscrapers built upon 24 layers of hell,' wrote Chinese author Xia Yan.

The city was often a place of horrific cruelty and brutal violence. After the Small Swords Rebellion, 66 heads, even those of elderly women and children, were stuck up on the city walls. In 1927 striking workers were beheaded and their heads displayed in cages. Up to 80,000 rickshaw pullers worked the littered streets until they dropped, while overcrowded factory workers routinely died of lead and mercury poisoning. In 1934 the life expectancy of the Chinese in Shànghăi stood at 27 years. In 1937 municipal sanitation workers picked up 20,000 corpses off the streets.

Shànghăi offered the purely synthetic pleasures of civilisation. Prostitution ran the gamut from the high-class escorts in the clubs of the International Settlement and 'flowers' of the Fuzhou Rd teahouses to the *yějī*, or 'wild chickens', of Hóngkŏu, who prowled the streets and back alleys. The 'saltwater sisters' from Guăngdōng specialised in foreigners fresh off the boats. Lowest of the low were the 'nail sheds' of Zhapei, so called because their services were meant to be as fast as driving nails. Lists of the city's 100 top-ranking prostitutes were drawn up annually and listed next to the names of 668 brothels, which went by such names as the 'Alley of Concentrated Happiness'.

Prostitution was not the exclusive domain of the Chinese. The traditional roles were reversed when White Russians turned to prostitution and Chinese men could be seen flaunting Western women. An American madam ran Gracie's, the most famous foreign brothel in town, at 52 Jiangsu Rd, in a strip of brothels called 'The Line'.

Linked to prostitution was opium. At the turn of the century Shànghăi boasted 1500 opium dens (known locally as 'swallows' nests') and 80 shops openly selling opium. Even some hotels, it is said, supplied heroin on room service. Opium financed the early British trading houses and most of the buildings on the Bund. Later it funded Chinese gangsters, warlord armies and Kuomintang military expeditions. It was true that the police in the French Concession kept a close eye on the drug trade, but only to ensure that they got a reasonable slice of the profits. Not that there was much they could do even if they had wanted to; it was said that a wanted man in 1930s Shànghăi need only pop into the neighbouring concession to avoid a warrant for his arrest.

were conscripted to make umbrellas; monks were sent to labour in the countryside, where they often perished; and believers were prohibited from worship. Amid all the chaos, Shànghăi's concession architecture stood largely preserved, their wealthy occupants merely fading memories of a vanished era.

1945

After the Japanese surrender, the Kuomintang takes back Shànghăi, closing treaty ports and revoking foreign trading and self-governing rights.

1949

Hyperinflation means that one US dollar is worth 23,280,000 yuan. Communist forces take Shànghăi and the establishment of the People's Republic of China is proclaimed.

1966

The Cultural Revolution is launched from Shànghăi; eventually one million Shanghainese are sent to the countryside. St Ignatius Cathedral finds new employment as a grain store.

1972

US President Nixon visits Shànghăi as China rejoins the world.

In 1976, after the death of Mao, the Gang of Four was overthrown and imprisoned. Accused of everything from forging Mao's statements to hindering earthquake relief efforts, the gang's members were arrested on 6 October 1976 and tried in 1980. Jiang Qing remained unrepentant, hurling abuse at her judges and holding famously to the line that she 'was Chairman Mao's dog – whoever he told me to bite, I bit'. Jiang Qing's death sentence was commuted and she lived under house arrest until 1991, when she committed suicide by hanging.

When the Cultural Revolution lost steam, pragmatists such as Zhou Enlai began to look for ways to restore normalcy. In 1972 US president Richard Nixon signed the Shanghai Communiqué at the Jinjiang Hotel. The agreement provided a foundation for increased trade between the US and China, and marked a turning point in China's foreign relations. With the doors of China finally reopened to the West in 1979, and with Deng Xiaoping at the helm, China set a course of pragmatic reforms towards economic reconstruction, which would result in consistently strong annual growth rates.

In communist China, however, the rush of economic reform generated very little in the way of political reform. Corruption and inflation led to widespread social unrest, which in 1989 resulted in the demonstrations in Běijīng's Tiān'ānmén Square.

The demonstrations overtaking the capital spread to Shànghǎi. In the days leading up to 4 June 1989 tens of thousands of students – holding banners demanding, among other things, democracy and freedom – marched from their universities to People's Square. Hundreds went on hunger strike. Workers joined students to bring chaos to the city by instigating road blocks across more than 100 Shànghǎi streets. But city mayor Zhu Rongji was praised for his handling of events. In contrast to leaders in Běijīng, he didn't take a heavy-handed approach. 'The municipal government was careful: The rallies continued. Police disappeared from the streets, and no tanks came. The city government sent a message by doing nothing.' (*Unstately Power,* Lynn T White, 1999). According to White, the only serious incident during the unrest was on 6 June when a train outside Shanghai Station ran into demonstrators who were trying to block it. Eight people were killed and 30 were injured.

PEOPLE'S COMMUNE

In 1966 a People's Commune, modelled on the Paris Commune of the 19th century, was set up in Shànghǎi. Led by Zhang Chunqiao from headquarters in the Peace Hotel, it lasted just three weeks before Mao, sensing that the anarchy had gone too far, ordered the army to put an end to it.

INTO THE 21ST CENTURY

In 1990 the central government began pouring money into Shànghǎi, beginning the city's epic turnaround. The process was simply staggering in scale and audacity. By the mid-1990s more than a quarter (some sources say half) of the world's high-rise cranes were rising over

1976

Mao Zedong dies in September – the same year as the Tángshān earthquake – preparing the way for a rehabilitated Deng Xiaoping to assume leadership of the PRC.

GAVIN HELLIER / GETTY IMAGES ©

Mao Zedong

1989

Antigovernment demonstrations in Shànghǎi's People's Square mirror similar protests in Běijīng's Tiān'ānmén Square; the demonstrations are broken up.

Shànghǎi. A huge proportion of the world's concrete was shipped into Shànghǎi as China sucked up a staggering 50% of world production.

Towering over Lùjiāzuǐ, the Oriental Pearl TV Tower was completed in 1994, establishing an architectural template for Pǔdōng that survives today. What followed was a roll-call of skyscraper heavyweights: the Jinmao Tower (1999), Tomorrow Square (2003), Shimao International Plaza (2005) and the Shànghǎi World Financial Center (2008). Shànghǎi's vertical transformation mirrored its growing stature as an international city.

A 2012 survey discovered that fewer than 40% of the city's elementary school children speak the Shànghǎi dialect (Shànghǎihuà) at home (even then it may be mixed with Mandarin).

Before the 1990s were out, the city had already built two metro lines, a light-railway system, a US$2 billion international airport in Pǔdōng, a US$2 billion elevated highway, several convention centres, two giant bridges, several underground tunnels and a whole new city (Pǔdōng).

Always a byword for excess, Shànghǎi had effortlessly outstripped every other city in China by the dawn of the new millennium, except for southern rival Hong Kong. The government deliberately sought to make Shànghǎi the financial centre of Asia, replacing Hong Kong as China's frontier of the future, swinging the spotlight of attention from the ex-colony on to a home-grown success story.

The Shànghǎi Chinese obsessively compare themselves to Hong Kong and the Huángpǔ River city was catching up at breathtaking speed during the noughties. Served by two airports and the world's first Maglev train (2004), Shànghǎi now commanded some of the highest salaries in

TOP SHÀNGHǍI HISTORICAL BIOGRAPHIES

- *Captive in Shanghai*, Hugh Collar (1991) – A fascinating personal account of life in the Japanese internment camps in the early 1940s. It's published by Oxford University Press, but is pretty hard to get your hands on.
- *Daughter of Shanghai*, Tsai Chin (1989) – This book has less to say about Shànghǎi but is still a good read. Daughter of one of China's most-famous Běijīng opera stars, Chin left Shànghǎi in 1949 and later starred in the film *The World of Suzie Wong* (as the original 'China doll') and in *The Joy Luck Club*. This memoir bridges two worlds during two different times.
- *Life and Death in Shanghai*, Nien Cheng (1987) – A classic account of the Cultural Revolution and one of the few biographies with a Shànghǎi angle.
- *The Life, Loves and Adventures of Emily Hahn*, Ken Cuthbertson (1998) – A look at the unconventional life of Emily Hahn, who passed through Shànghǎi in 1935 (with her pet gibbon), got hooked on opium and became the concubine of a Chinese poet.
- *Red Azalea*, Anchee Min (2006) – A sometimes racy account of growing up in Shànghǎi in the 1950s and 1960s amid the turmoil of the Cultural Revolution.

1990

Pǔdōng discovers it will become a Special Economic Zone (SEZ), converting it, over the next decade, from flat farmland into one of the world's most ultramodern urban landscapes.

1995

Line 1 of the Shànghǎi metro commences operation, with Line 2 opening five years later.

2004

The world's first commercially operating Maglev train begins scorching across Pǔdōng. Plans to connect Běijīng and Shànghǎi are later put to rest.

2008

World markets crash, finally slowing down Shànghǎi's previously stratospheric rates of economic growth.

China with per capita incomes around four times the national average. The metro system was massively expanded, and is to date the world's largest (running to 11 lines) at 434km in length. Pǔdōng was built from the soles up, creating mainland China's most electrifying skyline. Skyscraping residential towers irrepressibly sprouted across the city while car ownership trebled between 2007 and 2012. Swelling numbers of residents dwelled in gated villa communities, rewarding a life of hard graft with an enviably middle-class standard of living.

Feeding much of this growth was a vast, multimillion-strong army of cheap labour and migrant workers from rural areas. The Bund was redesigned and spruced up while other areas – the Old Town, for example – underwent irreversible overdevelopment.

Despite draconian property taxes designed to hit speculators and purchasers of second flats, Shànghǎi property prices went through the roof in the noughties. The authorities were determined to tame property prices to avoid a long-term Japanese-style stagnation, but measures were hit-and-miss and prices continue to soar.

The Shànghǎi Chinese are proud of their city, even though it lacks the *bon vivant* romantic allure of Paris, the multicultural vibrancy of London or the creative zest of New York. Shànghǎi can certainly be spectacular and highly modern in parts, but is also a work in progress, if not a metropolitan-sized construction site. Shànghǎi's triumphant skyline is staggering, but the city's creative flatline and aversion to spontaneity still guarantee that many expats arrive to make money, and move on.

There is, though, an allure and energy to Shànghǎi. Popping Shànghǎi into any conversation abroad prompts a flood of superlatives, agitated adjectives and breathless hyperbole. Reading the international papers, the city can do no wrong, and wherever you look, the smart money has flooded into town.

Despite propaganda to the contrary, the future isn't necessarily endlessly bright for Shànghǎi. Many pundits see the city, and China, as reaching a fork in the road. The formula that served China so well for so long – a cheap workforce, hefty stimulus packages, high investment, endless property price increases and round-the-clock construction – is losing its potency. With the Hu Jintao and Wen Jiabao era over, the task of the new Chinese leadership under President Xi Jinping is to balance the economy, root out corruption and narrow the chasm dividing low-wage earners from the wealthy elites. It's no small task. The Chinese Communist Party's legitimacy depends heavily on economic growth. Keeping the economy on track while coping with the global downturn and matching the expectations of Chinese who are pushing for a fairer society could constitute a daunting challenge.

Having grown faster than virtually any other Chinese city in the past two decades, Shànghǎi remains the pot of gold at the end of the rainbow for China's swarming migrant workers, who now constitute almost four million of the city's total population of 23 million, and around 40% of the workforce.

When the clean-up of Sūzhōu Creek was finally completed in 2012, a total of more than a hundred wartime bombs had been dredged from the muck at the river bottom, many dating to the Japanese occupation.

2010

Shànghǎi hosts the 2010 World Expo, drawing 73 million visitors.

2009

Approval is finally given to plans to build a Disneyland in Shànghǎi, scheduled to open in 2015.

2011

The Shànghǎi–Běijīng high-speed rail line enters service, shrinking journey times to 5½ hours.

2012

Shànghǎi and other cities across China see anti-Japanese demonstrations in response to Japanese claims to the Diaoyu (Senkaku) Islands.

Arts

You won't be tripping over street-side performance artists, sidestepping wild-haired poets handing out flyers or spraycan-toting graffiti artists, but you can track down enough creativity in Shànghǎi to keep you fired up (and traditional Chinese arts are well covered).

VISUAL ARTS

Even if the city's artistic output remains limited, a growing gallery and art museum scene makes Shànghǎi a vibrant place to join the contemporary Chinese art learning curve. For political and cultural reasons (p224), Shànghǎi is rather straight-laced and it's rare to see much art (eg graffiti art) outside of the well-defined gallery environment.

A well-known graffiti wall at Moganshan Rd (M50) – one of the few places in Shànghǎi where you could actually see graffiti and wall art – was due to be demolished in 2012. For info on other sites where you can find graffiti and wall art in town see graffitipark .weebly.com.

Contemporary & Modern Art

Notable contemporary Shanghainese artists working across a large spectrum of styles include Pu Jie, with his colourful pop-art depictions of Shànghǎi, video-installation artists Shi Yong and Hu Jieming, and Hángzhōu-born Sun Liang. Wu Yiming creates calmer, more impressionistic works, while Ding Yi is a significant abstract artist whose works employ a repetitive use of crosses. Others to look out for are graphic-design artist Guan Chun, and the diverse works of Chen Hangfeng and Yang Yongliang, which draw inspiration from the techniques and imagery of traditional Chinese painting.

After sizing up contemporary directions in art at the Bund-side Rockbund Art Museum, your next stop should be M50, Shànghǎi's most cutting-edge art district, housed in warehouses across the river from Shànghǎi Railway Station. Put aside at least half a day for exploration. In People's Park, the Shànghǎi Museum of Contemporary Art (MOCA Shànghǎi) is a stimulating environment for art-watching. The nearby Shànghǎi Art Museum, housed in a fabulous neoclassical clock-tower building, also has some good exhibitions.

A stroll around the quaint alleys of Tiánzǐfáng, with its cafes, boutiques and smattering of decent small galleries, is always rewarding. This is where you can find the Deke Erh Art Centre, a fantastic warehouse exhibit space set up by Shànghǎi's cultural tour de force, Deke Erh, and the excellent Beaugeste.

Controversial artist Ai Weiwei's Shànghǎi studio was torn down in January 2011, a move the artist said was prompted by his activism. Local authorities said the building was 'illegal'.

Another art centre, focusing more on contemporary sculpture, is the huge complex known as Red Town, near Jiāotōng University. Also in West Shànghǎi are the thought-provoking displays at the Mínshēng Art Museum. The **Shanghai Chinese Painting Institute** (上海中国画院; Shànghǎi Zhōngguó Huàyuàn; ☎6474 9977; 197 Yueyang Rd; 岳阳路197号; ⓂHengshan Rd) also occasionally hosts major exhibitions.

Further afield, check to see what's on at the Shànghǎi Duōlún Museum of Modern Art in Hóngkǒu and earmark a trip to the Gallery Magda Danysz.

In Pǔdōng, the Himalayas Art Museum, in the organically designed Himalayas Center, is a neat environment for contemporary-art trends. Due to open in late 2012, the China Art Palace in the former World Expo site was tipped to become one of Shànghǎi's premier modern-art venues.

Now held in the cavernous Power Station of Art (the 41,000-sq-metre former Nánshì Power Plant), the **Shanghai Biennale** (www.shanghaibiennale.org) has been held in November every two years since 1996. Related fringe shows spring up around the same time, and are often of more interest. Outside Biennale years, the China International Arts Festival is an event held in November that brings traditional and modern (Western and Chinese) art, artists and galleries together. For the lowdown on the best art galleries in town, see p66.

Traditional Art

For traditional Chinese art, the Shànghǎi Museum is a must-visit, with a simply magnificent collection of ancient bronzes, Buddhist sculpture, ceramics, paintings, calligraphy, furniture, ancient jade and ethnic culture. The Shànghǎi Arts & Crafts Museum has displays of embroidery, paper cutting, lacquer work and jade cutting. For iridescent glassware, the Liúli China Museum is exquisite. Brash propaganda art from the Mao era is the riveting focus of the excellent Propaganda Poster Art Centre, while the foyer of the Jumeirah Himalayas Hotel in Pǔdōng is a virtual art gallery of traditional Chinese paintings.

More traditional art comes from the southern suburb of Jīnshān, which has its own school of untrained 'peasant' painters who have been turning out colourful and vibrant paintings for years. Their works have their roots in local embroidery designs and contain no perspective; the themes are mostly rural and domestic scenes full of details of everyday life. You can see a selection of paintings from the Jīnshān area in several shops in the Old Town's Old Street, or you can head out to Jīnshān itself.

POSTERS

Click on www.chineseposters.net for a breathtaking collection of Chinese propaganda posters from 1925 to 2006.

LITERATURE

Energised by a vibrant literary scene, Shànghǎi in the 1920s and '30s cast itself as a veritable publishing-industry hub. Sheltered from the censorship of Nationalists and warlords by the foreign settlements, and stimulated by the city's new-fangled modernity and flood of foreign ideas, Shànghǎi hosted a golden era in modern Chinese literature.

Birth of Modern Literature

Although born in Shàoxīng, Lu Xun, China's greatest modern writer, lived in Shànghǎi from 1927 until his death of tuberculosis in 1936. One of the first founders of the Shànghǎi-based League of Left-Wing Writers, the highly influential modernist author dragged Chinese literature into the modern era.

Until Lu Xun's radical *Diary of a Madman* in 1918, literary Chinese had been conceived in classical Chinese, a language that represented not Chinese as it was spoken or thought, but as it was communicated by the educated scholarly class. Classical Chinese was a terse, dry and inflexible language that bore little relevance to the real lives of Chinese people. Lu Xun's decision to write his story in vernacular Chinese was a revolutionary act that instantly transformed the literary paradigms of the day, and helped underpin the New Culture Movement (新文化运动; Xīn Wénhuà Yúndòng) which sought to challenge traditional Chinese culture.

Lu Xun's most famous work, the 1921 novella *The True Story of Ah Q* (阿Q正传, *Ā Q zhèngzhuàn*) – a satirical look at early 20th-century China – is considered a modern masterpiece and was the first piece of literature to entirely utilise vernacular Chinese. Admirers of Lu Xun can visit his Shànghǎi residence (p151).

A dark and Gothic image in the West, the bat is commonly used in Chinese porcelain, wood designs, textiles and artwork as a good-luck omen.

Mao Dun (real name Shen Yanbing), an active leftist writer in the 1930s, penned *Midnight (Zǐyè),* one of the most famous novels about Shànghǎi (see the boxed text, p223). *Rainbow* (1929), by the same author, tells the tale of a young girl from a traditional family background who travels to Shànghǎi on a journey of political awakening.

Ding Ling, whose most famous oeuvre is *The Diary of Miss Sophie,* lived in Shànghǎi, as did for a time the writers Yu Dafu and Ba Jin. Writers were not immune to political dangers; Lu Xun's friend Rou Shi was murdered by the Kuomintang in February 1931.

Eileen Chang (Zhang Ailing, 1920–95) is one of the writers most closely connected to Shànghǎi, certainly among overseas Chinese. Born in Shànghǎi, she lived in the city only from 1942 to 1948 before moving to Hong Kong and then the USA. Seeped in the city's details and moods, her books capture the essence of Shànghǎi. Chang's most famous books include *The Rouge of the North, The Faded Flower, Red Rose and White Rose, The Golden Lock* and *Love in a Fallen City*. Her 1979 novella *Lust, Caution* was made into an award-winning film directed by Ang Lee (director of *Crouching Tiger, Hidden Dragon* and *Brokeback Mountain*) in 2007.

LU XUN

A selection of Lu Xun's books in English, French and German translation can be found in the museum bookshop at the Lu Xun Memorial Hall.

Contemporary Directions

Contemporary voices are more sparse. The most respected Shànghǎi writer today is Wang Anyi, whose bestselling novels (in China) include *Love on a Barren Mountain, Baotown* and *Song of Everlasting Sorrow,* the latter following a Shanghainese beauty pageant winner through four decades from the 1940s. Wang also co-wrote the script for Chen Kaige's film *Temptress Moon.*

More recently, several high-school dropouts gained notoriety, beginning with Mian Mian, who vividly described the marginalised underbelly of China in *Candy* (see the boxed text, p223). To date this remains her only novel translated into English.

Increasingly known in the West is writer/rally driver/musician/blogger Han Han, who skyrocketed to fame before his 18th birthday with his novel *The Third Gate,* a searing critique of China's educational system. He inspired awe and disgust simultaneously by turning down a scholarship to the prestigious Fùdàn University in order to race cars in Běijīng. Today, Han Han's highly influential blogs are among the most widely read in China.

For a taste of contemporary Chinese short-story writing with both English and Chinese, buy a copy of *Short Stories in Chinese: New Penguin Parallel Text* (2012).

Sprinkled with snippets from the Shànghǎi dialect (but as yet untranslated), Wang Xiaoying's *Song of a Long Street* (2010) is a vivid portrait of the textures and grain of everyday life in a Shànghǎi backstreet.

Translated into English, *Vicissitudes of Life* (2010) is a collection of stories from contemporary Shànghǎi writers, including Wang Xiaoying, Qiu Maoru and Wang Jiren.

As with Chinese film, fiction dealing with contemporary Shànghǎi is far less successful at filling bookstore shelves than historically set novels. Historical fiction is a safer and far more popular publishing choice, meaning voices on contemporary issues are more marginalised.

Shànghǎi writers today share a common despair about the loss of the Shànghǎi dialect while having to compose in Mandarin (Shanghainese is not written down).

MUSIC

Shànghǎi had a buzzing live-music scene in the 1930s, featuring everything from jazz divas to émigré Russian troubadours, but the contemporary scene has long been dominated by Filipino cover bands and

SHÀNGHĂI FICTION

- *Candy,* Mian Mian (2003) – A hip take on modern Shànghǎi life, penned by a former heroin addict musing on complicated sexual affairs, suicide and drug addiction in Shēnzhèn and Shànghǎi. Applauded for its urban underground tone, but sensational more for its framing of post-adolescent themes in contemporary China.
- *Death of a Red Heroine,* Qiu Xiaolong (2000) – Despite some stilted dialogue, this well-received crime novel offers a street-level view of the social changes engulfing Shànghǎi in 1990. It is the first mystery in the Inspector Chen series, which had expanded to seven titles in 2012.
- *Empire of the Sun,* JG Ballard (1984) – An astonishingly well-written and poignant tale based on the author's internment as a child in a Japanese prisoner-of-war camp in Shànghǎi, and subsequently made into a film by Steven Spielberg.
- *Master of Rain,* Tom Bradby (2003) – Atmospheric, noir-ish detective story set in the swinging Shànghǎi of the '20s. 'Pockmarked' Huang, a brutally murdered Russian prostitute, and a naive British investigator come together for a real page-turner.
- *Midnight,* Mao Dun (1933) – In the opening scene of *Midnight,* conservative Confucian Old Man Wu visits his son's home in Shànghǎi. The sight of modern women in high-slit skirts and revealing blouses literally shocks him to death. A famed presentation of the social mores of 1920s Shànghǎi.
- *Shanghai: Electric and Lurid City,* Barbara Baker (1998) – An excellent anthology of more than 50 passages of writing about Shànghǎi, from its pre-treaty port days to the eve of the 21st century.
- *Shanghai Girls,* Lisa Lee (2010) – A moving novel about two beautiful sisters whose lives as high-flying models in 1930s Shànghǎi are transformed when their father decides to repay his gambling debts by selling the pair to a family in Los Angeles.
- *The Distant Land of My Father,* Bo Caldwell (2002) – A moving portrayal of the relationship between a daughter and father, and of betrayal and reconciliation, commencing in 1930s Shànghǎi.
- *The Painter from Shanghai,* Jennifer Cody Epstein (2008) – Highly acclaimed debut novel based on the remarkable life of child-prostitute-turned-painter Pan Yuliang.
- *The Sing-Song Girls of Shanghai,* Han Bangqing (1892) – Delving deeply into the lives of courtesans and prostitutes in fin-de-siècle Shànghǎi, this absorbing novel was first published in 1892 but only recently translated into English.
- *When Red is Black,* Qiu Xiaolong (2004) – A realistic detective story that packs plenty of literary muscle. This is a follow-up Inspector Chen novel (see *Death of a Red Heroine*) and a great snapshot of the changing city seen through Chinese eyes.
- *When We Were Orphans,* Kazuo Ishiguro (2000) – Subtle and absorbing portrayal of an English detective who sets out to solve the case of his parents' disappearance in Shànghǎi, climaxing in war-shattered Hóngkǒu.

saccharine-sweet Canto-pop. Things are changing, though, and while Shànghǎi's live-music scene still lags behind Běijīng's, there are some cracking venues in town where you can catch local bands, the best of which are Yùyīntáng and MAO Livehouse. Look out for the **JUE Festival** (www.juefestival.com), a music and art festival held in Běijīng and Shànghǎi in March.

Rock

Top Floor Circus, who play anything from folk to punk, are legendary on the Shànghǎi music scene. If they're playing while you're in town, do your best to get a ticket. Others worth checking out include Pinkberry (rock), indie popsters/rockers Candie Shop, Da Fresh, all-girl band Bigger Xifu and FAF (Forget & Forgive). Torturing Nurse, meanwhile, who make unusual and extremely loud sounds rather than music as such, are China's leading 'noise' band. Check out www.noishanghai.org to find out where they're playing.

For the lowdown on who's playing where, grab a free copy of the monthly entertainment magazines *Time Out Shanghai* (www.timeout shanghai.com), *That's Shanghai* (www.urbanantomy.com) and *City Weekend* (www.cityweekend.com.cn/shanghai), or check their websites. Also check out Smart Shanghai (www.smartshanghai.com).

The Fairmont Peace Hotel Jazz Bar has been serenading punters for decades, with an average customer age of 77.

Jazz

Shànghǎi's once world-famous jazz scene isn't quite as snappy as it was, but there are still a number of places around town where you can sample the sounds of the 1930s. Cotton Club and JZ Club are the best choices; the latter has a popular branch in Hángzhōu.

Traditional Chinese Music

The *èrhú* is a two-stringed fiddle that is tuned to a low register, providing a soft, melancholy tone. The *húqín* is a higher-pitched two-stringed viola. The *yuèqín*, a sort of moon-shaped four-stringed guitar, has a soft tone and is used to support the *èrhú*. Other instruments you may come across are the *shēng* (reed flute), *pípá* (lute), *gǔzhēng* (zither) and *xiāo* (vertical flute). A good place to hear free traditional music performances is the Shànghǎi Gǔqín Cultural Foundation or at a performance of Chinese opera.

AESTHETICS AND POLITICS

In reflection of the Chinese character, Chinese aesthetics have traditionally been marked by restraint and understatement, a preference for oblique references over direct explanation, vagueness in place of specificity and an avoidance of the obvious in place of a fondness for the veiled and subtle. Traditional Chinese aesthetics sought to cultivate a reserved artistic impulse, principles that compellingly find their way into virtually every Chinese art form, from painting to sculpture, ceramics, calligraphy, film, poetry, literature and beyond.

As one of the central strands of the world's oldest civilisation, China's aesthetic tradition is tightly embroidered within Chinese cultural identity. For millennia, Chinese aesthetics were highly traditionalist and, despite coming under the influence of occupiers from the Mongols to the Europeans, defiantly conservative. It was not until the fall of the Qing dynasty in 1911 and the appearance of the New Culture Movement that China's great artistic traditions began to rapidly transform. In literature the stranglehold of classical Chinese loosened to allow breathing space for *báihuà* (colloquial Chinese) and a progressive new aesthetic began to flower, ultimately leading to revolutions in all of the arts, from poetry to painting, theatre and music.

It is hard to square China's great aesthetic traditions with the devastation inflicted upon them since 1949. Confucius advocated the edifying role of music and poetry in shaping human lives, but 5th-century philosopher Mozi was less enamoured with them, seeing music and other arts as extravagant and wasteful. The communists took this a stage further, enlisting the arts as props in their propaganda campaigns and permitting the vandalism and destruction of much traditional architecture and heritage. Many of China's traditional skills (such as martial-arts lineages) and crafts either died out or went into decline during the Cultural Revolution. Many of the arts have yet to recover fully from this deterioration, even though 'opening up' and reform have prompted a vast influx of foreign artistic concepts.

Classical Music

The Shanghai Conservatory of Music is a prestigious clearing house of Chinese talent. One of its most famous former students is Liao Changyong, a world-class baritone who has performed with Placido Domingo, among others. Other famous classical music venues include the Shanghai Concert Hall and the Oriental Art Center.

CHINESE OPERA

Contemporary Chinese opera, of which the most famous is Běijīng opera (京剧; *Jīngjù*), has a rich and continuous history of some 900 years. Evolving from a convergence of comic and ballad traditions in the Northern Song period, Chinese opera brought together a disparate range of forms: acrobatics, martial arts, poetic arias and stylised dance.

Over 100 varieties of opera exist in China today and many are performed in Shànghǎi. Shanghainese opera (沪剧; *Hùjù*), sometimes called flower-drum opera, is performed in the local dialect and has its origins in the folk songs of Pǔdōng. Yueju opera (越剧; *Yuèjù*) was born in and around Shàoxīng County in neighbouring Zhèjiāng (the ancient state of Yue) in the early 20th century. *Yuèjù* roles are normally played by women. Kunju opera (昆剧; *Kūnjù*) or Kunqu opera (昆曲; *Kūnqǔ*) originates from Kūnshān, near Sūzhōu in neighbouring Jiāngsū.

Operas were usually performed by travelling troupes, who had a low social status in traditional Chinese society. Chinese law forbade mixed-sex performances, forcing actors to act out roles of the opposite sex. Opera troupes were frequently associated with homosexuality in the public imagination, contributing further to their lowly status.

Formerly, opera was performed mostly on open-air stages in markets, streets, teahouses or temple courtyards.

The actors take on stylised stock characters who are instantly recognisable to the audience. Most stories are derived from classical literature and Chinese mythology and tell of disasters, natural calamities, intrigues or rebellions. The musicians usually sit on the stage in plain clothes and play without written scores.

China's most legendary 20th-century opera star was Mei Lanfang, who allegedly performed privately for several of Shànghǎi's gangland bosses in the 1930s. The most central venue for appreciating Chinese opera in Shànghǎi is the Yìfū Theatre on Fuzhou Rd.

The lower Yangzi region has a long tradition of storytelling, farce, comic talk and mimicking, all of which were traditionally performed in teahouses. Hángzhōu and Sūzhōu have their own variants. *Píngtán* balladry is a mix of *pínghuà* (Sūzhōu-style storytelling) and *táncí* (ballad singing), accompanied by the *pípá* (lute) and *sānxián* (banjo). You can hear samples of various Chinese operas and *píngtán* at the Shànghǎi History Museum in Pǔdōng, or at the Píngtán Museum in Sūzhōu.

CALLIGRAPHY

The character 永, which means 'eternal', contains the five fundamental brushstrokes necessary to master calligraphy.

The shrill singing and loud percussion of Chinese opera were designed to be heard over the public throng, prompting American writer PJ O'Rourke to say it was 'as if a truck full of wind chimes collided with a stack of empty drums during a birdcall contest'.

CINEMA

Early Film

The first screening of any film in China illuminated the garden of a Shànghǎi teahouse in 1896, when Spanish entrepreneur Galen Bocca showed a series of one-reel films to astonished audiences. The city's first cinema opened up in 1908, but before films could reach their glamorous peak in the 1930s, filmmakers had to convince the distrustful Shanghainese that it was worth their hard-earned cash. Soon hooked, the city boasted more than 35 cinemas and over 140 film companies by

1930. Shànghǎi's teahouse culture began to feel the pinch, along with a host of traditional performing arts.

The Golden Age

The 1932 Japanese bombing of the Shànghǎi district of Hóngkǒu had a big effect on the industry, prompting a patriotic fervour epitomised by films coming out of the Lianhua Studio, with its close connections to Chiang Kaishek's Nationalist Party.

Shànghǎi's golden age of filmmaking reached its peak in 1937 with the release of *Street Angel*, a powerful drama about two sisters who flee the Japanese in northeast China and end up as prostitutes in Shànghǎi, and *Crossroads*, a clever comedy about four unemployed graduates. There was still time, however, after WWII and before the CCP took over in 1949, for a final flowering. *A Spring River Flows East*, dubbed the *Gone with the Wind* of Chinese cinema, and *Springtime in a Small Town*, another wartime tear jerker, remain popular films today.

The Old Film Café in Hóngkǒu, housed in a beautiful three-storey brick building with charming wooden interior, shows old Shànghǎi films on demand, although few have English subtitles.

Shànghǎi Cinema Today

China's film industry was stymied after the Communist Revolution, which sent filmmakers scurrying to Hong Kong and Taiwan, where they played key roles in building up the local film industries that flourished there. Today's moviegoers are scarce, as DVD piracy and internet downloads upset the economics of domestic filmmaking. Bucking the trend, however (but perhaps reflecting the Shànghǎi passion for cars), a drive-in cinema opened in Pǔdōng in 2012.

More innovative film studios in Xī'ān and Běijīng have captured much of the international acclaim of contemporary Chinese film. Coproductions have been more successful for the Shanghai Film Studios, which in 2001 moved from its central location in Xújiāhuì to the far-western city district of Sōngjiāng.

One critical success was *The Red Violin*, a coproduction between Canada and Shànghǎi. Shànghǎi-born Vivian Wu (Wu Junmei; *The Last Emperor*, *The Pillow Book*) returned to her native city with her husband, director Oscar L Costo, in order to focus on their production company, MARdeORO Films. It produced the well-received *Shanghai Red*, starring Wu and Ge You *(Farewell My Concubine, To Live)*, in 2006. Another actress hailing from Shànghǎi is Joan Chen (Chen Chong), who started her career at the Shanghai Film Studios in the late 1970s.

Shànghǎi's independent films are scarce. Look out for Ye Lou's *Suzhou River (Sūzhōu Hé)* and Andrew Chen's *Shanghai Panic (Wǒmen Hàipà)*. Both were shot with digital cameras and are notable for showing a decidedly unglamorous and more realistic side of the city.

Chen Yifei's 1920s period drama, *The Barber* (aka *The Music Box*), was released posthumously in 2006, while Taiwanese-born Oscar-winning director Ang Lee *(Crouching Tiger, Hidden Dragon* and *Brokeback Mountain)* released *Lust, Caution* in 2007. A controversial tale of sex and espionage set in WWII Shànghǎi, based on the 1979 novella by Eileen Chang, the award-winning film was heavily censored for its mainland China release.

FILM

The Shanghai International Film Festival (www.siff.com) celebrates international and locally produced films in June every year.

FASHION

The Shanghainese have the reputation of being the most fashionable people in China. 'There's nothing the Cantonese won't eat,' one version of a popular Chinese saying goes, 'and nothing the Shanghainese won't wear.' The generation gap is perhaps starker here, though, than anywhere else: you're still quite likely to see locals wandering around their neighbourhood dressed in very comfortable (but extremely uncool) pyjamas and slippers, but Shànghǎi has breathtaking, voguish pockets while the petite figures of young Shànghǎi women ooze glamour in even the cheapest skirts and blouses.

On the street, Chinese-language lifestyle magazines such as *Shanghai Tatler*, *Elle*, *Vogue*, *Harper's Bazaar* and *Marie Claire* crowd every corner newsstand. Christian Dior, Gucci and Louis Vuitton shops glut Shànghǎi's top-end malls, while trendy boutiques line French Concession streets such as Changle Rd, Xinle Rd and Nanchang Rd.

> As well as being an annual gay festival, Shanghai Pride is a week-long celebration of creativity across all media.

However, Shànghǎi still has a long way to go just to catch up with its own 1930s fashion scene, when images of Chinese women clad in figure-hugging *qípáo* (cheongsam) gave rise to its epithet as the 'Paris of the East'.

Shanghai Fashion Week (www.shanghaifashionweek.com) is a biannual event showcasing the work of local, national and international designers. There is also the city-sponsored, month-long International Fashion Culture Festival in March or April.

MARTIAL ARTS

China lays claim to a bewildering range of martial-arts styles, from the flamboyant and showy, inspired by the movements of animals or insects (such as Praying Mantis Boxing), to schools empirically built upon the science of human movement (eg Wing Chun). Some pugilists stress a mentalist approach while others put their money on physical power. On the outer fringes are the esoteric arts, abounding with metaphysical feats, arcane practices and closely guarded techniques.

Many fighting styles were once secretively handed down for generations within families and it is only relatively recently that outsiders have been accepted as students. Some schools, especially the more obscure styles, have been driven to extinction partly due to their exclusivity.

> An art salon on Moganshan Rd, Image Tunnel (www.imagetunnel.com) screens absorbing independent Chinese films on Saturday afternoons; browse films clips and photos on its website.

Unlike Western fighting arts – Savate, kickboxing, boxing, wrestling etc – Chinese martial arts are deeply impregnated with religious and philosophical values. Closely linked to martial arts is the practice of *qìgōng*, a technique for cultivating and circulating *qì* around the body. *Qì* can be developed for use in fighting to protect the body, as a source of power or for curative and health-giving purposes.

Shànghǎi's parks are good places to go to look for teachers of taichi and *wǔshù* (martial arts), although language may be a barrier. Check the listings of entertainment magazines such as *That's Shanghai*, *City Weekend* or *Time Out Shanghai* for classes, or check for courses at the Lóngwǔ Kungfu Center, the Wǔyì Chinese Kungfu Centre or the Míngwǔ International Kungfu Club.

Architecture in Shànghǎi

Shang-high

Jaw-dropping panoramas of glittering skyscrapers are its trump card, but Shànghǎi is no one-trick pony: the city boasts a diversity of architectural styles that will astound most first-time visitors.

Charm and panache indeed ooze from every crevice of its concession-era villas, *shíkùmén* buildings, *lǐlòng* lanes and art-deco marvels – perfect for sipping lattes and musing on yester-century Shànghǎi – but for the wow factor, look to the city's vertical skyline.

Like Hong Kong before it, Shànghǎi has filled its horizons with forests of soaring towers that define a brash and sophisticated zeitgeist. The grandiose Bund may forever recall the indignity of foreign encroachment, but Pǔdōng – and more specifically Lùjiāzuǐ – concerns itself with the future.

Pǔdōng only dates to the early 1990s, so don't expect the sheer variety of New York skyscraper architecture. But some of the world's very tallest buildings erupt from Shànghǎi's notoriously boggy terrain, including the breathtaking Shànghǎi World Financial Center (SWFC) in Lùjiāzuǐ, the world's fourth-tallest building (at the time of writing). Metallic, glass, uncompromising and audaciously designed, the tower is an awe-inspiring testament to money and ambition. The original design incorporated a circle at its top, where the 'bottle-opener' trapezoid aperture is (reducing the wind pressure), but this design was shouted down by local fears that it would recall the Japanese flag.

The SWFC replaced the Jinmao Tower as the tallest building in Shànghǎi. Replete with Chinese symbolism, the pagoda-like 421m-high Jinmao Tower has 88 floors (eight is *the* lucky number), while its 13 stepped bands allude to Buddhist imagery.

With a completion date of 2014, the dominant edifice in Lùjiāzuǐ will be the twisting form of the Shànghǎi Tower, all 632m of it. When finished, it will be China's tallest building and the second tallest in the world (but not for long, no doubt).

Don't overlook Pǔxī on the far side of the river, where there's a vigorous collection of modern architecture, including claw-like Tomorrow Square, rocketing nefariously over People's Square.

With such a meteoric construction agenda and an anything-goes attitude, designs can sometimes misfire: Shànghǎi is littered with cheesy disappointments such as the naff Oriental Pearl TV Tower, the curious crown atop the Bund Center (88 Middle Henan Rd) and the Radisson Blu Hotel Shanghai New World (88 West Nanjing Rd; another '88'!).

Clockwise from top left
1 Jinmao Tower (p139; at left) and Shànghǎi World Financial Center (p140) **2** Oriental Pearl TV Tower (p138

1

2

Shang-low

Shànghǎi's tall towers are lavished with media attention, but many of the city's most iconic contemporary buildings are low-rise.

In the Pǔdōng-side World Expo site, the staggering flying-saucer shaped Mercedes-Benz Arena looks like it's refuelling after a warp-speed voyage from Alpha Centauri. The nearby upturned red pyramid design of the China Art Palace (the former China Pavilion) is another distinctive architectural icon of the site. In 2012 the pavilion was reinvented as a modern-art museum, guaranteeing it a second wind. Unfortunately, most of the other World Expo pavilions – including the staggeringly inventive UK Pavilion – were dismantled after the event, but a few are still standing.

Also in Pǔdōng, the Arata Isozaki-designed Himalayas Center – attached to the Jumeirah Himalayas Hotel – is a highly complicated, organic-looking and challenging form in an otherwise uniform neighbourhood of Shànghǎi.

A stroll around People's Square in Pǔxī introduces you to three of the city's most eye-catching designs. The Shànghǎi Urban Planning Exhibition Hall is capped with a distinctive roof with four 'florets'. The nearby Shànghǎi Grand Theatre combines Chinese sweeping eaves with a futuristic employment of plastic and glass. Opposite this pair is the wonderfully designed Shànghǎi Museum, resembling an ancient Chinese vessel known as a *dǐng*.

Other low-rise modern Shànghǎi structures with spectacular interiors or exteriors include Pǔdōng International Airport Terminal 1 and Shànghǎi Hóngqiáo Railway Station. Elsewhere, conversions of industrial buildings have breathed new life into disused structures: in 2012, the Nánshì Power Plant was repurposed as the Power Station of Art, a huge contemporary art museum.

Don't overlook Shànghǎi's vast bridges, including the enormous Lúpǔ Bridge, which combine length and height in equal measure.

Clockwise from top left
1 China Art Palace (p141) **2** Shànghǎi Hóngqiáo Railway Station (p243) **3** Shànghǎi Grand Theatre (p72)

1

A TALL STOREY

At the time of writing, Shànghǎi's tallest buildings (in order of height):

➡ **Shànghǎi Tower** (p15) Aiming for a 2014 completion date and rising supreme over Lùjiāzuǐ; 121 storeys.

➡ **Shànghǎi World Financial Center** (p140) A colossal, shimmering bottle-opener at the heart of Lùjiāzuǐ; 101 storeys.

➡ **Jinmao Tower** (p139) Crystalline, art-deco-inspired pagoda and Shànghǎi's most attractive tower; 88 storeys.

➡ **Plaza 66 Tower One** (p135) Pǔxī's tallest building, best known for its exclusive mall slung out below; 66 storeys.

➡ **Tomorrow Square** (p66) Dramatically futuristic aluminium-and-glass tower climbing into the skies above People's Square; 55 storeys.

LU / VIEWSTOCK / CORBIS © ARCHITECT HE JINGTANG

MIGUEL SAYAGO / ALAMY ©

WIN INITIATIVE / GETTY IMAGES © ARCHITECT JEAN-MARIE CHARPENTIER

Concession Architecture

For many foreign visitors, Shànghǎi's modern architectural vision is a mere side salad to the feast of historic architecture lining the Bund and beyond. Remnants of old Shànghǎi, these buildings are part of the city's genetic code, inseparable from its sense of identity as the former 'Paris of the East'.

Neoclassical

Although the Bund contains the lion's share of Shànghǎi's neoclassical designs, arguably the most impressive is the Shànghǎi Art Museum in People's Square. This beautiful red-brick building with a clock tower once formed part of the main stand at the old racecourse.

In the 1920s the British architectural firm of Palmer & Turner designed many of Shànghǎi's major buildings (13 structures on the Bund alone), including the neoclassical Hongkong and Shanghai Banking Corporation (HSBC) building, the Yokohama Specie Bank, the Custom House and other gems.

A triumphant example of Soviet neoclassical architecture is the Shànghǎi Exhibition Center.

Villa Architecture

The tree-lined streets of the French Concession house a delightful collection of magnificent residential early-20th-century villa architecture, much of which has been well preserved. Standout examples include the Mansion Hotel, the Moller House, the Ruìjīn Hotel, Āntíng Villa Hotel and Fu 1039. See our French Concession walking tour for more (p93).

Art Deco

The late 1920s saw the Shànghǎi arrival of art deco and its sophisticated, modish

1

3

Clockwise from top left
1 Dome mosaics of HSBC Building (p56) **2** Fairmont Peace Hotel (p53) **3** Paramount Ballroom (p133)

LONELY PLANET / GETTY IMAGES ©

NICK BONETTI / EYE UBIQUITOUS / CORBIS ©

expressions of the machine age. It was one of Shànghǎi's architectural high-water marks, with the city boasting more art-deco buildings than any other city in the world. For a comprehensive lowdown on the style, read *Shanghai Art Deco* by Deke Erh and Tess Johnston.

Art-deco buildings of note include the Fairmont Peace Hotel, the Woo Villa, the Paramount Ballroom, Broadway Mansions, the Cathay Theatre, the Liza Building at 99 East Nanjing Rd, the Savoy Apartments at 209 Changshu Rd, the Picardie Apartments (now the Hengshan Hotel) on the corner of Hengshan Rd and Wanping Rd, the Embankment Building and the Bank of China building, but there are dozens of others.

Strongly associated with art deco (although he also used earlier styles), Ladislaus Hudec (1893–1958) was a Hungarian who came to Shànghǎi in 1918 after escaping en route to a Russian prisoner-of-war camp in Siberia. The Park Hotel, Grand Theatre, China Baptist Publication Society, the Green House and other art-deco buildings all owe their creation to Hudec.

BUILDING THE BUND

The Bund – Shànghǎi's most famous esplanade of concession buildings – was built on unstable foundations due to the leaching mud of the Huángpǔ River. Bund buildings were first built on concrete rafts that were fixed onto wood pilings, which were allowed to sink into the mud. Because of the lack of qualified architects, some of the earliest Western-style buildings in Shànghǎi were partially built in Hong Kong, shipped to Shànghǎi, then assembled on site.

Lòngtáng & Shíkùmén

Even though Shànghǎi is typified by its high-rise and uniform residential blocks, near ground level the city comes into its own with its low-rise *lòngtáng* and *shíkùmén* architecture. Here, both Western and Asian architectural motifs were synthesised into harmonious, utilitarian styles that still house a large proportion of Shànghǎi's residents.

Lòngtáng

In the same way that Běijīng's most authentic features survive among its homely (but far older) *hútòng* alleyways, so Shànghǎi's *lòngtáng* (or *lǐlòng*) lanes are the historic city's principal indigenous urban architectural feature. *Lòngtáng* (弄堂) are the back alleys that form the building blocks of living, breathing communities, supplying a warm and charming counterpoint to the abstract and machinelike skyscrapers rising over the city. Sadly, these alleys and their signature buildings, the *shíkùmén*, have offered little more than a feeble resistance against developers who have toppled swathes of *shíkùmén* to make way for more glittering projects. But if you want to find Shànghǎi at its most local, community-spirited, neighbourly and also at its quietest, more than enough *lòngtáng* survive off the main drag for you to savour their slow-moving tempo.

Shíkùmén

Following the devastation of the Taiping Rebellion in 1853, some 20,000 Chinese fled into the International Settlements. Sensing a newly arrived cash cow, the British decided to scrap the law forbidding Chinese from renting property in the concessions, and foreigners from developing real estate. British and French

Clockwise from top left
1 Bar in Tiánzǐfáng (p90) **2** Alley cafe in Tiánzǐfáng (p90)
3 *Shíkùmén* housing

LO MAK / REDLINK / CORBIS ©

2

LO MAK / REDLINK / CORBIS ©

speculators built hundreds of houses in what became Shànghǎi's biggest real-estate boom. The result was *shíkùmén* (石库门) – literally 'stone gate' – referring to the stone porticos that fronted these buildings and the alleys that led to them.

Such buildings made up 60% of Shànghǎi's housing between the 1850s and the 1940s; they can be found across historic Shànghǎi, but are most prevalent in the French Concession, Jìng'ān, Hóngkǒu and parts of the Old Town. One of the most charming *shíkùmén* areas is in the boutique-littered Tiānzǐfáng area in the French Concession. Xīntiāndì is also a restored, but more synthetic, *shíkùmén* area housing the absorbing Shíkùmén Open House Museum.

SHÍKÙMÉN STYLE

Shànghǎi *shíkùmén* architecture is a unique mixture of East and West, a blend of the Chinese courtyard house and English terraced housing. Typical *shíkùmén* houses were two to three storeys tall and fronted by an imposing stone-gate frame topped with a decorated lintel enclosing two stout wooden doors (frequently black), each decorated with a bronze handle. The lintel was sometimes elaborately carved with a dictum in Chinese, usually four characters long. At the entrance to the alley there was usually a *yānzhǐdiàn* (烟纸店) – literally a 'tobacco and paper shop' – where residents could pick up provisions round the clock.

Shíkùmén were originally designed to house one family, but Shànghǎi's growth and socialist reorientation led to them being sublet to many families, each of which shared a kitchen and outside bathroom to complement the *mǎtǒng* (chamber pot). For the Shanghainese, a single-family kitchen and separate bedrooms remained a dream until the 1990s.

Religious Architecture

Following the tumultuous destruction of religious beliefs, practices and architecture that characterised the Mao era, religion has enjoyed a powerful resurgence in Shànghǎi (as it has nationwide) from the 1980s to the present day. The city's most standout buildings may be dedicated to Mammon, but many of Shànghǎi's most impressive religious buildings are once again active places of worship.

Temples

The place of prayer for Buddhist, Taoist or Confucian worshippers, Chinese *sìmiào* (寺庙; temples) tend to follow a strict, schematic pattern. Most importantly, all are laid out on a north–south axis in a series of halls, with the main door of each hall facing south.

One striking difference from Christian churches is the open-plan design of temples, with buildings interspersed with breezy open-air courtyards. This allows the climate to permeate; seasons therefore play an essential role in defining the mood. The open-air layout furthermore allows the *qì* (气; energy) to circulate, dispersing stale air and allowing incense to be burned liberally.

Buddhist temples of architectural note include the Jade Buddha Temple, with its striking yellow-and-red walls; the Jìng'ān Temple, a recent rebuild of one of Shànghǎi's first temples (c AD 247); and the Old Town's Chénxiānggé Nunnery.

Standout Taoist temples include the Temple of the Town God, with its fine carvings, and the Báiyún Temple, rebuilt in 2004 with attractive port-red walls. Both are in the Old Town, which is also home to the large Confucian Temple, lovingly

Clockwise from top left
1 Jade Buddha Temple (p122) **2** St Ignatius Cathedral (p158) **3** Menorah in Ohel Moishe Synagogue (p151) **Over page** Balconies in the atrium of the Jinmao Tower (p139)

PETER ADAMS / CORBIS ©

LONELY PLANET / GETTY IMAGES ©

restored in the 1990s after taking a hammering during the Cultural Revolution.

Churches

Churches in Shànghǎi reflect the long Christian presence in this historically cosmopolitan city. After St Ignatius Cathedral and Shěshān Basilica, other churches of note are the beautiful Russian Orthodox Mission Church, with its blue domes; the pretty Dǒngjiādù Cathedral, Shànghǎi's oldest church (c 1853); the empty St Nicholas Church (1934); and the delightful St Joseph's Church (c 1862; *36 South Sichuan Rd*), with its Gothic spires, now located within the grounds of a school.

Mosques

The main active mosque in Shànghǎi is the Peach Garden Mosque, built in the Old Town in 1917. While not particularly impressive architecturally, it is nevertheless an interesting mix of styles with its neoclassical-like facade, Islamic green domes and mixture of Arabic lettering and Chinese characters.

Synagogues

Of the seven synagogues once built in Shànghǎi, only two remain. The recently renovated Ohel Moishe Synagogue is now the absorbing Shànghǎi Jewish Refugees Museum. Of more authentic charm is the rather neglected, ivy-cloaked Ohel Rachel Synagogue in Jìng'ān, which was Shànghǎi's first synagogue (1920).

SHÀNGHǍI'S BEST TEMPLES, CHURCHES & SYNAGOGUES

➡ **Jade Buddha Temple** (p122) Shànghǎi's best-known shrine, housing a serene effigy of Sakyamuni (Buddha).

➡ **Jìng'ān Temple** (p124) Now impressively restored, this Buddhist temple is a major Jìng'ān landmark.

➡ **Chénxiānggé Nunnery** (p77) One of the Old Town's most sacred sites.

➡ **Shěshān Basilica** (p188) Standing sublimely atop a hill just outside town.

➡ **Ohel Moishe Synagogue** (p151) Jewish Shànghǎi's most significant chunk of religious heritage.

JOSE FUSTE RAGA / CORBIS © ARCHITECT

Survival Guide

Transport

GETTING TO SHÀNGHĂI

Most passengers reach Shànghǎi from abroad by air. The city has two airports: Pǔdōng International Airport to the east and Hóngqiáo International Airport on the other side of the city to the west, with most international passengers arriving at the former. Shànghǎi is China's second-largest international air hub (third-largest including Hong Kong) and if you can't fly direct, you can go via Běijīng, Hong Kong or Guǎngzhōu.

Figure on a 13- to 14-hour flight from the US west coast to Shànghǎi or Běijīng, an hour or more extra for Hong Kong. It's about an 11-hour flight to Běijīng from London Heathrow and 12 to 13 hours to Shànghǎi and Hong Kong

➡ Daily (usually several times a day) domestic flights connect Shànghǎi to every major city in China.

➡ Shànghǎi is linked to the rest of China by an efficient rail network (with numerous high-speed lines) and, to a lesser extent, long-distance buses.

➡ Shànghǎi can be reached by ferry from Osaka, Kobe and (suspended at the time of writing) Nagasaki in Japan.

Beyond internet travel websites – **Expedia** (www.expedia.com) and **Travelocity** (www.travelocity.com), for example – flight comparison websites weigh up the best prices from airline websites, travel agents, search engines and other online sources and are highly versatile, but tend to quote similar fares. They include:

Fly.com (www.fly.com)

Kayak (www.kayak.co.uk)

Lastminute.com (www.lastminute.com)

Momondo (www.momondo.com)

Travelsupermarket (www.travelsupermarket.com)

Skyscanner (www.skyscanner.net)

Flights, tour and rail tickets can be booked online at lonely planet.com/bookings.

Pǔdōng International Airport

Pǔdōng International Airport (PVG; 浦东国际机场; Pǔdōng Guójì Jīchǎng; ☎6834 1000, flight information 96990; www.shairport.com) is located 30km southeast of Shànghǎi, near the East China Sea. All international flights (and some domestic flights) operate from here (other domestic flights fly from Hóngqiáo airport). If you're making an onward domestic connection from Pǔdōng International Airport, it's essential that you find out whether the domestic flight leaves from Pǔdōng or Hóngqiáo (the latter has two terminals), as it will take at least an hour to cross the city.

Simple and easy to navigate, there are currently two main passenger terminals, with a satellite terminal due to start operating in 2015. Departures are on the upper level and arrivals on the lower level, where there is a tourist information counter.

Banks and ATMs are easily located throughout the airport, on both sides of customs. The Shànghǎi Pǔdōng Development Bank, at the international end of the lower level, can cash travellers cheques and give Visa credit-card cash advances. There are China Post offices in the arrival and departures hall.

Left Luggage Located in the arrival and departure halls and open from 6am to 9.30pm. Charges are ¥20 for one hour or ¥30 for a day.

Hotel The **Merry Lin Air Terminal Hotel** (大众美林阁空港宾馆; Dàzhòng Měilín Gékōng Gǎng Bīnguǎn; ☎3879 9999; 6hr from ¥198, 24hr from ¥298) is located between terminals 1 and 2, in front of the Maglev ticket office.

Shuttle Buses Connect the terminals, stopping at doors 1 and 8 (terminal 1) and doors 23 and 27 (terminal 2).

Wi-fi Available, but you have to purchase time.

Maglev

The warp-speed **Maglev** (磁浮列车; Cífú Lièchē; www.smtdc.com; economy single/return ¥50/80, with same-day air ticket ¥40, children under/over 1.2m free/half-price) runs to Longyang Rd metro stop (just south of Century Park) on metro line 2 in eight minutes, running every 20 minutes in both directions roughly between 6.45am and 9.40pm. See also p242.

Metro

Metro line 2 runs from Pǔdōng airport to Hóngqiáo airport (Map p302), passing through central Shànghǎi. It is convenient, though not for those in a hurry. From Pǔdōng airport, it takes about 1¼ hours to People's Square (¥7, Map p280) and 1¾ hours to Hóngqiáo airport (¥8).

Airport Buses

Numerous airport buses take between 60 and 90 minutes to run to their destinations in Pǔxī, on the west side of the Huángpǔ River. Buses drop off at all departures halls and pick up outside arrivals, at both terminals 1 and 2, leaving the airport roughly every 15 to 30 minutes from 7am to 11pm and heading to the airport from roughly 5.30am to 9.30pm (bus 1 runs till 11pm).

The most useful buses are **airport bus 1** (¥30), linking Pǔdōng airport with Hóngqiáo airport (Terminals 1 and 2), and **airport bus 2** (¥22), linking Pǔdōng airport with the **Airport City Terminal** (Shànghǎi Jīchǎng Chéngshì Hángzhàn Lóu, Map p294; West Nanjing Rd), east of Jìng'ān Temple. **Airport bus 5** (¥16-22) links Pǔdōng airport with Shànghǎi Railway Station (Map p293) via People's Square (Map p280). **Airport bus 7** (¥22) runs to Shànghǎi South Railway Station. A **midnight line** (¥16-30) operates from 11pm to the last arrival, running to Hóngqiáo airport via Longyang Rd metro station to Shimen No 1 Rd and Huashan Rd.

Taxi

Rides into central Shànghǎi cost around ¥160 and take about an hour; to Hóngqiáo airport it costs around ¥200. Most Shànghǎi taxi drivers are honest, though ensure they use the meter; avoid monstrous overcharging by using the regular taxi rank outside the arrivals hall.

Hotel Shuttle Buses

Most top-end and some midrange hotels operate shuttle buses to and from their hotels at fixed times (roughly ¥40 to Pǔdōng International Airport). Enquire at the rows of hotel desks in the arrivals hall or contact your hotel beforehand.

Long-Distance Buses

Regular buses run to Sūzhōu (苏州; ¥84, three hours, 17 per day) and Hángzhōu (杭州; ¥100, three hours, six per day) from the long-distance bus stop at the airport.

Hóngqiáo International Airport

Eighteen kilometres west of the Bund, **Hóngqiáo International Airport** (SHA; 虹桥国际机场; Hóngqiáo Guójì Jīchǎng; Map p302; ☎6268 8899, flight information 5260 4620; www.shairport.com) has two terminals, the older and less-used **Terminal 1** (east terminal; halls A and B) and the brand-new and very sophisticated **Terminal 2** (west terminal; attached to Shànghǎi Hóngqiáo Railway Station), where most flights arrive. If flying domestically within China from Shànghǎi, consider flying from here, which is closer to central Shànghǎi; if flying in from one airport and transferring to the other, remember that they are a long way apart. Both stations are accessible on the Shànghǎi metro.

The **information counters** (⏲5.30am-11pm) are useful, booking discounted accommodation, providing free maps, offering advice on transportation into town and writing the Chinese script for a taxi. A China Post office is located in the departure halls. ATMs taking international cards are located at most exits.

Luggage storage is available in the departure halls and arrivals hall of both terminals, operating between 7am and 8.30pm. Bags must be locked and a passport or ID is required. Wi-fi is available; however, you'll

CLIMATE CHANGE & TRAVEL

Every form of transport that relies on carbon-based fuel generates CO_2, the main cause of human-induced climate change. Modern travel is dependent on aeroplanes, which might use less fuel per kilometre per person than most cars but travel much greater distances. The altitude at which aircraft emit gases (including CO_2) and particles also contributes to their climate change impact. Many websites offer 'carbon calculators' that allow people to estimate the carbon emissions generated by their journey and, for those who wish to do so, to offset the impact of the greenhouse gases emitted with contributions to portfolios of climate-friendly initiatives throughout the world. Lonely Planet offsets the carbon footprint of all staff and author travel.

need to ask for the password at an information counter.

Shuttle Buses Run frequently (6am to 10.30pm) between Terminal 2 and Terminal 1.

Terminal 2

METRO
Terminal 2 is connected to downtown Shànghǎi by lines 2 and 10 (30 minutes to People's Square, Map p280) from Hóngqiáo Airport Terminal 2 metro station; both lines run through East Nanjing Rd station (Map p280; for the Bund). Line 2 runs to Pǔdōng and connects with Pǔdōng International Airport (¥8; 1¾ hours) and Longyang Rd metro station, south of Century Park (for Maglev details, see the boxed text). The next stop west from Hóngqiáo Airport Terminal 2 is Hóngqiáo Railway Station (connected to the airport and accessible on foot).

TAXI
A taxi to the Bund will cost around ¥70; to Pǔdōng International Airport, around ¥160. Avoid taxi sharks.

BUS
Airport bus 1 (¥30, 6am to 9.30pm) runs to Pǔdōng International Airport; **bus 941** (¥6, 5.30am to 11pm) runs to the main Shànghǎi Railway Station (Map p293). **Night buses 316** (11am to 5pm) and **320** (11am to 5pm) run to East Yan'an Rd near the Bund (Map p280).

LONG-DISTANCE BUS
The long-distance bus station at Terminal 2 runs to myriad destinations, including Sūzhōu, Nánjīng, Qīngdǎo, Túnxī (for Huángshān), Hángzhōu and Dēngfēng (for the Shaolin Temple).

TRAIN
Attached to Terminal 2, Shànghǎi Hóngqiáo Railway Station has high-speed G-class trains to Hángzhōu, Sūzhōu, Nánjīng and Běijīng.

Terminal 1

METRO
Hóngqiáo Airport Terminal 1 is the next stop east on line 10 from Hóngqiáo Airport Terminal 2 metro station. Change to line 2 for the metro to Pǔdōng International Airport (¥8).

BUS
From Hóngqiáo Airport Terminal 1, an **airport shuttle bus** (¥4, 7.50am to 11pm) runs to the **Airport City Terminal** (Map p294; West Nanjing Rd). **Airport bus 1** (¥30, 6am to 9.30pm) runs to Pǔdōng International Airport; **bus 941** (¥6) links Hóngqiáo Airport with the main Shànghǎi Railway Station (Map p293) and **bus 925** (¥4) runs to People's Square (Map p280) via Hongmei Rd and Shimen No 1 Rd. Other buses include **bus 938** (¥7) to Yángjiādù (Map p296) in Pǔdōng via Hongxu Rd, North Caoxi Rd (Map p300) and South Xizang Rd and **bus 806** (¥5) to Lùpǔ Bridge in the south of Pǔxī.

TAXI
If arriving at Hóngqiáo Airport Terminal 1, taxi queues can be long (it can be quicker to take the metro or the bus). Avoid taxi sharks.

Train

China's rail service is gargantuan, excellent and more than a little mind-boggling, while colossal investment over recent years has pumped up the high-speed network. The only 'international' train to arrive in Shànghǎi is the T99 from Kowloon in Hong Kong. The train is, however, an excellent way to arrive in Shànghǎi from other parts of China. The network was due to total 110,000km by the end of 2012. The railway to Lhasa

OFF THE RAILS

If you need to reach or depart Pǔdōng International Airport chop-chop, Shànghǎi's futuristic Maglev train (磁浮列车) comes with a top speed of 430km/hr. It's the world's sole Maglev (magnetic levitation) train in commercial operation; in place of conventional wheels, the Sino-German train's carriages are supported above the tracks by a magnetic field. With ample legroom, carriages have simple interiors and, perhaps tellingly, no seatbelts. LED meters notch up the rapidly escalating velocity, although the train starts to decelerate around five minutes into its eight-minute cruise, in preparation for arrival.

Launched in 2003, the Maglev train may be a wonder of the modern world but it's of limited use in getting into central Shànghǎi, as the train only takes you as far as the terminus at Longyang Rd station (off Map p297) in Pǔdōng, from where you'll have to lug your luggage a few hundred metres to the metro station of the same name to continue your journey. Nonetheless, a trip on the train is thrilling and a return trip to the airport is a fun outing for kids and the family. From a transportation point of view, the Maglev has run into competition from metro line 2, which travels into town from Pǔdōng International Airport and on to Hóngqiáo Airport Terminal 2, via the city centre.

in Tibet began running in 2006, despite scepticism that it could ever be laid, so you can climb aboard a train in Shànghǎi and alight in Tibet's capital (when Tibet is accessible).

Stations

The city has three principal stations: the main Shànghǎi Railway Station, Shànghǎi Hóngqiáo Railway Station and Shànghǎi South Railway Station. All stations are easily accessed on the metro system. Left-luggage facilities exist at all train stations.

Shànghǎi Hóngqiáo Railway Station (上海虹桥站; Shànghǎi Hóngqiáo zhàn; off Map p302; Ⓜ Hongqiao Railway Station) is located at the western end of Line 10 of the metro (also on line 2). Very new and sophisticated and the largest train station in Asia, Shànghǎi Hóngqiáo Railway Station is the terminus for the high-speed G-class trains from Běijīng and Hángzhōu (as well as other trains):

Běijīng (G-class) 2nd/1st class seat ¥555/935, 5½ hours, very regular (7am to 7.55pm)

Hángzhōu (G-class) 2nd/1st class seat ¥78/124, one hour, very regular (6.38am to 9.32pm)

Nánjīng South (G-class) 2nd/1st class seat ¥135/230, 70 minutes to two hours, frequent

Sūzhōu (D-class) 2nd/1st class seat ¥26/31, 30 minutes, regular

Shànghǎi Railway Station (上海火车站; Shànghǎi Huǒchē Zhàn; Map p293; ☎6317 9090; 385 Meiyuan Rd; Ⓜ Shanghai Railway Station) Most trains depart from here, with destinations including:

➡ **Běijīng (D-class)** seat/sleeper ¥311/¥698, 8 to 11½ hours, three daily

➡ **Hángzhōu (G-class)** 2nd/1st class seat ¥93/148, 1½ hours, four daily

➡ **Hong Kong** seat/hard sleeper ¥226/409, 18½ hours, one daily (6.24pm)

➡ **Huángshān** seat/hard sleeper ¥94/175, 11½ hours, two daily

➡ **Nánjīng (G-class)** 2nd/1st class seat ¥140/220, two hours, frequent

➡ **Sūzhōu (G-class)** 2nd/1st ¥40/60, 30 minutes, frequent services

➡ **Xī'ān** seat/hard sleeper ¥182/333, 16 to 20 hours, 10 daily

Shànghǎi South Railway Station (上海南站; Shànghǎi Nánzhàn; off Map p300; ☎9510 5123; 200 Zhaofeng Rd). Has trains largely to southern and southwestern destinations, including:

➡ **Guìlín** hard/soft sleeper ¥353/539, 22 hours, four daily

➡ **Hángzhōu** ¥29, 2½ to three hours, frequent

A few trains also leave from the renovated West Station (上海西站; Shànghǎi Xīzhàn), including trains to Nánjīng; however, it's less convenient.

Tickets

Although procuring tickets for nearby destinations (Sūzhōu, Hángzhōu etc) and high-speed train tickets is reasonably straightforward, never assume you can casually stroll to the train station and hand over your credit card for a hard-sleeper ticket for a same-day departure to distant destinations.

➡ You will need your passport when buying a ticket (the number is printed on your ticket) at all train ticket offices.

➡ Never aim to get a hard-sleeper (or increasingly, soft-sleeper) ticket on the day of travel – plan a few days ahead.

➡ Most tickets can be booked in advance between two and 10 days (and sometimes longer) prior to your intended date of departure.

➡ Automated ticket machines at Shànghǎi Railway Station require Chinese ID and your passport will not work; you will need to queue at the ticket window.

➡ Prepare to queue for a long time at the train station.

➡ Tickets purchases can only be made in cash.

➡ As with air travel, buying tickets around Chinese New Year and during the 1 May and 1 October holiday periods can be very hard, and prices increase on some routes.

➡ Tickets on many routes (such as to Lhasa) can be very hard to get in July and August so prepare to take a flight to distant destinations.

➡ Try to use train ticket offices outside of the station.

➡ Avoid black-market tickets – your passport number must be on the ticket.

➡ There are no refunds for lost train tickets, so hold on to them tightly.

DOMESTIC AIR TICKETS

Tickets can be purchased from hundreds of airline offices and travel agencies (including hotel travel agents) around town (though few take credit cards); try to book several days in advance of your flight. Tickets are often substantially discounted, so shop around. Buy tickets at a discount online at **CTrip** (☎400 619 9999; http://english.ctrip.com) or **eLong** (www.elong.net). Discounts can be harder to come by during the main holiday seasons (Chinese New Year, first week of May and October) and on weekends.

Ticket Offices

There are several options for getting hold of train tickets in Shànghǎi. You can queue at the ticket offices (售票厅; *shòupiàotīng*) at train stations, but brace for a long wait. There are two ticket halls at the Shànghǎi Railway Station, one in the main building (same-day tickets) and another on the east side of the square (advance tickets). One counter should have English-speakers.

Alternatively, your hotel will be able to obtain a ticket for you, albeit sometimes for a hefty surcharge. Tickets can also be purchased for a small surcharge from travel agencies (see p248).

Hard-seat and hard-sleeper train tickets can also be purchased for a small ¥5 commission from the following train ticket offices (火车票预售处; *huǒchēpiào yùshòuchù*):

Bund (Map p280; 384 Middle Jiangxi Rd; 江西中路384号; ⌚8am-8pm)

French Concession (Map p290; 12 Dongping Rd; ⌚8am-noon & 1-6pm Mon-Fri, 9am-noon & 1-5.30pm Sat & Sun)

Jìng'ān North (Map p293; Hengfeng Rd, west of Shànghǎi Railway Station; 恒丰路)

Jìng'ān South (Map p294; 77 Wanhangdu Rd; 万航渡路77号; ⌚8am-5pm)

Pǔdōng (Map p296; 1396 Lujiazui Ring Rd; 陆家嘴环路1396号; ⌚8am-7pm)

Hóngkǒu (Map p298; 106 Huangpu Rd; 黄浦路106号; ⌚8-11.30am & 12.30-6pm)

Train information is available over the phone in Chinese only (☎800 820 7890).

Classes

The most comfortable way to get to destinations around Shànghǎi (such as Sūzhōu and Hángzhōu) is by high-speed train, which assures you a comfortable seat and regular and punctual departures.

On swish high-speed G-class, D-class and C-class trains seating classes are straightforward:

- 1st class (一等; *yīděng*)
- 2nd class (二等; *èrděng*)
- Business class (商务座; *shāngwù zuò*)
- VIP class (特等座; *tèděng zuò*)

For most other slower (T-class, K-class, some Z-class and other) Chinese trains, you have the following choice of ticket types:

- Hard seat (硬座; *yìngzuò*)
- Hard sleeper (硬卧; *yìngwò*)
- Soft seat (软座; *ruǎnzuò*)
- Soft sleeper (软卧; *ruǎnwò*)

On non-high-speed trains, numbered soft seats are more comfortable than hard seats. Hard-seat class is not available on the high-speed C-, D- and G-class trains, and is only found on T- and K-class trains and trains without a number prefix; a handful of Z-class trains have hard seats. Hard-seat class generally has padded seats, but it's hard on your sanity: often unclean and noisy, and painful on the long haul. Since hard seat is the only class most locals can afford, it's packed to the gills.

For overnight trips to farther destinations, hard sleepers are easily comfortable enough, with only a fixed number of people allowed in the sleeper carriage. They serve very well as an overnight hotel.

The hard-sleeper carriage consists of doorless compartments with half a dozen bunks in three tiers and fold-away seats by the windows. Sheets, pillows and blankets are provided. Carriages are nonsmoking, although smokers congregate between carriages. Competition for hard sleepers is keen, so reserve early (see p244). Prices vary according to which berth you get: upper (cheapest), middle or lower berth.

Soft sleepers are expensive (about twice the hard-sleeper price), with four comfortable bunks in a closed, carpeted compartment.

Travelling by Train

- Trains are generally highly punctual and are usually a safe way to travel.
- Train stations are often conveniently close to the centre of town.
- Travelling in sleeper berths at night often means you can arrive at your destination first thing in the morning, saving a night's hotel accommodation.

Timetables

Paperback train timetables for the entire country (¥7) are published every April and October, but are available in Chinese only. Online English-language timetables:

Travel China Guide (www.travelchinaguide.com)

China Highlights (www.chinahighlights.com)

China Train Timetable (www.china-train-ticket.com)

Useful Websites

www.12306.cn For buying tickets online; however, it's Chinese-language only and only accepts Chinese bank cards and credit cards.

Seat 61 (www.seat61.com/china.htm)

Travel China Guide (www.travelchinaguide.com)

Tielu (www.tielu.org, in Chinese)

Bus

As trains are fast, regular and efficient, and traffic on roads unpredictable, travelling by bus is not a very useful way to leave or enter Shànghǎi, unless you are visiting local water towns. Buses to Běijīng take between 14 and 16 hours: it is far faster and more comfortable (but more expensive of course) to take the 5½-hour high-speed G-class trains to the capital, or even the eight-hour D-class trains.

The vast **Shànghǎi South Long-Distance Bus Station** (上海长途客运南站; Shànghǎi Chángtú Kèyùn Nánzhàn; www.ctnz.net; ☎5436 2835; 666 Shilong Rd; Ⓜ Shanghai South Railway Station) serves cities in south China, including:

Hángzhōu (Jiǔbǎo, Hángzhōu north bus station and Hángzhōu south bus station) ¥68, two hours, very regular (7.10am to 7.20pm).

Nánjīng ¥105, four hours.

Nánxún ¥47, 2½ hours, eight per day, take the bus for Húzhōu (湖州; 6.50am to 7.28pm).

Sūzhōu (south and north bus stations) ¥38, 90 minutes, regular (6.27am to 7.30pm).

Wūzhèn ¥49, two hours, eight daily (7.44am to 6.17pm).

Xītáng ¥32, 90 mins, 12 daily.

Zhōuzhuāng ¥25, two daily.

Although it appears close to Shànghǎi Railway Station, the vast **Shànghǎi Long-Distance bus station** (上海长途汽车客运中心; Shànghǎi Chángtú Qìchē Kèyùn Zǒngzhàn; Map p293; ☎6605 0000; 1666 Zhongxing Rd; 中兴路1666号; Ⓜ Shanghai Railway Station) is a pain to get to, but has buses to everywhere, including very regular buses to Sūzhōu and Hángzhōu, as well as Nánjīng (12 daily), Zhōuzhuāng (¥25, six daily) and Běijīng (¥311, 4pm). It's easiest to catch a cab here.

Regular buses also depart for Hángzhōu (¥100, two hours) and Sūzhōu (¥84, two hours) from Pǔdōng International Airport. Buses for Hángzhōu, Sūzhōu and a host of destinations also leave from the **Hóngqiáo Long-Distance bus station** (长途客运虹桥站; Chángtú Kèyùn Hóngqiáozhàn) at Hóngqiáo Airport Terminal 2.

From the **Shànghǎi Sightseeing Bus Centre** (上海旅游集散中心; Shànghǎi Lǚyóu Jísàn Zhōngxīn; Map p300) at Shànghǎi Stadium, you can join tours to Sūzhōu, Hángzhōu, Tónglǐ, Zhōuzhuāng, Zhūjiājiǎo and other destinations around Shànghǎi; see the Day Trips chapter (p169) for details.

Boat

Shànghǎi Port International Cruise Terminal (上海港国际客运中心; Shànghǎi Gǎng Guójì Kèyùn Zhōngxīn; Map p298; 500 Dongdaming Rd; 东大明路500号) Located north of the Bund and mostly serves cruise ships. A few international passenger routes serve Shànghǎi, with reservations recommended in July and August (passengers must be at the harbour three hours before departure to get through immigration). At the time of writing, the recently opened 26-hour ferry route between Shànghǎi and Nagasaki had been suspended.

China-Japan International Ferry Company (中日国际轮渡有限公司; Zhōngguó Guójì Lúndù Yǒuxiàn Gōngsī; Map p298; ☎6595 6888/6325 7642; www.chinajapanferry.com; 18th fl, Jin'an Bldg, 908 Dongdaming Rd; 东大明路908号金岸大厦) Has staggered departures (44 hours) every week to either Osaka or Kobe in Japan on Saturdays at 12.30pm. Fares range from ¥1300 in an eight-bed dorm to ¥6500 in a deluxe twin cabin.

Shànghǎi International Ferry Company (Map p298; ☎6595 8666; www.shanghai-ferry.co.jp; 15th fl, Jin'an Bldg, 908 Dongdaming Rd; 东大明路908号金岸大厦) Has departures (44 hours) to Osaka on Tuesdays at 11am. Fares range from ¥1300 in an eight-bed dorm to ¥6500 in a deluxe twin cabin.

GETTING AROUND SHÀNGHĂI

The best way to get around town is either by taxi or metro. The rapidly expanding metro and light railway system works like a dream; it's fast, efficient and inexpensive. Rush hour on the metro operates at overcapacity, however, and you get to savour the full meaning of the big squeeze. Taxis are ubiquitous and cheap, but flagging one down during rush hour or during a rainstorm requires staying power of a high order. With a wide-ranging web of routes, buses may sound tempting, but that's before you try to decipher routes and stops or attempt to squeeze aboard during the crush hour. Buses also have to contend with the increasing solidity of Shànghǎi's traffic, which can slow movement to an agonising crawl. Bicycles are good for small neighbourhoods but distances are too colossal for effective transport about town. Walking around Shànghǎi is only really possible within neighbourhoods, and even then the distances can be epic and tiring.

Metro

The best way to get about town, the **Shànghǎi metro** (上海地铁; Shànghǎi Dìtiě; www.shmetro.com) is fast, cheap, clean and easy, though hard to get a seat at the best of times (unless you get on at the terminus). The rush hour sees carriages filled to overcapacity, but trains are frequent and the system is being rapidly expanded to envelop more and more of the city.

At the beginning of 2003 there were only three lines in operation, at the time of writing there were 11 lines. New extensions to lines 11 and 13 (formerly the Expo Line) and additional lines (12 and 22) were expected to open by the end of 2012 or in 2013, and a further line (16) in 2013. An extra 175km are planned to be added to the network by 2015.

Metro maps are available at most stations; the free tourist maps also have a small metro map printed on them and there's an English section on the website. The most useful lines for travellers are 1, 2 and 10. Lines 1 and 2 connect at People's Square interchange (Map p280), the busiest station.

Line 1 (一号线; yīhào xiàn) Runs from Fujin Rd in the north, through Shànghăi Railway Station and People's Square, along Middle Huaihai Rd, through Xújiāhuì and Shànghăi South Railway Station to Xīnzhuāng in the southern suburbs.

Line 2 (二号线; èrhào xiàn) Runs from Xujing Dong in the west via Hóngqiáo Railway Station and Hóngqiáo Airport Terminal 2 to Pŭdōng International Airport in the east, passing through Jìng'ān, People's Square, East Nanjing Rd (and the Bund district) in the centre of town, going under the Huángpŭ River and on to Longyang Rd, the site of the Maglev terminus, before terminating at Pŭdōng International Airport.

Line 10 (十号线; shíhào xiàn) Runs from Hóngqiáo Railway Station in the west through Hóngqiáo Airport Terminal 2 and Hóngqiáo Airport Terminal 1 before zipping through the French Concession, the Old Town, the Bund area and Hóngkŏu before terminating at Xinjiangwancheng.

Metro station exits can be complicated so look for a street map (usually easy to find) before exiting. To find a metro station look for the red M.

Fares & Tickets

➡ Tickets range from ¥3 to ¥10, depending on the distance.

➡ Tickets are sold only from coin- and note-operated machines (except in rare cases).

➡ Service counters will provide you with change if your bills are not accepted.

➡ Keep your ticket until you exit.

➡ When entering the metro, swipe your card across the turnstile sensor for access; when exiting, enter it into the slot, where it will be retained.

➡ The rechargeable Transport Card (see the boxed text, p248) can be used on the metro, some buses, ferries, and all taxis.

➡ The one-day and three-day tourist pass (see the boxed text, p248) is also for use on the metro.

➡ There can be huge distances between different lines at interchange stations, such as between line 9 and 1 at Xújiāhuì station.

➡ A growing number of stations have coin-operated toilets.

Operating Hours

There's one main shortcoming to the metro system: it stops running relatively early in the night. Most lines begin their final run between 10pm and 10.30pm (some earlier), so anyone out later than 11pm will need to catch a cab home.

Taxi

Shànghăi has around 45,000 taxis. Most are Volkswagen Santanas, though some are Volkswagen Passats, there's a fleet of Mercedes-Benz taxis and a new 4000-strong fleet of spacious and comfortable white Volkswagen Touran taxis.

Shànghăi's taxis are reasonably cheap, hassle-free and easy to flag down outside rush hour (exept during summer storms). Taxis may not have rear seatbelts, in which case sit up front. On many taxis the rear left-hand door is locked, so board by the doors on the right side. Most taxi drivers (mostly male) are honest, though you should always go by the meter. The driver should push this down to start the meter when you get in the cab. Note that taxis can't take the tunnel to Lùjiāzuĭ in Pŭdōng from 8am to 9.30am and 5pm to 6.30pm.

➡ Fares are metered. Flag fall is ¥14 for the first 3km, and ¥2.4 per kilometre thereafter; there is no need to tip. A ¥1 fuel surcharge is included in the price.

➡ A night rate operates from 11pm to 5am, when the flag fall is ¥18, then ¥3.10 per kilometre.

➡ Pay by cash *(xiànjīn)* or use a Transport Card (see the boxed text, p248).

➡ At night you can tell if a taxi is empty by the red 'for hire' sign on the dashboard of the passenger side.

➡ Ask for a printed receipt, which gives the fare and the driver and car number, the distance travelled, waiting time and the number to call if there are any problems or if you left something in the taxi.

➡ If you don't speak Chinese, take a Chinese-character map, have your destination written down in characters, or pack your destination's business card.

➡ Use your mobile to phone your local contact (or the 24-hour tourist hotline – ☎962 288) in Shànghăi and ask him or her to give instructions to the driver.

➡ It also helps if you have your own directions and sit in the front with a map, looking knowledgeable (to deter circuitous, looping detours).

➡ Shànghǎi's main taxi companies include turquoise-coloured **Dazhong Taxi** (☎96822), **Qiangsheng** (☎6258 0000) and **Bashi** (☎96840).

➡ For taxi complaints, phone ☎962 000.

Many drivers are immigrants and can be inept at finding their way around, even to the most obvious of places. Some stick to the main roads and have little grasp of short-cuts. To avoid total novices, examine (if you have a choice between taxis) the number of stars below the driver's photo on the dashboard; stars range from one to five in order of expertise (and English-language skills). Motorcycle taxis wait at some intersections and metro stations to whisk travellers off to nearby destinations. Most trips cost less than ¥10.

Bus

Although sightseeing buses (see the boxed text) can be extremely handy, the huge Shànghǎi public bus system is unfortunately very hard for non-Chinese-speaking or -reading foreigners to use. Bus-stop signs and routes are in Chinese only and drivers and conductors speak little, if any, English, although on-board announcements in English will alert you to when to get off. The conductor will tell you when your stop is arriving, if you ask. Bus stops are widely spaced and your bus can race past your destination and on to the next stop up to a kilometre away. Suburban and long-distance buses don't carry numbers – the destination is in characters.

➡ Air-con buses (with a snowflake motif and the characters 空调 alongside the bus number) cost ¥2 to ¥3 (¥1.5 on far rarer buses without air-con).

➡ For buses without conductors, drop your cash (no change given) into the tray by the driver (always carry exact money).

➡ The swipeable Transport Card (see boxed text, p248) works on many but not all bus routes.

➡ Try to get on at the terminus (thus guaranteeing yourself a seat), avoid rush hours, and stick to a few tried-and-tested routes.

➡ Be alert to pickpockets, especially during the rush-hour squeeze.

➡ Buses generally operate from 5am to 11pm, except for 300-series buses, which operate all night.

➡ For English language bus routes in town, go to http://msittig.wubi.org/bus.

Bicycle

If you can handle the fumes and menace of Shànghǎi's intimidating traffic, cycling is a good way to get around town, but you will need to link it in with public transport.

➡ Bikes are banned from major roads, so cyclists often surge down the pavements (sidewalks) of busy streets.

➡ Cars will give you little room; if you're new to Shànghǎi, allow a few days to adjust.

➡ Bicycle repairmen dot the side streets, charging around ¥1 to pump up your tyres.

➡ Make sure that you have your own bicycle cable lock and try to leave your bike at bike parks (available at most shopping areas and subway stations for ¥0.50): an attendant will keep an eye on your wheels.

➡ Cyclists never use lights at night and Chinese pedestrians favour dark clothing, so ride carefully.

➡ Several hostels around town, including Le Tour Traveler's Rest (p199), can rent you a bike.

You can pick up a cheap mountain bike for as little as ¥250 at supermarkets and hypermarkets such as Carrefour. Purchased bikes need to be taxed, with a disc (available at bike shops) displayed.

Giant (捷安特; Jiéāntè; Map p300; ☎6426 5119; 666 Tianyaoqiao Rd; ⏲9am-8pm) Has a good collection of bikes.

Oyama (欧亚马折叠车; Ōuyāmǎ Zhédiéchē; Map p300; ☎6426 5218; 666 Tianyaoqiao Rd; ⏲10am-8pm) Has lightweight fold-up bikes starting from ¥678 and kicking off from around 8.5kg.

GOING FOR A RIDE

Tickets for the hop-on, hop-off, open-top **City Sightseeing Buses** (都市观光; Dūshì Guānguāng; www.springtour.com; ☎6252 0000; tickets ¥30; ⏲9am-8.30pm summer, to 6pm winter) last 24 hours and are, besides touring Shànghǎi's highlights, a great way to get around the centre of town and Pǔdōng. A recorded commentary runs in eight languages; just plug in your earphones (supplied). Buses have their own stops across central Shànghǎi, including the Bund, the Old Town (Map p284) and People's Square. **Big Bus Tours** (www.bigbustours.com; ☎6351 5988; adult/child US$44/29) also operates hop-on, hop-off services, lassoing the sights along 22 stops across two routes. Tickets are valid for 48 hours and include a one-hour boat tour of the Huángpǔ River plus admission to the 88th-floor observation tower of the Jinmao Tower.

TRANSPORT CARDS & TOURIST PASSES

If you are making more than a fleeting trip to Shànghǎi, it's worth getting a Transport Card (交通卡; *Jiāotōng Kǎ*). Available at metro stations and some convenience stores, cards can be topped up with credits and used on the metro, some buses and ferries, and in taxis. Credits are electronically deducted from the card as you swipe it over the sensor, equipped at metro turnstiles and near the door on buses; when paying your taxi fare, hand it to the taxi driver, who will swipe it. They don't save you money, but they are much more convenient than fishing through your pockets for change every time you want to go somewhere. A deposit of ¥20 is required; refunds are available at the East Nanjing Rd metro station (Map p280).

Other handy cards include a one-day tourist pass (¥18), offering unlimited travel on the metro for one day, and the three-day travel pass (¥45), also for use on the metro system. Both passes are available at metro stations.

BOHDI and SISU (see Tours) also sell and rent quality bikes.

The city has a public bike-hire scheme (Forever Public Bike Hire Scheme; bikes ¥4 per hour) with stations for the orange bikes dotted around the city, but it has not proved popular with visitors. To register for a card (¥300 deposit and ¥100 credit), you will need to take your passport to the **Xujiahui Tourist Information Center** (徐家汇旅游咨询中心; Xújiāhuì Lǚyóu Zīxún Zhōngxīn; Map p300; 1068 Zhaojiabang Rd; ⏲9.30am -4.30pm) or the **Wukang Road Tourist Information Center** (武康路旅游咨询中心; Wǔkāng Lù Lǚyóu Zīxún Zhōngxīn; Map p290; 393 Wukang Rd; ⏲9am-5pm).

Car

It is possible to hire a car in Shànghǎi, but the bureaucratic hurdles are designed to deter would-be foreign drivers – you can't just pick up a car at Pǔdōng International Airport. You will need a temporary or long-term Chinese driving licence and a residency permit. If your visa is for less than 90 days, **Hertz** (☎6085 1900; www.hertzchina.com) or **Avis** (☎6229 1118; www.avischina.com) can help you apply for a temporary Chinese driving licence, but this takes up to a week to arrange and includes a physical exam. If your visa exceeds 90 days, you can apply for a long-term Chinese driving licence, but this takes up to a month to arrange and includes a theory text plus medical exam. Residents can apply for a Chinese licence at their local Public Security Bureau or the **Shànghǎi Transport Bureau** (www.jt.sh.cn). For most visitors, it is more advisable to hire a car and a driver. A Volkswagen Santana with driver and petrol starts at around ¥600 per day – it may be cheaper to hire a taxi. Ask for more information at your hotel.

Ferry

Ferries cross the Huángpǔ River between Pǔxī on the west bank and Pǔdōng on the east. The most useful ferry operates between the southern end of the Bund and Dongchang Rd in Pǔdōng from the **Jinling Road Ferry** (金陵路轮渡站; Jīnlíng Dōnglù Dùkǒu; Map p280; ☎6326 2135; 127 East Zhongshan No 2 Rd; 中山东二路127号), running every 15 minutes from 7am to 10pm. Tickets (¥2) are sold at the kiosks out front. The **Fuxing Road Ferry** (复兴路轮渡站; Fùxīng Lù Lúndù Zhàn; Map p284) runs from Fuxing Rd north of the Cool Docks in the South Bund to Dongchang Rd as well. Ferries (¥2) run every 10 to 20 minutes from 5am to 11pm.

TOURS

Fun and handy bus tours of Shànghǎi that cover the top sights of Pǔxī and Pǔdōng include City Sightseeing Buses and Big Bus Tours (see the boxed text, p247). Other intriguing tours:

China Cycle Tours (☎1376 111 5050; www.chinacycletours.com; half-day tours from ¥400) City and rural tours in Shànghǎi and Sūzhōu.

Shanghai Sideways (www.shanghaisideways.com; from ¥800) Unusual motorcycle-sidecar tours of the city for up to two passengers, setting off from the Peninsula Hotel.

BOHDI (☎5266 9013; www.bohdi.com.cn; tours ¥220) Night-time cycling tours on Tuesdays (March to November) and trips around the region.

SISU (☎5059 6071; www.sisucycling.com; tour ¥150) Night-time cycling tours on Wednesdays and trips out of town.

TRAVEL AGENCIES

The following agencies can help with travel bookings.

CTrip (☎400 619 9999; http://english.ctrip.com) An excellent online agency, good for hotel and flight bookings.

eLong (www.elong.net) Hotel and flight bookings.

Directory A–Z

Business

Business Cards

Business name cards are absolutely crucial, even if you don't do business. You could be left high and dry when name cards are being dealt around and you are empty-handed. Try to get your name translated into (simplified) Chinese and have it printed on the reverse of the card. Remember that the Chinese pay particular attention to the quality of business cards so aim for a good finish if you want to impress. When proffering and receiving business cards, emulate the Chinese method of respectfully using the thumb and forefinger of both hands. Buying a name-card wallet is also recommended.

Useful Organisations

American Chamber of Commerce (AmCham; Shànghǎi Měiguó Shānghuì; Map p294; ☎6279 7119; www.amcham-shanghai.org; room 568, Shànghǎi Centre, 1376 West Nanjing Rd; 南京西路1376号568室) This office only helps members.

Australian Chamber of Commerce (AustCham Shanghai; Map p284; ☎6248 8301; www.austchamshanghai.com; suite 1101B, Silver Court, 85 Taoyuan Rd; 桃源路85号永银大厦1101B室)

British Chamber of Commerce (BritCham; 上海英国商会; Shànghǎi Yīngguó Shānghuì; Map p294; ☎6218 5022; www.britishchambershanghai.org; 5th fl, 863 West Nanjing Rd; 南京西路863号5楼) Inside the Marks & Spencer building.

China Britain Business Council (英中贸易协会; Yīngzhōng Màoyì Xiéhuì; Map p294; ☎6218 5183; www.cbbc.org; room 1701-1702, Westgate Tower, 1038 West Nanjing Rd; 南京西路1038号1701-1702室)

European Union Chamber of Commerce in China (中国欧盟商会; Zhōngguó Ōuméng Shānghuì; Map p286; ☎6385 2023; www.euccc.com.cn; room 2204, Shui On Plaza, 333 Middle Huaihai Rd; 淮海中路333号2204室)

US Commercial Center (Map p294; ☎6279 7640; room 631, Shànghǎi Centre, 1376 West Nanjing Rd; 南京西路1376号631室) The overseas office of the US Department of Commerce; can assist US businesses with finding Chinese business partners.

US-China Business Council (Map p294; ☎6288 3840; www.uschina.org; room 1301, 1701 West Beijing Rd; 北京西路1701号1301室)

Business Hours

Businesses in China close for the week-long Chinese New Year (usually in February) and National Day (beginning 1 October). The reviews in this book don't list business hours for the following unless they differ significantly from these standards.

Bank of China Branches are usually open weekdays from 9.30am to 11.30am and 1.30pm to 4.30pm. Some branches also open on Saturday mornings. Most Bank of China branches have 24-hour ATMs.

Bars Some bars may open in the morning; otherwise, from around 5pm to 2am.

China Post Most major China Post offices open daily from 8.30am to 6pm, and sometimes until 10pm. Local branches of China Post close on the weekend.

Museums Most museums are open on weekends; a few close on Monday. They usually stop selling tickets 30 minutes before they close.

Offices & Government Departments Normally open Monday to Friday from 9am to noon and about 2pm to 4.30pm.

Restaurants Most restaurants open from 11am to 10pm or later; some open from 10am to 2.30pm, with an afternoon break before opening again from 5pm to 11pm or later.

Shops Shopping malls and department stores are generally open from 10am to 10pm.

Cultural Centres

The following are useful places to keep you culturally connected to your home country and fellow expats, and are also a good place to meet internationally minded Shanghainese.

Alliance Française (上海法语培训中心; Shànghǎi Fǎyú Péixùn Zhōngxīn; Map p298; ☎6357 5388; www.afshanghai.org; 5th & 6th fl, 297 Wusong Rd; 吴淞路297号5 & 6楼) There's fantastic French cinema at the *ciné-club* on the last Friday of each month at 6.30pm; admission is free. On hand is a large French library with magazines, newspapers, DVDs and music CDs; exhibitions, music concerts and literary events are also held. The centre also offers French-language courses and internet access. There is a **branch** (Map p302; ☎6226 4005; 2nd fl, 155 Wuyi Rd) in the west of town and another **branch** (☎6782 7961; 20-22, Lane 58, Longteng Rd) in Sōngjiāng.

British Council (英国文化教育处; Yīngguó Wénhuà Jiàoyù Chù; Map p290; Cultural and Education Section of the British Consulate-General, unit 18-19, 20/F the Center, 989 Changle Road; 长乐路989号; ☎6192 2626; Ⓜ Changshu Rd) Of interest mainly to Chinese wishing to study in the UK, but also supports arts and cultural programs in China. Phone ahead as the office does not offer drop-in access.

Goethe Institute (歌德学院; Gēdé Xuéyuàn; Map p280; ☎6391 2068; www.goethe.de/china; room 102A, Cross Tower, 318 Fuzhou Rd; 福州路318号102A室) Has a useful library, film screenings, internet access and German courses.

US Consulate Bureau of Public Affairs (Map p294; ☎6279 7662; room 532, Shànghǎi Centre, 1376 West Nanjing Rd; 南京西路1376号532室) Has a reading room with American newspapers and periodicals.

Customs Regulations

Chinese customs generally pay tourists little attention. There are clearly marked green channels and red channels. Importation of fresh fruit or cold cuts is prohibited. Pirated DVDs

PRACTICALITIES

Entertainment Magazines

Stacked up in bars, restaurants and cafes, free expat entertainments and listings magazines cover all bases:

- **City Weekend** (www.cityweekend.com.cn/shanghai) Glossy bimonthly.
- **That's Shanghai** (www.urbanatomy.com) Info-packed monthly.
- **Time Out Shanghai** (www.timeoutshanghai.com) Well-written and authoritative monthly.

Newspapers

Imported English-language newspapers can be bought from five-star hotel bookshops or read online. The Shànghǎi-published English-language newspaper the **Shanghai Daily** (www.shanghaidaily.com) is a better read than the insipid national **China Daily** (www.chinadaily.com.cn), but censored ,of course.

Radio

Websites can be jammed but you can listen to the following:

- **BBC World Service** (www.bbc.co.uk/worldservice/tuning)
- **Voice of America** (www.voa.gov)

TV

Your hotel may have ESPN, Star Sports, CNN or BBC News 24. Otherwise you can tune into the (censored) English-language channel, **CCTV9** (Chinese Central TV).

Weights & Measures

China officially subscribes to the international metric system, but you will encounter the ancient Chinese weights and measures system in markets, which features the *liǎng* (tael, 37.5g) and the *jīn* (catty, 0.6kg). There are 10 *liǎng* to the *jīn*.

and CDs are illegal exports from China as well as illegal imports into most other countries. If they are found they will be confiscated. Duty-free, you can bring in:

- 400 cigarettes (or 100 cigars or 500g of tobacco)
- 1.5 litres of alcoholic drink
- 50g of gold or silver
- ¥20000 in Chinese currency (there are no restrictions on foreign currency but declare any cash that exceeds US$5000, or its equivalent in another currency)

Objects considered to be antiques require a certificate and a red seal to clear customs when leaving China. Anything made before 1949 is considered an antique, and if it was made before 1795 it cannot legally be taken out of the country.

Electricity

Embassies & Consulates

Most consulates defer to their embassies in Běijīng; the offices listed below are consulates-general. Most consulates have efficient websites with useful information, from doing business in Shànghǎi to cultural relations, events and downloadable maps of town.

If you are planning a trip to Southeast Asia, you'll have to go to Běijīng or Hong Kong for a visa for Vietnam, Laos or Myanmar (Burma). There is a Vietnamese consulate in Kūnmíng (in Yúnnán province), as well as Thai, Lao and Myanmar consulates in Kūnmíng.

Australia (澳大利亚领事馆; Àodàlìyà Lǐngshìguǎn; Map p294; ☎2215 5200; www.shanghai.china.embassy.gov.au; 22nd fl, Citic Sq, 1168 West Nanjing Rd; 南京西路1168号22楼)

Canada (加拿大领事馆; Jiānádà Lǐngshìguǎn; Map p294; ☎3279 2800; www.shanghai.gc.ca; 8th fl, 1788 West Nanjing Rd; 南京西路1788号8楼)

France (法国领事馆; Fǎguó Lǐngshìguǎn; Map p280; ☎6103 2200; www.consulfrance-shanghai.org; room 201, 2nd fl, Hai Tong Securities Bldg, 689 Guangdong Rd; 广东路689号2楼201室)

Germany (德国领事馆; Déguó Lǐngshìguǎn; Map p290; ☎3401 0106; www.shanghai.diplo.de; 181 Yongfu Rd; 永福路181号)

Ireland (爱尔兰领事馆; Ài'ěrlán Lǐngshìguǎn; Map p294; ☎6279 8729; www.embassyofireland.cn/ireland/consulate.htm; suite 700A, West Tower, Shànghǎi Centre, 1376 West Nanjing Rd; 南京西路1376号700A室; ⊙9.30am-12.30pm & 2-5.30pm)

Japan (日本领事馆; Rìběn Lǐngshìguǎn; Map p302; ☎5257 4766; fax 6278 8988; www.shanghai.cn.emb-japan.go.jp; 8 Wanshan Rd; 万山路8号)

Netherlands (荷兰领事馆; Hélán Lǐngshìguǎn; Map p302; ☎2208 7288; www.hollandinchina.org; 10th fl, Tower B, Dawning Center, 500 Hongbaoshi Rd; 红宝石路500号东银中心东塔10楼; ⊙9am-noon & 1-5.30pm Mon-Fri)

New Zealand (新西兰领事馆; Xīnxīlán Lǐngshìguǎn; Map p290; ☎5407 5858; www.nzembassy.com; room 1605-1607A, The Centre, 989 Changle Rd; 长乐路989号1605-1607A室; ⊙8.30am-5pm Mon-Fri)

Russia (俄罗斯领事馆; Éluósī Lǐngshìguǎn; Map p298; ☎6324 8383; fax 6306 9982; www.rusconshanghai.org.cn; 20 Huangpu Rd; 黄浦路20号; ⊙9.30am-noon Mon, Wed & Fri)

Singapore (新加坡领事馆; Xīnjiāpō Lǐngshìguǎn; Map p302; ☎6278 5566; www.mfa.gov.sg/shanghai; 89 Wanshan Rd; 万山路89号; ⊙8.30am-noon & 1-5pm)

Thailand (泰王国领事馆; Tàiwángguó Lǐngshìguǎn; Map p294; ☎6288 3030; www.thaishanghai.com; 15th fl, 567 Weihai Rd; 威海路567号15楼; ⊙visa office 9.30-11.30am Mon-Fri)

UK (英国领事馆; Yīngguó Lǐngshìguǎn; Map p294; ☎3279 2000, visa office 6279 8130; http://ukinchina.fco.gov.uk; room 301, Shànghǎi Centre, 1376 West Nanjing Rd; 南京西路1376号301室; ⊙8.30am-5pm Mon-Thu, to 5.30pm Fri)

USA consulate-general (美国领事馆; Měiguó Lǐngshìguǎn; Map p290; http://shanghai.usembassy-china.org.cn; 1469 Middle Huaihai Rd, entrance on Wulumuqi Rd; 淮海中路1469号乌鲁木齐路); US Citizen Services & Visas (Map p294; ☎3217 4650, after-hours emergency for US citizens 6433 3936; 8th fl, Westgate Tower, 1038 West Nanjing Rd; 南京西路1038号8楼; ⊙8.15-11.30am & 1.30-3.30pm Mon-Fri)

Emergency

Ambulance (☎120)

Fire (☎119)

Police (☎110)

Gay & Lesbian Travellers

Local law is ambiguous on this issue; generally the authorities take a dim view of gays and lesbians but there's a growingly confident scene, as evinced by gay bars and the annual event-stuffed **Shanghai Pride** (www.shpride.com), going since 2009. Young Chinese men sometimes hold hands; this carries no sexual overtones in China.

For up-to-date information on the latest gay and lesbian hotspots in Shànghǎi and elsewhere throughout China, try the **Utopia website** (www.utopia-asia.com/chinshan.htm). *City Weekend* also runs a bimonthly gay and lesbian column.

Health

Health concerns for travellers to Shànghǎi include pollution, traveller's diarrhoea and winter influenza. You can find a more-than-adequate standard of medical care here, providing you have good travel insurance.

If you have arrived from South America or Central Africa, you are required to show proof of a yellow-fever vaccination within the last 10 years.

It's a good idea to consult your own government's official travel-health website before departure.

Australia (www.dfat.gov.au/travel)

Canada (www.travelhealth.gc.ca)

New Zealand (www.mfat.govt.nz/travel)

UK (www.dh.gov.uk) Search for travel in the site index.

USA (www.cdc.gov/travel)

Recommended Vaccinations

You should see your doctor at least three months before your trip in order to get your vaccinations in time. The following immunisations are recommended for Shànghǎi.

Diphtheria & tetanus (DT) Booster of 0.5ml every 10 years. It will cause a sore arm and redness at the injection site.

Hepatitis A & B (combined in Twinrix) The dose is 1ml at day one, day 30 and six months. Minimal soreness at injection site. You are not immune until after the final shot. If you don't have time for the six-month booster you will be fully immune for one year for hepatitis A after the second shot and have some immunity for hepatitis B. You may be able to get the third shot at an international medical clinic while travelling.

Influenza Dose of 0.5ml is recommended if you are travelling in the winter months, and especially if you are over 60 years of age or have a chronic illness. It should not be given if you are allergic to eggs. Immunity lasts for one year.

Japanese encephalitis A series of three shots over one month; get only if you plan on being in rural areas for longer than a month. Immunity will last for three years. As there is a risk of an allergic reaction to the second and third shots, you must remain close to medical care after you receive these.

Polio Dose of 0.5ml syrup orally every 10 years. There are no side effects.

Typhoid Booster of 0.5ml every three years. Minimal soreness at the injection site.

Do not have any of these immunisations if you are pregnant or breastfeeding. It is possible to have a shot of gamma globulin in pregnancy, which gives short-term (four to five months) protection against hepatitis and other viral infections. It is not a common thing to do because it is derived from blood products.

HEPATITIS A

This virus is common in Shànghǎi and is transmitted through contaminated water and shellfish. It is most commonly caught at local seafood restaurants. Immunisation and avoiding suspicious restaurants will help prevent it. If you do get hepatitis A, it means six to eight weeks of illness and future intolerance to alcohol.

HEPATITIS B

While this is common in the Shànghǎi area, it is transmitted only by unprotected sex, sharing needles, treading on a discarded needle or receiving contaminated blood. Always use a condom, never share needles and always protect your feet on commonly used beaches. Vaccination against hepatitis B before you travel is a wise option as it can be a chronic, debilitating illness.

JAPANESE ENCEPHALITIS

Mosquitoes that feed on birds carry this potentially fatal virus, hence it is limited to rural areas of China, particularly near rice fields. It is most common in summer and autumn. Vaccination is recommended if you are travelling in rural areas for longer than one month.

TRAVELLER'S DIARRHOEA

This is the most common disease that a traveller will encounter throughout Asia. Many different types of organisms, usually bacteria (eg *E. coli*, salmonella), are responsible and the result is sudden diarrhoea and vomiting or both, with or without fever. It is caught from contaminated food or water.

TYPHOID FEVER
Otherwise known as salmonella, typhoid fever is common throughout China and is caught from faecally contaminated food, milk and water. It manifests as fever, headache, cough, malaise and constipation or diarrhoea. Treatment is with quinolone antibiotics, and a vaccine is recommended before you travel.

Environmental Hazards

POLLUTION
The air quality in Shànghǎi is dreadful, especially on still days. If you suffer from asthma or other allergies, you may anticipate a worsening of your symptoms here and you may need to increase your medication. Eye drops may be a useful addition to your travel kit, and contact-lens wearers may have more discomfort here.

WATER
Don't drink tap water or eat ice. Bottled water is readily available. Boiled water is OK.

Online Resources

There is a wealth of travel-health advice on the internet. The Lonely Planet website (www.lonelyplanet.com) is a good place to start. The WHO publishes a book called *International Travel and Health*, which is revised annually and is available online at no cost at www.who.int/publications/en.

Internet Access

The Chinese authorities remain highly mistrustful of the internet, and censorship here is heavy-handed, employing an army of 30,000 censors. The authorities block around 10% of websites; sites like Google may be slow, while social-networking sites such as Facebook and Twitter are blocked (as is YouTube). Some users get around blocked websites by using a proxy like g-proxy.com, downloading an add-on such as Gladder (for Firebox browsers) or using a VPN (Virtual Private Network) service.

Occasionally email providers can go down, so having a backup email address is advised.

The majority of hostels and hotels have broadband internet access and many hotels, cafes, restaurants and bars are wi-fi enabled. Remember that wi-fi is generally unsecured, so take care what kind of information you enter if you're using a wireless connection.

Email Centres & Internet Cafes

Internet cafe charges start at around ¥3 per hour; the cafes are typically either open 24 hours or from 8am to midnight.

You will need some form of ID to register; take your passport. Some internet cafes in Shànghǎi and surrounding provinces may require Chinese ID to get online, thus barring foreign users (which can leave you stuck if you need to respond to emails), so be prepared.

Internet cafes are now scarce in touristy areas – it's more convenient to get online at your hotel or at a wi-fi hotspot. Besides the places listed below, many bars and cafes are wi-fi-equipped. The easiest way to find the nearest internet cafe is to ask someone if there is a *wǎngbā* (网吧) nearby. Some Tourist and Information Service Centres allow you to go online for free.

Bùlè Internet Cafe (布乐网吧; Bùlè Wǎngba; Map p293; 2nd fl, Moling Rd; per hr ¥3; ⏲24hr) Corner of Moling Rd by the main Shànghǎi Railway Station.

Eastday Bar (东方网点; Dōngfāng Wǎngdiǎn; Map p294; 30 East Yuyuan Rd; per hr ¥4; ⏲24hr)

Internet Cafe (网吧; Wǎngbā; Map p296; 3rd fl, 565 Dongchang Rd; per hr ¥4; ⏲8am-midnight) Just off South Pudong Rd.

Internet Cafe (网吧; Wǎngbā; Map p293; per hr ¥5; ⏲24hr) Down the escalator across the road opposite the main Shànghǎi Railway Station.

Internet Cafe (网吧游艺城; Wǎngbā Yóuyìchéng; Map p298; 5th fl, eastern entrance to Duolun Rd; per hr ¥3; ⏲24hr)

Jídù Internet Cafe (极度网络; Jídù Wǎngluò; Map p286; 2nd fl, cnr Changle Rd & North Xiangyang Rd; per hr ¥3; ⏲24hr)

Shànghǎi Library (上海图书馆; Shànghǎi Túshūguǎn; Map p290; 1555 Middle Huaihai Rd; 淮海中路1555号; per hr ¥4; ⏲8.30am-8.30pm) Has an internet room (open from 9am to 8.30pm) and is the cheapest and most pleasant place in the city for internet use (minimum one hour). Bring your passport or ID if you have no library card. Connections are generally pretty fast. Wi-fi access is available from 3.30pm to 8.30pm.

Tàshí Internet Cafe (拓实网吧; Tàshí Wǎngbā; 3rd fl, 18 Yuyuanzhi Rd; 愚园支路18号3楼; per hr ¥4; ⏲24hr)

Xīwàng Internet Cafe (夕旺网吧; Xīwàng Wǎngbā; Map p280; 515 Fuzhou Rd; per hr ¥4; ⏲24hr)

Legal Matters

China does not officially recognise dual nationality or the foreign citizenship of children born in China if one of the parents is a PRC national. If you have Chinese and another nationality you may, in theory, not be allowed to visit China on your foreign passport. In practice, Chinese authorities are not switched on enough to know if you own two passports, and will accept you on a foreign passport. Dual-nationality citizens who enter China on a Chinese passport are subject to Chinese laws and are legally not allowed consular help.

China takes a particularly dim view of opium and all its derivatives; trafficking in more than 50g of heroin can lead to the death penalty. Foreign-passport holders have been executed in China for drug offences.

The Chinese criminal justice system does not ensure a fair trial and defendants are not presumed innocent until proven guilty. China conducts more judicial executions than the rest of the world combined, up to 10,000 per year according to some reports. If arrested, most foreign citizens have the right to contact their embassy.

Medical Services

Clinics

Shànghǎi is credited with the best medical facilities and most advanced medical knowledge in mainland China. The main foreign embassies keep lists of the English-speaking doctors, dentists and hospitals that accept foreigners.

Huáshān Hospital (Huáshān Yīyuàn; Map p290; ☎5288 9998; www.sh-hwmc.com.cn; 12 Middle Wulumuqi Rd; 乌鲁木齐中路12号) Hospital treatment and outpatient consultations are available at the 8th-floor foreigners' clinic, the **Huashan Worldwide Medical Center** (☎6248 3986; ⏲8am-10pm), with 24-hour emergency treatment on the 15th floor in Building 6.

Parkway Health (以极佳医疗保健服务; Yǐjíjiā Yīliáo Bǎojiàn Fúwù; ☎24hr hotline 6445 5999; www.parkwayhealth.cn) Hóngqiáo (Map p302; unit 30, Mandarine City, 788 Hongxu Rd; 虹许路788号30室); Jìng'ān (Map p294; suite 203, Shànghǎi Centre, 1376 West Nanjing Rd; 南京西路1376号203室) There are six locations around town. Offers comprehensive private medical care from internationally trained physicians and dentists. Consultation fees are around ¥800 to ¥1800. Members can access after-hours services and an emergency hotline.

Shànghǎi First People's Hospital/International Medical Care Centre (IMCC) (上海市第一人民医院; Shànghǎi Shì Dìyī Rénmín Yīyuàn; Map p298; ☎6306 9480, 6324 0090, ext 2101; 585 Jiulong Rd; 九龙路585号)

Shànghǎi United Family Hospital (上海和睦家医院; Shànghǎi Hémùjiā Yīyuàn; ☎2216 3900, 24hr emergency 2216 3999; www.ufh.com.cn; 1139 Xianxia Rd; 仙霞路1139号) This Western-owned and -managed hospital is a complete private hospital, staffed by doctors trained in the West. Medical facilities run to inpatient rooms, operating rooms, an intensive-care unit and birthing suites.

Other contacts for medical assistance include:

Huádōng Hospital (华东医院外宾门诊; Huádōng Yīyuàn Wàibīn Ménzhěn; Map p290; ☎6248 3180, ext 63208; Foreigners Clinic, 2nd fl, Bldg 3, 221 West Yan'an Rd; 延安西路221号3号楼2层; ⏲24hr emergency)

International Peace Maternity Hospital (国际妇幼保健院; Guójì Fùyòu Bǎojiànyuàn; Map p300; ☎6407 0434; 910 Hengshan Rd; 衡山路910号)

Ruìjīn Hospital (瑞金医院; Ruìjīn Yīyuàn; Map p286; ☎6437 0045; 197 Ruijin No 2 Rd; 瑞金二路197号)

Shànghǎi Chiropractic & Osteopathic Clinic (上海脊椎医疗中心; Shànghǎi Jǐzhuī Yīliáo Zhōngxīn; Map p290; ☎5213 0008; www.spine.sh.cn; 7th fl, 937 West Yan'an Rd, cnr Jiangsu Rd; 延安西路937号7层)

Dental Services

Arrail Dental (瑞尔齿科; Ruì'ěr Chǐkē; Map p286; ☎5396 6539; www.arrail-dental.com; 2nd fl, 2 Corporate Ave, 202 Hubin Rd; 湖滨路202号企业天地商业中心2号楼2楼)

Dr Harriet Jin's Dental Surgery (金医生口腔诊所; Jīn Yīshēng Kǒuqiāng Zhěnsuǒ; Map p300; ☎6448 0882; www.drharrietdental.com; room 1904, South Bldg, Huiyin Plaza, 2088 Huashan Rd; 华山路2088号汇银广场南楼1904室)

Shànghǎi Dental Medical Centre (上海口腔医疗中心; Shànghǎi Kǒuqiāng Yīliáo Zhōngxīn; ☎6445 5999; 7th fl, 9th People's Hospital, 639 Zhizaoju Rd; 制造局路639号第九人民医院7层)

Shànghǎi United Family Hospital (上海和睦家医院; Shànghǎi Hémùjiā Yīyuàn; ☎2216 3999; www.unitedfamilyhospitals.com; 1139 Xianxia Rd; 仙霞路1139号)

Shēndà Dental Clinic (申大齿科; Shēndà Chǐkē; Map p300; ☎6437 7987; 8th fl, 807 Zhaojiabang Rd; 肇嘉浜路807号8楼)

Pharmacies

The Hong Kong store **Watson's** (Qūchénshì; Map p286; ☎6474 4775; 787 Middle Huaihai Rd; 淮海中路787号) can be found in the basements of malls all over town (there's a branch in Westgate Mall; Map p294), mainly selling imported toiletries and a limited range of simple, over-the-counter pharmaceuticals.

For harder-to-find foreign medicines, try any pharmacy (药房; *yàofáng*), easily identified by a green cross outside; some have service through the night (via a small window). Nearly all pharmacies stock both Chinese and Western medicines.

Traditional Chinese Medicine

Traditional Chinese medicine (TCM) is extremely popular in Shànghǎi, both for prevention and cure. There are many Chinese medicine shops, but English is not widely spoken. Chiropractic care, reflexology and acupuncture are popular, but check that disposable needles are used.

Body and Soul TCM Clinic (Map p284; ☎5101 9262; www.tcm-shanghai.com; suite 5, 14th fl, Anji Plaza, 760 South Xizang Rd; 西藏南路760号安基大厦14层5室) International staff integrating TCM and Western medical practices; four clinics in town. Acupuncture and *tuīná* (traditional) massage available.

Dr Li Jie's Chinese Medical Clinic (李洁中医诊所; Lǐjié Zhōngyī Zhěnsuǒ; Map p300; ☎3424 1989; 5c, No 28, Lane 18, Hongqiao Rd; 虹桥路18弄28号5C)

Lónghuá Hospital (龙华中医院; Lónghuá Zhōngyīyuàn; Map p300; ☎6438 5700; 725 South Wanping Rd; 零陵路725号) A kilometre northeast of Shànghǎi Stadium.

Shànghǎi Qìgōng Institute (上海气功研究所; Shànghǎi Qìgōng Yánjiūsuǒ; Map p286; ☎6387 5180, ext 220; top fl, 218 Nanchang Rd; 南昌路218号; ⏲8am-4.30pm) Part of Shànghǎi's TCM school, the Qìgōng Institute offers *qìgōng* (*qì*-energy development) treatments and massage (¥280), as well as acupuncture sessions (¥280). No English is spoken; call for an appointment.

Shǔguāng Hospital (曙光医院; Shǔguāng Yīyuàn; Map p286; ☎6385 5617; 185 Pu'an Rd; 普安路185号) Next to Huaihai Park.

Money

The Chinese currency is known as renminbi (RMB), or 'people's money'. Officially, the basic unit of RMB is the yuan (¥), which is divided into 10 jiao, which again is divided into 10 fen. In spoken Chinese the yuan is referred to as *kuài* and jiao as *máo*. The fen has so little value that it is rarely used these days. It's generally a good idea to keep ¥1 coins on you for the metro (some ticket machines frequently take only coins) and buses.

The Bank of China issues RMB bills in denominations of one, two, five, 10, 20, 50 and 100 yuan. Coins come in denominations of one yuan; five and one jiao; and one, two and five fen (the last are rare). Paper versions of the coins circulate, but are disappearing.

For information regarding exchange rates, see the inside front cover. Check p16 for some idea of the costs you are likely to incur during your stay in Shànghǎi.

ATMs

ATMs that take foreign cards are very plentiful, but it's generally safest to use Bank of China (中国银行), the Industrial and Commercial Bank of China (工商银行; ICBC) and HSBC (汇丰银行) ATMs, many of which are 24-hour. Many top-end hotels also have ATMs, as do malls, department stores and some metro stations. All ATMs accepting international cards have dual language ability.

Changing Money

You can change foreign currency and travellers cheques at money-changing counters at almost every hotel and at many shops, department stores and large banks such as the Bank of China and HSBC, as long as you have your passport; you can also change money at the international airport. Some top-end hotels will change money only for their guests. Exchange rates in China are uniform wherever you change money, so there's little need to shop around. The Bank of China charges a 0.75% commission to change cash and travellers cheques.

Whenever you change foreign currency into Chinese currency you will be given a money-exchange voucher recording the transaction. You need to show this to change your yuan back into any foreign currency. Changing Chinese currency outside China is a problem, though it's quite easily done in Hong Kong.

There's a branch of **American Express** (Měiguó Yùntōng Gōngsī; Map p294; ☎6279 8082; room 455, Shànghǎi Centre, 1376 West Nanjing Rd; 南京西路1376号455室; ⏲9am-noon & 1-5.30pm Mon-Fri), but Amex cardholders can also cash personal cheques with their card at branches of the Bank of China, China International Trust & Investment Corporation (Citic), the Bank of Communications or ICBC.

Counterfeit Bills

Very few Chinese will accept a ¥50 or ¥100 note without first checking to see if it's a fake. Many shopkeepers will run notes under an ultraviolet light looking for signs of counterfeiting; visually checking for forged notes is hard unless you are very familiar with bills, but be aware that street vendors may try to dump forged notes on you in large-denomination change.

Credit Cards

Credit cards are more readily accepted in Shànghǎi than in other parts of China. Most tourist hotels will accept major credit cards (with a 4% processing charge) such as Visa, Amex, MasterCard, Diners and JCB, as will banks, upper-end restaurants and tourist-related shops. Credit hasn't caught on among most Chinese, and most local credit cards are in fact debit cards. Always carry enough cash (for buying train tickets and just in case).

Check to see if your credit-card company charges a foreign transaction fee (usually between 1% and 3%) for purchases in China.

The following are emergency contact numbers in case you lose your card.

American Express (☎6279 8082; ⌚9am-noon & 1-5.30pm) Out of business hours, call the 24-hour **refund line** (☎852-2811 6122) in Hong Kong.

MasterCard (☎108-00-110 7309)

Visa (☎108-00-110 2911)

Tipping

Tipping is generally not expected, although staff are becoming used to it in fancy restaurants, where most people round up the bill. In general there is no need to tip if a service charge has already been added. Hotel porters may expect a tip; taxi drivers do not.

Travellers Cheques

As ATMs are so plentiful and easy to use in Shànghǎi, travellers cheques are far less popular than they once were. Stick to the major companies such as Thomas Cook, American Express and Citibank.

Post

The larger tourist hotels and business towers have convenient post offices from where you can mail letters and small packages. China Post offices and post boxes are green.

Useful branches of China Post:

Main China Post office (Map p298; ☎6393 6666; 276 North Suzhou Rd; 苏州北路276号; ⌚7am-10pm) Just north of Sūzhōu Creek in Hóngkǒu.

China Post branch (Map p286; Xingye Lu) Opposite Site of the 1st National Congress of the CCP in Xīntiāndì.

Shànghǎi Centre branch (Map p294; 1376 West Nanjing Rd)

Letters and parcels take about a week to reach most overseas destinations; Express Mail Service (EMS) cuts this down to three or four days. Courier companies can take as little as two days. Ubiquitous same-day courier companies (快递; *kuàidì*) can express items within Shànghǎi from around ¥6 within the same district.

Courier Companies

Several foreign courier companies operate in China with fairly standard prices. The following companies offer door-to-door pick-up and delivery.

DHL (☎landline toll-free 800 810 8000, mobile phone toll-free 400 810 8000; www.dhl.com)

FedEx (☎landline toll-free 800 988 1888, mobile phone toll-free 400 886 1888; www.fedex.com)

UPS (☎800 820 8388; www.ups.com)

Public Holidays

Many of the entries below are nominal holidays and do not qualify for a day off work. For more holidays and festivals, see p23.

New Year's Day (Yuándàn) 1 January.

Spring Festival (Chūn Jié) 31 January 2014, 19 February 2015, 8 February 2016. Also known as Chinese New Year. Officially three days, but generally a week-long break.

Tomb Sweeping Day (Qīngmíng Jié) First weekend in April. A three-day weekend.

International Labour Day (Láodòng Jié) 1 May. Three-day holiday.

Dragon Boat Festival (Duānwǔ Jié) 12 June 2013, 2 June 2014, 20 June 2015.

Mid-Autumn Festival (Zhōngqiū Jié) 19 September 2013, 8 September 2014, 27 September 2015.

National Day (Guóqìng Jié) 1 October. Officially three days, but often morphs into a week-long vacation.

Safe Travel

Shànghǎi feels very safe, and crimes against foreigners are rare; even taxi drivers don't try to rip you off. Don't, however, end up in an ambulance: Chinese drivers never give way.

If you do have something stolen, you need to report the crime at the district Public Security Bureau (PSB) office and obtain a police report.

Crossing the road is probably the greatest danger: develop avian vision and a sixth sense to combat the shocking traffic. The green man at traffic lights does not mean it is safe to cross. Instead, it means it is *slightly safer* to cross, but you can still be run down by traffic allowed to turn on red lights. Bicycles and scooters regularly flout all traffic rules, as do many cars. Bicycles, scooters, mopeds and motorbikes freely take to the pavements (sidewalks), as occasionally do cars. Older taxis only have seatbelts in the front passenger seat. Watch out for scooters whizzing down Shànghǎi roads – especially on streets without lighting – without lights at night.

Other street hazards include spent neon-light tubes poking from litter bins, open manholes with plunging drops, and welders showering pavements with burning sparks. Side streets off the main drag are sometimes devoid of street lights at night, and pavements can be crumbling and uneven.

Scams

See our Top Tip on p51 for detailed info on Shànghǎi's most common scam.

Watch out for taxi scams, especially at Pudong International Airport and outside the Maglev terminal at Longyang Rd metro station. A registered taxi should always run on a meter and have a licence displayed on the dashboard.

Taxes

All four- and five-star hotels and some top-end restaurants add a service charge of 10% or 15%, which extends to the room and food; all other consumer taxes are included in the price tag.

Telephone

Using a mobile phone is naturally most convenient. If you have the right phone (eg BlackBerry, iPhone, Android) and are in a wi-fi zone, **Skype** (www.skype.com) and **Viber** (www.viber.com) can make calls either very cheap or free.

Long-distance phone calls can be placed from hotel-room phones, though this is expensive without an internet phonecard. You may need a dial-out number for a direct line. Local calls should be free.

Phones are also sometimes attached to magazine kiosks or small shops. Just pick up the phone, make your call, and then pay the attendant (usually five *máo* for a local call). If dialling long-distance within China from Shànghǎi, prefix the number with 17909 for cheaper rates.

Shànghǎi has plentiful 24-hour phone bars (话吧; *huàbā*), where international calls can be made at cheap rates.

Most international calls cost ¥8.20 per minute or ¥2.20 to Hong Kong. You are generally required to leave a ¥200 deposit for international calls.

Note the following country and city codes:

Běijīng (☎010)

People's Republic of China (☎00 86)

Shànghǎi (☎021)

If calling Shànghǎi or Běijīng from abroad, drop the first zero.

The following numbers are useful:

Enquiry about international calls (☎106)

Local directory enquiries (☎114)

Weather (☎12121)

Mobile Phones

You can certainly take your mobile phone to China, but ensure it is unlocked, which means you can use another network's SIM card in your phone. Purchasing a SIM card in Shànghǎi is straightforward: pick one up from a branch of China Mobile (Zhōngguó Yídòng; 中国移动); branches are widespread.

Mobile-phone shops (*shǒujīdiàn;* 手机店) can sell you a SIM card, which will cost from ¥60 to ¥100 and will include ¥50 of credit. SIM cards are also available from newspaper kiosks (报刊亭; *bàokāntíng*). When this runs out, you can top up the number by buying a credit-charging card *(*充值卡*; chōngzhí kǎ*) for ¥50 or ¥100 worth of credits.

The Chinese avoid the number four (*sì;* which sounds like but has a different tone from the word for death – *sǐ*) and love the number eight *(bā)*. Consequently, the cheapest numbers tend to contain numerous fours and the priciest have strings of eights.

Buying a mobile phone in Shànghǎi is also an option as they are generally inexpensive. Cafes, restaurants and bars in larger towns and cities are frequently wi-fi enabled.

Phonecards

The internet phonecard (IP card; IP卡) connects via the internet and is much cheaper than dialling direct. You can use any home phone, some hotel and some public phones (but not card phones), or a mobile phone to dial a special telephone number and follow the instructions (there is usually an English option).

Cards can be bought at newspaper kiosks, but are far less available than they used to be. Cards come in denominations of ¥50, ¥100, ¥200 and ¥500 – but they are always discounted, with a ¥100 card costing in the region of ¥35 to ¥40. Check that you are buying the right card. Some are for use in Shànghǎi only, while others can be used around the country. Check that the country you wish to call can be called on the card.

Generally, a safe bet is the CNC *guójì shíguókǎ* (10-country card; 国际十国卡), which can be used for calls to the USA, Canada, Australia, New Zealand, Hong Kong and Macau, Taiwan, England, France, Germany and some East Asian countries. Check the expiry date.

Time

Time throughout China is set to Běijīng local time, which is eight hours ahead of GMT/UTC. There is no daylight-saving time.

When it's noon in Shànghǎi, it's 8pm (the day before) in Los Angeles, 11pm (the day before) in Montreal and New York, 4am (the same day) in London, 5am in Frankfurt, Paris and Rome, noon in Hong Kong, 2pm in Melbourne and 4pm in Wellington. Add one hour to these times during the summer.

Toilets

Shànghǎi has plenty of public toilets. Often charging a small fee, they run from the sordid to coin-operated portaloos and modern conveniences. The best bet is to head for a top-end hotel, where someone will hand you a towel, pour you some aftershave or exotic hand lotion and wish you a nice day.

- Fast-food restaurants can be lifesavers.
- Always carry an emergency stash of toilet paper, as many toilets are devoid of it.
- Growing numbers of metro stations have coin-operated toilets.
- Toilets in hotels are generally sitters, but expect to find squatters in many public toilets.
- Remember the Chinese characters for men (男) and women (女).

Tourist Information

The best place for tourist information or possibly a map of town should be from your hotel concierge. For competent English-language help, call the **Shànghǎi Call Centre** (☎962 288), a free 24-hour English-language hotline that can respond to cultural, entertainment or transport enquiries (even providing directions for your cab driver).

Shànghǎi has about a dozen or so rather useless **Tourist Information and Service Centres** (旅游咨询服务中心; Lǚyóu Zīxún Fúwù Zhōngxīn) where you can at least get free maps and (sometimes) information. Branches:

The Bund Beneath the Bund promenade, opposite the intersection with East Nanjing Rd.

The Bund (Map p280; ☎6357 3718; 518 Jiujiang Rd; 九江路518号; ⌚9.30am-8pm; ⓂEast Nanjing Rd)

French Concession (Map p286; ☎5386 1882; 138 South Chengdu Rd, just off Middle Huaihai Rd; 成都南路138号; ⌚9am-8.30pm)

Huángpǔ (Map p280; ☎6357 3718; 518 Jiujiang Rd; 九江路518号; ⌚9.30am-8pm)

Jìng'ān (Map p294; ☎6248 3259; Lane 1678, 18 West Nanjing Rd;南京西路1678弄18号; ⌚9am-5pm)

Pǔdōng (Map p296; ☎3878 0202; 1st fl, Superbrand Mall, 168 Lujiazui Rd; 陆家嘴路168号1楼; ⌚9am-6pm)

Old Town (Map p284; ☎6355 5032; 149 Jiujiaochang Rd; 旧校场路149号; ⌚9am-7pm) Southwest of Yùyuán Gardens.

There is also the useful **Shanghai Information Centre for International Visitors** (Map p286; ☎6384 9366; Xīntiāndì South Block, Bldg 2, Xingye Rd; ⌚10am-10pm).

The **tourist hotline** (☎962 020) offers a limited English-language service.

Travellers with Disabilities

Shànghǎi's traffic and the city's overpasses and underpasses are the greatest challenges to disabled travellers. Many metro stations have lifts to platforms but escalators only go up from the ticket hall to the exit, and not down. Pavements on lesser roads may be cluttered with obstacles.

That said, an increasing number of modern buildings, museums, stadiums and most new hotels are wheelchair accessible. Try to take a lightweight chair for navigating around obstacles and for collapsing into the back of taxis. **Bashi taxis** (☎6431 2788) has wheelchair-accessible minivan taxis. Top-end hotels have wheelchair-accessible rooms but budget hotels are less well prepared. Disabled travellers are advised to travel with at least one able-bodied companion.

China's sign language has regional variations, as well as some elements of American Sign Language (ASL), so foreign signers may have some problems communicating in sign language.

Visas

For everyone apart from citizens of Japan, Singapore, Brunei and San Marino, a visa is required for visits to the People's Republic of China (although 48-hour visa-free transit in Shànghǎi is available, see p260).

Visas are easily obtainable from Chinese embassies, consulates or Chinese Visa Application Service Centres abroad. Getting a visa in Hong Kong is also an option. Most tourists are issued with a single-entry visa for a 30-day stay, valid for three months from the date of issue. Your passport must be valid for at least six months after the expiry date of your visa (nine months for a double-entry visa) and you'll need at least two entire blank pages in your passport for the visa. For children under the age of 18, a parent must sign the application form on their behalf.

At the time of writing, the visa application process had become more rigorous and applicants were required to provide the following:

➡ A copy of your flight confirmation showing onward/return travel.

➡ For double-entry visas, you need to provide flight confirmation showing all dates of entry and exit.

➡ If staying at a hotel in China, you must provide confirmation from the hotel (this can be cancelled later if you stay elsewhere).

➡ If staying with friends or relatives, you must provide a copy of the information page of their passport, a copy of their China visa and a letter of invitation from them.

At the time of writing, prices for a standard single-entry 30-day visa (not including Chinese Visa Application Service Centre administration fees) were as follows:

➡ £30 for UK citizens

➡ US$130 for US citizens

➡ US$30 for citizens of other nations

Double-entry visas:

➡ £45 for UK citizens

➡ US$130 for US citizens

➡ US$45 for all other nationals

Six-month multiple-entry visas:

➡ £90 for UK citizens

➡ US$130 for US citizens

➡ US$60 for all other nationals

A standard 30-day single-entry visa can be issued in three to five working days. With China becoming increasingly popular as a travel and business destination, queues at Chinese embassies and consulates are getting longer. In many countries, the visa service has been outsourced from the Chinese embassy to a **Chinese Visa Application Service Centre** (www.visaforchina.org), which levies an extra administration fee. In the case of the UK, a single-entry visa costs £30, but the standard administration charge levied by the centre is an additional £36 (three-day express £48, postal service £54). In some countries, such as the UK, France, the US and Canada, there is more than one service centre nationwide, so check the website for your nearest centre. Visa Application Service Centres are open Monday to Friday. You generally pay for your visa in cash when you collect it.

At least one passport-sized photo of the applicant is required. When asked about your itinerary on the application form, if you are planning on travelling from Shànghǎi, list standard tourist destinations. Many travellers planning trips to Tibet or western Xīnjiāng leave them off the form as the list is nonbinding, but their inclusion may raise eyebrows; those working in media or journalism often profess a different occupation to avoid having their visa refused or being given a shorter length of stay than requested.

A growing number of visa-arranging agents can do the legwork and deliver your visa-complete passport to you. In the US, many people use the **China Visa Service Center** (☎in the USA 800 799 6560; www.mychinavisa.com), which offers prompt service. The procedure takes around 10 to 14 days. **CIBT** (www.uk.cibt.com) offers a global network and a fast and efficient turnaround.

A 30-day visa is activated on the date you enter China, and must be used within three months of the date of issue. Longer-stay visas are also activated upon entry into China. Officials in China are sometimes confused over the validity of the visa and look at the 'valid until' date. On most 30-day visas, however, this is actually the date by which you must have *entered* the country, not left.

Although a 30-day length of stay is standard for tourist visas, six-month and 12-month multiple-entry visas are also available. If you have trouble getting more than 30 days or a multiple-entry visa, try a local visa-arranging service or a travel agency in Hong Kong.

A business visa is multiple-entry and valid for three to six months from the date of issue, depending on how much you paid for it.

Note that if you go to China, on to Hong Kong or Macau and then to Shànghǎi, you will need a double-entry visa to get 'back' into China from Hong Kong or Macau, or you will need to reapply for a fresh visa in Hong Kong.

When you check into a hotel, there is usually a question on the registration form asking what type of visa you have. The letter specifying your visa category is usually stamped on the visa itself. There are eight categories of ordinary visas, as follows:

TYPE	DESCRIPTION	CHINESE NAME
L	travel	*lǚxíng*
F	business or student (less than 6 months)	*fǎngwèn*
D	resident	*dìngjū*
G	transit	*guòjìng*
X	long-term student	*liúxué*
Z	working	*rènzhí*
J	journalist	*jìzhě*
C	flight attendant	*chéngwù*

Residence Permit

The 'green card' is a residence permit issued to English teachers, businesspeople, students and other foreigners who are authorised to live in the PRC. Green cards are issued for a period of one year.

To get a residence permit you first need to arrange a work permit (normally obtained by your employer), health certificate and temporary 'Z' visa. If your employer is organised, you can arrange all of this before you arrive in Shànghǎi.

You then go to the PSB with your passport, health certificate, work permit, your employer's business registration licence or representative office permit, your employment certificate (from the Shanghai Labour Bureau), the temporary residence permit of the hotel or local PSB where you are registered, passport photos, a letter of application from your employer and around ¥400 in RMB. In all, the process usually takes from two to four weeks. Expect to make several visits and always carry multiple copies of every document. Each member of your family needs a residence permit and visa. In most cases, your employer will take care of much of the process for you. If not, check expat websites for the latest updates to the process.

Shànghǎi Visa-Free Transit

Citizens from a number of countries including the USA, Australia, Canada, New Zealand, Germany, Sweden and France can transit through Shànghǎi between Hóngqiáo Airport and Pǔdōng International Airport for up to 48 hours (due to be extended to 72 hours) without a visa as long as they have visas for their onward countries and proof of seats booked on flights out of China.

Travel in China

Most of China is accessible on a standard Chinese visa. A small number of restricted areas in China require an additional permit from the PSB. In particular, permits are required for travel to Tibet, a region that the authorities can suddenly bar foreigners from entering.

Visa Extensions

Extensions of 30 days are given for any tourist visa. You may be able to wrangle more with reasons such as illness or transport delays, but second extensions are usually only granted for a week, on the understanding that you are leaving. Visa extensions take three days and cost ¥160 for most nationalities and ¥940 for Americans (reciprocity for increased US visa fees). The fine for overstaying your visa is up to ¥300 per day.

To extend a business visa, you need a letter from a Chinese work unit willing to sponsor you. If you're studying in China, your school can sponsor you for a visa extension.

Visa extensions in Shànghǎi are available from the **PSB** (公安局; Gōng'ānjú; ☎2895 1900; 1500 Minsheng Rd; 民生路1500号; ⏲9am-5pm Mon-Sat).

Women Travellers

Female travellers will encounter few problems in Shànghǎi, as Chinese men are neither macho nor generally disrespectful of women. Shànghǎi is very cosmopolitan, so women can largely wear what they like.

Tampons can be bought everywhere, although it is advisable for you to bring your own contraceptive pills.

Work

It's not too difficult to find work in Shànghǎi, though technically you will need a work visa. You should arrive in Shànghǎi with enough funds to keep you going for at least a few weeks until a job opens up. Examine the classified pages of the expat magazines for job opportunities. Modelling and acting can be quite lucrative – especially if you find a decent agent – and teaching English is perennially popular. Bear in mind that most big companies tend to recruit from home, offering comfortable expat packages. See also Residence Permit, p259.

Language

Discounting its many ethnic minority languages, China has eight major dialect groups: Pǔtōnghuà (Mandarin), Yue (Cantonese), Wu (Shanghainese), Minbei (Fuzhou), Minnan (Hokkien-Taiwanese), Xiang, Gan and Hakka. Each of them also divides into subdialects.

Mandarin, which the Chinese themselves call Pǔtōnghuà (meaning 'common speech') is considered the official language of China. Most of the population speaks Mandarin, so you'll find that knowing a few basics in Mandarin will come in handy in Shànghǎi (as well as in many other parts of the country) which is why we've included it in this chapter.

For some more information about Shanghainese, see the boxed text, p264.

Writing

Chinese is often referred to as a language of pictographs. Many of the basic Chinese characters are highly stylised pictures of what they represent, but around 90% are compounds of a 'meaning' element and a 'sound' element.

A well-educated, contemporary Chinese speaker might use between 6000 and 8000 characters. To read a Chinese newspaper you need to know 2000 to 3000 characters, but 1200 to 1500 would be enough to get the gist.

Theoretically, all Chinese dialects share the same written system. In practice, Cantonese adds about 3000 specialised characters and many dialects don't have a written form at all.

WANT MORE?

For in-depth language information and handy phrases, check out Lonely Planet's *China Phrasebook* and *Mandarin Phrasebook* You'll find it at **shop.lonelyplanet.com**, or you can buy Lonely Planet's iPhone phrasebooks at the Apple App Store.

Pinyin & Pronunciation

In 1958 the Chinese adopted Pinyin, a system of writing Mandarin using the Roman alphabet. The original idea was to eventually do away with Chinese characters, but over time this idea was abandoned.

Pinyin is often used on shop fronts, street signs and advertising billboards. However, in the countryside and the smaller towns you may not see a single Pinyin sign anywhere, so unless you speak Chinese you'll need a phrasebook with Chinese characters.

In this chapter we've provided Pinyin alongside the Mandarin script. Below is a brief guide to the pronunciation of Pinyin letters.

Vowels

a	as in 'father'
ai	as in 'aisle'
ao	as the 'ow' in 'cow'
e	as in 'her' (without 'r' sound)
ei	as in 'weigh'
i	as the 'ee' in 'meet' (or like a light 'r' as in 'Grrr!' after c, ch, r, s, sh, z or zh)
ian	as the word 'yen'
ie	as the English word 'yeah'
o	as in 'or' (without 'r' sound)
ou	as the 'oa' in 'boat'
u	as in 'flute'
ui	as the word 'way'
uo	like a 'w' followed by 'o'
yu/ü	like 'ee' with lips pursed

Consonants

c	as the 'ts' in 'bits'
ch	as in 'chop', with the tongue curled up and back
h	as in 'hay', articulated from further back in the throat
q	as the 'ch' in 'cheese'
sh	as in 'ship', with the tongue curled up and back
x	as the 'sh'in 'ship'
z	as the 'ds' in 'suds'
zh	as the 'j' in 'judge', with the tongue curled up and back

The only consonants that occur at the end of a syllable are n, ng and r. In Pinyin, apostrophes are occasionally used to separate syllables in order to prevent ambiguity, eg the word píng'ān can be written with an apostrophe after the 'g' to prevent it being pronounced as pín'gān.

Tones

Mandarin is a language with a large number of words with the same pronunciation but a different meaning. What distinguishes these homophones (as these words are called) is their 'tonal' quality – the raising and the lowering of pitch on certain syllables. Mandarin has four tones – high, rising, falling-rising and falling, plus a fifth 'neutral' tone that you can all but ignore. Tones are important for distinguishing meaning of words – eg the word ma has four different meanings according to tone: mā (mother), má (hemp, numb), mǎ (horse), mà (scold, swear). Tones are indicated in Pinyin by the following accent marks on vowels: ā (high), á (rising), ǎ (falling-rising) and à (falling).

Basics

When asking a question it is polite to start with qǐng wèn – literally, 'May I ask?'.

Hello.	你好。	Nǐhǎo.
Goodbye.	再见。	Zàijiàn.
How are you?	你好吗？	Nǐhǎo ma?
Fine. And you?	好。你呢？	Hǎo. Nǐ ne?
Excuse me.	劳驾。	Láojià.
Sorry.	对不起。	Duìbùqǐ.
Yes./No.	是。/不是。	Shì./Bùshì.
Please ...	请……	Qǐng ...
Thank you.	谢谢你。	Xièxie nǐ.
You're welcome.	不客气。	Bù kèqi.

What's your name?
你叫什么名字？ Nǐ jiào shénme míngzi?

My name is ...
我叫…… Wǒ jiào ...

Do you speak English?
你会说英文吗？ Nǐ huìshuō Yīngwén ma?

I don't understand.
我不明白。 Wǒ bù míngbái.

Accommodation

Do you have a single/double room?
有没有(单人/套)房？ Yǒuméiyǒu (dānrén/tào) fáng?

How much is it per night/person?
每天/人多少钱？ Měi tiān/rén duōshǎo qián?

KEY PATTERNS

To get by in Mandarin, mix and match these simple patterns with words of your choice:

How much is (the deposit)?
(押金)多少？ (Yājīn) duōshǎo?

Do you have (a room)?
有没有(房)？ Yǒuméiyǒu (fáng)?

Is there (heating)?
有(暖气)吗？ Yóu (nuǎnqì) ma?

I'd like (that one).
我要(那个)。 Wǒ yào (nàge).

Please give me (the menu).
请给我(菜单)。 Qǐng gěiwǒ (càidān).

Can I (sit here)?
我能(坐这儿)吗？ Wǒ néng (zuòzhèr) ma?

I need (a can opener).
我想要(一个开罐器)。 Wǒ xiǎngyào (yīge kāiguàn qì).

Do we need (a guide)?
需要(向导)吗？ Xūyào (xiàngdǎo) ma?

I have (a reservation).
我有(预订)。 Wǒ yǒu (yùdìng).

I'm (a doctor).
我(是医生)。 Wǒ (shì yīshēng).

air-con	空调	kōngtiáo
bathroom	浴室	yùshì
bed	床	chuáng
campsite	露营地	lùyíngdì
guesthouse	宾馆	bīnguǎn
hostel	招待所	zhāodàisuǒ
hotel	酒店	jiǔdiàn
window	窗	chuāng

Directions

Where's a (bank)?
(银行)在哪儿？ (Yínháng) zài nǎr?

What's the address?
地址在哪儿？ Dìzhǐ zài nǎr?

Could you write the address, please?
能不能请你把地址写下来？ Néngbunéng qǐng nǐ bǎ dìzhǐ xiě xiàlái?

Can you show me where it is on the map?
请帮我找它在地图上的位置。 Qǐng bāngwǒ zhǎo tā zài dìtú shàng de wèizhi.

Go straight ahead.
一直走。 Yīzhí zǒu.

Turn left/right.
左/右转。 Zuǒ/Yòu zhuǎn.

Question Words

What?	什么?	Shénme?
When?	什么时候	Shénme shíhòu?
Where?	哪儿	Năr?
Which?	哪个	Năge?
Who?	谁?	Shuí?
Why?	为什么?	Wèishénme?

at the traffic lights	在红绿灯	zài hónglǜdēng
behind	背面	bèimiàn
far	远	yuǎn
in front of ...	……的前面	... de qiánmian
near	近	jìn
next to	旁边	pángbiān
on the corner	拐角	guǎijiǎo
opposite	对面	duìmiàn

Eating & Drinking

What would you recommend?
有什么菜可以推荐的? Yǒu shénme cài kěyǐ tuījiàn de?

What's in that dish?
这道菜用什么东西做的? Zhèdào cài yòng shénme dōngxi zuòde?

That was delicious.
真好吃。 Zhēn hǎochī.

The bill, please!
买单! Mǎidān!

Cheers!
干杯! Gānbēi!

I'd like to reserve a table for ...	我想预订一张……的桌子。	Wǒ xiǎng yùdìng yīzhāng ... de zhuōzi.
(eight) o'clock	(八) 点钟	(bā) diǎn zhōng
(two) people	(两个) 人	(liǎngge) rén

I don't eat ...	我不吃……	Wǒ bùchī ...
nuts	果仁	guǒrén
poultry	家禽	jiāqín
red meat	牛羊肉	niúyángròu

Key Words

bar	酒吧	jiǔbā
bottle	瓶子	píngzi
bowl	碗	wǎn
breakfast	早饭	zǎofàn
cafe	咖啡屋	kāfēiwū
(too) cold	(太)凉	(tài) liáng
dinner	晚饭	wǎnfàn
food	食品	shípǐn
fork	叉子	chāzi
glass	杯子	bēizi
hot (warm)	热	rè
knife	刀	dāo
local specialties	地方小吃	dìfāng xiǎochī
lunch	午饭	wǔfàn
market	菜市	càishì
menu (in English)	(英文) 菜单	(Yīngwén) càidān
plate	碟子	diézi
restaurant	餐馆	cānguǎn
(too) spicy	(太)辣	(tài) là
spoon	勺	sháo
vegetarian food	素食食品	sùshí shípín

Meat & Fish

beef	牛肉	niúròu
chicken	鸡肉	jīròu
duck	鸭	yā
fish	鱼	yú
lamb	羊肉	yángròu
pork	猪肉	zhūròu
seafood	海鲜	hǎixiān

Fruit & Vegetables

apple	苹果	píngguǒ
banana	香蕉	xiāngjiāo
carrot	胡萝卜	húluóbo
celery	芹菜	qíncài
cucumber	黄瓜	huángguā
fruit	水果	shuǐguǒ
grape	葡萄	pútáo
green beans	扁豆	biǎndòu
mango	芒果	mángguǒ
mushroom	蘑菇	mógū
onion	洋葱	yáng cōng
orange	橙子	chéngzi

Signs

入口	Rùkǒu	**Entrance**
出口	Chūkǒu	**Exit**
问讯处	Wènxùnchù	**Information**
开	Kāi	**Open**
关	Guān	**Closed**
禁止	Jìnzhǐ	**Prohibited**
厕所	Cèsuǒ	**Toilets**
男	Nán	**Men**
女	Nǚ	**Women**

pear	梨	lí
pineapple	凤梨	fènglí
plum	梅子	méizi
potato	土豆	tǔdòu
radish	萝卜	luóbo
spring onion	小葱	xiǎo cōng
sweet potato	地瓜	dìguā
vegetable	蔬菜	shūcài
watermelon	西瓜	xīguā

Other

bread	面包	miànbāo
butter	黄油	huángyóu
egg	蛋	dàn
herbs/spices	香料	xiāngliào
pepper	胡椒粉	hújiāo fěn
salt	盐	yán
soy sauce	酱油	jiàngyóu
sugar	砂糖	shātáng
tofu	豆腐	dòufu
vinegar	醋	cù
vegetable oil	菜油	càiyóu

Drinks

beer	啤酒	píjiǔ
coffee	咖啡	kāfēi
(orange) juice	(橙)汁	(chéng) zhī
milk	牛奶	niúnǎi
mineral water	矿泉水	kuàngquán shuǐ
red wine	红葡萄酒	hóng pútáo jiǔ
rice wine	米酒	mǐjiǔ
soft drink	汽水	qìshuǐ
tea	茶	chá
(boiled) water	(开)水	(kāi) shuǐ
white wine	白葡萄酒	bái pútáo jiǔ
yoghurt	酸奶	suānnǎi

SHANGHAINESE

Shanghainese has around 14 million speakers. As one of the dialects of Wu Chinese, it is similar to the dialects of Níngbō, Sūzhōu and Kūnshān. It is not mutually intelligible with other Wu dialects nor with Standard Mandarin. Nonetheless, it is infused with elements of Mandarin. The younger generation of Shànghǎi residents uses Mandarin expressions and, with government campaigns to encourage the use of Mandarin only, some fear for the future of the dialect. However, while it is rarely heard in schools or in the media, it remains a source of pride and identity for many Shànghǎi natives. Travellers will be perfectly fine using Mandarin in Shànghǎi.

Emergencies

Help!	救命!	Jiùmìng!
I'm lost.	我迷路了。	Wǒ mílù le.
Go away!	走开!	Zǒukāi!

There's been an accident.
出事了。 Chūshì le.

Call a doctor!
请叫医生来! Qǐng jiào yīshēng lái!

Call the police!
请叫警察! Qǐng jiào jǐngchá!

I'm ill.
我生病了。 Wǒ shēngbìng le.

Where are the toilets?
厕所在哪儿? Cèsuǒ zài nǎr?

Shopping & Services

I'd like to buy ...
我想买…… Wǒ xiǎng mǎi ...

I'm just looking.
我先看看。 Wǒ xiān kànkan.

Can I look at it?
我能看看吗? Wǒ néng kànkan ma?

I don't like it.
我不喜欢。 Wǒ bù xǐhuan.

How much is it?
多少钱? Duōshǎo qián?

That's too expensive.
太贵了。 Tàiguì le.

Can you lower the price?
能便宜一点吗? Néng piányi yīdiǎn ma?

There's a mistake in the bill.
帐单上有问题。 Zhàngdān shàng yǒu wèntí.

ATM	自动取款机	zìdòng qǔkuǎn jī
internet cafe	网吧	wǎngbā
post office	邮局	yóujú
tourist office	旅行店	lǚxíng diàn

Time & Dates

What time is it?
现在几点钟? Xiànzài jǐdiǎn zhōng?

It's (10) o'clock.
(十)点钟。 (Shí) diǎn zhōng.

Half past (10).
(十)点三十分。 (Shí) diǎn sānshífēn.

Numbers

1	一	yī
2	二/两	èr/liǎng
3	三	sān
4	四	sì
5	五	wǔ
6	六	liù
7	七	qī
8	八	bā
9	九	jiǔ
10	十	shí
20	二十	èrshí
30	三十	sānshí
40	四十	sìshí
50	五十	wǔshí
60	六十	liùshí
70	七十	qīshí
80	八十	bāshí
90	九十	jiǔshí
100	一百	yībǎi
1000	一千	yīqiān

morning	早上	zǎoshang
afternoon	下午	xiàwǔ
evening	晚上	wǎnshàng
yesterday	昨天	zuótiān
today	今天	jīntiān
tomorrow	明天	míngtiān
Monday	星期一	xīngqī yī
Tuesday	星期二	xīngqī èr
Wednesday	星期三	xīngqī sān
Thursday	星期四	xīngqī sì
Friday	星期五	xīngqī wǔ
Saturday	星期六	xīngqī liù
Sunday	星期天	xīngqī tiān

Transport

boat	船	chuán
bus (city)	大巴	dàbā
bus (intercity)	长途车	chángtú chē
plane	飞机	fēijī
taxi	出租车	chūzū chē
train	火车	huǒchē
tram	电车	diànchē

I want to go to ...
我要去⋯⋯ Wǒ yào qù ...

Does it stop at ...?
在⋯⋯能下车吗？ Zài ... néng xià chē ma?

At what time does it leave?
几点钟出发？ Jǐdiǎnzhōng chūfā?

At what time does it get to ...?
几点钟到⋯⋯？ Jǐdiǎnzhōng dào ...?

I want to get off here.
我想这儿下车。 Wǒ xiǎng zhèr xiàchē.

When's the first/last (bus)?
首趟/末趟(车)几点走？ Shǒutàng/Mòtàng (chē) jǐdiǎn zǒu?

A ... ticket to (Dàlián).	一张到(大连)的⋯⋯票。	Yīzhāng dào (Dàlián) de ... piào.
1st-class	头等	tóuděng
2nd-class	二等	èrděng
one-way	单程	dānchéng
return	双程	shuāngchéng

aisle seat	走廊的座位	zǒuláng de zuòwèi
ticket office	售票处	shòupiàochù
timetable	时刻表	shíkè biǎo
window seat	窗户的座位	chuānghu de zuòwèi

bicycle pump	打气筒	dǎqìtóng
child seat	婴儿座	yīng'érzuò
helmet	头盔	tóukuī
mechanic	机修工	jīxiūgōng
petrol	汽油	qìyóu
service station	加油站	jiāyóu zhàn

I'd like to hire a ...	我要租一辆⋯⋯	Wǒ yào zū yīliàng ...
4WD	四轮驱动	sìlún qūdòng
bicycle	自行车	zìxíngchē
car	汽车	qìchē
motorcycle	摩托车	mótuochē

Does this road lead to ...?
这条路到⋯⋯吗？ Zhè tiáo lù dào ... ma?

How long can I park here?
这儿可以停多久？ Zhèr kěyi tíng duōjiǔ?

The car has broken down.
汽车是坏的。 Qìchē shì huài de.

I have a flat tyre.
轮胎瘪了。 Lúntāi biě le.

I've run out of petrol.
没有汽油了。 Méiyou qìyóu le.

GLOSSARY

arhat – Buddhist, especially a monk who has achieved enlightenment
běi – north
biéshù – villa
bīnguǎn – tourist hotel
bówùguǎn – museum
cāntīng – restaurant
CCP – Chinese Communist Party; founded in Shànghǎi in 1921
cheongsam – see *qípáo*
Chiang Kaishek – (1887–1975) leader of the Kuomintang, anticommunist and head of the nationalist government from 1928 to 1949
chop – carved name seal that acts as a signature
Confucius – (551–479 BC) legendary scholar who developed the philosophy of Confucianism, which defines codes of conduct and patterns of obedience in society
Cultural Revolution – a brutal and devastating purge of the arts, religion and the intelligentsia by Mao's *Red Guards* and later the *PLA* from 1966 to 1970
dàdào – boulevard, avenue
dàfàndiàn – large hotel
dàjiē – avenue
dàjiǔdiàn – large hotel
dàshà – hotel, building
Deng Xiaoping – (1904–97) considered to be the most powerful political figure in China from the late 1970s until his death; Deng's reforms resulted in economic growth, but he also instituted harsh social policies and authorised the military force that resulted in the Tiān'ānmén Square incident in Běijīng in 1989
dōng – east
fàndiàn – hotel, restaurant
fēn – one-tenth of a *jiǎo*
fēng – peak
fēng shuǐ – geomancy, literally 'wind and water'; the art of using ancient principles to maximise the flow of *qì* (universal energy)
Gang of Four – members of a clique, headed by Mao's wife, Jiang Qing, who were blamed for the *Cultural Revolution*
gé – pavilion, temple
gōngyuán – park
gùjū – house, home, residence
gǔzhèn – ancient town
hé – river
hú – lake
huā – flower tea
jiāng – river
jiǎo – unit of currency, one-tenth of a *yuán*
jiē – street
jié – festival
jīn – unit of measurement (500g)
jìniànguǎn – memorial hall
jiǔdiàn – hotel
jū – residence, home
kuài – in spoken Chinese, colloquial term for the currency, *yuán*
Kuomintang – *Chiang Kaishek's* Nationalist Party; the dominant political force after the fall of the Qing dynasty
liǎng – unit of measurement (50g)
lǐlòng – alleyway
lòngtáng – narrow alleyway, or *lǐlòng*; lòngtáng is the preferred term used in Shànghǎi
lóu – tower
lǜ – green tea
lù – road
luóhàn – see *arhat*
máo – in spoken Chinese, colloquial term for the *jiǎo*
Mao Zedong – (1893–1976) leader of the early communist forces, he founded the *PRC* and was party chairman until his death
mǎtou – dock
mén – gate
miào – temple
nán – south
PLA – People's Liberation Army
pǔ'ěr – post-fermented, dark tea from Yúnnán (pu-erh)
PRC – People's Republic of China
PSB – Public Security Bureau; the arm of the police force set up to deal with foreigners
qiáo – bridge
qípáo – the figure-hugging dress worn by Chinese women (also called a cheongsam)
Red Guards – a pro-Mao faction that persecuted rightists during the *Cultural Revolution*
renminbi – literally 'people's money', the formal name for the currency; shortened to RMB
RMB – see *Renminbi*
shān – mountain
shì – city
shìchǎng – market
shíkùmén – stone-gate house; a blend of Chinese courtyard housing and English terraced housing
sì – temple, monastery
Sun Yatsen – (1866–1925) first president of the Republic of China; loved by republicans and communists alike
tǎ – pagoda
taichi – slow-motion shadow-boxing
Taiping Rebellion – rebellion (1850–64) that attempted to overthrow the Qing dynasty
tíng – pavilion
wūlóng – oolong tea
xī – west
yuán – Chinese unit of currency, the basic unit of RMB; garden
zhōng – middle
Zhou Enlai – an early comrade of Mao's, Zhou exercised the most influence in the day-to-day governing of China following the *Cultural Revolution*

MENU DECODER

bīng 冰 ice
bīngqílín 冰淇淋 ice cream
cù 醋 vinegar
dòufu 豆腐 tofu
hànbǎobāo 汉堡包 hamburger
huángguā 黄瓜 cucumber
huángyóu 黄油 butter
hújiāofěn 胡椒粉 pepper
jiàngyóu 酱油 soy sauce
jīdàn 鸡蛋 egg
jīròu 鸡肉 chicken
làjiāo 辣椒 chilli
lāmiàn 拉面 pulled noodles
miànbāo 面包 bread
niúròu 牛肉 beef
pángxiè 螃蟹 crab
qiézi 茄子aubergine
qíncài 芹菜 celery
qīngcài 青菜 green vegetables
sèlā 色拉 salad
shāokǎo 烧烤barbecue
shǔtiáo 薯条 chips
sùcài 素菜 vegetables
tāng 汤 soup
táng 糖 sugar
tǔdòu 土豆 potato
wèijīng 味精 MSG
xīhóngshì 西红柿 tomato
yán 盐 salt
yángròu 羊肉 lamb
yángròuchuàn
羊肉串
lamb kebab
yāzi 鸭子 duck
yóuyú 鱿鱼 squid
zhōu 粥 rice porridge (congee)
zhūròu 猪肉 pork

Rice Dishes 米饭

báifàn 白饭
steamed white rice
chǎofàn 炒饭 fried rice
jīdàn chǎofàn 鸡蛋炒饭
fried rice with egg

Soup 汤

húntun tāng 馄饨汤
won ton (dumpling) soup
jīdàn tāng 鸡蛋汤
egg drop soup
sānxiān tāng 三鲜汤
three kinds of seafood soup
suānlà tāng 酸辣汤
hot and sour soup
xīhóngshì jīdàntāng
西红柿鸡蛋汤
tomato and egg soup

Vegetable Dishes 素菜

báicài xiān shuānggū
白菜鲜双菇
bok choy and mushrooms
cuìpí dòufu 脆皮豆腐
crispy skin bean curd
dìsānxiān 地三鲜
cooked potato, aubergine and green pepper
háoyóu xiāngū 蚝油鲜菇
mushrooms in oyster sauce
hēimù'ěr mèn dòufu
黑木耳焖豆腐
bean curd with mushrooms
jiǔcài jiǎozi 韭菜饺子
chive dumplings
shāo qiézi 烧茄子
cooked aubergine (eggplant)
tángcù ǒubǐng
糖醋藕饼
lotus root cakes in sweet-and-sour sauce

Seafood 海鲜

chāngyú 鲳鱼 pomfret
chǎo huángshàn 炒黄鳝
fried eel
cōngsū jìyú 葱酥鲫鱼
braised carp with onion
dàzhá xiè 大闸蟹
hairy crabs
fúróng yúpiàn
芙蓉鱼片
fish slices in egg white
gānjiān xiǎo huángyú
干煎小黄鱼
dry-fried yellow croaker
guōbā xiārén 锅巴虾仁
shrimp in sizzling rice crust
héxiāng báilián 荷香白鲢
lotus-flavoured silver carp
hóngshāo shànyú
红烧鳝鱼
eel soaked in soy sauce
huángyú 黄鱼
yellow croaker
jiāng cōng chǎo xiè
姜葱炒蟹
stir-fried crab with ginger and scallions
jiǔxiāng yúpiàn 酒香鱼片
fish slices in wine
mìzhī xūnyú 蜜汁熏鱼
honey-smoked carp
níngshì shànyú 宁式鳝鱼
stir-fried eel with onion
qiézhī yúkuài 茄汁鱼块
fish fillet in tomato sauce
qīngzhēng guìyú
清蒸鳜鱼
steamed Mandarin fish
sōngjiānglúyú 松江鲈鱼
Songjiang perch
sōngshǔ guìyú 松鼠鳜鱼
squirrel-shaped Mandarin fish
sōngzǐ guìyú 松子鳜鱼
Mandarin fish with pine nuts
suānlà yóuyú 酸辣鱿鱼
hot-and-sour squid
yóubào xiārén 油爆虾仁
fried shrimp
zhá hēi lǐyú 炸黑鲤鱼
fried black carp
zhá yúwán 炸鱼丸
fish balls

Home-Style Dishes 家常菜

biǎndòu ròusī 扁豆肉丝
shredded pork and green beans
fānqié chǎodàn 番茄炒蛋
egg and tomato
hóngshāo qiézi 红烧茄子
red-cooked aubergine

huíguō ròu 回锅肉
double-cooked fatty pork

jiācháng dòufu 家常豆腐
'home-style' tofu

jīngjiàng ròusī 精酱肉丝
pork cooked with soy sauce

níngméng jī 柠檬鸡
lemon chicken

niúròu miàn 牛肉面
beef noodles in soup

páigǔ 排骨 ribs

sùchǎo biǎndòu 素炒扁豆
garlic beans

sùchǎo sùcài 素炒素菜
fried vegetables

tiěbǎn niúròu 铁板牛肉
sizzling beef platter

yángcōng chǎo ròupiàn
洋葱炒肉片
pork and fried onions

yúxiāng qiézi 鱼香茄子
fish-flavoured aubergine

Shanghainese Dishes 上海菜

hǔpíjiānjiāo 虎皮尖椒
tiger skin chillies

jīngcōng ròusī jiá bǐng
京葱肉丝夹饼
soy pork with scallions in pancakes

jīngdū guō páigǔ 京都锅排骨
Mandarin-style pork ribs

sōngrén yùmǐ 松仁玉米
sweet corn and pine nuts

sōngzǐ yā 松子鸭
duck with pine nuts

xiāngsū jī 香酥鸡
crispy chicken

xiánjī 咸鸡
cold salty chicken

xiǎolóngbāo 小笼包
little steamer buns

xièfěn shīzitóu 蟹粉狮子头
lion's head meatballs with crab

yóutiáo niú ròu 油条牛肉
fried dough sticks with beef

zuìjī 醉鸡 drunken chicken

Hángzhōu Dishes 杭州菜

dōngpō bèiròu 东坡焙肉
Dongpo pork

héyè fěnzhēng ròu
荷叶粉蒸肉
steamed pork wrapped in lotus leaf

jiào huā jī 叫化鸡
beggar's chicken

lóngjǐng xiārén 龙井虾仁
Longjing stir-fried shrimp

shāguō yútóu dòufu
沙锅鱼头豆腐
earthenware-pot fish-head tofu

xīhú chúncài tāng
西湖莼菜汤
West Lake water shield soup

xīhú cùyú 西湖醋鱼
West Lake fish

Cantonese Dishes 粤菜

chǎomiàn 炒面 chow mein

chāshāo 叉烧 cha siu

diǎnxīn 点心 dim sum

guōtiē 锅贴 fried dumplings

háoyóu niúròu 蚝油牛肉
beef with oyster sauce

kǎo rǔzhū 烤乳猪
crispy suckling pig

mìzhī chāshāo
蜜汁叉烧
roast pork with sweet syrup

tángcù lǐjī/gǔlǎo ròu
糖醋里脊/古老肉
sweet-and-sour pork fillets

xiāngsū jī 香酥鸡
crispy chicken

Sichuanese Dishes 川菜

dàndànmiàn 担担面
Dandan noodles

gōngbào jīdīng 宫爆鸡丁
spicy chicken with peanuts

málà dòufu 麻辣豆腐
spicy tofu

mápó dòufu 麻婆豆腐
Granny Ma's tofu

shuǐ zhǔ niúròu 水煮牛肉
fried and boiled beef, garlic sprouts and celery

suāncàiyú 酸菜鱼
boiled fish with pickled vegetables

yuānyāng huǒguō
鸳鸯火锅
Yuanyang hotpot

yúxiāng ròusī 鱼香肉丝
fish-flavoured meat

Běijīng & Northern Dishes 京菜和北方菜

běijīng kǎoyā 北京烤鸭
Peking duck

jiǎozi 饺子 dumplings

mántou 馒头 steamed buns

ròu bāozi 肉包子
steamed meat buns

shuàn yángròu huǒguō
涮羊肉火锅 lamb hotpot

sùcài bāozi 素菜包子
steamed vegetable buns

Drinks 饮料

báijiǔ 白酒 white spirits

dòunǎi 豆奶 soya milk

hóngchá 红茶
Western (black) tea

júhuā chá 菊花茶
chrysanthemum tea

lǜ chá 绿茶 green tea

mǐjiǔ 米酒 rice wine

nǎijīng 奶精 coffee creamer

yézi zhī 椰子汁 coconut juice

zhēnzhū nǎichá 珍珠奶茶
bubble tea

Behind the Scenes

SEND US YOUR FEEDBACK

We love to hear from travellers – your comments keep us on our toes and help make our books better. Our well-travelled team reads every word on what you loved or loathed about this book. Although we cannot reply individually to postal submissions, we always guarantee that your feedback goes straight to the appropriate authors, in time for the next edition. Each person who sends us information is thanked in the next edition – and the most useful submissions are rewarded with a selection of digital PDF chapters.

Visit **lonelyplanet.com/contact** to submit your updates and suggestions or to ask for help. Our award-winning website also features inspirational travel stories, news and discussions.

Note: We may edit, reproduce and incorporate your comments in Lonely Planet products such as guidebooks, websites and digital products, so let us know if you don't want your comments reproduced or your name acknowledged. For a copy of our privacy policy visit lonelyplanet.com/privacy.

OUR READERS

Many thanks to the travellers who used the last edition and wrote to us with helpful hints, useful advice and interesting anecdotes: Michael Campbell, Tom Connelly, Eric Danziger, Roland Dussart-desart, Zhang Fan, Rachel Diane Field, Crystal Isabel Fischetti, Thomas Grant, Katharina Guth, David Hartsuiker, Jace Labrenz, Matthias Landsberger, Holger Lichau, Monica Luo, Jesse Mandell, Peter Uftring, Viktoria Urbanek, Jeroen van de Weijer, Toon van der Hoorn, Marie-Claude Vinette, Oxana Vom Brocke, Stephanie Wang

AUTHOR THANKS

Damian Harper

Thanks first and foremost to Dai Min, Dai Lu, Li Jianjun, Chris Pitts, Katarina Nilsson, Edward Li, Maggie Zhang, Grace Wu and Henry Zhao. Thanks also to Jiale and Jiafu for their constant good humour and support. Gratitude moreover to the irrepressibly hard-working people of Shànghǎi, Zhèjiāng and Jiāngsū for making my journey so enjoyable and absorbing.

Christopher Pitts

As always, thanks to everyone who offered valuable insight or who provided company along the way. Much gratitude is due to Gerald and May Neumann for their hospitality and great suggestions. Thanks as well to Miranda Yao, Wang Xinhai, Laure Romeyer, Sandy Chu, Lynn Ye, Caroline and Antoine Lebouc, Sam Maurey and Claudio Valsecchi.

Special thanks also to *Shanghai* co-author Damian Harper, Emily Wolman, Barbara Delissen, Annelies Mertens, Mark Griffiths and all those who work behind the scenes.

And love to Perrine, Elliot and Celeste, who provide more inspiration than they'll ever know.

ACKNOWLEDGMENTS

Cover photograph: Shànghǎi World Financial Center and Jinmao Tower with Yùyuán Gardens & Bazaar in foreground. Grant Faint/Getty Images©.

THIS BOOK

This 6th edition of Lonely Planet's *Shanghai* guidebook was researched and written by Damian Harper and Christopher Pitts. The 5th edition was written by Christopher Pitts and Daniel McCrohan, and the 4th edition was written by Damian Harper and David Eimer. This guidebook was commissioned in Lonely Planet's Oakland office, and produced by the following:

Commissioning Editors Emily Wolman, Kathleen Munnelly

Coordinating Editors Carolyn Bain, Monique Perrin

Coordinating Cartographer Mark Griffiths

Coordinating Layout Designer Mazzy Prinsep

Managing Editors Barbara Delissen, Annelies Mertens

Senior Editors Catherine Naghten, Andi Jones

Managing Cartographer Alison Lyall

Managing Layout Designer Jane Hart

Assisting Editors Janet Austin, Ali Lemer, Anne Mulvaney

Assisting Cartographers Corey Hutchison, Eve Kelly

Cover Research Naomi Parker

Internal Image Research Kylie McLaughlin

Illustrator Michael Weldon

Language Content Branislava Vladisavljevic

Thanks to Lucy Birchley, Lauren Egan, Ryan Evans, Lorna Goodyer, Eva Murphy, Trent Paton, Kerrianne Southway, Phillip Tang, John Taufa, Diana Von Holdt, Gerard Walker, Juan Winata

See also separate subindexes for:
- EATING P274
- DRINKING & NIGHTLIFE P275
- ENTERTAINMENT P276
- SHOPPING P276
- SPORTS & ACTIVITIES P277
- SLEEPING P277

Index

Sights 000
Map Pages **000**
Photo Pages **000**

Sights 000
Map Pages **000**
Photo Pages **000**

Sights 000
Map Pages **000**
Photo Pages **000**

EATING

DRINKING & NIGHTLIFE

SPORTS & ACTIVITIES

SLEEPING

Shànghǎi Maps

Map Legend

Sights
- Beach
- Buddhist
- Castle
- Christian
- Hindu
- Islamic
- Jewish
- Monument
- Museum/Gallery
- Ruin
- Winery/Vineyard
- Zoo
- Other Sight

Eating
- Eating

Drinking & Nightlife
- Drinking & Nightlife
- Cafe

Entertainment
- Entertainment

Shopping
- Shopping

Sleeping
- Sleeping
- Camping

Sports & Activities
- Diving/Snorkelling
- Canoeing/Kayaking
- Skiing
- Surfing
- Swimming/Pool
- Walking
- Windsurfing
- Other Sports & Activities

Information
- Post Office
- Tourist Information

Transport
- Airport
- Border Crossing
- Bus
- Cable Car/Funicular
- Cycling
- Ferry
- Monorail
- Parking
- S-Bahn
- Taxi
- Train/Railway
- Tram
- Tube Station
- U-Bahn
- Underground Train Station
- Other Transport

Routes
- Tollway
- Freeway
- Primary
- Secondary
- Tertiary
- Lane
- Unsealed Road
- Plaza/Mall
- Steps
- Tunnel
- Pedestrian Overpass
- Walking Tour
- Walking Tour Detour
- Path

Boundaries
- International
- State/Province
- Disputed
- Regional/Suburb
- Marine Park
- Cliff
- Wall

Geographic
- Hut/Shelter
- Lighthouse
- Lookout
- Mountain/Volcano
- Oasis
- Park
- Pass
- Picnic Area
- Waterfall

Hydrography
- River/Creek
- Intermittent River
- Swamp/Mangrove
- Reef
- Canal
- Water
- Dry/Salt/Intermittent Lake
- Glacier

Areas
- Beach/Desert
- Cemetery (Christian)
- Cemetery (Other)
- Park/Forest
- Sportsground
- Sight (Building)
- Top Sight (Building)

MAP INDEX

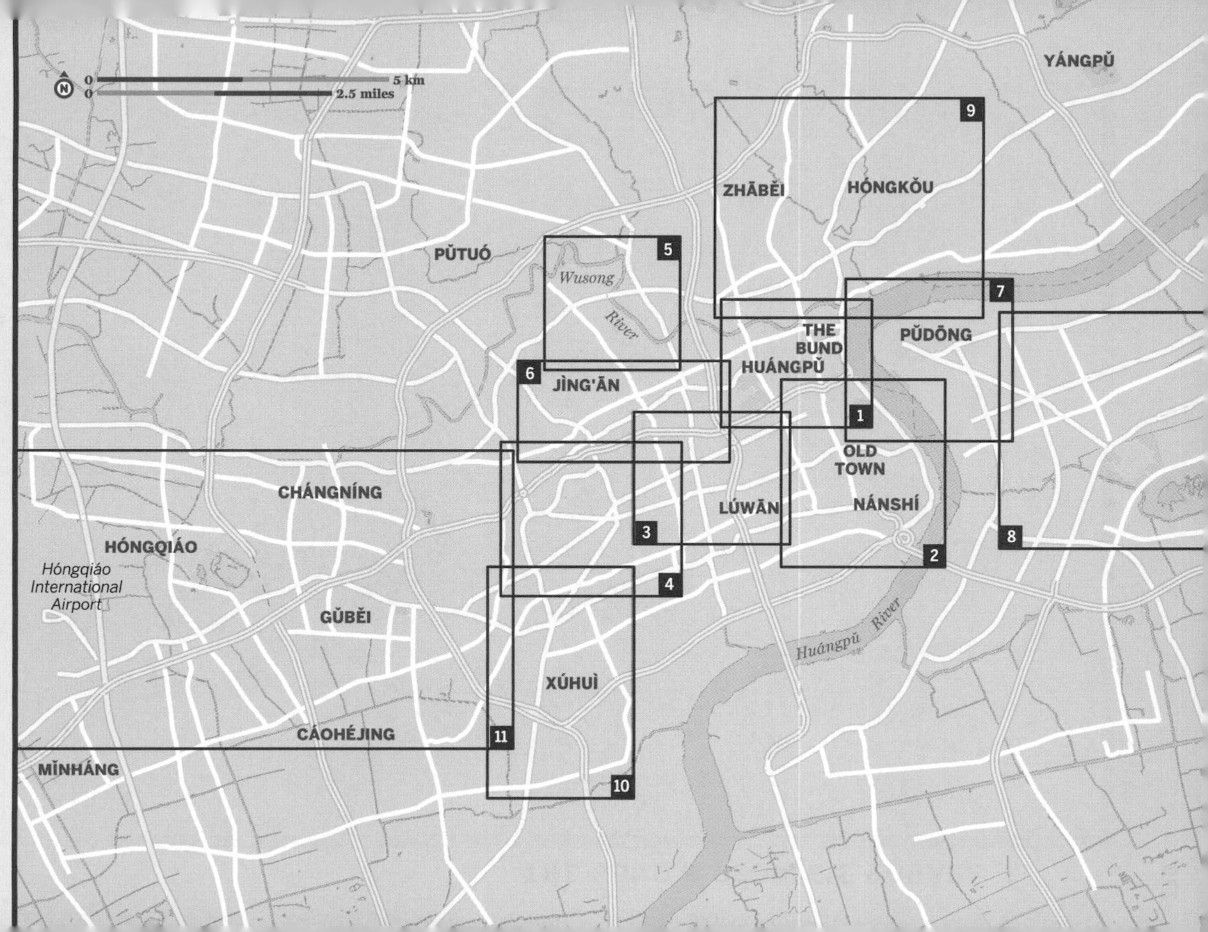

0
5 km
0
2.5 miles
N
YÁNGPǓ
9
ZHĀBĚI
HÓNGKǑU
5
PǓTUÓ
Wusong
River
7
THE
BUND
PǓDŌNG
HUÁNGPǓ
6
JÌNG'ĀN
1
OLD
TOWN
CHÁNGNÍNG
LÚWĀN
NÁNSHÍ
HÓNGQIÁO
3
8
Hóngqiáo
International
Airport
2
4
GǓBĚI
Huángpǔ River
XÚHUÌ
CÁOHÉJING
11
MǏNHÁNG
10

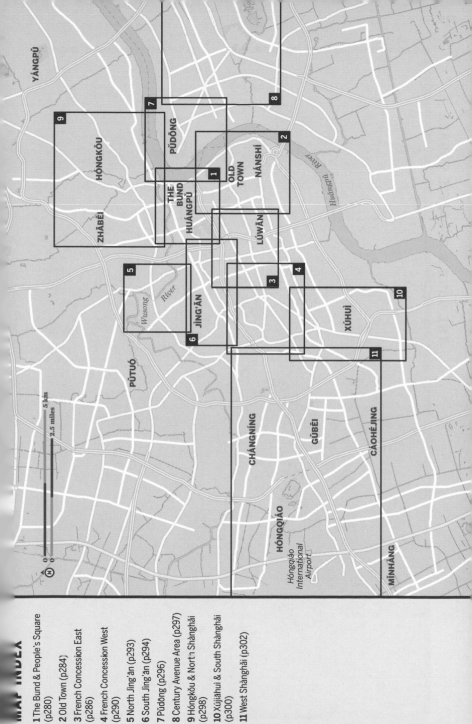

Key on p282

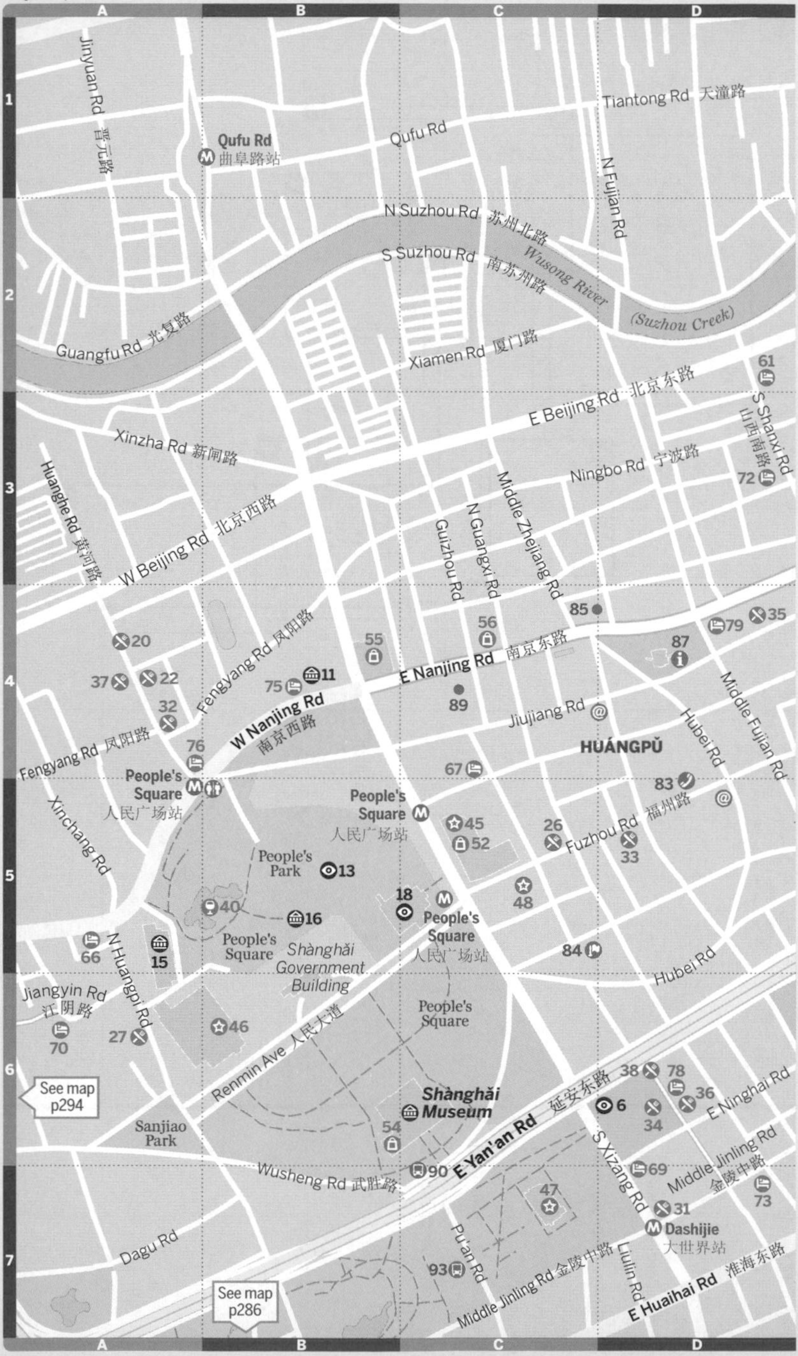
A
B
C
D
1
2
3
4
5
6
7
Jinyuan Rd 晋元路
Qufu Rd 曲阜路站
Qufu Rd
Tiantong Rd 天潼路
N Fujian Rd
N Suzhou Rd 苏州北路
S Suzhou Rd 南苏州路
Wusong River
(Suzhou Creek)
Guangfu Rd 光复路
Xiamen Rd 厦门路
E Beijing Rd 北京东路
S Shanxi Rd 山西南路
Xinzha Rd 新闸路
Ningbo Rd 宁波路
Huanghe Rd 黄河路
W Beijing Rd 北京西路
Middle Zhejiang Rd
N Guangxi Rd
Guizhou Rd
Fengyang Rd 凤阳路
E Nanjing Rd 南京东路
W Nanjing Rd 南京西路
Jiujiang Rd
HUÁNGPŬ
Hubei Rd
Middle Fujian Rd
Fengyang Rd 凤阳路
People's Square 人民广场站
Xinchang Rd
People's Square 人民广场站
Fuzhou Rd 福州路
People's Park
People's Square 人民广场站
People's Square
Shànghǎi Government Building
N Huangpi Rd
Jiangyin Rd 江阴路
People's Square
Renmin Ave 人民大道
Hubei Rd
E Ninghai Rd
See map p294
Shànghǎi Museum
Sanjiao Park
E Yan'an Rd 延安东路
S Xizang Rd
Middle Jinling Rd 金陵中路
Wusheng Rd 武胜路
Dashijie 大世界站
Dagu Rd
Pu'an Rd
Liulin Rd
Middle Jinling Rd 金陵中路
E Huaihai Rd 淮海东路
See map p286
61
72
85
79
35
56
55
87
20
37
22
11
75
32
89
76
67
83
45
52
26
33
13
40
16
18
48
66
15
84
27
46
70
38
78
6
36
34
54
90
69
47
73
31
93

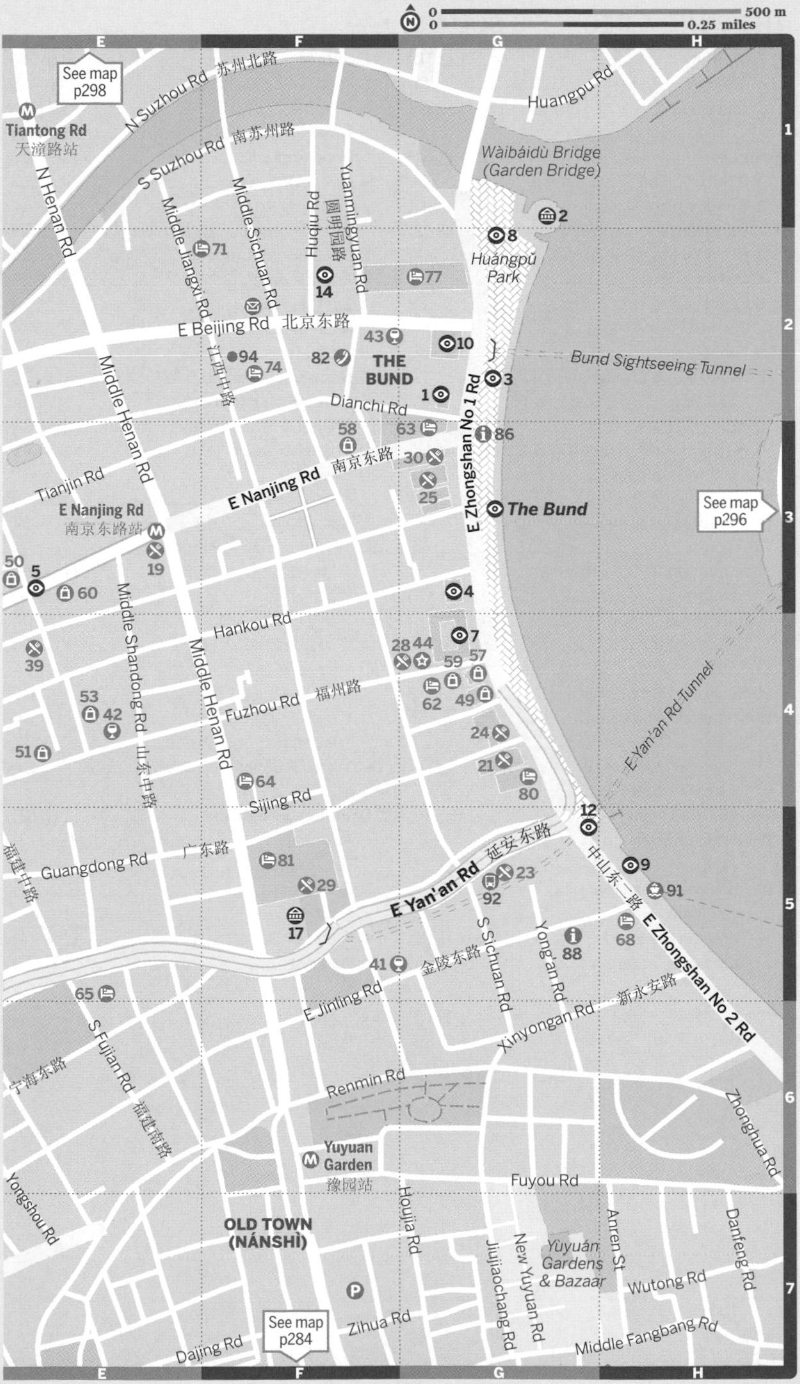

0 500 m
0 0.25 miles
E
F
G
H
See map p298
Tiantong Rd
天潼路站
N Suzhou Rd 苏州北路
S Suzhou Rd 南苏州路
Huangpu Rd
Wàibáidù Bridge (Garden Bridge)
N Henan Rd
Middle Jiangxi Rd
Middle Sichuan Rd
Huqiu Rd
Yuanmingyuan Rd 圆明园路
Huángpǔ Park
E Beijing Rd 北京东路
江西中路
THE BUND
Bund Sightseeing Tunnel
Dianchi Rd
E Zhongshan No 1 Rd
Middle Henan Rd
Tianjin Rd
E Nanjing Rd
南京东路站
E Nanjing Rd 南京东路
The Bund
See map p296
Hankou Rd
Middle Shandong Rd
山东中路
Middle Henan Rd
Fuzhou Rd 福州路
E Yan'an Rd Tunnel
Sijing Rd
福建中路
Guangdong Rd 广东路
E Yan'an Rd 延安东路
中山东二路
S Sichuan Rd
Yong'an Rd
E Jinling Rd 金陵东路
E Zhongshan No 2 Rd
Xinyongan Rd 新永安路
宁海东路
S Fujian Rd
福建南路
Renmin Rd
Zhonghua Rd
Yuyuan Garden
豫园站
Fuyou Rd
Yongshou Rd
OLD TOWN (NÁNSHÌ)
Houjia Rd
Jiujiaochang Rd
New Yuyuan Rd
Yùyuán Gardens & Bazaar
Anren St
Danfeng Rd
Wutong Rd
Zihua Rd
See map p284
Dajing Rd
Middle Fangbang Rd
1
2
3
4
5
6
7

THE BUND & PEOPLE'S SQUARE *Map on p280*

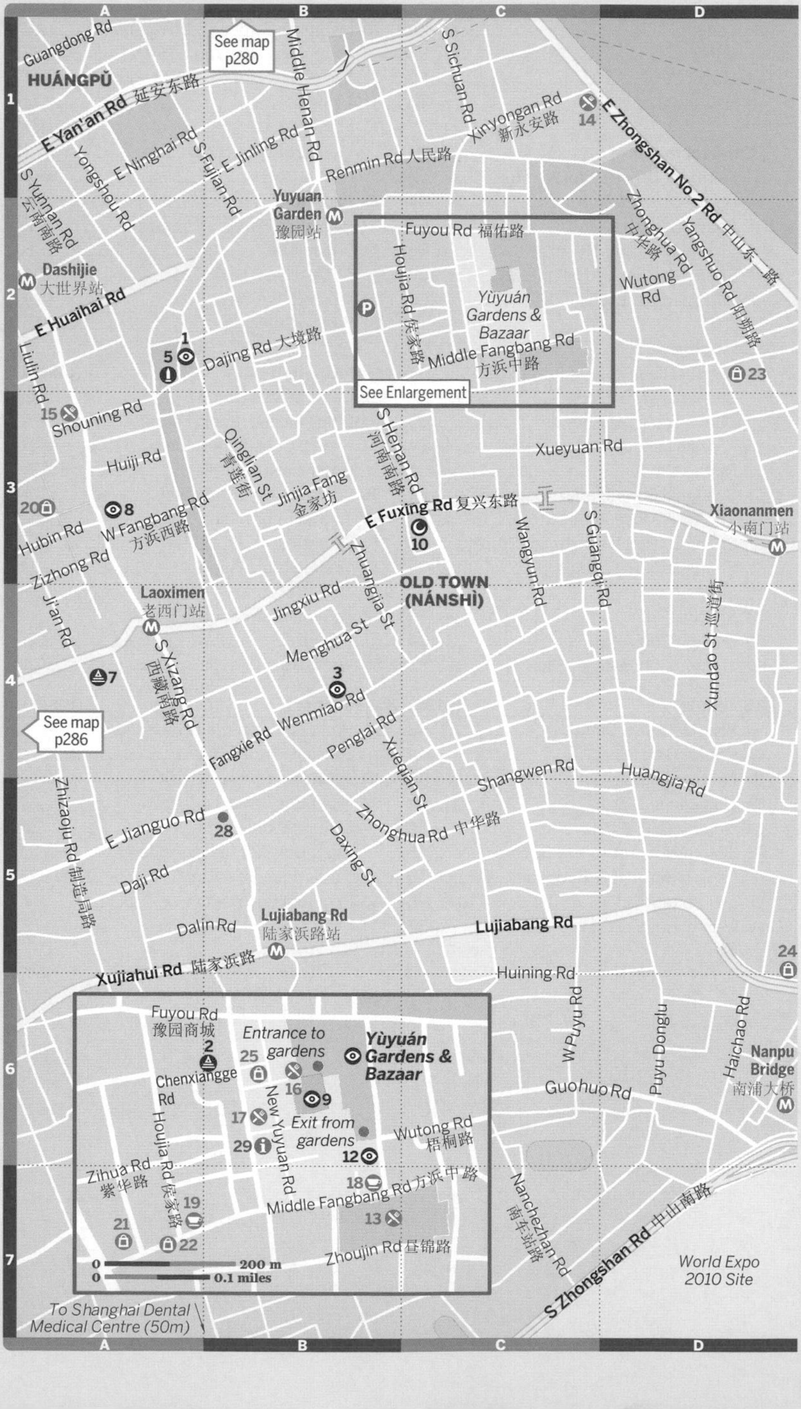
A
B
C
D
1
2
3
4
5
6
7
See map p280
See map p286
See Enlargement
HUÁNGPŮ
Guangdong Rd
E Yan'an Rd 延安东路
Middle Henan Rd
S Sichuan Rd
Xinyongan Rd 新永安路
E Zhongshan No 2 Rd 中山东二路
Yongshou Rd
E Ninghai Rd
S Fujian Rd
E Jinling Rd
Renmin Rd 人民路
S Yunnan Rd 云南南路
Yuyuan Garden 豫园站
Fuyou Rd 福佑路
Houjia Rd 侯家路
Yùyuán Gardens & Bazaar
Middle Fangbang Rd 方浜中路
Zhonghua Rd 中华路
Yangshuo Rd 阳朔路
Wutong Rd
Dashijie 大世界站
E Huaihai Rd
Dajing Rd 大境路
Liulin Rd
Shouning Rd
Huiji Rd
Qinglian St 青莲街
Jinjia Fang 金家坊
S Henan Rd 河南南路
Xueyuan Rd
E Fuxing Rd 复兴东路
Hubin Rd
W Fangbang Rd 方浜西路
Zizhong Rd
Zhuangjia St
Wangyun Rd
S Guangqi Rd
Xiaonanmen 小南门站
OLD TOWN (NÁNSHÌ)
Laoximen 老西门站
Ji'an Rd
S Xizang Rd 西藏南路
Jingxiu Rd
Menghua St
Xundao St 巡道街
Wenmiao Rd
Fangxie Rd
Penglai Rd
Xueqian St
Shangwen Rd
Huangjia Rd
Zhizaoju Rd 制造局路
E Jianguo Rd
Zhonghua Rd 中华路
Daxing St
Daji Rd
Dalin Rd
Lujiabang Rd 陆家浜路站
Lujiabang Rd
Xujiahui Rd 陆家浜路
Huining Rd
W Puyu Rd
Puyu Donglu
Haichao Rd
Nanpu Bridge 南浦大桥
Guohuo Rd
Nanchezhan Rd 南车站路
S Zhongshan Rd 中山南路
World Expo 2010 Site
Fuyou Rd 豫园商城
Entrance to gardens
Yùyuán Gardens & Bazaar
Chenxiangge Rd
New Yuyuan Rd
Exit from gardens
Wutong Rd 梧桐路
Zihua Rd 紫华路
Houjia Rd 侯家路
Middle Fangbang Rd 方浜中路
Zhoujin Rd 昼锦路
0 200 m
0 0.1 miles
To Shanghai Dental Medical Centre (50m)
1
2
3
5
7
8
9
10
12
13
14
15
16
17
18
19
20
21
22
23
24
25
28
29

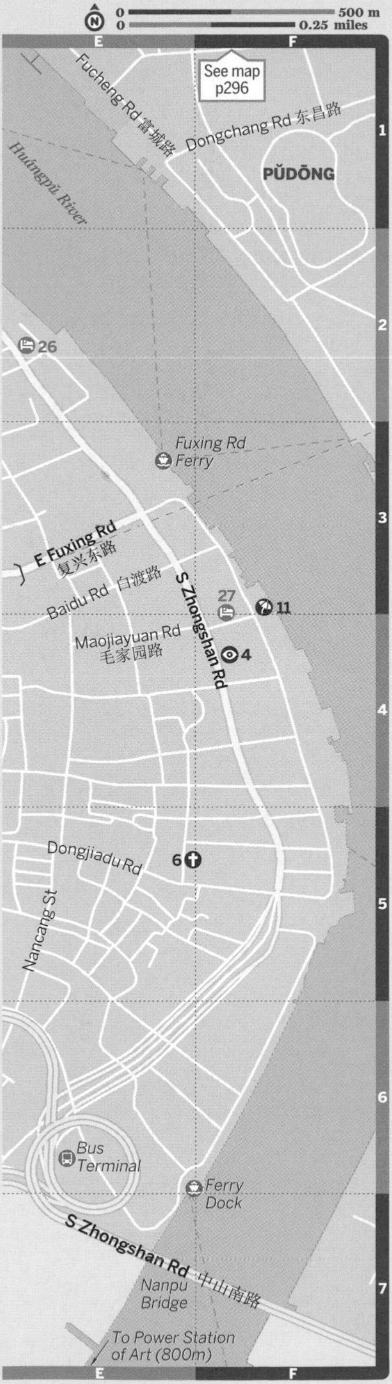

Top Sights (p76)

Yùyuán Gardens & Bazaar B6

Sights (p77)

1 Báiyún Temple A2
2 Chénxiānggé Nunnery B6
3 Confucian Temple B4
4 Cool Docks F4
5 Dàjìng Pavilion A2
6 Dǒngjiādù Cathedral E5
7 Fǎzàngjiǎng Temple A4
8 Flower, Bird, Fish & Insect Market A3
9 Mid-Lake Pavilion Teahouse B6
10 Peach Garden Mosque C3
11 Sunny Beach F3
12 Temple of the Town God B6

Eating (p82)

Char .... (see 26)
Din Tai Fung .... (see 13)
13 Dragon Gate Mall B7
14 El Willy C1
Element Fresh .... (see 15)
15 Fat Olive A3
Kebabs on the Grille .... (see 4)
16 Nánxiáng Steamed Bun Restaurant B6
17 Sōngyuèlóu B6
Stiller's Restaurant & Cooking School (see 4)
Table No 1 by Jason Atherton .... (see 27)

Drinking & Nightlife (p84)

Brix .... (see 14)
Char Bar .... (see 26)
18 Moonlight Teahouse B7
19 Old Shanghai Teahouse A7
Yawaragi .... (see 14)
Zeal .... (see 14)

Shopping (p86)

20 Dongtai Road Antique Market A3
21 Fúyòu Antique Market A7
22 Old Street A7
23 Shíliùpù Fabric Market D2
24 South Bund Fabric Market D5
25 Tóng Hán Chūn Traditional Medicine Store B6

Sleeping (p195)

26 Hotel Indigo E2
27 Waterhouse at South Bund F3

Information (p249)

Australian Chamber of Commerce ... (see 15)
28 Body and Soul TCM Clinic B5
29 Tourist Information & Service Centre B6

Key on p288

FRENCH CONCESSION EAST

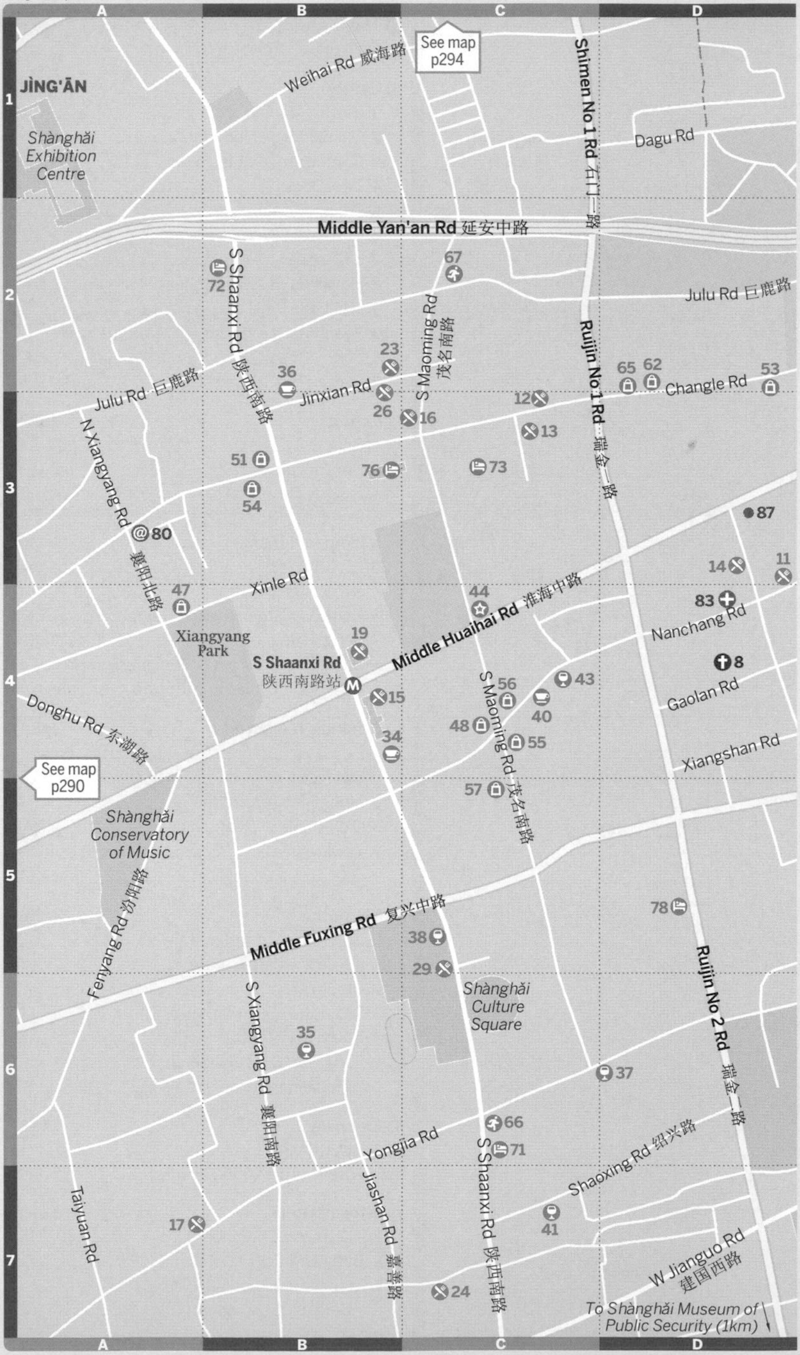
A
B
C
D
1
2
3
4
5
6
7
See map p294
See map p290
JÌNG'ĀN
Shànghǎi Exhibition Centre
Weihai Rd 威海路
Shimen No 1 Rd 石门一路
Dagu Rd
Middle Yan'an Rd 延安中路
Julu Rd 巨鹿路
S Shaanxi Rd 陕西南路
S Maoming Rd 茂名南路
Ruijin No 1 Rd 瑞金一路
Jinxian Rd
Changle Rd
N Xiangyang Rd 襄阳北路
Xinle Rd
Xiangyang Park
S Shaanxi Rd 陕西南路站
Middle Huaihai Rd 淮海中路
Nanchang Rd
Gaolan Rd
Donghu Rd 东湖路
Xiangshan Rd
Shànghǎi Conservatory of Music
Fenyang Rd 汾阳路
Middle Fuxing Rd 复兴中路
Ruijin No 2 Rd 瑞金二路
S Xiangyang Rd 襄阳南路
Shànghǎi Culture Square
Yongjia Rd
Jiashan Rd 嘉善路
Shaoxing Rd 绍兴路
Taiyuan Rd
W Jianguo Rd 建国西路
To Shànghǎi Museum of Public Security (1km)
67
72
23
36
26
16
65
62
53
12
13
51
76
73
54
87
80
14
11
47
44
83
19
8
43
15
56
40
48
55
34
57
78
38
29
35
37
66
71
17
41
24

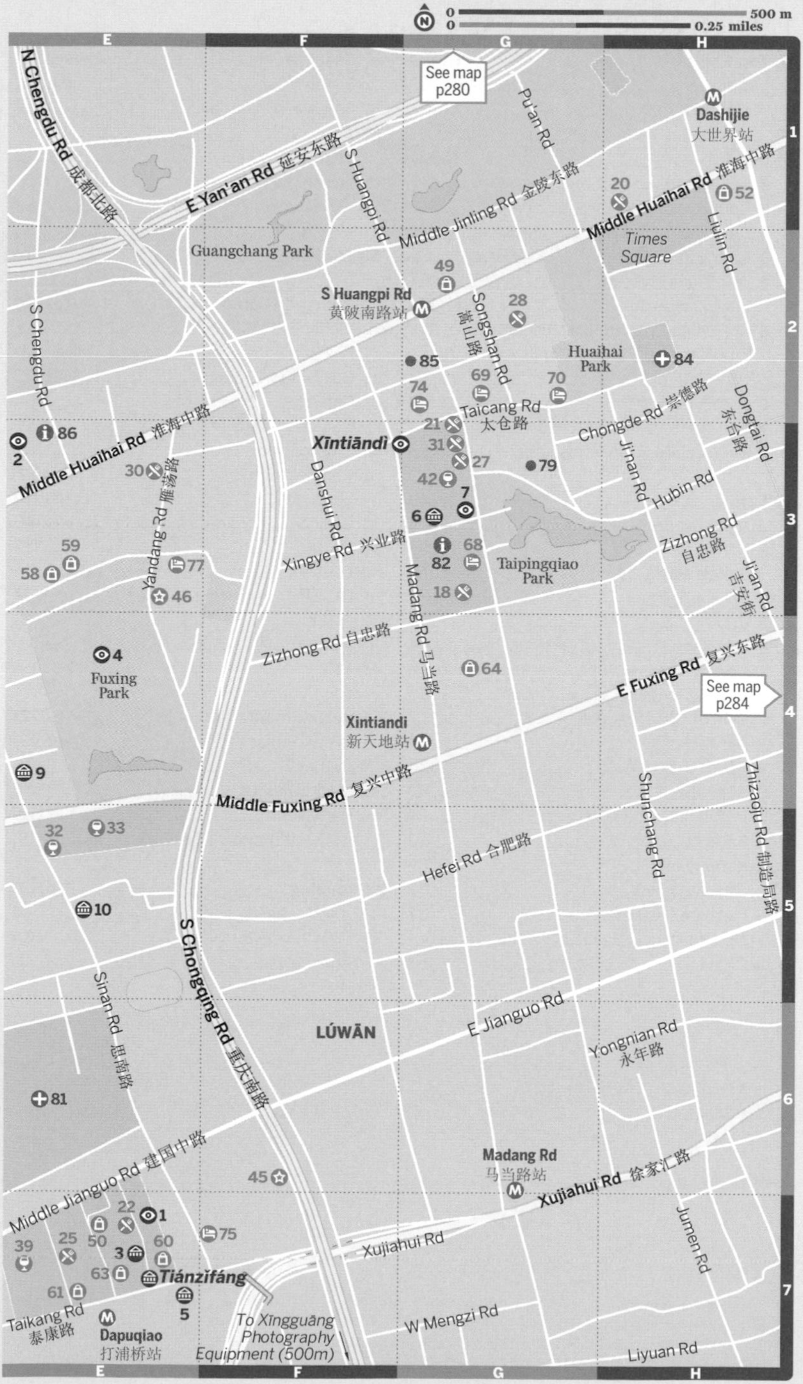
0 500 m
0 0.25 miles
E
F
G
H
1
2
3
4
5
6
7
See map p280
See map p284
N Chengdu Rd 成都北路
E Yan'an Rd 延安东路
S Huangpi Rd
Pu'an Rd
Dashijie
大世界站
Middle Huaihai Rd 淮海中路
Middle Jinling Rd 金陵东路
Guangchang Park
Times Square
Liulin Rd
S Huangpi Rd
黄陂南路站
Songshan Rd
嵩山路
S Chengdu Rd
Huaihai Park
Dongtai Rd
东台路
Taicang Rd
太仓路
Chongde Rd 崇德路
Xīntiāndì
Ji'nan Rd
Hubin Rd
Middle Huaihai Rd 淮海中路
Danshui Rd
Yandang Rd 雁荡路
Xingye Rd 兴业路
Taipingqiao Park
Zizhong Rd
自忠路
Ji'an Rd
吉安街
Madang Rd 马当路
Zizhong Rd 自忠路
Fuxing Park
E Fuxing Rd 复兴东路
Xintiandi
新天地站
Middle Fuxing Rd 复兴中路
Shunchang Rd
Zhizaoju Rd 制造局路
Hefei Rd 合肥路
S Chongqing Rd 重庆南路
Sinan Rd 思南路
LÚWĀN
E Jianguo Rd
Yongnian Rd
永年路
Middle Jianguo Rd 建国中路
Madang Rd
马当路站
Xujiahui Rd 徐家汇路
Jumen Rd
Xujiahui Rd
Tiánzǐfáng
Taikang Rd
泰康路
Dapuqiao
打浦桥站
To Xīngguāng Photography Equipment (500m)
W Mengzi Rd
Liyuan Rd
1
2
3
4
5
6
7
9
10
18
20
21
22
25
27
28
30
31
32
33
39
42
45
46
49
50
52
58
59
60
61
63
64
68
69
70
74
75
77
79
81
82
84
85
86

FRENCH CONCESSION EAST *Map on p286*

Top Sights **(p90)**

Tiánzǐfáng E7
Xīntiāndì F3

Sights **(p92)**

1 Beaugeste E7
2 Centre of Jewish Studies Shanghai E3
3 Deke Erh Art Centre E7
4 Fùxīng Park E4
5 Liúli China Museum E7
Moller House .... (see 72)
6 Shíkùmén Open House Museum G3
7 Site of the 1st National Congress of the CCP G3
8 St Nicholas Church D4
9 Sun Yatsen's Former Residence E4
10 Zhou Enlai's Former Residence E5

Eating **(p97)**

11 Art Salon Restaurant D3
12 Bankura C3
Bellagio Café .... (see 70)
13 Bì Fēng Táng C3
14 Chá's D3
15 City Shop B4
Crystal Jade .... (see 18)
16 Dī Shuǐ Dòng C3
17 Diǎn Shí Zhāi Xiǎo Yàn A7
18 Din Tai Fung G3
19 Food Fusion B4
Hǎijīnzī .... (see 36)
20 Infiniti Plaza H1
21 Kabb G3
22 Kommune E7
23 Lánxīn Cāntīng B2
24 Melange Oasis C7
New York Style Pizza .... (see 50)
25 Origin E7
Shànghǎi Min .... (see 18)
Simply Thai .... (see 6)
26 Southern Barbarian B3
27 T8 .... G3
28 Vegetarian Lifestyle G2
29 Vivi Kitchen C5
30 Wèixiāng Zhāi E3
Xīnjíshì .... (see 21)
31 Yè Shànghǎi G3

Drinking & Nightlife **(p105)**

32 Alchemist E5
Bell Bar .... (see 63)
33 Boxing Cat Brewery E5
34 Café 85°C B4
35 Café des Stagiaires B6
36 Citizen Café B2
37 Constellation 2 .... D6
Enoterra .... (see 70)
38 Geisha C5
39 Kāibā E7
40 Lòushì C4
41 Old China Hand Reading Room C7
42 TMSK G3
Vienna Cafe .... (see 41)
43 YY's C4

Entertainment **(p112)**

Brown Sugar .... (see 42)
44 Cathay Theatre C4
45 MAO Livehouse F6
46 Partyworld E3
UME International Cineplex .... (see 18)

Shopping **(p113)**

47 100 Change & Insect A4
48 100 Change & Insect C4
Annabel Lee .... (see 21)

Key on p292

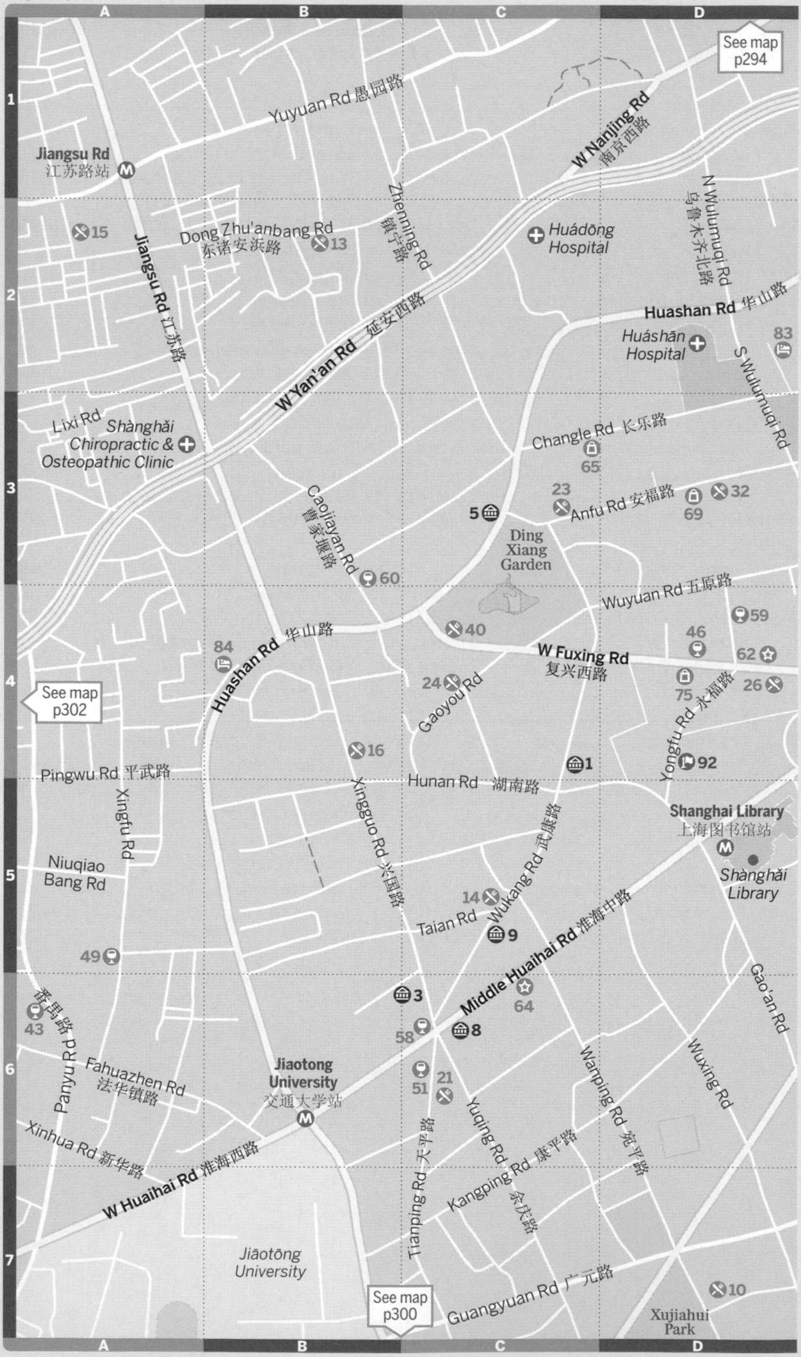
A
B
C
D
1
2
3
4
5
6
7
See map p294
See map p302
See map p300
Yuyuan Rd 愚园路
W Nanjing Rd 南京西路
Jiangsu Rd 江苏路站
Jiangsu Rd 江苏路
Dong Zhu'anbang Rd 东诸安浜路
Zhenning Rd 镇宁路
Huádōng Hospital
N Wulumuqi Rd 乌鲁木齐北路
W Yan'an Rd 延安西路
Huashan Rd 华山路
Huáshān Hospital
S Wulumuqi Rd
Lixi Rd
Shànghǎi Chiropractic & Osteopathic Clinic
Changle Rd 长乐路
Caojiayan Rd 曹家堰路
Anfu Rd 安福路
Ding Xiang Garden
Wuyuan Rd 五原路
W Fuxing Rd 复兴西路
Gaoyou Rd
Yongfu Rd 永福路
Pingwu Rd 平武路
Xingfu Rd
Hunan Rd 湖南路
Xingguo Rd 兴国路
Wukang Rd 武康路
Shanghai Library 上海图书馆站
Shànghǎi Library
Niuqiao Bang Rd
Taian Rd
Middle Huaihai Rd 淮海中路
Gao'an Rd
番禺路
Panyu Rd
Fahuazhen Rd 法华镇路
Jiaotong University 交通大学站
Wanping Rd 宛平路
Wuxing Rd
Xinhua Rd 新华路
Tianping Rd 天平路
Yuqing Rd 余庆路
Kangping Rd 康平路
W Huaihai Rd 淮海西路
Jiāotōng University
Guangyuan Rd 广元路
Xujiahui Park
1
3
5
8
9
10
13
14
15
16
21
23
24
26
32
40
43
46
49
51
58
59
60
62
64
65
69
75
83
84
92

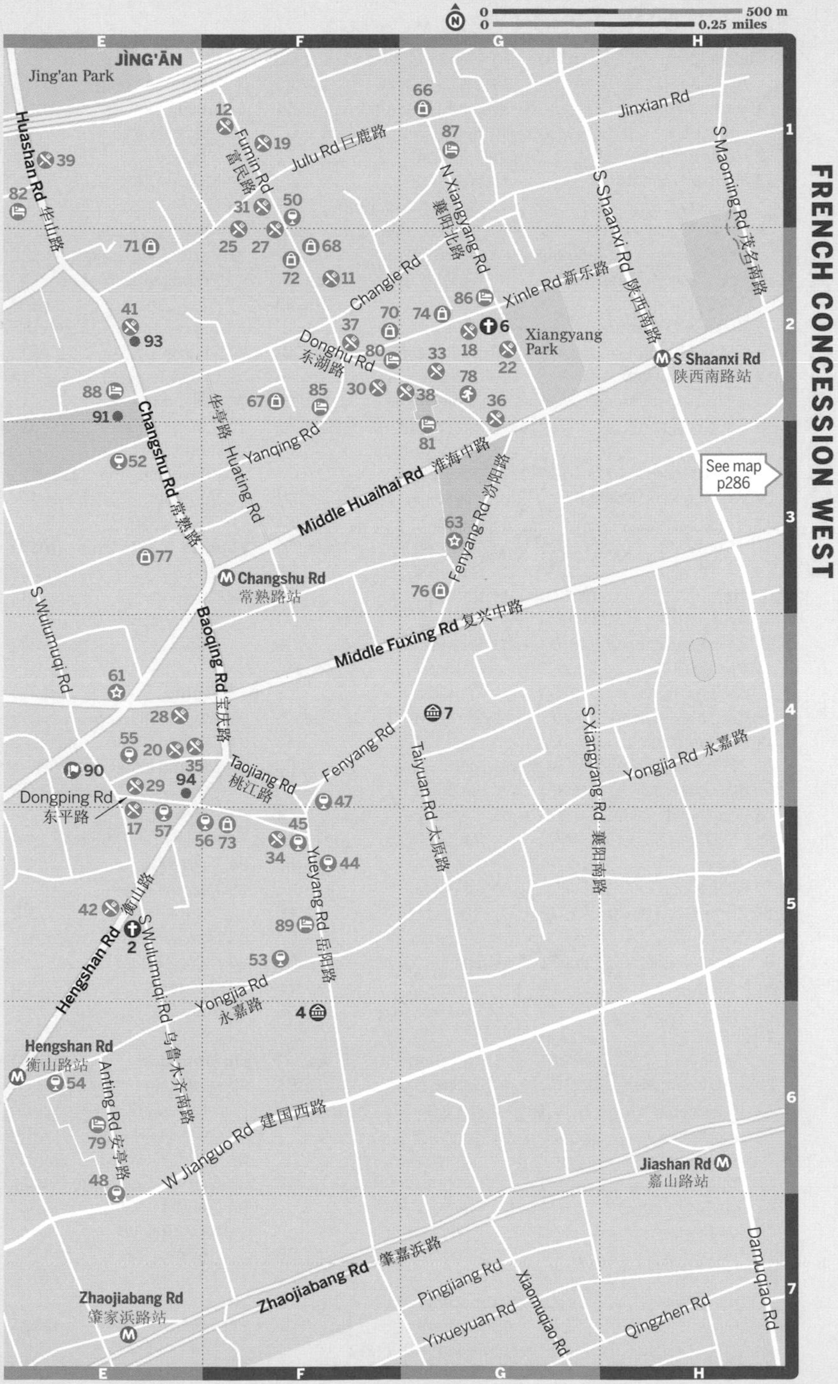
FRENCH CONCESSION WEST
0 500 m
0 0.25 miles
JÌNG'ĀN
Jing'an Park
Huashan Rd 华山路
Fumin Rd 富民路
Julu Rd 巨鹿路
Jinxian Rd
N Xiangyang Rd 襄阳北路
S Shaanxi Rd 陕西南路
S Maoming Rd 茂名南路
Changle Rd
Xinle Rd 新乐路
Xiangyang Park
Donghu Rd 东湖路
S Shaanxi Rd 陕西南路站
Changshu Rd 常熟路
华亭路 Huating Rd
Yanqing Rd
Middle Huaihai Rd 淮海中路
Fenyang Rd 汾阳路
See map p286
Changshu Rd 常熟路站
S Wulumuqi Rd
Baoqing Rd 宝庆路
Middle Fuxing Rd 复兴中路
Taojiang Rd 桃江路
Fenyang Rd
Taiyuan Rd 太原路
S Xiangyang Rd 襄阳南路
Yongjia Rd 永嘉路
Dongping Rd 东平路
Yueyang Rd 岳阳路
Hengshan Rd 衡山路
S Wulumuqi Rd 乌鲁木齐南路
Yongjia Rd 永嘉路
Hengshan Rd 衡山路站
Anting Rd 安亭路
W Jianguo Rd 建国西路
Jiashan Rd 嘉山路站
Zhaojiabang Rd 肇嘉浜路
Pingjiang Rd
Xiaomuqiao Rd
Darnuqiao Rd
Zhaojiabang Rd 肇家浜路站
Yixueyuan Rd
Qingzhen Rd

FRENCH CONCESSION WEST *Map on p290*

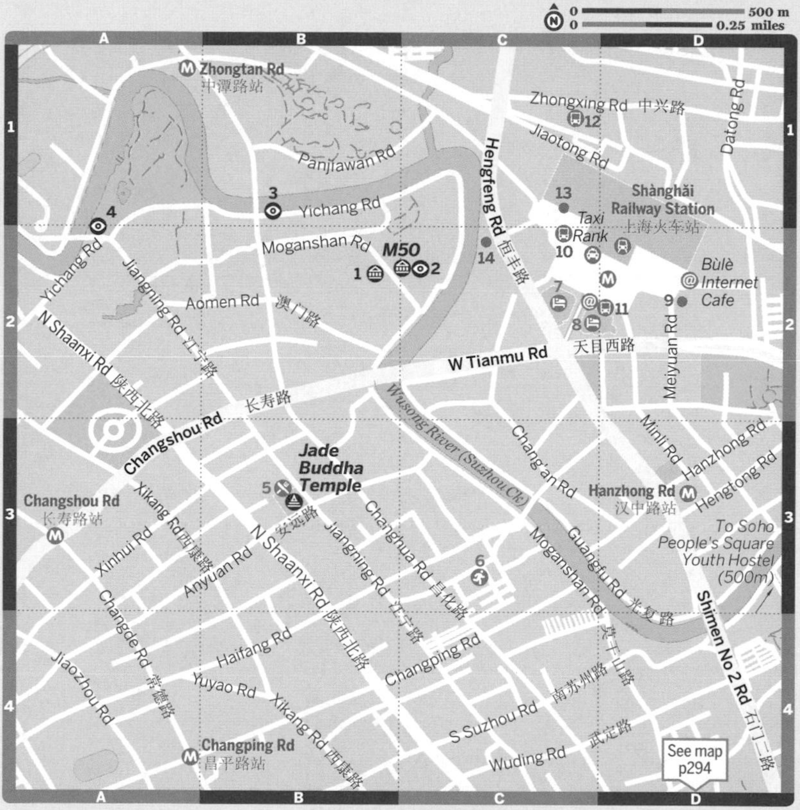

Top Sights (p122)
Jade Buddha Temple B3
M50 .... C2

Sights (p124)
island6 .... (see 2)
1 m97 .... B2
OFoto .... (see 2)
Other Gallery .... (see 2)
2 ShanghART C2
3 Sūzhōu Creek Boat Tours (Changhua Rd Dock) B1
4 Sūzhōu Creek Boat Tours (Xikang Rd Dock) A2
twocities .... (see 2)

Eating (p125)
5 Jade Buddha Temple Vegetarian Restaurant B3

Drinking & Nightlife (p131)
Bandu Cabin .... (see 2)
Roof Club .... (see 2)

Entertainment (p133)
Image Tunnel .... (see 2)

Shopping (p134)
Art Deco .... (see 2)

Sports & Activities (p135)
6 Oz Body Fit C3

Sleeping (p198)
7 Holiday Inn Downtown (Great Wall Wing) C2
8 Holiday Inn Downtown (Plaza Wing) C2

Transport (p240)
9 Advance Train Ticket Booking Office D2
10 Bus 941 to Hóngqiáo International Airport C2
11 Bus to Pǔdōng International Airport D2
12 Shànghǎi Long-Distance Bus Station C1
13 Ticket Office C1
14 Train Ticket Office C2

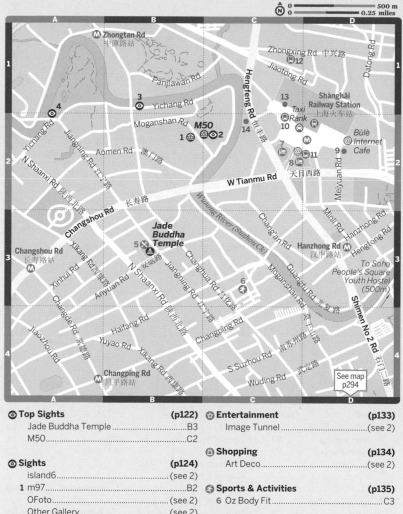

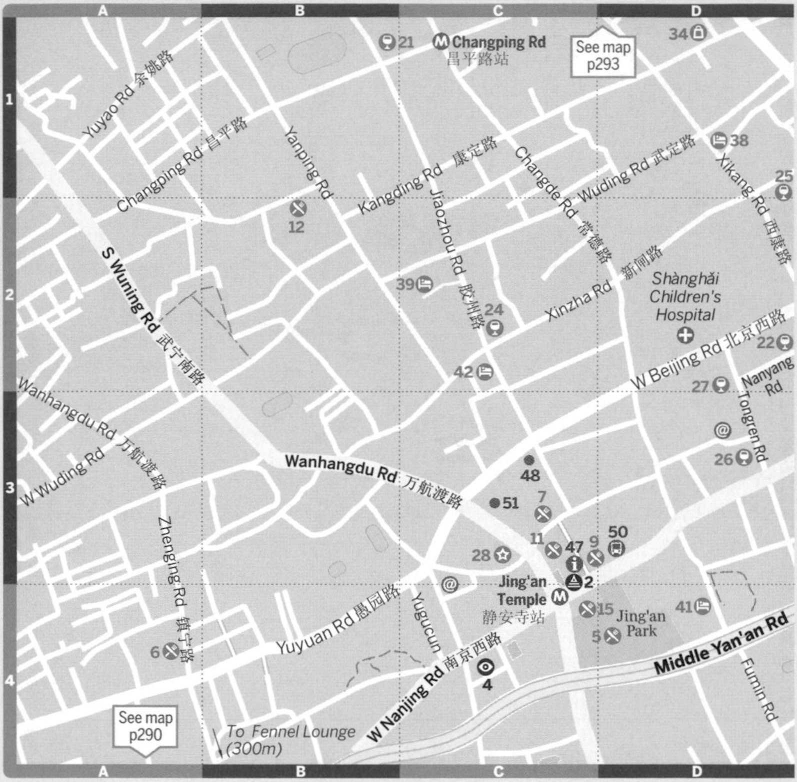

Sights (p124)

1 Former Residence of Mao Zedong.......F3
2 Jìng'ān Temple.......C3
3 Ohel Rachel Synagogue (former).......E1
4 Shànghǎi Children's Palace.......C4

Eating (p125)

Baker & Spice.......(see 29)
5 Bali Laguna.......D4
City Shop.......(see 29)
Crystal Jade.......(see 49)
Din Tai Fung.......(see 29)
Element Fresh.......(see 29)
6 Fu 1088.......A4
7 Golden Pot.......C3
8 Gōngdélín.......H2
9 Gǔyì Húnán Restaurant.......C3
10 Hǎi Dǐ Lāo.......E2
11 Jen Dow Vegetarian Restaurant.......C3
12 Legend Taste.......B2
13 Lynn.......E2
14 Méilóngzhèn Jiǔjiā.......F2
Nánxiáng Steamed Bun Restaurant (see 20)
15 New York Style Pizza.......C4
Pǐnchuān.......(see 33)
Pizza Marzano.......(see 29)
16 Qímín Organic Hotpot.......E2
17 Vegetarian Lifestyle.......F2
18 Wagas.......E2
19 Wujiang Rd Food Street.......G2
20 Yang's Fry Dumplings.......F2

Drinking & Nightlife (p131)

21 B&C.......B1
22 Big Bamboo.......D2
23 Café 85°C.......E2
24 I Love Shànghǎi.......C2
25 Kāibā.......D1
26 Malone's.......D3
27 Spot.......D2

Entertainment (p133)

28 Paramount Ballroom.......C3
29 Shànghǎi Centre Theatre.......E3
30 Shànghǎi Cultural Information & Booking Centre.......F2
Studio City.......(see 49)

Shopping (p134)

Amy Lin's Pearls...(see 31)
31 Han City Fashion & Accessories Plaza.......H2

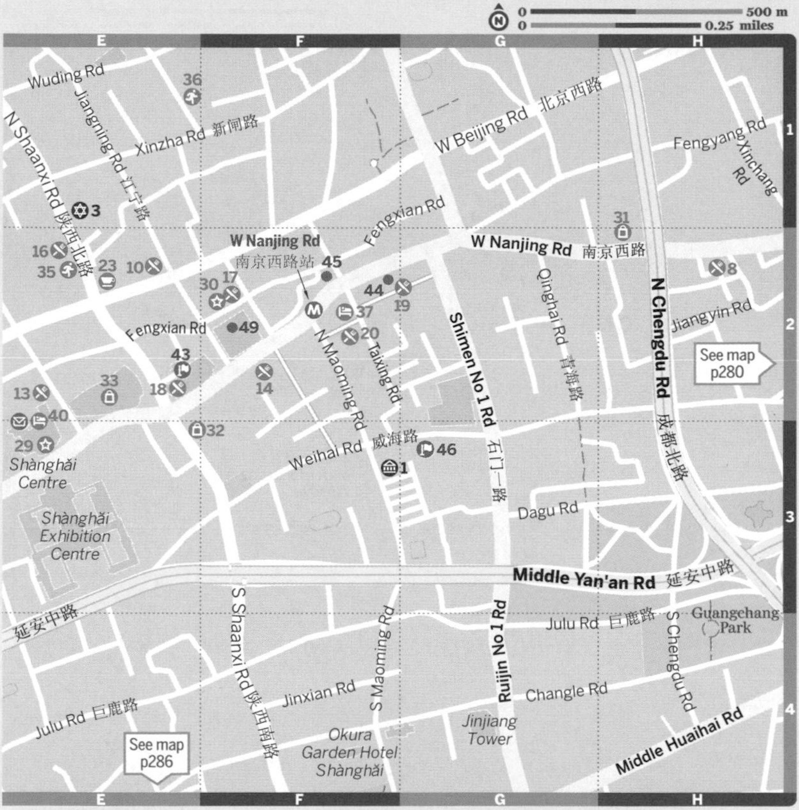

32 Jǐngdézhèn Porcelain Artware E3
33 Plaza 66 .... E2
34 Spin D1
Zhang's Textiles .. (see 29)

Sports & Activities (p135)
35 Apsara Spa E2
36 Aromassage E1
Green Massage ... (see 29)
One Wellness .... (see 30)

Sleeping (p198)
37 Jia Shànghǎi F2
38 Jǐnjiāng Inn D1
39 Le Tour Traveler's Rest C2
40 Portman Ritz-Carlton E3
41 Púlì D4
42 Urbn C2

Information (p249)
American Chamber of Commerce (AmCham) .... (see 29)
American Express (see 29)
43 Australian Consulate-General E2
44 British Chamber of Commerce F2
British Consulate-General .... (see 29)
British Visa Office (see 29)
Canadian Consulate-General .... (see 29)
China Britain Business Council .... (see 49)
45 China Mobile F2
Irish Consulate-General .... (see 29)
New Zealand Visa Office .... (see 29)
Parkway Health ... (see 29)
46 Thai Consulate-General G3
Thai Visa Office ... (see 46)
47 Tourist Information & Service Centre C3
US Citizen Services & Visas .... (see 49)
US Commercial Center .... (see 29)
US Consulate Bureau of Public Affairs .... (see 29)
48 US-China Business Council C3
Watson's .... (see 49)
49 Westgate Mall F2

Transport (p240)
50 Airport City Terminal D3
51 Train Ticket Office C3

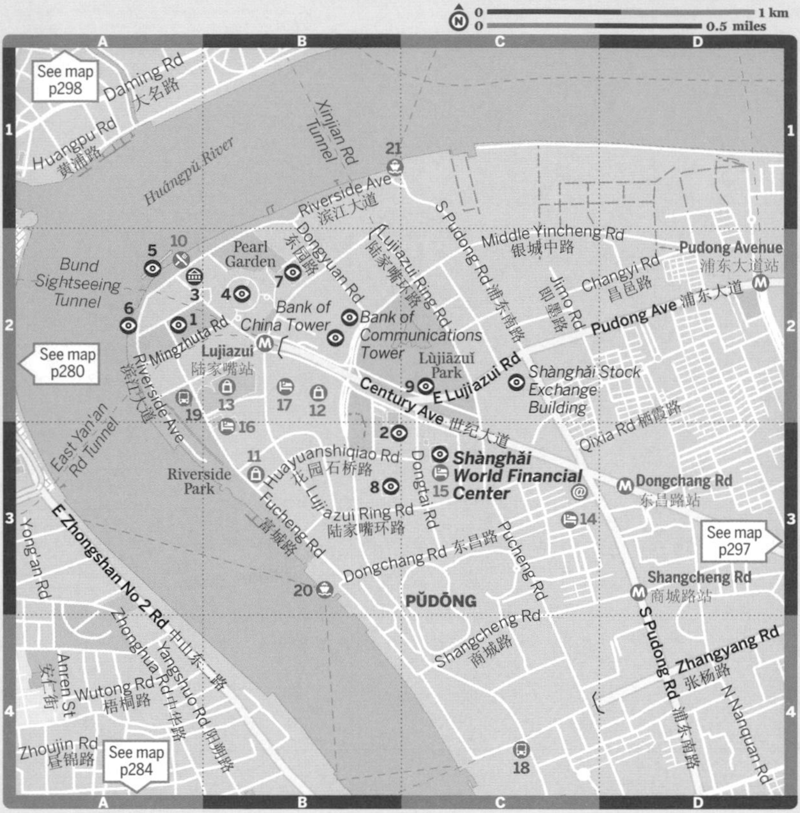

Top Sights (p140)
Shànghǎi World Financial Center C3

Sights (p138)
1 Bund Sightseeing Tunnel A2
2 Jinmao Tower B3
3 Natural Wild Insect Kingdom A2
4 Oriental Pearl TV Tower B2
5 Pearl Dock A2
6 Riverside Promenade A2
Shànghǎi History Museum .... (see 4)
7 Shànghǎi Ocean Aquarium B2
8 Shànghǎi Tower B3
9 Wú Chángshuò Memorial Hall C2

Eating (p140)
Din Tai Fung .... (see 13)
Element Fresh .... (see 13)
10 Kitchen Salvatore Cuomo A2
On 56 .... (see 2)
South Beauty .... (see 13)
Yi Café .... (see 16)

Drinking & Nightlife (p144)
100 Century Avenue .... (see 15)
Blue Frog .... (see 15)
Cloud 9 .... (see 2)
Flair .... (see 17)

Shopping (p146)
11 City Shop B3
12 IFC Mall B2
Shanghai Tang .... (see 16)
13 Superbrand Mall B2

Sleeping (p200)
14 Beehome Hostel C3
Grand Hyatt .... (see 2)
15 Park Hyatt C3
16 Pǔdōng Shangri-La B3
17 Ritz-Carlton Shànghǎi Pǔdōng B2

Information (p249)
Tourist Information & Service Centre .... (see 13)

Transport (p240)
18 Bus 938 to Hongqiao Airport C4
19 Bus Station A2
20 Ferry Dock B3
21 Ferry Dock B1
Train Ticket Office .... (see 7)

Sights (p139)
1 Century Park D4
2 Himalayas Art Museum D4
3 Qīncìyǎng Temple B1
4 Shànghǎi Science & Technology Museum C3

Eating (p144)
5 Hǎi Dǐ Lāo A2

Drinking & Nightlife (p144)
6 Brew D4

Entertainment (p146)
Daguan Theater .... (see 2)
7 Oriental Art Center C3

Shopping (p146)
Amy Lin's Pearls .... (see 8)
8 AP Xīnyáng Fashion & Gifts Market C3

Sleeping (p200)
Jumeirah Himalayas Hotel .... (see 2)

HÓNGKǑU & NORTH SHÀNGHǍI

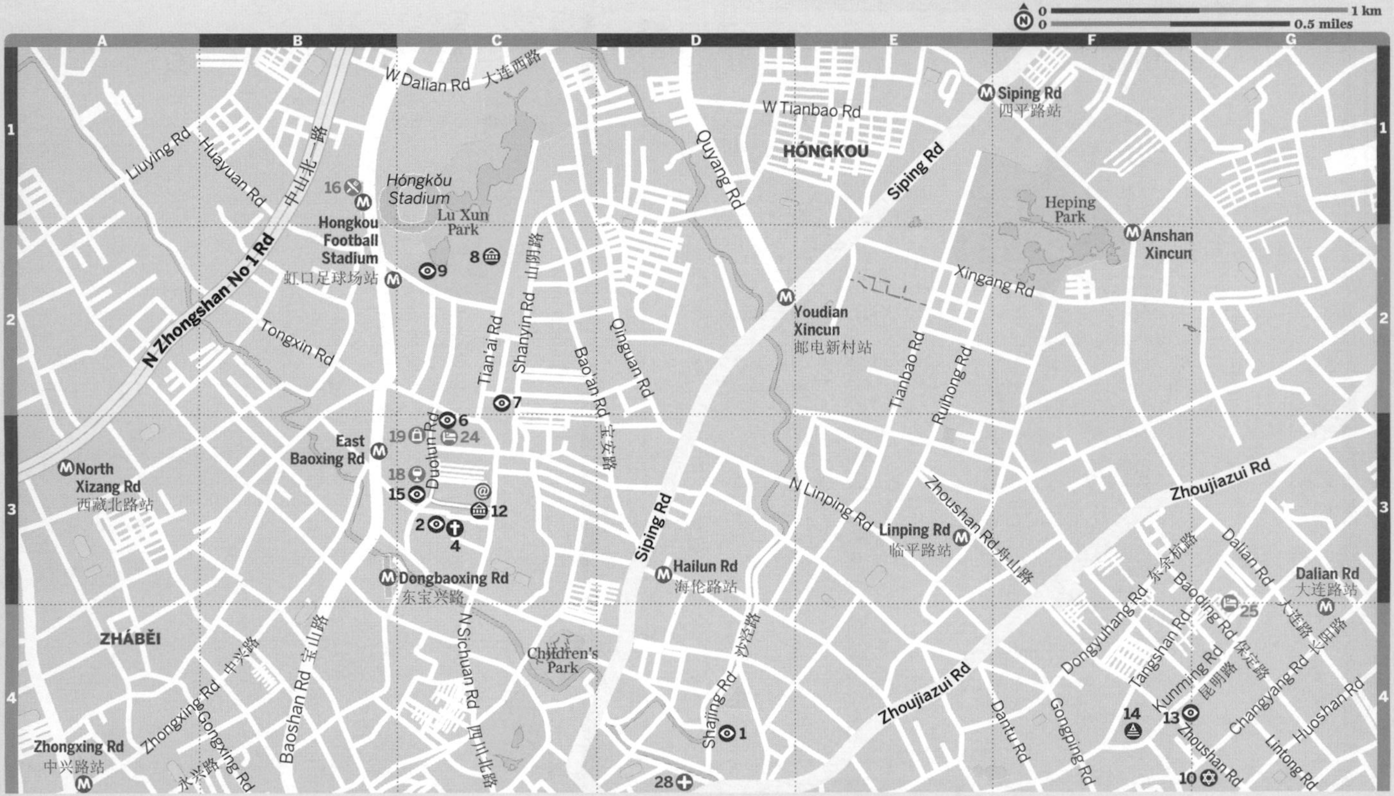

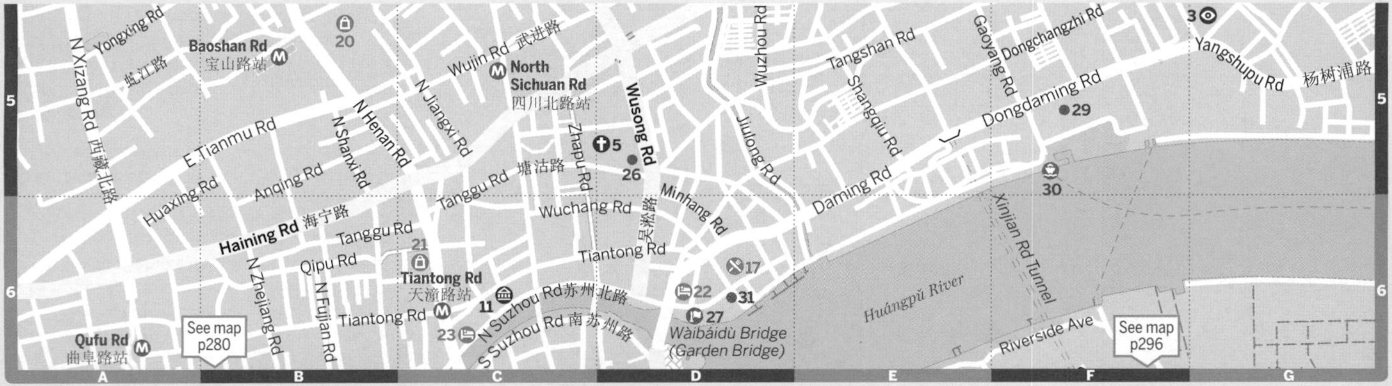

Sights (p150)

1 1933 D4
2 Duolun Road Cultural Street C3
Embankment Building (see 23)
3 Former Broadway Theatre G5
4 Hóngdé Temple C3
5 Hongkew Methodist Church D5
6 Kong Residence C3
7 Lu Xun Former Residence C2
8 Lu Xun Memorial Hall C2
9 Lu Xun Park C2
Main Post Office (see 11)
10 Ohel Moishe Synagogue G4
Political Museum (see 19)
11 Post Museum C6
12 Shànghǎi Duōlún Museum of Modern Art C3
13 Ward Road Jail F4
14 Xiàhǎi Buddhist Monastery F4
15 Xīshí Bell Tower C3

Eating (p152)

16 San Gines B1
17 Xīndàlù D6

Drinking & Nightlife (p154)

Bites Lounge (see 23)
18 Old Film Café C3
Vue (see 17)

Shopping (p154)

19 Dàshànghǎi C3
Details Gallery (see 23)
20 Electronics Market B5
21 Qīpǔ Market C6

Sleeping (p201)

22 Astor House Hotel D6
23 Chai Living Residences C6
24 Koala Garden House C3
25 Naza International Youth Hostel G4

Information (p249)

26 Alliance Française D5
International Medical Care Centre (IMCC) (see 28)
27 Russian Consulate-General D6
28 Shànghǎi First People's Hospital D4

Transport (p240)

29 China-Japan International Ferry Company F5
Shànghǎi International Ferry Company (see 29)
30 Shànghǎi Port International Cruise Terminal F5
31 Train Ticket Office D6

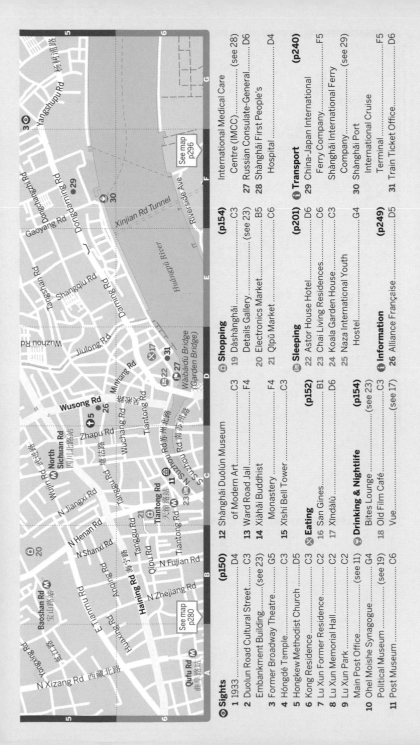

XÚJIĀHUÌ & SOUTH SHÀNGHĂI

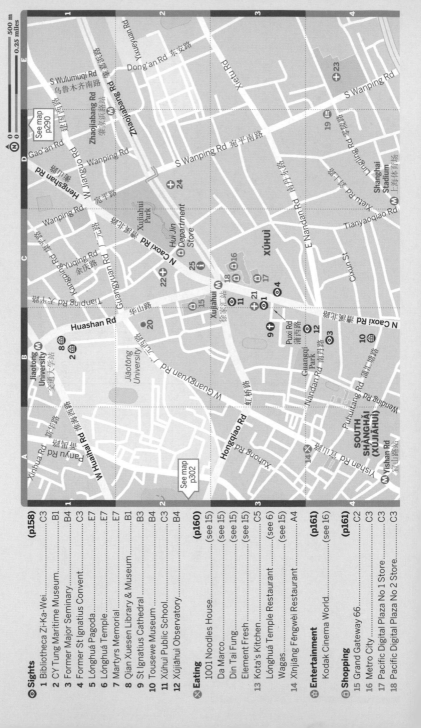

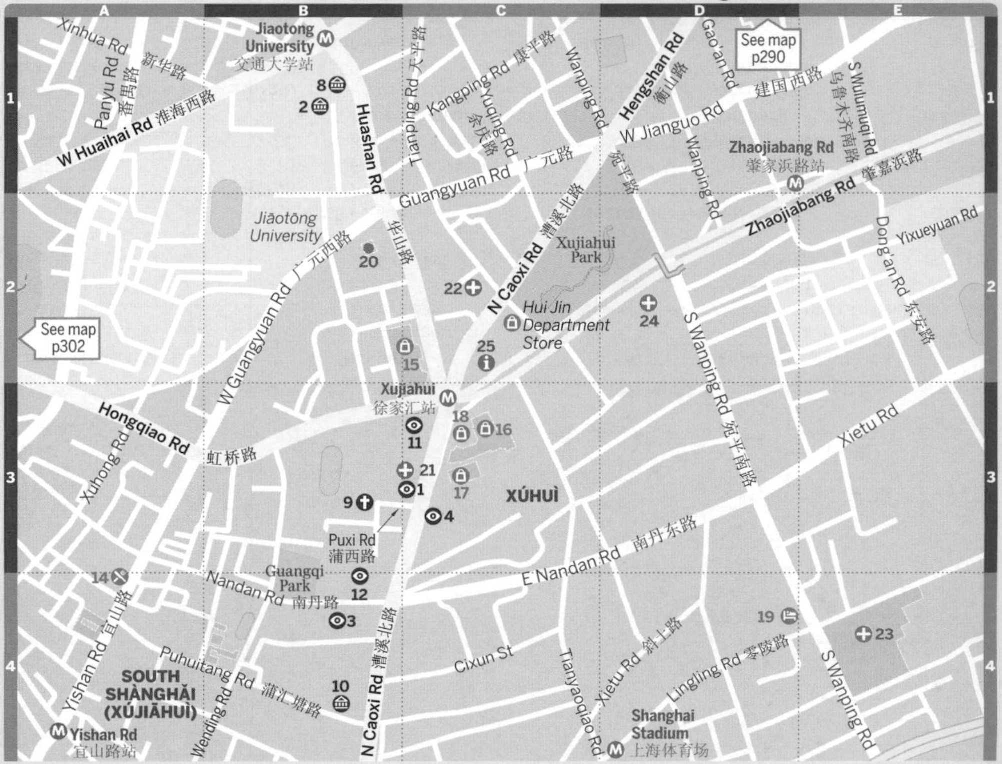

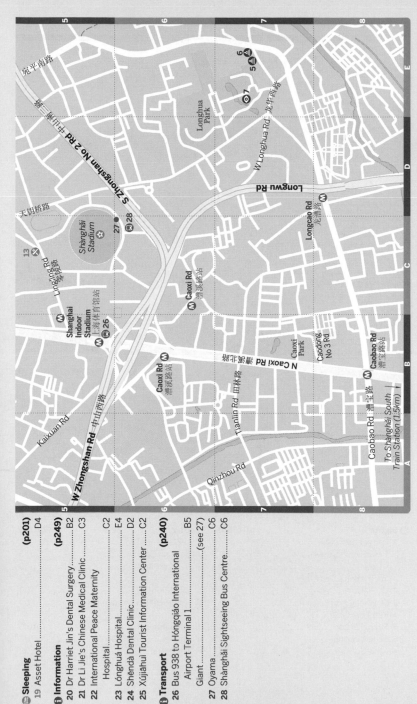

XÚJIĀHUÌ & SOUTH SHÀNGHĂI

Sleeping **(p201)**
19 Asset Hotel D4

Information **(p249)**
20 Dr Harriet Jin's Dental Surgery B2
21 Dr Li Jie's Chinese Medical Clinic C3
22 International Peace Maternity Hospital C2
23 Lónghuá Hospital E4
24 Shēndà Dental Clinic D2
25 Xújiāhuì Tourist Information Center C2

Transport **(p240)**
26 Bus 938 to Hóngqiáo International Airport Terminal 1 .... B5
Giant .... (see 27)
27 Oyama C6
28 Shànghǎi Sightseeing Bus Centre C6

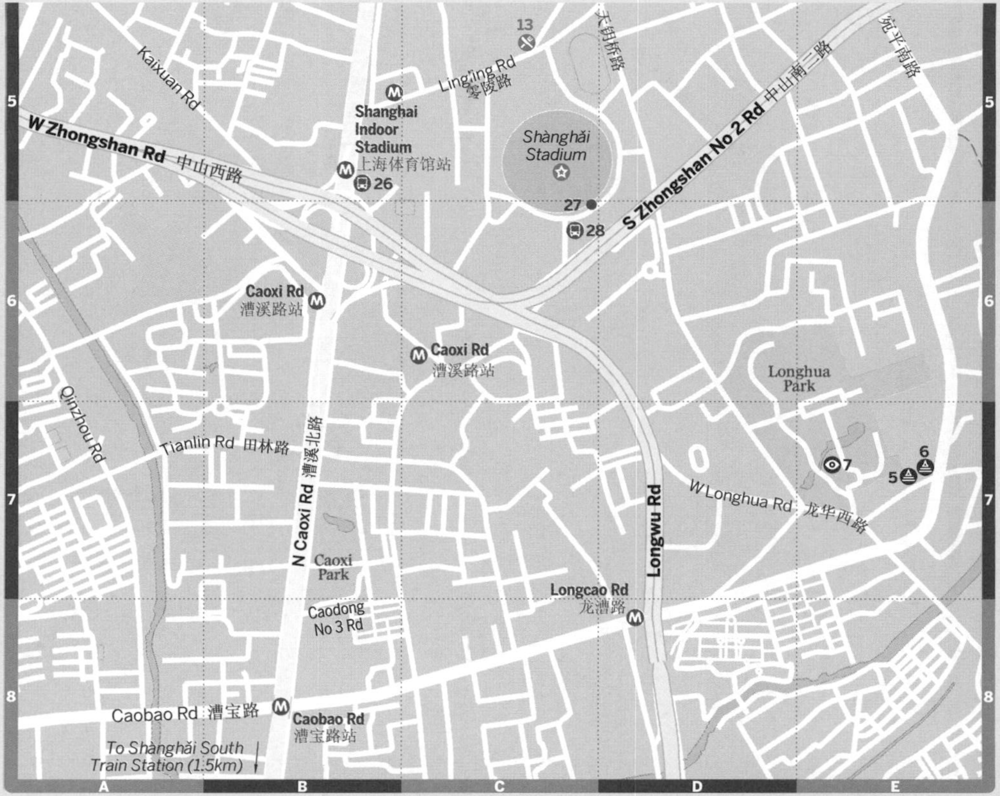

Sights (p165)

1 Former Sassoon Mansion (Cypress Hotel)....B4
International Cemetery....(see 6)
2 Liu Haisu Art Gallery....E3
3 Mínshēng Art Museum....H3
4 Red Town....H3
5 Shànghǎi Zoo....B3
6 Song Qingling Mausoleum....F3

Eating (p166)

7 1221....H2
8 Bellagio Café....E3
9 Bì Fēng Táng....E3
10 Carrefour....E3
11 City Shop....D4
12 Hongmei Rd Entertainment Street....D4

Entertainment (p167)

13 Shànghǎi Film Art Centre....H2
14 Yùyīntáng....G2

Shopping (p167)

15 Foreign Languages Bookstore........E3
16 Henry Antique Warehouse........D4
17 Hóngqiáo International Pearl City........D4
18 Tiānshān Tea City........G2

Sports & Activities (p167)

19 Mandarine City........E4
20 Míngwǔ International Kungfu Club........D4

Sleeping (p202)

21 Hóngqiáo State Guest House........E2
22 Hotel Carolina........G2
23 Marriott Hotel Hóngqiáo........C4
24 Xījiāo State Guest House........D3

Information (p249)

25 Alliance Française........H1
26 Dutch Consulate-General........F3
27 Japanese Consulate-General........F2
28 Parkway Health........E4
29 Singapore Consulate-General........F2

Our Story

A beat-up old car, a few dollars in the pocket and a sense of adventure. In 1972 that's all Tony and Maureen Wheeler needed for the trip of a lifetime – across Europe and Asia overland to Australia. It took several months, and at the end – broke but inspired – they sat at their kitchen table writing and stapling together their first travel guide, *Across Asia on the Cheap*. Within a week they'd sold 1500 copies. Lonely Planet was born.

Today, Lonely Planet has offices in Melbourne, London and Oakland, with more than 600 staff and writers. We share Tony's belief that 'a great guidebook should do three things: inform, educate and amuse'.

Our Writers

Damian Harper

Coordinating Author, Old Town, Pǔdōng, Hóngkǒu & North Shànghǎi, Xújiāhuì & South Shànghǎi, Day Trips from Shànghǎi After graduating with a degree in modern and classical Chinese from London's School of Oriental and African Studies, guidebook writer Damian has lived and worked in Shànghǎi, Běijīng and Hong Kong, travelling the highways and byroads of China. Fascinated by China's coming of age, relishing Shànghǎi's finest *xiǎolóngbāo* dumplings and *shíkùmén* buildings, and while hounded by deadlines, Damian has worked on multiple editions of *Shanghai*. For this edition, Damian also wrote Need to Know, Top Itineraries, Sleeping, the Understand Shànghǎi section, and the Transport and Directory chapters.

Read more about Damian at:
lonelyplanet.com/members/damianharper

Christopher Pitts

The Bund & People's Square, French Concession, Jìng'ān, West Shànghǎi Chris started his university years studying classical Chinese poetry before a week in 1990s Shànghǎi (en route to school in Kūnmíng) abruptly changed his focus to the idiosyncrasies of modern China. Several years in Asia memorising Chinese characters got him hooked, and he returns whenever he can to immerse himself in what is surely one of the world's most fascinating languages. He's written for Lonely Planet's *Shanghai* since 2005 and also contributes to the *China* guide. Visit him online at www.christopherpitts.net. For this edition, Christopher also wrote Welcome to Shànghǎi, What's New, If You Like, Month by Month, With Kids, Like a Local, For Free, Neighbourhoods at a Glance, the Eating, Drinking & Nighlife, Entertainment and Shopping overviews and Sleeping.

Read more about Chris at:
lonelyplanet.com/members/christopherpitts

Published by Lonely Planet Publications Pty Ltd
ABN 36 005 607 983
6th edition – April 2013
ISBN 978 1 74179 901 9

10 9 8 7 6 5 4 3 2 1
Printed in China